W9-BUJ-901

DICTIONARY OF FOREIGN QUOTATIONS

Compiled by Robert and Mary Collison

Facts on File
119 West 57 Street,
New York, N.Y. 10019

First published in the United States in 1980 by
FACTS ON FILE INC.

ISBN 0 87196 428 7

Filmset by Vantage Photosetting Co. Ltd.
Southampton and London

Printed in Great Britain

CONTENTS

FOREWORD

How to use this Dictionary

The quotations in this volume are arranged in alphabetical order of subjects. In many cases the subject classification of individual quotations was necessarily arbitrary, since even a short quotation may refer to more than one subject; in such cases the quotation is placed under one subject and a cross-reference provided to other(s). See the list of subject headwords at the end of the book.

Within each subject the quotations are arranged alphabetically by language – Arabic, Danish, French, Greek, etc. To most quotations a literal English translation has been added, but where a particularly well-known or successful translation exists, this has sometimes also been included.

In the case of languages such as Greek, Russian, Arabic and Japanese which do not use the Roman alphabet, there seemed no point in giving quotations in their original script as they would be meaningless to the majority of readers. The original quotation is therefore given in transliterated form, with some guidance as to pronunciation, so that the bold reader can still quote in the original language. For those who read Arabic, however, it should be noted that the quotations are in colloquial and not classical form.

INTRODUCTION

Next to the originator of a good sentence is the first quoter of it.
Ralph Waldo Emerson: *Quotation and Originality*

The spirit of collecting is instinctive, and it is easy to understand how book-collectors, for example, can spend long leisure hours assembling and cataloguing mint-condition copies of the first editions of their favourite authors. The goal in such cases is well-defined, and rules can be made and observed concerning the inclusion or elimination of borderline material in so wide a field. The much narrower area of quotations selected from published sources presents the collector with a very different set of problems: he must decide for whom he is collecting, from what sources he should select, and in what form he should present the results of his research.

In the case of the present Dictionary we assembled quotations which, once found, we wanted to be able to trace again. In this we feel we have much in common with a very large number of people; it is not unusual, for example, to hear public speakers refer – with varying degrees of accuracy – to the opinions of earlier writers when they wish to underline the point which they themselves are making. This type of quotation differs widely from statements made in a textbook, which must be reinforced by a scholarly footnote to some previous authority; but undoubtedly audiences would be grateful if speakers' quotation sources were also more precisely given.

We have tried to select a variety of quotations that will have an appeal and an interest for people of many differing tastes, and for many different occasions. We have not, however, tried to be comprehensive in any one area. Thus readers will find that only a few mottos, of schools and regiments and other organisations, and only a few striking inscriptions, have been included.

The collection is arranged alphabetically by subject-matter, in the belief that the majority of people are more interested in a variety of opinions on a specific subject, than in the author of a specific quotation or its place of origin. Nevertheless, an index of authors and their works has been included to help those who may be searching for items whose origin they partly know. From the first we found the subject approach rewarding, for the differences in national attitudes to any particular subject were impossible to ignore. Friendship is a particularly good instance of this. It was highly prized among the Romans, and the value they placed on it was well expressed by Cicero when he wrote 'Man's best support is a very dear friend'. The Greeks were more critical, their opinion being reflected in Sophocles' judgment that human friendships can scarcely be trusted. The Spanish attitude, on the other hand, is reflected in their proverb 'Better a friend of bad repute than an untried acquaintance', and in the philosopher Baltasar Gracián's firm assurance that there is no wilderness like a life without friends.

The variety of national approaches to any subject thus proved an unexpected reward as we noted interesting passages in the works we were reading, but the contrasts would have eluded us had we not classified our quotations immediately. We were convinced that many people are interested in the wide variety of what has been said or written on particular subjects. Without excluding, therefore, the memorable and more widely known quotations, we searched for the unusual and unexpected opinions that occur from time to time like flashes of light among the millions of published words that will never have more than a fleeting impact.

We were always conscious of the fact that our selection must supply the needs of late twentieth-century society, and must necessarily differ from that which might have been made for the needs of a society between the two World Wars or even a century earlier, just as we realise that collections made by future generations will naturally be different again. Changing tastes are very clearly shown, for example in the successive editions of anthologies of literature. We did not therefore feel compelled to include all the well-known Greek and Latin lines that have so frequently adorned English prose in the past. We have preferred to range more widely over the classical writings of the various European countries in search of passages more in keeping with present needs. And in re-reading them we have had the good fortune to find such gems as the passage on ideas in Alexandre Dumas' *La Dame de Monsoreau*.

Reference works are usually purchased for reference libraries, and few people can afford the space or the money to own more than a handful of reference books. To have selected a very large collection of quotations would have defeated the object, which is to compile a work, modest in size and price, within the means of those who prefer to have their own choice of reference works at hand. We do not claim that this Dictionary is a definitive collection of quotations, but even a limited number of items can offer a wider scope by judicious indexing, and this has been provided in the form of numerous cross-references that may lead the reader from the subject-heading he has originally looked up, to others where he may find equally relevant quotations, for each quotation has been inserted under only one subject-heading, and secondary allusions might otherwise be overlooked. This method, we hope, will also lead the reader to explore the less familiar items and, in some cases, to be tempted to read the works from which they have been selected.

The compiling of this Dictionary began some ten years ago in Los Angeles, where we were able to make use of one of the great libraries of the world in the University of California at Los Angeles. As is the case in the history of all great libraries, the University Research Library there is the result of the inspired librarianship and book selection of a series of University Librarians and their staffs, and it is to be regretted that the unique atmosphere of this three-million-volume library can only be fully appreciated by those who are able to work in it. The whole of the collection is on the open-stack principle, so that formalities of use are reduced to a minimum and students and research workers can easily and quickly obtain what they want. An added advantage is that, in being given the freedom of the shelves, a reader may find books and collections of material of whose existence he might otherwise remain in ignorance. For example, in the course of one afternoon we came across a collection of more than a thousand works on Napoleon, and a better range of books and pamphlets on English local history than is likely to be found in any English library except the British Library.

Access to such a library, most of whose contents could be borrowed without difficulty, offered the initial range from which we selected possible entries for inclusion in this Dictionary. Later, when we returned to England, we were able to pursue our research among the million-volume contents of the London Library in St James's Square, that astonishingly comprehensive collection, founded by Thomas Carlyle and his contemporaries, and built up and administered by a series of outstanding Librarians. Here again the stacks are open to all members, and the simple classification in use makes it extraordinarily easy to satisfy one's needs.

Two libraries, six thousand miles apart, thus provided the answer to the problem of sources. It remained to determine in what form the results should be presented. Since we were selecting quotations from works in a number of different languages, it appeared that it would be essential to sub-divide each subject-heading by language. Initially we thought of placing first those quotations in classical languages, *e.g.*, Greek, Latin, Pali, etc., followed by the modern language entries arranged in alphabetical order of language. However, it appeared that there was no adequate reason for doing so, except that of convention. It could not be said that the classical entries we had selected were antiquated in meaning; indeed, some of them are as relevant today as many of the more modern entries in the Dictionary. On the advice of the publishers we rearranged the entries so that all the languages are arranged in one alphabetical sequence under each subject entry – which has the result, in a number of cases, of offering an Arab proverb as a kind of *hors d'oeuvre*.

Within each language sequence we have not attempted to provided any specific arrangement, for the entries in the majority of cases are not numerous for any one language. We believe that the reader will thus be persuaded to consider *all* the entries for a specific language – and perhaps those under neighbouring languages as well. The translations offered are mainly fairly literal, though we have taken the precaution of providing an idiomatic English translation as well as a literal translation wherever there is a significant difference between the two. Occasionally it has been necessary to indicate the circumstances that gave rise to a remark, or to provide a reminder that another writer gives another version. Where variations in the form of names exist – *e.g.*, Vergil, Virgil, etc. – we have used the form most generally in current use.

Though the present lists are closed, we continue to discover and record quotations that must be considered for any revised edition of the Dictionary in the future. Readers who are similarly interested will find that margins and blank pages will probably accommodate only a very limited number of new items; we suggest that a loose-leaf volume, with each page devoted to a separate subject, will give better scope for the inevitable expansion of the collection. This can prove a rewarding pastime, for out of it may grow a new approach to each subject, and a new enjoyment in quotation. There is the reward too of discovering authors in unfamiliar roles, such as the remarkable verse of the author of the popular *Emil and the Detectives*.

'By necessity, by proclivity – and by delight, we all quote', said Emerson in his *Quotation and Originality*, and by widening the choice beyond the boundaries of the English language, a still broader and richer terrain is revealed. We hope this Dictionary will bring to the attention of readers quotations both unfamiliar and interesting, and perhaps lead them to investigate further the work of the many different writers in non-English-speaking countries whom we have tried to represent.

July 1980
R.C. and M.C.

A

ABILITY
see also Achievement, Effort, Faults.

Illī rijlay-h tuwāl yimshī qawām

ARAB PROVERB

He that has long legs travels fast.

ABSENCE

N'écris pas! Je suis triste, et je voudrais m'éteindre;
Les beaux étés, sans toi, c'est l'amour sans flambeau.

MARCELINE DESBORDES-VALMORE:
Les Séparés (French)

Don't write! I am sad and would like just to fade away.
These beautiful summers without you are like love without a torch.

L'absence est le plus grand des maux.

JEAN DE LA FONTAINE:
Les Deux Pigeons (French)

Absence is the greatest of evils.

L'absence diminue les médiocres passions et augmente les grandes, comme le vent éteint les bougies et allume le feu.

FRANÇOIS, DUC DE LA ROCHEFOUCAULD:
Réflexions (French)

Absence lessens mediocre passions but augments great ones, just as the wind blows out candles but starts conflagrations.

ABUSE
see also Calumny, Mockery.

La pelle se moque du fourgon.

FRENCH PROVERB

The shovel mocks the poker.

Belua multorum es capitum.

HORACE:
Epistles (Latin)

You are a many-headed monster.

Dijo la sartén a la caldera: 'Quitate allá, culinegra!'

SPANISH PROVERB

Said the frying-pan to the kettle: 'Get away from there, black bottom!'

ACCURACY

Nous mourons de la correction!

COUTELI, FRENCH HUMORIST:
Remarks

We are dying of accuracy!

Die barbarische Genauigkeit; winselnde Demut.

GEORG CHRISTOPH LICHTENBERG:
Aphorismen (German)

Barbaric accuracy – whimpering humility!

ACHIEVEMENT
see also Aspiration, Faults, Greatness, Meditation, Single-mindedness, Success, Work.

Ta gloire est dégagée, et ton devoir est quitte.

PIERRE CORNEILLE:
Le Cid (French)

Your duty is discharged, your glory redeemed.

A vaincre sans péril on triomphe sans gloire.

PIERRE CORNEILLE:
Le Cid (French)

A victory without danger is a triumph without glory.

Plutôt ce qu'ils ont fait que ce qu'ils ont été.

JEAN RACINE:
Andromaque (French)

What they have done is of more interest than what they have been.

Das Ganz macht, nicht das Einzelne.

GERMAN PROVERB

It's the whole, not the detail, that matters.

Entsagung und Verkümmerung, die wohnen nahe beisammen, und all Wirklichkeit und Werk ist eben nur das verkümmerte Mögliche.

THOMAS MANN:
Lotte in Weimar (German)

Renunciation and atrophy are near neighbours, and all reality and enterprise are only rudimentary forms of what is possible.

Wenn ich nicht morgen nachmittag Sieger bin, bin ich ein toter Mann!

ADOLF HITLER:
at Munich, 8 November 1923 *(German)*

If I have not won by tomorrow afternoon, I shall be a dead man.

Tēn kreittō ta sungrammata deixei

ERASMUS:
inscription added by Erasmus to his portrait on a medal designed by Quentin Metsys (*Greek*)

His writings will show the better picture.

Dokō men, ouden rhēma sun kerdei kakon

SOPHOCLES:
Electra (Greek)

The end justifies even illicit means.

Ti gar moi kai makrois aulois?

SUETONIUS:
Otho (Greek)

How can I achieve something so far beyond my ability? (*lit.* what concern have I with long pipes?)

Kreitton gar pou smikron eu ē polu mē hikanōs peranai

PLATO:
Theaetetus (Greek)

Better to complete a small task well, than do much imperfectly.

Pherei karpon kai anthrōpos kai theos kai ho kosmos. En tais oikeiais hōrais hekasta pherei

MARCUS AURELIUS:
Meditations (Greek)

Everyone and everything – man, God, and the universe – bears fruit in due season.

Ogni sublime acquisto
Va col suo rischio insieme;
Questo incontrar chi teme,
Quello non dee sperar.

PIETRO METASTASIO:
Il Trionfo di Clelia (Italian)

Every sublime conquest contains its own perils; one man encounters what he fears, another what he dare not hope for.

Qui e nuce nuculeum esse volt, frangit nucem.

PLAUTUS:
Curculio (Latin)

To get the kernel, you must crack the nut.

Habet, peractum est, fata se nostra explicant.

SENECA:
Dialogues (Latin)

It is finished; our fates reveal themselves.

Si finis bonus est, totum bonum erit.

LATIN PROVERB

If the end is good the whole will be good.

Finis coronat opus.   LATIN PROVERB

The end crowns the work.

Explicit, Deo gratis!
Medieval scribe's note at the end of the book he has just been copying (*Latin*)

Thank God, that's done!

ACTION
see also Advice, Decision, Hesitation, Loquacity, Meditation, Melancholy, Procrastination.

Ainsi dit, ainsi fait!

FRENCH PROVERB

No sooner said than done!

Ne faut-il que délibérer,
La Cour en conseillers foisonne;
Est-il besoin d'exécuter,
L'on ne rencontre plus personne.

JEAN DE LA FONTAINE:
Conseil Tenu par les Rats (French)

When it is only a question of policy, the Court

bristles with advisers; but once it is a question of action, no-one can be found.

Un premier mouvement ne fut jamais un crime.
PIERRE CORNEILLE:
Horace (French)

An impulsive action has never been classed as a crime.

Toutes actions hors les bornes ordinaires sont sujettes à sinistre interprétation.
MICHEL DE MONTAIGNE:
De l'Ivrognerie (French)

All unusual actions are liable to sinister interpretation.

Nostre nature est dans le mouvement; le repos entier est la mort.
BLAISE PASCAL:
Pensées (French)

Our nature lies in movement; absolute rest is death.

Es war getan fast eh' gedacht.
J. W. VON GOETHE:
Willkommen und Abschied (German)

It was done almost as soon as thought of.

Die Tat ist alles, nichts der Ruhm.
GERMAN PROVERB

It is the deed that matters, not the fame.

Es muss etwas geschehen!
HEINRICH BÖLL:
'Es wird etwas geschehen', in his
Doktor Murkes Gesammeltes Schweigen,
und Andere Satiren (German)

Something must happen! (The efficiency motto which the tyrant Wunsredel impressed daily on his employees).

Mein Geist dürstet nach Taten, mein Atem nach Freiheit.
J. C. F. VON SCHILLER:
Die Räuber (German)

My spirit yearns for action, my breath for freedom.

Das wahre Leben ist des Handelns
Ewige Unschuld
J. W. VON GOETHE:
Der Deutsche Dankt (German)

True life is the eternal innocence of action.

Ou bouleuesthai eti hōra alla bebouleusthai
GREEK PROVERB

It is no longer the time of day for making plans, but for having them.

Ē phusin ekhei praxin lexeōs hētton alētheias ephaptesthai;
PLATO:
The Republic (Greek)

Is it not natural that action cannot be as near to truth as thought is?

Auto deixei
GREEK PROVERB

You can only find out by trying (*lit.* the event itself will show).

Onasthai, mē mathein boulou, teknon
EURIPIDES:
Hippolytus (Greek)

Content yourself with practical aid, not theory.

To de zētoumenon
Halōton ekpheuge in de tameloumenon
SOPHOCLES:
Oedipus Tyrannus (Greek)

Look, and you will find it – what is unsought will go undetected.

Hōs entauth' emen,
Hin' ouket' oknein kairos, all' ergōn akmē
SOPHOCLES:
Electra (Greek)

The time for hesitation is past – let us act!

Semper enim honorabilius est agens patiente.
ARISTOTLE:
De Animae (Latin)

The active is always more noble than the passive (*tr.* James of Venice).

Strenui nimio plus prosunt populo quam arguti et cati.

TERENCE:
Truculentus (Latin)

Men of action are much more use to the people than smooth, clever chaps.

Factis ut credam facis.

TERENCE:
Hecyra (Latin)

Words gain credibility by deeds.

Ego quippe ne in homine quidem non stulte fieri puto quod inutiliter factum est.

BOETHIUS:
Contra Eutychen (Latin)

To my mind a human action that is useless is also foolish.

Age si quid agis.

PLAUTUS:
Persa (Latin)

If you want to do something, do it!

Ad vitam agendam non ad ostentationem.

CORNELIUS NEPOS:
Atticus (Latin)

Choose a life of action, not one of ostentation.

Res non verba.

Motto of the McRarie family *(Latin)*

Deeds, not words.

Sat celeriter fieri quidquid fiat satis bene.

SUETONIUS:
Divus Augustus (Latin)

Whatever is done well enough is done quickly enough (favourite saying of the Emperor Augustus).

Sed medicinae . . . tempus est quam querelae.

BOETHIUS:
Consolatio Philosophiae (Latin)

Better to mend our bridges than go on complaining.

Es fácil el decir y difícil el obrar.

SPANISH PROVERB

Talking is easy, action difficult.

ACTIVITY

To men ara agathon kinēsis kata te psukhēn kai kata sōma, to de tounantion?

PLATO
Theaetetus (Greek)

Is not activity good for both body and soul, and inactivity bad for them?

Panta dē pasan kinēsin aei kineitai

PLATO
Theaetetus (Greek)

Everything is always engaged in all forms of motion.

ADAPTABILITY

Hou gar toioutōn dei, toioutos eim' egō

SOPHOCLES:
Philoctetes (Greek)

I can adapt my humour to the needs of the hour.

En men mainomenois mala mainomai, en de dikaiois pantōn anthrōpōn eimi dikaiotatos

THEOGNIS:
Fragment (Greek)

Among the wild I am indeed wild, but among the righteous I am the most righteous of all men.

Omnium mulierum vir et omnium virorum mulier.

SUETONIUS:
Divus Iulius (Latin)

Every woman's man, and every man's woman. (speaking of Julius Caesar – a remark ascribed to the elder Curio).

ADORATION
see also Love.

Cet empire que tient la raison sur les sens
Ne fait pas renoncer aux douceurs des encens.

MOLIÈRE:
Les Femmes Savantes (French)

The sway that reason maintains over the senses does not mean that we must reject the sweet incense [of adoration].

ADULTERY
see also Cuckoldry, Honour.

Misō de kai tas sōphronas men en logois,
Lathrai de tolmas ou kalas kektēmenas

EURIPIDES:
Hippolytus (Greek)

I loathe women who boast of their chastity,
while secretly daring every sin.

Fundum alienum arat, incultum familiarem
deserit.

PLAUTUS:
Asinaria (Latin)

He tills another's field and leaves his own un-
tended (speaking of adultery).

ADVANTAGE
see also Blessings.

Le profit de l'un est le dommage de l'autre.

MICHEL DE MONTAIGNE:
Essays (French)

One man's advantage is another's loss.

Denn nur vom Nutzen wird die Welt regiert.

J. C. F. VON SCHILLER:
Wallensteins Tod (German)

The world is ruled only by considerations of
advantage.

En tierra de ciegos, el tuerto es rey.

SPANISH PROVERB

In the land of the blind, the one-eyed man is
king.

ADVENTURE
see also Youth.

La mer promet monts et merveilles;
Fiez-vous-y, les vents el les voleurs viendront.

JEAN DE LA FONTAINE:
Le Berger et la Mer (French)

The ocean promises mountains and marvels,
but beware! there are tempests and pirates as
well.

ADVERSITY
see also Difficulty, Disaster, Friendship, Misery, Misfortune, Rebuke, Sorrow.

Ne soyez pas un vaincu!

ARTHUR RIMBAUD:
L'Impossible (French)

Never admit defeat!

Le monde est rempli de beaucoup de traverses.

MOLIÈRE:
L'Etourdi (French)

The world is full of troubles.

A raconter ses maux souvent on les soulage.

PIERRE CORNEILLE:
Polyeucte (French)

By speaking of one's woes, one often assuages
them.

Grâce aux dieux! Mon malheur passe mon espérance!

JEAN RACINE:
Andromaque (French)

The gods be praised! My misfortunes surpass
even my expectation!

C'est donc estre misérable que de se connoistre
misérable; mais c'est estre grand que de connoistre qu'on est misérable.

BLAISE PASCAL:
Pensées (French)

It is a misery to know one's misery, but to
recognise it is to be great.

Le plus souvent,
Quand on pense sortir d'une mauvaise affaire,
On s'enfonce encore plus avant.

JEAN DE LA FONTAINE:
La Vieille et les Deux Servantes (French)

Very often, when one thinks of a way to get out of
a difficulty, one gets into still greater difficulties.

Staub soll er fressen, und mit Lust.

J. W. VON GOETHE:
Faust (prologue to Heaven) *(German)*

Dust shall he eat, and that with zest.

Wan daz daz wazzer fliuzet als uz wilent flôz
Für wâr ich wânde min unglucke wurde grôz.

WALTHER VON DER VOGELWEIDE:
Owê war sint verswunden allui minui jâr (German)

If the streams did not flow as they did in my youth, I should think my misfortune great.

Ob er heilig, ob er böse,
Jammert sie den Unglücksmann.

J. W. VON GOETHE:
Faust (German)

Whether he's holy or wicked, they pity this woeful man.

Wer den Schaden hat, braucht für den Spott nicht zu sorgen.

GERMAN PROVERB

The laugh is always on the loser.

Apōlomesth' ar', ei kakon prosoisomen
Neon palaiōi, prin tod' exēntlekenai

EURIPIDES:
Medea (Greek)

If we are to be faced with yet more difficulties before solving these, then we are done for.

To gar esleussein oikeia pathē,
Mēdenos allou parapraxantos,
Megalas odunas hupoteinei

SOPHOCLES:
Ajax (Greek)

The keenest sorrow is to recognise ourselves as the sole cause of all our adversities.

Gnōsēi d' anthrōpous authaireta pēmat' ek hontas

PYTHAGORAS:
Golden Verses (Greek)

Know that men suffer under the evils they have brought upon themselves.

Endustukhēsai tounom' epitēdeios ei

EURIPIDES:
The Bacchae (Greek)

You bear an apt name for calamity (Dionysus to the doomed Pentheus; *penthos*, grief).

Triste lupus stabulis, maturis frugibus imbres,
Arboribus venti.

VIRGIL
Eclogues (Latin)

The flocks fear the wolf, the ripe crops the storm and the trees the wind.

Nullumne malorum finem adeo poenaque dabis?

C. VALERIUS FLACCUS
Opera (Latin)

Will you make no end at all to calamity and punishment?

Sed quem felicitas amicum fecit, infortunium faciet inimicum.

BOETHIUS:
Consolatio Philosophiae (Latin)

He whom prosperity makes our friend, adversity shall make him our enemy.

Dies atri.

LATIN EXPRESSION

Unlucky days.

Fortes simus adversus fortuita.

SENECA:
Epistles (Latin)

Let us be brave in the face of adversity.

Ne sis miser ante tempus.

SENECA:
Epistles (Latin)

Don't worry before it's time to do so.

Nulla autem causa vitae est ... si timeatur quantum potest.

SENECA:
Epistles (Latin)

If we let things terrify us, life will not be worth living.

Omnes, quibu' res sunt minu' secundae, mage sunt nescioquo modo

Suspiciosi; ad contumeliam omnia accipiunt magis.

TERENCE:
Adelphoe (Latin)

Anyone who has bad luck always seems to get suspicious and to take offence at the slightest thing.

Enim fortuna malignior unquam
Eripiet nobis quod prior hora dedit.

PETRONIUS:
Satyricon (Latin)

Ill-luck can never take away those experiences the past has given us.

Miseros prudentia prima relinquit.

OVID:
Ex Ponto (Latin)

Prudence is the first to abandon the wretched.

Quocirca vivite fortes,
Fortiaque adversis opponite pectora rebus.

HORACE:
Satires (Latin)

Live bravely and present a brave front to adversity!

Miserrimum est timere, cum speres nihil.

SENECA:
Troades (Latin)

When the situation is hopeless, it is wretched to be afraid.

Nulla lux umquam mihi secura fulsit.

SENECA:
Hercules Furens (Latin)

No untroubled day has ever dawned for me.

Quem saepe transit casus, aliquando invenit.

SENECA:
Hercules Furens (Latin)

Calamity may pass you by time and again, but she will eventually find you.

Illic homo a me sibi malam rem arcessit jumento suo.

PLAUTUS:
Amphitruo (Latin)

That man brings misfortune on his own head!

Sequitur varam vibiam.

LATIN PROVERB
quoted by Ausonius

Misfortunes never come singly (*lit.* the table-top follows the trestle, *i.e.* one evil brings another in its train).

Quem deus vult perdere dementat prius.

LATIN PROVERB
deriving from Euripides: *Alcestis*

Whom the gods would destroy they first make mad.

Multum nuper amisimus.

QUINTILIAN:
Institutiones Oratoriae (Latin)

Lately we have had many losses.

Finis alterius mali gradus est futuri.

SENECA:
Hercules Furens (Latin)

The end of one ill is only a step toward the next.

Quem males sentiu
Saiba já temer,
E pelo que viu
Julgue o que ha de ser.

LUIS DE CAMÕES:
Vae o bem Fugindo (Portuguese)

He who has seen misery, let him learn to fear, and judge what is to come from what has already happened.

No hay más chinches que la manta llena.

SPANISH PROVERB

You can't have more bedbugs than a blanket-full.

Dios no nos envía más carga que la que poder-
mos cargar!

> PALACIO VALDÉS:
> *Santa Rogelia (Spanish)*

God send us no more burdens than we can
endure!

ADVERTISEMENT

Letras de luz pronuncian,
Silabario del vértigo,
Palabrerías bruscas.

> JORGE GUILLÉN:
> *Noche Céntrica (Spanish)*

Letters of light pronounce – grammar of vertigo
– their fretful rigmarole.

ADVICE
see also Action, Candour, Example, Problems, Time, Wisdom.

Qu'il est difficile de proposer une chose au
jugement d'un autre sans corrompre son jugement par la manière de la luy proposer.

> BLAISE PASCAL:
> *Pensées (French)*

What a difficult thing it is to ask someone's
advice on a matter without colouring his judgment by the way in which we present our
problem.

On ne donne rien si libéralement que ses con-
seils.

> FRANÇOIS, DUC DE LA ROCHEFOUCAULD:
> *Réflexions (French)*

There is nothing so liberally offered as advice.

On peut couper à Samson sa chevelure, mais il
ne faut pas lui conseiller de prendre perruque.

> FRENCH PROVERB

You can cut off Samson's hair, but you must not
advise him to wear a wig.

Ach, bitter bereut, wer des Weisen Rat scheut
Und vom Alter sich nicht lässen beraten!

> BERTOLT BRECHT:
> *Die Ballade von dem Soldaten (German)*

How you will regret that you spurned good
advice, and ignored the counsel of your elders!

Onōi tis elege muthon, ho de ta ōta ekinei

> GREEK PROVERB

To preach to deaf ears (*lit.* someone told a story
to an ass and he moved his ears).

Phronein gar hoi takheis ouk asphaleis

> SOPHOCLES:
> *Oedipus Tyrannus (Greek)*

Hasty advice is unreliable.

Hē de kakē boulē tōi bouleusanti kakistē

> HESIOD:
> *Works and Days (Greek)*

Bad advice harms him most who gives it.

Kai mēn touto ge auto, hē euboulia, dēlon hoti
epistēmē tis estin. Ou gar pou amathiai ge all'
epistēmēi eu bouleuontai

> PLATO:
> *The Republic (Greek)*

Good advice is a form of wisdom, and it cannot
be derived from ignorance or stupidity.

Grave errore è de' giovani Signori,
Che i consigli de' vecchi habbiano a schifo,
E i giovanili pregino, et che paia,
Che come lor va un huom canuto innanzi,
Di veder comparer' un lor nemico.

> GIAMBATTISTA CINTHIO GIRALDI:
> *Arrenopia (Italian)*

Young rulers make a serious mistake in ignoring
the advice of the old and preferring that of the
young; and in thinking that the white-haired
men who approach them are their enemies.

Malum consilium consultori pessimum est.

> LATIN PROVERB

Bad counsel is most ruinous to the giver.

Consiliarium est quod cogitanti factum est.

> SENECA:
> *Natural Questions (Latin)*

Advice is for those contemplating action.

Accipite haec animis laetasque advertite mentes.

VIRGIL:
Aeneid (Latin)

Heed these words cheerfully and take them to heart.

Quot homines, tot sententiae.   TERENCE:
Phormio (Latin)

You will find as many opinions as there are men.

Narrare asello fabellam surdo.   HORACE:
Epistles (Latin)

To preach to deaf ears (*lit.* to tell a tale to a deaf donkey).

Non verba me adnumerare lectori putavi oportere, sed tamquam appendere.

CICERO:
De Optimo Genere Oratorum (Latin)

It has seemed to me more necessary to have regard to the weight of words rather than to their number.

Facile omnes quom valemu' recta consilia aegrotis damus.

TERENCE:
Andria (Latin)

It is easy for a man in good health to offer advice to the sick.

No me den consejos, sino dineros!

SPANISH PROVERB

Don't offer me advice, give me money!

AESTHETICS

Ethik und Ästhetik sind Eins.

LUDWIG WITTGENSTEIN:
Tractatus Logico-philosophicus (German)

Ethics and aesthetics are one and the same.

AFFINITY

Hōs aiei ton homoion agei theos hōs ton homoion

HOMER:
Odyssey (Greek)

How God always brings like to like!

AFRICA

Semper Africa aliquid novi affert.

PLINY:
Natural History (Latin)

There's always something new coming out of Africa.

Teneo te, Africa!

SUETONIUS:
Divus Iulius (Latin)

Africa, I hold thee fast! (Julius Caesar's words as he stumbled, on disembarking on the African coast).

AGE
see also Mankind, Old age, Wisdom.

A los veinte años será pavón, a los treinta león, a los cuarenta camello, a los cincuenta serpiente, a los sesenta perro, a los setenta mona, y a los ochenta nada.

BALTASAR GRACIÁN:
Oráculo Manual y Arte de Prudencia (Spanish)

At twenty a man will be a peacock, at thirty a lion, at forty a camel, at fifty a serpent, at sixty a dog, at seventy a monkey, and at eighty, nothing at all!

A los veinte años reina la voluntad, a los treinta el ingenio, a los cuarenta el juicio.

BALTASAR GRACIÁN:
Oráculo Manual y Arte de Prudencia (Spanish)

At twenty the will is in command, at thirty the intellect, and at forty the judgement.

AGGRAVATION

Oleum adde camino.

HORACE:
Satires (Latin)

Pour oil on the fire (*i.e.* aggravate the issue).

AGREEMENT AND DISAGREEMENT
see also Unity.

Ast alii sex
Et plures uno conclamant ore.

JUVENAL:
Satires (Latin)

Six more at least voice their agreement.

Concordia discors.

> LUCAN:
> *The Civil War (Latin)*

Ha ionious discord.

Dissentientibus principibus, consequens est ut in multitudine sequatur dissensio.

> ST. THOMAS AQUINAS:
> *On Princely Government (Latin)*

If the rulers disagree, the result will be general dissension.

AMBITION
see also Achievement, Anger, Aspiration, Moderation, Money, Second-best, Single-mindedness, Virtue.

Quel vicaire de village ne voudrait pas être Pape?

> VOLTAIRE:
> *Lettres Philosophiques (French)*

What parish priest would not wish to be pope? (This passage was omitted from editions published after 1739.)

L'ambition prend aux petites âmes plus facilement qu'aux grandes, comme le feu prend plus aisément à la paille aux chaumières qu'aux palais.

> S. R. N. CHAMFORT:
> *Maximes et Pensées (French)*

Ambition gains control of little men more easily than of great, just as fire sets the straw alight more easily in thatched cottages than in palaces.

On passe souvent de l'amour à l'ambition, mais on ne revient guère de l'ambition à l'amour.

> FRANÇOIS, DUC DE LA ROCHEFOUCAULD:
> *Réflexions (French)*

From love we often pass to ambition, but we rarely return from ambition to love.

Heftigen Ehrgeiz und Misstrauen habe ich noch allemal beisammen gesehen.

> GEORG CHRISTOPH LICHTENBERG:
> *Aphorismen (German)*

I have always seen unbridled ambition accompanied by distrust.

Die Bahn ist breit genug, um vielen Bewerbern Um den Preis neben einander Raum zu geben

> CONRAD BURSIAN:
> *Geschichte der klassischen Philologie in Deutschland (German)*

The way is wide enough for many aspirants for the prize to make room for each other.

Ou pantos andros es Korinthon esth' ho plous

> GREEK PROVERB

Not everyone achieves his goal in life (*lit.* not everyone's journey is to Corinth – *i.e.* a very rich city).

Mēdeis zētēsēi meropōn pote kai theos einai, mēd' arkhēn megalēn, kompon huperphialon

> PALLADAS OF ALEXANDRIA:
> *Epigrams (Greek)*

It is not fitting for mankind to aspire to the attributes of the gods, or even to those of high office.

Eikē gar ouden poiēteon

> MARCUS AURELIUS:
> *Meditations (Greek)*

Without a purpose nothing should be done.

Li uomini mutano volontieri signore credendo migliorare.

> NICCOLÒ MACHIAVELLI:
> *The Prince (Italian)*

In the hope of bettering themselves, men willingly change masters.

Si quantum cuperem, possem quoque.

> PORPHYRY:
> *Letters to Horace (Latin)*

I may desire great things, but I also have the power.

Nec semper feriet quodcunque minabitur arcus.

> HORACE:
> *Ars Poetica (Latin)*

Nor will the arrow always hit the mark at which it is aimed.

Magnum iter ascendo, sed dat mihi gloria vires;
Non iuvat e facili lecta corona iugo.

PROPERTIUS:
Elegies (Latin)

Great is the road I climb, but ambition strengthens my task; the garland offered by an easier effort is not worth the gathering.

En gran río, gran pez; mas ahógase alguna vez.
SPANISH PROVERB

There are big fish in large rivers – but sometimes you'll get drowned.

Y mientras miserable –
mente se están los otros abrasando
en sed insacïable
del no durable mando,
tendido yo a la sombra esté cantando.

FRAY LUIS DE LEÓN:
Vida Retirada (Spanish)

Let me sing my song in the shade, while others miserably pledge themselves to the insatiable pursuit of ambition and brief power.

AMERICA

En Amérique, non seulement il existe des institutions communales, mais encore un esprit communal qui les soutient et les vivifie.

ALEXIS DE TOCQUEVILLE:
De la Démocratie en Amérique (French)

In America there are not only communal institutions, but also a community spirit that supports and enlivens them.

En Amérique l'homme n'obéit jamais à l'homme, mais à la justice ou à la loi.

ALEXIS DE TOCQUEVILLE:
De la Démocratie en Amérique (French)

In America people never obey people, but justice or the law.

L'habitant des Etats-Unis apprend dès sa naissance qu'il faut s'appuyer sur soi-même pour lutter contre les maux et les embarras de la vie.

ALEXIS DE TOCQUEVILLE:
De la Démocratie en Amérique (French)

Americans realise from the time of their birth that they must rely on their own efforts to combat the evils and vexations of life.

ANARCHY

Dame dynamite, que l'on danse vite . . .
Dansons et chansons et dynamitons!
French anarchist song of the 1880s

Dame Dynamite, let's dance quickly . . . let's dance and sing and blow up everything!

Le plus grand danger de la bombe est dans l'explosion de bêtise qu'elle provoque.

OCTAVE MIRBEAU:
Oeuvres (French)

The greatest danger of bombs is the explosion of stupidity that they provoke.

ANCESTORS

Le plus beau patrimoine est un nom révéré.
VICTOR HUGO:
Odes et Ballades (French)

The finest inheritance is a respected name.

Parmi les morts, il y en a toujours quelques-uns qui désolent les vivants.

DENIS DIDEROT:
Le Neveu de Rameau (French)

There are always some of the dead who will trouble the living.

Hēmeis toi paterōn meg' ameinones eukhometh' einai

HOMER:
Iliad (Greek)

We are far better men than our fathers.

Stemmata quid faciunt?

JUVENAL:
Satires (Latin)

What is the use of your pedigrees?

ANGELS
see also Insignificance, Mankind, Morals and morality, Patience.

Jeder Engel ist schrecklich.

RAINER MARIA RILKE:
Duineser Elegien (German)

Every angel is terrible.

ANGER

see also Cunning, Emotions, Indignation, Injustice, Life, Love, Time.

Awwil ghaḍab junūn wa-akhir-uh nadāma
ARAB PROVERB

Wrath begins in madness and ends in repentance.

La colère n'est bonne à rien.
P.A.C. DE BEAUMARCHAIS:
Le Mariage de Figaro (French)

Anger will get you nowhere.

J'enrage de bon coeur d'avoir tort, lorsque j'ai raison.
MOLIÈRE:
George Dandin (French)

It infuriates me to be wrong when I know I'm right.

Bezähme jeder die gerechte Wut
Und spare für das Ganze seine Rache:
Denn Raub begeht am allgemeinenen Gut,
Wer selbst sich hilft in seiner eignen Sache.
J. C. F. VON SCHILLER:
Works (German)

Each of us must restrain our righteous wrath and keep our revenge for the final reckoning. Anyone who acts by himself for himself alone harms our common cause.

Thumos de kreissōn tōn emōn bouleumatōn,
Hosper megistōn aitios kakōn brotois
EURIPIDES:
Medea (Greek)

I am overcome by anger, that source of lasting evil, in spite of my reason.

Kholou krateein!
GREEK PROVERB (attrib. Periander)

Control your anger!

Hōsper te hē lupē asthenous, outōs kai hē orgē
MARCUS AURELIUS:
Meditations (Greek)

Anger, like grief, is a weakness.

Quo quisque est maior, magis est placabilis irae.
OVID:
Tristia (Latin)

The greater the man, the more restrained his anger.

Pone irae frena modumque.
JUVENAL:
Satires (Latin)

Put a curb on and control your anger.

Procul omnis esto
Clamor et ira.
HORACE:
Odes (Latin)

Let all noise and anger be far off.

Iratus de re incerta contendere noli:
Impedit animum, ne possis cernere verum.
Catonis Disticha (Latin)

Control your anger until you know the facts. Anger clouds the soul, and impedes your judgment.

Ira furor brevis est.
HORACE:
Epistles (Latin)

Fury is a brief madness.

Non dico horrendam rabiem!
HORACE:
Satires (Latin)

To say nothing of your terrible temper!

In pectoribus ira considit: feras quidem mentes obsidet, eruditas praelabitur.
PETRONIUS:
Satyricon (Latin)

Anger dwells in our hearts; it takes root in savages, but slides over men of learning.

Eripere telum non dare irato decet.
LATIN PROVERB

Anger should be robbed of its weapon, not given one.

Bonum ad virum cito moritur iracundia.
LATIN PROVERB

In the good man anger quickly dies.

Legem solet obliviscier iracundia.
LATIN PROVERB

Anger usually forgets the law.

Atraviesan el cuerpo las jaras, pero las malas palabras el alma.
SPANISH PROVERB

Arrows pierce the body, but harsh words pierce the soul.

La codicia en las manos de la suerte
Se arroja al mar, la ira a las espadas,
Y la ambición se ríe de la muerte.
Epístola Moral (attrib. Andrés
Fernández de Andrada) (Spanish)

Greed in the hands of destiny braves the ocean,
Anger throws itself on the swords of the enemy,
And ambition laughs at death.

ANIMALS
see also Mankind.

Haben die Tiere weniger Angst, weil sie ohne Worte leben?
ELIAS CANETTI:
Aufzeichnungen, 1949 (German)

Is it possible that animals have less worries since they live without speech?

ANTICIPATION
see also Desire.

Lā tiqūl fūl ḥatta yiṣīr fi' l-makyūl
ARAB PROVERB

Don't count your chickens before they are hatched (lit. don't say beans until they are in the measure).

Hätte ich nicht die Welt durch Anticipation bereits in mir getragen, ich wäre mit sehenden Augen blind geblieben.
J. W. VON GOETHE:
Letter to J. P. Eckermann, 26 February 1824
(German)

If I had not already experienced the world in anticipation, I should have remained blind to what I saw.

. . . cum lux altera venit,
Iam cras hesternum consumpsimus.
PERSIUS:
Satires (Latin)

When tomorrow comes we shall already have spent yesterday's morrow.

ANTIQUITY
see also Renaissance.

Le moyen âge, si profond, si original, si poétique dans l'élan de son enthousiasme religieux, n'est, sous le rapport de la culture intellectuelle, qu'un long tâtonnement pour revenir à la grande école de la noble pensée, c'est-à-dire à l'antiquité.
ERNEST RENAN:
Averroès (preface) (French)

The Middle Ages, so profound, so original, so poetic in their surge of religious enthusiasm, were, as far as intellectual development is concerned, only feeling their way cautiously back to that great training-ground of high endeavour, antiquity.

APPEARANCE
see also Life, Merit.

. . . la plus forte apparence
Peut jeter dans l'esprit une fausse créance.
MOLIÈRE:
Sganarelle (French)

The most obvious appearances can give rise to false beliefs.

Garde-toi, tant que tu vivras,
De juger des gens sur la mine.
JEAN DE LA FONTAINE:
Le Cochet, le Chat et le Souriceau (French)

Beware, throughout your life, of judging people by their appearance.

De loin c'est quelque chose, et de près ce n'est rien.
JEAN DE LA FONTAINE:
Le Chameau et les Batons Flottants (French)

What from afar appears to be important, on nearer inspection can prove to be insignificant.

Les visages souvent sont de doux imposteurs.
PIERRE CORNEILLE:
Le Menteur (French)

[Women's] faces are often sweet imposters.

Tout ce qui brille n'est pas or.
FRENCH PROVERB

All that glitters is not gold.

L'insolent de caractère n'insulte que de temps en temps, l'insolent de physionomie insulte toujours.
DENIS DIDEROT:
Le Neveu de Rameau (French)

An overbearing character only offends from time to time, but a haughty expression always offends.

L'habit ne fait pas le moine.
FRENCH PROVERB

Clothes don't make the gentleman (lit. the monk).

C'est brutal, mais ça marche!
RENÉ PANHARD
commenting on the car gearbox
which he had invented (French)

It's crude, but it works!

Das Ärgste weiss die Welt von mir, und ich
Kann sagen, ich bin besser als mein Ruf.
J. C. F. VON SCHILLER:
Maria Stuart (German)

The world knows the worst about me, and I can say that I am better than my reputation (Maria Stuart speaking to Queen Elizabeth).

Was man scheint, hat jedermann zum Richter, was
Man ist, hat keinen.
J. C. F. VON SCHILLER:
Maria Stuart (German)

Everyone judges you by appearances, not by what you really are.

Ognuno vede quel che tu pari, pochi sentono quel tu sei.
NICCOLÒ MACHIAVELLI:
The Prince (Italian)

Everyone sees you as you appear to be, few realise what you really are.

Bisogna adunque essere volpe a conoscere i lacci, e lione a sbigottire i lupi.
NICCOLÒ MACHIAVELLI:
The Prince (Italian)

It is necessary to be a fox to recognise the snares, and a lion to terrorise the wolves.

El vulgo ne va preso con quello che para e con lo evento della cosa.
NICCOLÒ MACHIAVELLI:
The Prince (Italian)

People are always taken in by appearances and by the outcome of events.

Frontis nulla fides.
JUVENAL:
Satires (Latin)

Do not trust men's faces.

Si brevis es sedeas, ne stans, videare sedere.
OVID:
Ars Amatoria (Latin)

If you are short, sit, lest standing you appear to be seated.

Usque adhuc certe et animum meum probastis et vultum.
SUETONIUS:
Domitianus (Latin)

So far, at any rate, you have approved my heart and my countenance (Domitian was noted for the modesty of his expression).

APPETITE
see also Compromise, Hunger.

Meiri vil meiri hava.
FAROESE PROVERB

Appetite comes with eating (lit. more demands more).

L'homme qui mange est le plus juste des hommes.
PAUL VALÉRY:
L'Ame et la Danse (French)

The man who eats is the most just of men (referring to man's giving impartial sustenance to both his virtues and his vices).

On le mange, mais on ne le digère pas.
S. R. N. CHAMFORT:
Caractères et Anecdotes (French)

You eat it, but you don't digest it (speaking of a host who entertained well, but who was found very boring by his guests).

L'appétit vient en mangeant.
FRENCH PROVERB

Appetite grows with eating.

Quanto plura parasti
Tanto plura cupis.
HORACE:
Epistles (Latin)

The more you get, the more you want.

Ieiunus raro stomachus vulgaria temnit.
HORACE:
Satires (Latin)

Only a stomach that rarely feels hungry scorns common things.

Ingenii largitor venter.
LATIN PROVERB

The belly rules the mind.

No hay salsa como la buena gana.
SPANISH PROVERB

There's no sauce like a good appetite.

APPLAUSE
see also Success.

Epei de panu kalōs pepaistai, dote kroton kai pantes ēmas meta kharas propempsate
SUETONIUS:
Divus Augustus (Greek)

Since I have played my part well, all clap your hands and, with applause, dismiss me from this stage (Augustus's dying words to his friends).

Rumore secundo.
LATIN PHRASE

Amid shouts of support.

Aura popularis.
LIVY:
History (Latin)

Popular favour (*lit.* popular breeze).

ARGUMENT
see also Thought and thinking.

Hippeas eis pedion prokalei Sōkratē eis logous prokaloumenos
PLATO:
Theaetetus (Greek)

Inviting Socrates to join in an argument is like inviting the cavalry to battle on an open plain.

To gar homologēthen para beltionōn pou kuriōteron ē to para kheironōn
PLATO:
The Sophist (Greek)

What is confirmed by worthy men is more respected than that confirmed by less worthy men.

Pōs oun an pote tis pros ge ton epistamenon autos anepistēmōn ōn dunait' an hugies ti legōn anteipein?
PLATO:
The Sophist (Greek)

In arguing with an expert, how can any ignorant man contribute anything of worth?

Andra d' ouden' oid' egō
Dikaion hostis ex hapantos eu legei
SOPHOCLES:
Oedipus Coloneus (Greek)

No honest man can argue both sides well.

Amphēkēs glōtta
ARISTOTLE:
(Greek)

A tongue that will cut both ways (*i.e.* will maintain either right or wrong).

ARMS
See also Battles, Belligerence, Patriotism, War.

Des enfants de Japet toujours une moitié
Fournira des armes à l'autre.
JEAN DE LA FONTAINE:
L'Oiseau Blessé d'une Flèche (French)

One half of the children of Japhet [mankind] will always supply arms to the other (to fight it with). (Traditionally the Indo-European family is supposed to be descended from Japhet.)

Que ce soit pour le gouvernement, que ce soit pour les adversaires du gouvernement, les armes viennent toujours du même fournisseur. Les armes n'ont pas d'opinion.

JACQUES AUDIBERTI:
La Poupée (French)

Whether they are for the government or for the government's enemies, arms always come from the same suppliers. Arms have no political allegiance of their own.

Arma virumque cano.

VIRGIL:
Aeneid (opening words) (Latin)

I sing of arms and the man.

Arma relinque viris.

CLAUDIAN:
In Eutropium (Latin)

Leave arms to men of strength.

Occidat, immerita qui carpsit ab arbore vallum
Et struxit querulas rauca per ossa tubas.

PROPERTIUS:
Elegies (Latin)

He falls; he who turned the undeserving trees into ramparts, and wrought plaintive trumpets from harsh bones.

ART AND ARTISTS
see also Civilisation, Intellect, Painters and painting.

L'oeuvre d'art est une exagération.

ANDRÉ GIDE:
Journal, 1889–1939 (French)

A work of art is an exaggeration.

L'art est long, et le Temps est court.

CHARLES BAUDELAIRE:
Le Guignon (French)

Art is long, time is short.

A l'oeuvre on connaît l'artisan

JEAN DE LA FONTAINE:
Les Frelons et les Mouches à Miel (French)

You shall know an artist by his work.

L'Art est bête.

ARTHUR RIMBAUD:
(French)

Art is stupid.

L'art pour l'art.

FRENCH SLOGAN

Art for art's sake.

Nature diversifie et imite, artifice imite et diversifie.

BLAISE PASCAL:
Pensées (French)

Nature diversifies and imitates, art imitates and diversifies.

Certains ouvrages sont créés par leur public. Certains autres créent leur public.

PAUL VALÉRY:
Choses Tues (French)

Some works gain reputation through their public.
Others create their public.

C'est dommage qu'on ne puisse transposer de la peinture en la littérature.

STÉPHANE MALLARMÉ:
letter to Marius Roux *(French)*

What a pity one cannot transpose painting into literature!

L'homme ne se supporte vraiment lui-même que dans les activités les moins nécessaires à la vie.

VERCORS:
Ce que je Crois (French)

Man is only truly self-supporting in those activities least necessary to life.

Il faut prendre beaucoup sur soi pour vouloir s'établir dans ces régions reculées, où tout a d'abord l'air de se passer si mal, à plus forte raison pour vouloir y conduire quelqu'un.

ANDRÉ BRETON:
Manifeste du Surréalisme (French)

We have to take much on ourselves to want to establish ourselves in these recondite areas where at first everything seems to be going so badly – all the more so if we intend to take anyone there.

Die Kunstgebilde leiten die Augen auf sich.
ADALBERT STIFTER:
Der Nachsommer (German)

One's gaze is drawn to what has been created by art.

Sie sieht den Menschen in des Lebens Drang
Und wälzt die grössre Hälfte seiner Schuld
Den unglückseligen Gestirnen zu.
J. C. F. VON SCHILLER:
Prologue to the Wallenstein trilogy *(German)*

[Art] looks on man in life's struggle, exonerating him from the greater portion of blame and attributing it to the malign stars.

Mit der Wahrheit hat die Kunst doch nichts zu tun!
WOLFGANG BORCHERT:
Draussen vor der Tür (German)

Art has nothing to do with truth!

Die Kunst nur dadurch wahr ist, dass sie das Wirkliche ganz verlässt und rein ideell wird.
J. C. F. VON SCHILLER:
Über den Gebrauch des Chors
in der Tragödie (German)

Art only achieves truth by completely forsaking reality and becoming purely ideal.

Hier gilt's der Kunst.
Eva's motto from Richard Wagner's
opera *Die Meistersinger (German)*

Our aim is art.

. . . ewig ist die arme Kunst gezwungen,
Zu betteln von des Lebens Überfluss!
FRANZ GRILLPARZER:
Sappho (German)

Impoverished art is eternally forced to beg from life's plenty!

Die Kunst hat die Tendenz, wieder Natur zu sein.
ARNO HOLZ:
Works (German)

Art has a tendency to revert to nature.

Vor der Kunst wie vor dem Gesetz sind alle Menschen gleich.
GERHART HAUPTMANN:
Die Ratten (German)

Before art, as before the law, all men are equal.

Die Kunst ist eine verführerische, verbotene Frucht.
WILHELM HEINRICH WACKENRODER:
'Ein Brief Joseph Berglingers', in
Phantasien über die Kunst (German)

Art is a seductive, forbidden fruit.

Ek phuseōs tekhnē, ou gar phusin heureto tekhnē
JULIAN,
prefect of Egypt *(Greek)*

Art is the child of nature, for art did not invent nature.

Hē tekhnē ta men epitelei ha hē phusis adunatei apergasasthai ta de mimeitai
ARISTOTLE:
Physica (Greek)

Art not only imitates nature, but also completes its deficiencies.

Mē skhoinōi Persidi tēn sophiēn [krinete]
CALLIMACHUS:
Aetia (Greek)

Don't use a Persian rope (*i.e.* something unsuitable) to measure art.

Hai tekhnai tas phuseis mimountai
MARCUS AURELIUS:
Meditations (Greek)

Art mimics nature.

Hē te gar tekhnē pasa touto stokhazetai, hina to kataskeuasthen epitēdeiōs ekhēi pros to ergon pros ho kateskeuastai
MARCUS AURELIUS:
Meditations (Greek)

The aim of every art is to ensure that the thing designed should be suited to the work for which it is designed.

Gignetai de tekhnē, hotan ek pollōn tēs empeirias ennoēmatōn mia kath' holou genētai peri ton homoiōn hupolēpsis

> ARISTOTLE:
> *Metaphysics (Greek)*

Art is derived when a single universal judgment springs from many ideas born of experience.

Omne namque esse ex forma est.

> BOETHIUS:
> *De Trinitate (Latin)*

Everything owes its being to form.

Omnis ars naturae imitatio est.

> SENECA:
> *Epistles (Latin)*

The whole of art is only an imitation of nature.

Amor ingenii, neminem unquam divitem fecit.

> PETRONIUS:
> *Satyricon (Latin)*

Love of art has never yet enriched anyone.

Nulla ars absque magistro discitur.

> ST. JEROME:
> *Letter to Rusticus (Latin)*

No art is learnt without a master.

Ars longa, vita brevis.

> LATIN PROVERB

Art is long, life is short.

In quolibet artifice praeexistit ratio eorum quae constituuntur per artem.

> ST. THOMAS AQUINAS:
> *Summa Theologica (Latin)*

In every artist's mind there already exists the idea of what he will create by his art.

Ea, quae sunt secundum artem, imitantur ea, quae sunt secundum naturam.

> ST. THOMAS AQUINAS:
> *On Princely Government (Latin)*

That which is art imitates that which is nature.

Ars imitatur naturam.

> ST. THOMAS AQUINAS:
> *Commentary on the Politics of Aristotle (Latin)*

Art imitates nature.

Saepe bona materia cessat sine artifice.

> SENECA:
> *(Latin)*

Good material often stands idle for want of an artist.

Inventas aut qui vitam excoluere per artis.

> VIRGIL:
> *Aeneid (Latin)*

You may find people who refine life through the arts.

El arte es la misma Naturaleza.

> SPANISH PROVERB

Art is Nature herself.

Si cuando se admira a un artista, no debía una conocerle personalmente.

> JACINTO BENAVENTE Y MARTINEZ:
> *Lo Cursi (Spanish)*

When one admires an artist, it is important not to know him personally.

ARTIFICIALITY

Ich hab mich so an Künstliches verloren,
Dass ich die Sonne sah aus toten Augen
Und nicht mehr hörte als durch toten Ohren.

> HUGO VON HOFMANNSTHAL:
> *Der Tor und der Tod (German)*

I had so abandoned myself to artificiality that I saw the sun with dead eyes, and could no longer hear, save with deaf ears. (The aesthete Claudio bitterly regretting his misspent life).

ASPIRATION
see also Achievement, Ambition, Effort, Revelation.

Montons au plus haut de notre tour d'ivoire, sur la dernière marche, le plus près du ciel!

> GUSTAVE FLAUBERT:
> *Correspondance (French)*

Let's climb up to the top of our ivory tower, right up to the last step, close to the heavens!

mourut poursuivant une haute aventure;
e ciel fut son désir, la mer sa sépulture:
st-il plus beau dessin, ou plus riche tombeau?

PHILIPPE DESPORTES:
Icare (French)

e died in pursuit of a great adventure: the
eavens were his aim, the sea his tomb. Can
ere be a finer intent, or a finer sepulchre?

'homme est absurde par ce qu'il cherche;
rand par ce qu'il trouve.

PAUL VALÉRY:
Moralités (French)

Ian's aspiration is absurd; it is by what he
iscovers that he is great.

hacun tourne en réalités
utant qu'il peut ses propres songes.

JEAN DE LA FONTAINE:
Le Statuaire et la Statue de Jupiter (French)

veryone tries to realise his aspirations as far as
ossible.

ur rastlos betätigt sich der Mann.

J. W. VON GOETHE:
Faust (German)

Ian's restlessness makes him strive.

Ver immer strebend sich bemüht
en können wir erlösen.

J. W. VON GOETHE:
Faust (German)

Ve can redeem anyone who strives unceasingly.

er Zweck des Lebens ist das Leben selbst.

J. W. VON GOETHE:
(German)

he aim of living is life itself.

an zētēis kalōs, heurēseis

GREEK PROVERB

f you seek well, you will find.

Quod nimis miseri volunt hoc facile credunt.

SENECA:
Hercules Furens (Latin)

oor people willingly believe what they long for
eyond reason.

Superata tellus sidera donat.

BOETHIUS:
Consolatio Philosophiae (Latin)

Overcome the earth, and the stars shall be
yours.

Os homini sublime dedit caelumque videre
Iussit et erectos ad sidera tollere vultus.

OVID:
Metamorphoses (Latin)

God has uplifted man's countenance and demands that he keeps his gaze on the heavens.

Noctes atque dies niti praestante labore
Ad summas emergere opes rerumque potiri.

LUCRETIUS:
De Rerum Natura (Latin)

See how both night and day men strive with
outstanding effort to rise to utmost power and
seize the world.

Quicquid quaeritur, optimum videtur.

PETRONIUS:
Satyricon (Latin)

Whatever men aspire to, they deem best.

Nimio satiust, ut opust te ita esse, quam ut
animo lubet.

PLAUTUS:
Trinumnus (Latin)

Far better to be the man you ought to be, than
the man you incline to be.

ASSOCIATIONS

Quien con perros se acuesta con pulgas se
levanta.

SPANISH PROVERB

He who sleeps with dogs wakes up with fleas.

ASTRONOMY
see also Liberal, Stars, Zodiac.

Per varios usus artem experientia fecit
Exemplo mostrante viam.

MANILIUS:
Astronomica (Latin)

The art was learnt by experience gained
through practice, and the charts were based on
previous examples.

ATHEISM

Athéisme marque de force d'esprit, mais jusqu'à un certain degré seulement.

BLAISE PASCAL:
Pensées (French)

Atheism is a sign of mental strength, but only up to a certain point.

ATHLETICS

Citius, altius, fortius.
Official motto of the Olympic Games (*Latin*)

Swifter, higher, stronger.

Quis circum pagos et circum compita pugnax
Magna coronari contemnat Olympia, cui spes
Cui sit condicio dulcis sine pulvere palmae?

HORACE:
Epistles (Latin)

What local athlete would spurn the chance of an Olympic victory, if he could get it without the struggle involved?

Nemo athleta sine sudoribus coronatur.

ST. JEROME:
Letter to Heliodorus (Latin)

No athlete gains his crown without sweat.

ATONEMENT
see also Repentance.

Er büsst, er büsst gern, aber nur was er nicht verbrochen hat.

ELIAS CANETTI:
Aufzeichnungen, 1955 (German)

He makes no difficulty about making amends, but only for those things of which he is not guilty.

AUDIENCES

Ekousas ē ouk ēkousas, ē kōphēi legō?

AESCHYLUS:
The Seven against Thebes (Greek)

Are you listening, or am I talking to deaf ears?

Mēden, ē d' hos, oknei. Oute gar agnōmones oute apistoi oute dusnoi hoi akousomenoi

PLATO:
The Republic (Greek)

Don't be afraid! Your audience is not unsympathetic, nor is it unbelieving or hostile.

AUTHORITY
see also Kings, Obedience, Reason.

Hoti men presbuterous tous arkhontas dei einai, neōterous de tous arkhomenous, dēlon?

PLATO:
The Republic (Greek)

Is it not clear that the elders must rule, and the young must be ruled?

AUTHORSHIP
see also Books, Playwriting.

La main à plume vaut la main à charrue.

ARTHUR RIMBAUD:
Mauvais Sang (French)

The hand that guides the pen is as valuable as the hand that guides the plough.

Ne sachant m'expliquer sans paroles païennes, je voudrais me taire.

ARTHUR RIMBAUD:
Mauvais Sang (French)

If I cannot express myself without pagan words, I prefer to remain silent. (Rimbaud is trying to explain the words of an oracle).

L'acte d'écrire demande toujours un certain 'sacrifice de l'intellect'.

PAUL VALÉRY:
Monsieur Teste (preface) (*French*)

Writing always exacts a certain amount of intellectual sacrifice.

Il vaut mieux écrire de grandes choses que d'en exécuter de petites.

DENIS DIDEROT
Le Neveu de Rameau (French

Better to write great things than do small ones.

faut toujours couper le commencement et la
a de ce qu'on écrit. Pas d'introduction, pas de
ale.

STÉPHANE MALLARMÉ:
Propos sur la Poésie (French)

ne must always trim the beginning and the
ad of what one writes. Cut out the introduction
ad the ending.

a dernière chose qu'on trouve en faisant un
avrage, est de savoir celle qu'il faut mettre la
remière.

BLAISE PASCAL:
Pensées (French)

he last thing you find out in writing a book is
hat to put first!

n Auteur, homme de goût, est, parmi ce Public
asé, ce qu'une jeune femme est au milieu d'un
rcle de vieux libertins.

S. R. N. CHAMFORT:
Maximes et Pensées (French)

n author, a man of taste, is like a young woman
nong a group of old libertines in relation to
day's blasé audiences.

out écrit, extérieurement à son tresor, doit, par
gard envers ceux dont il emprunte, après tout,
our un objet autre, le langage, présenter, avec
s mots, un sens même indifférent.

STÉPHANE MALLARMÉ:
Le Mystère dans les Lettres (French)

hatever you write should, on the surface, out
respect for the sources from which you bor-
w, and for the sake of language, offer a sense of
rection however indifferent.

empéreur dicte ses ordres à ses capitaines, le
ape adresse des bulles à la chrétienté, et le fou
rit un livre.

ALOYSIUS BERTRAND:
Gaspard de la Nuit: A M. Sainte-Beuve (French)

n emperor issues his orders to his captains, the
ope addresses his bulls to the Christian world,
ad a fool writes a book.

Classique est l'écrivain qui porte un critique en
soi-même et qui l'associe étroitement à ses
travaux.

PAUL VALÉRY
(speaking of Baudelaire) *(French)*

The true author is his own critic, and is strict in
the application of criticism to his own works.

On décomposera l'homme en entier, l'on re-
trouvera peut-être les éléments de la pensée et de
la volonté; mais on recontrera toujours, sans
pouvoir le résoudre, cet x contre lequel je me
suis autrefois heurté. Cet x est la Parole, dont la
communication brule et dévora ceux qui ne sont
pas préparés à la reçevoir.

HONORÉ DE BALZAC:
Louis Lambert (French)

You can dissect man in his entirety, you can
perhaps retrieve elements of his thought and
will; but each time you will encounter – without
being able to deal with it – that 'x' I have
grappled with so often in the past. 'x' is The
Word whose communication burns and devours
those who are not prepared to receive it.

Polloi men boskontai en Aiguptōi poluphulōi
Bibliakoi kharakitai apeirita dērioōntes
Mouseōn en talarōi

TIMON OF ATHENS:
Fragments (Greek)

In the thronging lands of Egypt
There are many that are feeding,
Many scribblers on papyrus
Ever ceaselessly contending
In the bird-coup of the Muses (ie, the
Alexandrian Museum).
(*tr.* Sir John Sandys)

Homēron ex Homērou saphēnizein

GREEK SAYING
(sometimes attributed to Aristarchus)

Each author is his own best interpreter (*lit.*
Homer is the best interpreter of Homer).

Omne tulit punctum qui miscuit utile dulci,
Lectorem delectando pariterque monendo.

HORACE:
Ars Poetica (Latin)

He who has blended profit and pleasure,
delighting and instructing the reader at the
same time, wins all our votes.

Scribens est mortuus.

CICERO:
De Senectute (Latin)

He died while he was writing.

Mutavit mentem populus levis et calet uno
Scribendi studio.

HORACE:
Epistles (Latin)

Our fickle public has changed and burns with a
desire to write.

In verbis etiam tenuis cautusque serendis
Dixeris egregie.

HORACE:
Ars Poetica (Latin)

With a discriminating taste and with due care
in weaving your words together, you should
express yourself most pleasantly.

Mira mejor, que con el arte quiso
Vuestro ingenio sacar de la mentira
La verdad.

MARQUÉS DE ALCAÑICES:
Cervantes (Spanish)

Look more closely, see with what artistry this
talent extracts the truth from falsehood.

AUTOMATION

Jede Minute ein Ford kommt.

HAMILTON FISH ARMSTRONG
(in a speech to German businessmen, trying
to explain the American outlook) *(German)*

Every minute there's another Ford.

AUTUMN
see also Clouds, Moon, Sky.

Už jenom roztesknĕná elegie
z té zemĕ vlá zpod šlojiřových par.

J. S. MACHAR:
'Sonet řijnový' in *Podzimni Sonety (Czech)*

Now only a melancholy elegy wafts from this
earth from beneath veil-like mists.

L'automne souriait; les coteaux vers la plaine
Penchaient leurs bois charmants qui jaunis-
saient à peine;

Le ciel etait doré;
Et les oiseaux, tournés vers celui que tout
nomme,
Disant peut-être à Dieu quelque chose de
l'homme,
Chantaient leur chant sacré.

VICTOR HUGO:
Tristesse d'Olympio (French)

Autumn smiled; on the hillsides the delightful
woods, leaning towards the plain, had hardly
changed colour; the sky was golden; and the
birds, looking heavenwards to the meaning of all
this, spoke perhaps to God of mankind as they
sang their holy song.

Et chaque automne à flots versait tes feuilles
mûres,
Comme un manteau d'hiver, sur le coteau natal.

VICTOR DE LAPRADE
La Mort d'un Chêne (French)

Every autumn your mellow leaves fall in waves,
like a winter cloak on your native hillside.

Herr: Es ist Zeit. Der Sommer war sehr gross.
Leg deinen Schatten auf die Sonnenuhren,
Und auf den Fluren lass die Winde los.

RAINER MARIA RILKE
Herbsttag (German)

Lord, it is time! The summer was very fine. Now
let thy shadows lie across the sundial, and thy
winds across the fields.

Gewaltig endet so das Jahr
Mit goldnem Wein und Frucht der Gärten.
Rund schweigen Wälder wunderbar
Und sind des Einsamen Gefährten.

GEORG TRAKL
Verklärter Herbst (German)

Thus potently the year ends with golden wine
and garden fruits. Around us the woodlands are
silently wonderful and are the companions of the
solitary.

Noch immer stehen Blumen da,
Des Sommers letztes Gloria,
Zu schönem Strauss gebunden.

FRITZ DIETTRICH
In dieses Herbstes Stunden (German)

There are still flowers, tied up in fine bunches
from the last glories of summer.

Geheimnisvoll und düftig dehnte sich über alles
der Himmel aus, der geheimnisvolle Schoss der
Wunder Gottes.

JEREMIAS GOTTHOLF:
Uli der Knecht (German)

The sky stretched hazy and mysterious over
everything, the secret womb of God's wonders.

In seiner Fülle ruhet der Herbsttag nun.

FRIEDRICH HÖLDERLIN:
Mein Eigentum (German)

The autumn day reclines in its rich plenty.

Yama-gawa ni kaze no kaketaru shigarami wa
nagare mo ahenu momiji narikeri.

HARU-MICHI NO TSURAKI:
(Japanese)

Autumn's winds have piled up the withered
leaves in heaps, casting them in the mountain
torrents, the reddened leaves choking the spaces
among the rocks.

Hito mina wa
Aki wo oshimeri
Sono kokoro
Sora ni kayoite
Shigurekemu kamo.

TAYASU MUNETAKE:
Waga (Japanese)

We all hate to see autumn passing; the heavens
seem to agree, for now it is drizzling!

Pomifer autumnus fruges effuderit, et mox
Bruma recurrit iners.

HORACE:
Odes (Latin)

Autumn, the bringer of fruit, has poured out her
riches, and soon sluggish winter returns.

Uzh roshcha otryakhaet
Poslednie listȳ s nagikh svoikh vetveĭ;
Dokhnul osenniĭ khlad, doroga promerzaet,
Zhurcha eshchë bezhit za mel'nitsu rucheĭ,
No prud uzhe zastȳl.

ALEKSANDR SERGEEVICH PUSHKIN:
Osen' (Russian)

The grove is already shaking the last leaves from
its bare branches. The autumn cold has
breathed; the road is becoming frozen; the
stream still flows, murmuring, beyond the mill,
but ice has already formed on the pond.

Uzh nebo osen'yu dȳshalo,
Uzh rezhe solnȳshko blistalo,
Koroche stanovilsya den',
Lesov tainstvennaya sen'
S pechal'nȳm shumom obnazhalas',
Lozhilsya na polya tuman
Guseĭ kriklivȳkh karavan
Tyanulsya k yugu.

ALEKSANDR SERGEEVICH PUSHKIN:
Eugen Onegin (Russian)

The sky already breathed of autumn, the sun
already shone more seldom, the day was growing shorter, the woods' mysterious canopy bared
itself with a sad murmur, mist settled on the
fields, the noisy caravan of geese moved south-
ward.

I s kazhdoĭ osen'yu ya rastsvetayu vnov';
Zdorov'yu moemu polezen russkiĭ kholod.

ALEKSANDR SERGEEVICH PUSHKIN:
Osen' (Russian)

I blossom anew every autumn – the Russian
cold is good for my health.

Medlitel'noĭ chredoĭ niskhodit den' osenniĭ,
Medlitel'no krutitsya zhëltyĭ list,
I den' prozrachno svezh, i vozdukh divno chist –
Dusha ne izbezhit nevidimogo tlen'ya.

ALEKSANDR ALEKSANDROVICH BLOK:
The Autumn Day (Russian)

In slow succession the autumn days descend –
the yellow leaves slowly revolve. The air is
wonderfully pure, and the days deliciously cool.
The soul will not escape invisible decay.

Agudo el ramaje
Niega ya a las aves
Música escondida.

JORGE GUILLÉN:
El Otoño: Isla (Spanish)

The bare branches deny the birds their hidden
concerts.

Lo demás es lo otro: viento triste,
Mientras las hojas huyen en bandadas.

FEDERICO GARCIA LORCA:
Otoño (Spanish)

The rest happens otherwise: a sad wind, while
the leaves scatter in flurries.

En la copa de Otoño un vago vino queda
En que han de deshojarse, Primavera, tus rosas.
RUBÉN DARÍO:
Versos de Otoño (Spanish)

In autumn's cup lingers a cloudy wine in which
spring's roses must shed their petals.

AVARICE
see also Anger, Greed, Materialism, Money.

L'avarice perd tout en voulant tout gagner.
JEAN DE LA FONTAINE:
La Poule aux Oeufs d'Or (French)

Avarice, in wanting to gain everything, loses all.

L'avarice produit quelquefois la prodigalité, et
la prodigalité l'avarice.
FRANÇOIS DUC DE LA ROCHEFOUCAULD:
Réflexions (French)

Avarice sometimes gives rise to prodigality, and
sometimes prodigality gives rise to avarice.

D'una ren suy meravilhans
Qu'ades vey granar e florir
Escassetatz, oc! et Enjans.
MARCABRU:
Songs (French)

One thing always amazes me: I continually see
Avarice flourishing. Yes! and Deceit!

Quid iuvat immensum te argenti pondus et auri
Furtim defossa timidum deponere terra?
HORACE:
Satires (Latin)

What good does this huge weight of gold and
silver, if fear forces you to bury it secretly in the
ground?

Parcus ob heredis curam nimiumque severus
Adsidet insano.
HORACE:
Epistles (Latin)

He who is avaricious and too sparing, in the
interests of his heir, is near to madness.

Avarus nisi cum moritur nil recte facit.
PUBLILIUS SYRUS:
Sententiae (Latin)

The only right thing a miser can do is die.

Avaritia hians et imminens.
CICERO:
Actio in Verrem (Latin)

A gaping and eager avarice.

Nullus argento color est avaris
Abdito terris.
HORACE:
Odes (Latin)

Silver hidden in the greedy earth does not
gleam.

Avaritia pecuniae studium habet, quam nemo
sapiens concupivit.
SALLUST:
Catiline (Latin)

Avarice implies a desire for money which no
wise man covets.

In imperatore avaritiam esse acerbissimum
malum.
VULCACIUS GALLICANUS:
Vita Cassii (Latin)

In an emperor, avarice is the most hateful of
faults.

B

BANKRUPTCY

Solvendo non es!

SENECA:
Oedipus (Latin)

You're bankrupt! (quoting the classic Latin phrase for bankruptcy).

BARGAINS

Guten Kaufs macht den Beutel leer.

GERMAN PROVERB

Good bargains empty our pockets.

BATTLES
see also Bravery, Conquest, Courage, War.

Cette bataille offrira encore cela de remarquable, qu'on en a vu beaucoup mal commandées, mais ici on n'a pas commandé du tout.

GENERAL CHLAPOWSKI:
*Lettre sur les Événements Militaires en
Pologne et en Lithuanie (French)*

This battle was particularly remarkable since we have seen many battles poorly commanded, but this one was not commanded at all!

Le combat cessa faute de combattants.

PIERRE CORNEILLE:
Le Cid (French)

The battle ceased for want of combatants.

Schiesst! Schiesst! Und macht den Schoss der Erde bersten!
Der Riss soll eurer Leichen Grabmal sein.

HEINRICH VON KLEIST:
Prinz Friedrich von Homburg (German)

Fire! Fire! and make the earth explode with cannon. The breach they make shall be your bodies' monument.

. . . wie Paare ringender Männer

Fassen die Schiffe sich an, in die Woge taumelt das Steuer,
Unter den Streitern bricht der Boden, und Schiffer und Schiff sinkt.

FRIEDRICH HÖLDERLIN:
Der Archipelagos (German)

Like pairs of wrestlers, ship grapples with ship, rudders reel in the waves, decks break up under the strain, and ships and their crews go to the bottom.

Andr' apamunasthai, hote tis proteros khalepēnēi

HOMER:
Iliad (Greek)

Ward off stoutly whatever man is first to assail you!

Pange lingua gloriosi proelium certaminis.

VENANTIUS FORTUNATUS:
Hymn (Latin)

Record in words one battle of this glorious struggle.

Face feroque.

LATIN EXPRESSION

With fire and sword (*lit.* with torch and steel).

Professus ante inter suos, ire se ad exercitum sine duce et inde reversurum ad ducem sine exercitu.

SUETONIUS:
Divus Iulius (Latin)

I go to meet an army without a leader, and I shall return to meet a leader without an army (Caesar, to his friends, before setting out to attack Pompey).

Miles, faciem feri!

FLORUS:
Works (Latin)

Soldiers, strike the foe in the face! (Caesar to his men).

L'arena se tornó sangriento lago,
La llanura con muertos, aspereza;
Cayó en unos vigor, cayó denuedo,
Más en otros desmayo i torpe miedo.

FERNANDO DE HERRERA:
Canción por la Perdida del Rei Don Sebastian
(Spanish)

The battlefield became a bloody lake; the plain
harsh with corpses; there fell the brave and the
bold, there too the cowardly and the dismayed.

BEAUTY
see also Children, Enjoyment, Eyes, Life,
Love, Truth, Wealth, Wisdom, Youth.

Attarri as samāḥ daraja

ARAB PROVERB

Beauty is power.

Schoonheid, o, Gij, Wier naam geheiligd zij,
Uw wil geschiede; kóme Uw heerschappij;
Naast U aanbidde de aard geen andren god!

JACQUES PERK:
Sonnet (Dutch)

Beauty, O thou, may thy name always be blest,
thy will be done, thy kingdom come. Earth shall
worship thee and no other god!

La beauté n'est que vent, la beauté n'est pas
bien:
Les beautez en un jour s'en-vont comme les
Roses.

PIERRE DE RONSARD:
Sonnet (French)

Beauty is only a zephyr, it has no worth; beautiful women fade away as quickly as roses.

Les ruines d'une maison
Se peuvent réparer: que n'est cet avantage
Pour les ruines du visage!

JEAN DE LA FONTAINE:
La Fille (French)

A house in ruins can always be restored – what a
pity it is that nothing can be done for beauty
once passed!

Rien de beau n'est séparable de la vie, et la vie
est ce qui meurt.

PAUL VALÉRY:
Eupalinos (French)

Nothing beautiful can be separated from life,
and it is life itself that dies.

Ma beauté grandissait avec ma cruauté, l'une
épaulant l'autre

JEAN GIONO:
Les Paravents (French)

My beauty grew with my cruelty, the one nudg-
ing on the other.

Il ne sert de rien d'être jeune sans être belle, ni
d'être belle sans être jeune.

FRANÇOIS, DUC DE LA ROCHEFOUCAULD:
Refléxions (French)

It is no use being young without being beautiful,
nor beautiful without being young.

Mon nez? On dit que c'est la merveille des
merveilles. Mes pieds sont beaux, classiques.

LIANE DE POUGY:
Mes Cahiers Bleus (French)

They say my nose is a marvel among marvels;
and my feet are classically beautiful!

Die Schönheit ist für ein glückliches Geschlecht,
aber ein unglückliches muss man erhaben zu
rühren suchen.

J. C. F. VON SCHILLER:
Letters (German)

A fortunate race deserves beauty; an unhappy
one we must strive to stir in a sublime way.

. . . das Schöne ist nichts
Als des Schrecklichen Anfang, den wir noch
grade ertragen.

RAINER MARIA RILKE:
Duineser Elegien (German)

Beauty is nothing but the beginning of a terror
we can hardly bear.

Swaz ich noch freuden zer werlde ie gewan,
Daz hât ir schoene und ir güete gemachet,
Und ir rôter munt, der sô lieplîchen lachet.

WALTHER VON DER VOGELWEIDE:
Wol mich der Stunde (German)

Whatever happiness I have had in this world
has been due to her beauty, her goodness, and
her red mouth that smiles so sweetly.

Auch das Schöne muss sterben!

J. C. F. VON SCHILLER:
Nänie (German)

Even beauty must die!

Die Schönheit gibt schlechterdings kein einzelnes Resultat weder für den Verstand noch für den Willen, sie führt keinen einzelnen, weder intellektuellen noch moralischen Zweck aus, sie findet keine einzige Wahrheit, hilft uns keine einzige Pflicht erfüllen und ist, mit einem Worte, gleich ungeschickt, den Charakter zu gründen und den Kopf aufzuklären.

J. C. F. VON SCHILLER:
Works (German)

Beauty does not provide our intellect or our will with any single result; it does not fulfil a single intellectual or moral purpose; it does not uncover a single truth; it does not help us to carry out any duty; thus, in a word, it is equally unfit to form character or to enlighten the mind.

Kallos aneu kharitōn terpei monon, ou katekhei de, hōs ater ankistrou nēkhomenon delear

GAIUS ATEIUS CAPITO:
Fragments (Greek)

Beauty without charm only pleases us, but it does not hold us. It is like a bait floating without a hook.

To kalon an idou psukhē mē kalē genomenē

PLOTINUS:
Enneads (Greek)

The soul cannot behold beauty before it has become beautiful.

Che il crin s'è un Tago e son due Soli i lumi
Prodigio tal non rimirò Natura:
Bagnar coi Soli e rasciugar coi fiumi.

ARTALE:
Sonnet (Italian)

With hair like the river Tago and eyes like two suns, nature never before saw such a miracle – to wet with suns and dry with rivers!

Carmina erunt formae tot monumenta tuae.

PROPERTIUS:
Elegies (Latin)

My poems will be so many memorials of your beauty.

Dum vernat sanguis, dum rugis integer annus,
Utere, ne quid cras libet ab ore dies.

PROPERTIUS:
Elegies (Latin)

During the springtime of your blood, with your years still unwrinkled, seize the moment, for fear tomorrow may diminish your beauty.

Falsa est ista tuae, mulier, fiducia formae.

PROPERTIUS:
Elegies (Latin)

How wrong you are, woman, to have such confidence in your beauty.

Scias nec gratius quicquam decore nec brevius.

SUETONIUS:
Domitianus (Latin)

Be assured that nothing is more pleasing than beauty, but nothing is shorter-lived.

Suus rex reginae placet.

PLAUTUS:
Stichus (Latin)

Each man thinks his woman the most beautiful (*lit.* to the queen her own prince pleases).

Arbiter formae.

OVID:
Heroides (Latin)

Beauty's judge (referring to Paris).

Anceps forma bonum mortalibus,
Exigui donum breve temporis,
Ut velox celeri pede laberis!

SENECA:
Hippolytus (Latin)

Beauty! you dubious gift to mankind, lasting so little time, with what speed you slide out of our grasp!

Nocte latent mendae vitioque ignoscitur omni horaque formosam quamlibet illa facit.

OVID:
Remedia Amoris (Latin)

At night faults are unnoticed and every defect escapes censure; any woman can then pass as a beauty.

Raram fecit mixturam cum sapientia forma.
> PETRONIUS:
> *Satyricon (Latin)*

It is rare to see wisdom allied to beauty.

O matre pulchra filia pulchrior!
> HORACE:
> *Odes (Latin)*

O maiden more beautiful than your beautiful mother!

Men hvad er Skjønhed? En Vedtægt kun, –
En Mynt, som er gangbar till Sted og Stund.
> HENRIK IBSEN:
> *Peer Gynt (Norwegian)*

What is beauty? – A mere convention, a currency coined for a special purpose.

Todo lo que es hermoso tiene su instante, y pasa.
> LUIS CERNUDA:
> *Las Ruinas (Spanish)*

Everything beautiful has its moment and then passes away.

Si hablas, ó si ríes, ó si cantas,
Si muestras mansedumbre ó aspereza
(Efecto solo de tu gentileza),
Las potencias del alma nos encantas.
> CERVANTES:
> *La Ilustre Fregona (Spanish)*

If you speak, or laugh, or sing, whether you are mild or sharp – due only to your sweetness – the qualities of your soul enchant us.

¡Qué rostro! Qué hermoso brio!
Un hielo puede encender!
> LOPE DE VEGA:
> *El Gran Duque de Moscovia (Spanish)*

What a countenance! What spirited beauty! It could even set ice on fire!

BEES

Haec [apium] ut hominum civitates, quod hic est et rex et imperium et societas.
> MARCUS TERENTIUS VARRO:
> *De Re Rustica (Latin)*

The commonwealth of bees is like the state of mankind, for here are king, government, and fellowship.

As doces e solicitas abelhas
Com susurro agradavel vão voando.
> LUIS DE CAMÒES:
> *Canta Agora, Pastor (Portuguese)*

The sweet busy bees fill the air with their delightful murmur.

¡Cuánto gozo a la flor deja
Preciosamente la abeja!
> JORGE GUILLÉN:
> *Amor a una Mañana (Spanish)*

How much joy the honeybee leaves to the flower!

BEGGARS
see also Poverty

Bettler sind Könige.
> J. C. F. VON SCHILLER:
> *Die Räuber (German)*

Beggars are kings.

Malim moriri meos quam mendicarier:
Boni miserantur illum, hunc inrident mali.
> PLAUTUS:
> *Vidularia (Latin)*

I would rather my family died than begged. Dead people are mourned by good people; beggars are mocked by bad.

BEHAVIOUR
see also Conduct, Reputation

Hibb li-ghayr-ak zayy mā tiḥibb li-nafs-ak
> ARAB PROVERB

Do unto others as you would be done by (*lit.* do to yourself).

Toutes les bonnes maximes sont dans le monde; on ne manque qu'à les appliquer.
> BLAISE PASCAL:
> *Pensées (French)*

There are plenty of maxims in the world; all that remains is to apply them.

To mēden adikein pasin anthrōpois prepai
> GREEK PROVERB

It behoves all men to do no wrong.

Neois to sigan kreitton esti tou lalein
GREEK PROVERB

In the young, silence is better than speech.

Cosi fan tutte.
ITALIAN EXPRESSION
As everybody does.

Ab alio exspectes alteri quod feceris.
LATIN PROVERB

Do unto others as you would be done by.

Sic cum inferiore vivas, quemadmodum tecum
superiorem velis vivere.
SENECA:
Epistles (Latin)

Behave to your inferiors as you would wish your
betters to behave to you.

Quod tibi fieri non vis, alteri ne faceris.
Motto of John Tornasius (1504–64),
French printer and bookseller, whose
device was two vipers: the female devouring the
male, while her young devour her.

Do not do to others what you would not wish
them to do to you.

Kif tagħmel jagħmlulek.   MALTESE PROVERB

As you do to others, they will do to you.

En obrar mal o bien está el ser malo o ser bueno.
SPANISH PROVERB

Being great or mean consists in acting well or ill.

Obrar siempre como a vista.   SPANISH PROVERB

Behave as though you are under continual ob-
servation.

BELIEF
**see also Christianity, History, Last words,
Principles, Truth.**

On risque autant à croire trop qu'à croire trop
peu.
DENIS DIDEROT:
Etrennes des Esprits Forts (French)

You risk just as much in being credulous as in
being suspicious.

Allen zu glauben ist zu viel, keinen glauben zu
wenig.
GERMAN PROVERB

To believe everything is too much, to believe
nothing is not enough.

Der Glaube ist schwerer zu erschüttern als das
Wissen.
ADOLF HITLER:
Mein Kampf (German)

Belief is harder to shake than knowledge.

Phainetai moi doxa exienai ek dianoias ē
hekousiōs ē akousiōs, ekousiōs men hē pseudēs
tou metamanthanontos, akousiōs de pasa hē
alēthēs
PLATO:
The Republic (Greek)

Beliefs leave a man's mind willingly or unwil-
lingly. He willingly rejects a belief once he
knows it to be false, but he will not let go a true
belief.

BELLIGERENCE

Arma velit poscatque simul rapiatque juventus.
VIRGIL:
Aeneid (Latin)

Let youth desire, demand, and take up their
arms.

Quisnam audet stricto leges imponere ferro?
CLAUDIAN:
In Rufinum (Latin)

Who would dare to dictate to an army under
arms!

BELLS

Des cloches tout à coup sautent avec furie
Et lancent vers le ciel un affreux hurlement,
Ainsi que des esprits errants et sans patrie
Qui se mettent à geindre opiniâtrement.
CHARLES BAUDELAIRE:
Spleen et Idéal (French)

From the bells there suddenly leaps furiously
into the sky a hideous howling, just like those
exiled, wandering spirits who are given to per-
sistent whining.

Soll eine Stimme sein von oben
Wie der Gestirne helle Schar,
Die ihren Schöpfer wandelnd loben
Und führen das bekränzte Jahr.

> J. C. F. VON SCHILLER:
> *Das Lied von der Glocke (German)*

There shall be a voice from on high, like the
great crowd of stars that praise their creator as
they wander, leading the garlanded year.

Clocán binn
benar i n-aidchi gaíthe:
ba ferr lim dul ina dáil
indás i ndáil mná baíthe.

> Anonymous 9th-century Irish poet
> *(Irish Gaelic)*

Beautiful bell ringing through the night-wind.
I'd rather be with it than with a loose woman.

A grają im dzwony
Ze wszystkich kościołow
Ogromme, tętniące,
Wróżebne.

> STANISLAW WYSPIAŃSKI:
> *Kazimierz Wielki (Polish)*

From towers and steeples toll the bells, enor-
mous, pulsating and vast.

BENEFITS AND BENEFACTORS
see also Gratitude, Kindness.

E' benefizii si debbono fare a poco a poco, acciò
che si assaporino meglio.

> NICCOLÒ MACHIAVELLI:
> *The Prince (Italian)*

Benefits should be granted little by little, so that
they may be the better enjoyed.

La natura delli uomini è cosí obbligarsi per li
benefizii che si fanno come per quelli che si
recevano.

> NICCOLÒ MACHIAVELLI:
> *The Prince (Italian)*

It is in men's nature to be bound as much by the
benefits they confer, as by those they receive.

Beneficia eo usque laeta sunt dum videntur
exsolvi posse; ubi multum antevenere, pro
gratia odium redditur.

> TACITUS:
> *Annals (Latin)*

The benefits bestowed on us are welcome as
long as we believe they can be repaid. Once that
time has passed, gratitude is replaced by hate.

Ita non fit ex eo quod datur ut voluntas eius qui
dederit appareat.

> CICERO:
> *De Natura Deorum (Latin)*

The nature of the gift does not disclose the will of
the giver.

Amici, diem perdidi!

> SUETONIUS:
> *Divus Titus (Latin)*

Friends, I have lost a day! (Titus, on discovering
that he had done nothing for anyone all day).

BETRAYAL
see also Friendship, Murder.

Ovem lupo commisisti.

> TERENCE:
> *Eunuchus (Latin)*

You have thrown the sheep to the wolf.

Persuasae fallere rima sat est.

> PROPERTIUS:
> *Elegies (Latin)*

The smallest opportunity is sufficient for a
woman determined to betray you.

Más vale ir al presidio para toda la vida que no
denunciar a un hombre.

> PIO BAROJA:
> *La Dama Errante (Spanish)*

It is better to go to prison for life rather than
denounce someone.

BIRDS
see also Autumn, Dawn, Fountains, Misfortune, Rain and rainbows, Spring, Summer.

Oiseaux du plus long jour et du plus long repos.
ST-JOHN PERSE:
Oiseaux (French)

Birds of the longest day and the longest repose.

> . . . la terre n'a plus d'ombres,
Et les oiseaux du ciel, les rêves infinis,
Les blanches visions qui cherchent le lieux sombres,
Bientôt n'auront plus d'arbre où déposer leurs nids.
VICTOR DE LAPRADE:
Le Mort d'un Chêne (French)

There are no more shadows across the land, and the birds in the sky – infinite dreams, white visions seeking shady places – will soon have no more trees in which to build their nests.

Au printemps, l'oiseau naît et chante;
N'avez-vous pas ouï sa voix? . . .
Elle est pure, simple et touchante,
La voix de l'oiseau – dans les bois.
GÉRARD DE NERVAL:
Dans les Bois (French)

In spring birds are born and they sing – have you not heard them? Their songs are pure, simple and moving in the woods!

Frondiferasque novis avibus canere undique silvas.
LUCRETIUS:
De Rerum Natura (Latin)

The leafy forest everywhere resounds with the song of young birds.

Ptichka bozhiya ne znaet
Ni zabotȳ, ni truda;
Khlopotlivo ne svivaet
Dolgovechnogo gnezda;
V dolgu noch' na vetke dremlet;
Solntse krasnoe vzoïdët,
Ptichka glasu boga vnemlet,
Vstrepenëtsya i poët.
ALEKSANDR SERGEEVICH PUSHKIN:
The Gypsies (Russian)

God's little bird is free of work and care; it does not busy itself building a lasting nest, but makes do with a twig for its bed; at dawn it listens to God's voice, ruffles its feathers, and breaks forth into song.

BLASPHEMY

Les blasphémateurs, paradoxalement, font revivre le dieu jaloux que le christianisme voulait chasser de la scène de l'histoire.
ALBERT CAMUS:
L'Homme Revolté (French)

Paradoxically, the blasphemers give new life to the jealous god that Christianity is anxious to banish from the stage of history.

BLESSINGS
see also Advantage, Friendship, Contentment, Fortune

Heilige Gluten!
Wen sie umschweben,
Fühlt sich im Leben
Selig mit Guten.
J. W. VON GOETHE:
Faust (German)

Holy fires! He whom they enfold feels blessed throughout life with all that is good.

Singula ne referam, nil non mortale tenemus
Pectoris exceptis ingeniique bonis.
OVID:
Tristia (Latin)

In short, all our possessions are mortal, apart from the blessings of our heart and mind.

Dominus vobiscum.
LATIN GREETING

The Lord be with you!

Numquam sincera bonorum sors ulli concessa viro.
CLAUDIAN:
De Consulatu Stilichonis (Latin)

Not one human being has ever been granted all the blessings of the earth without alloy.

Ita me dii ament!
PLAUTUS:
Poenulus (Latin)

So may the gods love me!

Di te ament!

PLAUTUS:
Aulularia (Latin)

May the gods bless you!

Nihil est ab omni
Parte beatum.

HORACE:
Odes (Latin)

There is nothing that is wholly blessed.

Utatur enim suis bonis oportet et fruatur qui
beatus futurus est.

CICERO:
De Natura Deorum (Latin)

For a person who is to be happy must actively
enjoy his blessings.

Multa bona nostra nobis nocent.

SENECA:
Epistles (Latin)

Our many advantages do us harm.

Nemo autem sollicito bono fruitur.

SENECA:
Epistles (Latin)

No man enjoys blessings that bring anxiety in
their wake.

BOASTING
see also Love

Non laudandust cui plus credit qui audit quam
ille qui videt.

PLAUTUS:
Truculentus (Latin)

He whose feats impress the listener more than
those who actually saw them will get little
praise.

Aku bĕsi Tulang aku tĕmbaga!
Aku bĕrnama harimau Allah!
　　Malay medicine-man's charm for courage

Of iron am I! My bones are of brass! My name is
the Tiger of God!

BOOKS
see also Authorship, Bookworms, Dedications, Libraries, Mankind.

Tout, au monde, existe pour aboutir à un livre.

STÉPHANE MALLARMÉ:
Le Livre, Instrument Spirituel (French)

Everything in the wold exists to end up in a
book.

La plupart des livres d'à présent ont l'air d'avoir
été faits en un jour avec les livres lus de la veille.

S. R. N. CHAMFORT:
Maximes et Pensées (French)

Most of the books nowadays seem to have been
made in a day out of the books one read
yesterday.

Un livre n'est après tout qu'un extrait du monologue de son auteur.

PAUL VALÉRY:
Choses Tues (French)

After all, a book is nothing but an extract from
its author's monologue.

Les récits vrais traitent de la faim, et les récits
imaginaires de l'amour.

RAYMOND QUENEAU:
Une Histoire Modèle (French)

True stories treat of hunger, imaginary ones of
love.

Il est plus nécessaire d'étudier les hommes que
les livres.

FRANÇOIS, DUC DE LA ROCHEFOUCAULD:
Réflexions (French)

It is more important to study people than books.

Pâli comme un vieux livre.

STÉPHANE MALLARMÉ:
Hérodiade (French)

Faded as an old book.

Acht Bände hat er geschrieben. Er hätte gewiss
besser getan, er hätte acht Bäume gepflanzt oder
acht Kinder erzeugt.

GEORG CHRISTOPH LICHTENBERG:
Aphorismen (speaking of himself) *(German)*

He has written eight books. He would have done

better to have planted eight trees, or begotten eight children!

Meine Qual und meine Klagen
Hab ich in dies Buch gegossen.
> HEINRICH HEINE:
> *(German)*

Into this book I have poured my anguish and my outrage.

Ohne Bücher verfaulen die Freuden.
> ELIAS CANETTI:
> *Aufzeichnungen,* 1960 *(German)*

Pleasures rot away without books.

Das Buch ist ein Spiegel; wenn ein Affe hinein-guckt, so kann freilich kein Apostel heraus-sehen.
> GEORG CHRISTOPH LICHTENBERG:
> *Aphorismen (German)*

Books are like mirrors; if a monkey peeps into one, you can't expect an angel to be reflected.

Eine seltsamere Ware als Bücher gibt es wohl schwerlich in der Welt. Von Leuten gedruckt, die sie nicht verstehen; von Leuten verkauft, die sie nicht verstehen; gebunden, rezensiert und gelesen von Leuten, die sie nicht verstehen; und nun gar geschrieben von Leuten, die si nicht verstehen.
> GEORG CHRISTOPH LICHTENBERG:
> *Aphorismen (German)*

Anything as strange as books would be hard to find in this world! Printed by people who don't understand them; sold by people who don't understand them; bound, corrected, and proof-read by people who don't understand them; and now, even written by people who don't under-stand them!

Ei lupēs krateein etheleis,
Tēnde makairan anaptussōn
Biblon eperkheo endukeōs
> Epigram (attrib. archbishop Arethas of
> Caesarea) *(Greek)*

If you want to master care and pain, open this book and read its blessed pages again and again (referring to Marcus Aurelius's meditations).

Aphes ta biblia. Mēketi spō. Ou dedotai
> MARCUS AURELIUS:
> *Meditations (Greek)*

Away with books! No longer be distracted by them – it is not allowed!

To mega biblion ison tōi megalōi kakōi
> CALLIMACHUS:
> *Epigrams (Greek)*

The making of large books is a great evil.

Ad lividum de futura eius
Desperatione ob absolutum opus,
Stat liber.
> AMBROSIUS NOVIDIUS:
> *Sacri Fasti (Latin)*

For the person pale with anxiety over the future unavailability of this work because of its flaw-lessness, this book stands readily to hand.

Frustra palletis aut connivetis oculis; vigilan-dum est, lucubrandum est. Frustra quietem meditamini, laborandum est.
> FRANCESCO PETRARCH:
> *Familiarium Rerum (Latin)*

In vain you grow pale and blink your eyes, you must watch and labour. In vain you meditate rest, you must toil on. (Petrarch thanking Boc-caccio for the gift of a book that has kept him up half the night).

Nullum est librum tam malum ut non ex aliqua parte prodesset.
> PLINY THE ELDER:
> *Natural History (Latin)*

There is no book so bad that we cannot get something useful from it.

Haurit aquam cribro, quicunque studet sine libro.
or
Haurit aquam cribro qui discere vult sine libro.
> MEDIEVAL SCHOOL POEM

He who would learn without a book is like the man who tries to draw water with a sieve.

Distringit librorum multitudo.

SENECA:
Epistles (Latin)

The multitude of books provides distraction.

Fodere quam vites melius est scribere libros,
Ille suo ventri serviet, iste animae.

ALCUIN:
Carmina (Latin)

Writing books is better than planting vines: the
latter serves only the needs of the stomach,
whereas the former feeds the soul.

BOOKWORMS
see also Books.

Er verbrannte alle seine Bücher und zog sich als
Eremit in eine öffentliche Bibliothek zurück.

ELIAS CANETTI:
Aufzeichnungen, 1949 *(German)*

He burnt all his books and installed himself, like
a hermit, in a public library.

Das Vielsinnige des Lesens: die Buchstaben
sind wie Ameisen und haben ihren eigenen
geheimen Staat.

ELIAS CANETTI:
Aufzeichnungen, 1944 *(German)*

The many meanings in reading: the letters are
like termites and have their own secret state.

BOREDOM
see also Meditation, Melancholy.

Les Anglais n'ont point de mot pour désigner
l'ennui, cependant nous ne pouvons douter
qu'ils ne connaissent la chose; d'où leur vien-
drait sans celà cette passion effrenée pour le
commerce qui ainsi que le spleen est si commune
à leur nation?

P. H. D. D'HOLBACH:
Apologie de l'Ennui et des Ennuyeux (French)

The English have no word for 'ennui', nevertheless, we can be certain that they are acquainted
with it; whence else is derived their unbridled
passion for trade which, like the spleen, is
prevalent in their nation?

Le loup le plus horrible, c'est l'ennui.

JEAN GIONO:
Le Déserteur

Boredom is the most horrible of wolves.

L'inertie seule est menaçante.

SAINT-JOHN PERSE:
Poésie (French)

The only menace is inertia.

L'extrême ennui sert à nous désennuyer.

FRANÇOIS, DUC DE LA ROCHEFOUCAULD:
Réflexions (French)

Extreme boredom is its own cure.

Ennui. C'est une maladie de l'âme dont nous
afflige la nature en nous donnant l'existence.

Madame du Deffand to Horace Walpole
(French)

Boredom is a sickness of the soul with which
nature afflicts us in bringing us into this world.

Jak się nie nudzić na scenie tak małej,
Tak niemistrzowsko zrobionej,
Gdzie wszystkie wszystkich Ideały grały,
A teatr życiem płacony.

CYPRYAN KAMIL NORWID:
Marjonetki (Polish)

How can we help being bored on an ill-set and
diminutive stage, where everyone's ideals are
acted out and life itself pays for the theatre?

BORES

Tous les genres sont bons, hors le genre ennuyeux.

VOLTAIRE:
L'Enfant Prodigue (preface) *(French)*

All kinds of people are good except those that are
boring.

Qui, aut tempus quid postulet non videt, aut
plura loquitur, aut se ostentat, aut eorum
quibuscum est rationem non habet, is ineptus
esse dicitur.

CICERO:
(Latin)

He who ignores the occasion, who hogs the
conversation, or talks only of himself, or pays
little regard to the company he is in, is guilty of
impertinence.

BORROWING
see also Friendship.

rêter de l'argent fait perdre la mémoire.

ending money to a man makes him lose his
emory.

i quieres ver cuanto vale un ducado, búscalo
restado.
SPANISH PROVERB

you want to know the value of a pound, try
orrowing one.

BRAVERY
see also Adversity, Courage, Death, Discretion, Foolhardiness, Heroes, Resolution.

'n équipage cavalier
ait les trois quarts de leur vaillance.
JEAN DE LA FONTAINE:
L'Âme Vêtu de la Peau du Lion (French)

uniform provides three-quarters of a man's
alour.

ui ne craint point la mort, ne craint point les
enaces.
PIERRE CORNEILLE:
Le Cid (French)

e who does not fear death has no fear of
reats.

. . . aux âmes bien nées
a valeur n'attend pas le nombre des années.
PIERRE CORNEILLE:
Le Cid (French)

mong wellborn spirits courage does not
epend on age.

Tou ponous gar agathoi
olmōsi
EURIPIDES:
Iphigeneia in Tauris (Greek)

he brave venture anything.

icatrices adversae.
LATIN PHRASE

onourable wounds (*lit.* wounds in front).

Audentes fortuna iuvat.
VIRGIL:
Aeneid (Latin)

Fortune helps the brave.

Virtus praemium est optimum.
PLAUTUS:
Amphitruo (Latin)

Courage is its own reward.

Facile sibi facunditatem virtus argutam invenit.
PLAUTUS:
Truculentus (Latin)

Courage easily finds its own eloquence.

Ingenio stat sine morte decus.
PROPERTIUS:
Elegies (Latin)

May noble deeds survive long after death's
conclusion.

Rebus angustis animosus atque
Fortis appare.
HORACE:
Odes (Latin)

In times of stress be bold and valiant.

Post multa virtus opera laxari solet.
SENECA:
Hercules Furens (Latin)

After considerable effort, valour usually relaxes.

Hic est ille situs cui nemo civis neque hostis
Quivit pro factis reddere opis pretium.
ENNIUS:
Scipio Africanus Maior (Latin)

Here lies a man to whom no-one, friend or foe,
was able to pay due reward for his deeds.

Inflammata semel nescit mitescere virtus.
CLAUDIAN:
In Rufinum (Latin)

Valour once aroused knows no abatement.

Intumuit virtus et lucis prodigus arsit impetus.
CLAUDIAN:
In Rufinum (Latin)

Hearts beat high, and courage is lavish with life.

BREAD
see also Contentment.

Brod ist der Erde Frucht, doch ists vom Lichte
geseegnet.
FRIEDRICH HÖLDERLIN:
Brod und Wein (German)

Bread is the fruit of the earth, but it is blessed by
the sun's rays.

BRIBERY
see also Corruption, Money.

Donnez de l'argent, et bientôt vous aurez des
fers.
J. J. ROUSSEAU:
Du Contrat Social (French)

Make gifts of money and, very soon, you will find
yourself in chains.

. . . nec verbis victa patescit
Ianua, sed plena percutienda manu.
TIBULLUS:
To Delia (Latin)

The door will not open to words, and it is only a
well-filled palm that should do the knocking.

BUCCANEERS

Semperque recentes
Convectare juvat praedas, et vivere rapto.
VIRGIL:
Aeneid (Latin)

Hunting their sport, and plund'ring was their
trade (*tr.* Dryden).

BUSINESS
see also Hope.

Ash-sharṭ qabl al-ḥarth
ARAB PROVERB

Make your bargain before beginning to plough.

Ṣabāḥ al-khayr yā jār-ī inta fī dār-ak wa anā
dār-ī
ARAB PROVER

Mind your business (*lit.* good-day, neighbou
you are in your house and I am in mine).

Les affaires sont les affaires.
FRENCH PROVER

Business is business.

Der Druck der Geschäfte ist schön der Seel
wenn sie entladen ist, spielt sie freier un
geniesst des Lebens.
J. W. VON GOETH
Diary (German

Business pressures are good for the soul – whe
it is free of them, it is all the more ready to enjo
itself.

Ianus summus ab imo.
LATIN PHRAS

All the big businessmen (*lit.* every part of th
forum).

BUSTLE
see also Restlessness.

Nam illa tumultu gaudens non est industria, se
exagitatae mentis concursatio.
SENEC
Epistles (Latin

Glorying in bustle indicates a restless min
rather than industry.

BUSYBODIES
see also Interference.

Tua quod nil refert, ne cures.
PLAUTUS
Stichus (Latin

Don't meddle with that which does not concer
you.

¡No hazañero, sino hazañoso!
SPANISH PROVER

Be busy, but not a busybody!

C

CALUMNY

see also Abuse, Fame, Gossip, Rumour.

a calomnie, Monsieur? Vous ne savez guère ce
ue vous dédaignez; j'ai vu les plus honnêtes
ens près d'en être accablés. Croyez qu'il n'y a
as de plate méchanceté, pas d'horreurs, pas de
onte absurde, qu'on ne fasse adopter aux oisifs
'une grande Ville, en s'y prenant bien: et nous
vons ici des gens d'une adresse!... D'abord un
ruit léger, rasant le sol comme hirondelle avant
orage, *pianissimo* murmure et file, et sème en
ourant le trait empoisonné. Telle bouche le
cueille, et *piano*, *piano* vous le glisse en l'oreille
droitement. Le mal est fait, il germe, il rampe,
chemine, et *rinforzando* de bouche en bouche il
a le diable; puis tout a coup, ne sais comment,
ous voyez Calomnie se dresser, siffler, s'enfler,
randir à vue d'oeil; elle s'élance, étend son vol,
ourbillonne, enveloppe, arrache, entraîne,
clate et tonne, et devient, grâce au Ciel, un cri
énéral, un *crescendo* public, un *chorus* universel
e haine et de proscription.

P. A. C. DE BEAUMARCHAIS:
Le Mariage de Figaro (French)

Calumny, Sir? You hardly know what it is that
ou scorn; I have seen the most honest of men
verwhelmed by it. Believe me, there is no inane
ickedness, no horror, no ridiculous tale so
tupid that the idlers of the town will not accept
.... First there is a light breeze, skimming the
round like a swallow before the storm; *pianis-
imo*, it murmurs and slides past, laying as it goes
ne poisoned bait. Picked up and *piano piano* this
r that mouth will slip it adroitly in your ear.
he harm is done: it sprouts, sidles, creeps, and
inzforzando it plays the very devil from mouth to
nouth. Then, all of a sudden, I don't know how,
ou see Calumny itself stand up, blow, swell,
nd grow tall before our very eyes; it surges up,
idens its flight, whirls and eddies, envelops,
proots, sweeps along, thunders and bursts, and
ecomes, Heaven be praised, a general cry, a
ublic *crescendo*, and a universal *chorus* of hate
nd condemnation!

ed aliud est maledicere aliud accusare. Ac-
usatio crimen desiderat.... Maledictio autem
nihil habet propositi praeter contumeliam.

CICERO:
Pro Caelio (Latin)

It is one thing to slander a person, another to
accuse. Accusation requires a charge. Slander
has only one objective – abuse.

El bueno no siempre se escapa de la calumnia.

SPANISH PROVERB

The good man cannot always escape calumny.

CANDOUR

Terre à terre.

FRENCH EXPRESSION

Down to earth.

Il n'y a rien à gagner avec un Enthousiaste: il ne
faut point s'aviser de dire à un homme les
défauts de sa Maîtresse, ni à un Plaideur le faible
de sa Cause, ni des raisons à un Illuminé.

VOLTAIRE:
Lettres Philosophiques (French)

You cannot get anywhere with a fanatic: you
must never point out to anyone the defects of his
mistress, nor should you show the feebleness of a
cause to those who are advocating it, nor offer
reasons to one who is inspired.

Aimez qu'on vous conseille, et non pas qu'on
vous loue.

NICOLAS BOILEAU:
Art Poétique (French)

It is better to be advised than praised.

CAPRICE

Heut dies und morgen das.

GERMAN PROVERB

One thing today, another tomorrow.

CARE
see also Consolation, Worry.

O quid solutis est beatius curis!

CATULLUS:
Poems (Latin)

What can be more delightful than to put care aside!

CAREERS

La chose la plus importante à toute la vie, est le choix du mestier: le hazard en dispose.

BLAISE PASCAL:
Pensées (French)

The most important thing in life is the choice of a calling, but that is left to chance.

Il n'y a que Dieu et quelques génies rares pour qui la carrière s'étend à mesure qu'ils y avancent.

DENIS DIDEROT:
Le Neveu de Rameau (French)

It is only God and a few rare spirits for whom their careers extend as they advance.

CATHEDRALS AND CHURCHES

Alors ils croiront voir la vieille basilique,
Toute ainsi qu'elle était puissante et magnifique,
Se lever devant eux comme l'ombre d'un mort!

GÉRARD DE NERVAL:
Nôtre-Dame de Paris (French)

Then they will believe they see the old cathedral just as it was when it was powerful and magnificent, rising up in front of them like the shades of the dead!

Cloîtres silencieux, voûtes des monastères,
C'est vous, sombres caveaux, vous qui savez aimer.

ALFRED DE MUSSET:
Rolla (French)

Silent cloisters, monastic arches, it is you, sombre vaults, who know how to love.

... das strebende Stemmen,
Grau aus vergehender Stadt oder aus fremde
des Doms.

RAINER MARIA RILKI
Duineser Elegien (Germa

The grey cathedral striving upwards, out some foreign or derelict city.

Leva in roseo fulgor la cattedrale
Le mille guglie bianche e i santi d'oro
Osannando irraggiata.

GIOSUE CARDUCC
Sole e Amore (Italia

All rose-red stands the great cathedral, seemin to shout hosannas with its thousand spires an saints of gold.

Sorgono e in agili file dilungano
Gl' immani ed ardui steli marmorei,
E ne la tenebra sacra somigliano
Di giganti un esercito
Che guerra mediti con l'invisibile.

GIOSUE CARDUCC
In una Chiesa Gotica (Italia

These huge marble columns, with their syn metrical and cleancut lines, rise up, loomin mysteriously in the shadows, like giants pla ning war on the invisible.

CAUSE AND EFFECT
see also Fate, Understanding, Words

Numquam edepol temere tinnit tintinnabulu
Nisi qui illud tractat aut movet, mutumst, tace

PLAUTU
Trinummus (Lati

A bell doesn't ring on its own – if someo doesn't pull or push it, it will remain silent.

Sublata causa tillitur effectus.

LATIN PROVEF

Remove the cause and you remove the effect.

Homo causas rerum videt earumque progressu et quasi antecessiones non ignorat.

CICER
De Officiis (Lati

Man sees the causes of things and understand their course backwards and forwards (*i.e.* he ca reason from cause to effect, and from effect cause).

Non sine solo iris.
>Motto written on the 'Rainbow' portrait of
>Queen Elizabeth I at Hatfield House

There can be no rainbow without the sun.

CAUTION
see also Distrust, Impetuosity, Prudence, Resourcefulness.

Lā tiftī sh as-sirr quddām al-khaddām
>ARAB PROVERB

Do not tell secrets in front of the servant!

Zallit al-qadam wa-lā zallit al-qalam
>ARAB PROVERB

A slip of the foot is less dangerous [*lit.* rather] than a slip of the pen.

Al bekharram min ar-rā's, yasmo' an nās
>ARAB PROVERB

Walls have ears (*lit.* what comes out of your head, people hear).

En toute chose il faut considérer la fin.
>JEAN DE LA FONTAINE:
>*Le Renard et le Bouc (French)*

In every undertaking we must keep the outcome in mind.

On apprehende plus de blesser ceux dont l'affection est plus utile et l'aversion plus dangereuse.
>BLAISE PASCAL:
>*Pensées (French)*

We are more afraid to wound those whose friendship is most useful and whose dislike is most dangerous.

Hora ge mēn. Ou smikros, oukh, hagōn hode
>SOPHOCLES:
>*Oedipus Coloneus (Greek)*

Think carefully! This is an important problem.

Mē kinein ta akinēta
>GREEK PROVERB

Let sleeping dogs lie! (*lit.* do not move the immovable).

Logisai de pro ergou
>PYTHAGORAS:
>*Golden Verses (Greek)*

Think before you leap! (*lit.* reflect before acting).

Cave canem!
>LATIN TAG

Beware of the dog!

Nec procul a stabulis audet discedere, si qua excussa est avidi dentibus agna lupi.
>OVID:
>*Tristia (Latin)*

A lamb, once rescued from the teeth of the ravenous wolf, does not venture far from the fold.

Cautus adito:
Neu desis operae neve immoderatus abundes.
>HORACE:
>*Satires (Latin)*

Be cautious in your approach; show neither too little not too much zeal.

Via trita est tutissima.
>LATIN PROVERB

The worn path is the safest.

Las paredes oyen.
>SPANISH PROVERB

Walls have ears.

Antes moral que almendro.
>SPANISH PROVERB

Better to be slow than rash (*lit.* rather a mulberry (*i.e.* a slow-growing tree) than an almond (*i.e.* a quick-growing tree)).

CELEBRATION

Hoc agitemus convivium vino et sermone suavi.
>PLAUTUS:
>*Asinaria (Latin)*

Let us celebrate the occasion with wine and sweet words.

CENSORSHIP
see also Freedom.

Indignor quicquam reprehendi, non quia crasse
Compositum illepideve putetur, sed quia nuper,
Nec veniam antiquis, sed honorem et praemia
posci.

HORACE:
Epistles (Latin)

It annoys me that any work should be censored
not on account of its coarseness or inelegance,
but because it is modern; and that what is
claimed for the classics should be not indulgence
but honours and awards.

I malo gorya mne, svobodno li pechat'
Morochit olukhov, il' chutkaya tsenzura
V zhurnal'nȳkh zamȳslakh stesnyaet balagura.

ALEKSANDR SERGEEVICH PUSHKIN:
From Pindemonte (Russian)

Little does it matter to me whether the press is
free to mystify fools; or whether a sensitive
censorship does cramp the style of some super-
ficial journalist.

CERTAINTY
see also Truth.

Un tiens vaut mieux que deux tu l'auras.

FRENCH PROVERB

A bird in the hand is worth two in the bush (*lit.*
one of what you have is worth more than two
that you will have).

. . . un sou quand il est assuré
Vaut mieux que cinq en espérance.

JEAN DE LA FONTAINE:
Le Berger et la Mer (French)

One coin that you have is worth more than five
you hope for.

Il n'est pas certain que tout soit incertain.

BLAISE PASCAL:
Pensées (French)

It's not certain that everything is uncertain.

CHANCE
see also Destiny, Providence, Fate.

La Providence est le nom de baptême du
Hasard.

FRENCH PROVERB

Providence is the baptismal name of chance.

Un coup de dés jamais n'abolira le hazard.

STÉPHANE MALLARMÉ
(*French*)

One throw of the dice will never abolish chance.

Unsre Taten sind nur Würfe
In des Zufalls blinder Nacht.

FRANZ GRILLPARZER:
Die Ahnfrau (German)

Our actions are only throws of the dice in the
sightless night of chance.

Epi de tōn exōthen sumbainontōn, hoti ētoi kat'
epitukhian ē kata pronoian. Oute de tēi
epitukhiai mempteon oute tēi pronoiai enklē-
teon

MARCUS AURELIUS:
Meditations (Greek)

Everything that happens to you from without is
due either to chance or providence; nor have you
any reason to blame chance or to impeach providence.

Fors dubia aeternumque labans: quam blanda
fovet Spes.

AUSONIUS:
Ephemeris (Latin)

Chance, unstable and ever-changing, which
fond hope favours.

Res hominum fragiles alit et regit et perimit
Fors.

AUSONIUS:
Ephemeris (Latin)

The frail affairs of men are prospered, guided
and destroyed by chance.

Est autem fortuna; rerum igitur fortuitarum nulla praesensio est.

CICERO:
De Divinatione (Latin)

Yet chance does exist, therefore there is no foreknowledge of things that happen by chance.

Caput aut navia.

LATIN EXPRESSION

Heads or tails (*lit.* head or ship, referring to the images on coins of the head of Janus, and a ship).

CHANGE
see also Life, Temperament, Women.

Nous avons changé tout cela!

MOLIÈRE:
Le Médecin Malgré Lui

We've changed all that!

Panta en metabolēi. Kai autos su en diēnekei alloiōsei kai kata ti phthorai. Kai ho kosmos de holos

MARCUS AURELIUS:
Meditations (Greek)

There is change in all things. You yourself are subject to continual change and some decay – and this is common to the entire universe.

Phobeitai tis metabolēn? Ti gar dunatai khōris metabolēs genesthai?

MARCUS AURELIUS:
Meditations (Greek)

Do we shrink from change? Why, what can come into being save by change?

Panta rhei

GREEK EXPRESSION

Everything is in a state of flux.

Sempre una mutazione lascia l'addentellato per lo edificazione dell' altra.

NICCOLÒ MACHIAVELLI:
The Prince (Italian)

One change always leaves the way open for the introduction of others.

Plerumque gratae divitibus vices.

HORACE:
Odes (Latin)

In change even luxury finds a zest.

Naviget hinc alia jam mihi linter aqua.

OVID:
Fasti (Latin)

In other waters let my bark now sail (*i.e.* let me turn to something else).

CHARACTER
see also Appearance, Beauty, Destiny, Individualism, Personality, Temperament, Understanding, Wisdom.

Ordinairement la grandeur de caractère résulte de la balance naturelle de plusieurs qualités opposées.

DENIS DIDEROT:
Le Neveu de Rameau (French)

Usually greatness of character is due to nature's balance of many conflicting qualities.

Quiconque n'a pas de caractère, n'est pas un homme, c'est une chose.

S. R. N. CHAMFORT:
Maximes et Pensées (French)

He who has no character is not a man but only a thing.

C'est un grand malheur de perdre, par notre caractère, les droits que nos talents nous donnent sur la société.

S. R. N. CHAMFORT:
Maximes et Pensées (French)

It is a great pity to lose, by our character, the rights that our talents give us in society.

Ich bin nun wie ich bin;
So nimm mich nur hin!

J. W. VON GOETHE:
Liebhaber in allen Gestalten (German)

I am what I am, so take me as I am!

Touto ekhei hē teleiotēs tou ēthous, to pasan hēmeran hōs teleutaian diexagein kai mēte sphuzein mēte narkan mēte hupokrinesthai

MARCUS AURELIUS:
Meditations (Greek)

This is the mark of a perfect character – to pass through each day as though it were the last, without agitation, without torpor, and without pretence.

Non viribus aut velocitate aut celeritate corporum res magnae geruntur, sed consilio auctoritate sententia.

CICERO:
De Senectute (Latin)

Great things are accomplished not by strength, speed or physical dexterity, but by reflection, force of character and judgment.

Multum mutatus ab illo.

LATIN EXPRESSION

Much changed from his former self.

Quantum mutatus ab illo Hectore.

VIRGIL:
Aeneid (Latin)

How much changed from that Hector (*i.e.* that we used to know).

Sui cuique mores fingunt fortunam hominibus.

LATIN PROVERB

Each man's character shapes his fortunes.

Vulpes pilum mutat, non mores.

LATIN PROVERB

The leopard does not change his spots (*lit.* the fox changes his fur, but not his nature).

CHARITY
see also Benefits and benefactors, Gratitude.

Il est bon d'être charitable;
Mais envers qui, c'est la le point.

JEAN DE LA FONTAINE:
Le Villageois et le Serpent (French)

Charity is good, providing the recipient is worthy of it (*lit.* it is good to be charitable; but to whom, that's the point).

L'unique objet de l'Escriture est la charité.

BLAISE PASCAL:
Pensées (French)

The sole object of the Scriptures is charity.

Die Haut ist allweg näher als das Hemd.

GERMAN PROVERB

Charity begins at home (*lit.* the skin is nearer than the shirt).

Engion gonu knēmēs

GREEK PROVERB
(quoted in Seneca's *Apocolocyntosis Divi Claudii*)

Charity begins at home (*lit.* the knee is nearer than the shin).

Ti gar pleon theleis eu poiēsas anthrōpon? Ouk arkei touto, hoti kata phusin tēn sēn ti epraxas, alla toutou misthon zēteis?

MARCUS AURELIUS:
Meditations (Greek)

What more do you want when you have done a kindness? Does it not suffice that you have done something in accordance with your nature? Do you therefore look for recompense for it?

Deus Caritas est.

LATIN PROVERB

God is Love.

Titulis olim maior habebatur donandi gloria.

JUVENAL:
Satires (Latin)

Charity was once held in higher esteem than even the awarding of titles.

Más cerca están mis dientes que mis parientes.

SPANISH PROVERB

Charity begins at home (*lit.* my teeth are nearer than my relations).

Quien al pobre dió, a Dios prestó.

SPANISH PROVERB

Who gives to the poor, lends to God.

CHARLATANS

Le monde n'a jamais manqué de charlatans.
> JEAN DE LA FONTAINE:
> *Le Charlatan (French)*

We have never lacked for charlatans in this world.

CHASTITY
see also Adultery, Modesty, Poets and poetry, Purity.

To sōphronein timōsa tou biou pleon
> AESCHYLUS:
> *The Suppliant Maidens (Greek)*

Set chastity above life itself.

Caute, si non caste!
> LATIN PROVERB

If you can't be chaste, be careful!

CHILDREN
see also Families, Genius, Mothers, Parents, Punishment, Relations, Women.

Al-qird fī 'ayn umm-uh ghazāl
> ARAB PROVERB

A child is the apple of its mother's eyes (*lit.* the ape, in its mother's eyes, is a gazelle).

Qalb-ī 'alá walad-ī wa-qalb walad-ī 'alayya ḥajar
> ARAB PROVERB

I love my son, but he is indifferent to me (*lit.* is a stone to me).

On trouve son semblable
Beau, bien fait, et sur tous aimable.
> JEAN DE LA FONTAINE:
> *L'Aigle et le Hibou (French)*

We always believe those who resemble us [*i.e.* our own children] to be beautiful, well proportioned and, above all, delightful.

C'est abuser lâchement de sa force que de maltraiter un enfant.
> MME LA COMTESSE DE SÉGUR:
> *Un Bon Petit Diable (French)*

It is a cowardly abuse of power to ill-treat a child.

Si'il n'y avait pas d'enfants sur la terre, il n'y aurait rien de beau.
> REJEAN DUCHARME:
> *L'Avalée des Avalés* (preliminary note) (French)

If there were no children on this earth, there would be no beauty here.

L'enfance est un papillon qui se hâte de brûler ses blanches ailes aux flammes de la jeunesse.
> ALOYSIUS BERTRAND:
> *Gaspard de la Nuit* (foreword) *(French)*

Childhood is like a butterfly intent on burning its white wings in the flames of youth.

Nieman kan mit gerten
Kindes zuht beherten:
Den man zêren bringen mac,
Dem ist ein wort als ein slac.
> WALTHER VON DER VOGELWEIDE:
> *Nieman kan mit Gerten (German)*

No-one can make a child behave well with a switch. If the child is capable of being trained, a word will mean as much to him as a blow.

In Arme der Götter wuchs ich gross.
> FRIEDRICH HÖLDERLIN:
> *Da Ich ein Knabe war (German)*

In arms divine I grew to manhood.

O agathon kai pais epi gērai
> THEAETETUS SCHOLASTICUS:
> Fragment *(Greek)*

What a blessing is a child in our old age!

E kalon hokka pelēi tekna goneusin isa
> NOSSIS:
> *Epigrams (Greek)*

How delightful when children resemble their parents!

Egli è bene ubidire
A padri certo. Ma deono anchi i padri
Non esser duri a compiacere i figli.
> GIAMBATTISTA CINTHIO GIRALDI:
> *Gli Antivalomeni (Italian)*

Certainly children should obey their fathers. But fathers, also, should not be reluctant to humour their children.

Amor de niño, agua en cesto.

SPANISH PROVERB

A child's affection is like water in a sieve.

CHIVALRY

Car il est jeune et joliz
Doulx et Courtois de hault prise
Le plus bel des Fleurs de Liz.

CHRISTINE DE PISAN:
Fragments (French)

For he is young and handsome, gentle and chivalrous, of high rank, and the finest of the Fleurs de Lys.

Oh gran bontà de' cavalieri antiqui!
Eran rivali, eran di fé diversi,
E si sentian degli aspri colpi iniqui
Per tutto la persona anco dolersi;
E pur per selve oscure e calli obliqui
Insieme van senza sospetto aversi.

ARIOSTO:
Orlando Furioso (Italian)

Ah, the great generosity of knights of old! They were rivals, of different faiths, still smarting from the cruel and vicious blows they had dealt each other. Yet they continued together in mutual trust through the dark woods and crooked paths.

CHRISTIANITY
see also Blasphemy.

La communion et l'excommunication sont le pacte social du clergé, pacte avec lequel il sera toujours le maitre des peuples et des rois.

J. J. ROUSSEAU:
Du Contrat Social (footnote) *(French)*

Communion and excommunication are the social compact of the clergy, a compact that will always make them masters of peoples and monarchs.

Un vrai chrétien n'examine point ce qu'on lui ordonne de croire.

S. R. N. CHAMFORT:
Caractères et Anecdotes (French)

A true Christian never questions what he has been told to believe.

Der schwerste Schlag den die Menschheit je erlebte, war die Einführung des Christentume.

ADOLF HITLER:
Testament (German)

The worst blow mankind ever experienced was the introduction of Christianity.

CITIES
see also Civilisation, Night.

Fourmillante cité, cité pleine de rêves.

CHARLES BAUDELAIRE:
Les Sept Vieillards (French)

Swarming city, full of dreams.

In den Asphaltstädten bin ich daheim.

BERTOLT BRECHT:
Vom Armen B.B. (German)

The asphalt cities are my home.

Von diesen Städten wird bleiben: der durch sie hindurchging, der Wind!

BERTOLT BRECHT:
Vom Armen B.B. (German)

All that will be left of these cities will be the wind that blew through [their streets].

Die grossen Städte strecken ihre Gelenke (sie sind austauschbar) über die alte Landschaft.

BERTOLT BRECHT:
Baal (1926 version) *(German)*

The great cities stretch their joints (they are interchangeable) over the old landscape.

Hen gar ti pragma kai sunekhes hē polis hōsper zōion

PLUTARCH:
Moralia (Greek)

A city, like a living thing, is a united and continuous whole.

To gar kaukhēma tōn hapantakhou tēs oikoumenes khristianōn, to stērigma, ho hagiasmos kai hē doxa hē polis estin autē hē hagia

The Patriarch of Constantinople,

writing to the Metropolitan Cyprian for funds for the defence of Constantinople.
(Acta Patriarchatus Constantinopolitani) *(Greek)*

This holy city is the pride, the support, the sanctification and the glory of Christians throughout the whole inhabited world.

Poiché voi, cittadine infauste mura,
Vidi e conobbi assai, là dove segue
Odio al dolor compagno.
GIACOMO LEOPARDI:
La Vita Solitaria (Italian)

For I have seen and known you too much, black city walls where pain and hatred follow hatred and pain.

Est enim civitas principalissimum eorum quae humana ratione constitui possunt.
ST. THOMAS AQUINAS:
Commentary on the Politics of Aristotle (Latin)

The city is, in fact, the most important thing constituted by human reason.

Multitudo hominum iure sociata.
LEONARDO BRUNI:
Fragment *(Latin)*

A group of people united by a common law (referring to the Italian city-state).

Omnis civitas corpus est.
ST. AUGUSTINE:
De Civitate Dei (Latin)

Every city is a living body.

Est enim civitas conversatio populi assidua ad iure vivendum collecti.
Regesto del Codice Palavicino (Latin)

For a city is a continuous association of people gathered together to live according to law.

At man lukker sig inde i de store Stæder,
Blot for at rendes af Pakket paa Dør.
HENRIK IBSEN:
Peer Gynt (Norwegian)

To think that I should live cooped up in a great city, just to be pestered and plagued by people!

Ciudades que un tiempo fueron heroicas, esforzadas, activas, abundantes, hoy sólo tienen una existencia imaginaria y soporífera.
PEREZ DE AYALA:
La Caida de los Limones (Spanish)

Cities that once were heroic, courageous, active and flourishing, now have only an imaginary and sleepy existence.

CITIZENSHIP
see also Commonwealth, Duty, Eloquence, Law, Patriotism, Service, the State.

Né citoyen d'un Etat libre, et membre du souverain, quelque faible influence que puisse avoir ma voix dans les affaires publiques, le droit d'y voter suffit pour m'imposer le devoir de m'en instruire.
J. J. ROUSSEAU:
Du Contrat Social (introduction) *(French)*

Born a citizen and member of a free sovereign state, and with whatever feeble influence my voice can have in public affairs, my right to vote compels me to accept the duty of informing myself of these things.

Maior privato visus, dum privatus, et omnium consensu capax imperii, nisi imperasset.
TACITUS:
History (Latin)

When he was a commoner he seemed too big for his station, and had he never been emperor, no-one would have doubted his ability to reign (said of Servius Galba) *(tr.* Fyfe).

CIVIL WAR

La guerre civile est le règne du crime.
PIERRE CORNEILLE:
Sertorius (French)

Crime is rife in civil war.

La guerre civile est le plus grand des maux.
BLAISE PASCAL:
Pensées (French)

Civil war is the greatest of evils.

Le fruit des guerres civiles à Rome a été l'esclavage, et celui des troubles d'Angleterre la liberté.
VOLTAIRE:
Lettres Philosophiques (French)

In Rome civil strife led to slavery, in England to liberty.

Iusto magnoque triumpho
Civiles abolete notas.
CLAUDIAN:
De Bello Gildonico (Latin)

Wash out the stain of civil war by means of a great and well-deserved triumph.

Optime olere occisum hostem et melius civem est.
SUETONIUS:
Vitellius (Latin)

The odour of a dead enemy is sweet, but that of a fellow-citizen is sweeter still (Vitellius commenting on the evidence of the civil strife that had brought him to power).

Armaque fraternae tristia militae.
PROPERTIUS:
Elegies (Latin)

Brother confronts brother in war's grim service.

CIVILISATION
see also Cities, Knowledge, Life, Mankind, Possessions, Renaissance, World.

J'ai reçu au coeur le coup de la grâce.
ARTHUR RIMBAUD:
Mauvais Sang (French)

My heart has received its death blow (*i.e.* through the arrival of 'civilisation').

La civilisation ne réside pas dans un degré plus ou moins haut de raffinement. Mais dans une conscience commune à tout un peuple.
ALBERT CAMUS:
Carnets, 1935–37 *(French)*

Civilisation does not result from a particular level of sophistication, but from the common conscience of a whole nation.

Notre vie est devenue une vie de bureau,

l'homme perd le contact expérimental avec la nature.
ST.-JOHN PERSE:
speaking to Pierre Mazars *(French)*

Our life has become an office routine and has lost the experimental contact with nature.

Que la civilisation est loin de procurer les jouissances attribuable à cet état!
STÉPHANE MALLARMÉ:
Un Spectacle Interrompu (French)

How far civilisation is from providing the joys to be expected from that condition!

Du haut de nos pensers vois les cités serviles
Comme les rocs fatals de l'esclavage humain.
ALFRED DE VIGNY:
La Maison du Berger (French)

Look from the height of our thoughts down on the servile cities, fatal rocks of human slavery.

Nicht bloss wissen, sondern auch für die Nachwelt tun, was die Vorwelt für uns getan hat, heisst ein Mensch sein.
GEORG CHRISTOPH LICHTENBERG:
Aphorismen (German)

Being a man is not just knowing, but also doing for posterity what our ancestors have done for us.

Pax, jus, ars.
Motto of the Royal Niger Company's Medal
(Latin)

Peace, justice, and art.

CLARITY

Was sich überhaupt sagen lässt, lässt sich klar sagen.
LUDWIG WITTGENSTEIN:
Tractatus Logico-philosophicus (preface) *(German)*

What can be said at all can be said clearly.

CLASSICS
see also the Renaissance

Nous ne saurions aller plus avant que les anciens.
JEAN DE LA FONTAINE:
(in a note to *La Mort et le Malheureux*) *(French)*

We cannot improve on the classics.

CLEMENCY
see also Fear, King, Mercy.

La clémence est, au fait, un moyen comme un autre.

VICTOR HUGO:
Cromwell (French)

Clemency is, after all, only another means of accomplishing something.

En la alegría del hallazgo de los desposados se enterró la venganza y resucitó la clemencia.

MIGUEL DE CERVANTES:
La Gitanilla (closing words) *(Spanish)*

In the joy of discovering the betrothed, vengeance was buried and clemency revived.

CLEVERNESS
see also Learning, Wisdom.

Klegt, paa Spidsen satt, er Dumhed.

HENRIK IBSEN:
Peer Gynt (Norwegian)

Too much cleverness is folly.

CLOUDS
see also Dawn, Sky, Summer, Winter.

Quand on regarde les nuages, on pense à beaucoup de choses, mais ce sont des choses qui ressemblent à des nuages.

J.-M. LE CLÉZIO:
L'Inconnu sur la Terre (French)

When we look at clouds we think of many things, but they are things that resemble clouds.

Die finstern Wolken lagern
Schwer auf dem greisen Land,
Die welken Blätter rascheln,
Was glänzt, ist Herbstes-Tand.

OTTO ERICH HARTLEBEN:
Trutzlied (German)

The lowering clouds lie heavily over the ancient land; the withered leaves rustle, and what glitters is autumn's jewels.

Ouraniai te dinai nephelas dromaiou

EURIPIDES:
Alcestis (Greek)

O packs of clouds, racing heavenwards across the sky!

Lievi e bianche a la plaga occidentale
Van le nubi.

GIOSUE CARDUCCI:
Sole e Amore (Italian)

Fleecy and white the clouds westward stream.

Nube solet pulsa candidus ire dies.

OVID:
Tristia (Latin)

Once the clouds are scattered, the day is wont to brighten.

Poslednyaya tucha rassenyannoï buri!
Odna tỹ nesësh'sya po yasnoï lazuri,
Odna tỹ navodish' unỹluyu ten',
Odna tỹ pechalish' likuyushchiï den'.

ALEKSANDR SERGEEVICH PUSHKIN:
Tucha (Russian)

Last cloud of the scattered thunderstorm! you alone course across the clear azure sky, you alone cast a gloomy shadow, you alone sadden the jubilant day!

COLOUR

Ce qui serait vraiment surprenant, c'est que le son ne pût *pas* suggérer la couleur, que les couleurs ne pussent *pas* donner l'idée d'une mélodie, et que le son et la couleur fussent impropres à traduire les idées.

CHARLES BAUDELAIRE:
Wagner (French)

What would really be surprising would be if sounds could *not* suggest colours, if colours could *not* convey the idea of a melody, and if sound and colour were inappropriate for the expression of ideas.

COMEDY
see also Conclusions, Laughter, Playwriting.

C'est une étrange entreprise que celle de faire rire les honnêtes gens.

MOLIÈRE:
La Critique de l'Ecole des Femmes (French)

Making decent people laugh is a strange business.

La bonne comédie est la peinture parlante des ridicules d'une nation.

VOLTAIRE:
Lettres Philosophiques (French)

Good comedy is the speaking likeness of a nation's absurdities.

COMMON INTERESTS
see also Companionship, Self-interest, Service, Sympathy.

Qui gruge le vilain gruge le seigneur.

FRENCH PROVERB

He who harms a peasant harms his lord (*lit.* who eats the peasant out of house and home does the same to his master).

Hēlix hēlika terpei

GREEK PROVERB

Like goes with like.

Similes cum similibus facile congregantur.

LATIN PROVERB

Birds of a feather flock together (*lit.* like with like easily come together).

COMMON SENSE
see also Desire, Order, the State, Wisdom.

Raghupati Raghava Raja Ram,
Patita pavana Sita Ram.
Ishwara Allah Tere nam,
Sabko Sanmati de Bhagavan.
  Favourite prayer of Mahatma Gandhi *(Hindi)*

O King of Raghu clan, Rama, you and Sita are the purifiers of sinners! Ishwar and Allah both are your names. Give us good sense, O Lord!

COMMONPLACE

La generalidad de los hombres nadamos en el océano de la vulgaridad.

PIO BAROJA:
Las Inquietudes de Shanti Andía (Spanish)

Most of us swim in the ocean of the commonplace.

COMMONWEAL
see also Law, the People.

Chacun de nous met en commun sa personne et toute sa puissance sous la suprême direction de la volonté générale; et nous recevons encore chaque membre comme partie indivisible du tout.

J. J. ROUSSEAU:
Du Contrat Social (French)

Everyone subordinates himself and all his abilities to the supreme control of the general will, and is accepted as an indivisible part of the whole.

Consulite in medium, et rebus succurrite fessis.

VIRGIL:
Aeneid (Latin)

Consult the common good and help the sickly state.

Summum bonum multitudinis est pax.

REMIGIO GIROLAMI:
De Bono Pacis (Latin)

The highest common good is peace.

Sicut estis facti et positi in officio per commune, ita laboretis pro communi bono.

REMIGIO GIROLAMI
to the Priors of Florence *(Latin)*

Since you have been appointed to your office by the commune, you must work for the common good.

Quanto bonum est communius, tanto est magis amandum.

REMIGIO GIROLAMI:
De Bono Communi (Latin)

The more general the common good, the more desirable it is.

Maius autem et divinius est bonum multitudinis quam bonum unius.

ST. THOMAS AQUINAS:
On Princely Government (Latin)

The good of the community is greater and more divine than the good of the individual.

COMMONWEALTH
see also Citizenship, Duty.

Coetus multitudinis iuris consensu et utilitatis communione sociatus.

CICERO:
De Republica (Latin)

[The Commonwealth is] a union of the people linked by a common recognition of rights and by a community of interests.

COMPANIONSHIP
see also Common interests.

Dis-moi qui tu hantes, je te dirai qui tu es.

FRENCH PROVERB

Tell me whom you frequent and I will tell you who you are.

Quecx d'eis semblan trobar son par.

PEIRE D'ALVERNHE:
Be M'es Plazen (French)

Each man finds his equal among those of his like.

Comes jucundus in via pro vehiculo est.

PUBLILIUS SYRUS:
Fragments (Latin)

On the road a pleasant companion is as good as a coach.

Ma' min rajtek xebbahtek.

MALTESE PROVERB

I likened you to those I saw you with.

COMPARISONS

Comparer, c'est comprendre.

FRENCH PROVERB

To compare is to understand.

COMPASSION
see also Hardships, Sympathy.

Nam huius demum miseret, cuius nobilitas miserias nobilitat.

ACCIUS:
Fragments (Latin)

He whose very nobleness ennobles misery evokes compassion most.

COMPETITION

Rira bien qui rira le dernier.

FRENCH PROVERB

He laughs best who laughs last.

Kai kerameus keramei koteei kai tektoni tektōn,
Kai ptōkhos ptōkhōi phthoneei kai aoidos aoidōi

HESIOD:
Works and Days (Greek)

Potters compete with potters, hewers of wood with hewers of wood, beggars envy other beggars, and minstrels other minstrels.

Meliust te minis certare mecum quam minaciis.

PLAUTUS:
Truculentus (Latin)

Competition with me calls for cash, not bluster.

COMPLIMENTS

Equidem pol vel falso tamen laudari multo malo,
Quam vero culpari.

PLAUTUS:
Mostellaria (Latin)

I much prefer lying compliments to sincere criticisms.

COMPROMISE
see also Second-best.

Quand on n'a pas ce que l'on aime, il faut aimer ce que l'on a.

FRENCH PROVERB

When we cannot get what we love, we must love what is within our reach.

Faute de grives, on mange des merles.

FRENCH PROVERB

Beggars can't be choosers (*lit.* if there are no thrushes, we eat blackbirds).

Ersatz für's Unersatzliche.

GERMAN PHRASE

A substitute for the irreplaceable.

Der Weisheit erster Schritt ist: alles anzuklagen.
Der letzte: sich mit allem zu vertragen.
GEORG CHRISTOPH LICHTENBERG:
Aphorismen (German)

One's first step in wisdom is to question everything – and one's last is to come to terms with everything.

Man kann doch Menschen nicht für ein leeres Wort sterben lassen!
WOLFGANG BORCHERT:
Draussen vor der Tür (German)

We can't let men die for the sake of an empty word!

Ut quimus, aiunt, quando ut volumu' non licet.
TERENCE:
Andria (Latin)

He who cannot do what he wants must make do with what he can.

Contenti simus hoc Catone.
SUETONIUS:
Divus Augustus (Latin)

Let's be satisfied with the Cato we have (*i.e.* rather than with Cato's austere grandfather).

Cuando se tiene sed, se agradece el agua.
SPANISH PROVERB

When you're thirsty you welcome water.

Más vale mal ajuste que buen pleito.
SPANISH PROVERB

Better a bad settlement than a successful lawsuit.

A buena hambre no hay mal pan.
GABRIEL GARCÍA MÁRQUEZ:
El Coronel no Tiene quien le Escriba (Spanish)

When you have a healthy appetite there is no such thing as bad bread.

CONCEIT
see also Poets and poetry.

Gott weiss alles, aber Herr A. weiss alles besser!
GERMAN PROVERB

God knows everything, but so-and-so knows everything better!

CONCLUSIONS

Baissez le rideau, la farce est jouée.
Title of Daumier's satirical lithograph of Louis Philippe as a clown lowering the curtain on the mock spectacle of a representative Parliament (and no doubt alluding to the final words in Ruggiero Leoncavallo's opera *I Pagliacci*: La commedia è finita – The comedy is finished).
(French)

Lower the curtains, the comedy is finished.

CONDESCENSION

Neu fastidire minores.
CLAUDIAN:
Panegyricus de Quarto Consulatu Honorii Augusti (Latin)

Show no scorn of inferiors.

CONDUCT
see also Behaviour, Reputation.

Si tu veux qu'on t'épargne, épargne aussi les autres.
JEAN DE LA FONTAINE:
L'Oiseleur, l'Autour, et l'Alouette (French)

Do unto others as you would be done by (*lit.* if you want mercy for yourself, show mercy to others).

Ce que peut la vertu d'un homme ne se doit mésurer par ses efforts, mais par son ordinaire.
BLAISE PASCAL:
Pensées (French)

The worth of a man must be measured not by his efforts but by his ordinary life.

Optima sit vitae quae formula quaritis: haec est:
Mens hilaris faciens quod licet, idque loquens.
RODOLPHUS AGRICOLA:
Epigram (Latin)

You are looking for the best rule for life. Here it is: To maintain a cheerful disposition to do and and say what is right.

brar bien, que Dios es Dios.
SPANISH PROVERB

o right, for God is God.

CONFIDENCE

d-dīk al-faṣīḥ min al-bayḍa yiṣīḥ
ARAB PROVERB

n eloquent cock crows as soon as it comes out
f the egg.

ull dīk 'alā mazbalit-uh yiṣīḥ
ARAB PROVERB

very cock crows on his own dung-hill.

e trop de confiance attire le danger.
PIERRE CORNEILLE:
Le Cid (French)

verconfidence invites danger.

. . . qui sibi fidet,
ux reget examen.
HORACE:
Epistles (Latin)

Ie who has confidence in himself will lead the
est.

uid times? Caesarem vehis!
FLORUS:
Works (Latin)

Vhy are you afraid? You have Caesar aboard!
Caesar to the captain of his ship, during the
'ivil War).

CONFORMITY

oujours au plus grand nombre on doit
accomoder.
MOLIÈRE:
L'Ecole des Maris (French)

ne should always conform to the ways of the
ajority.

hrē de xenon men karta proskhōrein polei
EURIPIDES:
Medea (Greek)

 stranger must conform to his host's customs.

CONFUSION

Es geht, geht alles durcheinander
Wie Mäusedreck und Coriander.
J. W. VON GOETHE:
Peter Brey (German)

Everything is all mixed up, like mouse-
droppings and coriander.

Der Kopf steht mir wie eine Wetterfahne, wenn
ein Gewitter heraufzieht und die Windstösse
veränderlich sind.
J. W. VON GOETHE:
Letter to J. D. Salzmann, 1771 (German)

My head whirls like a weathercock when a
thunderstorm is brewing and the winds are
shifting and gusty.

CONQUEST
see also Achievement, Victory.

Tout vainqueur insolent à son perte travaille.
JEAN DE LA FONTAINE:
Les Deux Coqs (French)

Every insolent conqueror digs his own grave.

Qui se vainc une fois peut se vaincre toujours.
PIERRE CORNEILLE:
Tite et Bérénice (French)

He who masters himself once can always master
himself.

Besiegen könnt ihr uns, aber täuschen nicht
mehr.
LUDWIG BÖRNE:
Briefe aus Paris (German)

You can conquer us but you will never be able to
deceive us again.

Nel pigliare uno stato, debbe l'occupatore di
esso discorrere tutte quelle offese chi li è necessario fare, e tutto farle a un tratto per non le
avere a rinnovare ogni dì.
NICCOLÒ MACHIAVELLI:
The Prince (Italian)

When taking a country the conqueror must be
careful to commit all his cruelties at once, to
avoid being obliged to be cruel every day.

Veni, vidi, vici.
>Julius Caesar's inscription displayed
>at his Pontic triumph
>(Suetonius: *Divus Iulius*) *(Latin)*

I came, I saw, I conquered.

Vae victis!
>LATIN EXPRESSION

Woe to the vanquished!

CONSCIENCE
see also Integrity, Pardon.

Toute personne d'honneur choisit de perdre plutôt son honneur que de perdre sa conscience.
>MICHEL DE MONTAIGNE:
>*Essays (French)*

Any person of honour would prefer to lose his honour rather than lose his conscience.

La voix de la conscience et de l'honneur est bien faible, lorsque les boyaux crient.
>DENIS DIDEROT:
>*Le Neveu de Rameau (French)*

When one's guts cry out for food, how feeble are the voices of conscience and honour!

La conscience regne et ne gouverne pas.
>PAUL VALÉRY:
>*Mauvaises Pensées (French)*

Conscience reigns, but it does not govern.

Je ne vois rien dans l'ordre de l'esprit, nulle production ou trouvaille, qui puisse être préférable à la souveraineté de la conscience et au gouvernement par l'attention.
>PAUL VALÉRY:
>*Variété (French)*

I can see nothing in the order of the mind – no product or discovery – which would be preferable to the sovereignty of the conscience and government by vigilance.

Hapanti daimōn andri sumparistatai euthus genomenōi mustagōgos tou biou
>GREEK PROVERB

There stands an angel by every man, as soon as he is born, to guide him through the mystery of life.

Iudice nemo nocens absolvitur.
>JUVENAL
>*Satires (Latin)*

No guilty man can acquit himself at the bar of his own conscience.

Bona conscientia turbam advocat, mala etiam in solitudine anxia atque sollicita est.
>SENECA
>*Epistles (Latin)*

A clear conscience welcomes a crowd, but a bad conscience is disturbed and troubled even in solitude.

Nulla placida est quies, nisi quam ratio composuit.
>SENECA
>*Epistles (Latin)*

No sleep can be tranquil unless the mind is at rest.

Quisque suos patimur manes.
>VIRGIL
>*Aeneid (Latin)*

Each of us suffers from his own ghosts.

Etiam sine lege poena est conscientia.
>LATIN PROVERB

Even where there are no laws, conscience is its own punishment.

O tacitum tormentum animi conscientia!
>LATIN PROVERB

O conscience, silent torturer of the soul!

CONSEQUENCES
see also Cause and effect.

Ba'd aḍ-ḍīq faraj
>ARAB PROVERB

After sorrow, joy.

CONSOLATION
see also Dreams, Illusion.

Minuentur atrae
Carmine curae.
>HORACE
>*Odes (Latin)*

Let black care be diminished by song.

... omne malum vino cantuque levato,
:formis aegrimoniae dulcibus alloquiis.

> HORACE:
> *Epodes (Latin)*

ghten every ill with wine and song, sweet
nsolations for unlovely sorrow.

CONSTANCY
see also Faith.

, constance n'est bonne que pour des ridicules.

> MOLIÈRE:
> *Don Juan (French)*

>nstancy is only suitable for ridicule.

asuraruru mi wo ba omowads' chigai-teshi
to no inochi no oshiku mo aru kana.

> UKON, WIFE OF THE EMPEROR KOGUN:
> *Waga (Japanese)*

>u gave me your solemn word, and I was sure
u would be constant. I am moved to call down
you the penalty of death for abandoning me!

l Verdens Fald, imellem Havets Siv
ık ned, min Drøm – dig offrer jeg isteden.

> HENRIK IBSEN:
> *Love's Comedy (Norwegian)*

e low, my dream, deep down in the ocean – my
offered sacrifice until the end of the world!
vanhild, as she casts her lover's ring into the
a).

un ánimo constante
empre se halla igual semblante
ra el bien y el mal.

> PEDRO CALDERÓN DE LA BARCA:
> *El Príncipe Constante (Spanish)*

constant spirit always shows the same face to
·od and ill alike.

una constante mujer
ue es el mayor imposible.

> TIRSO DE MOLINA:
> *El Amor y el Amistad (Spanish)*

>constant woman – the greatest impossibility!

CONSTITUTION

La conséquence immédiate d'une constitution
est l'aplatissement des intelligences.

> HONORÉ DE BALZAC:
> *La Peau de Chagrin: 'Le Talisman' (French)*

The immediate result of the introduction of a
constitution is the levelling off of minds,

CONTENTMENT
see also Dissatisfaction, Enjoyment, Happiness, Home, Lies, Moderation, Oblivion, Poverty, Wealth.

Ḥelāt ad dunyā, 'aṣīd be-weik, arkab fok ḥumār,
martak tasūgah bēk

> ARAB PROVERB

The joys of life: porridge and soup, a donkey to
ride, and a wife to drive it.

Ḥeil et tākhuḍ bēah agana' bēah

> ARAB PROVERB

Be content with the strength you've got.

J'en ai conclu que le repos, l'amitié et la pensée
étaient les seuls biens qui convinssent à un
homme qui a passé l'âge de la folie.

> S. R. N. CHAMFORT:
> *Caractères et Anecdotes (French)*

I have come to the conclusion that rest, friendship and thought are the only treasures that suit
a man who has passed the age of madness.

J'aime mieux, n'en déplaise à la gloire,
Vivre au monde deux jours, que mille ans dans
l'histoire.

> MOLIÈRE:
> *La Princesse d'Elide (French)*

I prefer, if Heaven will forgive me, to live two
days in this world, than a thousand years in
history.

En mariage, comme ailleurs, contentement
passe richesse.

> MOLIÈRE:
> *Le Médecin Malgré Lui (French)*

In marriage, as in other things, contentment
surpasses wealth.

Que sont-ils devenus, les chagrins de ma vie?
Tout ce qui m'a fait vieux est bien loin main-
tenant;
Et rien qu'en regardant cette vallée amie,
Je redeviens enfant.
ALFRED DE MUSSET:
Souvenir (French)

Where have my life's vexations gone to? Everything that made me old is now far far away; and
just catching sight of this friendly valley makes
me a child once again.

Regarde sans frayeur la fin de toutes choses;
Consulte le miroir avec des yeux contents:
On ne voit point tomber ni tes lis ni tes roses,
Et l'hiver de ta vie est ton second printemps.
FRANÇOIS MAYNARD:
La Belle Vieille (French)

Look fearlessly on the end of all things; look into
your mirror with contented gaze; none will see
fall your lilies or your roses, and your life's
winter is now your second spring.

Zufriedenheit geht über Reichtum.
GERMAN PROVERB

Contentment is worth more than riches.

Peirasan pōs soi khōrei kai ho tou agathou an-
thrōpou bios tou areskomenou men tois ek tōn
holōn aponemomenois, arkoumenou de tēi idiai
praxei dikaiai
MARCUS AURELIUS:
Meditations (Greek)

Try to live the life of the good man who is more
than content with what is allocated to him out of
the whole, and is satisfied with his own acts as
just.

Monon philein to heautōi sumbainon kai sunk-
lōthomenon
MARCUS AURELIUS:
Meditations (Greek)

Love only what befalls you and is spun for you
by fate.

. . . è un' armonia
Ogni pensiero, ed ogni senso un canto.
GIOSUE CARDUCCI:
Sole e Amore (Italian)

Every thought is harmony, every song a sentiment.

Laetus sorte tua vives sapienter.
HORAC
Epistles (Lat

You will live wisely if you are happy in your l

Erit igitur pervagata inter suos gloria quisq
contentus.
BOETHI
Consolatio Philosophiae (Lat

Thus every man must be content with that glo
which he may have at home.

Et mihi vivam
Quod superest aevi, si quid superesse volunt
Sit bona librorum et provisae frugis in annu
Copia
HORA
Epistles (Lat

And may I live the remainder of my life – if t
gods will that any shall remain – for myself; m
there be plenty of books and a year's store of t
fruits of the earth!

Qua pote quisque, in ea conterat arte diem.
PROPERTI
Elegies (Lat

Let the cobbler stick to his last!

Dona praesentis cape laetus horae ac linque
Severa
HORA
Odes (Lat

Gladly accept the gifts of the present hour, a
abandon serious things.

Mens sana in corpore sano.
JUVEN
Satires (Lat

A sound mind in a sound body.

Glaðr ok reifr skyli gumna hverr,
Unz sinn biðr bana.
Sayings of the High One (Old Nors

Every man should be cheerful and glad, even
he suffers death.

Prekrasno v nas vlyublënnoe vino
I dobrÿï khleb, chto v pech' dlya nas saditsya

I zhenshchina, kotoroyu dano,
Sperva izmuchivshis', nam nasladit'sya.

NIKOLAI GUMILÉV:
Shestoe Chuvstvo (Russian)

Beautiful is the wine that loves us, the excellent bread that goes into the oven for our pleasure, and the woman we enjoy after she has had her fill of plaguing us!

Vivir quiero conmigo,
Gozar quiero del bien que debo al cielo
A solas, sin testigo,
Libre de amor, de celo,
De odio, de esperanzas, de recelo.

FRAY LUIS DE LEÓN:
Vida Retirada (Spanish)

I should like to live on my own and enjoy the blessings I owe heaven: a contemplative life, willingly forgoing love, and content not to know hope, hate, fear and jealousy

Un ángulo me basta entre mis lares,
Un libro y un amigo, un sueño breve,
Que no perturben deudas ni pesares

Epístola Moral (attrib. Andrés Fernández de Andrada) *(Spanish)*

For me it is sufficient to have a corner by my hearth, a book and a friend, and a nap undisturbed by creditors or grief.

Hoy la Nave del contento
Con viento en popa de gusto,
Donde jamas hay disgusto

LOPE DE VEGA:
Hoy la Nave del Deleite (Spanish)

Today the ship of contentment set sail with a favourable wind for a country where there are no troubles.

¡Ah, dormir gustoso y llano,
Sin cuidado y sin gobierno,
En la cocina en invierno
Y en las parvas en verano!

LOPE DE VEGA:
El Gran Duque de Moscovia (Spanish)

Ah, to sleep contentedly and plainly, without care or responsibility, in the kitchen in winter, and in the loft in spring!

CONTINUITY
see also Survival.

Quand nous voyons un effect arriver toujours de mesme, nous en concluons une nécessité naturelle, comme qu'il sera demain jour.

BLAISE PASCAL:
Pensées (French)

When we observe the same thing happening every day we come to the conclusion that a law of nature is involved, such as the certitude that there will be a tomorrow.

Continuatio est partium inter se non intermissa coniunctio.

SENECA:
Moral Questions (Latin)

Continuity is the uninterrupted joining of parts to each other.

CONVERSATION

Les conversations ressemblent aux voyages qu'on fait sur l'eau: on s'écarte de la terre sans presque le sentir, et l'on ne s'aperçoit qu'on a quitté le bord que quand on est déjà bien loin.

S. R. N. CHAMFORT:
Maximes et Pensées (French)

Conversations are like those trips we take on the water; we set sail almost without noticing it, and we do not realise that we have left the land until we are already far from it.

CO-OPERATION
see also Common interests.

Shayyil-nī wa ashayyil-ak

ARAB PROVERB

Scratch my back and I'll scratch yours (*lit.* mount me [on an animal's back] and I'll mount you).

Les hommes ne peuvent engendrer de nouvelles forces, mais seulement unir et diriger celles qui existent.

J.-J. ROUSSEAU:
Du Contrat Social (French)

Mankind cannot generate new forces – only unite and control those that already exist.

Kamuingi koiaga ndiri.
KIKUYU PROVERB

Even a little body of men, working in unison, can more easily lift a heavy load.

Serva me, servabo te.
PETRONIUS:
Satyricon (Latin)

Scratch my back, and I'll scratch yours (*lit.* serve me and I will serve you).

Tria juncto in uno.
Motto of the Order of the Bath

Three joined in one (*i.e.* England, Scotland, and Ireland).

Lehlaahlela le lla ka le leng.
SESOTHO PROVERB

One chain resounds by means of another.

COPYING
see also Printing.

Opus ab Authore bene scriptum, a Scriba male pictum.
RICHARD CRAKANTHORPE:
Defensio Ecclesiae Anglicanae (preface) *(Latin)*

A work well written by the author, but badly copied by the scribe.

CORRESPONDENCE

Al-mukātaba niṣf al-mushāda
ARAB PROVERB

Correspondence is equal to half a meeting in person.

CORRUPTION
see also Bribery, Law, Money.

Bestechlichkeit ist unsre einzige Aussicht. Solangs die gibt, gibts milde Urteilssprüche, und sogar der Unschuldige kann durchkommen vor Gericht.
BERTOLT BRECHT:
Mutter Courage und ihre Kinder (German)

Our only hope is corruption. As long as corruption lasts lenient judgments will continue, and even the innocent may get off scot free.

Das Edle schwindet von der weiten Erde,
Das Hohe sieht von Niedern sich verdrängt,
Und Freiheit wird sich nennen die Gemeinheit,
Als Gleichheit brüsten sich der dunkle Neid.
FRANZ GRILLPARZER:
Libussa (German)

Everything noble is vanishing from the world, and the lowest are supplanting the exalted. Vulgarity will call itself freedom, just as deep envy will boast of equality.

Criminibus debent hortos.
JUVENAL:
Satires (Latin)

A beautiful garden maintained by vice.

Omnia perversas possunt corrumpere mentes.
OVID:
Tristia (Latin)

Anything can corrupt a perverted mind.

Male rerum examinat omnis
Corruptus iudex.
HORACE:
Satires (Latin)

Every judge who has accepted bribes weighs truth badly.

Nisi ad regulam prava non corriges.
SENECA:
Epistles (Latin)

You can't straighten what is crooked without a ruler.

. . . velocius et citius nos
Corrumpunt vitiorum exempla domestica,
magnis Cum subeant animos auctoribus.
JUVENAL:
Satires (Latin)

No evil example corrupts us so soon and so rapidly as that which has been set at home, since it pervades the mind on the highest authority.

COST

Le coût fait perdre le goût.
FRENCH PROVERB

The price spoils the pleasure.

Cogitato, si nihil fiet, nihilo minus sumptum futurum.

MARCUS CATO:
De Agricultura (Latin)

Remember that even though work stops, nevertheless the expenses continue to mount up.

COUNTRYSIDE
see also Night, Peace.

Dort erblick' ich schöne Hügel
Ewig jung und ewig grün!
Hätt' ich Schwingen, hätt' ich Flügel,
Nach den Hügeln zög' ich hin!

J. C. F. VON SCHILLER:
Sehnsucht (German)

There I beheld beautiful hills, ever young and ever green! I'd make for them if I had wings!

Vocat ingenti clamore
Cithaeron,
Taygetique canes.

VIRGIL:
Georgics (Latin)

The echoing hills and chiding hounds invite (tr. Dryden) (*lit.* Cithaeron and the hounds of Taygetus call with a loud cry).

Tota natant crispis iuga motibus, et tremit absens
Pampinus, et vitreis vindemia turget in undis.

AUSONIUS:
Mosella (Latin)

The moving line of hills is reflected in the glassy stream; wherein the vintage swells, and the trembling tendrils of the absent vine yet sway.

COURAGE
see also Boasting, Bravery, Cowardice, Discretion, Fame, Foolhardiness, Fortune, Greatness, Integrity, Love.

Dhanna purukha asa navai na nāē;
Au supurusa hōi dēsa parāē.

MALIK MUHAMMAD JĀYASĪ:
Padumāvatī (Avadhi)

Blessed is he who does not succumb to tyranny and proves himself courageous in a foreign country.

Il y a tout de même une chose qui compte dans la la vie: c'est de ne pas être vaincu.

ANDRÉ MALRAUX:
Les Conquérants (French)

The one important thing in life is to see to it that you are never beaten.

La vraie épreuve de courage
N'est que dans le danger que l'on touche du doigt.
Tel le cherchait, dit-il, qui changeant de langage,
S'enfuit aussitôt qu'il le voit.

JEAN DE LA FONTAINE:
Le Pâtre et le Lion (French)

The true proof of courage is only in the danger which we can touch. He that talks of looking for it changes his mind and takes flight the moment he sees it.

Itel valor deit aver chevaler
Ki armes portet e en bon cheval set,
En bataille deit estre forz et fiers,
U altrement ne valt III deniers,
Einz deit monie estre en un de cez mustiers.

Le Chanson de Roland (French)

Such courage must a knight have who bears arms and rides a fine horse. In battle he must be strong and warlike; otherwise he's not worth tuppence.

Icare est chut ici, le jeune audacieux,
Qui pour voler au ciel eut assez de courage:
Ici tomba son corps dégarni de plumage,
Laissant tous braves coeurs de sa chute envieux.

PHILIPPE DESPORTES:
Icare (French)

Here fell the young brave Icarus who had courage enough to attempt the heavens; here fell his body bereft of its plumage, leaving all stout hearts envious of his fate.

On est souvent ferme par faiblesse, et audacieux par timidité.

FRANÇOIS, DUC DE LA ROCHEFOUCAULD:
Réflexions (French)

We are often firm through weakness, and audacious through timidity.

La parfaite valeur est de faire sans témoins ce qu'on serait capable de faire devant tout le monde.

> FRANÇOIS, DUC DE LA ROCHEFOUCAULD:
> *Réflexions (French)*

Perfect courage lies in doing without witnesses what we would be capable of doing in front of all the world.

Kosmon men andros outin' an tresaim' egō,
Oud' helkopoia gignetai ta sēmata

> AESCHYLUS:
> *The Seven against Thebes (Greek)*

No escutcheon terrifies me; heraldry unsupported by spears cannot harm me.

Makhōmeth', ouk atimon elpizō moron

> AESCHYLUS:
> *The Seven against Thebes (Greek)*

Into battle! – I seek only a worthy end.

Sōtērian egōg', eipon, legō tina einai tēn andreian

> PLATO:
> *The Republic (Greek)*

Courage, I said, means preserving something.

Nemo tam timidus est, ut malit semper pendere quam semel cadere.

> SENECA:
> *Epistles (Latin)*

No-one is so faint-hearted that he would rather hang for ever than drop once for all.

Militat spiritu, militat gladio.

> LATIN PROVERB

He fights with spirit as well as with the sword.

Nil desperandum.

> HORACE:
> *Odes (Latin)*

Never despair.

Sin miedo

> Motto inscribed on the figured blades
> of the daggers of old Toledo *(Spanish)*

Be always fearless! (*lit.* without fear).

COWARDICE
see also Death, Discretion, Fear, Fortune, Love, Memories.

Il n'est, je le vois bien, si poltron sur la terre
Qui ne puisse trouver un plus poltron que soi.

> JEAN DE LA FONTAINE:
> *Le Lièvre et les Grenouilles (French)*

No matter how cowardly a man may be, he can always find someone still more cowardly in this world.

Deilai toi deiloisin ephedrēssousi peleiai ammes
d' atrestois andrasi terpometha

> ANTIPATER OF SIDON:
> *Epigrams (Greek)*

Timid doves watch over cowards, but we delight in dauntless men.

Andras Arēs kteinei, deiloterous de nosos

> PHILIPPUS OF THESSALONICA:
> *Garland (Greek)*

Men perish by the sword, cowards by disease.

Ho pant' analkis houtos, hē pasa blabē,
Ho sun gunaixi tas makhas poioumenos

> SOPHOCLES:
> *Electra (Greek)*

The crawling villain, the creeping coward who, behind a woman's skirts, fights on.

Deiloi d' eisin ouden oudamou

> EURIPIDES:
> *Iphigeneia in Tauris (Greek)*

Cowards are of no avail.

Ta tōn philōn
Aiskhiston hostis katabalōn eis xumphoras
Autos sesōstai

> EURIPIDES:
> *Iphigeneia in Tauris (Greek)*

How cowardly to escape oneself and leave a friend in the lurch!

Arēs d' ouk agathōn pheidetai alla kakōn

> *Anacreontea (Greek)*

War is not sparing of the brave, but of cowards.

Fejgheds Knopp, i Blomst, er Grumhed.

HENRIK IBSEN:
Peer Gynt (Norwegian)

The fruit of cowardice in bloom is cruelty.

CREATION
see also Universe, World.

Jok' on taivoa takonut
Ilman kantta kalkutellut.

The Kalevala (Finnish)

He who hammered out the heavens and shaped the dome above the ether (referring to Ilmarinen the smith).

Joutsenen kynän nenästä,
Maholehmän maitosesta,
Ohran pienestä jyvästä,
Kesä-uuhen untuvasta.

The Kalevala (Finnish)

From the tip of the feather of a white swan, from the milk of a virgin heifer, from a tiny grain of barley, and from the fleece of a summer ewe-lamb (Ilmarinen the smith's recipe for the making of a Sampo – possibly a fortune-grinding mill).

Kein Mensch will begreifen, dass die höchste und einzige Operation der Natur und Kunst die Gestaltung sei.

J. W. VON GOETHE:
letter to K. F. Zelter, 1808 *(German)*

Nobody can grasp that creation is the highest and unique process of both nature and art.

Du wohnst bei mir Urquell der Natur
Leben und Freude der Creatur.

J. W. VON GOETHE:
Künstlers Erdewallen (German)

You dwell in me, primal source of nature, life and joy of creation.

CRICKETS

Serait-ce quelque grillon qui chante tapi dans la mousse et le lierre stérile, dont par pitié se chausse le bois?

ALOYSIUS BERTRAND:
Le Gibet (French)

Can it be the voice of some cricket, hidden in the moss and barren ivy, with which the woods compassionately bedeck themselves?

CRIME
see also Action, Civil war, Destiny, Faults, History, Life, Morals and morality, Nature, Pardon, Poverty.

Quelques crimes toujours précèdent les grands crimes.

JEAN RACINE:
Phèdre (French)

Great crimes are always preceded by crimes of some sort.

On crache sur un petit filou, mais on ne peut refuser une sorte de considération à un grand criminel: son courage vous étonne, son atrocité vous fait frémir.

DENIS DIDEROT:
Le Neveu de Rameau (French)

We spit on petty thieves, but we cannot repress a kind of respect for the great criminal – his courage astonishes us, while his atrocious deeds make us shudder.

Le crime fait la honte, et non pas l'échafaud.

THOMAS CORNEILLE:
Le Comte d'Essex (French)

It is the crime which causes shame, not the scaffold.

Un beau crime m'empoigne comme un beau mâle.

CÉLESTINE:
Le Journal d'une Femme de Chambre (French)

A good crime thrills me like a handsome man.

Cherche à qui le crime profite.

FRENCH PROVERB

In a crime seek those who profit from it.

Cherchez la femme.

FRENCH PROVERB

[In crime] look for the woman involved.

Les crimes engendrent d'immenses bienfaits, et les plus grandes vertus développent des conséquences funestes.

PAUL VALÉRY:
Eupalinos (French)

Crime gives birth to immense benefits, just as the greatest virtues are responsible for deadly consequences.

Il n'y a chose si innocente où les hommes ne
puissent porter du crime.

> MOLIÈRE:
> *Tartuffe* (preface) *(French)*

There is nothing so innocent that mankind cannot introduce crime there.

Li uomini offendono o per paura o per odio.

> NICCOLÒ MACHIAVELLI:
> *The Prince (Italian)*

People commit crimes either through fear or
hate.

Scelere velandum est scelus.

> SENECA:
> *Hippolytus (Latin)*

To conceal a crime, another must be committed.

> Qui sceleratus,
> Et furiosus erit.
> HORACE:
> *Satires (Latin)*

He who commits a crime must also be a
madman.

Nusquam facilius culpa quam in turba latet.

> LATIN PROVERB

Crime is nowhere more easily hidden than in a
crowd.

CRITICISM
see also Authorship, Compliments, Praise.

Je ne puis juger d'un ouvrage en le faisant; il faut
que je fasse comme les peintres et que je m'en
éloigne; mais non pas trop.

> BLAISE PASCAL:
> *Pensées (French)*

I cannot judge my work as it goes along; I have
to do what painters do – stand back, but not too
far!

Qui alterum incusat probri, sumpse enitere
oportet.

> PLAUTUS:
> *Truculentus (Latin)*

He who criticises another needs himself to be
outstanding.

CROWDS
see also Cities, Mankind, Suspicion.

Im Haufen steht die Tierwelt gar zu nah.

> FRANZ GRILLPARZER:
> *Ein Bruderzwist in Habsburg (German)*

In crowds the world of beasts is uncomfortably
close.

Odi profanum vulgus et arceo.

> HORACE:
> *Odes (Latin)*

I hate the uninitiate crowd and keep them far
away.

CUCKOLDRY

Il vaut mieux être encor cocu que trépassé!

> MOLIÈRE:
> *Sganarelle (French)*

Better cuckolded than dead!

CUCKOO

Hototogisu
Na ga naku sato no
Amata areba
Nao utomarenu
Omou mono kara.

> *Kokin shū (Japanese)*

Cuckoo, your sweet call comes from so many
villages that I always feel you are far away, but I
never cease to love you!

CULTURE
see also Education, Learning.

Es la cortesía la principal parte de la cultura.

> SPANISH PROVERB

Politeness is the chief ingredient of culture.

Nace bárbaro el hombre; redímese de bestia,
cultivándose.

> BALTASAR GRACIÁN:
> *Oráculo Manual y Arte de Prudencia (Spanish)*

Man is born a barbarian; but he is saved from
being a beast by acquiring culture.

CUNNING
see also Strategy.

Tou gar tekhnazein hēmeteros ho puramous
> ARISTOPHANES:
> *Thesmophoriazusae (Greek)*

For sheer cunning that takes the cake!

Gunē gar oxuthumos, hōs d' autōs anēr,
Rhaōn phulassein ē siōpēlos sophos
> EURIPIDES:
> *Medea (Greek)*

A woman – or a man – of hot temper is a less dangerous enemy than one quiet and clever.

Donde menos se piensa salta la liebre.
> SPANISH PROVERB

Up jumps the hare where least you expect it.

CURIOSITY
see also Fools, Intellectuals, Interference, Life.

Neugier nur beflügelt jeden Schritt.
> J. W. VON GOETHE:
> *Faust* (prologue) *(German)*

Mere curiosity adds wings to every step.

Curiosus nemo est quin sit malevolus.
> PLAUTUS:
> *Stichus (Latin)*

No-one is inquisitive without being malevolent.

D

DANCE

Bdiet iż-żifna meqjusa max-xejra
Tal-vjolini li tofrogh u tfur,
U l-iżwieġ fuq il-quiegħa bħal ħġieġa,
Bdiet titbandal, tizzengel u ddur.

DUN KARM:
Warda li Tgħid Grajjietha (Maltese)

The dance began, following the rhythm of the violins as they ebbed and flowed; the couples on the glassy floor began to rock and sway and revolve.

DANGER
see also Achievement, Adventure, Ambition, Caution, Confidence, Conquest, Courage, Liberty.

Le trop d'attention qu'on a pour le danger
Fait le plus souvent qu'on y tombe.

JEAN DE LA FONTAINE:
Le Renard et les Poulets d'Inde (French)

The more wary you are of danger, the more likely you are to meet it.

Toutes les balles ne tuent pas.

ALPHONSE DAUDET:
Tartarin sur les Alpes (French)

Not every bullet kills.

Le vent qui éteint une lumière allume un brasier.

P. A. C. DE BEAUMARCHAIS:
Le Barbier de Séville (French)

The same wind that extinguishes a light can set a brazier on fire.

Il ne faut pas mettre les étoupes trop près du feu.

FRENCH PROVERB

Don't put the tow too near the fire.

Le feu qui semble éteint souvent dort sous la cendre.

PIERRE CORNEILLE:
Rodogune (French)

The fire which seems out often sleeps beneath the cinders.

Mönchlein, Mönchlein, du gehst einen schweren Gang.

MARTIN LUTHER
(on the eve of his departure for Worms)
(German)

Little monk, you are embarking on a difficult journey.

Wehret den Anfängen.

GERMAN PROVERB

Nip in the bud! (*lit.* beware the beginnings).

Ecco un nuova periglio; il cor mi trema.

PIETRO METASTASIO:
Il Trionfo di Clelia (Italian)

Here is another peril! My heart shakes.

Citius venit periculum cum contemnitur.

LATIN PROVERB

When you underestimate danger it comes more quickly.

Numquam periculum sine periculo vincitur.

LATIN PROVERB

Danger can never be overcome without taking risks.

Numquam ubi diu fuit ignis defecit vapor.

LATIN PROVERB

There's no smoke without fire.

Nam ovis illius hau longe absunt a lupis.

PLAUTUS:
Truculentus (Latin)

Where there are sheep, the wolves are never very far away.

Lupum auribus tenere.

LATIN EXPRESSION

To hold a tiger by the tail (*lit.* to hold a wolf by the ears).

Cumque dedit paries venturae signa ruinae
Sollicito vacuus fit locus ille metus.

OVID:
Ex Ponto (Latin)

When a wall shows signs of its impending fall its neighbourhood is quickly emptied by fear.

Saepe enim ad limitem arboris radices sub vicini prodierunt segetem.

MARCUS TERENTIUS VARRO:
De Lingua Latina (Latin)

For often the roots of a tree that is close to the line of property reach out under a neighbour's cornfield.

Nam tua res agitur, paries cum proximus ardet,
Et neglecta solent incendia sumere vires.

HORACE:
Epistles (Latin)

When your neighbour's property is on fire your own safety is at stake, for neglected fires usually intensify.

Latet anguis in herba.

LATIN PROVERB

There's a snake in the grass.

Qui legitis flores, et humi nascentia fraga,
Frigidus, o pueri, fugite hinc, latet anguis in herba.

VIRGIL:
Eclogues (Latin)

Children, gathering flowers and wild strawberries, flee! a chill snake lies hidden in the grass!

Parcite, oves, nimium procedere; non bene ripae
Creditur; ipse aries etiam nunc vellera siccat.

VIRGIL:
Eclogues (Latin)

Beware, sheep! do not go too far, do not trust the banks! Even now the ram is drying his fleece.

Flamma fumo est proxima.

PLAUTUS:
Curculio (Latin)

Where there's smoke there's fire.

Anak dara dua sa-pasang,
Pakai baju pakai kěrosang,
Sa-biji nanas, sa-biji pisang,
Bělum tahu rězěki musang.

Sějarah Mělayu (Malay)

Two beautiful young maidens, decked in fine gold and rare silks, sit innocently there – unaware that when the fruit is ripe, the civet will be close by.

De sola una vez a incendio
Crece una breve pavesa.

PEDRO CALDERÓN DE LA BARCA:
El Alcalde de Zalamea (Spanish)

In a single instant a tiny spark can be fanned into a blaze.

Si el fuego está cerca de la estopa, llega el diablo y sopla.

SPANISH PROVERB

If the tow is near the fire, the Devil comes along and blows.

Vuélvete, paloma,
Que el ciervo vulnerado
Por el otero asoma,
Al aire de tu vuelo, y fresco toma.

ST. JOHN OF THE CROSS:
Canciones Entre el Alma y el Esposo (Spanish)

Turn back, my dove, that the wounded deer may reappear on the hillside and find new solace in the wake of your wings.

Escarba la gallina por su mal, y saca el cuchillo
que la ha de degollar.
SPANISH PROVERB

The hen scratches about on the ground, but
does herself no good, for she unearths the knife
that will cut her throat.

Casa con dos puertas mala es de guardar.
SPANISH PROVERB

A house with two doors is difficult to guard.

Con hijo de gato no se burlan los ratones.
SPANISH PROVERB

The mice do not mock at the cat's son.

DAUGHTERS
see also Families, Parents.

Le devoir d'une fille est en l'obéissance.
PIERRE CORNEILLE:
Horace (French)

Obedience is a daughter's duty.

DAWN
see also Night, Spring.

Na trávě skví se rosa,
Dech země vidím, v bílé páře stoupá
Jak tucha jitra k nebi.
JAROSLAV VRCHLICKÝ:
Noční Zpěv Merlina (Czech)

Dew glistens on the grass; I see earth's breath in
a milky haze rising skyward, like a promise of
morning.

Już ostatnie perły gwiazd zamierzchły, i na dnie
Niebios zgasły, i niebo środkiem czoła bladnie,
Prawą skronią złożone na węzgłowíu cieni,
Jeszcze smagławe, lewą coraz się rumieni.
ADAM MICKIEWICZ:
Pan Tadeusz (Czech)

The last pearls of the stars have already folded
slowly and gone out on the flow of the heavens;
the sky fades in the centre of its brow, as it lies
with its right temple on a pillow of shadow.

Die Sterne sind nicht immer da,
Es kommt ein Morgenrot.
BERTOLT BRECHT:
Legende vom Toten Soldaten (German)

The stars are not always there – eventually there
comes the rose-coloured dawn.

Aurora wie neukräfftig liegt die Erd um dich.
J. W. VON GOETHE:
Künstlers Erdewallen (German)

The dawn pervades the earth with new strength.

Existatai de nuktos aianēs kuklos
Tēi leukopōlōi phengos hēmerai phlegein
SOPHOCLES:
Ajax (Greek)

As dawn, drawn by white steeds, lights up the
heavens, night obediently withdraws.

Krokopeplos heōs
GREEK EXPRESSION

Saffron-mantled dawn.

Rhododaktulos heōs
HOMER:
Iliad (Greek)

Rosy-fingered dawn.

Hōs hēmin ēdē lampron hēliou selas
Heōia kinei phthegmat' ornithōn saphē
Melaina t' astrōn ekleloipen euphronē
SOPHOCLES:
Electra (Greek)

The black cloth of night, spangled with stars,
yields to the sun whose bright rays call forth the
songs of the birds.

E sorgo, e i lievi nugoletti, e il primo
Degli augelli susurro, e l'aura fresca,
E le ridenti piagge benedico.
GIACOMO LEOPARDI:
La Vita Solitaria (Italian)

I get up, and I bless the light thin clouds and the
first twittering of birds, and the breathing air
and the smiling face of the hills.

Ariake no
Tsurenaku mieshi
Wakare yori
Akatsuki bakari
Uki mono wa nashi.

MIFU NO TADAMINE:
Waga (Japanese)

To me she was as cold as the moon at dawn; and, since I have left her, the dawn is the sight I find most sad.

Aurora novo cum spargit lumine terras.

LUCRETIUS:
De Rerum Natura (Latin)

Dawn anew sprinkles the earth with light.

Nosque ubi primus equis Oriens afflavit anhelis,
Illic sera rubens accendit lumina Vesper.

VIRGIL:
Georgics (Latin)

When dawn breathes upon us with his panting steeds, the rosy Vesper afar off kindles the evening stars.

donde le pesa a la aurora
cuando se llega la hora
de venirnos a llamar.

LOPE DE VEGA:
Peribáñez (Spanish)

Whence it grieves the dawn when it is time to waken us.

Albor. El horizonte
Entreabre sus pestañas
Y empieza a ver.

JORGE GUILLÉN:
Los Nombres (Spanish)

Dawn: the horizon unlocks its eyelashes and begins to see.

Alba y lluvia se funden. Con informe,
Quizá penoso balbuceo
Tiende a se claro el día.

JORGE GUILLÉN:
Paso a la Aurora (Spanish)

Dawn and rain intermingle. With formless, perhaps painful babbling, day gropes towards clarity.

DEATH
see also Action, Anger, Bravery, Disgrace, Evil, Execution, Experience, Folly, Foolhardiness, Graves, Illness, Impermanence, Inheritance, Last words, Life, Mankind, Marriage, Mercy, Money, Mortality, Mourning, Old age, Pain, Pleasure, Suffering, Tyranny, War.

Fīh mathal fi 'ṣ-ṣīn yiqūl inn al-kafan mā fīh-sh jiyūb

ARAB PROVERB

A shroud has no pockets (*lit.* there is a proverb in China which says a shroud has no pockets).

Dood, o dood,
Sombere, somber geronnen rood,
Kom, o kom.

HERMAN GORTER:
De School der Poëzie (Dutch)

Death, o death, sombre one, sombre darkening red, come, o come!

J'ai perdu le souvenir
Du passé, de l'advenir,
Je ne suis que vaine masse
De bronze en homme gravé.

PIERRE DE RONSARD:
Hymne de la Mort (French)

My memory has gone, both of the past and the future, and I am nothing but a useless mass of bronze engraved in the likeness of a man.

Le plus semblable aux morts meurt le plus à regret.

JEAN DE LA FONTAINE:
La Mort et le Mourant (French)

Those who are nearly dead regret their approaching death the most.

La mort ne surprend point le sage;
Il est toujours prêt à partir.

JEAN DE LA FONTAINE:
La Mort et le Mourant (French)

The wise man is never surprised by death: he is always ready to depart.

Morte la bête, mort le venin.

FRENCH PROVERB

Dead men tell no tales (*lit.* the poison is dead when the beast is dead).

La mort est un remède à trouver quand on veut,
Et l'on s'en doit servir le plus tard que l'on peut.
MOLIÈRE:
Le Dépit Amoureux (French)

Death is a remedy always ready to hand, but
only to be used in the last extremity.

Pourrir sous du marbre ou pourrir sous de la
terre, c'est toujours pourrir.
DENIS DIDEROT:
Le Neveu de Rameau (French)

Whether you rot under marble or under earth,
the fact remains – you rot!

Ha Mort, ô douce mort, mort seule guerison
Des esprits oppressés d'une estrange prison!
ETIENNE JODELLE:
Cléopâtre Captive (French)

O death, sweet death, sole refuge of spirits confined in awful prisons!

Le mort n'entend sonner les cloches.
DENIS DIDEROT:
Le Neveu de Rameau (French)

The dead do not hear the funeral bells.

La mort entra comme un voleur.
VICTOR HUGO:
Le Revenant (French)

Death stole in like a thief.

Mon Dieu, accordez-moi, à l'heure de ma mort,
les prières d'un prêtre, un linceul de toile, une
bière de sapin et un lieu sec.
Les Patenôtres de M. le Maréchal (French)

Grant, oh God, that when I die I may have the
prayers of a priest, a linen winding-sheet, a
coffin of fir, and a dry grave.

Ce que j'ignore le plus est cette mort mesme que
je ne scaurais éviter.
BLAISE PASCAL:
Pensées (French)

Least of all do I know this very death whose
grasp I cannot avoid.

C'est une chose horrible de sentir s'écouler tout
ce qu'on possède.
BLAISE PASCAL:
Pensées (French)

It is dreadful to feel all one possesses slipping
away.

Mort soudaine seule à craindre.
BLAISE PASCAL:
Pensées (French)

It is only sudden death we need fear.

C'est qu'à la fin la mort toutes choses emmeine.
PIERRE DE RONSARD:
Tombeau de Charles IX (French)

Ultimately it is death that removes all.

Un homme mort n'est qu'un homme mort, et ne
fait point de conséquence.
MOLIÈRE:
L'Amour Médecin (French)

A dead man is only a dead man and is of no
importance.

La mort a des rigueurs à nulle autre pareilles.
On a beau la prier,
La cruelle qu'elle est se bouche ses oreilles
Et nous laisse crier.
FRANÇOIS DE MALHERBE:
Consolation à M. du Périer (French)

The harshness of death is unequalled. She closes
her ears to our prayers and lets us cry.

Comment on doit quitter la vie et tous ses maux,
C'est vous qui le savez, sublimes animaux!
ALFRED DE VIGNY:
La Mort du Loup (French)

Sublime animals, it is you who understand how
to depart this life and all its evils!

Aussi, quand tu parvins à ta saison dernière,
Vieux lion fatigué, sous ta blanche crinière,
Tu mourus longuement plein de glore et
d'ennui.
AUGUSTE BARBIER:
Michel-Ange (French)

You weary old lion, with that white mane of
yours, when you came to the final stage, you
died slowly, tired and renowned.

On meurt deux fois, je le vois bien:
Cesser d'aimer et d'être aimable,
C'est une mort insupportable;
Cesser de vivre, ce n'est rien.

VOLTAIRE:
A Madame du Châtelet (French)

I see clearly that there are two deaths: to cease loving and being loved is unbearable. But to cease to live is of no consequence.

L'ombre du sablier enterre la nuit.

RENÉ CHAR:
Aromates Chasseurs (French)

The shadow of the hourglass buries the night.

La mort nous parle d'une voix profonde pour ne rien dire.

PAUL VALÉRY:
Mauvaises Pensées (French)

Death speaks to us with a deep voice but has nothing to say.

La mort est dans la vie la vie aidant la mort
La vie est dans la mort la mort aidant la vie.

JACQUES PRÉVERT:
Art Abstrus (French)

Death is in life; life assisting death. Life is in death; death assisting life.

O mort! tu peux attendre; éloigne, éloigne-toi!

ANDRÉ CHÉNIER:
La Jeune Captive (French)

Oh Death, you can wait: keep your distance!

Je soutenais l'éclat de la mort toute pure.

PAUL VALÉRY

I maintained that the splendour of death lies in its purity.

Le lâche craint la mort, et c'est tout ce qu'il craint.

RACINE:
Andromaque (French)

The coward fears death and that's all he fears.

Les études littéraires nous permettent de dédaigner la mort.

MARCEL PROUST
(In an essay written when he was a pupil at the
Lycée Condorcet) *(French)*

Our literary studies allow us to scorn death.

Le soleil ni la mort ne se peuvent regarder fixement.

FRANÇOIS, DUC DE LA ROCHEFOUCAULD:
Réflexions (French)

We can stare in the face neither the sun nor death.

Tuer, pour rajeunir et pour créer;
Ou pour tomber et pour mourir, qu'importe!
Ouvrir, ou se casser les poings contre la porte!

EMILE VERHAEREN:
La Révolte (French)

Killing to rejuvenate and to create, or to fall and die, what does it matter! To open, or to bruise one's fists on the door!

L'avare Achéron ne lâche point sa proie.

JEAN RACINE:
Phèdre (French)

That miser Acheron never lets go of his victim (on hearing the false news of Theseus's death).

On ne meurt qu'une fois, et c'est pour si long-temps.

MOLIÈRE:
Le Dépit Amoureux (French)

One only dies once, and then it's for such a long time.

Komme, Tod, und raub mich, Tod, im Kusse!

CONRAD FERDINAND MEYER:
Der Kamerad (German)

Come, death, and snatch me away in your kiss!

Nun mag der Tod uns immerhin erscheinen,
Er trennt uns nicht, er kann uns nur vereinen!

FRANZ GRILLPARZER:
Blanka von Kastilien (German)

Come death, if you will: you cannot divide us; you can only unite us.

Aller Küsse Rausch,
Aller Lichter Schein,
Alle Glorie wird gegangen sein
PAULA VON PRERADOVIĆ:
Nach dem Tode (German)

The ecstasy of all kisses, the gleam of all light,
and all glories will be gone.

So weit im Leben, ist zu nah am Tod!
FRIEDRICH HEBBEL:
Sommerbild (German)

What is so far in life, is too near to death.

Wir wissen nichts von diesem Hingehn, das
Nicht mit uns teilt. Wir haben keinen Grund,
Bewunderung und Liebe oder Hass
Dem Tod zu zeigen, den ein Maskenmund
Tragischer Klage wunderlich entstellt
RAINER MARIA RILKE:
Todeserfahrung (German)

We know nothing of this journey that no-one
shares with us. We have no reason to look on
death with admiration, love or hate; since a
masked mouth strangely distorts it with tragic
lamentations.

Nur die Toten kommen nicht wieder.
GEORG BÜCHNER:
Dantons Tod (German)

Only the dead never return.

Ouwê daz wîsheit unde jugent,
Des mannes schoene noch sîn tugent
Niht erben sol, sô ie der lîp erstirbet!
WALTHER VON DER VOGELWEIDE:
Ouwê daz wîsheit (German)

How sad it is that when a man dies his wisdom,
his youth, his beauty, or his virtue cannot be
inherited!

Sterben, ach! sterben
Soll ich allein!   GERMAN FOLK SONG

In death shall I be alone!

Denn nah am Tod sieht man den Tod nicht
mehr.
RAINER MARIA RILKE:
Duineser Elegien (German)

As death draws near one sees it no more.

Der Tod ist kein Ereignis des Lebens. Den Tod
erlebt man nicht.
LUDWIG WITTGENSTEIN:
Tractatus Logico-philosophicus (German)

Death is not an event in life; we do not experience death.

Ach, noch weit entsetzlicher ist das einsame
Krankenbette, in das der Tod nach und nach
mit hineinkriecht, sich mit uns unter einer
Decke verbirgt und so vertraulich tut.
LUDWIG TIECK:
William Lovell (German)

Ah, yet more terrible is the lonely sickbed into
which death steals little by little, concealing
itself under our covers and behaving so inti-
mately.

Ja süss, himmlisch süss ists, eingewiegt zu werden in den Schlaf des Todes von dem Gesang
des Geliebten.
J. C. F. VON SCHILLER:
Die Räuber (German)

How sweet – heavenly sweet – it is to be lulled
into the sleep of death by one's beloved!

Kurz ist der Schmerz, und ewig ist die Freude!
J. C. F. VON SCHILLER:
Jungfrau von Orleans (German)

The pain is brief, but the joy eternal!

. . . der
Die dunkle Zukunft sieht, der muss auch
Sehen den Tod und allein ihn fürchten.
FRIEDRICH HÖLDERLIN:
Der Mensch (German)

He who can look into the dark future sees also
death, and he alone can fear it.

Todesangst ist ärger als Sterben.
J. C. F. VON SCHILLER:
Die Räuber (German)

Fear of death is worse than dying.

Der Leichnam ist nicht das *ganze* Tier.
J. W. VON GOETHE:
Letter to Herr Hetzler jr., 1770 *(German)*

The corpse is not the *whole* animal.

Tois gar thanousi mokhthos ou prosgignetai
SOPHOCLES:
Trachiniae (Greek)

No trouble comes to the dead.

Outoi nomizō sophon, hos an mellōn thanein
Oiktōi to deima toulethrou nikan thelēi
EURIPIDES:
Iphigeneia in Tauris (Greek)

How foolish is he who, facing death, thinks by
his cries to lessen its horror.

Ouk esti tous thanontas eis phaos molein
EURIPIDES:
Alcestis (Greek)

There is no return to life from death.

Brotois hapasi katthanein opheileta
EURIPIDES:
Alcestis (Greek)

No mortal can escape death.

Gignōske de
Hōs pasin hēmin katthanein opheiletai.
EURIPIDES:
Alcestis (Greek)

Know for certain that death is the one debt
everyone of us must settle.

Ōnthrōpe, mē dra tous tethnēkotas kakōs
SOPHOCLES:
Ajax (Greek)

Don't insult the dead.

Mia gar tōn biōtikōn praxeōn kai hautē esti,
kath' hēn apothnēskomen
MARCUS AURELIUS:
Meditations (Greek)

The act of dying is also one of the acts of life.

Pheugousi gar toi khoi thraseis, hotan pelas
Edē ton haidēn eisorōsi tou biou
SOPHOCLES:
Antigone (Greek)

Even the bravest will flee when closely pursued
by death.

Terma d'horain biotoio
GREEK PROVERB
(attrib. Solon)

Look at the end of life.

Monos theōn gar Thanatos ou dōrōn erai
AESCHYLUS:
Niobe (Greek)

Alone of the gods, death has no love of gifts.

Lathe biōsas
EPICURUS:
Precepts (Greek)

End your days unnoticed.

Auto to apothñeskein oudeis phobeitai
GREEK PROVERB

No-one fears death itself.

Pant' ethanen nekuessi
ST. GREGORY OF NAZIANZUS:
Opera (Greek)

For the dead all is dead.

Asson ith', hōs ken thasson olethrou peirath'
hikēai
HOMER:
Iliad (Greek)

Come near so that you can reach death's goal
more swiftly.

Ho thanatos toioutos, hoion genesis, phuseos
mustērion
MARCUS AURELIUS:
Meditations (Greek)

Death, like birth, is one of nature's secrets.

Thanatos anapaula aisthētikēs antitupias kai
hormētikēs neurospastias kai dianoētikēs diex-
odou kai tēs pros tēn sarka leitourgias
MARCUS AURELIUS:
Meditations (Greek)

Death is a release from the impressions of sense,
and from the impulses that make us their pup-
pets; from the vagaries of mind, and from the
hard service of the flesh.

O che bel morir è, quando la vita
È serena, et felice!
GIAMBATTISTA CINTHIO GIRALDI:
Euphimia (Italian)

How good it is to die when life is serene and
happy!

Al gener nostro il fato
Non donò che il morire.
GIACOMO LEOPARDI:
A Se Stesso (Italian)

What gift has fate brought man but dying?

Lasso! bèn sò che doloróse prède
Di nói fa quélla, ch'a null'uòm perdóna.
FRANCESCO PETRARCA:
Sonnets (Italian)

Alas! I know death makes us all his prey, and no
whit of mercy can be shown to man in his
destiny.

Il vivere è sventura,
Grazia il morir.
GIACOMO LEOPARDI:
Sopra un Basso Rilievo Antico Sepolcrale (Italian)

Living is a misfortune, death a kindness.

Wakete fuku kaze koso ukere hana tomo-ni,
Tsirade ko-no ha-va nado nokururan.
JAPANESE SONG

How is it that a breath of wind will carry away
the blossom but leave the leaves on a tree?
(referring to the lament of a lover for the death of
her child).

Kageri areba keo nugi sutetsu fudzi goromo
Hate naki mono-wa namida nari keri.
MITSINOBU:
Waga (Japanese)

There is a limit to the time mourning must be
worn, but my tears at least will never leave me.

Mortale igitur omne animal et dissolubile . . .
necesse est.
CICERO:
De Natura Deorum (Latin)

Thus every living thing is subject to death and
dissolution.

. . . sed omnes una manet nox,
Et calcanda semel via leti.
HORACE:
Odes (Latin)

There is a common night for all when the path to
death must at last be trodden.

Mors individua est.
SENECA:
Troades (Latin)

Death is indivisible.

Magnifica verba mors prope admota excutit.
SENECA:
Troades (Latin)

Proud words falter at the approach of death

Post mortem nihil est ipsaque mors nihil,
Velocis spatii meta novissima.
SENECA:
Troades (Latin)

After death there is nothing; even death is nothing but the end of a swift-run race.

Vixi, et, quem dederat cursum fortuna, peregi
VIRGIL:
Aeneid (Latin)

My life is ended for I have run through the span
fortune granted me.

Pulchrumque mori succurrit in armis.
VIRGIL:
Aeneid (Latin)

We are reminded how glorious it is to die with
sword in hand.

Pallida Mors aequo pulsat pede pauperum
Tabernas regumque turris.
HORACE:
Odes (Latin)

Wan death knocks impartially at the door of the
poor man's shop and the prince's palace.

Media vita in morte sumus.
NOTKER BALBULUS:
(opening words of hymn).
(Latin)

In the midst of life we are in death.

Scire mori sors prima viris.

LUCAN:
Imaginary Eulogy of Pompey by Cato (Latin)

Man's happiest lot is to know when to die.

Nec mea qui digitis lumina condat erit.

OVID:
Heroides (Latin)

There will be no-one to close my dying eyes with his fingers.

At vos incertam, mortales, funeris horam, quaeritis, et qua sit mors aditura via.

PROPERTIUS:
Elegies (Latin)

Yet, mortals, you want to know the uncertain hour of your death, and by what means your end will come.

Placidaque ibi demum morte quievit.

VIRGIL:
Aeneid (Latin)

At last he found his rest in peaceful death.

Felix opportunitate mortis.   LATIN PROVERB

Happy through death's intervention (implying being spared some misfortune by the chance of death).

Nemo praesumitur ludere in extremis.

LATIN PROVERB

It is assumed that a dying man will tell the truth.

Quicquid aetatis retro est, mors tenet.

SENECA:
Epistles (Latin)

Death holds whatever years lie behind us.

Non mortem timemus, sed cogitationem mortis.

SENECA:
Epistles (Latin)

It is not death we fear, but the thought of it.

Profunda super nos altitudo temporis veniet.

SENECA:
Epistles (Latin)

The deep flood of time will engulf us.

Mors sola fatetur quantula sint hominum corpuscula.

JUVENAL:
Satires (Latin)

Death alone proclaims the insignificance of our poor human bodies.

Vive memor leti.

PERSIUS:
Satires (Latin)

Live mindful of death.

Mortem igitur omnibus horis impendentem timens qui poterit animo consistere?

CICERO:
De Senectute (Latin)

With death threatening at every hour, how can we who fear it maintain our spirit steadfast?

[Sensi] mortem omni aetati esse communem.

CICERO:
De Senectute (Latin)

[I have learnt that] death is common to every age.

Moriendum enim certe est, et incertum an hoc ipso die!

CICERO:
De Senectute (Latin)

It is certain that we must die and, for aught we know, this very day!

Mors adeone parum est?

CICERO:
In Rufini (Latin)

Is death not enough?

Nobis cum semel occidit brevis lux,
Nox est perpetua una dormienda.

CATULLUS:
Poems (Latin)

Once our brief life is done, we must sleep throughout eternal night.

Usque adeone mori miserum est?

VIRGIL:
Aeneid (Latin)

Is it then so dreadful a thing to die?

Mors infanti felix, iuveni acerba, nimis sera est seni.

LATIN PROVERB

Death is luck for childhood, bitter for youth, too late for age.

Vsë pepel, prizrak, ten' i dȳm,
Ischeznet vsë kak vikhor' pȳl'nȳǐ,
I pered smert'yu mȳ stoim
I bezoruzhnȳ i bessil'nȳ.

ALEKSEǏ TOLSTOY:
Ioann Damaskin (Russian)

All is ashes, phantoms, shadows, smoke – everything will vanish like the dust of a whirlwind, and we shall stand before death unarmed and helpless.

V etoǐ zhizni umirat' ne novo,
No i zhit', konechno, ne noveǐ.

SERGEǏ ESENIN:
Do Svidan'ya (Russian)

In this life to die is nothing new; but then, there is nothing newer about living!

Edva uvidel ya seǐ svet,
Uzhe zubami smert' skrezheshchet,
Kak molnieǐ, kosoyu bleshchet
I dni moi, kak zlak, sechët.

GAVRIL ROMANOVICH DERZHAVIN:
On the Death of Prince Meshchersky (Russian)

Hardly have I seen anything of this world, but death is already grinding his teeth, and mows down my days with flashing scythe like a crop.

Lloraré mi muerte ya,
Y lamentaré mi vida
En tanto que detenida
Por mis pecados está.

ST. JOHN OF THE CROSS:
Coplas del Alma que Pena por ver a Dìos (Spanish)

I shall mourn my death now, and lament my life since it has been prolonged for my sins.

La muerte es una mujer.

SPANISH PROVERB

Death is a woman.

Los muertos en la huesa, y los vivos a la mesa.

SPANISH PROVERB

The dead to their graves, the living to their dinners.

Quien teme la muerte no goza la vida.

SPANISH PROVERB

He who fears death cannot enjoy life.

Muertos e idos no tienen amigos.

SPANISH PROVERB

The dead and the absent have no friends.

Al que ha de morir a oscuras, poco le importa ser cerero.

SPANISH PROVERB

To him who is going to die in the dark, it will not be much good being a candle-maker.

Y consiento en mi morir
Con voluntad plazentera,
Clara y pura,
Que querer ombre vivir
Cuando Dios quiere que muera,
Es locura.

JORGE MANRIQUE:
Coplas por la Muerte de su Padre (Spanish)

I acquiesce in my death with complete willingness, uncoloured by hesitation; how foolish to cling to life when God has ordained otherwise!

¡Oh hado esecutivo en mis dolores,
Cómo sentí tus leyes rigurosas!
Cortaste el árbol con manos dañosas,
Y esparciste por tierra fruta y flores.

GARCILASO DE LA VEGA:
Soneto (Spanish)

Ruthless fate, how I have suffered under your rigorous laws! with destructive hands you have felled my tree (*i.e.* his lover) and scattered its blossoms and fruit.

¡Oh, si acabase, viendo cómo muero,
De aprender a morir antes que llegue
Aquel forzoso término postrero

Epístola Moral (attrib. Andrés Fernández de Andrada) *(Spanish)*

Since I have to die, let me learn how to before the time of that final unavoidable end arrives.

¡Oh muerte! ven callada,
Como sueles venir en la saeta
                    Epístola Moral (attrib. Andrés Fernández
                              de Andrada) *(Spanish)*

Come silently, death, as by the arrow you are
used to come!

Del pecado y la invidia, pues, nací,
Porque dos furias en mi pecho estén:
Por la invidia caduca muerte di
A cuantos de la vida la luz ven.
                    CALDERON DE LA BARCA:
                    La Vida es Sueño (Spanish)

I was born of envy and sin – thus I have two
furies in my breast. Because of envy I gave
decrepit death to as many as had seen the light.

Tu historia, ¡qué naufragia en mar profundo!
¡Pero no importa,
porque ella es corta,
pasa, y la muerte es larga,
larga como el amor!
                    MIGUEL DE UNAMUNO:
                    En Gredos (Spanish)

Your (*i.e.* Spain's) history; what a shipwreck in
the ocean's deep! But it is of no importance for
history is short and it passes, whereas death is
long – long as love!

El mundo es un valle de lágrimas y mientras más
pronto salís de él.
                    PEREZ GALDÓS:
                    Miau (Spanish)

The world is but a vale of tears; the sooner we
leave it the better.

DECEIT
**see also Appearance, Avarice, Cuckoldry,
Flattery, Lies, Life, Love, Marriage,
Opinion, Praise, Self-deception, Sincerity,
Treachery, Women.**

Tel cuide engeigner autrui,
Qui souvent s'engeigne soi-même.
                    FRENCH PROVERB
            (cited in La Fontaine's *La Grenouille et le Rat*)

He who believes he is deceiving others often
deceives himself.

L'union qui est entre les hommes n'est fondée
que sur cette mutuelle tromperie.
                    BLAISE PASCAL:
                    Pensées (French)

The union binding mankind is based only on
mutual deceit.

Ce qu'on donne aux méchants, toujours on le
regrette.
                    JEAN DE LA FONTAINE:
                    La Lice et sa Compagne (French)

We always regret what we give to deceitful
people.

C'est double plaisir de tromper le trompeur.
                    JEAN DE LA FONTAINE:
                    Le Coq et le Renard (French)

It is doubly pleasing to deceive the deceiver.

Il n'est pas malaisé de tromper un trompeur.
                    JEAN DE LA FONTAINE:
                    L'Enfouisseur et son Compère (French)

It is not difficult to deceive a deceiver.

Chacun passe sa vie à jeter des petites pincées de
poudre dans l'oeil de son voisin.
                    LABICHE & MARTIN:
                    La Poudre aux Yeux (French)

Everyone makes a habit of throwing sand in his
neighbour's eyes.

Admirez l'artifice extrême
De ces moines ingénieux:
Ils vous ont habillé comme eux,
Mon Dieu, de peur qu'on ne vous aime.
                    Satire written on an eighteenth-century
                    print of Christ dressed as a Jesuit
                    (quoted in Voltaire:
                    Philosophical Dictionary: Convulsions) *(French)*

O Lord, you cannot but admire the extraordinary guilt of these wily monks – they have
dressed you in their garb, to prevent your being
loved!

Turpe est aliud loqui, aliud sentire.
                    SENECA:
                    Epistles (Latin)

It is ignoble to say one thing and mean another.

Bonitatis verba imitari maior malitia est.
PUBLILIUS SYRUS:
Sententiae (Latin)

To ape the accents of goodness is double-dyed villainy.

DECISION
see also Action, Battles, Deliberation, Dilemma, Hesitation, Leadership, Opportunity, Resolution.

Le trop d'expédients peut gâter une affaire.
JEAN DE LA FONTAINE:
Le Chat et le Renard (French)

Too many expedients can spoil a venture.

La nuit est bonne conseillère.
FRENCH PROVERB

Best to sleep on it (referring to making decisions).

Alles oder nichts!   GERMAN EXPRESSION

All or nothing!

Eatur quo deorum ostenta et inimicorum iniquitas vocat. Iacta alea esto!
SUETONIUS:
Divus Iulius (Latin)

Let us take the course which the signs of the gods and the false dealing of our enemies have indicated. Let the die be cast! (Caesar's memorable words when he finally decided to cross the Rubicon and march on Rome.)

Deliberandum est saepe: statuendum est semel!
LATIN PROVERB

Deliberate often – decide once!

Ad paenitendum properat, cito qui iudicat.
LATIN PROVERB

Precipitate judgment brings swift regret.

Aut agat aut desistat!   SUETONIUS:
Tiberius (Latin)

Let him take it or leave it! (A senator's protest when Tiberius hypocritically held back from accepting imperial authority).

Quae mora est? In hoc ego sinu bellum pacemque porto; utrum eligitis?
FLORUS:
Works (Latin)

Why this delay? In the folds of my robe I bear war and peace. Which do you choose? (The chief of the Roman embassy to the Carthaginians in the second Punic War).

El no y el sí son breves de decir, y piden mucho pensar
BALTASAR GRACIÁN:
Oráculo Manual y Arte de Prudencia (Spanish)

'No' and 'yes' are words quickly said, but they need a great amount of thought before you utter them.

DEDICATIONS

Treu und Fest.
Motto of the XI Hussars *(German)*

Loyal and Steadfast.

Pigli adunque vostra Magnificenzia questo piccolo dono con quello animo che io lo mando!
NICCOLO MACHIAVELLI:
The Prince (dedication) *(Italian)*

Accept, Your Highness, this little gift in the spirit in which it is offered! (addressed to Lorenzo de Medici).

Pro fide et pro utilitate hominum.
Motto of the Grand Order, Malta *(Latin)*

For the faith and for the service of mankind.

Sero sed serio
Motto of the Marquess of Salisbury *(Latin)*

Late, but seriously.

Ut prosim.
Motto of Ryde School *(Latin)*

That I may be useful.

Vade, liber, nostri fato meliore memento!
AEMILIUS PROBUS:
Epigram (Latin)

Go forth, little book, and under a better destiny be mindful of me!

Virginibus puerisque.
>Title of a book of essays by Robert Louis
Stevenson *(Latin)*

'or boys and girls.

DEFEAT
see also Adversity, Courage, Government, Night, Victory, War.

Wer den Schaden hat, braucht für den Spott
nicht zu sorgen.
GERMAN PROVERB

The laugh is always on the loser.

Quintili Vare, legiones redde!
SUETONIUS:
Divus Augustus (Latin)

Quintilius Varus, give me back my legions!
Augustus's frequent cry after hearing of
Varus's defeat in Germany).

DEFIANCE

No pasarán!
>Said by the Communist leader,
'La Pasionaria', at Republican public
meetings in the Spanish civil war.

They shall not pass!

DELIBERATION
see also Decision, Determination, Resolve.

Deliberando discitur sapientia.
LATIN PROVERB

Deliberation teaches wisdom.

Deliberando saepe perit occasio.
LATIN PROVERB

Deliberation often loses a good chance.

DEMOCRACY
see also America, England, Juries.

Romains, soyez vous-mêmes les auteurs des lois
qui doivent faire votre bonheur!
J. J. ROUSSEAU:
Du Contrat Social (French)

Romans, be yourselves the authors of the laws
that are to make you content! (Quoting, or
paraphrasing, the advice given by the decem-
virs).

Il n'y avait point de véritable democratie.
J. J. ROUSSEAU:
Du Contrat Social (French)

There was no such thing as a true democracy.

DEPENDENCE

Tout ce qui vit, sans l'excepter, cherche son
bien-être aux dépens de qui il appartiendra.
DENIS DIDEROT:
Le Neveu de Rameau (French)

There is no living being that does not look for his
wellbeing at the expense of those he belongs to.

On a souvent besoin d'un plus petit que soi.
JEAN DE LA FONTAINE:
Le Lion et Le Rat (French)

We often need someone smaller than ourselves.

Am Ende hängen wir doch ab
Von Kreaturen, die wir machten.
J. W. VON GOETHE:
Faust (German)

In the end we still depend on creatures of our
making.

DEPRIVATION

Mēt' emoi meli mēte melissa
SAPPHO:
Poems (Greek)

Neither honey nor bee for me.

DESIRE
**see also Ambition, Avarice, Emotion, Envy,
Fortune, Greatness, Greed, Immortality,
Love, Materialism, Moderation, Old age,
Reason.**

Sluit voor Begeerte uw graegh gezicht;
Zy loert, zy loert om in te vaeren
JOOST VAN DEN VONDEL:
Joseph in Egypten (Dutch)

Close to desire your eager sight; she lurks and
watches to invade you.

Vous êtes une femme pour qui on pourrait avoir
une grande passion!

> BENITO MUSSOLINI:
> (on first meeting Clare Sheridan)
> *(French)*

You are a woman whom I could love passionately.

Nous entreprenons tousjours choses defendues
et convoitons ce que nous est denié.

> RABELAIS:
> *Gargantua (French)*

We always long for forbidden things, and desire
what is denied us.

Il est bien plus aisé d'éteindre un premier désir
que de satisfaire tous ceux qui le suivent.

> FRANÇOIS, DUC DE LA ROCHEFOUCAULD:
> *Refléxions (French)*

It is much easier to allay an initial desire than to
satisfy all those that will follow.

Consir lo joi, et oblit la foudat,
E fuc mon sen, e sec ma voluntat

> ARNAUT DE MAREUIL:
> *Consir lo Joi (French)*

I think only of the joy and forget the folly – I lose
sight of common sense, and follow my desire.

Qu'enaissi s'aven de fin aman
Que.l sens non a poder contra.l talan

> GUI D'UISEL:
> *Qu'enaissi s'aven de Fin Aman (French)*

With sincere lovers, reason can do nothing
against desire.

Man darf das nicht vor keuschen Ohren nennen,
Was keusche Herzen nicht entbehren können.

> J. W. VON GOETHE:
> *Faust (Forest and Cave) (German)*

We cannot mention before ears so chaste what
chaste hearts cannot do without.

Folgte Begierde dem Blick, folgte Genuss der
Begier.

> J. W. VON GOETHE:
> *Roman Elegies (German)*

At a look, desire follows, with fulfilment close at
heel.

So tauml' ich von Begierde zu Genuss,
Und im Genuss verschmacht' ich nach Begierde.

> J. W. VON GOETHE:
> *Faust (Forest and Cave) (German)*

From desire I plunge to its fulfilment, where I
long once more for desire.

> ... unverständig ist
Das Wünschen vor dem Schicksaal.

> FRIEDRICH HÖLDERLIN:
> *Der Rhein (German)*

Desire stands foolishly in front of fate.

Kai potheō kai maomai

> GREEK PROVERB

I both yearn and seek.

Pothoblētois gar ep' ergois elpis alētheiēs esti
melikhroterē

> PAULUS SILENTIARIUS:
> *Epigrams (Greek)*

Anticipation is more delightful than realisation
in love.

El deseo es una pregunta cuya respuesta nadie
sabe.

> LUIS CERNUDA:
> *No Decía Palabras (Spanish)*

Desire is a question to which no-one has an
answer.

DESPAIR
see also Courage, Disaster, Disillusion, Fear, Fortune, Friendship, Hope, Marriage, Morals and morality, Poets and poetry, Poverty, Wisdom.

La vie commence au-delà du désespoir.

> JEAN-PAUL SARTRE:
> *(French)*

Life begins on the other side of despair.

Tan aut mespreis
Mon cor, car sai
Qu'enfol. M'aurei donc faz l'efan?

– Tot voll cant vei. – Respeit segrai.
– Respeitz loncs fai omen perir.
RAIMBAUT D'AURENGA:
Songs (French)

I despise myself so much, for I know I am going mad. Have I then made a fool of myself? I want everything I can see. I shall wait in patience. A long wait makes one perish!

Es ist ein Weinen in der Welt,
Als ob der liebe Gott gestorben wär,
Und der bleierne Schatten, der niederfällt,
Lastet grabesschwer.
ELSE LASKER-SCHÜLER:
Weltende (German)

There is a weeping in the world, as though our dear Lord were dead; and the leaden shadows that descend on us oppress us with the weight of the tomb.

Herr, ich kann nicht mehr beten!
Ich bin müde vom Elend des Menschen,
Vom Leiden der Kreatur.
Deine Schöpfung ist herrlich,
Aber erbarmungslos.
CHRISTINA BUSTA:
Salzgärten (German)

Lord! I can pray no more. I am tired of the misery of mankind, and of the suffering of all living creatures. Your creation is magnificent, but pitiless.

Oh, wär' ich nie geboren!
J. W. VON GOETHE:
Faust (Faust's cry of anguish when
he fails to rescue Gretchen) *(German)*

Oh, that I had never been born!

O sähst du, voller Mondenschein
Zum letztenmal auf meine Pein!
J. W. VON GOETHE:
Faust (Faust's opening monologue) *(German)*

Oh, if only this could be the last time, full moon, that you see my misery!

Lasso! non di diamante, ma d'un vétro
Véggio di man cadérmi ógni speranza:

E tutti mièi pénsièr rómper nél mèzzo.
FRANCESCO PETRARCA:
Sonnets (Italian)

Ah, wretched me! Now I can see only too well that each hope (unlike a diamond) is but a fragile mirror shattered into fragments.

Dolor non sente
Chi di speranza è nudo?
GIACOMO LEOPARDI:
Bruto Minore (Italian)

Who will not grieve when deprived of hope?

Nessun maggior dolore,
Che ricordarsi del tempo felice
Nella miseria.
DANTE:
Inferno (Italian)

There is no greater pain than, in wretchedness, to recall a happy time.

Lasciate ogni speranza, voi ch'entrate!
DANTE:
Inferno (Italian)

Abandon all hope, ye who enter here!

Perch'io no spero di tornar giammai.
GUIDO CAVALCANTI:
Canzone (first line) *(Italian)*

Because I do not hope to turn again (written just before his death in exile).

Ima wa tada omoi tahenan to bakari wo h'to-dsute narade if yoshi mo gana
SAKYO NO TAIFU MICHIMASA:
Waga (Japanese)

Despair overwhelms my mind, but I shall tell only you, for it is you I want to tell.

Du dejlige jord, vaer ikke vred
At jeg tramped dit græs til ingen nytte!
HENRIK IBSEN:
Peer Gynt (Norwegian)

Beautiful earth, do not be angry with me for traipsing your fields so uselessly!

Jak rozpacz – bez przytułku – bez celu – bez granic.

ANTONI MALCZEWSKI:
Marya (Polish)

Like despair – without refuge, without purpose, without end.

Los ojos tristes, de llorar cansados,
Alzando al cielo, su clemencia imploro;
Mas vuelven luego al encendido lloro,
Que el grave peso no les sufre alzados.

JUAN MENÉNDEZ VALDÉS:
El Despecho (Spanish)

Worn out with weeping, I raise my sad gaze to heaven, imploring its mercy; but then I begin to weep still more, so that my heavy sorrow prevents my looking upward longer.

DESTINY
see also Fate.

Parlez au diable; employez la magie,
Vous ne détournerez nul être da sa fin.

JEAN DE LA FONTAINE:
La Souris Métamorphosée en Fille (French)

Ask of the devil, use magic – still you cannot turn any human being from his destiny.

On n'a plus qu'à commettre tous les crimes imaginables, tromper, voler, assassiner, et dire, pour excuse, qu'on y a été poussé par sa destinée.

MOLIÈRE:
Les Fourberies de Scapin (French)

We can commit every imaginable crime – fraud, theft, assassination – and then excuse ourselves on the grounds that our destiny impelled us to do so.

L'homme contre la mer, comme l'arc tendu contre le destin, ou le violon gréé contre la nuit.

ST.-JOHN PERSE:
Amers (French)

Man against the sea, the bow stretched taut against destiny, or the violin strung against the night.

Altre honor te voldra atraire!

Le Mystère d'Adam (French

Surely God has some great honour in store fo you!

Immobile Destin, muette sentinelle,
Froide Nécessité! – Hasard qui, t'avançant
Parmi les mondes morts sous la neige éternelle,
Refroidis, par degrés, l'univers pâlissant.

GÉRARD DE NERVAL
Le Christ aux Oliviers (French

Rocklike destiny, silent sentinel, cold necessity – chance which, advancing through lifeles worlds beneath the eternal snow, graduall chills the fading universe.

Hominus autem est aliquis finis, ad quem tota vita eius et actio ordinatur.

ST. THOMAS AQUINAS
On Princely Government (Latin

Man has a destiny to which all his life and activities are directed.

Fata regunt homines, fatum est et partibus illis quas sinus abscondit.

JUVENAL
Satires (Latin

Man is ruled by destiny – even those parts of him that lie beneath his clothes.

Todos sueñan lo que son,
Aunque ninguno lo entiende.

PEDRO CALDERÓN DE LA BARCA:
La Vida es Sueño (Spanish

Everyone in the world dreams what he is, although none realises it.

Carácter es destino.

SPANISH PROVERE

Character is destiny.

DETACHMENT

Fais comme moi: vis du monde éloignée . . . resignée.

VICTOR HUGO:
A Ma Fille (French

Follow my example: live detached from the world, be resigned.

De moi à moi quelle distance!

ANDRÉ GIDE:
Journal, 1889–1939 *(French)*

What a distance there is between me and myself!
(i.e. a sense of separation from oneself, or difficulty in identifying oneself).

DETERMINATION

La volonté aussi est une solitude.

ALBERT CAMUS:
Carnets (French)

Determination is also a solitude.

Siempre le he hallado firme,
Como un gran peñasco opuesto.

TIRSO DE MOLINA:
El Condenado por Desconfiado (Spanish)

I have always found him firm, resisting like a giant crag.

DEVILS
see also Evil, Hell, Night.

Je n'ayme poinct les diables. Ilz me faschent, et sont mal plaisans.

RABELAIS:
Tiers Livre (French)

I don't like devils. They vex me and are most unpleasant.

Il parle italien avec un accent russe.
Verlaine's definition of the Devil's speech
(French)

He speaks Italian with a Russian accent.

Le Diable
Fait toujours bien tout ce qu'il fait!

CHARLES BAUDELAIRE:
L'Irrémédiable (French)

Anything the Devil does is always done well!

Ich möcht' mich gleich dem Teufel übergeben,
Wenn ich nur selbst kein Teufel wär!

J. W. VON GOETHE:
Faust (German)

I'd give myself up to the Devil, if I weren't a devil myself!

Lupus in fabula
or
Lupus in sermone.

LATIN EXPRESSIONS

Talk of the devil and he appears.

Vade retro, Satanas!

NEW TESTAMENT

Get thee behind me, Satan!

DEVOTION
see also Prayer.

La femme ne voit jamais ce que l'on fait pour elle, elle ne voit que ce qu'on ne fait pas.

GEORGES COURTELINE:
La Paix Chez Soi (French)

Women never notice what one does for them, only what is not done.

Vous estes ma morte et ma vie.

FRENCH PROVERB

You are my life, and my death.

Cest mon désir de Dieu Servir
Pour acquérir son doux Plaisir.

Motto of the fifteenth-century printer,
Michel le Noir, of Paris *(French)*

It is my desire to serve the Lord to gain his sweet favour.

Hare Ram, Hare Ram, Hare Ram, Hare;
Bhaj Man Nishidini Pyare.
Favourite prayer of Mahatma Gandhi *(Hindi)*

O God Ram, God Ram, God Ram, God; O mind, think of the beloved day and night.

DICTATORSHIP
see also Government, Tyranny.

Oderint, dum probent.

SUETONIUS:
Tiberius (Latin)

Let them hate me, providing they respect my conduct (favourite saying of Tiberius).

Oderint, dum metuant.

SUETONIUS:
Gaius Caligula (Latin)

Let them hate me, so they but fear me (a favourite saying of Caligula, quoted from Accius: *Tragedies*).

Memento omnia mihi et in omnis licere!

SUETONIUS:
Gaius Caligula (Latin)

Remember I have the right to do anything to anybody!

DICTIONARIES
see also Encyclopaedias, Words.

Zy zyn stomme Taalkundigen, die, naar de betekenis van eenig woord in eene andere Taale gevraagd zynde, terstont duidelyk en klaar antwoorden.

Evert Visscher's dedication of the third
edition of Willem Sewel's dictionary
to Joachim van Gent, 1727 *(Dutch)*

They are stupid linguists who, when asked the meaning of any word in another language, will answer at once, plainly and clearly.

Wat een moeijelyke en verdrietige arbeyd het is, een Woordenboek te maaken, weeten zulke best, die ooit de hand aan zodaanig een werk geslagen hebben.

WILLEM SEWEL:
De Boekzaal (Dutch)

How difficult and irksome a task it is to make a dictionary, is best known to those who have at some time turned their hand to such a labour.

O mes amis, ne faites jamais de dictionnaire!

EMILE LITTRÉ:
Comment J'ai fait mon Dictionnaire (French)

Friends, never undertake to compile a dictionary!

Le premier livre d'une nation est le Dictionnaire de sa langue.

CONSTANTIN, COMTE DE VOLNEY:
Sayings (French)

The most important book of a nation is the dictionary of its language.

Les mots dans le dictionnaire gisent, pareils ou de dates diverses, comme des stratifications; vite je parlerai de couches.

STÉPHANE MALLARMÉ:
Les Mots Anglais (French)

In the dictionary the words lie entombed with their equals or forebears, in stratifications: soon I shall be speaking of layers!

On connaît le petit jeu qui consiste à partir d'une définition, à rechercher le sens des mots de cette définition et l'on en arrive ainsi assez vite au mot d'où l'on était parti, après avoir acquis un savoir nul.

RAYMOND QUENEAU:
Présentation de l'Encyclopédie (French)

We all know the little game of starting off from a definition and examining the meaning of the words in that definition, whereby we return quickly enough to the word we started off with, having meanwhile learnt nothing.

Es steht noch nicht im Meyer,
Und auch im Brockhaus nicht.

CHRISTIAN MORGENSTERN:
Das Nasobēm (German)

It's not in Meyer – nor is it in Brockhaus! (Two standard German dictionaries.)

Si quem dira manet sententia judicis olim,
Damnatum aerumnis, suppliciisque caput:
Hunc neque fabrili lassent ergastula massa,
Nec rigidas vexent fossa metalla manus.
LEXICA contexat, Nam caetera quid moror? omnes
Poenarum facies, hic labor unus habet.

J. J. SCALIGER:
Epistles (Latin)

At one time if some terrible judgment were meted out, the condemned faced hard labour in the galleys or hewing rocks in the quarries with his stiff hands. But why bother about the rest? Dictionary-making alone contains all these different kinds of punishment in one.

I wolę z bladym srebrnej łzy świecznikiem
W podziemia schodzić, niż z waszym słownikiem.

CYPRYAN KAMIL NORWID:
Post Scriptum (Polish)

I would rather enter the darkness with only the

pale light of a single tear, than with your dictionary.

DIFFICULTIES
see also Adversity, Friendship, Integrity.

Li uomini sono sempre nimici delle imprese dove si vegga difficultà.
>   NICCOLÒ MACHIVELLI:
>   *The Prince (Italian)*

Men are always averse to enterprises in which they foresee difficulties.

Nec aspera terrent.
>   Motto of the Royal Guelphic Order

Difficulties do not terrify.

DIFFIDENCE

En khronôi d' apophthinei
To tarbos anthrôpoisin
>   AESCHYLUS:
>   *Agamemnon (Greek)*

In time we lose our diffidence.

DIGNITY
**see also Glory, Honour, Thought
and Thinking.**

Aquila non capit muscas.
>   LATIN PROVERB

Eagles do not hunt flies.

Elephas Indicus culices non timet.
>   Family motto of the Malatestas *(Latin)*

The elephant is not afraid of mosquitos.

DILATORINESS

Clipeum post vulnera sumo.
>   HORACE:
>   *Tristia (Latin)*

I am shutting the stable door after the horse has bolted (*lit.* I take up my shield when already wounded).

Por la calle de después se va a la casa de nunca.
>   SPANISH PROVERB

The street of by-and-by leads to the house of never.

DILEMMA
see also Decision, Deliberation.

Zudem gibt's Lagen, wo ein Schritt voraus
Und einer rückwärts gleicherweis verderblich.
>   FRANZ GRILLPARZER:
>   *Ein Bruderzwist in Habsburg (German)*

There are times when a step forward and a step backwards could prove equally disastrous.

Hic locus est, partis ubi se via findit in ambas.
>   VIRGIL:
>   *Aeneid (Latin)*

This is the place where the road forks (one way leading to Elysium, the other to Hades).

Hac urget lupus, hac canis angit.
>   HORACE:
>   *Satires (Latin)*

You can be caught between two fires (*lit.* here the wolf presses, there the hound).

Atter og fram, det er lige langt; –
Ud og ind, det er lige trangt!
>   HENRIK IBSEN:
>   *Peer Gynt (Norwegian)*

Backward or forward, it's just as far – out or in, the way's as narrow.

DISASTER
**see also Adversity, Danger, Despair,
History, Wealth.**

Min ad-dār ilạ 'n-nār
>   ARAB PROVERB

Out of the frying–pan into the fire.

La pire n'est pas toujours sûr, il est seulement bien probable!
>   FRENCH PROVERB

The worst is not always certain, but it's very likely!

Iou iou dustēnos, oikhomai talas
Olôl' olôla, phengos ouket' esti moi
>   SOPHOCLES:
>   *Trachiniae (Greek)*

Alas, I am done for; no light remains for me.

Men duro è il male
Che riparo non ha?

GIACOMO LEOPARDI:
Bruto Minore (Italian)

Where there is no remedy, is disaster the less harsh?

Non può piú senno in me, non può consiglio
Né posso piú non rimaner sommersa
Nel mortal golfo de gli affanni miei

GIAMBATTISTA CINTHIO GIRALDI:
Cleopatra (Italian)

Wisdom and advice are no longer of any help to me; no more can I avoid being submerged in the fatal gulf of my troubles.

Magnum   aliquid   instat,   efferum   immane impium.

SENECA:
Medea (Latin)

Something great is impending, wild, monstrous, impious.

Si vieres tu casa quemar, llégate a escalentar.

SPANISH PROVERB

If your house is on fire, go and warm yourself by it.

DISCORD

Nutrix Discordia belli

CLAUDIAN:
In Rufinum (Latin)

Discord, mother of war.

DISCRETION

Al-hurūb nuşş ash-shujā'a

ARAB PROVERB

Better to fight and run away, and live to fight another day (*lit.* flight is half bravery).

Oukh hai trikhes poiousin hai leukai phronein

GREEK PROVERB

It is not grey hairs that produce discretion.

Kalon toi glōss' hotōi pistē parēi

EURIPIDES
Iphigeneia in Tauris (Greek

A loyal tongue is a wonderful attribute.

Más vale que digan aquí huyó, que aquí murió

SPANISH PROVERB

It is better they should say 'Here he ran away' rather than 'Here he died'.

En la boca del discreto lo público es secreto.

SPANISH PROVERB

In the mouth of a discreet person even tha which is notorious remains secret.

DISCRIMINATION

Qui ne connait les noms de virtus ni de vices?

PIERRE DE RONSARD:
Complainte Contre Fortune (French)

Who can be ignorant of the names of both virtues and vices?

Malo bene facere tantundemst periculum
Quantum bono male facere.

PLAUTUS:
Poenulus (Latin)

There's as much danger in doing a good turn to a bad man, as in doing a bad turn to a good man.

Nam nihil aegrius est quam res secernere apertas ab dubiis.

LUCRETIUS:
De Rerum Natura (Latin)

Nothing is more difficult than separating things that are evident from those that are doubtful.

DISEASE
see also Evil, Illness.

Nousoi d' anthrōpoisin eph' hēmerēi, hai d' epi nukti automatoi phoitōsi kaka thnētoisi pherousai sigēi, epei phōnēn exeileto mētieta Zeus

HESIOD:
Works and Days (Greek)

Diseases come of their own volition night and day, silently attacking the human race, for Zeus the Counsellor has robbed these ills of speech.

DISGRACE
see also Avarice.

Nonne mori satius, vitae quam ferre pudorem?
CLAUDIAN:
De Bello Gildonico (Latin)

Is not death preferable to a life disgraced?

DISILLUSION
see also Despair, Love.

N'espérons plus, mon âme, aux promesses du
monde;
Sa lumière est un verre, et sa faveur une onde
Que toujours quelque vent empêche de calmer
FRANÇOIS DE MALHERBE:
Paraphrase du Psaume CXLV (French)

Let us no more put our trust in worldly promises, my soul! The world's light is only a glass, its
favour but a wave which some wind or other
always keeps it from calming.

De las domnas me dezesper;
Ja mais en lor no'm fiarai;
C'aissi com las solh chaptener,
Enaissi las deschaptenrai.
BERNARD DE VENTADOUR:
Can Vei la Lauzeta Mover (French)

I despair of women: I shall never again put my
trust in them. No matter how often I have
praised them, I have just as often had occasion
to despise them.

Vivo nel non volere
Del tramontato dopoguerra: amando
Il mondo per odio.
PIER PAOLO PASOLINI:
Le Ceneri di Gramsci (Italian)

I live in the apathy of the twilight of the postwar
period, loving a world I hate.

Vae o bem fugindo
Cresce o mal c' os annos,
Vão-se descobrindo
C' o tempo os enganos.
LUIS DE CAMÕES:
Vae o bem Fugindo (Portuguese)

Sorrow grows with the years, joy is swiftly spent,
and with time appears disillusion.

DISOBEDIENCE

Veteres fugiunt iuga saepe iuvenci
Et domitus freno saepe repugnat equus.
OVID:
Tristia (Latin)

Aged bullocks often shun the yoke, and the
well-trained horse often fights the bit.

DISSATISFACTION
see also Contentment.

Notre condition jamais ne nous contente;
La pire est toujours la présente.
JEAN DE LA FONTAINE:
L'Âne et ses Maîtres (French)

We are never content with our lot; the worst
time is always the present.

Optat ephippia bos, piger optat arare caballus.
HORACE:
Epistles (Latin)

No-one is content with his own lot (*lit.* the ox
longs for the trappings of a horse; the horse,
when lazy, longs to plough).

Nostri nosmet paenitet.
TERENCE:
Phormio (Latin)

None of us is ever satisfied with what we are.

Omne aevum curae, cunctis sua displicet aetas.
AUSONIUS:
Opuscula (Latin)

Every stage of life has its troubles, and no man is
content with his own age.

DISTRACTION

Mein armer Kopf
Ist mir verrückt,
Mein armer Sinn
Ist mir zerstückt.
J. W. VON GOETHE:
Faust (the spinning-wheel song) *(German)*

My poor head is in such a whirl, my mind is all in
bits.

DISTRUST
see also Ambition, Caution.

De tout inconnu le sage se méfie.

JEAN DE LA FONTAINE:
Le Renard, le Loup et le Cheval (French)

A wise man distrusts everyone he does not know.

Timeo Danaos, et dona ferentes.

VIRGIL:
Aeneid (Latin)

I distrust the Greeks – even when they bring gifts.

Antidotum adversus Caesarem?

SUETONIUS:
Gaius Caligula (Latin)

What! an antidote against Caesar? (Caligula, on learning that his brother was suspected of taking drugs as a precaution against being poisoned by him).

Ante la puerta del rezador, nunca eches tu trigo al sol.

SPANISH PROVERB

Never put your corn to dry in front of the door of the man of prayer.

DIVERSITY
see also Mankind.

Omnis diversitas discors, similitudo vero appetenda est.

BOETHIUS:
Quomodo Substantiae (Latin)

Diversity repels; likeness is to be eagerly sought.

DIVORCE

Le divorce est si naturel que, dans plusieurs maisons, il couche toutes les nuits entre deux époux.

S. R. N. CHAMFORT:
Maximes et Pensées (French)

Divorce is so natural that, in many houses, it sleeps nightly between husband and wife.

DOUBT
see also Jealousy, Philosophy.

Der Zweifel zeugt den Zweifel an sich selbst.

FRANZ GRILLPARZER
Ein Bruderzwist in Hapsburg (German

Doubt breeds doubt (Rudolph II addressing the citizens of Prague).

DREAMS
see also Illusion, Life, Sleep, World.

C'est en contraire sens qu'un songe s'interprète.

PIERRE CORNEILLE
Horace (French

Dreams should be interpreted by contraries.

J'ai rêvé tant et plus, mais je n'y entends note.

RABELAIS
Pantagruel (French

I've dreamed enough in my time, but I've never understood any of it.

Qui rêve, dîne.   FRENCH PROVERB

Who dreams has a feast.

Hēdu gar philous
Kan nukti leussein, hontin an parēi khronon

EURIPIDES:
Alcestis (Greek)

How pleasant to see a loved one, even in a short-lived dream!

Quanto piace al Mondo è breve sogno.

FRANCESCO PETRARCA:
Sonetto Primo (Italian)

How pleasing to the world is a short dream.

Pa rawa, i, e te tahakura
E homai tohu ki au
kia oho ake e te ngakau
Ko wai rawa koe e tahu nei i a au
Ka haramai e roto, ka kai kohau noa
Ka waitohu noa

TE IHU-NUI-O-TONGA:
Tangi (Maori)

An omen, a dream, has upset me. Its sign disturbs my being. Who are you who thus afflicts me, uttering in the vaguest way a wordless warning?

No se pierde
Obrar bien, aun entre sueños.
PEDRO CALDERÓN DE LA BARCA:
La Vida es Sueño (Spanish)

Doing good is not wasted, even in dreams.

Toda la vida es sueño,
Y los sueños sueños son.
PEDRO CALDERÓN DE LA BARCA:
La Vida es Sueño (Spanish)

The whole of life is a dream, and dreams are only dreams.

Si acaso recuerdo,
Me hallo entre las flores
Y de mis dolores
Apeñas me acuerdo.
OLD SPANISH SONG

If I awake surrounded by flowers, I can hardly remember my sad dreams.

Sueña el pobre que padece
Su miseria y su pobreza;
Sueña el que a medrar empieza.
PEDRO CALDERÓN DE LA BARCA:
La Vida es Sueño (Spanish)

The poor man dreams of the poverty and misery he bears; dreams that keen worries overwhelm.

DRINKING
See also Contentment, Mankind, Pleasure, Remedies, Temperance, Wine.

Il rugit, il déconne,
Il a bu trop d'alcool,
Il sombre, il est dément,
Il hurle à tout vent.
RAYMOND QUENEAU:
Zigzag (French)

He shouts and curses; he has drunk too much. He scowls, acts crazy, and roars with all his might.

Je boy eternellement. Ce m'est eternité de beuverye, et beuverye de eternité.
RABELAIS:
Gargantua (French)

I never stop drinking. For me there is an eternity of drinking, and a drinking of eternity.

Si quelqu'un ou quelqu'une disoit 'beuvons', tous beuvoient!
RABELAIS:
Gargantua (French)

If a lady or gentleman invited you to drink, why – naturally, everyone drank!

Les bouteilles que tu vides, tu les remplis de ton esprit.
GÉRARD DE NERVAL:
Sur un Carnet (French)

As you empty the bottles you refill them with your soul.

Wer Schnaps hat, ist gerettet!
WOLFGANG BORCHERT:
Draussen vor der Tür (German)

If you've got some schnaps you're saved!

Das Haupt ist frisch, der Magen ist gesund,
Die Beine aber wollen nicht mehr tragen.
J. C. F. VON SCHILLER:
Die Piccolomini (German)

My head is clear, my belly sound, but my legs don't seem to bear me any more.

Ich habe Leute gekannt, die haben heimlich getrunken und sind öffentlich besoffen gewesen.
GEORG CHRISTOPH LICHTENBERG:
Aphorismen (German)

I have known people who drank secretly and were besotted publicly.

Eins ist der Herr; Zwei ist das finstre Chaos;
Drei ist die Welt. Drei Gläser lob ich mir.
Im dritten trinkt man mit den Tropfen Sonnen
Und Firmamente mit den übrigen.
HEINRICH VON KLEIST:
Der Zerbrochene Krug (German)

First is the Lord; second, black Chaos; third, the world. There is nothing like three glasses. In the third, we drink the sun with every drop and the firmament in the others.

Kheimerias methuōn mēdama nuktos ieis
GREEK PROVERB

Never go out drunk on a winter night.

Misō mnamona sumpotan
GREEK PROVERB

I hate a boon-companion with a good memory.

Si bene quid memini causae sunt quinque
bibendi:
Hospitis adventus, praesens sitis atque futura,
Aut vini bonitas, aut quaelibet altera causa.
OLD LATIN SAYING

It is well to remember that there are five reasons
for drinking: the arrival of a friend; one's present
or future thirst; the excellence of the wine; or any
other reason.

Cujus finis bonus totum ipsum bonum.
Inscription on the cup of Stephen le Scrope,
archdeacon of Richmond *(Latin)*

A fine end to a fine drink.

DUPLICITY

Méfie-toi de celui qui rit avant de parler!
ALPHONSE DAUDET:
Tartarin sur les Alpes (French)

Beware of him who laughs before speaking!

DUTY
see also Achievement, Citizenship, Gods, Honour, Obedience, Patriotism, Pleasure, Service.

Voor Godt wil ick belijden
End zijner grooter Macht,
Dat ick tot gheenen tijden
Den Coninck heb veracht:
Dan dat ick Godt den Heere,
Der Hoochster Majesteyt,
Heb moeten obediëren
In der gherechticheyt.
WILHELMUS VAN NASSOUWE:
the National Anthem of the Netherlands

Before God and his great might, I will testify
that, while I have at no time repudiated the
King, I have had to obey God, the Highest
Majesty, as justice bade me.

Faites votre devoir, et laissez faire aux dieux.
PIERRE CORNEILLE:
Horace (French)

Do your duty, and leave the rest in the lap of the
gods (Horace's advice to his friend Curiace
before he battles with him).

Wie selig lebt ein Mann, der seine Pflichten
kennt!
C. F. GELLERT:
Der Menschenfreund (German)

Happy the man who knows his duties!

Pasi tois eunomoumenois ergon ti hekastōi en tēi
polei prostetaktai, ho anankaion ergazesthai
PLATO:
The Republic (Greek)

Each citizen in a well-ordered community has
his own task which it is his duty to carry out.

To gar dikaion ouk ekhei logon
Duoin erizein, all' epispeudein to dran
SOPHOCLES:
Electra (Greek)

We should not argue when duty calls – we
should act.

Mono-no fu wo omi-no otoko-wa oho-kimi-no
make-no mani-mani kiku-to-wo omono zo
Manyo Shū (Japanese)

The heroes charged with the orders of the army
must always conform to the Emperor's commands.

E

EARTH
see also Insignificance, Nature, World.

Unsere Erde ist vielleicht ein Weibchen.
> GEORG CHRISTOPH LICHTENBERG:
> *Aphorismen (German)*

Perhaps our earth is female.

Eine Kugel, die immer in die Höhe geworfen wird, um den Himmel zu ärgern, – die Erde.
> ELIAS CANETTI:
> *Aufzeichnungen, 1957 (German)*

The Earth: a globe ceaselessly hurled into the universe to annoy the heavens.

Munificat tacita mortalis muta salute.
> LUCRETIUS:
> *De Rerum Natura (Latin)*

With silent blessing she [Cybele, the Earth Mother] makes men rich.

EAVESDROPPING

Quien asecha por agujero ve su duelo.
> SPANISH PROVERB

Listeners never overhear good of themselves (*lit.* he who spies through a keyhole will see what will vex him).

ECHOES

O Widerhall
Wo lauschest du?
> CLEMENS BRENTANO:
> *O Kühler Wald (German)*

O Echo, where are you listening?

EDINBURGH

Mon amour est écrit sur les murs d'Edimbourg.
> PAUL GILSON:
> *Le Chant du Triste Commensal (French)*

My love is written on the walls of Edinburgh.

EDUCATION
see also Judgment, Learning, Pleasure, Teaching, Words.

Education, c'est délivrance.
> ANDRÉ GIDE:
> *Journal, 1889–1939 (French)*

Education is delivery from bondage.

Qu'est-ce qu'une bonne éducation, sinon celle qui conduit à toutes sortes de jouissances sans péril et sans inconvenient?
> DENIS DIDEROT:
> *Le Neveu de Rameau (French)*

What is a good education, if not the means of achieving all kinds of pleasure without danger and without hindrance?

Arkhē paideuseōs hē tōn onomatōn episkepsis
> ANTISTHENES:
> *Fragment (Greek)*

The investigation of the meaning of words is the beginning of education.

Ancora imparo.
> Motto of Monash University *(Italian)*

I continue to learn.

Litterae thesaurum est, et artificium nunquam moritur.
> PETRONIUS:
> *Satyricon (Latin)*

Education is a treasure, and culture never dies.

EFFORT
see also Action, Aspiration, Athletics, Bravery, Endurance, Human nature, Success, Work.

Kathīr an-naṭṭ qalīl aṣ-ṣayd
> ARAB PROVERB

Much pains, little gains (*lit.* much jumping, little game).

Le chemin est long du projet à la chose.

MOLIÈRE:
Le Tartuffe (French)

Long is the road from the idea to its completion.

Tout ce qui m'était facile m'était indifférent et presque ennemi. La sensation de l'effort me semblait devoir être recherchée.

PAUL VELÉRY:
Monsieur Teste (preface) *(French)*

Everything I found easy I was hostile and indifferent to; it seemed that I had to strive to achieve the sensation of effort.

Tout que je puis.

Motto of Enfield Grammar School
(French)

All that I can I will.

Ne vaut pas le détour.

FRENCH EXPRESSION

Hardly worth the effort (*lit.* not worth the detour).

Rien ne nous plaist que le combat, mais non pas la victoire.

BLAISE PASCAL:
Pensées (French)

It is the fight alone that pleases us, not the victory.

Se faire servir par l'obstacle est un grand pas vers la triomphe.

FRENCH PROVERB

To turn an obstacle to one's advantage is a great step towards victory.

Fais énergiquement ta longue et lourde tâche
Dans la voie où le sort a voulu t'appeler.

ALFRED DE VIGNY:
La Mort du Loup (French)

Carry out your long and heavy task energetically, in the way of life to which Fate has called you.

Wer recht sehen will, was der Mensch tun könnte, wenn er wollte, darf nur an die Personen denken, die sich aus Gefängnissen gerettet haben oder haben retten wollen. Sie haben mit einem einzigen Nagel so viel getan wie mit einem Mauerbrecher.

GEORG CHRISTOPH LICHTENBERG:
Aphorismen (German)

If we want to see what men are capable of when they wish, we need only think of the people who have escaped from prisons or who have attempted to escape. With a single nail they have achieved as much as if they had had a battering-ram!

Die Idee des Kampfes ist so alt wie das Leben selbst.

ADOLF HITLER,
at Kulmbach, 5 February 1928 *(German)*

The idea of struggle is as old as life itself.

Der Kampf hat den Menschen gross gemacht.

ADOLF HITLER,
in a letter to Heinrich Brüning (German)

Struggle has made mankind great.

Wer immer strebend sich bemüht,
Den können wir erlösen.

J. W. VON GOETHE:
Faust (conclusion) *(German)*

We can always redeem the man who aspires and strives.

Wie der Pfeil die Sehne besteht, um gesammelt im Absprung
Mehr zu sein er selbst.

RAINER MARIA RILKE:
Duineser Elegien (German)

As the arrow strains against the bowstring, in order to accumulate greater power when fired than it actually possesses, it becomes *more.*

Kathairein tēn kopron tou Augeion

GREEK EXPRESSION

To cleanse the Augean stables (one of the mythical labours of Hercules).

Arkhē hēmisu pantos

GREEK PROVERB

A beginning is half of the whole.

Tharrein, ō Theaitēte, khrē ton kai smikron ti dunamenon eis to prosthen aei proienai

> PLATO:
> *The Sophist (Greek)*

Never discourage anyone, Theaetetus, who continually makes progress, no matter how slow.

Dimidium facti qui coepit habet.

> LATIN PROVERB
> (quoted in Horace: *Epistles*)

Well begun is half done.

Laterem lavem.

> LATIN EXPRESSION

My effort is useless (*lit.* I shall be washing a brick).

Fiet sedulo.

> LATIN EXPRESSION

I'll do my best.

Moderatio modo virium adsit et tantum quantum potest quisque nitatur, ne ille non magno desiderio tenebitur virium.

> CICERO;
> *De Senectute (Latin)*

If only every man would make proper use of his strength and do his utmost, he need never regret his limited ability.

Ad supervacua sudatur.

> SENECA:
> *Epistles (Latin)*

It is for the superfluous things of life that men sweat.

Palmas non sine pulveri.

> LATIN PROVERB

No sweet without sweat.

Parturient montes, nascetur ridiculus mus.

> HORACE:
> *Ars Poetica (Latin)*

Mountains will labour and give birth to a ridiculous mouse.

... nil sine magno
Vita labore dedit mortalibus.

> HORACE:
> *Satires (Latin)*

Life gives nothing to mankind unless they strive mightily.

Clivo sudamus in ino.

> OVID:
> *Heroides (Latin)*

We are but at the beginning of our task.

Quomodo quisque potest.

> SENECA:
> *Epistles (Latin)*

Everyone does the best he can.

> Sua cuique exorsa laborem
Fortunamque ferent.

> VIRGIL:
> *Aeneid (Latin)*

Everyone must toil and endeavour until Fate declares its judgment.

Incipere multost quam impetrare facilius.

> PLAUTUS:
> *Poenulus (Latin)*

It is easier to begin well than to finish well.

Durate, et vosmet rebus servate secundis.

> VIRGIL:
> *Aeneid (Latin)*

Endure, and save yourselves for happier times.

Cloacas Augiae purgare.

> LATIN PROVERB
> (quoted in Seneca: *Apocolocyntosis divi Claudii*)

To cleanse the Augean stables (*i.e.* to do a difficult and unpleasant duty).

Catus amat pisces, sed non vult tingere plantas.

> LATIN PROVERB

Cats love fish but do not want to get their feet wet.

Multo magis opus est adiutorio illis qui pauca quam qui multa possunt.

DANTE:
De Vulgari Eloquio (Latin)

Small projects need much more help than great.

Ite et Romanae consulite historiae!

PROPERTIUS:
Elegies (Latin)

Give the historians something to write about! (*lit.* go off and do your best for Roman history)

Nil volentibus arduum.

Motto of the Dutch Poets' Society, founded 1669 *(Latin)*

Nothing is difficult to those who have the will.

Per ardua ad astra

LATIN EXPRESSION

To achieve the heights (*lit.* stars) through hard work.

Hvor løftende dog, at sætte sig et Maal,
Og drive det igjennem som Flint og Staal!

HENRIK IBSEN:
Peer Gynt (Norwegian)

To see one's goal and to drive toward it, steeling one's heart, is most uplifting!

¿Cúando descansaré, Dios mío? ¿Cuál será mi postrer anhelo?

MIGUEL DE UNAMUNO:
Recuerdos de Nĩnas y de Mocedad (Spanish)

When, O Lord, shall I rest? What will be my last effort?

No se toman truchas a bragas enjutas.

SPANISH PROVERB

You can't catch trout with dry breeches.

ELITE
see also Equality.

Ne nous associons qu'avecque nos égaux.

JEAN DE LA FONTAINE:
Le Pot de Terre et le Pot de Fer (French)

Let us associate only with our equals.

Le petit nombre des élus.

FRENCH EXPRESSION

The small number of the élite.

Polloi toi narthēkophoroi, pauroi de te bakhhoi

GREEK PROVERB

The thyrsus-bearers are many, the initiated few (thyrsus = staff tipped with a pine-cone and sometimes wreathed with ivy or vine branches, carried by votaries of Bacchus).

ELOCUTION

Elocution n'est autre chose qu'une propriété et splendeur de paroles bien choisies et ornées de graves et courtes sentences, qui font reluyre les vers comme les pierres précieuses bien enchassées les doigts de quelque grand Seigneur.

PIERRE DE RONSARD:
Abbregé de l'Art Poëtique François (French)

Elocution is nothing but the correctness and splendour of well-chosen words set in impressive but short sentences, which enhance verse in the same way as precious stones beautifully engraved set off the fingers of some nobleman.

ELOQUENCE
see also Love, Oratory, Sincerity, Speech, Words.

L'éloquence est une peinture de la pensée.

BLAISE PASCAL:
Pensées; Adversaria (French)

Eloquence is a reflection of thought.

L'éloquence est une sorte de mensonge, et rien de plus contraire à l'illusion que la poésie.

DENIS DIDEROT:
Les Deux Amis de Bourbonne (French)

Eloquence is a kind of lie, and nothing is more contrary to illusion than poetry.

L'art de la paranthèse est un des grands secrets de l'éloquence dans la Société.

S. R. N. CHAMFORT:
Maximes et Pensées (French)

The art of the parenthesis is one of the greatest secrets of eloquence in society.

La véritable éloquence consiste à dire tout ce qu'il faut, et à ne dire que ce qu'il faut.

FRANÇOIS, DUC DE LA ROCHEFOUCAULD:
Réflexions (French)

True eloquence comprises saying all that needs to be said, and only that.

Thrasei de dunatos kai legein hoios t' anēr
Kakos politēs gignetai noun ouk ekhōn

EURIPIDES:
The Bacchae (Greek)

The eloquent and influential speaker who lacks good sense may prove to be a bad citizen.

Ouk ho logos, alla ta erga peithei

GREEK PROVERB

Not speech but facts convince.

Ho gar kalōs legōn kalos te kai agathos

PLATO:
Theaetetus (Greek)

He who speaks well is both beautiful and good.

EMOTION
see also Despair, Feelings, Grief, Happiness, Motives, Reason, Self-control.

Een maeghdenhart is teder,
Zoo wel in rouw als blyschap weêr te staen.

JOOST VAN DEN VONDEL:
Jeptha (Dutch)

A young girl's heart is frail in resisting both grief and happiness.

Peu de chose nous console parce que peu de chose nous afflige.

BLAISE PASCAL:
Pensées (French)

We are easily consoled for we are easily distressed.

Le coeur a ses raisons que la raison ne connoist point.

BLAISE PASCAL:
Pensées (French)

The heart has its reasons which reason knows not.

Ceux qui sont accoustumés à juger par le sentiment ne comprennent rien aux choses de raisonnement.

BLAISE PASCAL:
Pensées (French)

Those who are accustomed to judge by feeling understand nothing of the rules of argument.

Dans le domaine de sentiments, le réel ne se distingue pas de l'imaginaire.

ANDRÉ GIDE:
(French)

In the realm of the emotions, it is impossible to separate the real from the imaginary.

La durée de nos passions ne dépend pas plus de nous que la durée de notre vie.

FRANÇOIS, DUC DE LA ROCHEFOUCAULD:
Réflexions (French)

The duration of our emotions depends no more on ourselves than does the duration of our lives.

Nous n'éprouvons pas des sentiments qui nous transforment, mais des sentiments qui nous suggèrent l'idée de transformation.

ALBERT CAMUS:
Carnets 1937–39 (French)

We don't experience feelings that transform us, but feelings that suggest to us the idea of transformation.

Jeder Affekt hat seine spezifiken Äusserungen und, so zu sagen, seinen eigentümlichen Dialekt, an dem man ihn kennt.

J. C. F. VON SCHILLER:
Werke (German)

Every emotion has its individual expression and, so to say, its particular dialect by which we can recognise it.

Gottseidank geht alles schnell vorüber
Auch die Liebe und der Kummer sogar.

BERTOLT BRECHT:
Nannas Lied (German)

Thank God everything is quickly over – both love and grief.

Dem Herzen folg' ich, denn ich darf ihm trauen.
J. C. F. VON SCHILLER:
Wallensteins Tod (German)

I follow my heart, for I can trust it.

Jeder Mensch ist ein Adam; denn jeder wird einmal aus dem Paradiese der warmen Gefühle vertrieben.
J. W. VON GOETHE:
Letter to J. C. Lobe, July 1820 *(German)*

Everyone is like Adam in that he is sooner or later expelled from the paradise of warm emotions.

Quoque magis tegitur, tectus magis aestuat ignis.
OVID:
Metamorphoses (Latin)

Hidden fires are fiercest.

Sukhasya duḥkhasya na kopi dātā
Paro dadātīti kubuddhir eṣā
Svayaṁ kṛtaṁ svena phalena yujyate
Sárīra he nistara yat tvayā kṛtam
Garuḍa Purāṇa (Pali)

No-one gives joy or sorrow. That others give them to us is an erroneous conception. We gather the consequences of our own deeds. Body of mine, repay what you have done!

Kāmato jāyatī soko, kāmato jāyatī bhayam
Kāmato vippamuttassa n'atthi soko, kuto bhayam?
Dhammapada: Piyavaggo (Pali)

Both grief and fear arise from desire. He who is free from desire does not grieve. How then can there be fear?

ENCOURAGEMENT

Ich brauche Thau und Nachtluft wie die Blumen.
GEORG BÜCHNER:
Leonce und Lena (German)

Like the flowers, I need dew and night-air.

Aut, si nox pluviam ne colligat ante veremur,
Cantantes licet usque (minus via laedet) eamus;

Cantantes ut eamus, ego hoc te fasce levabo.
VIRGIL:
Eclogues (Latin)

Or if we are afraid that the night will bring rain before we arrive, we may sing as we go – the way will be less tedious – and so that we may go on our way singing, I will relieve you of your burden.

[Dominus] pro beneficio gratiam referat, ut aliis recte facere libeat.
CATO:
De Agricultura (Latin)

[The master] should show his appreciation of good work, so that other workmen may also take pleasure in doing their work well.

Rex eris si recte facies, si non facies non eris!
LATIN CHILDREN'S VERSE

You will be king if you do right – if you don't, you won't!

Agite pugni!
PLAUTUS:
Amphitruo (Latin)

Up fists and at 'em!

Illegitimi non carborundum!
American dog-Latin saying

Don't let the bastards grind you down!

Bono animo estote! Nobis adluxit
SUETONIUS:
Vitellius (Latin)

Be of good cheer! Light has been granted us (Vitellius making light of the burning of his dining-room).

Saepe facias!
SUETONIUS:
Vitellius (Latin)

May you often do it! (Vitellius, congratulating Claudius on the presentation of the Secular Games).

La que es más humilde planta,
Si la subida endereza,

Por gracia ó naturaleza
A los cielos se levanta.

MIGUEL DE CERVANTES:
La Gitanilla (Spanish)

Even the most humble plant, set up by nature or good fortune, will lift its head to the heavens.

ENCYCLOPAEDIAS
see also Dictionaries, Philosophy.

Cet ouvrage immense et immortel semble accuser la brièveté de la vie des hommes.

VOLTAIRE:
Sur L'Encyclopédie (French)

This vast and immortal work seems to accentuate how brief is the life of man.

Le vray puys et abysme d'une encyclopédie

RABELAIS:
Pantagruel (French)

The very well and abyss of an encyclopaedia.

ENDURANCE
see also Effort, Pain, Survival, War.

Quo plura possis, plura patienter feras.

SENECA:
Troades (Latin)

The more you can do, the greater should be your patience to endure.

Lǫng es nótt, lǫng es ǫnnur,
Hvé mega ek þreyja þrjár?
Opt mér mána ǫr minni þótti
En sjá hálf hýnótt.

SNORRI STURLUSON:
Gylfaginning (Norse)

One night is long, so is a second. How shall I endure for three nights? Often a month has seemed less to me than this half bridal-night.

Tȳ govorila: 'Kamennȳe mȳ'.
Net,
    mȳ sil'nee kamnya,
        mȳ-zhivȳe

MARGARITA ALIGER:
Spring in Leningrad (Russian)

You used to say: We are made of stone. NO! we are stronger than stone, for we have survived! (referring to the siege of Leningrad in World War II).

ENEMIES
see also Flattery, Friendship, Gifts, Marriage, Peace.

. . . entre nos ennemis.
Les plus à craindre sont souvent les plus petits.

JEAN DE LA FONTAINE:
Le Lion et le Moucheron (French)

Among our enemies, the most to fear are often the lowliest.

Tous nos ennemis sont mortels.

PAUL VALÉRY:
Mauvaises Pensées (French)

All our enemies are mortal.

Phulattesthai ta zōia epistantai aph' hōn malista dei kai tauta eis oudenos didaskalou pōpote phoitēsanta

GREEK PROVERB

Animals are instinctively on their guard against their worst enemies, even though they have never been to school.

Mē dusōpou ton misounta mēd' hupaikalle pisteuein dokounta

PLUTARCH:
Moralia (Greek)

Do not let your enemy embarrass you – nor should you fawn on him when he appears to trust you.

Ē karta polloi nun philoi kauthis pikroi

SOPHOCLES:
Ajax (Greek)

Today's friend may be tomorrow's foe.

Epistamai gar artiōs hoti
Ho t' ekhthros hēmin es tosond' ekhtharteos
Hōs kai philēsōn authis, es te ton philon
Tosauth' hupourgōn ōphelein boulēsomai,
Hōs aien ou menounta

SOPHOCLES:
Ajax (Greek)

It is my rule, from experience, to remember my friend may become my enemy, and my enemy my friend.

... s'altri puote
Offender di nascosto, e gran sciocchezza
Il nemico assalir palesemente.
GIAMBATTISTA CINTHIO GIRALDI:
Altile (Italian)

It is very foolish to attack one's enemy openly, if one can injure him in secret.

... pol mavelim
Mihi inimicos invidere, quam med inimicis meis.
PLAUTUS:
Truculentus (Latin)

I'd rather my enemies envied me, than I my enemies!

Tandem vipera sibilare desisti!
FLORUS:
Works (Latin)

At last, you viper, you have ceased to hiss!

Extinguere hostem maxima est virtus ducis.
Octavia (attrib. Seneca) *(Latin)*

The greatest service of a leader is to destroy the enemy.

ENGLAND
see also Democracy, Law, Religion.

C'est une belle langue que l'anglais; il en faut peu pour aller loin.
P. A. C. DE BEAUMARCHAIS:
Le Mariage de Figaro (French)

English is a fine language; a little of it goes a long way.

Race ennemie, trop perfide Albion!
French song, 1809

Enemy nation, outrageously perfidous Albion! (*NB:* the expression *la perfide Albion* had previously been used in a poem by the Marquis de Ximenez in 1793; while *la perfide Angleterre* is attributed to Jacques Bossuet, bishop of Meaux, who is said to have used it in 1652).

Les Anglais sont le seul Peuple qui ait trouvé le moyen de limiter la puissance d'un homme dont la figure est sur un petit écu.
S. R. N. CHAMFORT:
Maximes et Pensées (French)

The English are the only nation to have dis-

covered the means of limiting the powers of the man whose portrait appears on their coins.

Englands Beherrscher brauchen nichts zu scheuen, als ihr Gewissen und ihr Parlament.
J. C. F. VON SCHILLER:
Maria Stuart (German)

England's rulers have nothing to fear apart from their conscience and their Parliament.

ENJOYMENT
see also Pleasure.

C'est la sagesse! Aimer le vin,
La beauté, le printemps divin,
Cela suffit. Le reste est vain.
THÉODORE DE BANVILLE:
A Adolphe Gaïffe (French)

This is wisdom: to love wine, beauty, and the heavenly spring. That's sufficient – the rest is worthless.

Wer am meisten geniesst, betet am meisten.
GEORG BÜCHNER:
Dantons Tod (German)

He who enjoys the most, prays the most.

Ich habe gerochen alle Gerüche
In dieser holden Erdenküche;
Was man geniessen kann in der Welt,
Das hab' ich genossen wie je ein Held!
HEINRICH HEINE:
Rückschau (German)

I have smelt all the aromas there are in this fragrant kitchen they call Earth; and what we can enjoy in this life, I surely have enjoyed just like a lord!

ENVY
see also Competition, Death, Enemies, Fortune, Merit, Vanity.

L'envie aux doigts crochus, au teint pâle et livide.
P. A. C. DE BEAUMARCHAIS:
Le Barbier de Séville (French)

Envy with its crooked fingers and its pale, livid face.

L'envie est une passion timide et honteuse que l'on n'ose jamais avouer.

FRANÇOIS, DUC DE LA ROCHEFOUCAULD:
Réflexions (French)

Envy is a timid and shameful feeling to which we never dare admit.

L'envie et le mépris sont les deux arrêts du tribunal de l'orgueil.

PAUL VALÉRY:
Choses Tues (French)

Envy and contempt are the two warrants for the Court of Arrogance.

Hoi dustukheis gar toisin eutukhesterois
Autoi kalōs praxantes ou phronousin eu

EURIPIDES:
Iphigeneia in Tauris (Greek)

Those who have fallen on evil days resent their luckier brethren.

Pephulaxo ge tauta poiein, hoposa phthonon iskhei

PYTHAGORAS:
Golden Verses (Greek)

Take care not to do anything that could provoke the envy of others.

Phthonos kai erōs enantia estin

GREEK PROVERB

Envy and love are opposite principles.

Pros gar ton ekhonth' ho phthonos herpei

SOPHOCLES:
Ajax (Greek)

Envy follows in the tracks of the wealthy.

Ho phthonos oiktirmou estin ameinōn

PINDAR:
Pythian Odes (Greek)

Envy is better than pity.

Ouden onēsei ho phthonos

GREEK PROVERB

Envy accomplishes nothing.

Perchè s'appuntan li vostri disiri

Dove per compagnia parte si scema,
Invidia move il mantaco ai sospiri.

DANTE:
Purgatorio (Italian)

Because your desires are centred upon what is desired by others, envy lends flames to your sighs.

Invidus alterius macrescit rebus optimis.

HORACE:
Epistles (Latin)

Envy sickens from the well-being of others.

Invidiam placare paras virtute relicta?

HORACE:
Satires (Latin)

Do you hope to placate envy by abandoning virtue?

Nam invidere alii bene esse, tibi mal esse, miseria est.

PLAUTUS:
Truculentus (Latin)

It is misery to envy someone else's well-being, when you yourself are not prospering.

Aliena nobis, nostra plus aliis placent.

LATIN PROVERB

We all envy other people's luck.

EPITAPHS
see also Graves, Last words, Prayer.

En toy qui est filz de dieu le pere
Sauvez soit que gist souz cest piere.

Inscription on the tomb of John Gower in
St. Saviour's Church, Southwark *(French)*

Thou, Son of God the Father, save him who lies beneath these stones.

Vous qe passez ov bouche close
Pries pur cely cy repose.

Inscription on the tomb of John Warren,
earl of Surrey, at Lewes *(French)*

Ye who pass with silent lips, pray for him who here lies at rest.

Tout cil qi pur moi prieront
Ou a Dieu m'acorderont

Dieu les mette en son paradys
Ou nul ne poet estre chetifs.
> Inscription of the brass of the Black Prince
> at Canterbury *(French)*

May God admit to his paradise, where evil is unknown, all those who pray for me or entrust me to him.

Dona, Jesu, ut grex pastoris calle sequatur.
> Epitaph on the tomb of Wilfrid,
> bishop of York *(Latin)*

Grant, Lord, his flock may tread their shepherd's path.

Suscippe, terra, tuo corpus de corpore sumtum.
> Epitaph on the tomb of St. Gregory *(Latin)*

Earth, take this corpse – 'tis dust of thine own dust.

EQUALITY
see also Elite, Honour, Right and wrong.

C'est un vin pur et généreux; mais nous avons bu trop du nôtre.
> H. A. TAINE;
> *Letters*, 2 January, 1867 *(French)*

[Equality] is a pure and noble wine; but we have drunk too much of ours.

Un chien regarde bien un évêque.
> FRENCH PROVERB

A cat can look at a king *(lit.* a dog can stare at a bishop).

L'égalité suggère à l'esprit humain plusiers idées qui ne lui seraient pas venues sans elle, et elle modifie presque toutes celles qu'il avait déjà.
> ALEXIS DE TOCQUEVILLE:
> *De la Démocratie en Amérique (French)*

Equality suggests to the human mind many ideas that would not have occurred to it otherwise, and modifies nearly every idea that it already possesses.

Quod ad ius naturale attinet, omnes homines aequales sunt.
> ROMAN LEGAL MAXIM *(Latin)*

As far as the law of nature is concerned, all men are equal.

ESCAPE
see also Sanctuary.

Ita fugias ne praeter casam.
> LATIN PROVERB
> (Quoted in Terence: *Phormio*) *(Latin)*

Do not overlook the most obvious means of escape (*lit.* do not run beyond the hut).

ETERNITY

Svět rozkládá se za světem,
za hvězdou hvězda, když půlnoc se tmí
> OTAKAR BŘEZINA:
> 'Zem?' in *Stavitelé Chrámn (Czech)*

In midnight's gloom world reaches out to world, and star to star.

Rien n'est si important à l'homme que son estat, rien ne luy est si redoutable que l'éternité.
> BLAISE PASCAL:
> *Pensées (French)*

Nothing is so important to man as his condition, nothing is so formidable to him as the idea of eternity.

In der Ewigkeit ist alles am Anfang, duftender Morgen.
> ELIAS CANETTI
> *Aufzeichnungen*, 1945 *(German)*

In eternity everything is just beginning, it is the fragrant dawn.

Ora y sempre.
> ITALIAN EXPRESSION

Now and always.

Quod non fuit primus homo, nec erit ultimus immo semper fuit et semper erit generati hominis ex homine.
> Etienne Tempier's condemnation of heresy
> 1277 (*Chartularium Universitatis Parisiensis*
> *(Latin)*

For man was not the first, nor will he be the last he has always existed from the beginning of the world, and each generation of mankind will derive from its predecessor.

Pregona eternidad tu alma de piedra
Y amor de vida en tu ragazo arraiga,

Amor de vida eterna, y a su sombra
Amor de amores.

MIGUEL DE UNAMUNO:
Salamanca (Spanish)

Your rocklike soul proclaims eternity; love of life
lies confidently in your lap; love of eternal life,
and – in its shadow – love of loves.

EVASION

Tout' au parōkheteusas eu kouden legōn

EURIPIDES:
The Bacchae (Greek)

Again a smooth answer, signifying nothing.

EVENING
see also Night, Twilight.

Schoon de dag nog marre
Schittert door 't azuur
Vast der avondstarre
Rozenkwistend vuur.

EVERHARDUS JOHANNES POTGIETER:
De Nalatenschap van den Landjonker: Gemijmer
(Dutch)

Though the day still lingers, the rose-scattering
fire of the evening star already scintillates
through the azure sky.

En ver, daar ginds, die zacht gekleurde lucht
Als perlemoer, waar ied're tint vervliet
In teêrheid.

WILLEM KLOOS:
Avond (Dutch)

Far away, the soft-coloured heavens are like
mother-of-pearl, dissolving every ethereal hue.

Que le jour est lent de mourir par ces soirs
démesurés de l'été!

MARCEL PROUST:
La Fugitive (French)

How slow the days are to die in these endless
summer evenings!

La soirée n'est jamais plus belle pour moi que
quand je suis content de ma matinée.

DENIS DIDEROT:
Le Neveu de Rameau (French)

The evenings are never more beautiful for me
than when I have been pleased with the
morning.

Les soleils couchants
Revêtent les champs
Les canaux, la ville entière
D'hyacinthe et d'or;
Le monde s'endort
Dans une chaude lumière.

CHARLES BAUDELAIRE:
Invitation au Voyage (French)

The setting sun sheaths the fields, canals and
the entire town in hyacinth and gold; the world
falls asleep in the warm twilight.

Mais le soir vermeil ressemble à l'aurore,
Et la nuit plus tard amène l'oubli!

GÉRARD DE NERVAL:
Ni Bonjour ni Bonsoir (French)

The rosy sky of evening resembles the dawn,
and later night will bring oblivion.

Will kein lieber Vogel singen?
Alle Büsche bleiben stumm.
Nur ein Falter mit bunten Schwingen
Tummelt sich im Roggenfeld herum.

THEODOR DÄUBLER:
Gegen Abend (German)

Will no bird sing? All the bushes are mute; only
a butterfly with coloured wings bustles about
the rye-field.

Der Abend wiegte schon die Erde,
Und an den Bergen hing die Nacht.

J. W. VON GOETHE:
Willkommen und Abschied (German)

Evening was already cradling the earth, and the
night hovered over the mountains.

I molcha zhizn' krugom blagoukhaet,
I v nepodvizhnoï krasote svoeï
Prokhladnȳï vecher molcha rastochaet
Poeziyu bez zvukov, bez recheï.

PËTR VYAZEMSKY:
Vecher (Russian)

And all around life silently spreads fragrance,
and the cool evening in its motionless beauty
silently diffuses a poetry without sounds, without speech.

La tarde en la montaña, moribunda se inclina,
Y el sol postrer un lampo, como una aguja fina,

Pasa por los quiméricos miradores de encaje.
JULIO HERRERA Y REISSIG:
El Teatro de los Humildes (Spanish)

The dying evening leans on the mountain, and the sun slips a needle of light through the incredible lacelike balconies of the heavens.

EVENTS
see also Familiarity, Law.

Les événements jouent avec nos pensées comme le chat avec la souris.
PAUL VALÉRY:
Mauvaises Pensées (French)

Events toy with our thoughts like a cat with a mouse.

Pas de nouvelles, bonnes nouvelles.
FRENCH PROVERB

No news is good news.

Quod hodie non est, cras erit.
PETRONIUS:
Satyricon (Latin)

What does not take place today, will tomorrow.

Quo evenat dis in manust.
PLAUTUS:
Bacchides (Latin)

The outcome lies in the hands of the gods.

EVIL
see also Adversity, Anger, Devils, Fools, Good, Gossip, Greatness, Happiness, Indifference, Ingratitude, Innocence, Joy, Philosophy, Redemption, Sin, Soul, Steadfastness.

An-nās al-baṭṭālin yi 'rafū ba'ḍ
ARAB PROVERB

Evil people know each other.

Il finit par croire à l'existence de Satan comme à la sienne, c'est-à-dire qu'il finit par croire qu'il est Satan.
ANDRÉ GIDE:
Les Faux-monnayeurs (French)

He finished by believing that Satan existed just as he did; that is to say, he finished up by believing he *was* Satan.

Le mal est toujours venu ici-bas par quelque homme de génie.
DENIS DIDEROT:
Le Neveu de Rameau (French)

Evil always turns up in this world through some genius or other.

Quand on cède á la peur du mal, on ressent déjà le mal de la peur.
P. A. C. DE BEAUMARCHAIS:
Le Barbier de Séville (French)

When we yield to the fear of evil, we already experience the evil of fear.

Le bon Dieu conserve les méchants gens pour leur donner le temps du repentir.
MME LA COMTESSE DE SÉGUR:
Un Bon Petit Diable (French)

God preserves the wicked to give them time to repent.

Une méchante vie amène une méchante mort.
MOLIÈRE:
Don Juan (French)

A wicked life leads to a wicked death.

S'il importe d'être sublime en quelque genre, c'est surtout en mal.
DENIS DIDEROT:
Le Neveu de Rameau (French)

If it is necessary to be sublime in some rôle or other, it is above all necessary in evil.

Prendre conscience de ce qui est atroce et en rire, c'est devenir maître de ce qui est atroce.
EUGÈNE IONESCU
La Démystification par l'Humeur Noir (French)

If we recognise what is atrocious and laugh at it we can master the atrocious.

La vipère engendre la vipère.
VICTOR HUGO
Cromwell (French)

Vipers breed vipers.

Mauvais herbe croît toujours.
ERASMUS
Adages (French)

Weeds always flourish.

Le mal est bon à tout.
FRENCH PROVERB

Evil is ready for anything.

Le mal est ce qui nuit.
FRENCH PROVERB

Evil is whatever does harm.

Le mal que nous faisons ne nous attire pas tant de persécution et de haine que nos bonnes qualités.
FRANÇOIS, DUC DE LA ROCHEFOUCAULD:
Réflexions (French)

The evil we do does not attract as much persecution and hate as do our good qualities.

La foule met toujours, de ses mains dégradées,
Quelque chose de vil sur les grandes idées.
VICTOR HUGO:
Cromwell (French)

The mob, with its vicious hands, will always tarnish any great idea.

Wer schmutzige Hände hat, dem ist alles Schmutz.
BERTOLT BRECHT:
Baal (1918 version) *(German)*

Everything is filthy to him who has filthy hands.

Wie anstrengend es ist, böse zu sein!
BERTOLT BRECHT:
Die Maske des Bösen (German)

How exhausting it is to be evil!

Überhaupt beobachtet man, dass die Bösartigkeit der Seele gar oft in kranken Körpern wohnt.
J. C. F. VON SCHILLER:
(German)

We observe in general that malignity of soul often dwells in diseased bodies.

Hoi d' akosmountes brotōn
Didaskalōn logoisi gignontai kakoi
SOPHOCLES:
Philoctetes (Greek)

The wrong that men do can all be traced to those who mistaught them.

Hōs apoloito kai allos hotis toiauta ge rhexoi
HOMER:
Odyssey (Greek)

So may everyone perish who does such things!

Kaka kerdea is' aatēisin
HESIOD:
Works and Days (Greek)

What is ill-gained can prove disastrous.

All' out' apolesthai ta kaka dunaton, ō Theodōre.
Hupenantion gar ti tōi agathōi aei einai anankē
PLATO:
Theaetetus (Greek)

You cannot do away with evil, Theodorus, for you must always have something to counterbalance good.

Ouden thaumaston to homilein tois ponērois tous ponērous
GREEK PROVERB

There is nothing surprising in bad men consorting with bad.

Kakon de kan en hēmerai gnoiēs miai
SOPHOCLES:
Oedipus Tyrannus (Greek)

You can spot a bad man in a day.

Epei ouden pō kakon g' apōleto
SOPHOCLES:
Philoctetes (Greek)

Evil never dies.

K'an hus dakoi andra ponēron
GREEK PROVERB

Even a pig would bite a bad man.

Oudeis anthrōpōn adikōn tisin ouk apotisei
GREEK PROVERB

No evil-doer can escape punishment.

Hubris pore pollaki kerdos
GREEK PROVERB

Outrage often produces profit.

Stasin ara kai noson tēs psukhēs ponērian
legontes orthōs eroumen
PLATO:
The Sophist (Greek)

Evil is a disrupter and a disease of the soul.

Thuraze kēres
ANCIENT GREEK SPELL

Spectres avaunt!

Hoi g' autōi kaka teukhei anēr allōi kaka
teukhōn
HESIOD:
Works and Days (Greek)

Those who have evil designs on others threaten
themselves.

Per mal' oprar mai non gioisce
Un animo malvagio.
GIAMBATTISTA CINTHIO GIRALDI:
Altile (prologue) *(Italian)*

An evil disposition never finds joy through
wrongdoing.

Abstineas igitur damnandis.
JUVENAL:
Satires (Latin)

Abstain from things that you must condemn.

Magna non latitant mala.
SENECA:
Medea (Latin)

Great evils cannot hide themselves.

Contumeliam si dices, audies.
PLAUTUS:
Pseudolus (Latin)

If you say evil things you will hear them.

Fons vitii et perjurii.
PLAUTUS:
Truculentus (Latin)

You source of vice and perjury.

[Malitia] mala bonis ponit ante.
CICERO:
De Officiis (Latin)

[Malice] puts evil before good.

Malus bonum malum esse volt, ut sit sui similis.
PLAUTUS:
Trinummus (Latin)

Evil people want good people to be evil and thus
resemble them.

Exemplo quodcumque malo comittitur, ipsi
displicet auctori.
JUVENAL:
Satires (Latin)

No deed that sets an evil example can bring joy
to the doer.

Ipse Deus mala esse in mundo non sineret,
nisi ex eis bona eliceret ad utilitatem et
pulchritudinem universi.
ST. THOMAS AQUINAS:
On Princely Government (Latin)

God himself would not permit evil in this world
if good did not come of it for the benefit and
harmony of the universe.

Nisi oderimus malum, bonum amare non
possumus.
ST. JEROME:
Letter to Rusticus (Latin)

We cannot love good, if we do not hate evil.

In omni condicione et gradu optimis mixta sunt
pessima.
ST. JEROME:
Letter to Rusticus (Latin)

In every rank and condition of life the very bad is
mixed with the very good.

Scelera conspectum sui reformidant.
SENECA:
Natural Questions (Latin)

Evil deeds shun the sight of themselves.

Da, pater, invictam contra omnia crimina
mentem.
AUSONIUS:
Opuscula (Latin)

Father, grant me a heart that can hold out
against all deeds of wrong.

EXAMPLE   101

Ex malis multis malum quod minimumst, id minimest malum.

> PLAUTUS:
> *Stichus (Latin)*

The best evil of the infinite number of evils of this world is that which harms us least.

Tuus malus genius!

> FLORUS:
> *Works (Latin)*

I am your evil genius! (Caesar's ghost appearing to Brutus).

Satis est enim, si hoc habemus ne quis nobis male facere possit.

> SUETONIUS:
> *Divus Augustus (Latin)*

We must be content if we can stop anyone from doing evil to us (Augustus to Tiberius).

Dobra za zlo isporchennoe serdtse –
Akh! – ne prostit.

> ALEKSEĬ TOLSTOY:
> *Ballada o Kamergere Delaryu (Russian)*

Alas! a depraved heart will not forgive the man who returns good for evil.

V ochakh lyudeĭ chitayu ya
Stranitsÿ zlobÿ i poroka.

> MIKHAIL LERMONTOV:
> *The Prophet (Russian)*

In people's eyes I read pages of malice and vice.

Bicho malo nunca muere.

> SPANISH PROVERB

A vicious beast never dies.

Muchas veces empeoran los malos con los remedios.

> SPANISH PROVERB

Evils are often aggravated by remedies.

EXAGGERATION
see also Oratory, Simplicity.

Arcem facere e cloaca.

> CICERO:
> *Oratio pro Plancio (Latin)*

To make a mountain out of a molehill (*lit.* to make a citadel out of a sewer).

Imponere Pelio Ossam.

> VIRGIL:
> *Georgics (Latin)*

To pile Pelion on Ossa.

cf. Involvite Pelion Ossae

> CLAUDIAN:
> *Panegyricu de Quarto Consulatu Honorii Augusti (Latin)*

Place Pelion on Ossa.

Olla que mucho hierve, sabor pierde.

> SPANISH PROVERB

The over-cooked stew loses its flavour.

El encarecer es ramo de mentir.

> BALTASAR GRACIÁN:
> *Oráculo Manual y Arte de Prudencia (Spanish)*

Exaggeration is an offshoot of lying.

EXAMPLE
see also Advice, Evil, Glory, Leadership, Prudence, Reticence.

L'exemple est un dangereux leurre.

> JEAN DE LA FONTAINE:
> *Le Corbeau Voulant Imiter l'Aigle (French)*

Example is a dangerous bait.

L'exemple souvent n'est qu'un miroir trompeur.

> PIERRE CORNEILLE:
> *Cinna (French)*

Example is often but a lying mirror.

Les vieillards aiment à donner de bons préceptes, pour se consoler de n'être plus en état de donner de mauvais exemples.

> FRANÇOIS, DUC DE LA ROCHEFOUCAULD:
> *Réflexions (French)*

Old men love to give good advice to console themselves for no longer being able to set a bad example.

Tel maître, tel valet.

> FRENCH PROVERB

Like master, like man.

Hotan gar aiskhra toisin esthloisin dokēi,
E karta doxei tois kakois g' einai kala
> EURIPIDES:
> *Hippolytus (Greek)*

When the noble choose evil, the lowly will surely do the same.

Respicere exemplar vitae morumque jubebo
Doctum imitatorem, et vivas hinc ducere voces.
> HORACE:
> *Ars Poetica (Latin)*

I would advise one who has learned the imitative art to look to life and manners for a model and draw from thence living words (*tr.* Fairclough).

Amore et virtute.
> Motto of the Raleigh family *(Latin)*

By love and virtue.

Como canta el abad, responde el sacristan.
> SPANISH PROVERB

As chants the abbot, so replies the clerk.

EXCELLENCE
see also Good, Greatness.

Selten wird das Treffliche gefunden, seltner geschätzt.
> J. W. VON GOETHE:
> *Wilhelm Meisters Lehrjahre (German)*

True excellence is rarely found; even more rarely is it cherished.

EXCESS
see also Judgment, Moderation.

Die Mutter der Ausschweifung ist nicht die Freude, sondern die Freudlosigkeit.
> FRIEDRICH NIETZSCHE:
> *Menschliches Allzumenschliches (German)*

The mother of excess is not pleasure, but the lack of it.

EXCUSES

Qui s'excuse, s'accuse.
> FRENCH PROVERB

He who excuses himself, accuses himself.

Male factum interpretando facias acrius.
> LATIN PROVERB

Least said, soonest mended.

Mortuus est, puto, licuit
> SUETONIUS
> *Divus Claudius (Latin)*

He's dead; I think the excuse is a lawful one (a explanation for why a witness had not appeare at a trial).

EXECUTION

Die Guillotine ist der beste Arzt!
> GEORG BÜCHNER
> *Dantons Tod (German)*

The guillotine is the best physician!

Welch Haupt steht fort, wenn dieses heil'ge fie
> J. C. F. VON SCHILLER
> *Maria Stuart (German)*

What head is safe if this blest one falls? (referrin to the execution of Mary Stuart).

Willst du grausamer sein als der Tod? Kanns du verhindern, dass unsere Köpfe sich auf der boden des Korbes küssen?
> GEORG BÜCHNER
> *Dantons Tod (German)*

Do you want to be more inhuman than death Can you prevent our heads kissing at the botton of that basket? (Danton's last words addressed, at the guillotine, to the executione who has prevented Hérault from embracin him).

Ita feri ut se mori sentiat!
> SUETONIUS
> *Gaius Caligula (Latin)*

Strike so that he can feel that he is dying (Caligula, referring to his favourite method c having people put to death by numerous sligh wounds).

EXILE
see also Fatherland, Parents, Solitude.

Quand reverrai-je, hélas, de mon petit village
Fumer la cheminée? et en quelle saison
Reverrai-je le clos de ma pauvre maison,

Qui m'est une province, et beaucoup davantage?
JOACHIM DU BELLAY:
Sonnet des 'Regrets' (French)

When shall I see again the smoke arising from the chimneys of my little village? When shall I see again the yard of my poor house which, to me, is a province and even more?

Il fit de son exil l'asile de son chant.
Robert Mallet, speaking of St-Jean Perse's
Exil (French)

He turned his exile into the refuge of his song.

J'emmène avec moi pour bagage
Cent villages sans lien sinon
L'ancienne antienne de leurs noms,
L'odorante fleur du langage.
LOUIS ARAGON:
Le Conscrit des Cents Villages (French)

For luggage I take with me a hundred villages with nothing in common save the age-old harmony of their names, and the fragrance of their language.

Livre, qu'un vent t'emporte
En France, où je suis né!
L'arbre déraciné
Donne sa feuille morte.
VICTOR HUGO:
Le Livre (French)

Dear book, may a wind carry you off to France, where I was born! The uprooted tree is giving up its last dead leaf.

Doch uns ist gegeben,
Auf keiner Stätte zu ruhn.
FRIEDRICH HÖLDERLIN:
Hyperions Schicksaalslied (German)

We are fated to find no resting-place.

O patris, o dōmata, mē
Det' apolis genoiman
Ton amēkhanias ekhousa
Dusperaton aiōn',
Oiktrotatōn akheōn
EURIPIDES:
Medea (Greek)

O my country, O my home, I pray that I may be spared that most pitiful fate – of leading the unbearable, poverty-stricken life of an exile!

Mokhthōn d' ouk allos huperthen ē
Gas patrias steresthai
EURIPIDES:
Medea (Greek)

There is no worse fate than to be exiled.

Exsul ubi ei nusquam domus est sine sepulcro est mortuus.
LATIN PROVERB

An exile with no home anywhere is a corpse without a grave.

Se a saudade
Ao proscripto sempre diz
Que não ha terra formosa
Sem o sol do seu paiz.
FRANCISCO GOMES DE AMORIM:
O Desterrado (Portuguese)

The heart of the exile tells him that the land alone is fair which the sun of his country knows.

Gorau Cymro, Cymro oddi cartref.
WELSH PROVERB

The best Welshman is the Welshman in exile.

EXISTENCE
see also Art, Change, Life, Mankind, Purpose, Solitude, Survival.

Les choses existent, nous n'avons pas à les créer!
STÉPHANE MALLARMÉ:
Réponses à des Enquêtes sur l'Évolution Littéraire (French)

Things exist – we don't have to create them!

Je pense donc je suis (Cogito ergo sum).
DESCARTES:
Discours de la Méthode (French)

I think therefore I am.

Alles
Ist nicht es selbst.
RAINER MARIA RILKE:
Duineser Elegien (German)

Nothing is anything.

Dadurch existieren wir,
Dass wir uns von unserem Existieren ablenken.
THOMAS BERNHARD:
Der Ignorant und der Wahnsinnige (German)

We can only exist by taking our minds off the fact that we exist.

Kein Ding sei wo das Wort gebricht!
STEFAN GEORGE:
Das Neue Reich (German)

Let nothing exist which violates the word!

Ho mē proteron ēn, husteron alla touto einai aneu tou genesthai kai gignesthai adunaton
PLATO:
Theaetetus (Greek)

What did not previously exist could not now exist without having come into existence.

To genomenon aei gegonen holon
PLATO:
The Sophist (Greek)

Whatever comes into existence always comes as a whole.

Tithemai gar horon horizein ta onta, hōs estin ouk allo ti plēn dunamis
PLATO:
The Sophist (Greek)

Existence is nothing else than power, as I define it.

Ou gar mē pote touto damēi, einai mē eonta
PARMENIDES:
Fragments (Greek)

Do not allow the belief that non-being is to continue.

Esser uomo fra gli umani,
Io non so più dolce cosa
UMBERTO SABA:
Esser Uomo (Italian)

I know of no sweeter thing than to be a man among men.

Det er dyrt at bøde med Livet for sin Fødsel.
HENRIK IBSEN:
Peer Gynt (Norwegian)

One's life is a heavy price to pay for being born.

Hvilket skyldberg der sig højner
Fra det lille ord: at leve.
HENRIK IBSEN:
Ghosts (Norwegian)

What a towering mound of sin rises from one small word – to be!

Soy, más, estoy. Respiro.
Lo profundo es el aire.
La realidad me inventa,
Soy su leyenda. ¡Salve!
JORGE GUILLÉN
Más Allá (Spanish)

I am. I continue to exist. I breathe. Profound is the atmosphere. Reality invented me. I am its legend. Hail!

No hay dolor más grande que el dolor de ser vivo,
Ni mayor pesadumbre que la vida consciente.
RUBÉN DARÍO:
Lo Fatal (Spanish)

There is no greater sorrow than that of being alive; no greater burden than conscious existence.

EXISTENTIALISM

Je consens à être existentialiste à la condition de ne pas le savoir.
ANDRÉ GIDE:
(French)

I will agree to be an existentialist as long as I may remain unaware of it.

L'Existentialisme est un humanisme.
JEAN-PAUL SARTRE:
L'Existentialisme est un Humanisme (French)

Existentialism is a form of humanism (the title of Sartre's famous lecture).

EXPECTATION
see also Certainty.

'Aṣfūr fi 'l-yad wa-lā 'ashara 'alā 'h-hajara
ARAB PROVERB

A bird in the hand is worth ten in the bush.

Ḥumār ḥayy aḥsan min ḥuṣanayn thalātha
mayyitīn
ARAB PROVERB
A live donkey is better than two or three dead
horses.

Aus Nichts wird Nichts.
GERMAN PROVERB
Nothing will come of nothing (*lit.* out of nothing,
nothing will come).

Non fumum ex fulgore, sed ex fumo dare lucem
Cogitat, ut speciosa dehinc miracula promat.
HORACE:
Ars Poetica (Latin)
He plans to give not smoke after flame, but light
after smoke, so that he may relate plausible and
wonderful tales.

El que espera lo mucho espera lo poco.
GABRIEL GARCÍA MÁRQUEZ:
El Coronel no Tiene quien le Escriba (Spanish)
He who awaits much can expect little.

EXPERIENCE
**see also Action, Anticipation, Caution,
Fortune, Fulfilment, Life, Mind.**

Wat dat de wereld is
Dat weet ick al te wis.
God betert! door 't verzoecken.
GERBRAND ADRIAENSZOON BREDERO:
Wat dat de Wereld is (Dutch)
I know too well what the world is like, God help
me! – from experience.

Je veux, sans que la mort ose me secourir,
Toujours aimer, toujours souffrir, toujours
mourir.
PIERRE CORNEILLE:
Suréna (French)
I want always to love, always to suffer, always to
die, without death daring to offer me his refuge.

Quiconque a beaucoup vu
Peut avoir beaucoup retenu.
JEAN DE LA FONTAINE:
L'Hirondelle et les Petits Oiseaux (French)
He who has seen much will have remembered
much.

Deux choses instruisent l'homme de toute sa
nature: l'instinct et l'expérience.
BLAISE PASCAL:
Pensées (French)
Two things reveal the whole of his nature to
man: instinct and experience.

Mais si tout m'est connu, vivre n'est-il que
revoir?
ST-JOHN PERSE:
Vents (French)
But if I know everything, is not living only a
repetition?

Tout esprit est façonné par les expériences les
plus banales.
PAUL VALÉRY:
Mauvaises Pensées (French)
Every mind is shaped by the most banal experiences.

Nourri dans le sérail, j'en connais les détours.
JEAN RACINE:
Bajazet (French)
Brought up as I was in the seraglio, I know all
the ins and outs.

Elle a tout vu, elle a tout lu, elle sait tout.
GABRIEL NAUDÉ,
speaking of Queen Christina of Sweden,
in a letter (1652) to Gassendi *(French)*
She has seen everything, read everything, knows
everything.

Und was der ganzen Menschheit zugeteilt ist,
Will ich in meinem innern Selbst geniessen.
J. W. VON GOETHE:
Faust (fragment of 1790) *(German)*
What is allotted to the whole of mankind I
would savour in my inner being.

Wer lange lebt, hat viel erfahren,
Nichts Neues kann für ihn auf dieser Welt ges-
chehn.
J. W. VON GOETHE:
Faust (German)
He who has lived long has experienced much.
There can be nothing new for him in this world.

Ich habe meine Lehrzeit
Hinter mir.
ERICH FRIED:
Fast Alles (German)

My time for learning is now behind me.

Ta mellonta tekmairomai tois gegenēmenois
GREEK PROVERB

I judge what will be by what has been.

Polla para gnōmēn epesen
GREEK PROVERB

Many things happen contrary to experience.

Tranquillas etiam naufragus horret aquas.
OVID:
Ex Ponto (Latin)

The shipwrecked man shrinks even from calm
waters.

Experto credite.
VIRGIL:
Aeneid (Latin)

Trust one who has tried.

In otio, in negotio, et docemus quod scimus et
addiscimus quod nescimus.
POPE SYLVESTER II (GERBERT):
Epistles (Latin)

In leisure and in labour we teach what we know,
and we learn what we did not know.

Discit enim citius meminitque libentius illud
Quod quis deridet, quam quod probat et ven-
eratur.
HORACE:
Epistles (Latin)

A man learns more quickly and remembers
more gladly what he scorns than what he
approves and esteems.

Quid est aetas hominis, nisi ea memoria rerum
veterum cum superiorum aetate contexitur?
CICERO:
Orator (Latin)

Of what value is man's life if it is not bound
together with the life of his predecessors by the
records of antiquity?

Posse taurum tollere, qui vitulum sustulerit.
LATIN PROVERB
(quoted in Petronius' *Satyricon*)

She'll bear the bull that bore the calf.

El gato escaldado del agua fria huye.
SPANISH PROVERB

The scalded cat flees even from cold water.

Non hay mula de alvarda que la troxa non
consienta.
SPANISH PROVERB

There is no pack-mule that won't take panniers.

EXPLANATION

All' ex huparkhēs authis aut' egō phanō
SOPHOCLES:
Oedipus (Greek)

I'll start again and explain everything.

EXPLOITATION

Humma yibarradū wa-ghayrhum yākul
ARAB PROVERB

Some work, but others enjoy the profits (*lit.* they
cool [the dishes], others eat [the food]).

EYES
see also Beauty, Sorrow, Tears, Widows and widowers.

Lajit ' eināthā
Shabah an-najma 'z-zahra
The Song of Zargā (Arabic)

Her eyes shine like Venus, brightest of the stars.

Tes yeux, illuminés ainsi que des boutiques
Ou des ifs flamboyant dans les fêtes publiques,
Usent insolemment d'un pouvoir emprunté,
Sans connaître jamais la loi de leur beauté.
CHARLES BAUDELAIRE:
Spleen et Idéal (French)

Your eyes, lit up like shop windows or illumina-
tions for public celebrations, insolently make
use of their borrowed power in permanent ignorance of the law of their beauty.

Tes yeux sont la citerne ou boivent mes ennuis.

CHARLES BAUDELAIRE:
Sed non Satiata (French)

Your eyes are the source from which my troubles drink.

C'est de tes jeunes yeux que mon ardeur est née,
C'est de leurs premiers traits que je fus abattu.

FRANÇOIS MAYNARD:
La Belle Vieille (French)

My ardour was born from your youthful eyes, and it was their first shafts that overthrew me.

. . . la gloire
Des yeux qui me semblent doux

PIERRE CORNEILLE:
Stances à la Marquise (French)

The glory of eyes that seem pleasing to me.

Et l'on voit de la flamme aux yeux des jeunes gens,
Mais dans l'oeil du vieillard on voit de la lumière.

VICTOR HUGO:
Booz Endormi (French)

In the eyes of youth we see a flame, but in the eyes of the aged we see light.

On dirait ton regard d'une vapeur couvert
Ton oeil mysterieux (est-il bleu, gris ou vert?)
Alternativement tendre, rêveur, cruel,
Réfléchit l'indolence et la paleur du ciel.

CHARLES BAUDELAIRE:
Ciel Brouillé (French)

One would say your look shrouded in a mist, your mysterious eyes (are they blue, grey or green?) alternatively tender, dreamy, cruel, reflect the pallor and indolence of the heavens.

Ton regard, c'est l'astre qui brille
Aux yeux troublés des matelots,
Dont la barque en proie au naufrage,
A l'instant où cesse l'orage,
Se brise et s'enfuit sous les flots.

GÉRARD DE NERVAL:
Laisse-Moi! (French)

Your gaze is like the star that shines in the worried eyes of the sailors whose boat is in danger of shipwreck; at the moment when the storm dies down, the boat breaks up and vanishes beneath the waves.

Quand le plaisir brille en tes yeux
Pleins de douceur et d'espérance.

GÉRARD DE NERVAL:
Mélodie (French)

When pleasure shines in your eyes filled with sweetness and hope.

Ancor negli occhi ond'escon le faville
Che mi fiammano il cor, ch'io porto anciso.

DANTE:
Canzone (Italian)

Still into those eyes, the source of those sparks that fire my conquered heart.

Speculum mentis est facies et taciti oculi cordis fatentur arcana.

ST. JEROME:
Letter to Furia, AD 394 (Latin)

The face is the mirror of the mind; and eyes, without speaking, confess the secrets of the heart.

Rosto singular!
Olhos socegados,
Pretos e cansados,
Mas não de matar!

LUIS DE CAMÕES:
A uma Cativa com quem Andava de Amores na India, chamada Barbara (Portuguese)

Her eyes are dark and still in her lovely face — eyes of languid grace, yet still keen to kill!

Lyublyu glaza tvoi, moï drug,
S igroï ikh plamneno-chudesnoï,
Kogda ikh pripodýmesh' vdrug
I, slovno molnieï nebesnoï,
Okinesh' beglo tselyï krug.

FÉDOR TYUTCHEV:
Lyublyu Glaza Tvoi (Russian)

Dearest, I love your eyes, with their fiery wonderful play, when suddenly you raise them a little and, like a flash of lightning, glance quickly around you.

F

FACTS
see also Eloquence, State, World.

Res ipsa testist.

> PLAUTUS:
> *Aulularia (Latin)*

Facts speak for themselves.

FAILURE
see also Faults.

In melius adversa, in deterius optata flectuntur.

> SENECA:
> *Natural Questions (Latin)*

Failure changes for the better, success for the worse.

FAITH
see also Fear, Fickleness, Piety, Pity, Steadfastness.

La foy est un don de Dieu.

> BLAISE PASCAL:
> *Pensées (French)*

Faith is a gift of God.

Fiez-vous donc à moi, la foi soulage, guide, guérit.

> ARTHUR RIMBAUD:
> *Mauvais Sang (French)*

Have faith in me, then; faith assuages, guides, restores.

La foi qui n'agit point, est-ce une foi sincère?

> JEAN RACINE:
> *Athalie (French)*

Can a faith that does nothing be called sincere?

Multo enim gravius est corrumpere fidem per quam est animae vita, quam falsare pecuniam. Temporali vitae subvenitur.

> ST. THOMAS AQUINAS:
> *Summa Theologica (Latin)*

Far graver is it to corrupt the faith that is the life of the soul than to counterfeit the money that sustains temporal life.

Improbo
Iracundior Adria
Tecum vivere amem, tecum obeam libens

> HORACE:
> *Odes (Latin)*

Rough as the Adriatic Sea, yet will I live with thee, or else for thee will die (*tr.* Robert Herrick)

. . . sua quemque moretur
Cura, neque assueto mutet amore locum

> PROPERTIUS:
> *Elegies (Latin)*

Let each man's darling hold him; and let him not shift from the love to which he is accustomed!

Troen gaar frit; den lægges ingen Told paa.

> HENRIK IBSEN:
> *Peer Gynt (Norwegian)*

Faith is quite free, and pays no duty.

Znayu, volya tvoya voln morskikh ne verneĭ

> VLADIMIR SOLOVIEV:
> *U Tsaritsÿ Moeĭ (Russian)*

I know that your resolve is not more constant than the waves of the sea.

FALLIBILITY

Ce qui m'estonne le plus est de voir que tout le monde n'est pas estonné de sa foiblesse.

> BLAISE PASCAL:
> *Pensées (French)*

Most of all it astonishes me to see that men are not astonished by their own weakness.

L'homme n'est qu'un sujet plein d'erreur, naturelle et ineffaçable sans la grâce.

> BLAISE PASCAL:
> *Pensées (French)*

Unless he has grace, man is only a caricature, full of natural and unredeemable sin.

FAME
see also Greatness, Reputation.

Les pierres parleroient pour luy.

ADRIEN BAILLET
(French)

The very stones will speak for him (speaking of John Selden)

On grave sur le marbre bien plus malaisément que sur le sable; mais les choses y sont conservées bien plus longtemps.

MOLIÈRE:
Le Malade Imaginaire (French)

It is harder to engrave on marble than on sand, but the inscription lasts much longer.

La gloire est une espèce de maladie que l'on prend pour avoir couché avec sa pensée.

PAUL VALÉRY:
Choses Tues (French)

Glory is a kind of sickness that we catch from sleeping with the thought of it.

La gloire expose à la calomnie.

FRENCH PROVERB

Glory makes us vulnerable to calumny.

Au pilori du temps n'expose pas mon ombre!
Je suis las des soleils, laisse mon urne à l'ombre!
Le bonheur de la mort, c'est d'être enseveli.

ALPHONSE DE LAMARTINE:
Au Comte d'Orsay (French)

Don't expose my memory to the pillory of time! I am tired of the sun's rays; leave my urn in the shade. The great fortune of death is to be buried!

La célébrité est le châtiment du mérite et la punition du talent.

S. R. N. CHAMFORT:
Maximes et Pensées (French)

Fame is the chastisement of merit and the punishment of talent.

Was unsterblich im Gesang soll leben,
Muss im Leben untergehn.

J. C. F. VON SCHILLER:
Die Götter Griechenlands (last lines) *(German)*

That which is immortalised in song must perish in life.

Als ihr Mund verstummte, wurde ihre Stimme gehört.

BERTOLT BRECHT:
Der Prozess der Jeanne d'Arc (German)

When her mouth was silenced, her voice began to be heard.

Könnten Sie nicht ein wenig vergessen, berühmt zu sein?

ROBERT WALSER:
to Hugo von Hofmannsthal, at a party *(German)*

Can't you forget to be famous just for a little while?

Pollai mēteres humnopolōn

ANTIPATER OF THESSALONICA:
Epigrams (Greek)

Famous men are claimed as sons by many cities (*lit.* minstrels have many mothers).

Che 'n nulla parte sì saldo s'intaglia,
Per far di marmo una persóna viva

FRANCESCO PETRARCA:
Sonnets (Italian)

In no part is it so firmly carved as to create a living being from the marble.

. . . il vago
Desio di gloria antico in me fia spento;
Vana Diva non pur, ma di fortuna
E del fato e d'amor, Diva più cieca.

GIACOMO LEOPARDI:
Al Conte Carlo Pepoli (Italian)

My old hunger for fame is quite gone; fame is a tarnished goddess, more blind than fortune, love or destiny ever were!

Latebrasque per omnes
Intrat et abstrusos explorat fama recessus.

CLAUDIAN:
Panegyricus de Quarto Consulatu Honorii Augusti (Latin)

Fame penetrates every hiding-place and discovers the inmost secrets of the heart.

Sed tamen innumeros homines sublimia facta
Et virtutis honos in tempora longa frequentant.
JUVENCUS:
Epic on the Gospel Story (Latin)

Noble deeds and the glory of a virtuous life
nevertheless keep the memory of countless men
alive for years to come.

Fama homines inter, coelum animus repetit.
AUSONIUS:
Opuscula (Latin)

His fame dwells among men, his spirit is returned above (speaking of a soldier who died in
the Trojan War).

Omni nobilior lustro, tibi gloria soli contigit.
CLAUDIAN:
Panegyricus de Probino et Olybrice (Latin)

An honour that no age has ever yet known is
thine alone.

. . . quem cepit vitrea fama,
Hunc circumtonuit gaudens Bellona cruentis.
HORACE:
Satires (Latin)

He who is dazzled by fame invites the blood-
thirsty attentions of the goddess of war.

Vixere fortes ante Agamemnona
Multi, sed omnes illacrimabiles
Urgentur ignotique longa
Nocte, carent quia vate sacra.
HORACE:
Odes (Latin)

Before Agamemnon's time there were many
men of courage, but all of them are unwept,
unknown and lost in the long night for lack of a
holy bard.

Prisca fides facto, sed fama perennis.
VIRGIL:
Aeneid (Latin)

Old is its faith, but deathless its fame.

Haec loca puer amavit, vir celebravit
Inscription on the plaque for Gavin Maxwell
on Craigower Hill *(Latin)*

These places he loved as a boy; as a man he
made them famous.

Hanchor-lah badan di-kandong tanah,
Budi yang baik di-kĕnang jua
Awang sulong (Malay)

Our bones lie hidden in the grave, but not the
memory of our good deeds.

Chto v imeni tebe moem?
Ono unret, kak shum pechal'nyĭ
Volnȳ, plesnuvsheĭ v bereg dal'nyĭ,
Kak zvuk nochnoĭ v lesu glukhom
ALEKSANDR SERGEEVICH PUSHKIN:
Sonnet (Russian)

How can my name be of interest to you? It will
die, just like the sad splash of a wave on a far-off
shore, or some sound in the night in a peaceful
copse.

FAMILIARITY
see also Reputation.

La familiarité engendre le mépris.
FRENCH PROVERB

Familiarity breeds contempt.

Unum quom noris, omnis noris.
LATIN EXPRESSION

When you know one, you know all.

Quod crebro videt non miratur, etiamsi cur fiat
nescit; quod ante non viderit, id si evenerit,
ostentum esse censet.
CICERO:
De Divinatione (Latin)

Even if he does not know the cause, whatever
happens repeatedly fails to surprise him. But
single happenings he regards as prodigies.

Nullumst iam dictum quod non dictum sit prius.
TERENCE:
Eunuchus (prologue) *(Latin)*

Nothing has been said that has not already been
said.

Inferior rescit quicquid peccat superior.
LATIN PROVERB

No man is a hero to his valet

La facilidad es ramo de vulgaridad.

> BALTASAR GRACIÁN:
> *Oráculo Manual y Arte de Prudencia (Spanish)*

Familiarity is an off-shoot of vulgarity.

FAMILIES
see also Ancestors, Children, Daughters, Home, Husbands, Parents, Relations, Wives, Women.

La plus ancienne de toutes les sociétés, et la seule naturelle, est celle de la famille.

> J. J. ROUSSEAU:
> *Du Contrat Social (French)*

The most ancient of all societies, and the only natural one, is that of the family.

Kai pais men arsēn pater' ekhei purgon megan

> EURIPIDES:
> *Alcestis (Greek)*

A father is a tower of strength to his sons.

Entre dos hermanos dos testigos y un notario.

> SPANISH PROVERB

Between two brothers you will find two witnesses and a lawyer. (Can also be read as: it is essential to have a lawyer and two witnesses even for agreements between brothers.)

FAMILY FRIENDS
see also Guests.

Toujours présent, rarement présenté, et jamais présentable.

> DON FULCO SANTO STEFANO,
> MARCHESE DELLA CERDA:
> *The Happy Summer Days* (Don Fulco's mother's opinion of an old family friend) *(French)*

Always present, rarely presented, and never presentable.

FANATICISM
see also Candour.

L'Enthousiasme est une maladie qui se gagne.

> VOLTAIRE:
> *Lettres Philosophiques (French)*

Fanaticism is a sickness that spreads.

Gefährlich ist's den Leu zu wecken,
Verderblich ist des Tigers Zahn,
Jedoch der schrecklichste der Schrecken,
Das ist der Mensch in seinem Wahn.

> J. C. F. VON SCHILLER:
> *Das Lied von der Glocke (German)*

It is dangerous to awaken a lion, the teeth of the tiger can prove fatal, but the most fearsome of all is the human fanatic.

Jetzt ergeht es ihm wie jedem Schwärmer, der von seiner herrschenden Idee überwältigt wird. Er kennt keine Grenzen mehr.

> J. C. F. VON SCHILLER:
> *Works (German)*

What happens to him now is what happens to every fanatic who is overwhelmed by his own ruling idea. He does not know where to stop.

FAREWELL
see also Exile, Last words, Parting.

Adieu, vendanges et adieu tous les paniers,
Adieu, paniers, vendanges sont faites.

> FRENCH FOLK-SONG
> (quoted by Rabelais)

Goodbye the grape gathering, goodbye the harvest, our business is done!

Ave, atque vale!

> LATIN EXPRESSION

Hail and farewell.

Bene ambula et redambula!

> PLAUTUS:
> *Captivi (Latin)*

Fare well, and fare well back.

Ipsae rursum concedite silvae.

> VIRGIL:
> *Eclogues (Latin)*

Once more, ye woods, adieu!

FARMING
see also Fertility, Oblivion.

O fortunatos nimium, sua si bona norint agricolae!

> VIRGIL:
> *Georgics (Latin)*

Oh, ye husbandmen, too happy would you be, did ye but know your own advantages!

Est operae pretium doctos spectare colonos.
DOMINICK MANCINI:
De Quattuor Virtutibus (Latin)

It is very pleasant to see skilled tillers of the soil.

El pie del dueño, estiércol para la heredad.
SPANISH PROVERB

The master's foot is manure to the estate (alluding to the necessity for the master to supervise his workmen).

FASHION

Si l'on n'a la tête levée,
Le poil de la barbe frisé,
Et la moustache relevée,
On est des dames méprisé.
C. C. D'ASOUCI;
Les Poésies (French)

Women scorn you if you don't hold up your head, have your beard curled, and your moustache turned up.

Le style c'est l'homme.
FRENCH PROVERB

Fashion makes the man.

FASTIDIOUSNESSS

Les délicats sont malheureux:
Rien ne saurait les satisfaire.
JEAN DE LA FONTAINE:
Contre Ceut qui ont le Goût Difficile (French)

How unhappy the fastidious – nothing will ever satisfy them.

Il più bel fior ne coglie.
Motto of the Accademia della Crusca
(founded in 1582) *(Italian)*

It collects only the finest flowers.

Nimioque sibi mulier meretrix repperit odium ocius
Sua immunditia, quam in perpetuom ut placeat muditia sua.
PLAUTUS:
Stichus (Latin)

It's much easier for a girl to lose her lovers by being dowdy than to hold them for ever by being dainty.

Post asellum diaria non sumo.
PETRONIUS
Satyricon (Latin

After a banquet I take no common food.

FATALISM
see also Fate.

On recontre sa destinée
Souvent par des chemins qu'on prend pour l'éviter.
JEAN DE LA FONTAINE
L'Horoscope (French

We often meet our fate on the road we take to avoid it.

Je consens ou plutôt j'aspire à ma ruine.
PIERRE CORNEILLE
Polyeucte (French,

I agree to – or rather I yearn for – my ruin.

FATE
see also Achievement, Death, Desire, Destiny, Disaster, Fortune, the Future, Gods, Love, Misfortune, Murder, Opportunity, Politics, Providence, Resignation, War, Wisdom.

Al-ḥadhar ma yanfa' fi-'l gadar
ARAB PROVERB

Care avails nothing against fate.

Netamassak bel-ḥadhar ḥattā yinzil al-gadar
ARAB PROVERB

Let's take care of ourselves until fate descends upon us!

Al-kharīf wa-'s-sulṭān, yagdaru yaqtulūk fi beitak
ARAB PROVERB

There's no escaping fate (*lit.* autumn and kings can kill you even in your own house).

Āju daiya hauṁ kīnha subhāgā;
Jasa dukha kīnha nīka saba lāgā
MALIK MUHAMMAD JĀYASĪ:
Padumāvatī (Avadhi,

Today destiny has made me fortunate: whatever suffering has been inflicted has all ended happily.

De roos bade 't hoofd in den stralenden gloed,
Wen eens haar de storrem ontluistert, verdoet,
Zoo moge z' in 't duister verflensen.

EVERHARDUS JOHANNES POTGIETER:
De Twintigjarige (Dutch)

Though the rose bathes her head in the sun's rays, she wilts in the darkness when she is defaced and overcome by the storms.

Ainsi va le monde; on travaille, on projette, on arrange d'un côté; la fortune accomplit de l'autre.

P. A. C. DE BEAUMARCHAIS:
Le Mariage de Figaro (French)

That's the way of the world: we work, we scheme, we plan one way. Fate finishes it all off in another.

A quoi que se soit que l'homme s'applique, la nature l'y destinait.

DENIS DIDEROT:
Le Neveu de Rameau (French)

Man proposes; God disposes (*lit.* whatever man turns to, nature planned it).

Rien de stable dans ce monde: aujourd'hui au sommet, demain au bas de la roue.

DENIS DIDEROT:
Le Neveu de Rameau (French)

There's nothing certain in this world; today we are on top, tomorrow we're at the bottom of the ladder.

Nos destins ténébreux vont sous des lois immenses
Que rien ne déconcerte et que rien n'attendrit.

VICTOR HUGO:
A Villequier (French)

Our shadowy fates are subject to vast laws that nothing can upset and nothing alleviate.

Il faut ce qu'il faut.

FRENCH PROVERB

What must be, must be.

Tout passe, tout lasse, tout casse.

FRENCH PROVERB

Everything passes; everything wears out; everything breaks.

Le vin est tiré, il faut boire.

Empress Eugénie of France to
Napoleon III's surgeon (Germain
Sée), on being told that the
Emperor was in no condition
to head his army

The wine is poured; we must drink it.

Der Zufall wohl pathetische, niemals aber tragische Situationen hervorbringen dürfe; das Schicksal hingegen müsse immer fürchterlich sein.

J. W. VON GOETHE:
Wilhelm Meisters Lehrjahre (German)

Chance can doubtless create pathetic, but never tragic, situations; fate, on the other hand, must always prove frightful.

Das Schicksal benutzt meistens doch unsere schwachen Punkte, um uns auf das uns Dienliche aufmerksam zu machen.

WILHELM RAABE:
Stopfkuchen (German)

Fate mostly uses our weaker points to make us attentive to what may be of service to us.

Einsam steigt er dahin, in die Berge des Ur-Leids,
Und nicht einmal sein Schritt klingt aus dem tonlosen Los.

RAINER MARIA RILKE:
Duineser Elegien (German)

Alone he climbs the mountains of primeval pain, nor does his footstep ring even once in this soundless doom.

Wir wissen, dass wir Vorläufige sind
Und nach uns wird kommen: nichts Nennenswertes.

BERTOLT BRECHT:
Vom armen B.B. (German)

We know that we are empheral and that after us there will be nothing worth mentioning.

Und so taumle ich beängstigt, Himmel und Erde und ihre webenden Kräfte um mich her.

J. W. VON GOETHE:
Werther (German)

Overwhelmed by the interwoven powers of the heavens and the earth, I reel, terrified.

Mags schnell geschehn was muss geschehn!
> J. W. VON GOETHE:
> *Faust (German)*

Let what must be happen speedily!

Wie man sich bettet, so liegt man.
> GERMAN PROVERB

As a man makes his bed, so shall he lie on it.

Der schmeichlerische Elende, ich möchte fast
sagen der Feigling, der unter jedem Streich des
Schicksals winselt.
> GEORG CHRISTOPH LICHTENBERG:
> *Aphorismen (German)*

The fawning wretch, I might even say coward,
who whimpers at every blow of fate.

Ein Grab ist doch immer die beste Befestigung
wider Stürme des Schicksals.
> GEORG CHRISTOPH LICHTENBERG:
> *Aphorismen (German)*

The tomb is still the best fortress against the
storms of destiny.

Viele Unternehmungen misslingen bloss, weil
man die Früchte davon noch gerne erleben
wollte.
> GEORG CHRISTOPH LICHTENBERG:
> *Aphorismen (German)*

Many undertakings miscarry simply because
people want to live to enjoy the results of their
efforts.

Diesen Sieg soll der Himmel nicht haben, diesen
Spott mir nicht antun die Hölle!
> J. C. F. VON SCHILLER:
> *Die Räuber (German)*

Heaven shall not have this triumph; Hell shall
not ruin me with its scorn!

Ich habe geliebt manch schönes Kind
Und manchen guten Gesellen.
Wo sind sie hin? Es pfeift der Wind,
Es schäumen und wandern die Wellen.
> HEINRICH HEINE:
> *Träumen (German)*

I have loved many a pretty girl, and some very
good fellows. Where are they all now? The wind
whistles, and the waves foam and wander.

Du danke Gott, wenn er dich presst,
Und dank' ihm, wenn er dich wieder entlässt.
> J. W. VON GOETHE:
> Conversations with J. P. Eckermann *(German)*

Thank God when he oppresses you, and again
when he releases you.

Es weiss vielleicht ein Gott, wohin wir ziehn.
Wir wissen nicht das Ziel und nicht zurück.
> FRITZ USINGER:
> *Grosse Elegie (German)*

It is possible that some god knows where we are
going, but we do not, nor do we know the way
back.

Kouk' esti thnētōn hostis exepistatai
Tēn aurion mellousan ei biōsetai
> EURIPIDES:
> *Alcestis (Greek)*

No-one can confidently say that he will still be
living tomorrow.

Lusin de kakōn paroi sunisasi
> PYTHAGORAS:
> *Golden Verses (Greek)*

Few people know how to liberate themselves
from evil.

Tēn peprōmenēn moirēn adunata estin
apophugeein kai theōi
> HERODOTUS:
> *History (Greek)*

Even the gods find it impossible to evade what
has been ordained by fate.

Kakōn gar dusalōtus oudeis
> SOPHOCLES:
> *Oedipus Coloneus (Greek)*

No man can escape his fate.

Ho ti toi morsimon estin, to genoit' an
> AESCHYLUS:
> *The Suppliant Maidens (Greek)*

What will be, will be.

Epi xurou histatai akmēs olethros ēe biōnai
> HOMER:
> *Iliad (Greek)*

Life and death are balanced on the edge of a razor.

Theōi makhesthai deinon esti kai tukhēi
> GREEK PROVERB

It is hard to fight with heaven and fate.

Hēxei gar auta, k'an egō sigēi stegō
> SOPHOCLES:
> *Oedipus Tyrannus (Greek)*

Even if I am silent, what will be will be.

Ou gar idois an athrōn broton hostis an,
Ei theos agoi,
Ekphugein dunaito
> SOPHOCLES:
> *Oedipus Coloneus (Greek)*

There is no man who, if God so wills, can escape destruction.

> Panta gar ta tōn theōn
Eis aphanes herpei, kouden oid' oudeis kakon
> EURIPIDES:
> *Iphigeneia in Tauris (Greek)*

The ways of the gods are a mystery; we can never foresee disaster.

Ho ti an soi sumbainēi, touto soi ex aiōnos prokateskeuazeto. Kai hē epiplokē tōn aitiōn suneklōthe tēn te sēn hupostasin ex aidiou kai tēn toutou sumbasin.
> MARCUS AURELIUS:
> *Meditations (Greek)*

Whatever may befall you was set in train from everlasting, and the interrelation of causes was derived from eternity's weaving into one fabric your existence and the coincidence of this event.

Tu non altro che il canto avrai del figlio,
O materna mia terra: a noi prescrisse
Il fato illacrimata sepoltura.
> UGO FOSCOLO:
> *A Zacïnto (Italian)*

Mother earth, from your son you can expect nought but a song; and our fate is but an unmourned grave!

Hyōtan kara koma ga deru.
> JAPANESE PROVERB

The unexpected often happens (*lit.* a pony comes out of a gourd).

Fatis agimur; cedite fatis!
> SENECA:
> *Oedipus (Latin)*

Since we are driven by fate, let us yield to it!

Nulli scriptum proferre diem licet.
> SENECA:
> *Hercules Furens (Latin)*

No-one can postpone the allotted day.

> Res humanas ordine nullo
Fortuna regit.
> SENECA:
> *Hippolytus (Latin)*

Fate rules the affairs of mankind with no recognisable order.

Omnia secto tramite vadunt.
> SENECA:
> *Oedipus (Latin)*

All things move along an appointed path.

Miserum populum Romanum, qui sub tam lentis maxillis erit!
> SUETONIUS:
> *Tiberius (Latin)*

Alas for the Roman people, to be ground by jaws that crunch so slowly (Augustus, speaking of his heir, Tiberius).

Ille est par superis deis
Et mortalibus altior
Qui fati ambiguum diem
Non optat levis, an timet.
> LIPSIUS:
> *Works (Latin)*

He who does not desire or fear the uncertain day of capricious fate, is equal to the gods above and loftier than mortals.

Omnia sunt hominum tenui pendentia filo.

OVID:
Ex Ponto (Latin)

All the affairs of men hang by a slender thread.

Ductores quondam, pulvis et umbra sumus.

AUSONIUS:
Opuscula (Latin)

Once we were champions; now we are but dust and shadows.

Iniqua raro maximis virtutibus
Fortuna parcit.

SENECA:
Hercules Furens (Latin)

Unrighteous fortune seldom spares the highest worth.

Hodie mihi, cras tibi.

LATIN PROVERB

Today me, tomorrow you!

Quid miser egi?

LATIN PHRASE

What have I done to deserve this?

Quod hodie non est, cras erit.

PETRONIUS:
Satyricon (Latin)

If not today, it will happen tomorrow.

Det er saa fælt at se Skjæbnen under Øjne;
Og saa vil en jo gjerne ryste Sorgerne af sig,
Og prøve som bedst at skyde Tankerne fra sig.
En bruger Brændevin, en anden bruger Løgne.

HENRIK IBSEN:
Peer Gynt (Norwegian)

It is very hard to face fate's onset. So we try to shake off our sorrows, or do our best to stop thinking. Some try drink; others lies.

O moshchnyï vlastelin sud'bÿ!

ALEKSANDR SERGEEVICH PUSHKIN:
Eugen Onegin (Russian)

O mighty master of fate!

Malo es tener pensado ni previsto nada en l[
vida.

JACINTO BENAVENTE Y MARTINEZ
Rosas de Otoño (Spanish

It is bad to plan or foresee anything in life.

Pisando la tierra dura
De continuo el hombre está,
Y cada paso que da
Es sobra su sepultura.

PEDRO CALDERÓN DE LA BARCA
El Príncipe Constante (Spanish

Man continually treads the hard earth, an[
every step he takes is on his grave.

FATHERLAND
see also Exile, Home, Kings, Patriotism, Revolution.

O patrie! ô patrie, ineffable mystère!
Mot sublime et terrible! inconcevable amour!
L'homme n'est-il donc né que pour un coin d[
terre,
Pour y bâtir son nid et pour y vivre un jour?

ALFRED DE MUSSET
Retour, Le Havre, sept. 1855 (French,

Fatherland, ineffable mystery! Sublime an[
awesome word! Inconceivable love! Are we no[
born for a plot of land where we may one day
build our home and live?

On tient toujours du lieu dont on vient.

JEAN DE LA FONTAINE
La Souris Métamorphosée en Fille (French,

We always hark back to the place we came from.

Il est doux de revoir les murs de la patrie.

PIERRE CORNEILLE:
Sertorius (French)

How good it is to see again the walls of one's own
city!

Ist dir ein Heiligtum ganz unbekannt,
Das, in dem Lager, Vaterland sich nennt?

HEINRICH VON KLEIST:
Prinz Friedrich von Homburg (German)

Are you quite unaware of a shrine which, in the
camp, is called Fatherland?

O wie die Tale glänzen
Durch die silberne Sommernacht,
Dort, wo der Mond am Himmel steht,
Muss meine ferne Heimat sein.

HANS BETHGE:
Heimwehlied (German)

How the dales glitter throughout the silver summer night; there, where the moon stands in the heavens must my far-off homeland be!

Gelebte ich noch die lieben zît
Daz ich daz lant solt aber schouwen,
Dar inne al min fröude lît
Nu lange an einer schoenen frouwen.

FRIEDRICH VON HAUSEN:
Heimweh (German)

Would that I yet lived in that happy time when I could see my homeland where all my joy lay in one fine woman.

Tōi gar kalōs prattonti pasa gē patris

GREEK PROVERB

To the prosperous any land is a native land.

Hōs ouden glukion hēs patridos

HOMER:
Odyssey (Greek)

Nothing is sweeter than a man's fatherland.

Dikos kai patrē biotou kharis

POLYAENUS:
Fragments (Greek)

The delight of life is in our home and country.

Non è quésto il terrén ch' i'toccai pria?
Non è questo 'l mio nido,
Ove nutrito fui sì dolceménte?
Non è questa la patria, in ch'io mi fido
Madre benigna e pia,
Che còpre l'uno e l'altro mio parènte?

FRANCESCO PETRARCA:
Canzone (Italian)

Is this the land where I was born? This the cradle where I was nurtured so affectionately? This my country in which I put my trust? Benign and pious mother who shelters all my kindred?

H'to wa iza-kokoro mo shirads furu-sato wa hana zo mukashi no ka ni nihoikeru

KI NO TSURAYUKI:
Waga (Japanese)

How indifferently do my boyhood companions look on me as I return to the village of my childhood! Only the fragrance of the flowers remains familiar to me.

Primum ad virtutem ut redeatis, abeatis ignavia
Domi patres patriam ut colatis potius quam peregri probra.

NAEVIUS:
Fragment (Latin)

To return to virtue, you must shun depravity and follow father and fatherland rather than foreign infamy.

Udruchënnÿĭ nosheĭ krestnoĭ,
Vsyu, tebya, zemlya rodnaya,
V rabskom vide Tsar' Nebesnÿí
Iskhodil, blagoslovlyaya.

FËDOR TYUTCHEV:
Eti Bednÿe Selen'ya (Russian)

The King of heaven, in the guise of a slave and weighted down by the burden of the cross, has walked throughout you, my native land, bestowing his blessings.

Lyublyu otchiznu ya, no strannoyu lyubov'yu!
Ne pobedit eë rassudok moĭ!

MIKHAIL LERMONTOV:
Rodina (Russian)

I love my country, but with a strange love; my reason cannot explain it!

FATIGUE

Omnia membra lassitudo mihi tenet.

PLAUTUS:
Stichus (Latin)

Fatigue has all my limbs in its custody.

Medullam lassitudo perbibit.

PLAUTUS:
Stichus (Latin)

Fatigue has sucked out my very bone-marrow.

FAULTS
see also Forgiveness, Greatness, Wives.

Il y a plus de défauts dans l'humeur que dans
l'esprit.

FRANÇOIS DUC DE LA ROCHEFOUCAULD:
Maxims (French)

There are more defects in temperament than in
the mind.

Chacun a son défaut où toujours il revient.
Honte ni peur n'y rémedie.

JEAN DE LA FONTAINE:
L'Ivrogne et sa Femme (French)

Everyone has his faults which he continually
repeats; neither fear nor shame can cure them.

Le bien nous le faisons; le mal, c'est la Fortune.

JEAN DE LA FONTAINE:
*L'Ingratitude et l'Injustice des Hommes envers la
Fortune (French)*

We attribute our successes to our own abilities,
our failures to fortune.

Si nous n'avions point de défauts, nous ne
prendrions pas tant de plaisir à en remarquer
dans les autres.

FRANÇOIS DUC DE LA ROCHEFOUCAULD:
Réflexions (French)

If we had no faults, we should not take so much
pleasure in noticing them in others.

Souvent de nos défauts nôtre oeil est écarté,
Et nous ne voyons que du meilleur côté.

VICTOR HUGO:
Cromwell (French)

We are often distracted from noticing our faults
and only see our best side.

Il n'appartient qu'aux grands hommes d'avoir
de grands défauts.

FRANÇOIS DUC DE LA ROCHEFOUCAULD:
Réflexions (French)

It is given only to great men to have great faults.

Alle Menschlichen Gebrechen
Sühnet reine Menschlichkeit.

J. W. VON GOETHE:
(German)

Genuine humanity atones for all human weak-
nesses.

Nam vitiis nemo sine nascitur;
Optimus ille est, qui minimis urgetur.

HORACE:
Satires (Latin)

No mortal is without faults – the best is he who is
burdened with the least.

Vitia enim flagitiis leviora sunt.

GELLIUS:
Attic Nights (Latin)

Faults are less serious than crimes.

Moriantur ante te vitia.

SENECA:
Epistles (Latin)

Let your faults die before you do.

Dum vitant stulti vitia, in contraria currunt.

HORACE:
Satires (Latin)

In avoiding errors, fools fall into other faults.

Nota mala res optumast.

LATIN PROVERB
(quoted by Plautus: *Trinummus*)

The ill that's known is the ill that's best.

Ipse mihi asciam in crus impegi.

PETRONIUS
Satyricon (Latin

I have only injured myself by my actions (*lit. I*
have stuck the axe into my own leg).

In vitium ducit culpae fuga.

HORACE
Ars Poetica (Latin

The fear of a fault makes one fall into a worse
one.

FEAR
**see also Adversity, Courage, Cowardice,
anger, Death, Dictatorship, Emotion, Evil,
Hope, Kings, Life, Misfortune, Pleasure,
Reason, Resolution, Terror.**

a bonne crainte joint à l'espérance, parce
uelle naist de la foy, et qu'on espère au Dieu
ue l'on croit.

BLAISE PASCAL:
Pensées (French)

rue fear is joined with hope, for it is born of
ith, and we derive hope from God in whom we
lace our trust.

timore à tenuto da una paura di pena che non
bandona mai.

NICCOLO MACHIAVELLI:
The Prince (Italian)

ear is maintained by a never failing dread of
unishment.

essimus in dubiis augur timor.

STATIUS:
Thebaid (Latin)

1 doubt, fear is the worst of prophets.

ec ipse timor caret periculo, cum ex nimio
more plurique in desperationem inciderint.

ST. THOMAS AQUINAS:
On Princely Government (Latin)

ear itself carries with it its own dangers;
ecause when fear is excessive it can make many
man despair.

etus cum venit, rarum habet somnus locum.

LATIN PROVERB

Vhere fear has come, sleep has scant place.

ecesse est multos timeat quem multi timent.

LATIN PROVERB

Ie needs must many fear whom many fear.

Ietus improbos compescit non clementia.

LATIN PROVERB

ear, not clemency, restrains the wicked.

El rostro feo
Les hice ver del temor.

JUAN RUIZ DE ALARCÓN Y MENDOZA:
No hay Mal que por Bien no Venga (Spanish)

I let them see the ugly face of fear.

FEASTS

Verecundari neminem apud mensam decet,
Nam ibi de divinis atque humanis cernitur.

PLAUTUS:
Trinummus (Latin)

Never hold back at a feast; since there you have
to fight for everything, human and divine.

FEELINGS
**see also Emotion, History, Motives,
Self-control.**

L'expression d'un sentiment est toujours
absurde.

PAUL VALÉRY:
La Soirée avec Monsieur Teste (French)

The expression of our feelings is always absurd.

J'ai détruit mes passions, à peu près comme un
homme violent tue son cheval, ne pouvant le
gouverner.

S. R. N. CHAMFORT:
Maximes et Pensées (French)

I have destroyed my passions, somewhat as a
man, being unable to control his horse, kills it.

Animo imperabit sapiens, stultus serviet.

LATIN PROVERB

Feelings are kept under control by the wise, but
are served by fools.

FERTILITY

Fertilis assiduo si non renovatur aratro
Nil nisi cum spinis gramen habebit ager.

OVID:
Tristia (Latin)

If you don't renew a fertile field by constant
ploughing, it will only yield grass and thorns.

FICKLENESS
see also Constancy.

Le coeur de l'homme est un grand fripon!
PIERRE CARLET DE CHAMBLAIN DE MARIVAUX:
La Fausse Suivante (French)

Man's heart is a great rascal!

De domnas m'es veyaire
Que gran falhimen fan
Per so car no son gaire
Amat li fan aman.
Eu no'n dei ges retraire
Mas so qu'elas volran,
Mas greu m'es c'us trichaire
A d'amor ab enjan
O plus o atretan
Com cel qu'es fis amaire
BERNARD DE VENTADOUR:
Can la Freid' aura Venta (French)

It seems to me that women commit a great fault,
in that they hardly ever love those who are their
most faithful lovers. I must not say of them what
they want to hear, but I find it painful to see a
knave get as much or more by his tricks than the
faithful lover.

Iro miede
Utsurou mono wa
Yo no naka no
Hito no kokoro no
Hana ni zo arikeru
ONO NO KOMACHI:
Waga (Japanese)

It is the fickle heart of man that unobtrusively
fades away.

Mulier cupido quod dicit amanti,
In vento et rapida scribere oportet aqua.
CATULLUS:
Poems (Latin)

What a woman says to the man she loves should
be written in the wind and in swift flowing
waters.

Koketka sudit khladnokrovno.
ALEKSANDR SERGEEVICH PUSHKIN:
Eugen Onegin (Russian)

Flirts are coldblooded in their choice of men.

FISH

C'était plaisir de voir sous l'eau limpide et bleue
Mille petits poissons faisant frémir leur queue,
Se mordre, se poursuivre, ou, par bandes
nageant,
Ouvrir et refermer leurs nageoires d'argent.
AUGUSTE BRIZEUX
Le Pont Kerlô (French)

How pleasing to see in the limpid blue water
thousand little fish flicking their tails, biting
pursuing, or swimming in clusters, opening an
closing their silver fins.

FISHERMEN
see also Sailors, Sea.

Ho d' ek pontoio mateuōn
Zōēn, ek pontou kai moron heilkusamēn
ANTIPATER OF SIDON
Fragments (Greek

It was from the sea that I made my living, an
from the sea I found my death.

Épeirōi gar enesti makros bios. Ein hali d' ou pō
eumares eis poliēn andros idein kephalēn
PHALAECUS
Fragments (Greek

Life can be lengthy on land, but you will see fev
people with grey hair at sea.

FLATTERY
see also Vanity.

Nous aimons à être trompés.
BLAISE PASCAL
Pensées (French

We like to be deceived (speaking of the flattery o
friends).

Tout flatteur
Vit aux dépens de celui qui l'écoute.
JEAN DE LA FONTAINE
Le Corbeau et le Renard (French

Every flatterer lives at the expense of those wh
listen to him.

On ne peut trop louer trois sortes de personnes:
Les dieux, sa maîtresse, et son roi.

JEAN DE LA FONTAINE:
Simonide Préservé par les Dieux (French)

We cannot praise too much three kinds of
people: the gods, our mistress, and our king.

La flatterie est une fausse monnaie qui n'a de
cours que par notre vanité.

FRANÇOIS, DUC DE LA ROCHEFOUCAULD:
Réflexions (French)

Flattery is counterfeit money that has no
currency except through our own vanity.

Non ci è altro modo a guardarsi dalle adula-
zioni, se non che li uomini intendino che non ti
offendino a dirti el vero.

NICCOLÒ MACHIAVELLI:
The Prince (Italian)

The only way to protect yourself against flattery
is to let it be known that no man will offend you
by speaking the truth.

Ornatur Fortuna viro.

CLAUDIAN:
Epithalamium de nuptiis Honorii Augusti (Latin)

You are the ornament of fortune.

La lisonja hace amigos, y la verdad enemigos.

SPANISH PROVERB

Flattery makes friends, truth enemies.

FLOWERS
see also Spring, Women.

De mille et mille et de mille couleurs,
Peignent le sein de la terre si gaye.

PIERRE DE RONSARD:
Sonnets (French)

Thousands and thousands of colours paint the
bosom of the earth so gaily.

Chaque fleur est une âme à la Nature éclose.

GÉRARD DE NERVAL:
Vers Dorés (French)

Each flower is a soul blossoming out to nature.

Éstas, que fueron pompa y alegría,
Despertando al albor de la mañana,

A la tarde serán lástima vana,
Durmiendo en brazos de la noche fría

PEDRO CALDERÓN DE LA BARCA:
Soneto (Spanish)

These flowers which were splendid and spright-
ly, waking in the morning's dawn, will be a
pitiful frivolity in the evening, falling asleep in
the night's cold arms.

FOLLY
see also Desire, Honour, Old age, Wisdom, Women, Youth.

Qui vit sans folie n'est pas si sage qu'il croit.

FRANÇOIS DUC DE LA ROCHEFOUCAULD:
Maximes (French)

He who lives without folly is not as wise as he
thinks.

Atēs aroura thanaton ekkarpizetai

AESCHYLUS:
The Seven against Thebes (Greek)

Death can be the only harvest of folly.

Quid volui?

LATIN EXPRESSION

What folly! (*lit.* what was I thinking of!).

Propugnat nugis armatus.

HORACE:
Epistles (Latin)

He takes up arms to fight for trifles.

Nemo stultitiam finget.

LATIN PROVERB

No-one feigns folly.

Non est cantandum.

LATIN SAYING

This is not the occasion for nonsense (*lit.*
singing).

El primer escalón de locura es creerse consciente.

SPANISH PROVERB

The first rung in the ladder of folly is to believe
oneself wise.

FOOLHARDINESS

Quo moriture ruis majoraque viribus audes?
VIRGIL:
Aeneid (Latin)

Where are you rushing to your death, with daring greater than your strength?

FOOLS
see also Jesters, Laughter, Mediocrity, Money, Wisdom.

Qui se fait brebis le loup le mange.
FRENCH PROVERB

Mugs always get fleeced (lit. if you make a lamb of yourself, the wolf will eat you).

Imprudence, babil, et sotte vanité,
Et vaine curiosité,
Ont ensemble étroit parentage;
Ce sont enfants tous d'un lignage.
JEAN DE LA FONTAINE:
La Tortue et les Deux Canards (French)

Imprudence, prattle, stupid vanity, and empty curiosity are very closely related; they are all offspring of the same family.

Belle tête, mais de cervelle point.
FRENCH PROVERB

A fine head, but no brains.

Un sot sera plus souvent un méchant qu'un homme d'esprit.
DENIS DIDEROT:
Le Neveu de Rameau (French)

A fool is more likely to be wicked than witty.

Un sot savant est sot plus qu'un sot ignorant.
MOLIÈRE:
Les Femmes Savantes (French)

A learned fool is more of a fool than an ignorant fool.

Il devrait être sourd aux aveugles souhaits.
JEAN DE LA FONTAINE:
La Tête et la Queue du Serpent (French)

One should be deaf to foolish requests.

Fols no tem, tro que pren.
MEDIAEVAL FRENCH PROVERB

Fools are only afraid when they are beaten.

Deinon sophistēn eipas, hostis eu phronein
Tous mē phronountas dunatos est' anankasai
EURIPIDES:
Hippolytus (Greek)

It would take a genius to turn a fool into a wise man.

Pollaki toi kai mōros anēr mala kairion eipen
GREEK PROVERB

Every so often a fool expresses himself to some purpose.

Istic est thensaurus stultis in lingua situs,
Ut quaestui habeant male loqui melioribus.
PLAUTUS:
Poenulus (Latin)

The treasure-house of a fool is in his speech, so that he can enrich himself by speaking ill of his betters.

Omnium fatuorum doctissimum!
Queen Christina of Sweden,
speaking of Salmasius (Latin)

The most learned of all fools!

Pudor . . . te malus angit,
Insanos qui inter vereare insanus haberi.
HORACE:
Satires (Latin)

You torture yourself unnecessarily, fearing to be thought a fool among fools.

Ne ista hercle magno iam conatu magnas nugas dixerit!
TERENCE:
Heauton Timorumenos (Latin)

Truly he makes a great effort to talk great nonsense!

Taciturnitas stulto homini pro sapientia est.
LATIN PROVERB

The fool is wise who holds his tongue.

Caranti bālā dummedhā amitten' eva attanā
Karontā pāpakaṁ kammaṁ yaṁ hoti kaṭukap-
phalam

Dhammapada: Balavaggo (Pali)

Fools, of little understanding, being their own
enemies, wander about committing evil deeds
that bear bitter fruits.

Quien asno nace, asno muere.

SPANISH PROVERB

He who is born an ass, will die an ass.

A los bobos se les aparece la Madre de Dios.

SPANISH PROVERB

It is to fools that the Mother of God appears.

Donde crece la escoba, nace el asno que la roe.

SPANISH PROVERB

Where the thistle grows, there lives the fool who
will eat it.

FORCE
see also Might, Motives, Obedience, Violence.

La force n'est jamais qu'un élément passager de
succès: après elle vient aussitôt l'idée du droit.

ALEXIS DE TOCQUEVILLE:
De la Démocratie en Amérique (French)

Force is never more than a fleeting element
of success; after it the concept of law follows
immediately.

La force est la reine du monde, et non pas
l'opinion. Mais l'opinion est celle qui use de la
force. C'est la force qui fait l'opinion.

BLAISE PASCAL:
Pensées (French)

Force, not opinion, is queen of the world. But
opinion makes use of force; and force forms
opinion.

Zerstücke den Donner in seine einfache Silben,
und du wirst Kinder damit in der Schlummer
singen; schmelze sie zusammen in einen
plötzlichen Schall, und der monarchische Laut
wird den ewigen Himmel bewegen.

J. C. F. VON SCHILLER:
Fiesco (Fiesco's monologue) (German)

Divide up the thunder into its individual parts
and you can use them to lull children to sleep;

but, welded together in one sudden burst, their
royal crash can shake the very heavens.

Mē to kratos aukhei dunamin anthrōpois
ekhein,
Mēd', ēn dokēis men, hē de doxa sou nosēi,
Phronein dokei ti

EURIPIDES:
The Bacchae (Greek)

Human affairs are not controlled by force.
Should you believe that they are, do not mistake
your belief for wisdom.

Vis consili expers mole ruit sua.

HORACE:
Odes (Latin)

Brute force, bereft of wisdom, rushes to its doom
by its own weight.

Fit via vi.

VIRGIL:
Aeneid (Latin)

Force finds a way.

Hic faciet, si vos non feceritis

SUETONIUS:
Divus Augustus (Latin)

This will do it, if you don't! (The centurion
Cornelius showing his sword to the Senate when
they hesitated to make Augustus a consul).

FORESTS
see also Birds, Nature, Night, Summer.

En moi de la forêt le calme s'insinue;
De ses arbres sacrés, dans l'ombre enseveli,
J'apprends la patience aux hommes inconnue,
Et mon coeur apaisé vit d'espoir et d'oubli.

VICTOR DE LAPRADE:
La Mort d'un Chêne (French)

The peace of the forest pervades me; from its
revered trees, buried in the shadows, I learn a
patience unknown to mankind, and my soothed
heart lives on in hope and oblivion.

Tant de forêts sacrifiées pour la pâte à papier.

JACQUES PRÉVERT:
Tant de Forêts ... (French)

So many forests sacrificed for the sake of paper
pulp!

FORGIVENESS

Qui pardonne aisément invite à l'offenser.
PIERRE CORNEILLE:
Cinna (French)

He who forgives easily invites insult.

. . . aequum est
Peccatis veniam poscentem reddere rursus.
HORACE:
Satires (Latin)

It is only fair that he who seeks indulgence for his own faults should grant it in return.

Multa ignoscendo fit potens potentior.
LATIN PROVERB

By forgiving much, power grows more powerful.

FORTUNE
**see also Bravery, Envy, Failure, Fate,
Greatness, Happiness, Honesty, Life,
Moderation, Pride, Providence, Religion,
Resolution, the Unexpected, Villains,
Words.**

Ad-dahar sā'a ma'ak wa-'ashara 'alay-k
ARAB PROVERB

Fortune is with you for an hour, and against you for ten!

Le bien de la fortune est un bien périssable;
Quand on bâtit sur elle, on bâtit sur le sable;
Plus on est elevé, plus on court de dangers.
MARQUIS DE RACAN:
Stances sur la Retraite (French)

The profits of good luck are perishable; if you build on fortune, you build on sand; the more advancement you achieve, the more dangers you run.

Il faut de plus grandes vertus pour soutenir la bonne fortune que la mauvaise.
FRANÇOIS DUC DE LA ROCHEFOUCAULD:
Réflexions (French)

Greater virtues are required to maintain good fortune than to maintain bad fortune.

Quelques grands avantages que la natur donne, ce n'est pas elle mais la fortune qui fai les héros.
FRANÇOIS DUC DE LA ROCHEFOUCAULD
Réflexions (French

Whatever great advantages nature grants, it i not she but chance who makes heroes.

Le malheur succède au bonheur le plus doux.
PIERRE CORNEILLE
Horace (French

Unhappiness follows even the sweetest of good fortune.

La Fortune a toujours tort.
JEAN DE LA FONTAINE
La Fortune et le Jeune Enfant (French

Fortune is always to blame (*i.e.* man always blames fortune for his own stupidities).

Fortune aveugle suit aveugle hardiesse.
JEAN DE LA FONTAINE:
Les Deux Aventuriers et le Talisman (French)

Blind fortune follows blind audacity.

Denn Schwer ist zu tragen
Das Unglück, aber schwerer das Glück.
FRIEDRICH HÖLDERLIN:
Der Rhein (German)

Hard though misfortune is to bear, even harder is good fortune.

Wer hat, dem wird gegeben.
GERMAN PROVERB

To him who has, more shall be given.

Wie in verwehte Jugendtage blickst du zurück,
Und irgendeiner sagt dir weise: 'Es ist dein Glück!'
Da denkt man, dass es vielleicht so ist,
Wundert sich still, dass man doch nicht froh ist!
PETER ALTENBERG:
Sehnsucht (German)

As one looks back on the thoughtless days of youth, and someone sententiously comments: 'You were happy then!', one thinks that perhaps one really was, and is secretly surprised that one is not happy still!

Gnōma d' hois men akairos
Olbou, tois d' eis meson hēkei
EURIPIDES:
Iphigeneia in Tauris (Greek)

Fortune slips through one man's grasp to fall,
unasked, into another man's lap.

Tēs anankaias tukhēs
Ouk estin ouden meizon anthrōpois kakon
SOPHOCLES:
Ajax (Greek)

Dreadful are the ills that cruel fortune brings on
mankind.

Tois tropois gar hai tukhai,
Emplēktos hōs anthrōpos, allot' allose
Pēdōsi
EURIPIDES:
Troades (Greek)

Fortune is like a senseless fool in her ways, going
first this way and then that.

Anankaion esti pherein ta tēs tukhēs
GREEK PROVERB

We must endure what fortune sends.

Ou panu moiras eudaimonisai
Prōtēs
SOPHOCLES:
Oedipus Coloneus (Greek)

You need not envy me – I am no child of fortune!

Andra gar kalōs
Prassont' anankē khrēsta kerdainein epê
SOPHOCLES:
Trachiniae (Greek)

The fortunate deserve a kind welcome.

Hai de tōn eutukhēmatōn huperokhai kai lam-
protētes pollakis ton phthonon katasbennuousin
PLUTARCH:
Moralia (Greek)

Supreme and resplendent, good fortune often
extinguishes envy.

Ne le cose, che noi ci diamo a fare,
Si tosto che veggiam, che n'è seconda
La Sorte, non dobbiam lasciare adietro

Quell', onde ci pensiamo pienamente
Potere esser contenti
GIAMBATTISTA CINTHIO GIRALDI:
Altile (Italian)

As soon as we see that fortune favours our
endeavours, we must not fail to do whatever we
think may bring us complete fulfilment of our
desires.

Tum denique homines nostra intellegimus
bona,
Quom quae in potestate habuimus, ea
amisimus.
PLAUTUS:
Captivi (Latin)

It is only when we have lost them that we fully
appreciate our blessings.

Neque . . . admiratus fortunam sum alterius, ut
me meae poeniteret.
CICERO:
De Divinatione (Latin)

I never admired another's fortune so much that
I became dissatisfied with my own.

Te, bona dum splendet fortuna, sequuntur
amici
Ut te, dum lucet sol, solet umbra sequi.
JOHN OWEN:
Epigrammata (Latin)

Attracted by the glitter of good fortune, your
friends will follow you, just as your shadow will
follow you as long as the sun shines.

Diligitur nemo, nisi cui fortuna secunda est.
OVID:
Ex Ponto (Latin)

There is love for none save him whom fortune
favours.

Fortis fortuna adiuvat.
TERENCE:
Phormio (Latin)

Fortune favours the strong.

Fortuna vitrea est: tum cum splendet frangitur.
PUBLILIUS SYRUS:
Sententiae (Latin)

Fortune is like glass – amid its glitter it breaks.

Haud est virile terga fortunae dare.

SENECA:
Oedipus (Latin)

It is not manly to turn one's back on fortune.

Fortuna fortes metuit, ignavos premit.

SENECA:
Medea (Latin)

Fortune reveres the brave, and overwhelms the cowardly.

Fortuna opes auferre, non animum potest.

SENECA:
Medea (Latin)

Fortune can rob me of my wealth, but not my soul.

Quod non dedit fortuna, non eripit.

SENECA:
Epistles (Latin)

What fortune has not given, she cannot take.

Audentes fortuna iuvat.

VIRGIL:
Aeneid (Latin)

Fortune helps the brave.

Superat quoniam fortuna sequamur,
Quoque vocat, vertamus iter.

VIRGIL:
Aeneid (Latin)

Since fortune is all-powerful, let us follow her whither she calls.

[Appius ait] Fabrum esse suae quemque fortunae.

CLAUDIUS CAECUS (PSEUDO SALLUST):
Ad Caesarem (Latin)

Every man is the architect of his own fortune.

Alumnus fortunae.

PLINY:
Epistles (Latin)

A child of fortune.

Levis est Fortuna: cito reposcit quod dedit.

LATIN PROVERB

Fortune is fickle: she soon demands back what she has given.

Vivo et regno.

HORACE:
Epistles (Latin)

I live like a king.

Amor e alegria
Menos tempo dura
Triste de quem fia
Nos bens da ventura!

LUIS DE CAMÕES:
Vae o bem Fugindo (Portuguesse)

Love soon slips away, happiness sinks to the dust. How unhappy they are who put their trust in fortune!

No hay mal que por bien no venga.

SPANISH PROVERB

It's an ill wind that blows no good.

Es desventura para unos la que suele ser ventura para otros.

SPANISH PROVERB

One man's misfortune is another man's luck.

Cánsare la fortuna de llevar a uno a cuestas tan a la larga.

BALTASAR GRACIÁN:
Oráculo Manual y Arte de Prudencia (Spanish)

Fortune soon tires of carrying us too long on her shoulders.

Que bienes son de Fortuna
Que rebuelve con su rueda
Presurosa,
La cual no puede ser una
Ni estar estable ni queda
En una cosa.

JORGE MANRIQUE:
Coplas por la Muerte de su Padre (Spanish)

These riches are Fortune's: they revolve swiftly on her wheel which cannot be or remain firm, nor stay in one place.

Más triunfos, más coronas dió al prudente
Que supo retirarse, la fortuna,
Que al que esperó obstinada y locamente.
Attrib. ANDRÉS FERNÁNDEZ DE ANDRADA:
Epístola Moral (Spanish)

Fortune has awarded more victories and prizes to those who knew when to withdraw, than to those who foolishly and obstinately waited in expectation.

No hay más fortuna que Dios.
SPANISH PROVERB

There is no fortune, only God.

FOUNTAINS

Au calme clair de lune triste et beau
Qui fait rêver les oiseaux dans les arbres
Et sangloter d'extase les jets d'eau,
Les grands jets d'eau sveltes parmi les marbres
PAUL VERLAINE:
Claire de Lune (French)

In the peaceful light of the sad and beautiful moon, which makes the birds dream in the trees and the fountains sob rapturously, the great slim jets among the marble statuary.

Aufsteight der Strahl, und fallend giesst
Er voll der Marmorschale Rund,
Die, sich verschleiernd, überfliesst
In einer zweiten Schale Grund;
Die zweite gibt, sie wird zu reich,
Der dritten wallend ihre Flut,
Und jede nimmt und gibt zugleich
Und strömt und ruht
CONRAD FERDINAND MEYER:
Der Römische Brunnen (German)

The jet of water mounts, and falling fills full the round marble bowl which mistily overflows into the bottom of a second bowl. The second bowl, overflowing, yields to the third its bubbling torrent, and each at the same time takes and gives and pauses in its stream.

Smotri, kak oblakom zhivým,
Fontan siyayushchiĭ klubitsya
FÈDOR TYUTCHEV:
The Fountain (Russian)

Look how the shining fountain swirls like a living cloud!

Fonte-frida, Fonte-frida,
Fonte-frida y con amor,
Do todas las avecicas
Van tomar consolación.
Romance de Fonte-frida y con Amor (Spanish)

Fountain of freshness and of love, where all the little birds come for comfort.

FRANKNESS
see also Honesty, Truth.

L'important n'est pas tant d'être franc que de permettre à l'autre de l'être.
ANDRÉ GIDE:
Les Faux-monnayeurs (French)

The important thing is not so much to be frank oneself, as to let the other man be frank.

Je veux montrer à mes semblables un homme dans toute la vérité de la nature; et cet homme, ce sera moi.
J. J. ROUSSEAU:
Les Confessions (opening words) (French)

I want to show my fellow-men a man in all the honesty of nature; and that man is myself!

Ce n'est pas ce qui est criminel qui coûte le plus à dire; c'est ce qui est ridicule et honteux.
J. J. ROUSSEAU:
Les Confessions (French)

It is not criminal admissions that are hardest to make, but those that are ridiculous and shameful.

Und wenn's euch Ernst is was zu sagen,
Ista nöthig Worten nachzuiagen?
J. W. VON GOETHE:
Faust (German)

When you really have something to say, do you find it necessary to hunt for the right words?

FREEDOM
see also Action, Juries, Law, Liberal arts, Liberty, Mind, Patriotism, Permissiveness, Resolution, Right and wrong, Slaves, Soldiers, Suffering, Wind.

Je suis mon Roy, mon directeur et guide,
Entreteneur de ma franchise, et cuide

Que loy ne peult en oster ou distraire.
BÉRANGER DE LA TOUR D'ALBÉNAS:
Le Siècle d'Or (French)

I am my own king, my leader and my guide, guardian of my freedom, and may no law ever remove or alter these rights.

Nur der verdient sich Freiheit wie das Leben,
Der täglich sie erobern muss.
J. W. VON GOETHE:
Faust (final monologue) (German)

He alone deserves liberty and life who daily must win them anew.

Sehen Sie sich um
In seiner herrlichen Natur! Auf Freiheit
Ist sie gegründet – und wie reich ist sie
Durch Freiheit!
J. C. F. VON SCHILLER:
Don Carlos (German)

Look around at God's splendid world of nature! It is founded on freedom – and, through freedom how rich it has become!

Das freie Meer befreit den Geist.
GERMAN PROVERB

The free ocean makes the spirit free.

Frei aber einsam.
Personal motto of Joseph Joachim,
violinist and composer *(German)*

Free but alone.

Ou thnaskei zalos eleutherias
GREEK PROVERB

The passion for freedom never dies.

Eimi penēs anthrōpos, eleutheriēi de sunoikō
PALLADAS OF ALEXANDRIA:
Epigrams (Greek)

I may be poor, but I live with freedom.

Libero, dritto e sano è tuo arbitrio,
E fallo fora non fare a suo senno.
DANTE:
Purgatorio (Italian)

Your will is free, upright and whole, and it would be a pity not to do as its says.

Multo maioris alapae mecum veneunt.
PHAEDRUS
Epilogues (Latin

With me freedom is much more dearly purchased.

Ubi libertas cecidit, audet libere nemo loqui.
LATIN PROVERB

Where freedom has fallen, none dare freely speak.

Nasha svoboda
Tol'ko ottuda b'yushchii svet,
Lyudi i teni stoyat u vkhoda
V zoologicheskii sad planet.
NIKOLAÏ GUMILÉV
Zabludivshiïsya Tramvaï (Russian,

Our freedom is only a light breaking through from another world – people and shadows stand at the entrance to the zoo of the planets.

El día que cada uno fuéramos un tirano para nosotros mismos, todos los hombres seríar igualmente libres.
JACINTO BENAVENTE Y MARTINEZ:
La Escuela de las Princesas (Spanish,

The day each of us becomes his own tyrant, everyone will be free and equal.

FRIENDSHIP
see also Contentment, Enemies, Family friends, Flattery, Love, Loyalty, Modesty, Neighbours, Possessions, Relations, Self-help, Wine.

'Adduww 'āqil khayr min sadīq jāhil
ARAB PROVERB

An intelligent enemy is preferable to an ignorant friend.

Illī mā luh-sh hadd luh rabbu-nā
ARAB PROVERB

God looks after the friendless.

Si tous les hommes scavoient ce qu'ils disent les uns des autres, il n'y auroit pas quatre amys dans le monde.

BLAISE PASCAL:
Pensées (French)

If everyone knew what they all said about each other, there would not be four friends left in the world.

Rien n'est si dangereux qu'un ignorant ami;
Mieux vaudrait un sage ennemi.

JEAN DE LA FONTAINE:
L'Ours et l'Amateur des Jardins (French)

Better to have a wise enemy than to undergo the dangers of having an ignorant friend.

Qu'un ami véritable est une douce chose!
Il cherche vos besoins au fond de votre coeur;
Il vous épargne la pudeur
De les lui découvrir vous-même.

JEAN DE LA FONTAINE;
Les Deux Amis (French)

What a wonderful thing it is to have a good friend. He identifies your innermost desires, and spares you the embarrassment of disclosing them to him yourself.

En ce monde il se faut l'un l'autre secourir.

JEAN DE LA FONTAINE:
Le Cheval et l'Âne (French)

In this world we must help one another.

Il est plus honteux de se défier de ses amis que d'en être trompé.

FRANÇOIS DUC DE LA ROCHEFOUCAULD:
Réflexions (French)

It is more shameful to mistrust one's friends than to be deceived by them.

L'amitié delicate et vraie ne souffre l'alliage d'aucun autre sentiment.

S. R. N. CHAMFORT:
Maximes et Pensées (French)

True sensitive friendship will not stand the alloy of any other feeling.

J'ai toujours distingué deux sortes d'amis: ceux qui exigent des preuves et ceux qui n'en exigent pas. – Les uns m'aiment pour moi-même et les autres pour eux. – Tous ont raison, mais je n'ai pas tort.

GÉRARD DE NERVAL:
Sur un Carnet (French)

I have always differentiated between two types of friends: those who want proofs of friendship, and those who do not. One kind love me for myself, and the others for themselves. Both are right, but I am not wrong.

Alle Kreatur braucht Hilf von allen.

BERTOLT BRECHT:
Von der Kindermörderin, Marie Farrar (German)

Everyone needs help from everyone.

Meine Freunde sind schwank wie Rohr,
Auf ihren Lippen sitzt ihr Herz,
Keuschheit kennen sie nicht;
Tanzen möchte ich auf ihren Häuptern.

ALBERT EHRENSTEIN:
Freunde (German)

My friends are as pliant as reeds, their hearts are on their sleeves (*lit.* lips); they know nothing of purity; I could dance on their heads.

Den letzten Spruch behalt ich,
Dass Feuer nicht fresse dein Haus;
Das letzte Wort verschweig ich,
Dass nicht am Balken du hangst
Den letzten Fluch spar ich
Als Waffe gegen deinen Feind,
Den letzten Segen hüt ich
Für ein Kind, das du liebst.

ERNST BERTRAM:
Aus dem Nornenbuch (German)

I decree my last verdict that fire should not devour your home; my last word I conceal, that you should not hang from a beam; my last curse I save as a weapon against your enemies; and my last blessing I cherish for a child that you love.

Tois polloisi gar
Brotōn apistos esth' etaireias limēn

SOPHOCLES:
Ajax (Greek)

Human friendships can scarcely be trusted.

Khrēn gar metrias eis allēlous
Philias thnētous anakirnasthai,
Kai mē pros akron muelon psukhēs

EURIPIDES:
Hippolytus (Greek)

Since we are mortal, friendships are best kept to
a moderate level, rather than sharing the very
depths of our souls.

Oudeis alastōr tois philois ek tōn philōn

EURIPIDES:
Hercules Furens (Greek)

Nothing can come between true friends.

Aretēi poieu philon hostis aristos

PYTHAGORAS:
Golden Verses (Greek)

Choose for your friend the one who is most
virtuous.

Hōs oudeis ouden ekhonti philos

GREEK PROVERB

He who has nothing has no friends.

En tais anankais khrēmatōn kreittōn philos

GREEK PROVERB

It is better in times of need to have a friend
rather than money.

Philon gar esthlon ekbakein ison legō
Kai ton par' hautōi bioton, hon pleiston philei

SOPHOCLES:
Oedipus Tyrannus (Greek)

Rather throw away that which is dearest to you
– your own life – than turn away a good friend.

Ti gar
Genoit' an helkos meizon ē philos kakos?

SOPHOCLES:
Antigone (Greek)

What can wound more deeply than a false
friend?

Makarios hostis tunkhanei gennaiou philou

GREEK PROVERB

Happy the man who finds a generous friend.

Eunoia kairōi krinetai

GREEK PROVERB

In times of difficulty friendship is on trial.

Pollōi kreitton estin emphanēs philos ē ploutos
aphanēs

GREEK PROVERB

Better the friend we can see than the money we
cannot!

Pōs gar tis aiskhunoit' an ōphelōn philous?

SOPHOCLES
Philoctetes (Greek)

Should he who helps his friends be afraid?

Nadzumi nisi ka-'i koso nakere tabi-goromo
Kino okumi-no keo ya tatsuran

JAPANESE PROVERB

He who puts on the clothes of a traveller will
seek in vain the links of friendship – here today,
gone tomorrow!

Nimium difficilest reperiri amicum ita ut nomen
cluet,
Quoi tuam quom rem credideris, sine omni cura
dormias.

PLAUTUS:
Trinummus (Latin)

How difficult it is to find a friend worthy of the
name, one to whom you can entrust your property and sleep soundly afterwards.

Si quoi mutuom quid dederis, fit pro proprio
perditum:
Quom repetas, inimicum amicum beneficio
invenias tuo.

PLAUTUS:
Trinummus (Latin)

What is lent is lost: try to get it back and by your
kindness your friend becomes your enemy.

Quod est facillimum, facis. Quid id est? Amico
iniuriam.
Neque meumst neque facere didici. Indoctus
quam docte facis.

PLAUTUS:
Trinummus (Latin)

What you are doing is the easiest of all things.
What is that? Hurting a friend. I never could do

that; I wouldn't know how. Then, for an amateur, you are very skilled.

Est enim amicitia nihil aliud nisi omnium divinarum humanarumque rerum cum benevolentia et caritate consensio.

CICERO:
De Amicitia (Latin)

Friendship is nothing else but an accord in all things, human and divine, conjoined with mutual goodwill and affection.

Sentio nisi in bonis amicitiam esse non posse.

CICERO:
De Amicitia (Latin)

I believe friendship can only exist among good men.

Est enim quatenus amicitiae dari venia possit.

CICERO:
De Amicitia (Latin)

There are limits to the indulgence which friendship allows.

Vive et amicitias semper cole.

AUSONIUS:
Opuscula (Latin)

Live your life and always practise friendship.

Non enim debent esse amicitiarum, sicut aliarum rerum, satietates; veterrima quaeque, ut ea vina quae vetustatem ferunt, esse debent suavissima.

CICERO:
De Amicitia (Latin)

Friendships should never be allowed to cloy as other things do; and, as in the case of wines that improve with age, the oldest freindships ought to be the most delightful.

Adminiculum in amicissimo quoque dulcissimum est.

CICERO:
De Amicitia (Latin)

Man's best support is a very dear friend.

Virtutum amicitia adiutrix a natura data est, non vitiorum comes.

CICERO:
De Amicitia (Latin)

Friendship was given by nature to be an assistant to virtue, not a companion in vice.

Ut matrona meretrici dispar erit atque
Discolor, infido scurrae distabit amicus.

HORACE:
Epistles (Latin)

As matron and mistress will differ in temper and tone, so will the friend be distinct from the faithless parasite.

Vilis amicorum est annona, bonis ubi quid deest.

HORACE:
Epistles (Latin)

The price of friends is cheap when good men are in need.

Archetypi amici.

MARTIAL:
Epigrams (Latin)

Friends that cost nothing (*lit.* original friends).

Ut cuique homini res paratast, perinde amicis utitur.

PLAUTUS:
Stichus (Latin)

A man's standing with his friends depends on his financial position.

Detrahit amicitiae maiestatem suam, qui illam parat ad bonos casus.

SENECA:
Epistles (Latin)

He who looks for advantage out of friendship, strips it of all its nobility.

Inter mundana omnia nihil est quod amicitiae digne praeferendum videatur.

ST. THOMAS AQUINAS:
On Princely Government (Latin)

There is nothing on this earth more to be prized than true friendship.

Ipsa [amicitiae] est quae maximas delectationes
affert, in tantum ut quaecumque delectabilia in
taedium sine amicis vertantur.
ST. THOMAS AQUINAS:
On Princely Government (Latin)

Friendship is the source of the greatest pleasures, and without friends even the most agree-
able pursuits become tedious.

Haec facetiast, amare inter se rivalis duos,
Uno cantharo potare, unum scortum ducere.
PLAUTUS:
Stichus (Latin)

How marvellous to have your rival for your
mate, drinking from one cup, and sharing the
same girl.

Amicum cum vides, obliviscere miserarias.
PRISCIAN:
Fragment (quoting a Saturnian) *(Latin)*

Forget your woes when you see your friend.

Foederis aequas
Dicamus leges.   VIRGIL:
Aeneid (Latin)

Let us settle fair terms of treaty.

Certe hercle quam veterrimus, tam homini op-
timust amicus.
PLAUTUS:
Truculentus (Latin)

The older a friend the better.

Is est amicus, qui in re dubia re iuvat, ubi rest
opus.   PLAUTUS:
Epidicus (Latin)

A friend in need is a friend indeed.

Ubi amici ibidem sunt opes.
LATIN PROVERB, quoted in PLAUTUS:
Truculentus

Your wealth is where your friends are.

Más vale mal conocido que bueno por conocer.
SPANISH PROVERB

Better a friend of bad repute than an untried
acquaintance.

No hay desierto como vivir sin amigos: la amis-
tad multiplica los bienes y reparte los males; es
único remedio contra la adversa fortuna, y un
desahogo del alma.
BALTASAR GRACIÁN
Oráculo Manual y Arte de Prudencia (Spanish)

There is no wilderness like a life without friends:
friendship multiplies blessings and minimises
misfortunes; it is a unique remedy against adversity, and it soothes the soul.

FRUGALITY

Simplex eius prandium,
Margarina, panis;
Modicum stipendium,
Domus haud immanis.
G. HERBERT FOWLER:
The Archivist (Latin)

His breakfast is simple – margarine and bread;
he has a modest salary, and his house could
never be called large.

Vivitur exiguo melius.
CLAUDIAN:
In Rufinum (Latin)

The frugal life is best.

Frugalitas miseria est rumoris boni.
LATIN PROVERB

Frugality is wretchedness with a good name.

FULFILMENT
see also Desire, Experience.

Stirb und werde!
J. W. VON GOETHE:
Selige Sehnsucht (German)

Die, and become!

Die ewigen Götter sind
Voll Lebens allzeit; bis in den Tod
Kann aber ein Mensch auch
Im Gedächtnis doch das Beste behalten,
Und dann erlebt er das Höchste.
FRIEDRICH HÖLDERLIN:
Der Rhein (German)

The eternal gods are ever full of life; but man too
can also keep in mind the best he remembers,
and thus experience the utmost right up to the
time of his death.

THE FUTURE
see also Fate, History, Life, Oracles,
Thought, Time, Women.

Ne penche plus ton front sur les choses qui
meurent;
Tourne au levant tes yeux, ton coeur à l'avenir.
Les arbres sont tombés, mais les germes demeurent;
Tends sur ceux qui naîtront tes bras pour les
bénir.

VICTOR DE LAPRADE:
La Mort d'un Chêne (French)

Do not mourn over dying things; look to the east,
give your heart to the future. The trees have
fallen, but the shoots remain. Reach out your
arms to bless those yet to be born.

La postérité n'est pas autre chose qu'un public
qui succède à un autre.

S. R. N. CHAMFORT:
Caractères et Anecdotes (French)

Posterity is nothing more than a new public that
has succeeded its ancestors.

Quand l'esprit te conduit sur le bord d'une
tombe,
De vie et d'avenir c'est pour nous y parler.

VICTOR DE LAPRADE:
La Mort d'un Chêne (French)

When the spirit brings you to the edge of the
tomb, it is to speak to us of life and the future.

Nach drüben ist die Aussicht uns verrannt.

J. W. VON GOETHE:
Faust (Auerbach's wine-cellar) *(German)*

Prospects over there are prejudiced against us.

Niemand kann sagen, ob die kommende Generation eine Generation von Giganten sein wird.

ADOLF HITLER, 1943
(German)

No-one can tell whether or not the coming
generation will be a race of giants.

Erst in dem Doppelbereich
Werden die Stimmen
Ewig und mild.

RAINER MARIA RILKE:
Sonnets to Orpheus (German)

It is only in the double-zone that the voices grow
eternal and mild.

Ta mellonta mē tarassetō. Hēxeis gar ep' auta,
ean deēsēi pherōn ton auton logon, hōi nun pros
ta paronta khrai

MARCUS AURELIUS:
Meditations (Greek)

Don't worry about the future – if you have to
come here, you will come armed with the same
reasoning that you apply to the present.

Il domani velato che non fa orrore.

EUGENIO MONTALE:
Le Occasioni (Italian)

The veiled tomorrow that does not make us
shudder.

Istuc est sapere, non quod ante pedes modost
Videre sed etiam illa quae futura sunt
Prospicere.

TERENCE:
Adelphoe (Latin)

What wisdom not only to see clearly the present
situation, but also to foresee what will be the
outcome!

Quis scit an adiciant hodiernae crastina
summae
Tempora di superi?

HORACE:
Odes (Latin)

Who knows if the gods above will add tomorrow's span to this day's sum?

Futura pugnant ne se superari sinant.

LATIN PROVERB

The future struggles against being mastered.

G

GAIN
see also Greed, Ill-gotten Gains, Money, Profit, Risk, War, Work.

> ... lucri bonus est odor ex re
> Qualibet.
>
> JUVENAL:
> *Satires (Latin)*

Whatever its source, the smell of gain is good.

Lucrum sine damno alterius fieri non potest.
LATIN PROVERB

Gain cannot be made without another's loss.

GAMBLING

C'est dans le jeu qu'on voit les plus grands coups de sort.
MOLIÈRE:
Les Fâcheux (French)

It's in gambling that we see the most amazing strokes of luck.

Il y a deux grands plaisirs dans le jeu, celui de gagner et celui de perdre.
FRENCH PROVERB

There are two great pleasures in gambling: winning, and losing.

Yo no siento que mi marido juegue, sino que pierda.
SPANISH PROVERB

My only worry about my husband's gambling is that he may lose.

Saberse dejar ganando con la fortuna i es de talures de reputación.
BALTASAR GRACIÁN:
Oráculo Manual y Arte de Prudencia (Spanish)

Knowing how to abandon a game when their luck is in is characteristic of good gamblers.

GARDENS
see also Flowers.

Non defit hortis et voluptas maxima
Multisque mixta commodis jocunditas.
ASMENIUS
Fragment *(Latin)*

It is in gardens that the greatest delight, mixed with much profit, is to be found.

> Qui cultus habendo
> Sit pecori?
>
> VIRGIL:
> *Georgics (Latin)*

What manner of breeding cattle should be used? (adopted as the motto of The Good Gardeners' Association).

Hortus deliciarum.
THE ABBESS HERRAD OF HOHENBURG
(Latin)

The garden of delights (adopted as the title of the Abbess Herrad's encyclopaedia).

GENEROSITY
see also Charity, Clemency, Kindness, Liberality.

La generosité n'est que la pitié des âmes nobles.
S. R. N. CHAMFORT:
Maximes et Pensées (French)

Generosity is only the pity of noble hearts.

Toute aultre science est dommageable à celuy qui n'a la science de la bonté.
MONTAIGNE:
Essays (French)

All other knowledge is harmful in someone who does not know generosity.

Lo spendere quello d'altri no ti toglie reputazione, ma te ne aggiugne.
NICCOLÒ MACHIAVELLI:
The Prince (Italian)

You will increase rather than diminish your reputation by spending the wealth of others.

Quippe velut denso currentia
Munera nimbo cernere semper erat.
> CLAUDIAN:
> *Panegyricus de Probino et Olybrice (Latin)*

The thick cloud of his generosity was ever thronged with gifts.

Benignitas enim mea me ad caelestem gloriam efferet.
> SUETONIUS:
> *Divus Augustus (Latin)*

My generosity will exalt me to immortal glory (Augustus, in a letter to Tiberius).

Benignus etiam causam dandi cogitat.
> LATIN PROVERB

Even the generous man considers the reason for giving.

Bis dat qui cito dat.
> LATIN PROVERB

He gives twice who gives quickly.

GENIUS
see also Evil, Law, Simplicity, Thought.

Saluez-moi, car je suis tout simplement en train de devenir un génie.
> Honoré de Balzac, to his sister,
> autumn 1833 *(French)*

Salute me! I am about to become a genius!

Je puis en un quart d'heure faire vingt ducs et pairs; il faut des siècles pour faire un Mansart.
> Louis XIV of France, ordering Mansart
> to cover his head in his presence for
> fear of the sun. *(French)*

In a quarter of an hour I can make twenty dukes and peers; it takes centuries to produce a Mansart.

Grand parmi les petits, libre chez les serviles,
Si le génie expire, il l'a bien mérité;
Car nous dressons partout aux portes de nos villes
Ces gibets de la gloire et de la vérité.
> ALPHONSE DE LAMARTINE:
> *Ferrare (French)*

Great among the little, free among slaves, if his genius dies it is well deserved; for we set up at the gates of our cities these gibbets, glory and truth.

Il faut qu'il y ait un grand nombre d'hommes qui s'y appliquent pour faire sortir l'homme de génie.
> DENIS DIDEROT:
> *Le Neveu de Rameau (French)*

It takes the effort of a great many people to produce a single man of genius.

Homme ou Dieu, tout génie est promis au martyre:
Du supplice plus tard on baise l'instrument.
> ALPHONSE DE LAMARTINE:
> *Ferrare (French)*

Every genius, whether God or man, is doomed to martyrdom; he kisses that which will later be the instrument of his torture.

Les progrès du génie étaient en proportion avec ceux du langage.
> E. B. DE M. DE CONDILLAC
> *(French)*

The progress of genius has kept pace with that of language.

Wüchsen die kinder in der Art fort, wie sie sich andeuten, so hätten wir lauter Genies.
> J. W. VON GOETHE:
> *Dichtung und Wahrheit (German)*

If children continued to grow in the spirit of their first promise, they would all be geniuses.

Amor ingenii neminem unquam divitem fecit.
> PETRONIUS:
> *Satyricon (Latin)*

The worship of genius never made any man rich.

At non ingenio quaesitum nomen ab aevo
Excidet: ingenio stat sine morte decus
> PROPERTIUS:
> *Elegies (Latin)*

Renown gained by genius will never be forgotten; the glory genius gains is deathless.

Ab Jove principium Musae.

VIRGIL:
Eclogues (Latin)

The foundation of genius belongs to Jove.

GENTLEMEN
see also Honour.

Un gentilhomme qui vit mal est un monstre dans la nature.

MOLIÈRE:
Don Juan (French)

A gentleman who acts badly is one of nature's monsters.

On n'apprend pas aux hommes à estre honnestes hommes et on leur apprend tout le reste.

BLAISE PASCAL:
Pensées (French)

Men are taught everything else but how to be gentlemen.

On dict bien vray qu'un honneste homme c'est un homme meslé.

MONTAIGNE:
Essays (French)

It is truly said that a gentleman is a busy man.

Le seul honnête homme est celui qui ne se paique de rien.

FRANÇOIS, DUC DE LA ROCHEFOUCAULD:
Réflexions (French)

A well-bred man has no pretensions.

Il y a longtemps qu'il est honnête homme.

B. J. Saurin, speaking of the historian
E. L. de Foncemange in his old age *(French)*

He's been a gentleman for a long time.

Virum bonum natura non ordo facit.

PUBLILIUS SYRUS:
Sententiae (Latin)

Nature, not rank, makes the gentleman.

Sólo consiste en obrar
Como caballerro, el serlo.

JUAN RUIZ DE ALARCÓN Y MENDOZA:
La Verdad Sospechosa (Spanish)

Being a gentleman consists simply in behaving like one.

GIFTS
see also Benefits and Benefactors, Distrust Gods, Greatness, Sympathy.

La façon de donner vaut mieux que ce qu'on donne.

FRENCH PROVERB

The way in which something is given is worth more than the gift itself.

Ekhthrōn adōra dōra kouk' onēsima

SOPHOCLES
Ajax (quoting an ancient adage) *(Greek)*

Gifts from an enemy are not gifts but fatal blows.

Parva munera diutina, locupletia non propria esse consuerunt.

LATIN PROVERB

Small gifts are lasting; lavish ones are impermanent.

GLORY
see also Achievement, Bravery, Fame, Greatness, Greece, Heroes, History, Kings, Solitude, Women.

Quand la gloire nous enfle, il sait bien comme il faut
Confondre notre orgueil qui s'élève trop haut.

PIERRE CORNEILLE:
Horace (French)

When we swell with glory, our overweening pride is soon abashed.

Un homme tel que moi voit sa gloire ternie
Quand il tombe en péril de quelque ignominie.

PIERRE CORNEILLE:
Horace (French)

Such a man as I am, once in danger of ignominy, regards his glory as tarnished (Horace, defending his action in killing his sister).

J'ai vécu pour ma gloire autant qu'il fallait vivre,
Et laisse un grand exemple à qui pourra me suivre.

PIERRE CORNEILLE:
Suréna (French)

I have lived as much as possible for my glory, and leave a fine example for my successor.

Aucun chemin de fleurs ne conduit à la gloire.

JEAN DE LA FONTAINE:
Les Deux Aventuriers et le Talisman (French)

The road to glory is not strewn with flowers.

La plus grande bassesse de l'homme est la recherche de la gloire.

BLAISE PASCAL:
Pensées (French)

Man's deepest abasement is his pursuit of glory.

Triste comme la gloire.

NAPOLEON I
(French)

Sad as glory itself.

O bienheureux celui qui peut de sa mémoire
Effacer pour jamais ce vain espoir de gloire,
Dont l'inutile soin traverse nos plaisirs

MARQUIS DE RACAN:
Stances sur la Retraite (French)

How lucky he is who can obliterate for ever from
his memory the vain pursuit of glory, that useless aim which thwarts our happiness.

Ō doxa doxa muriosi dē brotōn
Ouden gegōsi bioton ōnkōsas megan

EURIPIDES:
Andromeda (Greek)

O glory! countless worthless mortals have been
raised to honour and dignity by you!

No e Gloria il principio, ma il seguire.

LODOVICO DEGLI ARRIGHI:
*La Operina da Imparare di Scrivere
Littera Cancellaresca (Italian)*

Glory comes at the end, not at the beginning [of
life].

Pertinet enim ad boni viri officium, ut contemnat gloriam, sicut alia temporalia bona.

ST. THOMAS AQUINAS:
On Princely Government (Latin)

It is a just man's duty to despise glory, together
with all other temporal rewards.

GOD

**see also Blasphemy, Charity, Death, Fate,
Greatness, Humility, Justice, Kings,
Laughter, Loyalty, Mankind, Merit,
Money, Nature, Pain, the People, Piety,
Pity, Prayer, Providence, Religion,
Revelation, Sin, Sky, Truth, Universe,
Wealth, Wine, Women.**

Innamā illī yittaqi Allāh huwa 'l-baṭal

ARAB PROVERB

The only hero is he who fears God.

Mānusa citta āna kachu bītā;
Karai gusāīṁ jō mana cītā

MALIK MUHAMMAD JĀYASĪ:
Padumāvatī (Avadhi)

Man proposes, but God disposes.

Le Seigneur contient tout dans ses deux bras
immenses,
Son Verbe est le séjour de nos intelligences,
Comme ici-bas l'espace est celui de nos corps.

ALFRED DE VIGNY:
La Maison du Berger – Lettre à Eva (French)

The Lord embraces all in his great arms; His
Word is the source of our understanding, just as
on earth space is provided for our bodies.

Dieu est le lieu des esprits comme l'espace est le
lieu des corps.

NICOLAS DE MALEBRANCHE:
Recherche de la Vérité (French)

God is the home of the mind, just as space is the
home of the body.

Chaque créature indique Dieu, aucune ne le
révèle.

ANDRÉ GIDE:
Les Nourritures Terrestres (French)

Every living creature gives some glimpse of God,
but none reveals him.

Dieu fait bien ce qu'il fait.

JEAN DE LA FONTAINE:
Le Gland et la Citrouille (French)

What God does he does well.

Vous Empereurs, vous Princes, et vous Roys,
Vous qui tenez le peuple sous vos lois,
Oyez icy de quelle providence
Dieu regit tout par sa haulte prudence.
>> PIERRE DE RONSARD:
>> *Discours au Duc de Savoie (French)*

Emperors! Princes! Monarchs! You who govern
your peoples by your laws, take notice how God
rules everything by his care and providence.

Qui Dieu vielt aidier, nuls hom ni li puet nuire.
>> GEOFFROI DE VILLEHARDOUIN:
>> *Histoire de la Conquête de Constantinople (French)*

None can harm God's protégés.

Qu'il y a loin de la connaissance de Dieu à
l'aimer!
>> BLAISE PASCAL:
>> *Pensées, Adversaria (French)*

What a distance there is between knowing God
and loving him!

Je ne sais point où Dieu commence, et moins
encore où il finit. Même j'exprimerai mieux ma
pensée si je dis qu'il n'en finit jamais de com-
mencer.
>> ANDRÉ GIDE:
>> *Thésée (French)*

I cannot tell where God begins, still less where
he ends. But my belief is better expressed if I say
that there is no end to God's beginning.

Vers quoi tendre sinon vers Dieu?
>> ANDRÉ GIDE:
>> *Thésée (French)*

Whither should we aim if not towards God?

Vouloir ce que Dieu veut est la seule science
Qui nous met en repos
>> FRANÇOIS DE MALHERBE:
>> *Consolation à M. du Perier (French)*

Wanting what God wants is the only learning
that can give us peace of mind.

Je ne reconnaîtrai de souverain que celui qui
alluma la flamme des soleils et qui d'un seul
coup de sa main fit rouler tous les mondes.
>> FRANÇOIS RENÉ, VICOMTE DE CHATEAUBRIAND:
>> *Voyage en Amérique (French)*

The only sovereign I recognise is he who sets fire
to the suns and, with one blow of his hand, can
send the worlds rolling in space.

Il ne peut être question de deux Dieux.
>> ANDRÉ GIDE:
>> *Attendu que . . . (French)*

There can be no question of there being two
Gods.

C'est Dieu qui le veut.
>> VICTOR HUGO:
>> *Réponse à un Acte d'Accusation (French)*

It is God's will.

Toute puissance vient de Dieu, je l'avoue; mais
toute maladie en vient aussi.
>> J. J. ROUSSEAU:
>> *Du Contrat Social (French)*

I admit that all power derives from God; but so
does all sickness.

Le gentilhomme d'en haut.
>> The Marshal of France, the duc de
>> Brissac's euphemism for God *(French)*

The gentleman upstairs.

En cherchant l'oeil de Dieu, je n'ai vu qu'une
orbite
Vaste, noire et sans fond, d'où la nuit qui
l'habite
Rayonne sur le monde et s'épaissit toujours.
>> GÉRARD DE NERVAL:
>> *Le Christ aux Oliviers (French)*

In seeking the eye of God, I have seen a vast
sphere, black and fathomless, whence the night
that inhabits it shines forth on the world and
continually deepens.

Es lebt ein Gott, zu strafen und zu rächen.
>> GERMAN PROVERB

There is a God who punishes and avenges.

>> Ein Gott bewegt die Wunderuhr
>> Der Welt, die er erfand, beseelet die Natur.
>> CHRISTOPH MARTIN WIELAND:
>> *Die Natur der Dinge (German)*

A god keeps in motion the miraculous clock of
the world which he invented, and gives nature a
soul.

Gott schuf den Menschen nach seinem Bilde, das heisst vermutlich, der Mensch schuf Gott nach dem seinigen.
GEORG CHRISTOPH LICHTENBERG:
Aphorismen (German)

God fashioned man after his own image; in other words man probably fashioned God in his own image.

Nicht das macht frei, das wir nichts über uns erkennen wollen, sondern eben, dass wir etwas verehren, das über uns ist.
J. W. von Goethe to J. P. Eckermann, 18 January 1827 *(German)*

It does not make us free if we do not recognise that there is something over us, but that we venerate what is over us.

La gloria di colui che tutto move
Per l'universo penetra, e risplende
In una parte più, e meno altrove.
DANTE:
Paradiso (Italian)

The glory of Him who controls all things, pervades the universe, and illuminates its parts with varying light.

Jovis omnia plena.
VIRGIL:
Eclogues (Latin)

God permeates everything.

Nemo contra deum nisi deus ipse.
J. W. VON GOETHE:
Dichtung und Wahrheit (Latin)

None can be against God, unless it be God himself.

Quod mullum gaudium sit extra Deum sed totum in Deo, et ipse Deus totus sit gaudium, consequens est quod primus loquens primo et ante omnia dixisset, *Deus*
DANTE:
De Vulgari Eloquio (Latin)

Since there is no joy without God, and all joy is in God, and God himself is all joy, it follows that he who spoke first, said first and before all other things, 'God!'

Est deus in nobis, agitante calescimus illo.
OVID:
Fasti (Latin)

God is within us – we glow with his inspiration.

Vocatus atque non vocatus Deus aderit.
Inscription carved by C. G. Jung on the lintel of his house *(Latin)*

Whether invoked or not, God will be present.

Paucorum est intellegere quid donet deus.
LATIN PROVERB

It is the privilege of few to understand what God gives.

Deus escreve direito por linhas tortas.
PORTUGUESE PROVERB

God moves in mysterious ways . . . (*lit.* God uses crooked lines to write straight).

Da Dios nueces al que no tiene muelas.
SPANISH PROVERB

God gives nuts to the toothless.

GODS
see also Adversity, Events, Fate, Greece, Human nature, Illusion, Impermanence, Life, Love, Mercy, Poets and poetry, Prayer, Reason, Self-help, Worship.

Es fürchte die Götter
Das Menschengeschlecht!
J. W. VON GOETHE:
Iphigenie auf Tauris (German)

May mankind fear the gods!

Zwar leben die Götter,
Aber über dem Haupt droben in anderer Welt.
FRIEDRICH HÖLDERLIN:
Brod und Wein (German)

Of course the gods still live, but right up there in another world!

Alles Höchste, es kommt frei von den Göttern
herab.
J. C. F. VON SCHILLER:
Das Glück (German)

All that is highest freely derives from the gods.

Polus taragmos en te tois theiois eni
K'an tois broteiois
EURIPIDES:
Iphigeneia in Tauris (Greek)

There is as much confusion in the world of the
gods as in ours.

Ta d' huperballont'
Oudena kairon dunatai thnētois
Meizous d' atas, hotan orgisthēi
Daimōn, oikois apedōken
EURIPIDES:
Medea (Greek)

When the anger of the gods is incurred, wealth
or power only bring more devastating punishment.

Peithein dōra kai theous logos
EURIPIDES:
Medea (Greek)

Even the gods, they say, can prove susceptible to
gifts.

Tōn d' adokētōn poron hēure theos
EURIPIDES:
Medea (Greek)

It is the gods who can disclose the hidden
pathway.

Phthonos de mē genoito tis theōn
EURIPIDES:
Alcestis (Greek)

Pray the gods do not envy your happiness!

Ei de tis theōn
Blaptoi, phugoi t'an khō kakos ton kreissona
SOPHOCLES:
Ajax (Greek)

When the gods do mischief, the wicked man may
escape the better.

Ou miaineis thnētos ōn ta tōn theōn
EURIPIDES:
Hercules Furens (Greek)

Man cannot defile the divine.

Kēdomenoi gar
Athanatōn autoi pleion ekhousi brotoi
THEOCRITUS:
Poems (Greek)

Mankind can benefit by cherishing the gods.

Athanatous men prōta theous, nomōi hōs
diaketai
Tima
PYTHAGORAS:
Golden Verses (Greek)

Worship first the immortal gods, in obedience to
the custom of the country.

. . . cui non risere parentes,
Nec deus hunc mensa, dea nec dignata cubili
est.
VIRGIL:
Eclogues (closing words) *(Latin)*

A god will refuse a meal, a goddess a bed, to him
on whom his parents have not smiled.

Di bene!
CLAUDIAN:
De Bello Gildonico (Latin)

Thanks be to the gods!

Ego deum genus esse semper dixi et dicam
caelitum,
Sed eos non curare opinor, quid agat humanum
genus.
ENNIUS:
Telamon (quoted in Cicero:
De Divinatione) (Latin)

I always have said and always shall say there are
gods in the heavens, but I believe they don't care
what happens to mankind.

Nihil deos ignorare quod omnia sint ab eis
constituta.
CICERO:
De Divinatione (quoting a Stoic
syllogism) *(Latin)*

The gods know all, since all was ordained by
them.

Quem di diligunt
Adulescens moritur.

PLAUTUS:
Bacchides (Latin)

Whom the Gods love die young.

Vilkat goð geyja: grey þykkjumk Freyja
ARI THORGILSSON:
Libellus Islandorum (Norse)

I don't want to blaspheme the gods, but I think
Freyja is a bitch! (Hjalti's remark to the
heathen).

Tak khram ostavlennyǐ – vsĕ khram,
Kumir poverzhennyǐ – vsĕ bog!
MIKHAIL LERMONTOV:
I Do Not Love You (Russian)

An abandoned temple is still a temple – a
dethroned idol is still a god!

THE GOLDEN AGE
see also Law, Simplicity.

L'âge d'or du genre humain n'est point derrière
nous, il est au-devant, il est dans la perfection de
l'ordre social, nos pères ne l'ont point vu, nos
enfants y arriveront un jour: c'est à nous de leur
en frayer la route.
CLAUDE HENRI, COMTE DE SAINT-SIMON
AND AUGUSTIN THIERRY:
De la Réorganisation de la Société Européenne (French)

The golden age of mankind is not behind, but
before us; and it lies in the perfection of the social
order. Our fathers have not seen it; our children
will one day reach it. It is up to us to prepare the
way for them.

Et lors on n'oyoit point ce mot de tien ne mien
Tous vivoient en commun, car tous n'avoient
qu'un bien.
PIERRE DE RONSARD:
Les Armes (French)

And when we no longer hear talk of 'mine' and
'thine', we shall all live as a community, for
everyone will have but one common inheritance.

Le grand Pan est mort.
BLAISE PASCAL:
Pensées (French)

Great Pan is dead.

O bienheureux le siecle où le peuple sauvage
Vivoit par les forests de gland et de fruitage!
PIERRE DE RONSARD:
Elegie au Seigneur Baillon (French)

Happy the age when the savage people lived on
the acorns and the fruits of the forest!

Ma ci fu dunque un giorno
La dolce giovinezza,
La gloria e la bellezza,
Fede, virtude, amor?
GIOSUE CARDUCCI:
Tedio Invernale (Italian)

Was there really a golden age when everyone
was young? When young men and women sang
of courage, faith and love?

Non acies, non ira fuit, non bella, nec ensem
Immiti saevus duxerat arte faber.
TIBULLUS:
Elegies (Latin)

There were no battle lines, no atrocities, no
wars, and the cruel armourer had not yet grimly
fashioned swords.

Siquidem simplex illā aurei seculi gens,
nullis armata disciplinis, solo naturae ductu
instinctuque vivebat.
ERASMUS:
Moriae Encomium (Latin)

The simple folk of the Golden Age, unequipped
with any arts, lived only by the guidance and
promptings of nature.

GOOD
see also Evil, Haste, Honour, Indifference, Ingratitude, Intentions, Kings, Politics, Redemption, the Soul, Steadfastness, Virtue.

Jeg har altid prøvet at vaere god
Det er meget kraevende.
BENNY ANDERSEN:
Godhed (Danish)

I have always tried to be good – it's very
demanding!

Le mal est aisé, il y en a une infinité; le bien presque unique.

> BLAISE PASCAL:
> *Pensées: Adversaria (French)*

Evil is easy, its forms are infinite; good is almost unique.

On aime toujours ce qui est beau ou ce qu'on trouvre tel; mais c'est sur ce jugement qu'on se trompe.

> J. J. ROUSSEAU:
> *Du Contrat Social (French)*

We always love what is good or what we think is good; it is in our judgment of what is good that we can make mistakes.

Aiai. Tôn agathôn hôs moros ôkuteros

> ST. GREGORY OF NAZIANZUS:
> *Poems (Greek)*

Alas! how soon do the good die!

Eis telos gar hoi men esthloi tunkhanousin axiôn

> EURIPIDES:
> *Ion (Greek)*

In the end the good will triumph.

Lege iustitiae boni homines malis angelis, praeferantur.

> ST. AUGUSTINE:
> *De Civitate Dei (Latin)*

Under the law of righteousness, good men are rated above bad angels.

Felix qui potuit boni
Fontem visere lucidum

> BOETHIUS:
> *Consolatio Philosophiae (Latin)*

How happy the man who can see the clear fountain of good.

Musicae occultae nullum respectum est.

> LATIN PROVERB

Hidden music counts for nothing.

GOOD WISHES
see also Friends.

Deos obsecro, ut te nobis conservent et valere nunc et semper patiantur.

> SUETONIUS:
> *Tiberius (Latin)*

I pray the gods will preserve you for us and grant you good health now and forever!

Abite laeti, abite locupletes!

> SUETONIUS:
> *Gaius Caligula (Latin)*

Go your way happily, go your way rich!

GOSSIP
see also Calumny, Rumour.

Al-fitine ashadd min al-muḳātala

> ARAB PROVERB

Gossip is worse than fighting.

Nescit vox missa reverti.

> HORACE:
> *Ars Poetica (Latin)*

A word once uttered can never be recalled.

Se complace en decir a todo el mundo todo lo malo que ella dice que dicen de uno.

> JACINTO BENAVENTE Y MARTÍNEZ:
> *Titania (Spanish)*

She enjoys telling everyone all the evil she says they say about them.

¡Qué hombres hay, Señor! ¡Cuánta lengua venenosa!

> RAMON PÉREZ DE AYALA:
> *Luz de Domingo (Spanish)*

What people there are, Lord! How great a number of poisonous tongues!

GOVERNMENT
see also Citizenship, Kings, Monarchy, Philosophers, Power, Punishment, Tyranny.

Les gouvernements périssent ordinairement par impuissance ou par tyrannie. Dans le premier cas, le pouvoir leur échappe; on le leur arrache dans l'autre.

ALEXIS DE TOCQUEVILLE:
De la Démocratie en Amérique (French)

Governments perish usually through impotence or tyranny. In the first case power eludes them; in the second it is seized from them.

Un gouvernement réduit à ne pouvoir atteindre ses ennemis que sur le champ de bataille serait bientôt détruit.

ALEXIS DE TOCQUEVILLE:
De la Démocratie en Amérique (French)

Any government reduced to meeting its enemies only on the battlefield would soon be destroyed.

Il est impossible d'assujettir un peuple à une règle qui ne convient qu'à quelques hommes mélancoliques, qui l'ont calquée sur leur caractère.

DENIS DIDEROT:
Entretien d'un Philosophe avec le Maréchale de . . . (French)

It is impossible to subject a whole people to some law that only suits a few gloomy individuals who have it engraved in their disposition.

On voit que de tout temps
Les petits ont pâti des sottises des grands.

JEAN DE LA FONTAINE:
Les Deux Taureaux et une Grenouille (French)

We can see that throughout history the common people have suffered for the follies of great men.

Qu'importe qu'il y ait sur le Trône un Tibère ou un Titus, s'il a des Séjan pour Ministres?

S. R. N. CHAMFORT:
Maximes et Pensées (French)

What does it matter whether a Tiberius or a Titus reigns if we have a Sejanus as minister?

Estin gar dē tis phonē tōn politeiōn hekastēs kathaperei tinōn zōiōn

PLATO:
Epistles (Greek)

Every kind of government has its own voice, just as though it were an animal.

Ouk agathon polukoiraniē, eis koiranos
Estō eis basileus

HOMER:
Iliad (Greek)

A state cannot be well governed when there are many in authority.

Ita mihi salvam ac sospitem rem publicam sistere in sua sede liceat atque eius rei fructum percipere, quem peto, ut optimi status auctor dicar et moriens ut feram mecum spem, mansura in vestigio suo fundamenta rei publicae quae iecero.

SUETONIUS:
Divus Augustus (Latin)

May it be my privilege to establish the State in a firm and secure position, and reap the fruit of that which I desire; so that I may be called the author of the best possible government, and bear with me the hope when I die that the foundations which I have laid for the State will remain unshaken (Augustus's hopes, expressed in an edict).

[Haec tibi erunt artes] pacisque imponere morem,
Parcere subiectis et debellare superbos.

VIRGIL:
Aeneid (Latin)

These shall be your arts: to set the law of peace, to spare the vanquished, and to quell the proud.

Divide ut regnes.

LATIN PROVERB

Divide and rule (*lit.* divide, so that you may rule).

In singulis enim operatur natura, quod optimum est; omne autem naturale regimen ab uno est.

ST. THOMAS AQUINAS:
On Princely Government (Latin)

Nature always works in the best way; but in nature, government is always by one individual.

Sicut autem regimen regis est optimum, ita regimen tyranni est pessimum.

ST. THOMAS AQUINAS:
On Princely Government (Latin)

Government by a king is best, but government by a tyrant is the worst form of rule.

GRACE AND FAVOUR

Hic tibi copia
Manabit ad plenum benigno
Ruris honorum opulenta cornu.

HORACE:
Odes (Latin)

Here to thee shall plenty flow, and all her riches show, to raise the honour of the quiet plain (*tr.* Creech).

GRAMMAR
see also Dictionaries, Language, Liberal arts, Philology.

Les erreurs des hommes sont presque toujours des erreurs de grammaire.

CHARLES POUGENS:
Plan du Dictionnaire Complet de la Langue française (French)

Mankind's errors are nearly always grammatical ones.

La plupart des occasions des troubles du monde sont grammairiennes

MONTAIGNE:
Essays (French)

The majority of causes of trouble in this world are due to grammar.

Grammatikē estin empeira tōn para poiētais te kai sungrapheusin hōs epi to polu legomenōn

DIONYSIUS THRAX:
Ars Grammatica (Greek)

Grammar is the empirical knowledge of what is for the most part being said by poets and prose writers.

Grammatica . . . necessaria pueris, iucunda senibus, dulcis secretorum comes, et quae vel sola in omni studiorum genere plus habeat operis quam ostentationis.

QUINTILIAN:
Institutiones Oratoriae

Grammar is a necessity for boys, a source of enjoyment for old men, the sweet companion of the solitary; and, almost alone among every type of study it possesses more usefulness than vulgar ostentation.

GRATITUDE
see also Benefits and benefactors, Ingratitude.

Tak for sidst.

DANISH GREETING

Thanks for the last time we were together.

La reconnaissance est un fardeau, et tout fardeau est fait pour être secoué.

DENIS DIDEROT:
Le Neveu de Rameau (French)

Gratitude is a burden – and all burdens are made to be shaken off.

Les hommes ne s'attachent point à nous en raison des services que nous leur rendons, mais en raison de ceux qu'ils nous rendent.

LABICHE ET MARTIN:
Le Voyage de M. Perrichon (French)

It is not the services we render them, but the services they render us that attaches people to us.

Dieu a donc oublié tout ce que j'ai fait pour lui!

Louis XIV of France (after the disastrous battle of Ramillies, 1706) *(French)*

So God has forgotten all that I have done for him!

Dieu a recommandé le pardon des injures, il n'a point recommandé celui des bienfaits.

S. R. N. CHAMFORT:
Caractères et Anecdotes (French)

God has recommended that we should pardon injuries; but he has not recommended that we should pardon good deeds.

O combien le péril enrichirait les dieux,
Si nous nous souvenions des voeux qu'il nous fait faire!

JEAN DE LA FONTAINE:
Jupiter et le Passager (French)

How wealthy the gods would be if we remembered the promises we made when we were in danger.

On n'aime point à voir ceux à qui l'on doit tout.
PIERRE CORNEILLE:
Nicomède (French)

We never like to see those to whom we owe everything.

Swes brot ich ezz', des liet ich sing'.
GERMAN MINSTRELS' MOTTO

If I eat a man's bread, I'll sing his song.

Ōkeiai kharites glukerōterai
GREEK PROVERB

Swift gratitude is the sweetest.

Parve culex, pecudum custos tibi tale merenti
Funeris officium vitae pro munere reddit.
VIRGIL:
Culex (attribution doubtful) *(Latin)*

To you, tiny, well-deserving gnat, the flock's grateful keeper now offers for the gift of his life due funeral rites in requital (inscription on a tomb set up by a grateful shepherd to a gnat who had saved his life).

Cum meruero.
SUETONIUS:
Nero (Latin)

Wait until I deserve them (Nero, acknowledging the Senate's vote of thanks).

Una cosa es el agradecimiento, y otra el amor.
SPANISH PROVERB

Gratitude is one thing, love another.

GRAVES
see also Epitaphs.

Ouden ho tumbos
ST. GREGORY OF NAZIANZUS:
Poems (Greek)

The tomb is nothing.

Lakhoi nu se bōlos elaphrē
Sumphōnon pinutōi skhonta logōi bioton
MELEAGER:
Garland (Greek)

May the earth that covers you prove light, for you led your life in moderation and wisdom.

Asbeston kleos hoide philēi peri patridi thentes
Kuaneon thanatou amphebalonto nephos
SIMONIDES:
Epigrams (Greek)

These men, having caparisoned their fatherland in undying glory, themselves put on the dark cloud of death.

Ourea men kai ponton huper tumboio kharasse
ALPHEIUS OF MITYLENE:
Fragment (Greek)

Carve the mountains and the sea on my tomb.

GREATNESS
see also Anger, Character, Envy, Faults, Government, Honour, Inspiration, Kings, Law, Politics, Problems, Reticence, Society, Success.

La grandeur d'âme et les hautes qualités sont de toutes les conditions et de tous les pays.
DENIS DIDEROT:
Les Deux Amis de Bourbonne (French)

Great hearts and noble qualities occur in all countries and in all classes of mankind.

Pensée fait la grandeur de l'homme.
BLAISE PASCAL:
Pensées (French)

The greatness of mankind derives from thought.

Je diray que des Grands la vie est incertaine.
PIERRE DE RONSARD:
Tombeau de Marguerite de France (French)

In my opinion the survival of any great person is uncertain.

Il n'y a pas de grands esprits sans un grain de folie.
FRENCH PROVERB

There's a pinch of the madman in every great man.

Un Grand nous fait assez de bien quand il ne nous fait pas de mal.
P. A. C. DE BEAUMARCHAIS:
Le Barbier de Séville (French)

The great are sufficiently benevolent to us when they do us no harm.

Voilà un homme!
>NAPOLEON I's comment on Göethe after
meeting him in 1808 *(French)*

What a man!

C'est une chose admirable que tous les grands
hommes ont toujours du caprice, quelque petit
grain de folie mêlé à leur science.
>MOLIÈRE:
>*Le Médecin Malgré Lui (French)*

It is remarkable that every great man always has
some caprice, some little madness mingled with
his learning.

Grand homme est celui qui laisse après soi les
autres dans l'embarras.
>PAUL VALÉRY:
>*Choses Tues (French)*

The great man is he who leaves his successors in
difficulties.

C'était un si grand homme que j'ai oublié ses
vices.
>LORD BOLINGBROKE, speaking of the Duke of
>Marlborough (according to Voltaire:
>*Lettres Philosophiques*) *(French)*

He was such a great man that I have forgotten
his faults.

Le riche parle bien des richesses, le roy parle
froidement d'un grand don qu'il vient de faire, et
Dieu parle bien de Dieu.
>BLAISE PASCAL:
>*Pensées (French)*

The rich speak authoritatively of wealth, the
king speaks calmly of a great gift he has just
made, and God speaks divinely of God.

Il y a une mélancolie qui tient à la grandeur de
l'esprit.
>S. R. N. CHAMFORT:
>*Maximes et Pensées* (Appendix I) *(French)*

There is a melancholy that stems from greatness
of mind.

La gloire des grands hommes se doit toujours
mesurer aux moyens dont ils se sont servir pour
l'acquérir.
>FRANÇOIS, DUC DE LA ROCHEFOUCAULD:
>*Réflexions (French)*

The glory of great men should always be measured by the means they have used to acquire it.

Il y a des héros en mal comme en bien.
>FRANÇOIS, DUC DE LA ROCHEFOUCAULD:
>*Réflexions (French)*

There are heroes of evil as well as of good.

Gross kann man sich im *Glück*, erhaben nur im
Unglück zeigen.
>J. C. F. VON SCHILLER:
>*Von Erhabenen (German)*

You can be great when you are in good fortune;
only in misfortune can you be sublime.

Ein edler Mensch kann einem engen Kreise
Nicht seine Bildung danken. Vaterland
Und Welt muss auf ihn wirken.
>J. W. VON GOETHE:
>*Tasso (German)*

A man of noble mind cannot owe his culture to a
narrow circle. His country and the world must
have influenced him too.

Der kann sich manchen Wunsch gewähren,
Der kalt sich selbst und seinem Willen lebt;
Allein wer andre wohl zu leiten strebt,
Muss fähig sein, viel zu entbehren.
>J. W. VON GOETHE:
>*Ilmenau (German)*

A cold and selfish man, living only for himself,
can plentifully indulge his own desires; but he
who would be a good leader must be prepared to
deny himself much.

Ta akra tois akrois apodidonai
>PLATO:
>*The Republic (Greek)*

The highest places should go to great men.

All' ē kalōs zēn ē kalōs tethnēkenai
Ton eugenē khrē
>SOPHOCLES:
>*Ajax (Gretk)*

The well-born must live with honour or die with
glory.

Nessuna cosa fa tanto stimare uno principe, quanto fanno le grande imprese e dare di sé rari esempli.

NICCOLÒ MACHIAVELLI:
The Prince (Italian)

Nothing causes a prince to be so much esteemed as great enterprises and proofs of prowess.

Quo quisquam optimus sit, pessimus, si hoc ipsum, quod optimus sit, adscribat sibi.

ST. BERNARD:
In Cantica Sermones (Latin)

A man becomes worst from being best, if he ascribes his best to his own efforts.

Ab humana cessit in astra via.

PROPERTIUS:
Elegies (Latin)

A man who stepped from human paths to dwell among the stars.

Nihil tetigit quod non ornavit.

LATIN PROVERB

He nothing touched that he did not adorn.

Omnium horarum homo.

ERASMUS:
Epistles (Latin)

A man for all seasons (a classical phrase applied by Erasmus to Thomas More; the phrase also occurs in Suetonius: *Tiberius,* and Quintilian)

Boni sibi haec expetunt, rem, fidem, honorem, Gloriam et gratiam: hoc probis pretiumst.

PLAUTUS:
Trinummus (Latin)

Good men seek wealth, trust, honour, glory and public favour: this is the prize integrity earns.

Quidquid delirant reges plectuntur Achivi.

HORACE:
Epistles (Latin)

Whatever errors the great commit, the people must pay for (*lit.* whatever folly the kings commit, the Acheans pay the penalty).

Neminem excelsi ingenii virum humilia delectant et sordida.

SENECA:
Epistles (Latin)

Base and squalid things have no appeal for men of noble virtue.

No hay hombre grande para su ayuda de cámara.

LUIS COLOMA:
Pequeñeces (Spanish)

No man is great in his valet's eyes.

El saber y el valor alternan gradenza.

BALTASAR GRACIÁN:
Oráculo Manual y Arte de Prudencia (Spanish)

Wisdom and courage make mutual contributions to greatness.

GREECE
see also Slaves.

Seeliges Griechenland! du Haus der Himmlischen alle!

FRIEDRICH HÖLDERLIN:
Brod und Wein (German)

Blessed land of Greece! You home of all the immortals!

Die edle Einfalt und stille Grösse der griechischen Statuen ist zugleich das wahre Kennzeichen der griechischen Schriften aus den besten Zeiten.

J. J. WINCKELMANN:
Werke (German)

The noble simplicity and serene greatness of Greek statues are also the true characteristics of Greek writing of the best period.

Kai mallon Hellēnas kaleisthai tous tēs paideuseōs tēs hēmeteras ē tous tēs koinēs phuseōs metekontas

ISOCRATES:
Panegyricus (Greek)

Those who share our Athenian culture – rather than those who belong to the same race – are worthy of being called Greeks.

. . . di Grecia i numi
Non sanno occaso; ei dormon ne'materni

Tronchi e ne'fiori, sopra i monti i fiumi
I mari eterni.

GIOSUE CARDUCCI:
Primavere Elleniche (Italian)

The gods of Greece know no decay; they sleep in the flowers, the streams, the mountains; in their native trees, and in the eternal deep.

Graecum est, nec potest legi.

Attrib. ACCURSIUS *(Latin)*

This is Greek and is not included in our lectures (possibly referring to the danger of being accused of heresy if he admitted to a knowledge of Greek).

Graecia capta ferum victorem cepit.

HORACE:
Epistles (Latin)

Greece the captive made her savage victor captive.

GREED
see also Anger, Avarice.

'Ittāmah yiqilli mā gāmah

ARAB PROVERB

Greed lessens what is gathered.

La concupiscence est la source de tous nos mouvements, et l'humanité.

BLAISE PASCAL:
Pensées (French)

Greed is the source of all our actions – in addition, of course, to human nature!

Quand on met son coeur avec son argent, la malédiction de Dieu est dans la maison.

MME LA COMTESSE DE SÉGUR:
Un Bon Petit Diable (French)

The curse of God is on the house where heart and money go together.

On hasarde de perdre en voulant trop gagner.

JEAN DE LA FONTAINE:
Le Héron (French)

We risk all in being too greedy.

Wie ein Kind am Tischtuch zerrt, aber nichts gewinnt, sondern nur die ganze Pracht hinun-terwirft und sie sich für immer unerreichba macht.

FRANZ KAFKA
Das Schloss (German

Just like the child who tugs at the tablecloth; h gains nothing by pulling all the fine china on t the floor and putting it beyond his reach for ever

Das älteste Sprichwort ist wohl: Allzuviel is ungesund.

GEORG CHRISTOPH LICHTENBERG
Aphorismen (German

The oldest proverb is still good: Too much i unwholesome.

Quod satis est cui contingit, nihil amplius optet.

HORACE
Epistles (Latin,

Let him who has enough wish for nothing more.

Semper avarus eget: certum voto pete finem.

HORACE
Epistles (Latin,

He who is greedy is always in want; maintain a fixed limit to your desires.

Semper inops quicumque cupit.

CLAUDIAN.
In Rufinum (Latin)

The covetous man is always poor.

Avarus animus nullo satiatur lucro.

LATIN PROVERB

No gain satisfies a greedy mind.

Venum cuncta dari.

CLAUDIAN:
In Rufinum (Latin)

Everything has its price.

Nec tamen inviso pectus mihi carpitur auro,
Nec bibit e gemma divite nostra sitis

PROPERTIUS:
Elegies (Latin)

My heart does not hanker after gold, no matter how desirable, nor do I thirst to drink from a jewelled flask.

GREMLINS

Will ich mein Küchel gehn,
Will mein Süpplein kochen,
Steht ein bucklicht Männlein da,
Hat mein Töpflein brochen.

GERMAN FOLKTALE

When I go to the kitchen to make my soup, I find that the little hunchback there has broken my little saucepan.

Es gibt ein Gespenst,
Das frisst Taschentücher.

CHRISTIAN MORGENSTERN:
Gespenst (German)

There is a ghost that eats handkerchiefs (referring to the way in which handkerchiefs get lost on a journey).

GRIEF
see also Anger, Despair, Emotion, Life, Philosophy, Pleasure, Sorrow, Tears, Time, Widows and widowers, Youth.

Roi gaṁvāē bāraha māsā;
Sahasa sahasa dukha eka eka sāṁsā;
Tila tila barasa barasa jimi jāī;
Pahara pahara juga juga nisarāi

MALIK MUHAMMAD JĀYASĪ:
Padumāvatī (Avadhi)

Twelve months have I lost in weeping; a thousand sorrows in every sigh. Every moment becomes a year, and every watch stretches into an age.

Tā sauṁ dukha kahiē ē bīrā;
Jehi suni kai lāgai para pīrā

MALIK MUHAMMAD JĀYASĪ:
Padumāvatī (Avadhi)

We should tell our woes to him who, on hearing them, is moved by another's sorrow.

Mie sanon sinulle jällen,
Haastan mielihaikiani,
Sitte vaihamma vajoja,
Kahenkesken kaihojamme.

The Kanteletar (Finnish)

In sympathy I should like to tell you again of my bitter troubles so that, mutally, by recounting our grief, we can lighten each other's sorrow (the shepherd's song to the birds).

Haastan haavan lehtyisille,
Pakajan pajun vesoille;
Ne ei kerro kellenkänä,
Kuihkaele kullenkana.

The Kanteletar (Finnish)

The tale of my grief will stir the aspen and move a willow's tender shoots; they will keep my woe to themselves, and not even whisper anything of my sorrow.

Runo radalla rakettu.

BARTHOLDUS VHAEL:
Valitusruno (Finnish)

Sad the song from warfare welded.

La douleur est un fruit; Dieu ne le fait pas croitre
Sur la branche trop faible encor pour le porter.

VICTOR HUGO:
L'Enfance (French)

Sorrow is a fruit; God does not allow it to grow on a branch that is too weak to bear it.

La douleur trop contrainte aisément se redouble.

MOLIÈRE:
Le Dépit Amoureux (French)

If you suppress grief too much, it can well redouble.

Errōgen paga dakruōn

SOPHOCLES:
Trachiniae (Greek)

We could no longer hold back our tears.

All' oute klaiein out' oduresthai prepei
Mē kai teknōthēi dusphorōteros goos

AESCHYLUS:
The Seven against Thebes (Greek)

It is not fitting to grieve or weep, lest our sorrows grow still more unbearable.

Ti tauta penthein dei? Paroikhetai ponos

AESCHYLUS:
Agamemnon (Greek)

It's all over; why grieve over it?

Khronos gar eumarēs theos

SOPHOCLES:
Electra (Greek)

Gentle time will heal our sorrows.

It é saigthi gona súain,
cech trátha i n-aidchi adúair,
sercgoí.

Anonymous ninth-century Irish poet
(Irish Gaelic)

The arrows that murder sleep throughout the cold nights are our laments for love.

Levis est dolor qui capere consilium potest et clepere sese.

SENECA:
Medea (Latin)

Light is the grief that can take counsel and hide itself.

Non levat miseros dolor.

SENECA:
Hippolytus (Latin)

Grief is of no help to the wretched.

Sunt lacrimae rerum et mentem mortalia tangunt.

VIRGIL:
Aeneid (Latin)

They are not unacquainted with tears and the lot of mortals touches their heart.

Mortalis nemo est quem non attingit dolor.

CICERO:
paraphrasing Euripides *(Latin)*

There is no living man who has not experienced grief at one time or another.

Strangulat inclusus dolor atque exaestuat intus.
Cogitur et vires multiplicare suas.

OVID:
Tristia (Latin)

A suppressed grief chokes and seethes within, thereby multiplying its own strength.

Dolor aetatem iussit inesse suam.

BOETHIUS:
Consolatio Philosophiae (Latin)

Sorrow has stolen my youth.

Nec te tantus edat tacitam dolor.

VIRGIL:
Aeneid (Latin)

Feed not in silence on a grief so great.

Et tacitum vivit sub pectore vulnus.

VIRGIL:
Aeneid (Latin)

The wound festered silently in her breast.

Onde magoas levam alma
Vão tambem corpo levar.

BERNARDIM RIBEIRO:
Romance (Portuguese)

Wherever grief bears the soul, the body too must follow.

Bem sem fundamento
Tem certa a mudança,
Certo o sentimento
Na dôr da lembrança

LUIS DE CAMÕES:
Vae o Bem Fugindo (Portuguese)

Uncertain pleasure turns swiftly to certain sadness in our unhappy memories.

No hay dolor más grande que el dolor de ser vivo,
Ni mayor pesadumbre que la vida consciente.

RUBÉN DARÍO:
Lo Fatal (Spanish)

There is no greater grief than that of being alive, nor any greater affliction than conscious life.

El cielo en mis dolores
Cargó la mano tanto,
Que a sempiterno llanto
Y a triste soledad me ha condenado

GARCILASO DE LA VEGA:
Eclogues (Spanish)

Heaven has burdened me so heavily with grief that I am condemned to eternal weeping and sad solitude.

GUESTS

Lupoumenois okhlēros, ei moloi, xenos

EURIPIDES:
Alcestis (Greek)

On the day of a funeral no guests are welcome.

El huesped y el pez hieden al tercero dia.
SPANISH PROVERB

Guests and fish stink on the third day.

GUIDANCE
see also Leadership.

Ond'io per lo tuo me' penso e discerno,
Che tui mi segui, ed io sarò tua guida.
DANTE:
Inferno (Italian)

Wherefore I think and discern this for thy best,
that thou follow me; and I will be thy guide.

Viam qui nescit, qua deveniat ad mare,
Eum oportet amnen quaerere comitem sibi.
PLAUTUS:
Poenulus (Latin)

If you don't know the way to the sea, take a river
as your travelling companion.

GUIDES

Yā rayt kānū al-mutarjimīn kulla-hum yikhrasū
ARAB PROVERB

If only all guides were dumb!

H

HABITS
see also Fastidiousness.

Al-'āda khāmis ṭabi'a

ARAB PROVERB

Habits are second (*lit.* fifth) nature.

Das verzogene Treusein einer Gewohnheit.

RAINER MARIA RILKE:
Duineser Elegien (German)

The gnarled fidelity of an old habit.

Quem mater amictum dedit, sollicite custodire.

LATIN PROVERB

Do not give up the habits formed in early youth
(*lit.* take care to keep the cloak your mother gave
you).

Aegre reprendas quod sinas consuescere.

LATIN PROVERB
(quoted in St. Jerome's *Epistles*)

We resent reproof for the habits we have acquired.

HAIR
see also Beauty.

Et, pour mieux couronner ma jeune Fiancée,
Amour qui fait tout bien, docile à ma pensée,
Mêle à ses noirs cheveux quelque neige de fleurs.

CHARLES-AUGUSTIN SAINTE-BEUVE:
Sonnet (French)

And the better to crown my beloved, love that
does everything well, submissive to my thought,
has mixed a sprinkling of snowy blossoms in the
deep black of her hair.

Fuis le miroir séduisant
Où tu nattes à présent
L'or de tes cheveux de fée.

FRANÇOIS COPPÉE:
Sérénade du 'Passant' (French)

Leave that seductive mirror where you are plait-
ing your hair of fairy gold.

Cheveux bleus, pavillon de ténèbres tendues
Vous me rendez l'azur du ciel immense et rond.

CHARLES BAUDELAIRE:
La Chevelure (French)

Blue-black hair, tense frame of shadows, you
yield the vast dome of the azure heavens to me.

Hieros ho plokamos

EURIPIDES:
The Bacchae (Greek)

My hair is holy (a favourite passage for recita-
tion in Greek schools).

S'io avessi le belle treccie prese
Che fatte son per me scudiscio e ferza.

DANTE:
Canzone (Italian)

Had I only grasped the beautiful tresses that
have long been my lash and whip!

HANDS

Ses mains estoient blanches, longues, douil-
lettes,
Qui tressailloient en veines et rameaux,
Puis se fendoient en cinq frères jumeaux
Environnez de cinq bords de perlettes.

PIERRE DE RONSARD:
Elegie à Janet (French)

Long white and soft were her hands, throbbing
with veins and tiny delicate bones. They each
divided into five twin brothers crowned with
pearl-like fingernails.

C'était une main étrange, osseuse, aux fortes
jointures, aux veines noueuses, aux tendons sail-
lants, une main velue, surtout au bord externe
et cependant c'était une belle main.

MICHEL SERVIN
Les Réguliers (French

His hands were strange, bony, with strong
knuckles, knotty veins, prominent sinews –
hairy hands (particularly on the outer edges)
yet beautiful.

Desiderio delle tue mani chiare
Nella penombra della fiamma.
SALVATORE QUASIMODO:
Antico Inverno (Italian)

The desire of your hands, transparent in the penumbra of the flame.

HAPPINESS
see also Blessings, Common sense, Contentment, Despair, Disillusion, Emotion, Enjoyment, Fortune, the Golden age, Joy, Life, Love, Marriage, Nature, Oblivion, Pain, Pleasure, Principles, Sorrow, Wealth, Wisdom, Youth.

Ḥelu ad-dunyā, akhuḍ al-bitt, ag'od fī bulad abūk ummak mirid
ARAB PROVERB

The ideal life is to marry your girl and live in your parents' town for ever.

Al-jōza 'l-muṭī'ye, al-bulād ash-shibī'ye,
Ad-dābbe 's-sārī'ye, alkiswe 'l wāsī'ye,
Al-gamar ar-rābīḥe
ARAB PROVERB

Let your wife be obedient, your lands be rich, your cattle strong-limbed, your clothes ample, and a profitable moon [guide your steps].

De prijs blijft klein voor het mensche-geluk,
Al gaan duizendmall duizend harten stuk.
HENRIETTE ROLAND HOLST:
De Vrouw in het Woud (Dutch)

Yet the price is small for man's happiness, even though a thousand thousand hearts should break.

Tout bonheur que la main n'atteint pas n'est qu'un rêve.
JOSÉPHIN SOULARY:
Rêves Ambitieux (French)

Whatever good fortune we do not achieve is nought but a dream.

Il ne se faut jamais moquer des misérables:
Car qui peut s'assurer d'être toujours heureux?
JEAN DE LA FONTAINE:
La Lièvre et la Perdrix (French)

Never mock the unfortunate, for which of us can be certain of eternal happiness?

Oui, sans doute, tout meurt; ce monde est un grand rêve,
Et le peu de bonheur qui nous vient en chemin,
Nous n'avons pas plus tôt ce roseau dans la main,
Que le vent nous l'enlève.
ALFRED DE MUSSET:
Souvenir (French)

It is true that everything dies, and this world is but a dream. The little good fortune that we find on the way is like a slender reed which, no sooner in our hand, is wrested from us by the wind.

Chacun court après le bonheur.
P. A. C. DE BEAUMARCHAIS:
Le Barbier de Séville (French)

Everyone runs after happiness.

Nostre instinct nous fait sentir qu'il faut chercher nostre bonheur hors de nous.
BLAISE PASCAL:
Pensées (French)

Instinct teaches us to look for happiness outside ourselves.

Tous les hommes recherchent d'estre heureux; cela est sans exception.
BLAISE PASCAL:
Pensées (French)

Everyone, without exception, is searching for happiness.

La felicité est dans le goût, et non pas dans les choses.
FRANÇOIS, DUC DE LA ROCHEFOUCAULD:
Réflexions (French)

Happiness lies in taste and not in material things.

Nous nous tourmentons moins pour devenir heureux que pour faire croire que nous le sommes.
FRANÇOIS, DUC DE LA ROCHEFOUCAULD:
Réflexions (French)

We torture ourselves less to become happy than to make others believe that we are happy.

Le bonheur a ses tempêtes.
FELICIEN MARCEAU:
En de Secrêtes Noces (French)

Good luck has its storms.

D'aisi.m sent ric per bona sospeison,
Qu'en ioi m'afic e m'estau volentiers.
PEIRE D'ALVERNHE:
Sobre.l Vieill Trobar (French)

Through fine hopes I feel noble, for I cling to joy
and willingly remain with it.

All rennen nach dem Glück
Das Glück rennt hinterher.
BERTOLT BRECHT:
*Das Lied von der Unzulänglichkeit Menschlichen
Strebens (German)*

Everyone chases after happiness, [not noticing
that] happiness is at their heels.

Sei ewig glücklich,
Wie du mich liebst!
J. W. VON GOETHE:
Mailied (German)

If you love me, be happy for ever!

Die Welt des Glücklichen ist eine anders als die
des Unglücklichen.
LUDWIG WITTGENSTEIN:
Tractatus Logico-philosophicus (German)

The world of those who are happy is different
from the world of those who are not.

Oikoi menein dei ton kalōs eudaimona
GREEK PROVERB

He who would be happy should stay at home.

Eudaimones hoisi kakōn ageustos aiōn
SOPHOCLES:
Antigone (Greek)

Happy are those who have never tasted evil.

Thnētōn gar oudeis estin eudaimōn anēr
EURIPIDES:
Medea (Greek)

Happiness eludes the grasp of mankind.

En tōi phronein gar mēden ēdistos bios
SOPHOCLES:
Ajax (Greek)

Life's happiness is based on ignorance.

Halkuonides hēmerai
ARISTOPHANES:
The Birds (Greek)

Halcyon days.

Ita gaudiis gaudium suppeditat.
PLAUTUS:
Trinummus (Latin)

Joy is increased by other joys.

Quo modo enim potest beatus esse, si nihil sit?
ST. AUGUSTINE:
De Civitate Dei (Latin)

How can a man be happy if he is nothing?

Nemo tamen beatus est qui eo quod amat non
fruitur.
ST. AUGUSTINE:
De Civitate Dei (Latin)

No man is happy who does not come to enjoy
what he loves.

Laetitia est hominis transitio a minore ad
majorem perfectionem.
SPINOZA:
Ethics (Latin)

Happiness consists in man's progress from
minor to major perfection.

Felix qui potuit rerum cognoscere causas.
VIRGIL:
Georgics (Latin)

Happy is he who has been able to comprehend
the causes of things.

Gaudia
Sua si omnes homines conferant unum in locum,
Tamen mea exsuperet laetitia.
PUBLIUS JUVENTIUS CELSUS:
Fragment (Latin)

Even if everyone brought their happiness to one
single place, my joy would outweigh the whole of
theirs.

Alegria secreta candela muerta.

SPANISH PROVERB

Unshared joy is an unlighted candle.

¡Felicidad, no he de volver a hallarte
En la tierra, en el aire, ni en el cielo,
Aun cuando sé que existes
Y no eres vano sueño!

ROSALÍA CASTRO:
Ya No Sé (Spanish)

Happiness, I do not know where to turn to discover you on earth, in the air or the sky; yet I know you exist and are no futile dream.

Un ángulo me basta entre mis lares,
Un libro y un amigo, un sueño breve,
Que no perturben deudas ni pesares.

attrib. ANDRÉS FERNÁNDEZ DE ANDRADA:
Epístola Moral (Spanish)

Sufficient for me are a corner by the hearth, a book, a friend, and time enough for sleep, undisturbed by debts or sorrows.

HARDSHIPS
see also Distress, Sympathy.

Attenuatum te esse continuatione laborum cum audio et lego, di me perdant nisi cohorrescit corpus meum.

SUETONIUS:
Tiberius (Latin)

When I hear and read that you are worn out by constant hardships, may the Gods confound me if my own body does not wince in sympathy (Augustus in a letter to Tiberius).

HASTE
see also Hurry, Impetuousness.

Hâtez-vous lentement.

FRENCH PROVERB

Hasten slowly.

Eile mit Weile.

GERMAN PROVERB

More haste, less speed.

Gut Ding will nicht Eile haben.

GERMAN PROVERB

Good things are not done in a hurry.

Mēden agan speudein

THEOGNIS:
Fragment (Greek)

More haste, less speed.

Festina lente.

LATIN PROVERB

Hasten slowly.

Gratis anhelans, multa agendo nihil agens.

PHAEDRUS:
Fables (Latin)

Breathless for no reason and busy doing nothing.

HATRED
see also Benefits and benefactors, Calumny, Dictatorship, Evil, Ingratitude, Injustice, Justice, Kings, Reconciliation, Self–love, Truth, Women.

La perte que j'ai faite est trop irréparable,
La source de ma haine est trop inépuisable;
A l'egal de mes jours je la ferai durer;
Je veux vivre avec elle, avec elle expirer.

PIERRE CORNEILLE:
Pompée (Cornélie's closing speech) (French)

My loss is irreparable; the source of my hatred is inexhaustible; I shall make my hate last throughout my lifetime – I want to live with it, and die with it still unquenched.

Tous hommes se haïssent naturellement l'un l'autre.

BLAISE PASCAL:
Pensées (French)

It is natural for all men to hate each other.

Der Hass ist so gut erlaubt als die Liebe, und ich hege ihn im vollsten Masse gegen die, welche ihn verachten.

GEORG BÜCHNER:
letter to his family, February 1824

Hatred is just as permissible as love, and I cherish it in fullest measure against those who despise others.

Selig wer sich vor der Welt
Ohne Hass verschliesst.

J. W. VON GOETHE:
Der Mondlied (German)

Happy is he who can turn away from the world without hatred.

Deinē tis orgē kai dusiatos pelei,
Hotan philoi philoisi sumbalōs' erin

EURIPIDES:
Medea (Greek)

The worst, the least curable hatred is that which has superseded deep love.

Kai gar adikeisthai doxantes autoi pephukasi misein

PLUTARCH:
Moralia (Greek)

It is men's nature to hate when they believe they have been wronged.

Kreisson de moi nun pros s' apekhthesthai gunai,
Ē malthakisthenth' husteron mega stenein

EURIPIDES:
Medea (Greek)

I shall do far better to gain your hatred now, than to yield and bitterly regret it later.

Men her mod Slægten, slap og lad,
Ens bedste Kærlighed er Had!
Had! Had!

HENRIK IBSEN:
Brand (Norwegian)

This generation, slack as it is and slow, proves that hatred is the best love to bestow . . . Hate! Hate!

HEALTH
see also Moderation, Philosophy.

Ash-shidda 'alạ 'llah

ARAB PROVERB

Health comes from God (lit. health is God's responsibility).

Itg̲h̲addạ wa itmaddạ wa it'ashsha wa it-mashshạ

ARAB PROVERB

After dinner, rest awhile; after supper, walk a mile.

C'est une ennuyeuse maladie que de conserver sa santé par un trop grand régime.

FRANÇOIS, DUC DE LA ROCHEFOUCAULD:
Maximes (French)

What a troublesome affliction to have to preserve one's health by too strict a régime.

Ut sit mens sana in corpore sano.

JUVENAL:
Satires (Latin)

May a healthy mind dwell in a healthy body.

Pars sanitatis velle sanari fuit.

SENECA:
Hippolytus (Latin)

The desire to be healed has always been part of health.

Nihil interest valeam ipse necne, si tu non valebis.

SUETONIUS:
Tiberius (Latin)

It matters not whether I am well or not, if you are not well (Augustus, in a letter to Tiberius).

HELL

L'enfer ne peut attaquer les païens.

ARTHUR RIMBAUD:
Mauvais Sang (French)

Hell has no terrors for pagans.

Car sache que, dans les Enfers, il n'est pas d'autre châtiment que de recommencer toujours le geste inachevé de la vie.

ANDRÉ GIDE
(French)

You must understand that in Hell there is no other punishment than to begin over and over again the tasks left unfinished in your lifetime.

Lasciate ogni speranza, voi ch'entrate.

DANTE:
Inferno (Italian)

Abandon all hope, ye that enter here.

HEROES
see also Bravery, God, Greatness, Oblivion.

Nous, on a trop de héros. Et trop de gloire et d'or sur nos héros.

JEAN GENET:
Les Paravents (French)

We've got too many heroes – and we have heaped too much glory and gold on our heroes.

Man darf Heldentaten nicht in der Nähe betrachten.

THEODOR FONTAINE:
Ein Sommer in London (German)

Heroic acts should not be too closely examined.

. . . es erhält sich der Held, selbst der Untergang war ihm
Nur ein Vorwand, zu sein: seine letzte Geburt.

RAINER MARIA RILKE:
Duineser Elegien (German)

The hero keeps up the struggle. Even his destruction is only a pretext for achieving his final birth.

Wunderlich nah ist der Held doch den jugendlich Toten.

RAINER MARIA RILKE:
Duineser Elegien (German)

Strangely near is the hero to those who died young.

Hērōōn oligai men en ommasin, hai d' eti loipai patrides ou pollōi g' aiputerai pediōn

ALPHEIOS OF MYTILENE:
Anthologia Palatina (Greek)

Few heroes' homes have survived, and these hardly rise above the ground.

Unus homo nobis vigilando restituit rem.

SUETONIUS:
Tiberius (Latin)

One man alone, by his watchfulness, has saved our country from ruin.

HESITATION
see also Action, Procrastination.

C'est hasarder notre vengeance que de la reculer.

MOLIÈRE:
Don Juan (French)

We put our revenge at risk if we postpone it.

Mein Flügel ist zum Schwung bereit,
Ich kehrte gern zurück.

GERHARD SCHOLEM:
Gruss vom Angelus (German)

Though my wings are ready for flight, I would fain turn back.

At trahere, atque moras tantis licet addere rebus.

VIRGIL:
Aeneid (Latin)

Yet I may prolong the process and cause delay in events so momentous (*tr.* Jackson Knight).

Etiam nunc regredi possumus; quod si ponticulum transierimus, omnia armis agenda erunt.

SUETONIUS:
Divus Iulius (Latin)

Even now we can draw back – but once we cross that little bridge, we must settle things by the sword (Julius Caesar's words to his troops as they prepare to cross the Rubicon).

HISTORY
see also Life, Poets and poetry,
Prudence, Tradition.

Le passé n'est qu'un croyance.

> PAUL VALÉRY:
> *Lust (French)*

The past is only belief.

Les peuples heureux n'ont pas d'histoire. L'histoire est la science du malheur des hommes.

> RAYMOND QUENEAU:
> *Une Histoire Modéle (French)*

Happy nations have no history. History is the study of mankind's misfortunes.

Presque toute l'Histoire n'est qu'une suite d'horreurs.

> S. R. N. CHAMFORT:
> *Maximes et Pensées (French)*

Almost the whole of history is but a sequence of horrors.

L'histoire n'est que le tableau des crimes et des malheurs.

> VOLTAIRE:
> *L'Ingénu (French)*

History is nought but a list of crime and calamity.

Je veux faire parler les silences de l'histoire.

> JULES MICHELET:
> lecture, 1839 *(French)*

I want to make heard those aspects on which history has kept silent.

L'histoire ne servira à rien si on n'y met les tristesses du présent.

> JULES MICHELET:
> lecture, 1839 *(French)*

History is useless if one does not look at it in the light of current misfortunes.

Moi, avec un texte, je fais mieux que d'autres avec cinquante.

> JULES MICHELET:
> lecture, 1839 *(French)*

I can do more with a single text than others can do with fifty.

J'ai violé l'histoire, mais je lui ai fait des enfants

> ALEXANDRE DUMAS pè
> *(French*

I may have raped history, but at least I hav given her some children!

Geschichte berichtet, wie es gewesen. Er zählung spielt eine Möglichkeit durch.

> ALFRED ANDERSCH
> *Winterspelt (German*

History tells how it was. A story, how it migh have been.

Die Weltgeschichte ist das Weltgericht.

> J. C. F. VON SCHILLER
> *Resignation (German*

The history of the world is the verdict of th world.

Ein Mensch der kein Gefühl für Geschichte hat ist wie einer ohne Augen und Ohren.

> ADOLF HITLE
> *(German*

Anyone who has no feeling for history is like man who is both blind and deaf.

Die Geschichte der Welt ist sich selbst gleich wi die Gesetze der Natur und einfach wie die Seel des Menschen. Dieselben Bedingungen bringer dieselben Erscheinungen zurück.

> J. F. C. VON SCHILLER
> lecture, 1789 *(German*

The world's history is constant, like the laws o nature, and simple, like the souls of men. The same conditions continually produce the same results.

Amandae sunt artes, at reverenda est historia.

> F. A. WOLF
> *Homeri et Homeridarum Opera e*
> *Reliquiae* (preface) *(Latin*

The arts are to be loved, but history must be respected.

Quien mira lo pasado
Lo porvenir advierte.

> LOPE DE VEGA
> *Égloga a Claudio (Spanish*

To observe the past is to take warning for the future.

Cada edad tiene sus emociones.
>GREGORIO MARTÍNEZ SIERRA:
>*El Reino de Dios (Spanish)*

Every age has its own feelings.

Las brumas quedan de la falsa gloria
Que brota de la historia.
>MIGUEL DE UNAMUNO:
>*En Gredos (Spanish)*

The mists remain of the false glory that erupts
from history.

HOME
see also Fatherland, Marriage, Moderation, Oblivion, Patriotism.

Und wann ich hame geh
Scheint der Mond so scheh.
>GERMAN FOLK SONG:

When I go home, the moon shines so beautifully.

Da wo wir lieben,
Ist Vaterland;
Wo wir geniessen
Ist Hof und Haus.
>J. W. VON GOETHE:
>*Felsweihegesang an Psyche (German)*

The place we love is our fatherland; where we
enjoy ourselves, that is hearth and home.

Die Krähen schrein
Und ziehen schwirren Flugs zur Stadt:
Bald wird es schnein. –
Wohl dem, der jetzt noch Heimat hat!
>FRIEDRICH NIETZSCHE:
>*Vereinsamt (German)*

The crows screech, and make whirring swoops
over the city. Soon it will snow. Happy then he
who still has a home to go to.

Tu nidam servas.
>HORACE:
>*Epistles (Latin)*

You keep to your nest (*i.e.* home)

Plus habet hic vitae, plus habet ille viae.
>CLAUDIAN:
>*Poems (Latin)*

One [the wanderer] has more journeys, but the
other [the homedweller] has more of life.

HONESTY
see also Frankness, Temptation, Wealth.

Il y a peu de métiers honnêtement exercés, ou
peu d'honnêtes gens dans leurs métiers.
>DENIS DIDEROT:
>*Le Neveu de Rameau (French)*

Either there are too few professions conducted
honestly, or there are too few honest people in
their professions.

On m'a toujours appelé l'Ingénu, parceque je
dis toujours naïvement ce que je pense, comme
je fais tout ce que je veux.
>VOLTAIRE:
>*L'Ingénu (French)*

Everyone calls me the Naïve, because I always
innocently say what I think, just as I do everything I want to do.

Khronos dikaion andra deiknusin monos
>SOPHOCLES:
>*Oedipus Tyrannus (Greek)*

Honesty can only be proved in time.

Probitas laudatur et alget.
>JUVENAL:
>*Satires (Latin)*

Honesty is praised, but left to shiver.

Quaerenda pecunia primum est;
Virtus post nummos!
>HORACE:
>*Epistles (Latin)*

Honesty – after the first million! (*lit.* first get
after the money; virtue comes after coin).

Bonus sermo secreta non quaerit.
>ST. JEROME:
>*Letter to Pacatula (Latin)*

If you have nothing to hide, let your words be
heard by everyone (*lit.* honest words seek no
quiet retreat).

Nam si a me regnum, fortuna atque opes
Eripere quivit, at virtutem non quit.
>ACCIUS:
>*Fragment (Latin)*

Even if fortune has succeeded in robbing me of
my kingdom and my wealth, at least she cannot
steal my honesty.

Puras Deus non plenas aspicit manus.
                          LATIN PROVERB

God takes notice of clean hands, not full hands.

Non omne quod licet honestum est.
                          LATIN PROVERB

Not everything that is permitted is honest.

Verbum meum pactum.
              Motto of the London Stock Exchange

My word is my bond.

HONOUR

see also Bravery, Conscience, Fame, Glory,
Greatness, Honesty, Integrity, Loyalty,
Materialism, Money, Poverty, Smoking,
Truth, Virtue, War.

Mourant sans déshonneur, je mourrai sans
regret.
                    PIERRE CORNEILLE:
                          Le Cid (French)

If I die without dishonour, I have no regrets.

L'amour n'est qu'un plaisir, l'honneur est un
devoir.
                    PIERRE CORNEILLE:
                          Le Cid (French)

Love is only a pleasure, honour is a duty.

Elle me résistat, je l'ai assassinée.
                    ALEXANDRE DUMAS:
                          Antony (French)

She resisted me, and I killed her! (Antony's
words in the dénouement of the play, where
Antony kills his mistress to save her honour).

J'appelle un honnête homme celui à qui le récit
d'une bonne action rafraîchit le sang, et un
malhonnête celui qui cherche chicane à une
bonne action.
                    S. R. N. CHAMFORT:
Caractères et Anecdotes, Appendix 1 (French)

My definition of an honourable man is one who
is inspired by the story of a good deed; while a
dishonourable man is one who tries to quibble at
a good deed (attrib. M. de Mauran).

Eiper kakon pheroi tis, aiskhunēs ater
Estō. Monon gar kerdos en tethnēkosi
                          AESCHYLUS:
                    The Seven against Thebes (Greek)

If we fall on evil days, let us avoid dishonour –
for honour is our only gain in death.

                    Toisi gennaioisi toi
To t' aiskhron ekhthron kai to khrēston euklees
                          SOPHOCLES:
                          Philoctetes (Greek)

A noble soul will reject what is shameful, and
embrace what is good.

Aesopo ingentem statuam posuere Attici,
Servumque collocarunt aeterna in basi,
Patere honoris scirent ut cunctis viam.
                          PHAEDRUS:
                          Epilogues (Latin)

The Athenians erected a large statue to Aesop,
thus putting a slave on a permanent pedestal
and demonstrating that honour is within
everyone's grasp.

La honra el trono de la entereza.
                          SPANISH PROVERB

Honour is the throne of integrity.

¡Ay, honra, al fin sofística inventora
De tantas ceremonias y locuras!
                          LOPE DE VEGA:
              Los Comendadores de Córdoba (Spanish)

Honour! What is it in the end but the sophisti-
cated contrivance of so many ceremonies and
follies!

Más no hará, que el mundo alaba
Al marido varonil
Que la honra en sangre vil
De los adúlteros lava
                          TIRSO DE MOLINA:
                          El Celoso Prudente (Spanish)

There will be no more occasions when the world
praises the manly husband who cleanses his
honour in the vile blood of the adulterer.

El honor
s patrimonio del alma.
>PEDRO CALDERÓN DE LA BARCA:
>*El Alcalde de Zalamea (Spanish)*

Honour is the patrimony of the soul.

'uve amor y tengo honor.
>PEDRO CALDERÓN DE LA BARCA:
>*El Médico de su Honra (Spanish)*

Once I had love, now I have honour.

Honor
'engo y las palabras cumplo,
orque caballero soy.
>TIRSO DE MOLINA:
>*El Burlador de Sevilla (Spanish)*

Being a gentleman, I am honorable and I keep
my word.

HOPE
see also Chance, Despair, Fear, Hell, Last words, Life, Love, Mortality, Music, Old age, Patience, Wisdom, Women.

Dawām al-ḥāl min al-muḥāl
>ARAB PROVERB

It's a long lane that has no turning.

Onen i–Estel Edain, ú–chebin estel anim.
>J. R. R. TOLKIEN:
>*The Return of the King* (Appendix A) *(Elvish)*

I gave hope to the Dúnedain, I have kept no
hope for myself.

L'espérance n'est qu'un Charlatan qui nous
rompe sans cesse.
>S. R. N. CHAMFORT:
>*Maximes et Pensées (French)*

Hope is but a charlatan who always deceives us.

L'espérance et la crainte sont inséparables, et
il n'y a point de crainte sans espérance, ni
d'espérance sans crainte.
>FRANÇOIS, DUC DE LA ROCHEFOUCAULD:
>*Réflexions (French)*

Hope and fear are inseparable: you cannot have
fear without hope, and you cannot have hope
without fear.

Le seul espoir de l'homme est la découverte de
moyens d'action qui diminuent son mal et
accroissent son bien.
>PAUL VALÉRY:
>*Quelques Pensées de Monsieur Teste (French)*

Man's only hope is the discovery of some means
of action that will reduce his misfortunes and
increase his well-being.

Je parvins à faire s'évanouir dans mon esprit
toute l'espérance humaine.
>ARTHUR RIMBAUD:
>*Une Saison en Enfer (French)*

I contrived to purge my mind of all human hope.

L'illusion féconde habite dans mon sein.
D'une prison sur moi les murs pèsent en vain,
J'ai les ailes de l'espérance.
>ANDRÉ CHÉNIER:
>*La Jeune Captive (French)*

My heart is filled with fertile illusion; in my
prison the walls press hard on me in vain, for I
wear hope's wings.

Ich gesteh' es: ich
Habe keine Hoffnung.
>BERTOLT BRECHT:
>*Der Nachgeborene (German)*

I confess it – I have no hope.

Pas anēr k'an doulos ēi tis hēdetai to phōs
>GREEK PROVERB

Every man, even a slave, is glad to see the light.

Ha gar dē poluplanktos elpis pollois men onasis
andrōni
>SOPHOCLES:
>*Antigone (Greek)*

Tireless hope brings vantage to many.

Elpis aei biotou kleptei khronon
>JULIUS POLYAENUS:
>*Fragment (Greek)*

Hope keeps us going.

Tarbein men erga dein' anankaiōs ekhei,
Tēn d' elpid' ou khrē tēs tukhēs krinein paros
SOPHOCLES:
Trachiniae (Greek)

The situation is bad, but do not lose heart before
we know the outcome.

Spem iuvat amplecti.
OVID:
Ex Ponto (Latin)

It is good to embrace a hope.

Saepe aliquem sollers medicorum cura reliquit
Nec spes huic vena deficiente cadit.
OVID:
Ex Ponto (Latin)

Often has a man been abandoned by the skill
and care of his doctors but, though his pulse
fails, hope does not desert him.

Dum spiro spero.
Sir David Lindsay's motto
(Latin)

While there's life there's hope (*lit.* while I
breathe I hope).

THE HORIZON

Fugere ad puppim colles campique videntur.
LUCRETIUS:
De Rerum Natura (Latin)

The hills and fields seem to fly toward the ship.

HORROR

Horror ubique animos, simul ipsa silentia
terrent.
VIRGIL:
Aeneid (Latin)

All things were full of horror and affright,
And dreadful ev'n the silence of the night
(*tr.* Dryden).

HORSES
see also Leadership, Understanding.

Hippon   m' ōkupodōn amphi ktupos ouat
ballei
HOMER
Iliad (Greek

Listen! now I can hear the trampling hooves o
the swift-footed coursers!

Vedut ko mne konya; v razdolii otkrȳtom,
Makhaya grivoyu, on vsadnika nesët,
I zvonko pod ego blistayushchim kopȳtom
Zvenit promërzlȳĭ dol, i treskaetsya lëd.
ALEKSANDR SERGEEVICH PUSHKIN
Osen' (Russian

The horse they bring me shakes its mane an
carries me off through the wide open spaces
The frozen valley echoes the resonant clatter o
its hooves as they strike sparks from the cracking
ice.

HOSPITALITY

Au clair de la lune,
Mon ami Peirrot,
Prête-moi ta plume
Que j'écrive un mot.
Ma chandelle est morte,
Je n'ai plus de feu;
Ouvre-moi ta porte,
Pour l'amour de Dieu.
FRENCH FOLK-SONG

Lend me your pen, friend Pierrot, so that I can
write a note by moonlight. My candle has gone
out, and I have no more matches. Open your
door, for the love of God!

HUMAN NATURE
see also Faults, Mankind.

Ce qui m'estonne le plus est de voir que tout le
monde n'est pas estonné de sa faiblesse.
BLAISE PASCAL
Pensées (French

What astonishes me most of all is to see that men
are not astonished by their own frailty.

Être humain, c'est sentir vaguement, qu'il y a de tous dans chacun, et de chacun dans tous.

PAUL VALÉRY:
Mauvaises Pensées (French)

To be human is to feel vaguely that there is something of everyone in each of us, and something of each of us in everyone.

. . . ce n'est pas sur l'habit
Que la diversité me plaît, c'est dans l'esprit.

JEAN DE LA FONTAINE:
Le Singe et le Léopard (French)

Diversity of spirit rather than of clothing pleases me best.

Je te salue maria,
A qui dieu son filz maria
A humaine fragilité.

BODLEIAN MS. DOUCE: 252:
(French)

I hail thee, Mary! – God united his son with human frailty.

Je suis maître de moi comme de l'univers.

PIERRE CORNEILLE:
Cinna (French)

I am master of myself as of the universe.

Humanität ist der Schatz and die Ausbeute aller menschlichen Bemühungen.

J. G. HERDER:
Briefe zu Beförderung der Humanität (German)

Humanity is the wealth, the produce of all human efforts.

Was ist das, was in uns lügt, hurt, stielt, und mordet?

GEORG BÜCHNER:
Dantons Tod (German)

What is it inside us that lies, whores, steals and murders?

Je mehr du fühlst, ein Mensch zu sein,
Desto ähnlicher bist du den Göttern!

J. W. VON GOETHE:
Zahme Xenien (German)

The more you feel you are a human being, the more you resemble the gods!

Heut bedarf's der kleinsten Reise
Zum vollgütigen Beweise,
Dass wir mehr als Fische sind.

J. W. VON GOETHE:
Faust (German)

We have only to travel a little distance today to prove conclusively that we are more than fishes.

Ein Mensch bleibt was er ist.

J. W. VON GOETHE:
(German)

A man remains what he is.

. . . non ciascun segno
È buono, ancor che buona sia la cera.

DANTE:
Purgatorio (Italian)

Not every seal is good, even though the wax may be good.

Idque apud imperitos humanitas vocabatur, cum pars servitutis esset.

TACITUS:
Agricola (Latin)

What fools called 'humanity' was, in effect, a kind of slavery.

Det er underligt med den Menneskeart;
Den hænger i saa mærkværdigt længe.

HENRIK IBSEN:
Peer Gynt (Norwegian)

It's a funny thing, this human nature! it clings to a man with such persistence.

At være sig selv, er: sig selv at døde
HENRIK IBSEN:
Peer Gynt (Norwegian)

To be one's self is to slay one's self (*i.e.* to kill the base part of one's nature so that one's better self may live).

HUMILITY
see also Accuracy.

Jhesu Roy de tout le monde
En qui toute bonté habonde
Je suis ta povre creature.
BODLEIAN MS. DOUCE 252
(French)

Lord Jesus, ruler of the world, in whom dwells every bounty, I am your lowly creature.

Je vous supplie, ô Dieu! de regarder mon âme,
Et de considérer
Qu'humble comme un enfant et doux comme une femme,
Je viens vous adorer!
VICTOR HUGO:
A Villequier (French)

Oh God, I beg you to look into my soul where you will see that with the humility of a child and the compassion of a woman I come to worship you!

L'humilité est l'autel sur lequel Dieu veut qu'on lui offre des sacrifices.
FRANÇOIS, DUC DE LA ROCHEFOUCAULD:
Réflexions (French)

Humility is the altar on which God wants us to offer our sacrifices.

Herr, ich bin ein arm und kaum noch glühend Döchtlein am Altare deiner Gnade.
ANNETTE VON DROSTE-HÜLSHOFF:
Das Geistliche Jahr (German)

Lord, I am a poor, small, scarcely-glowing candle on the altar of thy grace.

Fuge magna: licet sub paupere tecto
Reges et regum vita praecurrere amicos.
HORACE:
Epistles (Latin)

Flee grandeur: though humble be your home, yet in life's race you may outstrip kings and the friends of kings.

Oblatio humilitatis. LATIN EXPRESSION

The offering of humility.

HUMOUR
see also Life.

Ne plaisantez pas avec l'humeur
L'humeur c'est sérieux!
JACQUES PRÉVERT:
Définir l'Humeur (French)

Don't joke about humour – humour is serious!

HUNGER
see also Appetite, Compromise, Conscience, Greed, Idleness, Integrity, Love, Poverty.

Maḍagh aḍ-ḍurūs mā bemla 'l kurūsh
ARAB PROVERB

Grinding one's teeth does not fill one's belly.

Quicumvis depugno multo facilius quam cum fame.
PLAUTUS:
Stichus (Latin)

I can fight anyone more easily than hunger.

Quis potest sine offula vivere?
SUETONIUS:
Divus Claudius (Latin)

Who can live without a snack?

HUNTERS AND HUNTING

Le gentilhomme croit sincèrement que la chasse est un plaisir grand et un plaisir royal; mais le piqueur n'est pas de ce sentiment-là.
BLAISE PASCAL:
Pensées (French)

The master is sincerely convinced that hunting is a great, nay, a royal pleasure; his beaters are not of that opinion.

J'aime le son du Cor, le soir, au fond des bois,
Soit qu'il chante les pleurs de la biche aux abois,
Ou l'adieu du chasseur que l'écho faible accueille,
Et que le vent du nord porte de feuille en feuille.
ALFRED DE VIGNY:
Le Cor (French)

I love to hear the sound of the horn deep in the woods – whether it records the whining of the cowering animal or the farewell of the hunter as he hears the distant sound, brought by the north wind through the foliage.

Aliter catuli longe olent, aliter sues.   PLAUTUS:
Epiducus (Latin)

Hounds and the hunted have different smells (*lit.* puppies and pigs have different smells).

Torva leaena lupum sequitur, lupus ipse capellam;
Florentem cytisum sequitur lasciva capella.
VIRGIL:
Eclogues (Latin)

The greedy lioness the wolf pursues, the wolf the kid, the wanton kid the browse (*tr.* Dryden).

HUSBANDS
see also Honour, Marriage, Widows and widowers, Wives.

Jinha ghara kaṁtā tē sukhī, tinha gārava tinha garaba;
Kaṁta piyarē bāhirai hama sukha bhūlā saraba
MALIK MUHAMMAD JĀYASĪ:
Padumāvatī (Avadhi)

Only those whose husbands are home are happy – theirs is the honour and the pride. My dearest husband is abroad, and I have forgotten all my happiness.

On peut changer d'amant, mais non changer d'époux.
PIERRE CORNEILLE:
Horace (French)

You can change one lover for another, but not a husband.

Pour aimer un mari l'on ne hait pas ses frères.
PIERRE CORNEILLE:
Horace (French)

Because you love your husband, you don't have to hate his brothers.

Vieux époux,
Vieux jaloux,
Tirez tous
Les verrous.   FRENCH SONG

Aged husband, jealous old man, mind you pull the bolts.

HYPOCRISY
see also Adultery, Argument.

Heureusement je n'ai pas besoin d'être hypocrite; il y en a déjà tant de toutes les couleurs, sans compter ceux qui le sont avec eux-mêmes.
DENIS DIDEROT:
Le Neveu de Rameau (French)

Fortunately I have no need to be a hypocrite; there are already so many hypocrites of all shapes and sizes, not to mention those who are even hypocritical to themselves.

La profession d'hypocrite a de merveilleux avantages!
MOLIÈRE:
Don Juan (French)

Being a hypocrite has marvellous advantages!

L'hypocrisie est un vice à la mode, et tous les vices à la mode passent pour vertus.
MOLIÈRE:
Don Juan (French)

Hypocrisy is a fashionable vice, and all fashionable vices pass for virtues.

Sois hypocrite, si tu veux; mais ne parle pas comme l'hypocrite!
DENIS DIDEROT:
Le Neveu de Rameau (French)

Be a hypocrite if you like; but don't talk like one!

L'hypocrisie est un hommage que le vice rend à la vertu.
FRANÇOIS, DUC DE LA ROCHEFOUCAULD:
Réflexions (French)

Hypocrisy is the homage that vice offers to virtue.

Hypocrita dicitur, qui alterius repraesentat personam, sicut in spectaculis fieri consuevit.
ST. THOMAS AQUINAS:
On Princely Government (Latin)

A hypocrite is one who pretends to take the part of another, as in a play.

I

IDEALISM
see also Poets and poetry, Politics.

Bestünde nur die Weisheit mit der Jugend
Und Republiken ohne Tugend,
So wär die Welt dem höchsten Ziele nah.

J. W. VON GOETHE:
Faust (subsequently omitted) *(German)*

If only there were wisdom with youth, and
republics without virtue, the world would be
close to its highest goal.

So geschieht es denn nicht selten, dass [der
Idealist] über dem unbegrenzten Ideale den
begrenzten Fall der Anwendung übersiehet
und, von einem Maximum erfüllt, das
Minimum verabsäumt, aus dem noch alles
Grosse in der Wirklichkeit erwächst.

J. C. F. VON SCHILLER:
*Über Naive und Sentimentalische
Dichtung (German)*

Thus, it frequently happens that [the idealist],
taken up with a boundless ideal, overlooks the
limited instances to which it is applicable and,
inspired by what is greatest, spurns what is
smallest, from which after all everything that is
great in reality derives.

IDEAS
see also Evil, Knowledge, Painters and
painting, Thought and thinking.

Une idée c'est un nain géant qu'il faut surveiller
nuit et jour; car l'idée qui rampait hier à vos
pieds, demain dominera votre tête. Une idée
c'est l'étincelle qui tombe sur le chaume; il faut
de bons yeux en plein jour pour deviner les
commencements de l'incendie.

ALEXANDRE DUMAS:
La Dame de Monsoreau (French)

An idea is a giant dwarf that one must keep one's
eyes on night and day, for the idea which today
crawls at your feet will dominate your head
tomorrow. An idea is like the spark that falls on
the thatch; you need to have good eyes even in
daylight to predict the outbreak of the blaze.

Les idées n'ont de valeur que transitive.

PAUL VALÉRY
Mauvaises Pensées (French

Ideas have only transitory worth.

Un homme sérieux a peu d'idées. Un homme à
idées n'est jamais sérieux.

PAUL VALÉRY
Mauvaises Pensées (French,

Serious-minded people have few ideas. People
with ideas are never serious.

Die Idee ist nicht so ohnmächtig es nur zu Idee
zu bringen.

FRIEDRICH HEGEL
(German)

An idea is not so powerless that it cannot make
itself into more than an idea.

Falsche Begriffe und schlechtes Wissen können
durch Belehrung beseitigt werden.

ADOLF HITLER
(German)

False ideas and poor knowledge can be set aside
by correction.

Serere arbores alteri fortasse saeculo profuturas.

HUGO GROTIUS:
Pax Christiana (Latin)

To sow trees (*i.e.* ideas) which may perhaps be
useful to another century.

Las cosas claras y el chocolate espeso.

SPANISH PROVERB

Ideas should be clear and chocolate thick.

Las cabezas toman también la forma de las ideas
que se les meten dentro.

CAMBA:
Aventuras de una Peseta (Spanish)

Heads also take the form of the ideas that are put
into them.

IDLENESS
see also Laziness, Love, Misery, Old age, Pleasure, Poverty, Purity, Work.

Tomaḵāt lel-maskīn khusāra

ARAB PROVERB

A poor man cannot afford to be lazy (lit. yawning means trouble to the poor man).

Ar-rijl ar-roāga, yabuddina tajīb as-sāha

ARAB PROVERB

Satan finds mischief for idle hands to do (lit. a wandering foot will surely bring its possessor to shame).

Nous avons plus de paresse dans l'esprit que dans le corps.

FRANÇOIS, DUC DE LA ROCHEFOUCAULD:
Réflexions (French)

We are lazier in our minds than in our bodies.

Il n'est pire eau que l'eau qui dort.

FRENCH PROVERB

There's no worse water than standing water.

Ich glaube, dass die Quelle des meisten menschlichen Elends in Indolenz und Weichlichkeit liegt. Die Nation, die die meiste Spannkraft hatte, war auch allezeit die freiste und glücklichste.

GEORG CHRISTOPH LICHTENBERG:
Aphorismen (German)

I believe that the source of most human misery is indolence and sloth. The nation that has the most vigour is also always the freest and the happiest.

Limos gar toi pampan aergōi sumphonos andri

HESIOD:
Works and Days (Greek)

Hunger is a suitable comrade for the work-shy.

La góla, e 'l sónno, e l'ozióse piume
Hanno del móndo ogni cirtù sbandita

FRANCESCO PETRARCA:
Sonnets (Italian)

Gluttony, sleep, and idleness have banished all virtue from this world.

Satius est otiosum esse quam nihil agere.

ERASMUS:
Adages (Latin)

Better to do something idle than nothing at all.

Nemo rationem otii sui reddere cogeretur.

SUETONIUS:
Galba (Latin)

No-one can be forced to render an account for doing nothing.

Min jorqod ma jaqbadx ħut.

MALTESE PROVERB

A sleepy man catches no fish.

Más vale bien holgar que mal trabajar.

SPANISH PROVERB

Better to idle well than to work badly.

IGNORANCE

L'ignorance vacille entre extrême audace et extrême timidité.

PAUL VALÉRY:
Choses Tues (French)

Ignorance vacillates between extreme audacity and extreme timidity.

Kaitoi ti meizon amathias tekmērion ē epeidan tis sophois andrasi diapherētai?

PLATO:
Hippias Minor (Greek)

What greater proof of ignorance is there than when we disagree with a wise man?

To ge mēn agnoein estin ep' alētheian hormōmenēs psukhēs, paraphorou suneseōs gignomenēs, ouden allo plēn paraphrosunē

PLATO:
The Sophist (Greek)

Ignorance is but the failure of the soul when, by error, it misses its target of truth.

En tōi phronein gar mēden hēdistos bios

SOPHOCLES:
Ajax (Greek)

To be ignorant is life's greatest joy!

Nec me pudet ut istos fateri nescire quid nesciam.

CICERO:
Tusculan Disputations (Latin)

I am not ashamed like them to confess ignorance of what I do not know.

Quantum est quod nescimus!

Motto of Daniel Heinsius of Ghent
(Latin)

What a lot of things we do not know!

Nescire quaedam, magna pars
Sapientiae est.

HUGO GROTIUS:
Docta Ignorantia (last lines) *(Latin)*

Not to know something is a great part of wisdom.

Nihil turpius quam cognitionem assertionem praecurrere.

CICERO:
Academica (Latin)

Nothing is more shameful than assertion without knowledge.

Nec dubitamus multa esse quae et nos praeterierint. Homines enim sumus, et occupati officiis; subsicivisque temporibus ista curamus.

PLINY:
Natural History (preface) *(Latin)*

We have no doubt that there are many things of which we are ignorant, for we are only human and we are fully occupied with our duties, and in our leisure time we are concerned with those same duties.

Non audiendi sunt homines imperiti, qui humano ingenio majorem, vel inutilem, et rebus gerendis adversam πολυμάθειαν criminantur.

DANIEL GEORG MORHOF:
Polyhistor (Latin)

Those ignorant men are not to be listened to, who find fault with wide and varied learning as being too much for the human intellect, or else useless and unfavourable to a life of action.

Todo tigre es un primer tigre; tiene que empezar desde el principio su profesión de tigre.

JOSÉ ORTEGA Y GASSET:
Misión del Bibliotecario (Spanish)

Every tiger believes it is the first tiger. It believes it is starting right at the beginning on its profession as a tiger.

Infeliz caballo cuyo amo no tiene ojos: mal engordará.

SPANISH PROVERB

Unhappy the horse whose owner has no eyes – it will certainly not grow fat!

ILL-GOTTEN GAINS
see also Evil, Possessions.

Non si può ancora chiamare virtú ammazzare li sua cittadini, tradire li amici, essere sanza fede, sanza pietà, sanza relligione; li quali modi possono fare acquistare imperio, ma no gloria.

NICCOLÒ MACHIAVELLI:
The Prince (Italian)

It cannot be called virtue to kill one's fellow-citizens, betray one's friends, be without faith, without pity, and without religion; by these means one may indeed obtain power, but not glory.

Male partum, male disperit.

PLAUTUS:
Poenulus (Latin)

Ill-gotten, ill-spent.

ILLNESS
see also Death, Disease, God, Remedies.

Vous avez un médecin – que vous fait-il?
Sire, nous causons ensemble; il m'ordonne des remèdes, je ne les fais point, et je guéris.

Molière's reply to Louis XIV *(French)*

You have a doctor – what does he do for you?
Sire, we chat; he writes a prescription for me, I don't take it, and I get well.

Il vaut mieux mourir selon les règles que de réchapper contre les règles.

MOLIÈRE:
L'Amour Médecin (French)

Its better to die according to the rules, than to recover in spite of the rules.

Les maladies suspendent nos vertus et nos vices.
LUC DE CLAPIERS, MARQUIS DE VAUVENARGUES:
Réflexions et Maximes (French)

When we are sick our virtues and our vices are in abeyance.

Kreissōn gar Haidai keuthōn ho nosōn matan,
Hos ek patrōias hēkōn geneas aristos
Poluponōn Akhaiōn
SOPHOCLES:
Ajax (Greek)

Better by far that he who was born to be the best of all the warring Greeks should die than endure the disease of madness.

Mortis arra.
PLINY:
Letters *(Latin)*

Money given to physicians (*lit.* the earnest – money of death).

Quae medicamenta non sanant, ferrum sanat, quae ferrum non sanat, ignis sanat.
LATIN PROVERB

Iron cures what drugs cannot, fire cures what iron cannot.

Per fretum febris.
Latin phrase quoted by John Donne in his *Hymn to God my God in my Sickness*

The vehemence of fever.

Dios es el que sana, y el médico lleva la plata.
SPANISH PROVERB

God cures the patient, and the doctor pockets the fee.

ILLUSION
see also Hope, Life.

Voyez combien ma vie est pleine de trespas,
Quand tout mon reconfort ne dépend que du songe.
PIERRE DE RONSARD:
Sonnets pour Helène (French)

Look how my life is nought but death when my only consolation lies in dreams.

Macht euch von Fabeln frei!
Eurer Götter alt Gemenge,
Lasst es hin, es ist vorbei.
J. W. VON GOETHE:
Faust (German)

Free yourself of fables! That ancient throng of gods are best left behind – they're out of date!

Hoc te
Crede modo insanum, nihilo ut sapientior ille,
Qui te deridet, caudam trahat.
HORACE:
Satires (Latin)

Believe yourself insane only insofar as he who mocks you drags a tail behind him, and is no whit the wiser man.

IMAGINATION

Imagination, o magie!
ALPHONSE DAUDET:
Tartarin sur les Alpes (French)

Imagination, what magic power you possess!

L'imagination dispose de tout; elle fait la beauté, la justice, et le bonheur, qui est le tout du monde.
BLAISE PASCAL:
Pensées (French)

Imagination governs everything; it creates beauty, justice, and happiness – everything that matters in the world.

Les hommes prennent souvent leur imagination pour leur coeur.
BLAISE PASCAL:
Pensées (French)

Men often mistake their imagination for the promptings of their hearts.

Quand la tête se monte, l'imagination la mieux reglée devient folle comme un rêve!
P. A. C. DE BEAUMARCHAIS:
Le Mariage de Figaro (French)

When one's blood is up, the best controlled imagination becomes as mad as a dream!

Les habiles par imagination se plaisent tout

autrement à eux mesmes que les prudents ne se peuvent raisonnablement plaire.

BLAISE PASCAL:
Pensées (French)

The satisfaction of men whose cleverness lies in their own imagination is quite different from that of sensible men.

Toute image a besoin d'être confrontée avec une autre image.

PAUL ELUARD:
Variété (French)

Every image should be confronted with another image.

Vous n'avez qu'à suivre les traits d'une imagination qui se donne l'essor, et qui souvent laisse le vrai pour attraper le merveilleux.

MOLIÈRE:
La Critique de l'Ecole des Femmes (French)

You have only to follow the tracks of an imagination that gives itself scope and often abandons the truth to capture the wonderful.

Quasi quidquam infelicius sit homine cui sua figmenta dominantur.

PLINY:
Natural History (Latin)

As if there were anything more wretched than a man ridden by his own imagination.

Saṁkalpaprabhavo rāgo dveṣo mohaś ca kathyate

Mādhyamika-kārikā (Pali)

Of imagination are born attachment, aversion, and delusion.

IMITATION
see also Example.

Tout art d'imitation a son modèle dans la nature.

DENIS DIDEROT:
Le Neveu de Rameau (French)

Every art of imitation has its model in nature.

Die Nachahmung ist uns angeboren, das Nachzuahmende wird nicht leicht erkannt.

J. W. VON GOETHE:
Wilhelm Meisters Lehrjahre (German)

Imitation is inborn in us; but it is not easy to determine what to imitate.

Sic enim se profecto res habet, ut nunquam perfecte veritatem casus imitetur.

CICERO:
De Divinatione (Latin)

There is no denying that no perfect imitation was ever made by chance.

IMMORALITY

Neque quicquam hic nunc est vile nisi mores mali.

PLAUTUS:
Trinummus (Latin)

The only cheap thing around here nowadays is immorality.

IMMORTALITY
see also Inspiration, the Soul, Survival.

Rien ne me serait trop cher pour l'éternité.

BLAISE PASCAL:
Pensées (French)

Nothing would be too much to pay for immortality.

Yadā sarve pramucyante kāmā, ye'sya hṛdi sthitāh
Atha martyo-mṛto bhavati

Bṛhad-āraṇyaka Upanishad (Pali)

When all the desires that enter one's heart are abandoned, then does the mortal become immortal.

IMPERFECTION

Toujours l'épine est sous la rose.

FRENCH PROVERB

No rose without a thorn.

Quia ubicunque dulce est, ibi et acidum invenies.

PETRONIUS:
Satyricon (Latin)

Sweetness is always tainted with bitterness.

La visija quebrantada es la que nunca se acaba de romper, que enfada con su durar.

BALTASAR GRACIÁN:
Oráculo Manual y Arte de Prudencia (Spanish)

It is the cracked vessel that never gets completely broken that annoys you by its durability.

IMPERMANENCE

Auf der Welt ist kein Bestand,
Wir müssen alle sterben,
Das ist uns wohlbekannt!
GERMAN FOLKSONG

Nothing in this world is permanent. We all have
to die – that we know very well!

Et deus et durus vertitur ipse dies.
PROPERTIUS:
Elegies (Latin)

Both god and cruel time change.

IMPETUOSITY
see also Caution, Haste, Leadership.

Al-me zādak, lā tabaddadah fī shān as-sarāb
ARAB PROVERB

Look before you leap (*lit.* don't pour away the
water you are travelling with because of a
mirage).

Le trop de promptitude à l'erreur nous expose.
MOLIÈRE:
Sganarelle (French)

Jumping to conclusions exposes us to error.

Ek puros es phloga
GREEK PROVERB

Out of the frying-pan into the fire (*lit.* out of the
fire into the flame).

Speude bradeōs
SUETONIUS:
Divus Augustus (Greek)

More haste, less speed (a favourite saying of the
Emperor Augustus).

Lu que luego se hace, luego se deshace.
SPANISH PROVERB

Soonest done, soonest undone.

THE IMPOSSIBLE
see also Endurance.

A l'impossible nul n'est tenu.
FRENCH PROVERB

No-one is expected to achieve the impossible.

Nur allein der Mensch vermag das Unmögliche.
J. W. VON GOETHE:
Das Göttliche (German)

Man alone can do the impossible.

Meglio oprando oblíar, senza indagarlo,
Questo enorme mister de l'universo!
GIOSUE CARDUCCI:
Idillio Maremmano (Italian)

Far better in one's work to forget than to seek to
solve the vast riddles of the universe.

Sane, cum mula pepererit.
SUETONIUS:
Galba (Latin)

Very likely, when a mule has a foal (Galba
commenting on the likelihood of his family
attaining the highest dignities).

Agnum lupe eripere velle.
LATIN PROVERB

To desire the impossible (*lit.* to wish to rescue a
lamb from a wolf).

No busques cinco pies al gato.
SPANISH PROVERB

Don't look for the fifth foot of a cat.

IMPRESSIONS

Quand on se fait entendre, on parle toujours
bien.
MOLIÈRE:
Les Femmes Savantes (French)

If we make ourselves understood, we are speaking correctly.

Haerent infixi pectore vultus
Verbaque.
VIRGIL:
Aeneid (Latin)

His words and countenance were deeply im-
printed in her heart.

INADEQUACY
see also Frailty.

La faiblesse est plus opposée à la vertu que le vice.

FRANÇOIS, DUC DE LA ROCHEFOUCAULD:
Maximes (French)

Weakness is more contrary to virtue than is vice.

La faiblesse est le seul défaut qu'on ne saurait corriger.

FRANÇOIS, DUC DE LA ROCHEFOUCAULD:
Maximes (French)

Weakness is the only fault that we do not know how to correct.

Das Unzulängliche ist produktiv.

J. W. VON GOETHE
(German)

The inadequate is productive.

INCOMPATIBILITY

Si vetustae [ulmo] vitem applicueris, coniugem necabit.

COLUMELLA:
De Re Rustica (Latin)

If you couple a vine with an old elm, it will kill its mate.

INDEPENDENCE
see also Self-help.

Chacun le sien, ce n'est pas trop.

MOLIÈRE:
Le Malade Imaginaire (French)

Everyone has a right to his own course of action – that's not too much to ask.

Jeder ist Kaiser in seiner Lage.

GERMAN PROVERB

Every man is master in his own house.

Debajo de mi manto al rey mando.

SPANISH PROVERB

Every man his own master (*lit.* beneath my cloak I command the king).

INDIFFERENCE
see also Moderation, Sympathy.

Le monde en marchant n'a pas beaucoup plus de souci de ce qu'il écrase que le char de l'idole de Jagarnata.

ERNEST RENAN:
(in the *Revue des Deux Mondes*, 1876) *(French)*

As the world progresses it has little more care for what it destroys than has the chariot of the Juggernaut.

So kann es Leute geben, die zuletzt mechanisch Gutes oder Böses tun.

J. C. F. VON SCHILLER:
Works (German)

There are people in this world who ultimately do mechanically what is good or evil.

Aware to mo if beki h'to wa omohohede, mi no itads'ra ni narinu-beki kana

KEN-TOKU KO
(Japanese)

You passed me with indifference, even though you could have had pity on me. What despair you have caused me!

Ergo ego nec amicum habeo nec inimicum?

SUETONIUS:
Nero (Latin)

Have I then neither friend nor foe? (Nero, on finding himself abandoned and ignored in his own palace).

INDIGNATION
see also Anger.

Magnum secum affert crimen indignatio.

LATIN PROVERB

Indignation comes accompanied with some serious charge.

Saeva indignatio.

LATIN EXPRESSION

Savage indignation.

INDIVIDUALISM
see also Character, Commonweal, Society.

Ta mē pateousin amaxai
Ta steibein

CALLIMACHUS:
Fragments (Greek)

Tread where the traffic does not go.

Og har jeg end sejlet min Skude på Grund,
O, så *var* det dog dejligt at fare!

HENRIK IBSEN:
Love's Comedy (Norwegian)

And what if I did run my ship aground – oh, still
it was splendid to sail it!

No se me da nada, que en muriéndome yo, todo
se acaba.

SPANISH PROVERB

I don't care for anything, because everything
finishes when I die.

INEXPERIENCE

Un jeune curé fait les meilleurs sermons.

FRENCH PROVERB

It's the young priests who make the best
sermons.

Je ne comprenais pas que je vivais.

ANDRÉ GIDE:
L'Immoraliste (French)

I did not understand that I was alive.

INFATUATION
see also Love.

Quicquid agit Rufus, nihil est, nisi Naevia Rufo,
Si gaudet, si flet, si tacet, hanc loquitur:
Coenat, propinat, poscit, negat, annuit, una est
Naevia; si non sit Naevia, mutus erit.
Scriberet hesterna patri cum luce salutem,
Naevia lux, inquit, Naevia numen, ave.

MARTIAL:
Epigrams (Latin)

Let Rufus weep, rejoice, stand, sit, or walk,
Still he can nothing but of Naevia talk;
Let him eat, drink, ask questions, or dispute,
Still he must speak of Naevia, or be mute.
He writ to his father, ending with this line:
I am, my lovely Naevia, ever thine. (*tr.* Steele)

THE INFINITE
see also the Universe.

Nous connoissons qu'il y a a un infiny, et
ignorons sa nature.

BLAISE PASCAL:
Pensées (French)

We are aware of the existence of the infinite, but
we know nothing of its nature.

INFLUENCES

Tout influe sur tout.

FRENCH PROVERB

Everything influences everything.

La forêt façonne l'arbre.

FRENCH PROVERB

The forest shapes the tree.

Non bagnarmi le polveri da sparo della mente!

TOMMASO TRINI:
title of his article in *Domus*, 1972 *(Italian)*

Don't wash the gunpowder of my mind!

INGRATITUDE
see also Gratitude.

L'ingratitude est une variété de l'orgueil.

LABICHE & MARTIN:
Le Voyage de M. Perrichon (French)

Ingratitude is a form of pride.

Il n'y a qu'un seul vice dont on ne voie personne
se vanter, c'est l'ingratitude.

GÉRARD DE NERVAL:
Paradoxe et Vérité (French)

There is only one vice of which no-one boasts –
ingratitude!

Hotou d' aporrei mnēstis eu peponthotos,
Ouk an genoit' eth' houtos eugenēs anēr

SOPHOCLES:
Ajax (Greek)

It is not noble to forget past services.

Men servasse, ut essent qui me perderent?

MARCUS PACUVIUS:
Armorum Iudicium (quoted in Suetonius:
Divus Iulius) *(Latin)*

Saved I these men that they might murder me?

Dixeris male dicta cuncta cum ingratum hominem dixeris.

LATIN PROVERB

Call a man ungrateful and you have no words of abuse left.

I vozdal esi mne zlÿe za blagie i za vozlyublenie moe – neprimiritel 'nuyu nenavist'

PRINCE ANDREĬ KURBSKIĬ:
Epistles to Ivan IV (Russian)

You have repaid my good actions with evil, and my love with implacable hatred.

La ingratitud humana no tiene límites.

GABRIEL GARCÍA MÁRQUEZ:
El Coronel no Tiene quien le Escriba (Spanish)

Man's ingratitude knows no limits.

Cría cuervos y te sacarán los ojos!

SPANISH PROVERB

Bring up crows and they'll peck your eyes out!

INHERITANCE

L'on a le temps d'avoir les dents longues, lorsqu'on attend, pour vivre, le trépas de quelqu'un.

MOLIERE:
Le Médecin Malgré Lui (French)

You can get very hungry while waiting, if your livelihood depends on someone's decease.

La mort n'a pas toujours les oreilles ouvertes aux vouex et aux prières de messieurs les héritiers.

MOLIÈRE:
Le Médecin Malgré Lui (French)

Death does not always listen to the promises and prayers of those who would inherit.

Li uomini sdimenticano piú presto la morte del padre che la perdita del patrimonio.

NICCOLÒ MACHIAVELLI:
The Prince (Italian)

Men forget more easily the death of their father than the loss of their patrimony.

Más han muerto porque hicieron testamento que porque enfermaron.

SPANISH PROVERB

More people have died because they made their will than because they were sick.

INJUSTICE
see also Justice, Law.

. . . der Zorn über das Unrecht
Macht die Stimme heiser.

BERTOLT BRECHT:
An die Nachgeborenen (German)

Anger over injustice makes one's voice harsh.

Kakourgian de tēn megistēn tēs heautou poleōs ouk adikaian phēseis einai?

PLATO:
The Republic (Greek)

Is not injustice the greatest of all threats to the state?

Perisca innanzi la città, che tante opere rie si sostengano.

GIANO DELLA BELLA:
thirteenth-century political reformer
of Florence (Italian)

Rather should the state be allowed to perish, than such things to be tolerated.

Iniqua numquam regna perpetuo manent.

SENECA:
Medea (Latin)

Injustice never rules for ever.

Sic odia fiunt.

SENECA:
Oedipus (Latin)

Thus is hatred engendered (when the guilty are freed).

INNOCENCE
see also Honesty, Injustice, Justice, Laments, Simplicity.

. . . piú d'ogni inganno
D'huomo malvagio l'innocente puote,

GIAMBATTISTA CINTHIO GIRALDI:
Selene (Italian)

Innocence has more power than all the deceits of an evil man.

Proxima puris
Sors est manibus nescire nefas.
SENECA:
Hercules Furens (Latin)

The next best to guiltless hands is ignorance of guilt itself.

Suum sequitur lumen semper innocentia.
LATIN PROVERB

Innocence always follows her own light.

A los párvulos se aparecen los santos.
SPANISH PROVERB

It is to little children that the saints appear.

INNS

Per un ladrón, pierden ciento en el mesón.
SPANISH PROVERB

For one man robbed on the road, a hundred are robbed in the inn.

Ventera hermosa, mal para la bolsa.
SPANISH PROVERB

The fairer the hostess, the fouler the reckoning.

INSIGNIFICANCE

La terre est au soleil ce que l'homme est à l'ange.
VICTOR HUGO:
Les Contemplations: Explication (French)

The earth is to the sun what man is to the angels.

Les petits en toute affaire
Esquivent fort aisément.
JEAN DE LA FONTAINE:
Le Combat des Rats et des Belettes (French)

In every trouble the little ones duck most easily.

INSOLENCE
see also Tyranny.

Hubris gar te kakē deilōi brotōi
HESIOD:
Works and Days (Greek)

Insolence ill becomes a poor man.

INSPIRATION
see also Poets and poetry.

Ces nymphes, je veux les perpétuer.
STÉPHANE MALLARMÉ:
L'Après-midi d'un Faune (French)

These nymphs – I should like to immortalise them!

Der du die weite Welt umschweiffst,
Geschäftiger Geist, wie nah fühl ich mich dir.
J. W. VON GOETHE:
Faust (German)

Busy spirit that roams through the world, how near I feel to you.

Nemo vir magnus sine aliquo adflatu divino umquam fuit.
CICERO:
De Natura Deorum (Latin)

No great man has ever existed who had not some spark of divine inspiration.

INTEGRITY
see also Greatness, Honour, Repentance.

Een hoofd vol kreucken, een geweten sonder rimpel.
J. van den Vondel's tribute to the memory of Pieter Corneliszoon Hooft *(Dutch)*

A face full of wrinkles, a conscience without a stain.

Tant vaut l'homme, tant vaut le métier, et réciproquement, à la fin, tant vaut le métier, tant vaut l'homme.
DENIS DIDEROT:
Le Neveu de Rameau (French)

Whatever a man is worth, so is his craft; and ultimately, by the same token, whatever his craft is worth, so is the man.

La voi de la conscience et d l'Honneur est bien faible, lorsque les boyaux crient.
DENIS DIDEROT:
Le Neveu de Rameau (French)

When one's guts are rumbling, how feeble is the voice of conscience and honour.

Monon de touto phas' hamillasthai biōi,
Gnōmēn dikaian k'agathēn hotōi tukhēi

EURIPIDES:
Hippolytus (Greek)

Integrity is essential if we are to cope with life's difficulties.

Primo avulso non deficit alter aureus.

CASSIODORUS:
Variae (Latin)

If the first gold piece is snatched away, there is always another.

Felix qui quod amat defendere fortiter audet.

OVID:
Amores (Latin)

Happy the man who ventures boldly to defend what he holds dear.

INTELLECT
see also Feelings, Sensations.

Principium autem eorum quae secundum artem fiunt est intellectus humanus.

ST. THOMAS AQUINAS:
Commentary on the Politics of Aristotle (Latin)

The human intellect is the origin of all things created by art.

Qua voluptate animi nulla certe potest esse maior.

CICERO:
De Senectute (Latin)

There can be no greater pleasures than those of the mind.

INTELLECTUALS

Les savants ne sont pas curieux.

FRENCH PROVERB

Learned people show little curiosity.

Ich kenne die Leute wohl, die ihr meint; sie sind bloss Geist und Theorie und können sich keinen Knopf annähen.

GEORG CHRISTOPH LICHTENBERG:
Aphorismen (German)

I know these people well: they are all intellect and theory and couldn't even sew on a button for themselves.

INTENTIONS

Je forme une entreprise qui n'eut jamais d'exemple, et dont l'exécution n'aura point d'imitateur.

J. J. ROUSSEAU:
Les Confessions (opening words) *(French)*

I am undertaking a unique enterprise whose treatment is unlikely to give rise to any imitations.

Multi enim et cum obesse vellent profuerunt et cum prodesse obfuerunt.

CICERO:
De Natura Deorum (Latin)

Plenty of people have done good when they meant to do harm, and harm when they intended to do good.

INTERFERENCE
see also Busybodies.

Es gibt Leute, die ihre Nase in gar alle Angelegenheiten hineinstecken müssen. Wenn man solchen Leuten den kleinen Finger reicht, nehmen sie gleich die ganze Hand.

BERTOLT BRECHT:
Mann ist Mann (German)

There are people who must stick their nose into everybody else's business. If you extend your little finger to such people, they will grasp your whole hand.

Invitum qui servat, idem facit occidenti.

HORACE:
Ars Poetica (Latin)

He who saves a man against his will, murders him.

INTRIGUE
see also Plots, Traps.

Dans le vaste champ de l'intrigue, il faut savoir tout cultiver.

P. A. C. DE BEAUMARCHAIS:
Le Mariage de Figaro (French)

You must know how to make use of everything in the vast field of intrigue.

Phōria d' amphadiōn lektra melikhrotera

> PAULUS SILENTIARIUS:
> *Epigrams (Greek)*

A secret love affair is much more enjoyable than an open one.

IRRESPONSIBILITY

Mē paidi makhairan

> GREEK PROVERB

Don't put a sword into a child's hands.

Mē puri pur epage

> GREEK PROVERB

Don't add fire to fire.

Cuando el gato va a sus devociones, bailan las ratones.

> SPANISH PROVERB

When the cat's away, the mice will play (*lit.* when the cat goes to mass, the mice begin to dance).

J

JEALOUSY
see also Husbands, Love.

La sombre Jalousie au teint pâle et livide
Suit d'un pied chancelant le Soupçon qui la
guide.

> VOLTAIRE:
> *La Henriade (French)*

Dark jealousy, pale and livid, follows with
unsteady tread suspicion, which is its guide.

Ah! si je suis cruel on me force de l'être,
Et de mes actions je ne suis pas le maître.

> JEAN RACINE:
> *La Thébaïde (French)*

If I am cruel, it is because I am forced to be so,
and I am not the master of my actions.

La jalousie n'est qu'un sot enfant de l'orgueil.

> P. A. C. DE BEAUMARCHAIS:
> *Le Mariage de Figaro (French)*

Jealousy is nothing but the foolish child of pride.

Je l'aimais en frère, mais j'en étois jaloux en
amant.

> J. J. ROUSSEAU:
> *Les Confessions (French)*

I loved her as though I were her brother, but
I was as jealous as though I were her lover.
(Writing of his childhood love for Mlle de
Vulson).

La jalousie se nourrit dans les doutes et elle
devient fureur, ou elle finit sitôt qu'on passe du
doute à la certitude.

> FRANÇOIS, DUC DE LA ROUCHEFOUCAULD:
> *Réflexions (French)*

Jealousy feeds on doubts and develops into passion – or it can finish just as soon as doubts
become certainties.

No hay más gloria que amor
Ni mayor pena que celos.

> LOPE DE VEGA
> *Cantorcillo de la Virgen (Spanish*

There is no greater glory than love, nor an
greater punishment than jealousy.

JESTERS
see also Fools.

Celui qui serait sage n'aurait point de fou; celu
donc qui a un fou n'est pas sage; s'il n'est pas
sage il est fou, et peut-être, fut-il le roi, le fou de
son fou.

> DENIS DIDEROT
> *Le Neveu de Rameau (French*

He who would be thought wise will not appoin
a fool; he who has one is unwise; if he is unwise
he must be a fool and, perhaps, if he is a king, the
fool of his fool.

Il n'y a pas de meilleur rôle auprès des grands
que celui de fou.

> DENIS DIDEROT
> *Le Neveu de Rameau (French*

There is no better rôle to play among the grea
than that of jester.

Longtemps il y a eu le fou du roi en titre, er
aucun il n'y a eu en titre le sage du roi.

> DENIS DIDEROT
> *Le Neveu de Rameau (French*

The position of court jester has existed for a very
long time – but we have never had a similar pos
for a king's Wise Man!

JOY
see also Desire, Disillusion, Evil, God, Happiness, Life, Pain, Spring.

Tot cant Jois genseis esclaira
Malvestatz roill' e tiura,

E enclau Joven en serca,
Per q'Ira Joi entrebresca.

RAIMBAUT D'AURENGA:
Cars Douz (French)

Everything that joy most graciously enhances, evil encrusts with rust and dross, encircling youth with a moat, so that sorrow entangles joy.

Freude heisst die starker Feder
In der ewigen Natur,
Freude, Freude treibt die Räder
In der grossen Weltenuhr.

J. C. F. VON SCHILLER:
An die Freude (German)

Joy is the coiled spring of eternal nature; joy drives the wheels in the great clock of the world.

Disce gaudere.

SENECA:
Epistles (Latin)

Learn how to feel joy.

Ripis superat mi atque abundat pectus laetitia.

PLAUTUS:
Stichus (Latin)

My heart brims over with joy.

Hermosas son las estaciones todas
Para el mortal que en sí guarda la dicha [*i.e.*, alegría];
Mas para el alma desolada y huérfana,
No hay estación risueña ni propicia.

ROSALÍA CASTRO:
Candente está la Atmósfera (Spanish)

All times are beautiful for those who maintain joy within them; but there is no happy or favourable time for those with disconsolate or orphaned souls.

JUDGMENT
see also Anger, Criticism, Decision, Justice, Injustice, Reputation.

Sire, on se défend mal contre l'avis d'un roi,
Et le plus innocent que le ciel ait vu naître,
Quand il le croit coupable, il commence de l'être.

PIERRE CORNEILLE:
Horace (French)

Sire, we have little defence against the opinion of a monarch, and even the most innocent man who ever lived will begin to be guilty if the king thinks him so.

Trop de jeunesse et trop de vieillesse empeschent l'esprit, trop et trop peu d'instruction.

BLAISE PASCAL:
Pensées (French)

Extreme youth and extreme age block the mind, like too much or too little education.

Die Waage sagt: das ist schwerer und das ist leichter; aber nicht, das ist Gold und das ist Silber.

GERMAN PROVERB

The scales can distinguish between weights but not values (*lit.* the scales will tell us what is heavy and what is light; but they cannot tell us what is gold, and what silver).

Am Jüngsten Tag, wenn die Posaunen schallen,
Und alles aus ist mit dem Erdeleben,
Sind wir verpflichtet Rechenschaft zu geben
Von jedem Wort, das unnütz uns entfallen.

J. W. VON GOETHE:
Warnung (German)

On the Day of Judgment, when the trumpets sound, and we are finished with life on earth, we shall be required to justify every word that has carelessly fallen from our lips.

Epeidan hapant' akousēte, krinate

GREEK PROVERB

Only judge when you have heard all.

Iudex damnatur cum nocens absolvitur.

The motto of *The Edinburgh Review (Latin)*

Acquittal of the guilty damns the judge.

Nihil (or Nil) admirari.

HORACE:
Epistles (from a Greek maxim) *(Latin)*

Marvel at nothing.

In trutina ponentur eadem.

Motto of the Scottish Certificate of
Education Examination Board *(Latin)*

These matters are to be weighed in the balance.

JURIES

Le jury, et surtout le jury civil, sert à donner à l'esprit de tous les citoyens une partie des habitudes de l'esprit du juge; et ces habitudes sont précisément celles qui préparent le mieux le peuple à être libre.

ALEXIS DE TOCQUEVILLE:
De la Démocratie en Amérique (French)

Juries, above all civil juries, help every citizen to share something of the deliberations that go on in the judge's mind; and it is these very deliberations which best prepare the people to be free.

JUSTICE
see also Juries, Law, Might.

Il existe une loi générale qui a été faite ou du moins adoptée, non pas seulement par la majorité de tel ou tel peuple, mais par la majorité de tous les hommes. Cette loi, c'est la justice. La justice forme la borne du droit de chaque peuple.

ALEXIS DE TOCQUEVILLE:
De la Démocratie en Amérique (French)

There is one universal law that has been formed or at least adopted not only by the majority of such and such a nation, but by the majority of mankind. That law is justice. Justice forms the corner-stone of each nation's law.

Une nation est comme un jury chargé de représenter la société universelle et d'appliquer la justice qui est sa loi.

ALEXIS DE TOCQUEVILLE:
De la Démocratie en Amérique (French)

A nation is like a jury that has been charged to represent universal society and to administer the justice which is its law.

Nous faisons justice les uns des autres sans que la loi s'en mêle.

DENIS DIDEROT:
Le Neveu de Rameau (French)

We dispense justice to each other without the law's intervention.

L'affection ou la haine change la justice de face
BLAISE PASCAL
Pensées (French

Both love and hatred are capable of changin the face of justice.

Mettez le plus glacé des Juges à plaider dans s propre cause, et voyez-le expliquer la loi!
P. A. C. DE BEAUMARCHAIS
Le Mariage de Figaro (French

Set the sternest of judges to plead in his own cas and then see how he expounds the law!

Il n'est pas permis au plus équitable homme d monde d'estre juge en sa cause.
BLAISE PASCAL
Pensées (French

The most just man in the world may still not ac as judge in his own case.

Selon que vous serez puissant ou misérable,
Les jugements de cour vous rendront blanc o noir.
JEAN DE LA FONTAINE
Les Animaux Malades de la Peste (French

A court will declare you innocent or guilt according to your high or low station in life.

La justice n'est pas une vertu d'Etat.
PIERRE CORNEILLE
Pompée (French

Justice is not one of the virtues of the state.

La Justice n'a rien à voir avec la Loi, qui n'en es que la déformation, la charge et la parodie. C sont là deux demi-soeurs, qui, sorties de deu pères, se crachent à la figure en se traitant d bâtardes et vivent à couteaux tirés, tandis qu les honnêtes gens, menacés de gendarmes, s tournent les pouces et le sang en attendan qu'elles se mettent d'accord.
GEORGES COURTELINE
L'Article 330 (French

Justice has nothing to do with the law, of whicl it is only a distortion, a burden and a parody Justice and the law are two half-sisters witl different fathers who spit in each others' faces treat each other as bastards and live at daggers drawn, while decent people, menaced by the

ɔlice, twiddle their thumbs and keep their cool
aiting for these two to come to some agree-
ent.

'amour de la justice n'est en la plupart des
ɔmmes que la crainte de souffrir l'injustice.
FRANÇOIS, DUC DE LA ROCHEFOUCAULD:
Réflexions (French)

ɔve of justice in most men is really the fear of
ıffering injustice.

'oute justice vient de Dieu, lui seul en est la
ɔurce.
J. J. ROUSSEAU:
Du Contrat Social (French)

ll justice comes from God – he is its sole source.

hè cima di giudizio non s'avvalla.
DANTE:
Purgatorio (Italian)

he height of justice is not abased.

eges per iustitiam adipiscuntur divitias, quam
er rapinam tyranni.
ST. THOMAS AQUINAS:
On Princely Government (Latin)

ings gain greater riches through justice than
ɔ tyrants by rapacity.

Iustitia est constans et perpetua voluntas ius
suum cuique tribuendi.
JUSTINIAN:
Institutiones (Latin)

Justice is a constant and perpetual desire to
grant each man his due.

Fiat justitia, ruat coelum.
ROMAN JURIST'S SAYING

Let justice be done, even though the heavens
fall.

Quis judicat ipsos judices?
LATIN LEGAL TAG

Who judges the judges? (*cf.* Quis custodiet ipsos
custodies, Juvenal: *Satires*: who watches the
watchmen?)

Ius summum saepe summast malitia.
TERENCE:
Heauton Timorumenos (Latin)

Extreme justice can often be extreme injustice.

De jure divino.
LATIN TAG

A matter of divine law.

Bona causa nullum iudicem verebitur.
LATIN PROVERB

A good cause will fear no judge.

K

KINDNESS
see also Benefits and benefactors, Charity,
Generosity, Liberality, Poverty.

Al-jūd, lel ma jūd
ARAB PROVERB

Repay kindness with kindness.

La bonté attire, adoucit et corrige.
MME LA COMTESSE DE SÉGUR:
Un Bon Petit Diable (French)

Kindness attracts, pacifies and corrects.

Esthla legein aiei pantas, kalon
GREEK PROVERB

It is always good to speak well of all people.

Kharis kharin gar estin hē tiktous' aei
SOPHOCLES:
Ajax (Greek)

Kindness will always attract kindness.

Bono, ma pechare da troppo bontà.
AMBROGIO DE MAINO,
to the Duke of Milan, 1495 (concerning
a retiring commissioner) (Italian)

A good man, but he errs on the side of too much
kindness.

Quid enim melius aut quid praestantius boni-
tate et beneficentia?
CICERO:
De Natura Deorum (Latin)

What can be better or more admirable than
kindness and beneficence?

Faciles motus mens generosa capit.
OVID:
Tristia (Latin)

A noble spirit is capable of kindly impulses.

KINGS
see also Advice, Agreement, Authority,
Avarice, Dictatorship, Government,
Greatness, Judgment, Justice, Leadership,
Learning, Liberality, Loyalty, Monarchy,
Peace, Philosophers, Revolution,
Right and wrong, Royal prerogative,
Statesmen, Wine.

Wald al-mulūk yarīd aṭ-ṭari
ARAB PROVERB

Only the best for the sons of kings.

Al-baḥar wa-'s-sulṭān mā 'indhum amān
ARAB PROVERB

Rivers and kings are not to be trusted.

L'amour entre les rois ne fait pas l'hyménée,
Et les raisons d'Etat plus fortes que ces noeuds
Trouvent bien les moyens d'en éteindre les feux
PIERRE CORNEILLE:
Nicomède (French)

Love between monarchs never reaches the nup-
tial stage, for reasons of state – far stronger than
these knots – have no trouble in finding the
means of extinguishing these ardours.

Mieux vaut en bonne foi
S'abandonner a quelque puissant roi
Que s'appuyer de plusieurs petits princes.
JEAN DE LA FONTAINE
Le Bassa et le Marchand (French)

Better to rely on one powerful king than on
many little princes.

Il n'y a dans tout un royaume qu'un homme qui
marche. C'est le souverain. Tout le reste prend
des positions.
DENIS DIDEROT
Le Neveu de Rameau (French)

In a whole kingdom there is only one man who
makes the moves, that's the monarch; all the rest
just stand to attention.

Pour grands que soient les rois, ils sont ce que
nous sommes.
> PIERRE CORNEILLE:
> *Le Cid (French)*

Great though they are, kings are only human.

Le monarque prudent et sage
De ses moindres sujets sait tirer quelque usage.
> JEAN DE LA FONTAINE:
> *Le Lion s'en Allant en Guerre (French)*

A wise and prudent king knows how to make use
of even the least of his subjects.

A peu de gens convient le diadème.
> JEAN DE LA FONTAINE:
> *Le Renard, le Singe, et les Animaux (French)*

Few men are fit to wear a crown.

Il serait peut-être plus aisé de trouver un enfant
propre à gouverner un royaume, à faire un
grand roi qu'un grand violon.
> DENIS DIDEROT:
> *Le Neveu de Rameau (French)*

You would probably find it easier to choose a
child fit to govern a country and to make a great
king, than to discover a great violin.

Les rois n'aiment rien tant qu'une prompte
obéissance, et ne se plaisent point du tout à
trouver des obstacles.
> MOLIÈRE:
> *L'Impromptu de Versailles (French)*

There's nothing kings like more than prompt
obedience, and nothing that pleases them less
than discovering obstacles.

Par l'oreille, l'épaule et l'oeil,
La France eut trois rois au cercueil.
Par l'oreille, l'oeil, et l'épaule,
mourut trois rois dans la Gaule.
> FRENCH FOLK SONG

Ear, shoulder and eye put three French kings in
their coffins (referring to Antoine de Bourbon,
who was shot in the shoulder; Henri II, shot in
the eye; and François II, poisoned in the ear).

Nous nous faisons gloire de commander à une
nation libre et généreuse.
> Louis XIV of France, at the
> beginning of his reign *(French)*

By commanding so free and generous a nation,
we make ourselves glorious.

Jamais à son sujet, un roi n'est redevable.
> PIERRE CORNEILLE:
> *Le Cid (French)*

A king is never beholden to his subjects.

Un grand vilain lors ils élurent,
Le plus ossu qu'entr'eux ils eurent.
> *Roman de la Rose (French)*

For their monarch they chose the thickest head,
the most villainous among them.

Et d'un trône si saint la moitié n'est fondée
Que sur la foi promise, et rarement gardée.
> JEAN RACINE:
> *Bajazet (French)*

Of this sacred throne, half is founded only on the
faith of promises that are rarely kept.

Un homme sage ne se fait point d'affaires avec
les grands.
> P. A. C. DE BEAUMARCHAIS:
> *Le Mariage de Figaro (French)*

Wise men do not pick quarrels with the great.

La clémence des princes n'est souvent qu'une
politique pour gagner l'affection des peuples.
> FRANÇOIS, DUC DE LA ROCHEFOUCAULD:
> *Réflexions (French)*

Royal clemency is often but a political man-
oeuvre to gain the nation's affection.

Ein königliches Wort ist ein Ding – ein Ding –
ein Ding, das nichts ist.
> GEORG BÜCHNER:
> *Leonce und Lena (German)*

Put not your trust in princes! (*lit.* a king's word is
a thing that is worth nothing).

Die Worte der Könige sind Könige der Worte.
> GERMAN PROVERB

The words of kings are kings of words.

Was Grosshaus sündigt, muss Kleinhaus
büssen.

GERMAN PROVERB

When the nobility sin, the poor folk atone.

A uno principe è necessario avere e' sua fon-
damenti buoni; altrimenti conviene che rovini.

NICCOLÒ MACHIAVELLI:
The Prince (Italian)

How necessary it is for a prince to get his basic
principles right; otherwise he is certain to be
ruined.

[Uno principe] é necessario essere tanto
prudente, che sappia fuggire l'infamia di quelle
che li torrebbano lo stato.

NICCOLÒ MACHIAVELLI:
The Prince (Italian)

A prince should be prudent enough to avoid the
scandal of vices that could lose him the state.

Al è n prinssi? Ca fassa el prinssi!

Senator Agnelli (on being asked to
find a job at Fiat for an Austrian prince who
had married into his family) (Italian)

He's a prince, isn't he? So let him get on with
being a prince!

. . . i Re son detti de le patrie padri,
Per dar loro a veder, ch'esser benigni
Deono, e non crudi

GIAMBATTISTA CINTHIO GIRALDI:
Cleopatra (Italian)

Kings are called fathers of the fatherland, to
show them that they must be benevolent, not
cruel.

Che dee far'altro un Re, che cercar sempre
Di far maggior lo stato, di acquistarsi
Maggior potenza?

GIAMBATTISTA CINTHIO GIRALDI:
Euphimia (Italian)

What else should a king do, but always aim at
augmenting his state and acquiring greater
power for himself?

. . . nec posse dari regalibus usquam
Secretum vitiis.

CLAUDIA
Panegyricus de Quarto Consula
Honorii Augusti (Lat

The vices of monarchs can never remain hidde

Recte igitur faciendo regis nomen tenetur, pe
cando amittitur.

ISIDORE OF SEVILL
Etymologiae (Lati

A king retains his reputation by doing good; :
doing wrong he loses it.

Vivat rex! Vivat regina!

LATIN EXPRESSIO

Long live the king! Long live the queen!

Nemo potest innocenter regnare.

MEDIEVAL LATIN EXPRESSIC

It is not possible to reign without blame.

Plebei regem se salutanti Caesarem se, no
regem esse responderit

SUETONIU
Divus Iulius (Lati

Caesar, when the commons hailed him as kin
replied: 'I am Caesar and no king!'

Compos factus votorum meorum, p[atre
c[onscripti], quid habeo aliud deos immortal
precari, quam ut hunc consensum vestrum a
ultimum finem vitae mihi perferre licent?

SUETONIU
Divus Augustus (Lati

Having attained my highest hopes, Fathers
the Senate, what more have I to ask of th
immortal gods than that I may retain this sam
unanimous approval of yours to the very end
my life?

Condicionem principum miserrimam aieba
quibus de coniuratione comperta non cr
deretur nisi occisis

SUETONIUS
Domitianus (Latin

He used to say that the lot of princes wa
most unhappy, since, when they discovered

onspiracy, no-one believed them unless they
were killed.

'idesne, ut cinaedus orbem digito temperat?

SUETONIUS:
Divus Augustus (quoting from an
unidentified play) *(Latin)*

ee'st how a wanton's finger sways the world?

Regem se voluisse ait, videre, non mortuos.

SUETONIUS:
Divus Augustus (Latin)

Augustus said he wished to see a king, not
orpses! (on being asked if he wished to see
he tomb of the Ptolemies, as well as the
arcophagus of Alexander the Great).

Rex in regno suo est imperator.

LATIN PROVERB

The king is emperor in his own country.

Odere reges dicta quae dici iubent.

SENECA:
Oedipus (Latin)

Kings loathe the words whose utterance is
licited by force.

Mikit má konungs gæfa.

Óláfs Saga Helga (Norse)

A king's luck can do much.

bozhieĭ stikhieĭ tsaryam ne sovladet'

RUSSIAN PROVERB

Against God's element there is no prevailing for
emporal rulers.

Las esperanzas cortesanas
Prisiones son do el ambicioso muere
Y donde al más astuto nacen canas.

Attrib. ANDRÉS FERNÁNDEZ DE ANDRADA:
Epístola Moral (Spanish)

A courtier's hopes are a prison where the ambitious die, and the cleverest go grey.

Essos reyes poderosos
Que vemos por escrituras
Ya passadas.

Con casos tristes, llorosos,
Fueron sus buenas venturas
Trastornadas.

JORGE MANRIQUE:
Coplas por la Muerte de su Padre (Spanish)

Those powerful kings of the past that we have
read about, by sad lamentable fate saw their fine
ventures overthrown.

KISSES
see also Death, Love, Personality,
Self-Interest.

Partons, dans un baiser, pour un monde
inconnu.

ALFRED DE MUSSET:
La Nuit de Mai (French)

With a kiss let us set out for an unknown world.

Einer Kuss von rosiger Lippe,
Und ich fürchte nicht Sturm nicht Klippe!

OLD GERMAN SONG

One kiss from rosy lips, and I fear no storm or
rock!

Einen Kuss in Ehren kann niemand verwehren.

GERMAN PROVERB

No-one can forbid an honourable kiss.

Si nám sîn antlüt in ir hende wîz
Únde druhte ez an ir munt, ir wengel klâr:
Owê sô gâr wol kuste sîz

JOHANS HADLOUB:
Sie Küsst ein Kind (German)

With her fair white hands she held up the child's
face and pressed it to her mouth and bright
cheeks, and kissed it with sheer delight.

Questi, che mai da me non fia diviso,
La bocca mi baciò tutto tremante

DANTE:
Inferno (Italian)

He who shall never be divided from me kissed
my mouth all trembling.

Hoc osculum mihi facit bonum apud cor.
Possum volare super tria clocheria nunc!

GEORGE RUGGLE:
Ignoramus (Latin)

This kiss makes me feel good at heart. I could fly
over three clock-towers now!

Dame, Amor, besos sin cuento,
Asido de mis cabellos,
Y mil y ciento tras ellos,
Y tras ellos mil y ciento.

CRISTÓBAL DE CASTILLEJO:
Al Amor (Spanish)

Give me, love, innumerable kisses, fast-tied in
my hair, and then eleven hundred more, and
then still eleven hundred more!

KNOWLEDGE
see also Belief, Experience, Ignorance, Judgment, Leadership, Learning, Memory, Opinion, Poets and poetry, Reality, Thought and thinking, Wisdom.

Le savoir à son prix.

JEAN DE LA FONTAINE:
L'Avantage de la Science (French)

Knowledge has its own price.

L'invasion des idées a succedé à l'invasion des
barbares. La civilisation actuelle décompassée
se perde en elle même.

CHATEAUBRIAND:
Mémoires d'Outre-Tombe (French)

The invasion of barbarians has given place
to the invasion of ideas. Today our limitless
civilisation is lost in its own depths.

Le seul plaisir est de redécouvrir seul toute
connaissance.

MICHEL SERVIN:
Les Réguliers (French)

The only pleasure is to rediscover for oneself the
whole of knowledge.

La fin naturelle de la science, et par conséquent
des études, est, après s'estre rempli soy-mesme,
de travailler pour les autres.

JEAN MABILLON:
Etudes Monastiques (French)

The natural purpose of knowledge and conse-
quently of study, is, after satisfying oneself, to
work for others.

Je goute peu les plaisantaries quand elles
s'adressent à la science.

LABICHE ET MARTIN:
Les Vivacites du Capitaine Tic

I don't much care for jokes when they are about
knowledge.

Alles Wissen hat etwas Puritanisches; es gi
den Worten ein Moral.

ELIAS CANETT
Aufzeichnungen, 1945 (Germa

All knowledge has a touch of the puritanical –
provides words with a moral.

Ouk allo ti estin epistēmē ē aisthēsis

PLAT
Theaetetus (Gree

Knowledge is nothing else but perception.

Tēn alēthe doxan epistēmēn einai

PLAT
Theaetetus (Gree

Knowledge is true opinion.

Appassutāyam puriso balivaddo va jīrati
Māmsāni tassa vaḍḍhanti, paññā tasse na
vaḍḍhati

Dhammapada: Jarāvaggo (Pal

He who learns little grows old like an ox: hi
flesh increases, but his knowledge does no
grow.

Nadie nacemos zabijondos.

ALVAREZ QUINTERC
El Genio Alegre (Spanish

None of us is born knowing everything.

Más vale saber que haber.

SPANISH PROVER

Knowledge is worth more than riches.

No es ciencia la que vive de opiniones.

LOPE DE VEGA
Égloga a Claudio (Spanish

True knowledge is not dependent on opinion.

¿De qué sirve el saber si no es plático?

SPANISH PROVER

What is the use of knowledge if it serves no usefu
purpose?

L

LAKES

Chaque flot est un ondin qui nage dans le courant, chaque courant est un sentier qui serpente vers mon palais, et mon palais est bâti fluide, au fond du lac, dans le triangle du feu, de la terre, et de l'air.

ALOYSIUS BERTRAND:
Ondine (French)

Every wave is a watersprite who swims in the current, each current is a path which snakes towards my palace, and my palace is fluidly built at the bottom of the lake, in the triangle of earth, fire and water.

LAMENTS

Ore est ocys
La Flur de Pris
Qe taunt savoir de guerre.

Lament for the death of
Simon de Montfort *(French)*

Now is slain that priceless flower who knew so much of war.

Cuncti flete pro Willelmo
Innocente interfecto.

Lament for the death of William Longsword,
second duke of Normandy *(Latin)*

Now let us all weep for William, innocent yet done to death.

LANDSCAPES
see also the Countryside.

Un paysage pourra être beau, gracieux, sublime, insignificant ou laid; il ne sera jamais risible.

HENRI BERGSON:
Le Rire (French)

You can have a beautiful landscape, or one that is graceful, sublime, trivial, or ugly; but you will never find a comic landscape.

Houblons et vignes,
Feuilles et fleurs,
Tentes insignes
Des francs buveurs!

PAUL VERLAINE:
Paysages Belges, Walcourt (French)

Hops and vines, leaves and flowers, insignia on the tents of open drinkers!

LANGUAGE
see also Dictionaries, Genius, Grammar, Nationhood, Philology, Words.

Her kom jeg for at læse et rigere sprog,
For at lytte til uforfalskede stemmer

BENNY ANDERSEN:
Nye Stemmer (Danish)

I came here to learn a richer tongue, and to listen to unfalsified voices.

C'est abus, dire que ayons language naturel.

RABELAIS:
Tiers Livre (French)

To say that we have a natural language is to abuse our understanding.

La langue d'un peuple donne son vocabulaire, et le vocabulaire est un table assez fidèle de toutes les connaissances de ce peuple: sur la comparaison du vocabulaire d'un nation en différents temps, on se formerait une idée de ses progrès.

DENIS DIDEROT:
'Encyclopédie' in *L'Encyclopédie (French)*

Our vocabulary is derived from the nation's language; and the vocabulary provides a very good indication of the nation's knowledge: by comparing a nation's vocabulary at different times, we can get a pretty good idea of that nation's progress.

Pris dans son tout, le langage est multiforme et hétéroclite; à cheval sur plusieurs domaines, à la fois physique, physiologique et psychique, il appartient encore au domaine individuel et au domaine social; il ne se laisse classer dans aucune catégorie des faits humains, parce qu'on ne sait comment dégager son unité.

FERDINAND DE SAUSSURE:
Cours de Linguistique Generale, Introduction (French)

Taken as a whole language is irregular and assumes many forms; dominant in many areas, at one and the same time physical, physiological, and psychical, it nevertheless belongs to the individual and to the social domains; it does not lend itself to classification in any category of human experience, because we do not know how to isolate its unity.

Dans les sciences, la grammaire doit se prêter aux exigences des découvertes.

HONORÉ DE BALZAC:
La Peau de Chagrin: 'L'Agonie' (French)

In science, grammar must bend to the requirements of new discoveries.

Les sages qui veulent parler au vulgaire leur langage au lieu du sien n'en sauraient être entendus.

J. J. ROUSSEAU:
Du Contrat Social (French)

If wise men try to address the common herd in their own language, instead of using the common tongue, they cannot possibly make themselves understood.

Il y a mille sortes d'idées qu'il est impossible de traduire dans la langue du peuple.

J. J. ROUSSEAU:
Du Contrat Social (French)

There are thousands of ideas that it is impossible to translate into popular language.

Les gémissements de la douleur, les plaintes de la souffrance sont à l'origine du langage.

RAYMOND QUENEAU:
Une Histoire Modèle (French)

The groans of suffering, the cries of pain, are the very basis of language.

Notre langage maternelle, nous la savions virtuellement avant que de naître.

V. HENRY:
Antinomies Linguistiques (French)

We knew our mother-tongue practically before we were born.

Die Grenzen meiner Sprache bedeuten die Grenzen meiner Welt.

LUDWIG WITTGENSTEIN:
Tractatus Logico-philosophicus (German)

The limits of my language mean the limits of my world.

Jede Sprache hat ihr eigenes Schweigen.

ELIAS CANETTI:
Aufzeichnungen, 1942 *(German)*

Every language has its own silences.

Jeder Mensch glaubt, weil er spricht, über die Sprache sprechen zu durfen.

GERMAN PROVERB

Every human being thinks that, because he speaks, he is qualified to speak about language.

Das Wort baut Brücken in unerforschte Gebiete.

ADOLF HITLER
(German)

Language builds bridges in unexplored territories.

Man hört jetzt: in der Sprachwissenschaft kriselt es; das ist ein gutes Wort.

HUGO SCHUCHARDT BREVIER
(German)

There is talk just now of a 'crisis' in linguistics: That's a word we like to hear!

Quod non agnoscit glossa, non agnoscit curia.
Medieval maxim, referring to the almost universal authority of Accursius's
Glossa Ordinaria (Latin)

The papal curia does not recognise what is not in his glossary.

Notitia linguarum est prima porta sapientiae.

ROGER BACON:
Opus Tertium (Latin)

Knowledge of languages is the gateway to wisdom.

Et cum loquela non alitur sit necessarium instrumentum nostrae conceptionis quam equus militis; et optimis militibus optimi conveniant qui, optimis conceptionibus, ut dictum est, optima loquela conveniet

DANTE:
De Vulgari Eloquio (Latin)

As language is the instrument of our thought, so horse is the instrument of a soldier, and as the best horses are suited to the best soldiers, so the best language will, as has been said, be suited to the best thoughts.

Lyublyu iz roda v rod mne dannyï
Moï chelovecheskiï yazyk:
Ego surovuyu svobodu,
Ego izvilistyï zakon

VLADISLAV KHODASEVICH:
Zhiv Bog! (Russian)

love my human language, passed down through the generations to me; I love its stern freedom and sinuous laws.

LAST WORDS
see also Epitaphs, Farewell, Parting.

Adieu', dit le mourant au miroir qu'on lui tend, nous ne nous verrons plus . . .'

PAUL VALÉRY:
Mauvaises Pensées (French)

Farewell', says the dying man to his reflection in the mirror that is held up to him, 'we shall not meet again'.

Voilà le premier chagrin qu'elle m'ait jamais donné.

Louis XIV, at the death of his cousin
the Infanta Maria Teresa, to whom he had
been married for 23 years *(French)*

This is the first pain she has ever given to me.

Un homme d'une grande indifférence sur la vie disait en mourant: 'Le docteur Bouvard sera bien attrapé'.

S. R. N. CHAMFORT;
Maximes et Pensées, Appendix II *(French)*

A dying man who was completely indifferent to life, said: 'Doctor Bouvard has been thoroughly cheated this time!'

'Docteur, croyez-vous que c'est le saucisson?'

Paul Claudel's dying words *(French)*

'Doctor, do you think it could have been the sausage?'

Je m'en vais enfin de ce monde, où il faut que le coeur se brise ou se bronze.

S. R. N. DE CHAMFORT:
(committed suicide 1794) *(French)*

And so I leave this world where one's heart either breaks or turns to lead.

Nin, non, j'aurai des maîtresses.

George II, to his dying wife who had
urged him to consider marrying again *(French)*

No! I shall have mistresses!

Je le crois parce que je l'espère.

LÉON BLUM: *(French)*

My belief is rooted in hope.

Wer dunkel ist, bleibe dunkel, wer
Unrein ist, unrein. Lobet
Mangel, lobet Misshandlung, lobet
Die Finsternis.

BERTOLT BRECHT:
Leben Eduards des Zweiten von England
(Edward's last words) *(German)*

Whoever is dark, stay dark! Whoever is unclean, stay unclean! Commend need, commend abuse, commend the darkness!

Khairete kai memnēsthe ta dogmata

Epicurus' last words *(Greek)*

Farewell – and remember my teachings.

Kai su teknon

> SUETONIUS:
> *Divus Iulius (Greek)*

'You, too, my child!' (Julius Caesar's last words to Brutus as he struck).

Emou th' nontos gaia meikhthētō puri
> Believed to be a line from Euripides'
> long-lost play *Bellerophon (Greek)*

When I am dead, let the earth be consumed by fire!

Bene se habet imperator!
> FLORUS:
> *Works (Latin)*

All is well with the general! (Scipio Nasica, as he committed suicide at Thapsus).

Vixi! invictus enim morior!
> CORNELIUS NEPOS:
> *Epaminondas (Latin)*

I have lived long enough, since I die unconquered!

Livia, nostri coniugii memor vive, ac vale!
> SUETONIUS:
> *Divus Augustus* (Augustus's dying
> words to his wife) *(Latin)*

Live on, mindful of our wedlock, Livia, and farewell!

Haec est fides!
> SUETONIUS:
> *Nero (Latin)*

This is fidelity! (Nero's ironic comment on the centurion who came too late to save him).

Ego vester sum et vos mei.
> SUETONIUS:
> *Galba (Latin)*

I am yours, and you are mine (Galba's protest to the soldiers who came to kill him).

Qualis artifex pereo!
> SUETONIUS:
> *Nero (Latin)*

What an artist the world is losing! (*lit.* what an artist I perish; Nero, preparing for death).

Vae! Puto deus fio.
> SUETONIU
> *Divus Vespasianus (Lati*

Woe is me! I think I'm turning into a gc (Vespasian, as death draws near).

Mantua me genuit, Calabri rapuere, tenet nur Parthenope; cecini pascua rura duces.
> VIRGI
> (his own couplet for engravin
> on his tomb) *(Latir*

Mantua gave me light, Calabria slew me; no Parthenope holds me. I have sung of shepherd of the country and of heroes.

Adiciamus vitae et hanc noctem.
> SUETONIU:
> *Otho (Latir*

Let us add this one more night to our live (Otho, on the night before his suicide).

Vulpes intravit, tanquam leo pontificavit, exi ut canis.
> Epitaph for Pope Boniface VIII *(Latir*

He got in like a fox, played the pontiff like a lio and went out like a dog.

O Domine Deus, speravi in Te!
Chare mi, Jesu, nunc libera me
In dura catena
In misera poena
Mi Jesu, desidero Te!
Languendo
Gemendo
Genuflectendo
Adoro, imploro
Ut liberes Me!
> Mary, Queen of Scots, short
> before her execution *(Latir*

O Lord God, I have set my hope in thee! M dear Jesus, free me; in these harsh fetters, in th miserable punishment, I long for thee. Wear with sighs, on my knees I adore thee, an implore thee to set me free!

Tvert imod!
> HENRIK IBSE
> *(Norwegia*

Not at all! (Ibsen's retort on hearing his wife remark that he seemed to be getting better).

¡Diles que no me maten!

JUAN RULFO;
(from his short story of that name) *(Spanish)*

Tell them not to kill me! (The hero's last words as he stands bound to the stake, waiting to be shot).

LAUGHTER
see also Comedy, Duplicity, Endurance, Reactions, Ridicule.

Aḍ-ḍiḥk min g͟hayr sabab qillit adab

ARAB PROVERB

Meaningless laughter is a sign of ill breeding.

Aḍ-ḍiḥik samm fōq umm falaja

ARAB PROVERB

Laughter is good to see on a girl with white teeth.

Al-hizār luh waqt wa-l-jadd luh waqt

ARAB PROVERB

There is a time for levity, and a time for seriousness.

La plus perdue de toutes les journées est celle où l'on n'a pas ri.

S. R. N. CHAMFORT:
Maximes et Pensées (French)

The most wasted of all our days are those in which we have not laughed.

D'où vient que l'on rit si librement au théâtre, et que l'on a honte d'y pleurer?

JEAN DE LA BRUYÈRE:
Des Ouvrages de l'Esprit (French)

How is it that we laugh so freely at the theatre, but are ashamed of weeping there?

Le rire est un refus de penser.

PAUL VALÉRY:
Lust (French)

Laughter is a refusal to think.

Un homme qui rit ne sera jamais dangéreux.

LAURENCE STERNE:
A Sentimental Journey through France and Italy: 'The passport – Versailles' *(French)*

A man who laughs is never dangerous.

Das Lachen ist ein schöpferischer Akt, der die phantastische Spielwelt eröffnet: das Lachen ist auch eine schenkende Geste.

REINHARD TRACHSLER:
Lichtenbergs Aphorismen (German)

Laughter is a creative act that opens up the world of fantasy and amusement; it is also a generous gesture.

Xun toi theōi pas kai gelai kōduretai

SOPHOCLES:
Ajax (Greek)

Laughter or tears, both derive from God.

Risus abundat in ore stultorum.

LATIN PROVERB

Laughter abounds in the mouths of fools.

LAW
see also America, Cities, Conscience, Government, Injustice, Judgment, Juries, Justice, Language, Liberty, Might, Morals and morality, Necessity, Right and wrong, Royal prerogative, the State, Wisdom.

Il est dangereux de dire au peuple que les loix ne sont pas justes, car il n'y obéit qu'a cause qu'il les croit justes.

BLAISE PASCAL:
Pensées (French)

It is dangerous to tell people that their laws are not just, for they only obey them because they believe them to be just.

Un société ne devrait point avoir de mauvaises lois, et si elle n'en avait que de bonnes, elle ne serait jamais dans le cas de persécuter un homme de génie.

DENIS DIDEROT:
Le Neveu de Rameau (French)

Society should never have bad laws; and if it has only good laws, it should never be in danger of persecuting men of genius.

Il y a deux sortes de lois, les unes d'une équité, d'une généralité absolues, d'autres bizarres, qui ne doivent leur sanction qu'à l'aveuglement ou le nécessité des circonstances.

> DENIS DIDEROT:
> *Le Neveu de Rameau (French)*

There are two kinds of laws: those of equity, which are entirely general; the others bizarre, and which only owe their approval to blindness or the necessity of events.

La législation anglaise est comme un arbre antique, sur lequel les légistes ont greffé sans cesse les rejetons les plus étrangers, dans l'espérance que, tout en donnant des fruits différents, ils confondront du moins leur feuillage avec la tige vénérable qui les supporte.

> ALEXIS DE TOCQUEVILLE:
> *De la Démocratie en Amérique (French)*

English legislation is like an ancient tree on which the legislators have ceaselessly grafted the strangest cuttings in the hope that, while producing different kinds of fruit, they will at least blend their foliage with the venerable trunk that supports them.

Le loi fait des Citoyens.

> Attributed by Voltaire (*Lettres Philosophiques*)
> to Lord Bolingbroke *(French)*

The law creates citizens.

Des lois différentes n'engendrent que trouble et confusion.

> J. J. ROUSSEAU:
> *Du Contrat Social (French)*

Different laws only cause trouble and confusion.

Un peuple ne devient célèbre que quand sa législation commence à décliner.

> J. J. ROUSSEAU:
> *Du Contrat Social* (footnote) *(French)*

A nation only becomes famous when its legislation begins to decline.

Les lois sont toujours utiles à ceux qui possèdent et nuisibles à ceux qui n'ont rien.

> J. J. ROUSSEAU:
> *Du Contrat Social (French)*

The law is always useful to the haves and vexatious to the have-nots.

Die Gesetze der Welt sind Würfelspiel worden

> J. C. F. VON SCHILLE
> *Die Räuber (Germa*

The laws of the world have become a lottery (*l* a game of dice).

Das Gesetz hat noch keinen grossen Man gebildet, aber die Freiheit brütet Kolosse ur Extremitäten aus.

> J. C. F. VON SCHILLE
> *Die Räuber (Germa*

The law has yet to produce a great man, where as freedom breeds both giants and extremists.

Alle streben doch nach dem Gesetz.

> FRANZ KAFK*
> *Der Prozess (Germar*

Everyone strives after the law.

Recht is nur der ausgeschmückte Name
Für alles Unrecht, das die Erde hegt.

> FRANZ GRILLPARZE*
> *Libussa (German*

Law is only the fancy name for all the injustice i the world.

Hotan gar nomothetōmetha, hōs esomenou ōphelimous tous nomous tithemetha eis to epeita khronon

> PLATC
> *Theaetetus (Greek*

When laws are made they are made with th idea that they will be useful in the future.

Pas an homologoi nomothetoumenēn polin pol lakis anankēn einai tou ōphelimōtatou apotunk hanein

> PLATC
> *Theaetetus (Greek*

In making law the state often fails to secure th greatest use from it.

Ek tou proteros legein ho diōkōn iskhuei

> GREEK PROVER

A plaintiff's strength lies in his speaking first.

Ouk estin ouden kreitton ē nomoi polei
GREEK PROVERB

Nothing is better for a country than law.

E veruna cosa fa tanto onore a uno uomo che di
nuovo si vegga, quanto fa le nuove legge e li
nuovi ordini trovati da lui.
NICCOLÒ MACHIAVELLI:
The Prince (Italian)

Nothing does so much honour to a newly-risen
leader than the new laws and measures that he
introduces.

Neque istis quicquam lege sanctumst: leges
mori serviunt,
Mores autem rapere properant qua sacrum qua
publicum.
PLAUTUS:
Trinummus (Latin)

Nor are our laws sacrosanct; laws are subser-
vient to custom, and custom makes nothing of
voiding both the sacred and the public.

Aurea prima sata est aetas, quae vindice nullo,
Sponte sua, sine lege fidem rectumque colebat
OVID:
Metamorphoses (Latin)

First was the Golden Age when men, of their
own accord, with none to compel, and without
laws, cherished both faith and right.

Quid faciant leges, ubi sola pecunia regnat?
PETRONIUS:
Satyricon (Latin)

What use are laws where money alone holds
sway?

Leges bonae ex malis moribus procreantur.
MACROBIUS:
Satires (Latin)

Good laws derive from bad customs.

Utque antehac flagitiis ita tunc legibus
laborabatur.
TACITUS:
Annals (Latin)

As before they had laboured under their mis-
deeds, so now they laboured under their laws.

Lex humana intantum recte mutatur, inquan-
tum per eius mutationem communi utilitati pro-
videtur.
ST. THOMAS AQUINAS:
Summa Theologica (Latin)

Changes in human law are only justified to the
extent that they benefit the general welfare.

Ibi pote valere populus ubi leges valent.
LATIN PROVERB

Where laws prevail, there can the people
prevail.

Inter arma silent leges.
LATIN PROVERB

Laws are powerless (lit. silent) when men are at
war (cf. Cicero: Pro Milone, silent enim leges
inter arma).

De minimis non curat lex.
LEGAL MAXIM (Latin)

The law does not concern itself with trifles.

Ignorantia juris non excusat.
LEGAL MAXIM (Latin)

Ignorance of the law is no excuse.

Quod omnes tangit ab omnibus comprobetur.
LEGAL PRINCIPLE (Latin)

What touches everyone should be approved by
everyone.

Que si a la ley no te ajustas,
Quedó en la cuna labrada
La materia de la tumba.
PEDRO CALDERÓN DE LA BARCA:
La Vida es Sueño (Spanish)

If you cannot reconcile yourself to the law,
remain in the cradle.

Como telas de arañas son las leyes, que prenden
a las moscas y no al milano.
SPANISH PROVERB

Laws, like the spider's web, catch the fly and let
the hawk go free.

¡Qué de pleitos, qué de trapisondas!
JACINTO BENAVENTE Y MARTÍNEZ:
Los Malhechores del Bien (Spanish)

What a lot of lawsuits, what a lot of snarls!

LAZINESS
see also Idleness.

Hoi argoi tēn dianoian eiōthasin hestiasthai huph' heautōn, hotan monoi poreuōntai
PLATO:
The Republic (Greek)

People with lazy minds feast on their own thoughts when they are alone.

Inertia indicatur cum fugitur labor.
LATIN PROVERB

Work shunned is an index of laziness.

LEADERSHIP
see also Confidence, Kings, Law, Liberality, Monarchy, Office, the People, Politics, Statesmen, Violence, War.

Tous ont également besoin de guides.
J. J. ROUSSEAU:
Du Contrat Social (French)

All men stand equally in need of guidance.

Diviser pour régner.
FRENCH PROVERB

Divide and rule (*lit.* divide in order to rule).

Il n'est pour voir que l'oeil du maître.
JEAN DE LA FONTAINE:
L'Oeil du Maître (French)

No eye is as keen as the master's.

On ne choisit pas pour gouverner un vaisseau celuy des voyageurs qui est de la meilleure maison.
BLAISE PASCAL:
Pensées (French)

We do not choose as the skipper of the ship the best born among the passengers.

C'est moi seul qui fais la politique, et sous m seule responsabilité. Moi seul ai le pouvoir c décision.
Charles de Gaulle to his Minister of Financ
Antoine Pinay *(Frenc*

I alone conduct the nation's politics; it is m responsibility alone. I alone have comple power of decision.

Qui n'a fait qu'obéir saura mal commander.
PIERRE CORNEILL
Pulchérie (Frenc

He who has always been a subordinate w make a bad leader.

Ist es dem Land nicht egal, wer auf de Apfelschimmel sitzt, der es staubig stampft?
BERTOLT BRECH
Der Prozess der Jeanne d'Arc (German

Who cares who sits on the dapple-grey horse a it paws the dust with its hooves? (implying tha the leader can be recognised by the quality of h mount, but his identity arouses only indiffe ence).

Ich führe euch herrlichen Zeiten entgegen.
Kaiser Wilhelm II, to the German peopl
(German

I lead you toward glorious times.

Das gesamte Leben lässt sich in drei These zusammenfassen: der Kampf ist der Vater alle Dinge, die Tugend ist eine Angelegenheit de Bluts, Führertum ist primär und entscheidend
Adolf Hitler (in a letter t
Heinrich Brüning) *(German*

The whole of life can be summed up in thre postulates: struggle is the father of all thing virtue is the family's concern; leadership i primary and crucial.

Mega gar en kairois episphalesi pros sōtēria doxa kai pistis andros hēgemonikēn empeiria kai dunamin ekhontos
PLUTARCH
Moralia (Greek

In times of crisis, nearly everything may depen on the regard and confidence placed in som man who possesses the experience and qualitie of a leader.

Ouk agathon polukoiraniē
HOMER:
Iliad (Greek)

It is not good to have several rulers.

Asphalēs gar est' ameinōn ē thrasus stratēlatēs
SUETONIUS:
Divus Augustus (Greek)

Better a safe commander than a bold one (a favourite saying of the Emperor Augustus).

Toutou g' espomenoio kai ek puros aithomenoio
Amphō nostēsaimen, epei perioide noēsai
HOMER:
Iliad (Greek)

With him as my companion, we may both escape the burning fire and return home, since his wisdom and knowledge are so great.

... quando stat'è d'auttoridade
Un ne la sua republica, et i cori
Ha mossi de le genti a le sue voglie,
Sculpito resta ne le menti loro.
GIAMBATTISTA CINTHIO GIRALDI:
Cleopatra (Italian)

When a man has held authority in his country and has won the hearts of the people to his own will, he will always be remembered by them, even though he suffer the extremes of misfortune.

Si el prior juega a los naipes, ¿qué harán los frailes?
SPANISH PROVERB

If the prior plays cards, what will the monks get up to?

Es bueno mandar, aunque sea a un hato de ganado.
SPANISH PROVERB

It is pleasant to command, be it only a herd of cattle.

No honra la casa al señor mas el señor a la casa.
SPANISH PROVERB

It is the master who makes the house respected, not the house the master.

LEARNING
see also Cleverness, Education, Experience, Fools, Knowledge, Life, Philosophers, Teaching.

Apprendre à apprendre, c'est savoir s'orienter parmi une forêt de faits, d'idées et de théories, une prolifération de connaissances en transformations constantes. Apprendre à apprendre, c'est savoir ignorer, ne pas refuser la nouveauté, ne pas s'opposer à la recherche.
RAYMOND QUENEAU:
Présentation de l'Encyclopédie (French)

Learning to learn is to know how to navigate in a forest of facts, ideas and theories, a proliferation of constantly changing items of knowledge. Learning to learn is to know what to ignore but at the same time not rejecting innovation and research.

No. us fassatz de sen trop temer,
Per qu'om digua: 'trop es senatz'.
Peire Rogier to Raimbaut d'Aurenga
(French)

Do not make yourself too feared for your learning, in case people say 'He is too clever'.

Die Gelehrsamkeit kann auch ins Laub treiben, ohne Früchte zu tragen.
GEORG CHRISTOPH LICHTENBERG:
Aphorismen (German)

Learning can also put forth leaves without bearing fruit.

Ou gar aiskhunomai manthanōn
PLATO:
Hippias Minor (Greek)

I (*i.e.* Socrates) am not afraid to learn.

To gnōnai epistēmēn labein estin
GREEK PROVERB

Learning is acquiring knowledge.

Polumathiē noon ou didaskei
HERACLITUS:
Fragment (Greek)

Much learning does not make a scholar.

Khalepa ta kala estin hopêi ekhei mathein
PLATO:
Cratylus (Greek)

Knowledge of high things is hard to gain (an 'ancient saying' quoted by Socrates).

Doctrina sed vim promovet insitam.
HORACE:
Odes (Latin)

Learning increases native strength.

Non omnis aetas ad perdiscendum sat est.
PLAUTUS:
Truculentus (Latin)

Even the whole of life is not sufficient for thorough learning.

Discendo docebis, docendo disces.
LATIN PROVERB

By learning, you will teach; by teaching you will learn.

LEWDNESS

Luxus erit lubricis.
BEDE:
Hymn on Virginity (Latin)

Leave lewdness to the lewd.

LIBERAL ARTS

GRAM loquitur; DIA vera docet; RHET verba colorat;
MUS canit; AR numerat; GE ponderat; AST colit astra.
Late Latin couplet designed to remind students of the names of the seven liberal arts (quoted by Nicolaus de Orbellis).

Grammar speaks; Logic teaches the truth; Rhetoric colours words; Music sings; Arithmetic counts; Geometry measures; Astronomy studies the stars.

Las artes son liberales
Porque hacen que libre viva
A quien en ellas se emplea.
TIRSO DE MOLINA:
El Amor Médico (Spanish)

The arts are called liberal, because they enable those who practise them to live in freedom.

LIBERALITY
see also Generosity, Kindness.

E non ci è cosa che consumi sé stessa quanto la liberalità.
NICCOLÒ MACHIAVELLI:
The Prince (Italian)

Nothing destroys itself as much as liberality.

E quel principe che va con li eserciti, che si pasce di prede, di sacchi e di taglie, maneggia quel di altri, li è necessaria questa liberalità; altrimenti non sarebbe seguito da' soldati.
NICCOLÒ MACHIAVELLI:
The Prince (Italian)

Liberality is very necessary to a prince who marches with his armies, lives by plunder, pillage and ransom and is dealing with the wealth of others, for without it he would not be followed by his soldiers.

LIBERTY
see also Civil war, Freedom, Money, Permissiveness, Revolution, Tyranny.

Il n'est pas bon d'estre trop libre.
BLAISE PASCAL:
Pensées (French)

It is not good to be too free.

L'homme est né libre, et partout il est dans les fers.
J. J. ROUSSEAU:
Du Contrat Social (French)

Man is born free, but everywhere he is in chains.

La liberté est le droit de faire ce que les lois permettent.
CHARLES DE SECONDAT, BARON DE MONTESQUIEU:
Réflexions et Pensées (French)

Liberty is the right to do what the law permits.

Que sert la bonne chère
Quand on n'a pas la liberté?
JEAN DE LA FONTAINE:
Le Cheval s'étânt voulu venger du Cerf (French)

What's the use of the good life if you are not free?

'impulsion du seul appétit est esclavage, et
obéissance à la loi qu'on s'est prescrite est
berté.

J. J. ROUSSEAU:
Du Contrat Social (French)

he impulse of one's own desires is slavery,
while obedience to the law as laid down is
berty.

Jn peu d'agitation donne du ressort aux âmes,
t ce qui fait vraiment prospérer l'espèce est
noins la paix que la liberté.

J. J. ROUSSEAU:
Du Contrat Social (French)

A little disturbance gives the soul elasticity;
what makes the race truly prosperous is not so
much peace as liberty.

Jn peut acquérir la liberté mais on ne la
ecouvre jamais.

J. J. ROUSSEAU:
Du Contrat Social (French)

Liberty may be gained, but can never be
recovered.

La liberté, n'étant pas un fruit de tous les
limats, n'est pas à la portée de tous les peuples.

J. J. ROUSSEAU:
Du Contrat Social (quoting Montesquieu's
Esprit des Lois) (French)

Liberty, not being the fruit of every climate, is
not within the reach of all nations.

Dans la république, chacun est parfaitement
ibre en ce qui ne nuit pas aux autres.

J. J. ROUSSEAU:
Du Contrat Social
(quoting the marquis d'Argenson) *(French)*

In a republic everyone is perfectly free to do
anything that does not harm other people.

Ein freies Leben ist ein paar knechtischer Stunden wert.

J. C. F. VON SCHILLER:
Fiesco (German)

Freedom is worth the sacrifice of a few menial
hours.

Die Statue der Freiheit ist noch nicht gegossen,
der Ofen glüht, wir alle können uns noch die
Finger dabei verbrennen.

GEORG BÜCHNER:
Dantons Tod (German)

The Statue of Liberty is not yet cast. The oven is
glowing and we can all yet burn our fingers on it.

Ich glaube, der Mensch ist am Ende ein so freies
Wesen, dass ihm das Recht zu sein, was er
glaubt zu sein, nicht streitig gemacht werden
kann.

GEORG CHRISTOPH LICHTENBERG:
Aphorismen (German)

I believe that, in the end, man is so free a being
that his right to be what he wants to be cannot be
questioned.

Malo periculosam libertatem quam quietum
servitium.

The Palatine of Posnan (quoted in
J. J. Rousseau: *Du Contrat Social) (French)*

I prefer liberty with danger to peace with
slavery.

LIBRARIES
see also Books, Censorship, Protest.

Les livres tristes, innombrables, par hautes
couches crétacées.

ST.-JOHN PERSE:
Vents (French)

Sad books, innumerable, in high cretaceous
layers.

LIES
see also Compliments, Deceit,
Exaggeration, Modesty, Poets and poetry,
Truth, Untrustworthiness.

Ne point mentir, être content du sien,
C'est le plus sûr.

JEAN DE LA FONTAINE:
Le Bûcheron et Mercure (French)

It's best never to lie and to be content with one's
lot.

Un menteur est toujours prodigue de serments.

PIERRE CORNEILLE:
Le Menteur (French)

A liar is always prodigal of oaths.

Ontos de ge pseudous estin apatē

> PLATO:
> *The Sophist (Greek)*

If falsehood exists, deceit exists.

Calidum hercle esse audivi optimum mendacium.

> PLAUTUS:
> *Mostellaria (Latin)*

I've heard the best lie is a whopper!

. . . fallacia
Alia aliam trudit.

> TERENCE:
> *Andria (Latin)*

One lie gives birth to another.

Ja, en Løgn kan endevendes,
Stadses opp med Brask og Bram,
Klædes i en nygjort Ham,
Saa dens magre Skrott ej kjendes.

> HENRIK IBSEN:
> *Peer Gynt (Norwegian)*

Lies can be so furbished and disguised in gorgeous wrappings that not a soul would recognise their skinny carcases.

La mentira y la torta, gorda.

> SPANISH PROVERB

A cake should be big – and so should a lie!

LIFE
see also Action, Art, Aspiration, Beauty, Civilisation, Death, Despair, Effort, Eternity, Existence, Experience, Grief, Home, Love, Mercy, Mortality, Purpose, Sorrow, Vanity, Work, World.

Jeg beder om balance i tilværelsen,
Som kræmmeren der snyder med vaegten:
Måtte den bare *vise* rigtigt!

> BENNY ANDERSEN:
> *Skeptisk Bøn (Danish)*

I pray for balance in my life – just like a shopkeeper with his thumb on the scales – only let it *look* right!

Nimmer kan leven
Verlangen verlies zijn,
Maar dubble winst.

> PETER CORNELIS BOUTENS
> *Rustige Vaart (Dutch*

Life can never lose through longing – onl doubly gain!

Eeuwigh gaet voor oogenblick.

> DUTCH PROVER

Life eternal transcends time.

D'autres aiment la vie, et je la dois haïr.

> PIERRE CORNEILLE
> *Horace (French*

Others love life, but I must hate it.

Ne maudissons pas la vie!

> ARTHUR RIMBAUD
> *Matin (French*

Don't let's hate life!

J'ai toujours vécu mon âme fixée sur l'horloge.

> STÉPHANE MALLARMÉ
> *Vie d'Igitur (French*

I have always lived with my soul governed by the clock.

Notre vie n'est qu'un désir permanent de tremper curieusement les lèvres dans la coupe de toutes les sensations.

> STÉPHANE MALLARMÉ:
> *Les Poésies Parisiennes (French)*

Our life is only an unending desire to dip our lips curiously in the cup of every sensation.

L'homme arrive novice à chaque âge de la vie.

> S. R. N. CHAMFORT:
> *Caractères et Anecdotes* (Appendix I) *(French)*

Man enters each stage of life as a novice.

Le Passé, l'Avenir sont nos grands ennemis.

> PAUL VALÉRY:
> *Poème (French)*

The past and the future are our inveterate enemies.

La vie est belle
je me tue à vous le dire
dit la fleur
et elle meurt.

JACQUES PRÉVERT:
Soleil de Mars (French)

Life is beautiful; in telling you, I write my death warrant, says the flower. She dies.

Ah! je le répète sans cesse, il n'y a qu'un malheur, celui d'être né!

Mme du Deffand to Horace Walpole
(French)

I shall go on repeating that there is only one misfortune, that of being born!

Les sables balafrés issus des lents charrois de la terre.

RENÉ CHAR:
Afin qu'il n'y soit Rien Changé (French)

The scarred sands, born of the slow wagons of the earth.

Il faut glisser la vie.

Hugo von Hofmannsthal to Richard Beer-Hofmann *(French)*

We must hold life lightly.

L'emploi normal de la vie de l'homme est donc de travailler et d'imaginer.

RAYMOND QUENEAU:
Une Histoire Modèle (French)

Man's usual routine is to work and to dream.

Au matin de la vie
Par des rêves d'espoir notre âme poursuivie
Se balance un moment sur les flots du bonheur;
Mais, sitôt que le soir étend son voile sombre,
L'onde qui nous portait se retire, et dans l'ombre
Bientôt nous restons seuls en proie à la douleur.

GERARD DE NERVAL:
Mélodie Irlandaise (French)

In the morning of life our soul, haunted by dreams of hope, hovers for a moment on waves of happiness. But as soon as evening spreads its sombre shade, the wave that brought us recedes and in the shadow we soon find ourselves alone and a prey to sorrow.

La saturation, il y a un moment où cela vient dans ce repas qu'on appelle la vie; il ne faut qu'une goutte alors pour faire déborder la coupe du dégoût.

CHARLES AUGUSTIN SAINTE-BEUVE:
Causeries du Lundi (French)

There is a moment in this repast we call life where we reach saturation point; after that, it needs only a drop more to make the cup of disgust run over.

La fortune et l'humeur gouvernent le monde.

FRANÇOIS, DUC DE LA ROCHEFOUCAULD:
Réflexions (French)

Fortune and humour rule the world.

Nous ne voyons jamais qu'un seul côté des choses;
L'autre plonge en la nuit d'un mystère effrayant.
L'homme subit le joug sans connaître les causes,
Tout ce qu'il voit est court, inutile et fuyant.

VICTOR HUGO:
A Villequier (French)

We never see more than one side of things; the other side is submerged in the darkness of terrifying mystery. Mankind submits to the yoke without knowing the reasons; all that he can see is short, useless, and fleeting.

La vie aussi est une épidémic, ça s'attrape de père en fils ou de mèr en fille.

JACQUES PRÉVERT:
Entrées et Sorties (French)

Life too is an epidemic, sons catching it from fathers, daughters from mothers.

So lang man lebt, sei man lebendig!

J. W. VON GOETHE:
Maskenzug (German)

Let us live, while we are alive!

Alles, was über das Leben auf diesem Planeten zu sagen ist, könnte man in einem einzigen Satz von mittlerer Länge sagen.

BERTOLT BRECHT:
Baal (1926 version) (German)

Everything there is to say about life on this planet could be put into a single sentence of average length.

Leben – das heisst fortwährend etwas von sich
abstossen, das sterben will.
>   FRIEDRICH NIETZSCHE:
>   *Die Fröhliche Wissenschaft (German)*

Life – that means continually expelling from
ourselves something that desires death.

Des Menschen Leben ist ein ähnliches Gedicht:
Es hat wohl einen Anfang, hat ein Ende,
Allein ein Ganzes ist es nicht.
>   J. W. VON GOETHE:
>   announcement of the second part of *Faust*
>   *(German)*

Human life is like a poem: it has a beginning and
an end, but does not comprise a whole.

Der Mensch ist doch wie ein Nachtgänger; er
steigt die gefährlichsten Kanten im Schlafe.
>   J. W. von Goethe, in a letter to
>   Charlotte von Stein, 1780 *(German)*

Man is like a sleepwalker moving safely across
the most dangerous precipices.

Die Zeit hat ungeheuren Schwung
Paar Jahre bist du stark und jung
Dann sackst du langsam auf den Grund
Der Weltgeschichte.
>   WOLF BIERMANN:
>   *Bilanzballade im Dreissigsten Jahr (German)*

Life goes at such a terrible pace – a few years full
of youth and grace, and then you fall flat on your
face before world history.

Der Zweck des Lebens ist das Leben selbst.
>   J. W. VON GOETHE:

Life's objective is life itself.

Man löst sich nicht allmählich von dem Leben!
>   J. C. F. VON SCHILLER:
>   *Werke (German)*

Withdrawing from life is not a gradual process.

Wer sass nicht bang vor seiner Herzens
Vorhang?
>   RAINER MARIA RILKE:
>   *Duineser Elegien (German)*

Who has not sat anxiously in front of the stage-
curtain of his life?

Das Leben ist ein Tortur . . .
Andererseits kommen wir
Gerade in den Angstzuständen
Zu uns selbst.
>   THOMAS BERNHARD
>   *Die Jagdgesellschaft (German*

Life is a torment . . . On the other hand, we only
really face up to ourselves when we are afraid.

Gegeben in die ewige Huld,
Gebunden durch die ewige Schuld,
Den ewigen Tod zu Füssen:
Will ich mein Leben grüssen
>   BERTHOLD VIERTEL
>   *Gloria (German*

Accepted into eternal grace, obliged through
eternal sin to encounter eternal death, I shall
greet my life.

Gott hielt dein und mein Leben
Wie Blumen in seiner Hand.
>   AGNES MIEGEL:
>   *Blumen (German*

God held my life and your life like flowers in his
hand.

Gross ist das Leben und reich!
Ewige Götter schenkten es uns.
>   OTTO ERICH HARTLEBEN
>   *Gesang des Lebens (German*

How rich and great is the life given us by the
eternal gods.

Und was der ganzen Menschheit zugeteilt ist,
Will ich in meinem innern Selbst geniessen
>   J. W. VON GOETHE:
>   *Faust (German*

I shall enjoy within my innermost self all that
has been allotted to mankind.

Panta gar esthla biōi
>   METRODORUS
>   Fragment *(Greek*

Everything in life is excellent.

Kalon anthrōpinou biou katopton
>   ALCIDAMUS:
>   Fragment *(Greek)*

A fair mirror of human life (referring to Homer's
Odyssey).

kēnē pas ho bios kai paignion

PALLADAS:
Epigrams (Greek)

All life is a stage and a play.

'sukhēi miai zēn, ou duoin opheilomen

EURIPIDES:
Alcestis (Greek)

There is just one life for each of us – our own.

Ei su tēn sautou phileis
'sukhēn, philein hapantas

EURIPIDES:
Alcestis (Greek)

You love your life; but then, so do all men!

Hapanth' ho makros kanarithmētos khronos
Phuei t' adēla kai phanenta kruptetai

SOPHOCLES:
Ajax (Greek)

All things the long and countless years first draw
from darkness, then bury from the light (*tr.*
Jebb)

Ognuno sta solo sul cuore della terra
Trafitto da un raggio di sole:
Ed è subito sera.

SALVATORE QUASIMODO:
Ed è Subito Sera (Italian)

Each alone on the heart of the earth, impaled
upon a ray of the sun: and suddenly it's evening.

Il vivere è sventura,
Grazia il morir.

GIACOMO LEOPARDI:
Sopra un Basso Rilievo Antico-sepolcrale (Italian)

Living is misfortune, death a kindness.

Spesso il male di vivere ho incontrato:
Era il rivo straziato che gorgoglia.

EUGENIO MONTALE:
Ossi di Seppia (Italian)

I have often met the evil of living: it was the
strangled stream that gurgled.

La vita fugge e non s'arresta un'ora,
E la morte vien dietro a gran giornate.

FRANCESCO PETRARCA:
Sonnets (Italian)

Life flees and does not pause a single hour – and
death, with great strides, follows close behind.

Questo affanoso e travagliato sonno
Che noi vita nomiam.

GIACOMO LEOPARDI:
Al Conte Carlo Pepoli (Italian)

This wearisome and wretched sleep that we call
life.

Forse in qual forma, in quale
Stato che sia, dentro covile o cuna,
È funesto a chi nasce il di natale.

GIACOMO LEOPARDI:
*Canto Notturno di un Pastore Errante dell'Asia
(Italian)*

Perhaps in any form, under any condition,
whether in den or cradle, the day of birth is
mournful for him who is born.

Ikeru hito
Tsui ni mo shinuru
Mono nareba,
Kono yo naru ma wa
Tanoshiku wo ara na

OTOMO NO TABITO:
Waga (Japanese)

Since we must all die sooner or later, let us enjoy
life while we can!

Fuyu-no no-no ko-no ha-ni nitari wa-ga inotsi
Ae-naki kaze-ni tsiri ya yuki nan

JAPANESE SONG

My life resembles those dried-up leaves of
winter that have not yet fallen from the trees,
but will be carried off by the slightest wind.

Crastinum si adiecerit deus, laeti recipiamus.

SENECA:
Epistles (Latin)

If God adds another day to our life, let us receive
it gladly.

Flos aevi.

OVID:
Metamorphoses (Latin)

The bloom of life.

Flos aetatis.

Latin expression, used in Cicero:
Orationes Philippicae in M. Antonium

The bloom of life.

Breve et irreparabile tempus
Omnibus est vitae.

VIRGIL:
Aeneid (Latin)

Life's span is brief for all men and not to be restored.

Modo sic, modo sic.

PETRONIUS:
Satyricon (Latin)

Life has its ups and downs.

Vitae pars nulla perit.

CLAUDIAN:
Panegyricus dictus Manlio Theodoro Consuli (Latin)

No part of life is lost.

Dum quaerimus, aevum
Perdimus, et nullo votorum fine beati,
Victuros agimus semper, nec vivimus unquam.

MANILIUS:
Astronomica (Latin)

While we seek life we lose it and, without realising any of our desires, we always act as if we were going to live, and never do live.

Multis variationibus humana vita subiicitur et sic non sunt homines ad eadem officia peragenda aequaliter per totam vitam idonei.

ST. THOMAS AQUINAS:
On Princely Government (Latin)

Human life is subject to many changes, and we are not capable of fulfilling the same tasks in the same way throughout the span of our lifetime.

Ut tibi mors felix contingat, vivere disce:
Ut felix possis vivere, disce mori.

CELIO CALCAGNINI
Delitiae (Latin

If you want to die happily, learn to live; if you would live happily, learn to die.

O vita misero longa, felici brevis!

LATIN PROVERB

O life, long for woe but brief for joy!

Det er Liv! Det kan baade hærde og højne!

HENRIK IBSEN
Peer Gynt (Norwegian

This is life! It can harden and it can exalt!

Det er at svæve
Tørrskod nedad Tidens Elv,
Helt og holdent som sig selv.

HENRIK IBSEN
Peer Gynt (Norwegian)

Life means passing safe and dry-shod down the stream of time purely and simply as oneself.

Esli zhizn' tebya obmanet,
Ne pechal'sya, ne serdis'!
V den' unyniya smiris':
Den' vesel'ya ver', nastanet

ALEKSANDR SERGEEVICH PUSHKIN:
Sonnet (Russian)

Don't be sad, don't be angry, if life deceives you! Submit to your grief – your time for joy will come, believe me.

Il' vsya nasha
I zhizn' nichto, kak son pustoi
Nasmeshka neba nad zemlei?

ALEKSANDR SERGEEVICH PUSHKIN:
The Bronze Horseman (Russian)

Is all our life nought but an idle dream? – Is it only heaven's mockery of earth?

Zhizn' prozhit' – ne pole pereiti

RUSSIAN PROVERB

Going through life is not like crossing a field.

zhizn', kak posmotrish' s kholodnȳm vniman'
m vokrug,–
Takaya pustaya i glupaya shutka

MIKHAIL LERMONTOV:
I Skuchno, i Grustno (Russian)

Life, looked at dispassionately, is such a hollow
and a stupid farce.

La Nochebuena se viene
La Nochebuena se va
Y nosotros nos iremos
Y no volveremos más.

OLD SPANISH CAROL

Christmas eve comes, Christmas eve goes, and
we too shall pass and never more return.

El delito mayor del hombre es haber nacido.

PEDRO CALDERÓN DE LA BARCA:
La Vida es Sueño (Spanish)

The greatest crime of man is to have been born.

Nuestras vidas son los ríos
Que van a dar en la mar,
Que es el morir.

JORGE MANRIQUE:
Coplas por la Muerte de su Padre (Spanish)

Our lives are rivers whose outlet is the sea of
death.

Certidumbre de vida un ora non avemos;
Con llanto venimos, con llanto nos imos.

FERRANT SANCHEZ CALAVERA:
Dezir de las Vanidades del Mundo (Spanish)

Our lives are never certain, even for an hour;
with tears we come into this world, and with
tears we shall leave it.

Mas, ¿cómo perseveras,
Oh vida, no viviendo donde vives,
Y haciendo porque mueras,
Las flechas que recibes,
De lo que el Amado en ti concibes?

ST. JOHN OF THE CROSS:
Canciones entre el Alma y el Esposo (Spanish)

How can you thus continue
To live, my life, where your own life is not?
With all the arrows in you
And, like a target, shot
By that which in your breast he has begot.

(*tr.* Roy Campbell)

¿Qué es nuestra vida más que un breve día
Do apena sale el sol cuando se pierde
En las tinieblas de la noche fria?

Attrib. ANDRÉS FERNÁNDES DE ANDRADA:
Epístola Moral (Spanish)

What is our life more than a short day in which
the sun hardly rises before it is lost in the utter
darkness of the cold night?

Cualquier instante de la vida humana
Es nueva ejecución con que me advierte
Cuán fragil es, cuán mísera, cuán vana.

FRANCISCO DE QUEVEDO Y VILLEGAS:
Letrilla Lírica (Spanish)

Every instant of human existence is a new execution, warning me how fragile, miserable and
futile it is.

La vida, el mundo, el gusto y gloria vana
Son junto nada, humo, sombra y pena.

ANTONIO MIRA DE AMESCUA:
El Esclavo del Demonio (Spanish)

Life, the world, pleasure and vain glory, are but
nothing, smoke, shadow, and pain.

En vez de estudiar para vivir va a tener que vivir
para estudiar.

JOSÉ ORTEGA Y GASSET:
Misión de Bibliotecario (Spanish)

Instead of studying to live, it is possible to live
for study.

Falta la vida, asiste lo vivido,
Y no hay calamidad que no me ronde.

FRANCISCO DE QUEVEDO Y VILLEGAS:
Soneto (Spanish)

Life fails me, my past is present, and there is no
misfortune that does not haunt me.

¿Qué es la vida? Un frenesí.
¿Qué es la vida? Una ilusión,
Una sombra, una ficción,
Y el mayor bien es pequeño

PEDRO CALDERÓN DE LA BARCA:
La Vida es Sueño (Spanish)

What is life? Madness! What is life? Illusion, a
shadow, a fiction, where the greatest benefit is
trifling.

Al acaso
Cruzo el mundo, sin pensar
De dónde vengo, ni adónde
Mis pasos me llevaran

GUSTAVO ADOLFO BÉCQUER:
Rimas (Spanish)

Haphazardly I cross this world, without thinking where I have come from or where my steps may be leading me.

Es sueño,
Cristo, la vida, y es la muerte vela.

MIGUEL DE UNAMUNO:
El Cristo de Velazquez (Spanish)

O Christ, life is a dream and death a vigil.

LOGIC
see also Liberal arts, Money.

Die Logik erfüllt die Welt; die Grenzen der Welt sind auch ihre Grenzen.

LUDWIG WITTGENSTEIN:
Tractatus Logico-philosophicus (German)

Logic pervades the world; the limits of the world are also the limits of logic.

In der Logik ist nichts zufällig.

LUDWIG WITTGENSTEIN:
Tractatus Logico-philosophicus (German)

Nothing, in logic, is accidental.

Epei ou ti ge pseudē doxazonta tis tina husteron alēthē epoiēse doxazein

PLATO:
Theaetetus (Greek)

No-one has ever taught anyone to think truly who had previously thought falsely.

LONDON

Enfin, dans un amas de choses, sombre, immense,
Un peuple noir, vivant et mourant en silence.

HENRI AUGUSTE BARBIER:
Londres (French)

Finally, within a huge and sombre mass of things, a blackened people who live and die in silence.

LONGING
see also Life, Love.

Wabi-nureba ima hata onadji Naniwa naru mi wo tskush'te mo awan to zo omo'

MOTOYOSHI SHIN-WO:
Waga (Japanese)

How will it all end, when I am in such despair? If only I could see you once more, even though it should cost me my life!

Tawhiri-ma-tea!
Tukua a au kia eke
I te awhiowhio
I te pu-roro-hau
E tuku ki te muri

NGA-PUHI:
He Walata-putorino (Maori)

Lord of tempests! Let me ascend on the whirlwind, on the stormwind, and be carried to the north!

LOQUACITY
see also Action, Advice, Words.

Rhaion esti lalein ē siōpan

GREEK PROVERB

It is easier to talk than to hold one's tongue.

Khōris to t' eipein polla kai ta kairia

SOPHOCLES:
Oedipus Coloneus (Greek)

Talkativeness is one thing, speaking well another.

Poll' an su lexas ouden an pleon labois

EURIPIDES:
Alcestis (Greek)

You can talk well enough, but words will get you nowhere.

Hapas logos, ean apēi ta pragmata, mataion ti phainetai kai kenon

GREEK PROVERB

If deeds are wanting, all words appear mere vanity and emptiness.

LOVE

see also Absence, Ambition, Constancy, Death, Desire, Emotion, Faith, Fickleness, Fortune, Gratitude, Hatred, Honour, Infatuation, Ingratitude, Intrigue, Jealousy, Justice, Kisses, Longing, Loyalty, Mankind, Necessity, Parting, Passion, Peace, Pride, Reconciliation, Respect, Sacrifice, Self-control, Women.

Tā sauṁ kavana aṁtarapaṭa jō asa prītama piu;
Nevachāvari kai āi hauṁ tana, mana, jōbana, iu.

> MALIK MUHAMMAD JAYASI:
> *Padumāvatī (Avadhi)*

From my dear lover what secrets can I withhold? My body, my mind, my youth, and my life have I offered; and now I come myself.

In recht van Minnen es opghedreghen:
Die den slach sleet wert selve ghesleghen.

> HADEWIJCH:
> *Die Veertiende Sanc (Dutch)*

It is written in the code of love: He who strikes the blow is himself struck down.

Liefde moet bloeien. Door liefde groeien
De boom en struiken.

> JOOST VAN DEN VONDEL:
> *Koridon (Dutch)*

Love must blossom. Through love will grow the trees and the bushes.

Il est un nom caché dans l'ombre de mon âme,
Que j'y lis nuit et jour et qu'aucun oeil n'y voit.

> ALPHONSE DE LAMARTINE:
> *Un Nom (French)*

There is a name hidden in the shadow of my soul, where I read it night and day and no other eye sees it.

Mes amours durent en tout temps.

> CLEMENT MAROT:
> *Chant de Mai et de Vertu (French)*

My love lasts for ever.

Je serais sans feu, si j'étais sans amour.

> FRANÇOIS MAYNARD:
> *La Belle Vieille (French)*

Without love, I should be spiritless.

Les grimaces d'amour ressemblent fort à la vérité.

> MOLIÈRE:
> *Le Malade Imaginaire (French)*

Love's grimaces bear a strong resemblance to the truth.

La tranquillité en amour est un calme désagréable.

> MOLIÈRE:
> *Les Fourberies de Scapin (French)*

Tranquillity in love is a disagreeable calm.

L'amour est un sot qui ne sait ce qu'il dit.

> MOLIÈRE:
> *Le Dépit Amoureux (French)*

Love is a fool who knows not what he is saying.

On ne badine pas avec l'amour.

> FRENCH PROVERB;
> also the title of Alfred de Musset's famous play of 1834

Love is not to be trifled with.

D'un objet aimé tout est cher.

> P. A. C. DE BEAUMARCHAIS:
> *Le Mariage de Figaro (French)*

Everything belonging to a loved one is precious.

Quelque ravage affreux qu'étale ici la peste,
L'absence aux vrais amants est encore plus funeste.

> PIERRE CORNEILLE:
> *Oedipe* (opening speech) *(French)*

Whatever havoc the plague has wrought here absence is even more mournful to true lovers.

Vous aviez mon coeur,
Moi, j'avais le vôtre;
Un coeur pour un coeur,
Bonheur pour bonheur!

> MARCELLINE DESBORDES-VALMORE:
> *Qu'en Avez-vous Fait? (French)*

You had my heart, and I yours; a heart for a heart, good fortune for good fortune!

Je serai grand, et toi riche,
Puisque nous nous aimerons.

VICTOR HUGO:
Un Peu de Musique (French)

Since we shall love each other, I shall be great,
and you rich.

Vous ne connaissez point ni l'amour ni ses traits:
On peut lui résister quand il commence à naître,
Mais non pas le bannir quand il s'est rendu
maître.

PIERRE CORNEILLE:
Horace (French)

You know neither love nor its characteristics: it
can be resisted at the beginning, but it is impossible to withstand once it is your master.

En fait d'amour, vois-tu, trop n'est pas même
assez.

P. A. C. DE BEAUMARCHAIS:
Le Mariage de Figaro (French)

Where love is concerned, too much is not even
enough!

Votre coeur est à moi, j'y règne; c'est assez.

PIERRE DE CORNEILLE:
Tite et Bérénice (Berenice's final statement)
(French)

Your heart is mine; there I reign. I am content.

L'amour idéal est un mensonge des poètes.

ALPHONSE DAUDET:
Tartarin sur les Alpes (French)

Ideal love is a lie put forth by poets.

Ce n'est plus une ardeur dans mes veines
cachée,
C'est Vénus toute entière à sa proie attachée.

JEAN RACINE:
Phèdre (French)

This is no longer a passion concealed in my body
– it is Venus completely overwhelming her
victim.

La pire souffrance amoureuse n'est sans doute
pas d'être trompé par celle qu'on aime, mais
bien de la tromper soi-même.

ANDRÉ GIDE
Caractères (French

Doubtless love's worst affliction is not being
deceived by the woman one loves, but rather in
deceiving her oneself.

Amour est un étrange maître.
Heureux qui peut ne le connaître
Que par récit, lui ni ses coups!

JEAN DE LA FONTAINE
Le Lion Amoureux (French

Love is a strange master. Happy is he who
knows love and its wounds only by report.

Amour, amour, quand tu nous tiens,
On peut bien dire: Adieu prudence.

JEAN DE LA FONTAINE
Le Lion Amoureux (French,

Love, when you hold us in your grasp we can
well say, Farewell, caution!

Dans l'amour rien ne ressemble plus à un héros
qu'un pauvre type.

CHARLES PLISNIER
Faux Passeports, 'Maurer' (French

In love it is the victim who looks most like a hero.

L'amour est un tyran qui n'épargne personne.

PIERRE CORNEILLE
Le Cid (French,

Love is a tyrant who spares no-one.

La raison n'est pas ce qui règle l'amour.

MOLIÈRE:
Le Misanthrope (French,

Love is not ruled by reason.

Tout le plaisir de l'amour est dans le change-
ment.

MOLIÈRE.
Don Juan (French,

The whole pleasure in love lies in the variety.

L'amour est souvent un fruit de mariage.

MOLIÈRE:
Sganarelle (French)

Love is often a consequence of marriage.

C'est le coeur qui fait tout.

> MOLIÈRE:
> *Mélicerte (French)*

The heart can do anything.

Il n'est sécurité plus grande qu'au vaisseau de l'amour.

> SAINT-JOHN PERSE:
> *Amers (French)*

There is no safer refuge than in the vessel of love.

Je t'aime plus qu'hier, moins que demain.

> EDMOND ROSTAND:
> *Les Musardises (French)*

I love you more than yesterday, less than tomorrow.

Il y a l'un qui baise, et l'autre qui tend la joue.

> FRENCH PROVERB

There is one who kisses, and the other who offers a cheek.

Amors, sitot m'estau
De mon ami cara trop luein,
Ges mon cor de lui non desluelin,
Qu'el lo ten, si com dis, en gage.

> *Le Roman de Flamenca (French)*

Dear love, although I am far away from my friend, my heart is not distant from him, for he has it in hostage, as he himself has said. (Flamenca, speaking of her lover Guillaume de Nevers.)

Qui bien ayme tart oblie.

> FRENCH PROVERB

Who loves well, forgets slowly.

Souvent d'un faux espoir un amant est nourri:
Le mieux reçu toujours n'est pas le plus chéri.

> MOLIÈRE:
> *Le Dépit Amoureux (French)*

A lover often thrives on false hopes; the best welcomed is not always the favourite.

Il est bon de ne pas laisser un amant seul maître du terrain, de peur que, faute de rivaux, son amour ne s'endorme sur trop de confiance.

> MOLIÈRE:
> *La Comtesse d'Escarbagnas (French)*

It is best not to leave a lover sole master of one's affections, for fear that, in the absence of any rivals, his love slumbers through over-confidence.

L'amour avidement croit tout ce qu'il souhaite.

> JEAN RACINE:
> *Mithridate (French)*

Love eagerly believes everything it wants to.

Que nul ne meure qu'il n'ait aimé!

> SAINT-JOHN PERSE:
> *Strophe (French)*

No-one should be allowed to die before he has loved!

Je suis si persuadée que l'amour est une chose incommode, que j'ai de la joie que mes amis et moi en soyons exempts.

> Mme de La Fayette (at the age of twenty),
> in a letter to Gilles Ménage *(French)*

I am so convinced that love is a nuisance, that I am pleased that my friends and I are exempt.

L'amour est comme les maladies épidémiques. Plus on les craint, plus on y est exposé.

> S. R. N. CHAMFORT:
> *Maximes et Penseées (French)*

Love is like an epidemic – the more one is afraid, the more vulnerable one is.

L'amour, tel qu'il existe dans la Société, n'est que l'échange de deux fantaisies et le contact de deux épidermes.

> S. R. N. CHAMFORT:
> *Maximes et Pensées (French)*

Love, such as it is in society, is only the exchange of two fantasies, and the contact of two bodies.

Le flambeau de l'amour s'allume à la cuisine.

> FRENCH PROVERB

The torch of love is lit in the kitchen.

Il n'y a que d'une sorte d'amour, mais il y en a mille différentes copies.

FRANÇOIS, DUC DE LA ROCHEFOUCAULD:
Réflexions (French)

There is only one kind of love, but there are a thousand different versions.

Les femmes commencent vers trente ans à garder les lettres d'amour.

S. R. N. CHAMFORT:
Caractères et Anecdotes (Appendix I) *(French)*

When they get towards thirty, women start keeping their love letters.

J'aime mieux maintenant ce que j'ai aimé que ce que j'aime.

ALFRED DE MUSSET:
Bettine (French)

Now I love her whom I once loved more than her whom I love.

Je n'ai jamais conçu l'amour sans le mystère, et là où était la mystère, là pour moi déjà était l'amour.

C. A. SAINTE-BEUVE:
(French)

Love and mystery go together in my concept of love, and where the mystery existed there, for me, was love already.

La maison de mon coeur est prête
Et ne s'ouvre qu'à l'avenir.
Puisqu'il n'est rien que je regrette,
Amour nouveau, tu peux venir.

FRENCH FOLKSONG

My heart's dwelling is ready for occupation and will open only onto the future. Since there is nothing I regret, my new love can come.

Celui qui aime et qui est aimé est a l'abri des coups du sort.

FRENCH PROVERB

He who loves and is loved is safe from the dangers of fate.

Un homme amoureux qui plaint l'homme raisonnable me paraît ressembler à un homme qui lit des contes de fées, et qui raille ceux q? lisent l'histoire.

S. R. N. CHAMFOR?
Maximes et Pensées (French?

To my mind, a lovesick man who pities a ration? al man resembles a man who reads fairy tale? and scoffs at those who read history.

Cujatz vos qu'ieu non conosca
D'Amor s'es orba o losca?
Sos digz aplan' et entosca.

MARCABRU?
Songs (French?

Do you think I have failed to realise that love i? blind or one-eyed? It smoothes out and polishe? its words.

Plaisir d'amour ne dure qu'un instant;
Chagrin d'amour dure toute la vie!

OLD FRENCH SON?

Love's pleasure lasts but a moment; the pain o? love can last a lifetime.

Pour la douleur qu'Amour veut que je sente
Ainsi que moy Phoebus tu lamentois,
Quand amoureux et banny tu chantois
Pres d'Ilion sur les rives de Xante.
Pinçant en vain ta lyre blandissante
Fleuves et fleurs et bois tu enchantois,
Non la beauté qu'en l'ame tu sentois,
Qui te navroit d'une playe aigrissante.

PIERRE DE RONSARD?
Amours de Cassandre (French?

Thus Love desires that I sorrow just as, m? Phoebus, you lamented, when lovesick and banished you sang near Ilion on the banks ? Xante. You plucked in vain your alluring lyre enchanting rivers and flowers and woodlands? but not the beauty who was in your heart cutting you with a bitter wound.

Obre e lim
Motz de valor
Ab art d'Amor.

ARNAUT DANIEL?
Canzoni (French?

I shape and keep words of worth with the art o? love.

So.m met en cor q'ieu colore mon chan
D'un aital flor don lo fruitz si' amors.

ARNAUT DANIEL:
Canzoni (French)

I am careful to colour my song with such a
flower that its fruit will be love.

Ben es mortz qui d'amor no sen
Al cor cal que dousa sabor;
E que val viure ses amor
Mas per enoi far a la gen?

BERNARD DE VENTADOUR:
Non es Meravelha s'eu Chan (French)

He who cannot feel in his heart some sweet taste
of love is quite dead; for what is the use of living
without love, except to vex people!

C'amors, pois om per tot s'en vana,
Non es amors, mas es ufana.

BERNARD DE VENTADOUR:
Ja mos Chantars no m'er Onors (French)

The love of which a man boasts everywhere is
not love but boastfulness.

Amors, e cals onors vos es
Ni cals pros vo'n pot eschazer,
S'aucizetz celui c'avetz pres,
Qu'enves vos no s'auza mover?

BERNARD DE VENTADOUR:
Bel m'es qu'eu Chan en aquel Mes (French)

Love, what honour or advantage do you find if
you kill your prisoner who dares not make a
move against you?

Per son joy pot malautz sanar,
E per sa ira sas morir.

GUILHEM IX, DUKE OF AQUITANE:
Sonnet (French)

Through its joy love can cure evils, just as
through its anger love can kill.

Car d'una filla dos gendres
Pot hom greu far.

GIRAUT DE BORNELH:
Ans que Venia (French)

One lover cannot serve two mistresses (*lit.* a
man cannot make two sons-in-law from one
daughter).

On est aisément dupé par ce qu'on aime.

MOLIÈRE:
Le Tartuffe (French)

We are easily tricked by those we love.

O sink hernieder
Nacht der Liebe,
Gibt vergessen
Dass ich lebe.

RICHARD WAGNER:
Tristan und Isolde (German)

Night of love, descend! Make me forget that I am
alive!

Liebe ist nichts als Angst des sterblichen
Menschen vor dem Alleinsein.

THEODOR STORM:
Im Schloss (German)

Love is nothing but the fear of mortal man at the
thought of solitude.

Daz si dâ heizent minne, de ist niwan senede leit.

WALTHER VON DER VOGELWEIDE:
Das Sie da Heizent Minne (German)

What they call love is nothing but yearning
sorrow.

Swer guotes wîbes minne hât,
Der schamt sich aller missetât.

WALTHER VON DER VOGELWEIDE:
Einniuwer Sumer (German)

Whoever enjoys the love of a good woman will
be ashamed of any misdeed.

Minne ist minne, tuot si wol.

WALTHER VON DER VOGELWEIDE:
Saget mir Ieman (German)

Love is love when it gives pleasure.

Du bist verschlossen
In meinen Herzen,
Verloren ist das Schlüsselein.

OLD GERMAN SONG

You are the prisoner of my heart; the key is lost.

Selbst der Geringste unter den Menschen so gross ist, dass das Leben noch viel zu kurz ist, um ihn lieben zu können.

GEORG BÜCHNER:
Leonce und Lena (German)

Even the lowliest of mankind is important enough that life is much too short for him to be loved.

Ich seh sie dort, ich seh sie hier
Und weiss nicht auf der Welt,
Und wie und wo und wann sie mir
Warum sie mir gefällt.

J. W. VON GOETHE:
Auf Christiane R. (German)

I see her here, I see her there, and cannot for the life of me say how or where or when or why I like her so.

Sphären in einander lenkt die Liebe,
Weltsysteme dauern nur durch sie.

J. C. F. VON SCHILLER:
Phantasie an Laura (German)

Love guides the stars towards each other, the world plan endures only through love.

Doch alles, was dazu mich trieb
Gott, war so gut! ach, war so lieb!

J. W. VON GOETHE:
Faust (German)

O God, all that led me to it was so good and so tender! (Margarete, lamenting her surrender to Faust).

Ein Blick von dir, ein Wort, mehr unterhält
Als alle Weisheit dieser Welt.

J. W. VON GOETHE:
Faust (German)

One glance, one word from you gives more pleasure than all the wisdom of this world.

Wer so
Liebte, gehet, er muss, gehet zu Göttern die Bahn.

FRIEDRICH HÖLDERLIN:
Menons Klagen um Diotima (German)

He who loved so much must surely make his way to the gods.

Und doch, welch Glück, geliebt zu werden!
Und lieben, Götter, welch ein Glück!

J. W. VON GOETHE:
Willkommen und Abschied (German)

And yet, what luck to be loved! and, ye gods, what luck to be in love!

Wenige wissen
Das Geheimnis der Liebe,
Fühlen Unersättlichkeit
Und ewigen Durst.

NOVALIS:
Hymne (German)

Few know the secret of love; they are insatiable and have unending thirst.

Ich sprach, ich wolte ir iemer leben:
Daz liez ich wîte maere komen.
Mîn herze here ich ir gegeben:
Daz hân ich nû von ir genomen.

HARTMAN VON AUE:
Absage und Rückkehr (German)

I spoke, I wanted to love her for ever: I had given her my heart. Now I have taken it back again.

Philei me. Kai mē lupēthēis ēn tis ekhēi m' heteros

Greek inscription on a girdle

Love me! Don't be sad if I am another's!

Erōta pauei limos. Ei de mē, khronos

CRATES:
Fragments (Greek)

Hunger will kill love – if it does not, time will.

Esti kai en psukhrois sabbasi thermos Erōs

GREEK PROVERB

Love burns hot even on cold Sabbaths.

Palaia kainōn leipetai kēdeumatōn

EURIPIDES:
Medea (Greek)

The new love quickly supersedes the old.

Pheu, pheu, brotois erōtes hōs kakon mega

EURIPIDES:
Medea (Greek)

Alas, what an evil influence love has over mankind!

Tris lēistēs ho Erōs kaloit' an ontōs.
Agrupnei, thrasus estin, ekdiduskei

DIOPHANES OF MYRINA:
Fragment (Greek)

Truly love can be called thrice a brigand – he is wakeful, reckless, and strips us bare.

Lēgō d' oupot' erōtos. Aei de moi ex Aphroditēs
Algos ho mē krinōn kainon agei ti pothos

POSIDIPPUS:
Epigrams (Greek)

I never cease loving; and unending desire always brings me some new pain from Aphrodite.

Di cor gentile è segno, quando
Fiamma amorosa un giovanetto incende

GIAMBATTISTA CINTHIO GIRALDI:
Gli Antivalomeni (Italian)

It is a sign of a noble heart when a young man burns with the flame of love.

Donna mi priegha
    perch'i volglio dire
D'un accidente
    che sovente
      e fero
Ed e si altero
    ch'e chiamato amore.

GUIDO CAVALCANTI:
Canzone (Italian)

As I am asked by a lady, I can tell of a fierce and powerful mishap that often strikes – it is called love!

Amor, s'io posso uscir de' tuoi artigli, appena creder posso che alcuno altro uncin mai più mi pigli.

GIOVANNI BOCCACCIO:
Decameron (Italian)

Love, should I escape your entanglements, I doubt I can be trapped by any other hook.

Amore è un desio che vien dal core
Per l'abondanza di gran piacimento,
E gli occhi in prima generan l'amore,
E lo core li da nutricamento.

JACOPO DA LENTINO:
Amore è un Desio (Italian)

Love is a desire that comes straight from the heart with a wealth of exceeding pleasure. Our eyes first give birth to love, and our hearts give it sustenance.

Mamma mia, medicate
Questa piaga, per pietà!
Melicerto fu l'arciero
Perchè pace in cor non ho!

OLD ITALIAN SONG

Mother! for pity's sake help me to survive this wound! Melicerto was the archer through whom I have lost my peace of mind!

Amor, che al cor gentil ratto s'apprende.

DANTE:
Inferno (Italian)

Love which is quickly caught in the gentle heart.

Amor la spinge e tira,
Non per elezion ma per destino.

FRANCESCO PETRARCA:
Sonnets (Italian)

Love drives and draws him on, not by choice but through fate.

Amore,
Acceso di virtù, sempre altro accese,
Pur che la fiamma sua paresse fuore.

DANTE:
Purgatorio (Italian)

Love, kindled by virtue, always kindles another love, providing its flame shines forth.

Amore e'l cor gentil son una cosa.

DANTE:
Sonnet (Italian)

Love and the gentle heart are but a single thing.

Al cor gentil ripara sempre Amor.

GUIDO GUINIZELLI:
Al Cor Gentil (Italian)

Love always makes repair to the gentle heart.

Negli occhi porta la mia donna Amore;
Per che si far gentil ciò ch'ella mira.

DANTE:
Vita Nuova (Italian)

In her eyes my lady carries love, and so makes
gentle what she looks upon.

'Nè Creator nè creatura mai',
Cominciò ei, 'figliuol, fu senza amore,
O naturale o d'animo'.

DANTE:
Purgatorio (Italian)

Neither Creator nor creature, my son, was ever
without natural or rational love.

Ototsu-hi mo
Kinou mo kefu mo
Mi-tsuredomo,
Asu saye mi-maku-
Hoshiki kimi kamo.

MASUHITO:
Waga (Japanese)

I saw you two days ago; I saw you yesterday; I
saw you today; but I must see you tomorrow as
well!

Natsu no nu no
Shigemi ni sakeru
Hime-yuri no
Shirayenu koi wa
Kurushiki mono zo.

Manyō Shū (Japanese)

Love that does not reveal itself is as bitter as the
flowers that grow among the thickets on the
moors in summer.

Haru tateba
Kiyuru kōri no,
Nokori naku
Kimi ga kokoro mo
Ware ni toke-namu.

Kokin Shū (Japanese)

Let your heart melt toward me, just as the ice
that melts in spring leaves no trace of its chill.

Nec sine te [Venus] fit laetum neque amabile
quicquam.

LUCRETIUS:
De Rerum Natura (Latin)

Without thee, Venus, there is no joy nor love.

Illa, quibus superas omnes, cape tela, Cupido!

OVID:
Metamorphoses (Latin)

Take these arrows, Cupid, with which you
conquer all.

Numquam Amor quemquam nis cupidum
hominem
Postulat se in plagas conicere.

PLAUTUS:
Trinummus (Latin)

Love never hopes to trap anyone in his nets
apart from men of loose desires.

Difficile est humanam animam non amare et
necesse est, ut in quoscumque mens nostra
trahatur affectus.

ST. JEROME:
Letter to Eustochius (Latin)

It is hard for the human soul not to love something, and our mind must of necessity be drawn
to some kind of affection.

Amantium irae amoris integratiost.

TERENCE:
Andria (Latin)

When lovers fall out their love revives.

Quisquis amat valeat, pereat qui nescit amare
bis tanto pereat quisquis amare vetat.

POMPEIAN GRAFFITI

Blessed be he who loves; perish the man who
cannot love; a double death for him who forbids
love!

Nihil amantibus durum est, nullus difficilis
cupienti labor.

ST. JEROME
Letter to Eustochius (Latin)

Nothing is too difficult for lovers, no task too
hard for the passionate.

Sine Cere et Libero friget Venus.

LATIN PROVERB
quoted in TERENCE: *Eunuchus (Latin)*

Love grows cold without food and wine.

ras amet, qui nunquam amavit,
uique amavit, cras amet!
Pervigilium Veneris (Latin)

et him love tomorrow who never loved before;
t him who has, love tomorrow.

aritas omnia potest.
ST. JEROME:
Letter to Innocentius (Latin)

ove can do anything.

lilitat omnis amans, et habet sua castra
upido.
OVID:
Amores (Latin)

very lover is a soldier, and Cupid has his own
rmy.

d mala quisque animum referat sua, ponet
morem.
OVID:
Remedia Amoris (Latin)

o free himself of love, a man need only concen-
rate on his own problems.

incit amor omnia.
'Ianus annum circinat', in *Carmina Burana
(Latin)*

ove conquers all.

mor et melle et felle est fecundissimus.
PLAUTUS:
Cistellaria (Latin)

ove is a mixture of honey and bitterness.

n amore haec sunt mala, bellum,
ax rursum.
HORACE:
Satires (Latin)

ove has two evils: war and then peace.

Iaeret lateri lethalis arundo.
VIRGIL:
Aeneid (Latin)

The fatal dart sticks in his side, and rankles in
is heart (*tr.* Dryden)

Durius in terris nihil est quod vivat amante.
PROPERTIUS:
Elegies (Latin)

No life is harder than that of the lover on this
earth.

Errat, qui finem vesani quaerit amoris:
Verus amor nullum novit habere modum.
PROPERTIUS:
Elegies (Latin)

He is wrong who seeks the limit of mad love; true
love knows no bounds.

Quaelibet autem aspera facilia et prope nulla
facit amor.
ST. THOMAS AQUINAS:
On Princely Government (Latin)

Love makes difficult things easy and almost
unworthy of note.

Qui in amorem praecipitavit,
Peius perit quasi saxo saliat.
PLAUTUS:
Trinummus (Latin)

He who falls headlong in love suffers worse than
if he had jumped off a cliff.

Ita est amor, ballista ut iacitur: nihil sic celere
est neque volat.
PLAUTUS:
Trinummus (Latin)

Love is like a missile – nothing is so swift in
flight.

Qui amat, tamen hercle, si esurit, nullum esurit.
PLAUTUS:
Casina (Latin)

He who craves for food no longer hungers once
he is in love.

Quanto minu' spei'st tanto magis amo.
TERENCE:
Eunuchus (Latin)

The less my hope, the greater my love.

Auro contra cedo modestum amatorem, a me aurum accipe.

> PLAUTUS:
> *Curculio (Latin)*

Find me a rational lover and I'll give you his weight in gold.

Amor timere neminem verus potest.

> SENECA:
> *Medea (Latin)*

True love has no fear for anyone.

Qui regi non vult amor vincatur.

> SENECA:
> *Hippolytus (Latin)*

Let the love which will not be controlled be overcome.

Omnia vincit Amor: et nos cedamus Amori.

> VIRGIL:
> *Eclogues (Latin)*

Love conquers all; let us, too, yield to love!

Nunc scio, quid sit Amor.

> VIRGIL:
> *Eclogues (Latin)*

Now I know what love is.

Felix, quem Veneris certamina mutua perdunt!

> OVID:
> *Amores (Latin)*

Happy is he whom love's mutual strife has downed!

Amare et sapere vix deo conceditur.

> PUBLILIUS SYRIUS:
> *Sententiae (Latin)*

Both to be wise and to love is scarcely granted to the gods themselves.

Turpis amor surdis auribus esse solet.

> LATIN PROVERB

A shameful love is usually deaf.

Is poterit felix una remanere puella,
Qui numquam vacuo pectore liber erit.

> PROPERTIUS
> *Elegies (Latin*

To win lasting hapiness in one mistress, one heart must never be disengaged, one must neve be free.

Tu tamen amisso non numquam flebis amico;
Fas est praeteritos semper amare viros.

> PROPERTIUS
> *Elegies (Latin*

Weep sometimes for your friend, though he i lost; it is fitting always to love lovers gone.

Laus in amore mori, laus altera si datur uno
Posse frui; fruar o solus amore meo.

> PROPERTIUS
> *Elegies (Latin*

How glorious to die in love; how more glorious the gods grant us enjoyment of one love; may alone have the enjoyment of mine!

Fulsere quondam candidi tibi soles,
Cum ventitabas, quo puella ducebat
Amata nobis, quantam amabitur nulla.

> CATULLU
> *Poems (Latin*

The brilliant sun used to shine down on yo when you went where your girl led, loved by yo as no other girl will ever be loved.

Vinceris aut vincis: haec in amore rota est.

> PROPERTIUS
> *Elegies (Latin*

Either you conquer, or you are conquered: this i the wheel of love.

Quis fallere possit amantem?

> VIRGI
> *Aeneid (Latin*

Who can deceive a lover?

Omnia leuia sunt amanti.

> LATIN PROVER

All things are easy for a lover.

quis amat non laborat.

LATIN PROVERB

e who loves does not strive.

eternum sanctae foedus amicitiae.

LATIN EXPRESSION

he eternal bond of hallowed friendship.

utĕri yang baik buat mĕnantu,
ifat-nya lĕngkap tujoh laksana

Hikayat koraish mĕngindĕra (Malay)

o not mock my daughter, who is perfect. You
,ay not get a saint again!

'ikar ĕmas bantal suasa;
(ana sama bantal di-lĕngan

MALAY PANTUN

old be the sleeping-mat, gold the pillows, but
ıe arms of my beloved are the pillow for me.

ra Elskovs Standpunkt set,
an en Hankatt og Profet
omme hartad ud paa et.

HENRIK IBSEN:
Peer Gynt (Norwegian)

onsidered just as lovers, there's probably not
ıuch to choose between a tomcat and a
rophet.

Gdyby tylko na to
by się żegnać, warto brać amanty.

JULIUSZ SŁOWACKI:
Beniowski (Polish)

is worthwhile falling in love, if only for the
arting.

mor com brandas mostras apparece,
'udo possivel faz, tudo assegura,
1as logo no melhor desapparece.

DIOGO BERNARDES:
Horas Breves (Portuguese)

ove always comes with so fair a show; all is
ossible, all certain, reaches a pinnacle – and
anishes.

'esta altura vejo o Amor!
iver não foi em vão se é isto a vida,

Nem foi de mais o desengano e a dôr.

ANTHERO DE QUENTAL:
Solemnia Verba (Portuguese)

I can see love from this height. If this is life, then
living – with all its hurt and disillusion – was not
in vain.

Mỹ smolodu vlyublyaemsya i alchem
Utekh lyubvi, no tol'ko utolim
Serdechnÿi glad mgnovennÿm obladan'em,
Uzh, okhladev, skuchaem i tomimsya?

ALEKSANDR SERGEEVICH PUSHKIN:
Boris Godunov (Russian)

Do we not fall in love and hunger for love's joys
from early youth? But as soon as we slake the
hunger of our hearts with momentary possession, growing cold, we yearn and are tormented.

Mỹ p'ëm v lyubvi otravu sladkuyu;
No vsë otravu p'ëm mỹ v neĭ,
I platim mỹ za radost' kratkuyu
Eĭ bezvesel'em dolgikh dneĭ.

EVGENY BARATYNSKY:
Lyubov' (Russian)

In love we drink sweet poison; but yet it is poison
that we drink. And we pay for this brief joy with
long and cheerless days.

Gde net lyubvi, tam net veselĭi.

RUSSIAN PROVERB

Where love is not, there can be no pleasures.

Lyubit' . . . no kogo zhe? . . . na vremya – ne stoit
truda,
A vechno lyubit' nevozmozhno.

MIKHAIL LERMONTOV:
I Skuchno, i Grustno (Russian)

Fall in love? But with whom? It's not worth it
just for a time! – and it's impossible to love for
ever!

I vpryam, blazhen lyubovnik skromnÿi,
Chitayushchiĭ mechtÿ svoi
Predmetu pesen i lyubvi,
Krasavitse priyatno-tomnoĭ!

ALEKSANDR SERGEEVICH PUSHKIN:
Eugen Onegin (Russian)

How fortunate is the modest lover who reads his
daydreams to a sultry beauty, the object of his
verse and of his love.

Cuando amor no es locura
No es amor.

> PEDRO CALDERÓN DE LA BARCA:
> *El Mayor Monstruo los Celos (Spanish)*

When love is not madness, it is not love.

No hay criatura sin amor
Ni amor sin celos perfeto.

> GABRIEL TIRSO DE MOLINA:
> *La Gallega Mari-Hernández (Spanish)*

There is no creature without love, and no perfect
love without jealousy.

Amor no tiene elección.

> SPANISH PROVERB

In love there is no choosing.

En asuntos de amor cualquier niña es la mujer
eterna.

> SPANISH PROVERB

In matters of love the veriest slip of a girl is ever
the woman.

El amor es fuego, pero con él no se cuece el
puchero.

> SPANISH PROVERB

Love is a furnace, but it will not cook the stew.

Riñin dos amantes, hácese la paz,
Si el enojo es grande, es el gusto más.

> MIGUEL DE CERVANTES:
> *Rinconete y Cortadillo (Spanish)*

Two lovers quarrel, and then make it up. The
fiercer the conflict, the more pleasure in the end.

Amor es siempre vida, sólo vida.
No hay mirada amorosa que no alumbre
Su eternidad. Allí secreta anida.

> JORGE GUILLÉN:
> *Anillo (Spanish)*

Love is always life – and only life. There is no
gaze of love that does not give birth to its
eternity. It nests there, in secret.

Por vos espero la vida
Cuando la muerte me mata,

Y la gloria en el infierno,
Y en el desamor la gracia.

> MIGUEL DE CERVANTE[S]
> *La Tia Fingida (Spanis[h])*

I pray life for you when death strikes me dow[n]
and glory in Hell, and, in hatred, pardon.

El amor faz sotil al omme que es rrudo,
Ffázele fabrar fermoso al que antes es mudo,
Al omme que es covarde fázelo muy atrevudo,
Al perezoso faze ser presto e agudo.

> JUAN RUI[Z]
> *El Amor (Spanis[h])*

Love makes a subtle man out of a crude one,
gives eloquence to the mute; it gives courage [to]
the cowardly, and makes the idle quick an[d]
sharp.

Arroyos murmuradores
De la fe de amor perjura
Por hilos de plata pura
Ensartan perlas en flores.

> LOPE DE VEG[A]
> *Al Son de los Arroyuelos (Spanis[h])*

Streams murmuring of perjured love strin[g]
pearls on flowers with pure silver thread.

En la dueña pequeña yaze muy grand amor.

> JUAN RUI[Z]
> *De las Propiedades que las Dueñas Chicas ha[n]*
> *(Spanis[h])*

In a little woman great love can grow.

Rogáselo, madre,
Rogáselo al niño,
Que no tire más
Que matan sus tiros.

> *El Amor Esquivo (Spanis[h])*

Mother! ask Cupid not to shoot any more of hi[s]
arrows at me!

LOYALTY
see also Discretion, Patronage.

Grand Dieu sauvez le roi!
Grand Dieu vengez le roi!
Vive le roi
Qu'à jamais glorieux
Louis victorieux

oit ses ennemis toujours soumis.
ive le roi!

MADAME DE BRINON:
Grand Dieu Sauvez le Roi! (French)

od save the King! May God avenge the King!
ong live the King, for ever glorious, Louis
ictorious. May he see his enemies always
onfounded! Long live the King! (These lines
ispired the British national anthem.)

eyoulte me lie.

MOTTO OF RICHARD, DUKE OF GLOUCESTER
(French)

am bound by loyalty.

Ionorez Dieu, servez le roi.

FRENCH PROVERB

Ionour God, and serve the King.

Quam in amicitia quaerimus fides est.

CICERO:
De Amicitia (Latin)

oyalty is what we seek in friendship.

Vir haud magna cum re, sed plenus fidei.

CICERO:
De Senectute (Latin)

A man of little wealth, but rich in loyalty.

Vir, quo meliores liberos habere ne opto
quidem.

SUETONIUS:
Otho (Latin)

A man of greater loyalty than I can even pray for
n my own children (Claudius's comment on
Otho).

Nihil boni praeter causam.

CICERO:
Ad Familiares (Latin)

Nothing is good except our cause.

LULLABIES
see also Sleep.

Schlaf, mein Küken – Racker, schafe!
Kuck: im Spiegel stehn zwei Schafe,
Bläkt ein grosses, mäht ein kleines,
Und das kleine, das ist meines!

RICHARD DEHMEL:
Wiegenlied (German)

Sleep, my chick! – Rascal, go to sleep!
Look! in the mirror there are two sheep.
The big one is baa-ing, the little one is bleating.
And that little one is mine!

Schlummre, schlummre immer zu,
Engelein dich decken
Mit Flügelein zur Ruh!

FRIEDRICH MÜLLER:
Golo und Genoveva (German)

Slumber, slumber without break! Little angels
cover thee with little wings of sleep!

LUXURY
see also Change.

Saevior armis luxuria.

JUVENAL:
Satires (Latin)

Luxury is more deadly than any foe.

M

MAGIC

Eisin d'epōidai kai logoi thelktērioi

EURIPIDES:
Hippolytus (Greek)

There are spells and soothing words.

MANKIND
**see also Action, Ambition, Arms,
Aspiration, Belief, Civilisation, Culture,
Deceit, Despair, Destiny, Dissatisfaction,
Effort, Eternity, Experience, Fallibility,
Fate, Faults, Greatness, Human nature,
Insignificance, Life, Love, Mathematics,
Misfortune, Nature, Necessity, Suffering.**

Kull aṣ-ṣawābi' mish zayy ba'ḍ-hum

ARAB PROVERB

Everyone's different (*lit.* the five fingers are not
all the same).

O douce Providence! ô mère de famille
Dont l'immense foyer de tant d'enfants four-
mille,
Et qui les vois pleurer, souriante au milieu,
Souviens-toi, coeur du ciel, que la terre est ta
fille
Et que l'homme est parent de Dieu!

ALPHONSE DE LAMARTINE:
La Vigne et la Maison (French)

Beloved Providence, mother of a family whose
immense home teems with so many children,
and who smiling in their midst, sees them cry,
remember – heart of the heavens! – that the
earth is your daughter, and that mankind is
God's kin!

Nous jugeons. Nous dressons l'échafaud.
L'homme tue
Et meurt. Le genre humain, foule d'erreur vêtre,
Condamne, extermine, détruit,
Puis s'en va.

VICTOR HUGO:
Horror (French)

We are the judges. We set up the scaffolds. Man
kills and dies. The human race, a crowd decked
out in error, condemns, exterminates, destroys
and then goes on its way.

L'homme et la femme sont deux bêtes très ma
faisantes.

DENIS DIDERO⁻
Ceci n'est pas un Conte (Frencl

Man and woman are two very evil-minde
beasts.

Les bêtes sont au bon Dieu,
Mais la bêtise est à l'homme.

VICTOR HUGC
La Coccinelle (Frencl

Beasts belong to God, but stupidity to man.

L'homme n'est ni ange ni bête.

BLAISE PASCAI
Pensées (Frencl

Man is neither angel nor beast.

L'homme est proprement *omne animal.*

BLAISE PASCAI
Pensées (Frencl

Man is, in a strict sense, entirely animal.

Boire sans soif et faire l'amour en tout temps
Madame; il n'y a que ça qui nous distingue de
autres bêtes.

P. A. C. DE BEAUMARCHAI⁵
Le Mariage de Figaro (Frencl

The only things that distinguish us from the res
of the animals, Madam, is our habit of drinkin
when we are not thirsty and making love at an
time.

L'homme n'est rien qu'un jonc qui tremble a
vent.

VICTORHUGO
A Villequier (French

Man is nothing but a reed trembling in the wind

Chacun est un tout à soi mesure, car, lui mort, le tout est mort pour soy.

BLAISE PASCAL:
Pensées (French)

Each of us is all in all to himself, for when he is dead all is dead to him.

Tout homme est un livre où Dieu lui-meme écrit.

VICTOR HUGO:
La Vie aux Champs (French)

Every man is a book in which God himself writes.

Il est plus nécessaire d'étudier les hommes que les livres.

FRANÇOIS, DUC DE LA ROCHEFOUCAULD:
Réflexions (French)

It is more necessary to study men than books.

La nature a donné des termes à la stature d'un homme bien conformé.

J. J. ROUSSEAU:
Du Contrat Social (French)

Nature has set bounds to the stature of the well-made man.

Il était bâti en hommes.

ETIENNE PASQUIER:
Oeuvres (French)

It was built of people (referring to Budaeus' Corporation of the Royal Readers, founded 1530, which originally had no headquarters or public lecture rooms. The Corporation is now known as the Collège de France).

Je sens que je suis une parcelle animée de cette force motrice qui fait tourner tous ces rouages de cette inconcevable usine: l'univers.

OCTAVE MIRBEAU:
La 628-E-8 (French)

I feel I am an animated fragment of that driving power that propels all the wheels of this unimaginable factory – the universe.

L'homme n'est qu'un roseau, le plus faible de la nature; mais c'est un roseau pensant.

BLAISE PASCAL:
Pensées (French)

Man is but a reed, nature's feeblest; but he is a thinking reed.

A la racine du monde dans les berceaux des germes
L'homme nidifie ses sens et ses proverbes.

TRISTAN TZARA:
L'Homme Approximatif (French)

At the heart of the world where germs are cradled, mankind makes nests for its meanings and proverbs.

Für dieses Leben
Ist der Mensch nicht schlau genug.

BERTOLT BRECHT:
Das Lied von der Unzulänglichkeit
Menschlichen Strebens (German)

Mankind is not cunning enough for this world.

Ein Sohn der Erde
Schein' ich; zu lieben gemacht, zu leiden.

FRIEDRICH HÖLDERLIN:
Die Heimath (German)

I am a mortal, born to love and to suffer.

Der Mensch hat die Weisheit all seiner Vorfahren zusammengenommen, und seht, welch ein Dummkopf er ist!

ELIAS CANETTI:
Aufzeichnungen, 1942 (German)

Mankind has collected together all the wisdom of his ancestors, and can see what a fool man is!

Kein lebendiges ist ein Eins,
Immer ist's ein Vieles.   J. W. VON GOETHE:
Epirrhema (German)

No living creature is a single unit, it is always manifold.

Ohne Beweis ist der Mensch überhaupt kein Mensch, sondern ein Orang.

BERTOLT BRECHT:
Elephantenkalb (German)

After all, without proof man is no man, only an ape.

Er irrt der Mensch, solang' er strebt.
> J. W. VON GOETHE:
> *Faust (German)*

Man errs as long as he struggles.

Die Menschen sind im ganzen Leben blind.
> J. W. VON GOETHE:
> *Faust (German)*

Men are blind throughout the whole of their lives.

Phēsi gar pou pantōn khrēmatōn metron anthrōpon einai, tōn men ontōn, hōs esti, tōn de mē ontōn, hōs ouk estin
> PLATO:
> *Theaetetus (Greek)*

Man is the measure of all things, both of those that exist and those that do not (quoting from Protagoras).

Solum enim hominis exitium herbae et semitae fundamentum.
> MARCUS TERENTIUS VARRO:
> *De Re Rustica (Latin)*

The foot of man is death to the grass, and marks the beginning of a path.

Omnes eodem cogimur.
> HORACE:
> *Odes (Latin)*

We are all gathered to the same fold.

Homo lupus, et lupa hominis.
> LATIN PROVERB

Man is a wolf, and woman is the mistress of man.

In grege adnumeror.
> CICERO:
> *Oratio pro Quinto Roscio Amerino (Latin)*

I am counted with the multitude.

Homo est ... inferior angelis, superior pecoribus.
> ST. AUGUSTINE:
> *De Civitate Dei (Latin)*

Man is lower than the angels, but higher than the beasts.

Homo ex anima et corpore est.
> AULUS GELLIUS
> *Attic Nights (Latin)*

Man is made up of body and soul.

Homo est animal naturaliter sociale in multitudine vivens.
> ST. THOMAS AQUINAS:
> *On Princely Government (Latin)*

Man is by nature a social animal living in a community.

It cuique ratus prece non ulla mobilis ordo.
> SENECA:
> *Oedipus (Latin)*

Completely unmoved by prayer, each man's appointed life continues.

Homo naturaliter est animal sociale, utpote qui indiget ad vitam suam multis, quae sibi ipse solus praeparare non potest.
> ST. THOMAS AQUINAS:
> *Commentary on the Nicomachean Ethics (Latin)*

Man is by nature a social animal, being compelled to live in society because of the many needs he cannot satisfy out of his own resources.

Homo sum: humani nil a me alienum puto.
> TERENCE:
> *Heauton Timorumenos (Latin)*

I am a human being. I think nothing human to be foreign to me (Chremos discussing the problems of bringing up children).

Civium coetum cole.
> SENECA:
> *Hippolytus (Latin)*

Seek out the haunts of men.

Tiap-tiap yang hina itu sahaja pĕrhimpunan niat jahat dan fitnah
> *Hikayat Kalila dan Damina (Malay)*

Every common nature is a mixture of evil and slanderous intentions.

Cada uno es como lo hizo Dios, y un poquito peor.

SPANISH PROVERB

Everyone is as God made him, only a little worse.

MARRIAGE
see also Contentment, Cuckoldry, Divorce, Faults, Greatness, Human nature, Love, Mothers, Sorrow, Virtue, World.

Les bons maris font les bonnes femmes.

LABICHE & MARC-MICHEL:
Un Chapeau de Paille d'Italie (French)

Good husbands make good wives.

Il vaut mieux encore être marié qu'être mort!

MOLIÈRE:
Les Fourberies de Scapin (French)

Better to be married than dead!

Epouser une sotte, est pour n'être point sot.

MOLIÈRE:
L'Ecole des Femmes (French)

Marrying a stupid woman will prevent you from looking stupid.

Par un prompt désespoir souvent on se marie,
Qu'on s'en repent après tout le temps de sa vie.

MOLIÈRE:
Les Femmes Savantes (French)

A sudden fit of despair will often give rise to a marriage that will be repented for the rest of one's life.

Se marier, c'est apprendre à être seul.

FRENCH PROVERB

Marriage teaches you to live alone.

Il y a des mariages commodes, mais point des délicieux.

FRANÇOIS, DUC DE LA ROCHEFOUCAULD:
Réflexions (French)

There are marriages of convenience, but never of delight.

Un Mariage bien reglé ne ressemble pas a ces mariages d'interest ou d'Ambition; ce sont deux Amans qui vivent ensemble. Qu'un Prestre dit de certains paroles, qu'un Notaire signe de certains papiers: je regarde ces preparatifs dans la mesme vûe qu'un Amant, l'echelle de Corde qu'il attache a la fenestre de sa Maitresse.

LADY MARY WORTLEY MONTAGU:
Essay (French)

A real marriage bears no resemblance to these marriages of interest or ambition. It is two lovers who live together. A priest may well say certain words, a notary may well sign certain papers – I regard these preparations in the same way that a lover regards the rope ladder that he ties to his mistress's window.

La femme qu'il me faudrait, je ne la cherche point, je ne l'évite même pas.

S. R. N. CHAMFORT:
Caractères et Anecdotes (French)

I do not seek the kind of wife I need, but I do not avoid her.

Le Mariage et le Celibat ont tous deux des inconvénients; il faut préférer celui dont les inconvénients ne sont pas sans remède.

S. R. N. CHAMFORT:
Maximes et Pensées (French)

Both marriage and celibacy have their inconveniences; you must choose the one whose inconveniences are not without remedy.

Autant de mariages, autant de ménages.

FRENCH PROVERB

As many marriages – so many homes!

Morgen ist aller Duft und Glanz von mir gestreift.

GEORG BÜCHNER:
Leonce und Lena (German)

Tomorrow all fragrance and radiance will be stripped from me (Lena, speaking of her impending marriage).

Erschöpfung lügt Harmonie.
Was sind wir uns schuldig? Das.
Ich mag das nicht. Deine Haare im Klo.

GÜNTER GRASS:
Ehe (German)

Exhaustion gives the lie to harmony. What do we owe each other? This – I do not like your hairs in the toilet.

Meta pollōn de gamōn hade teleuta proteran
peloi gunaikōn

AESCHYLUS:
The Suppliant Maidens (Greek)

Let marriage be our fate, as it has been of so
many women in the past.

Despoina gar geronti numphiôi gunē

EURIPIDES:
Phoenix (quoted from this lost play in
Aristophanes' *Thesmophoriazusae*) *(Greek)*

Old men marry tyrants, not wives.

Hēper megistē gignetai sōtēria,
Hotan gunē pros andra mē dikhostatēi

EURIPIDES:
Medea (Greek)

The greatest salvation is when a woman does
not disagree with her husband.

Aith' ophelon agamos t' emenai agonos t'
apolesthai

HOMER:
Iliad (Greek)

Would that I had never married, and that I had
died without children! (Hector to Paris).

Epei tais ge ontōs maiais monais pou prosēkei
kai promnēsasthai orthōs

PLATO:
Theaetetus (Greek)

The true midwife is the only proper match-
maker.

Chi lontano va ammogliare
Sarà ingannato o vorrà ingannare.

ITALIAN PROVERB

He who goes far away to marry will be deceived
or is willing to deceive.

Tanta la virtude è del matrimonio,
Che non pur cosa sacra è tra mortali,
Ma nel Cielo è tenuta anco divina.

GIAMBATTISTA CINTHIO GIRALDI:
Euphimia (Italian)

So great is matrimony's virtue that not only is it
a sacred affair among mankind, but even in
heaven it is held divine.

Hostis est uxor, invita quae viro nuptum datur.

PLAUTUS:
Stichus (Latin)

He who marries an unwilling wife gains an
enemy.

Uxorem esse ducendam.
German parody of 'Delenda est Carthago'
(Latin)

A man must marry.

Perenne coniugium animus, non corpus, facit.

LATIN PROVERB

Mind, not body, makes a lasting marriage.

Var hon mjǫk gefin til fjár.
Eiriks Saga Rauða (Flateyjarbók) (Norse)

She was married to him mainly for his money.

En los ojos de los novios
Relucían dos luceros;
Ella es la flor de la ontina,
Y él es la flor del romero.

SPANISH FOLKSONG

In the eyes of the newly-weds there gleam two
stars: his is the flower of the rosemary, hers that
of white sage.

Antes que te cases mira lo que haces.

SPANISH PROVERB

Before you get married, think what you are
doing.

Para ser el casamiento apacible, había de ser el
marido sordo y la mujer ciega.

SPANISH PROVERB

For a marriage to prove happy, the husband
should be deaf and his wife blind.

MATERIALISM
see also Morals and morality.

J'ai vu, dans le monde, qu'on sacrifiait sans
cesse l'estime des honnêtes gens à la considération, et le repos à la celebrité.

S. R. N. CHAMFORT:
Maximes et Pensées (French)

I have noticed that in this world people invari-
ably sacrifice the esteem of honest men in order

get their own way, and sacrifice peace of mind
r celebrity.

onteux attachements de la chair et du monde.
PIERRE CORNEILLE:
Polyeucte (French)

he shameful ties of the flesh and the world.

à leider desn mac niht gesîn,
az guot und weltlich êre
Jnd gotes hulde mêre
esamene in ein herze komen.
WALTHER VON DER VOGELWEIDE:
Ich Saz ûf eime Steine (German)

Jnfortunately it is not possible for wealth and
vorldly honour and God's grace as well to come
ogether in one heart.

akheia gastēr lepton ou tiktei noon
GREEK PROVERB
(quoted in St. Jerome's *Letter to Nepotian*)

A fat paunch never breeds fine thoughts.

otto umbilico ne religione ne verità.
ITALIAN PROVERB

Below the navel there is neither religion nor
ruth.

Jmnes homines ad suom quaestum callent et
astidiunt.
LATIN PROVERB
(quoted in Plautus: *Truculentus*)

Everyone is squeamish or insensitive, according
o his own interests.

O quam contempta res est homo, nisi supra
iumana surrexerit!
SENECA:
Natural Questions (Latin)

How contemptible a thing is man, unless he can
rise above human concerns.

Adhaesit pavimento anima mea
DANTE:
Purgatorio (Italian)

I kept my desires on earthly things (the lament
of the avaricious and the prodigal).

Más días hay que longanizas.
SPANISH PROVERB

There is more to life than material things (*lit.*
there are more days than sausages).

MATHEMATICS

Le nombre est un témoin intellectuel qui
n'appartient qu'à l'homme, et par lequel il
peut arriver à la connaissance de la parole.
HONORÉ DE BALZAC:
Louis Lambert (French)

Numbers are intellectual witnesses that belong
only to mankind, and by whose means we can
achieve an understanding of words.

Je ne comprends pas qu'on ne comprenne pas
les mathématiques!
RAYMOND POINCARÉ
(French)

I cannot understand how it is that people cannot
understand mathematics!

MATURITY

Les arbres tardifs sont ceux qui portent les
meilleurs fruits.
MOLIÈRE:
Le Malade Imaginaire (French)

Those trees that are slow to grow bear the best
fruits.

Nihil non acerbum prius quam maturum fuit.
LATIN PROVERB

Everything ripe was once sour.

MEDIATION

Wa-mā yinūb al-mukhalliṣ illā taqtī' hidūm-uh
ARAB PROVERB

All that the intervener gets is torn clothes.

MEDIOCRITY
see also Praise.

Rien que la médiocrité n'est bon.
BLAISE PASCAL:
Pensées (French)

Nothing but mediocrity is good.

La dernière démarche de la raison est de reconnaître qu'il y a une infinité de choses qui la surpassent. Elle n'est que faible, si elle ne va jusqu'à reconnaître cela.

BLAISE PASCAL:
Pensées (French)

The last advance of reason is to recognise that it is surpassed by innumerable things; it is very feeble if it cannot realise that.

Il vaut mieux souffrir d'être au nombre des fous. Que du sage parti se voir seul contre tous.

MOLIÈRE:
L'Ecole des Maris (French)

It is better to be numbered among fools than to be isolated among the wise and to see oneself alone against everyone.

Quand il fait sombre, les plus beaux chats sont gris.

FRENCH PROVERB

The finest cats are grey in the dark.

Lieber ein kleiner Herr als ein grosser Knecht.

GERMAN PROVERB

Better to be a minor lord than an important menial.

In einem guten Land brauchts keine Tugenden, alle können ganz gewöhnlich sein, mittelgescheit und meinetwegen Feiglinge.

BERTOLT BRECHT:
Mutter Courage und ihre Kinder (German)

A good country needs no virtues – everyone can just be ordinary, moderately sensible and, for all I care, cowards.

Wie klein denken doch kleine Menschen!

ADOLF HITLER, 1924
(German)

How shallow are the thoughts of little men!

Ouden eōn genomēn. Palin essomai, hōs paros ouden

GREEK PROVERB

I came from nothing – I shall be nothing.

MEDITATION
see also Action, Decision, Thought and thinking.

La vie contemplative fait descendre au fond (sacrés précipices.

JEAN GION
Le Déserteur (Frenc.

Contemplation can compel you to plunge to th depth of terrible precipices.

La méditation est un vice solitaire, qui creu: dans l'ennui un trou noir que la sottise vie remplir.

PAUL VALÉR'
Lust (Frenc.

Meditation is a solitary vice that digs a blac hole in boredom which folly fills.

La vie contemplative est souvent misérable. I faut agir davantage, penser moins, et ne pas s regarder vivre.

S. R. N. CHAMFOR'
Maximes et Pensées (French

Contemplation often makes life miserable. W should be more active, think less, and sto watching ourselves live.

En renonçant au monde et à la fortune, j'a trouvé le bonheur, le calme, la santé, même l richesse; et, en dépit du proverbe, je m'aperçoi que 'qui quitte la partie la gagne'

S. R. N. CHAMFOR'
Maximes et Pensées (French

In renouncing the world and fortune, I hav found contentment, peace, health, even riches And all this in spite of the proverb – I can se that 'he who quits the game wins'!

Überlegung ist eine Kranckheit der Seele, un hat nur krancke Tahten getahn.

J. W. VON GOETHE
Götz von Berlichingen (first version) *(German*

Reflection is a sickness of the spirit, and neve leads to the right action.

Die Betrachtung (Reflexion) ist das erste liberale Verhältnis des Menschen zu dem Weltall, das ihn umgibt.

J. C. F. VON SCHILLER:
Werke (German)

Meditation is the first liberal relationship of mankind with the universe that surrounds him.

Wer gar zuviel bedenkt, wird wenig leisten.

J. C. F. VON SCHILLER:
Wilhelm Tell (German)

He who reflects too much will achieve little.

MELANCHOLY
see also Boredom, Greatness.

La mélancholie elle-même n'est qu'un souvenir qui s'ignore.

GUSTAVE FLAUBERT
(French)

Melancholy is only a recollection that one does not recognise.

Rien n'est si insupportable à l'homme que d'être dans un plein repos, sans passions, sans affaire, sans divertissement, sans application. Il sent alors son néant, son insuffisance, sa dépendance, son impuissance, son vide. Incontinent il sortira du fond de son âme l'ennui, la noirceur, la tristesse, le chagrin, le dépit, le désespoir.

BLAISE PASCAL:
Pensées (French)

There is nothing man finds so unbearable as being completely at rest, without passion, without business, without amusement, without purpose. It is then that he recognises that he is nothing, he is inadequate, powerless, empty, and far from independent. Now pour forth from the depths of his soul boredom, gloom, sorrow, chagrin, spite, and despair.

Je suis le Ténébreux – le Veuf – l'Inconsolé,
Le Prince d'Aquitaine à la Tour abolie:
Ma seule Etoile est morte – et mon luth constellé
Porte le Soleil noir de la Mélancholie.

GÉRARD DE NERVAL:
Je suis le Ténébreux (French)

I am the Sinister one – the Widower – the Disconsolate, the Prince of Aquitaine of the shattered tower; My only star is dead and my star-spangled lute bears Melancholy's black sun.

ahi, ma nel petto,
Nell'imo petto, grave, salda, immota
Come colonna adamantina, siede
Noia immortale, incontro a cui non puote
Vigor di giovanezza.

GIACOMO LEOPARDI:
Al Conte Carlo Pepoli (Italian)

Alas! deep down in his heart, hidden in his deepest self, there sits enthroned undying melancholy solid and immovable as a stone column.

Quantum est in rebus inane!

PERSIUS FLACCUS:
Satires (Latin)

How empty everything is!

Taedium vitae

LATIN EXPRESSION

Life's tedium

MEMORIES
see also Experience, Lies, Love, Nostalgia, Remembrance.

Og dog blir mit hjerte ofte lindt
Ved minderne om dengang
Da jeg aldrig blev overrældet af minder.

BENNY ANDERSEN:
Minderne (Danish)

My heart turns to jelly when I remember the times when I was never overwhelmed with memory.

J'ai plus de souvenirs que si j'avais mille ans

CHARLES BAUDELAIRE:
Spleen et Idéal (French)

I have more memories than if I were a thousand years old.

Les bons souvenirs sont des bijoux perdus.

PAUL VALÉRY:
Mauvaises Pensées (French)

Good memories are lost jewels.

Les mémoires excellentes se joignent volontiers au jugements débiles.

MONTAIGNE:
Essays (French)

Excellent memories combine willingly with weak judgments.

Feig, wirklich feig ist nur, wer sich vor seinen
Erinnerungen fürchtet.
ELIAS CANETTI:
Aufzeichnungen, 1954 *(German)*

He who is afraid of his own memories is cowardly, really cowardly.

Sukhoï tsvetok, lyubovnỹkh pisem svyazka,
Ulỹbka glaz, schastlivỹkh vstrechi dve,–
Puskaï teper' v puti temno i vyazko,
No tỹ vesnoï brodil po murave.
MIKHAIL KUZMIN:
O, Bỹt' Pokinutỹm (Russian)

A dried flower, some love-letters, smiling eyes
and two happy meetings – although your road is
now dark and treacherous, nevertheless you
once trod fresh-grown grass in springtime.

MEMORY
see also Fame, Oblivion, Old age, Tradition.

La mémoire est nécessaire pour toutes les opérations de la raison.
BLAISE PASCAL:
Pensées (French)

Memory is necessary for all operations of
reasoning.

Tantum quisque scit, quantum memoria tenet.
ISAAC CASAUBON:
Adversaria (Latin)

Each man knows as much as his memory
retains.

Dubitat anceps memoria.
SENECA:
Oedipus (Latin)

My doubtful memory falters.

MERCY
see also Clemency.

La Clemenza
Esser scesa mi par dal Cielo in Terra,
Perché l'huomo per lei simil sia a Dio
GIAMBATTISTA CINTHIO GIRALDI:
Cleopatra (Italian)

Mercy, I believe, comes down from heaven to
earth, so that man, by practising it, may resemble God.

Re ipsa repperi
Facilitate nil esse homini meliu' nequ
clementia.
TERENCE
Adelphoe (Latin

I have found that there is nothing better for
man than affability or mercy.

Iam statua tandem gravibus aerumnis modum
SENECA
Hercules Furens (Latin

Set a limit to our overwhelming troubles.

Sola deos aequat clementia nobis.
CLAUDIAN
*Panegyricus de Quarto Consulatu Honorii Augusi
(Latin*

Mercy alone makes us equal with the gods.

Mortem misericors saepe pro vita dabit.
SENECA
Troades (Latin,

The merciful often give death instead of life.

MERIT
see also Greatness, Leadership.

La marque d'un mérite extraordinaire est d
voir que ceux qui l'envient le plus sont contraints de le louer.
FRANÇOIS, DUC DE LA ROCHEFOUCAULD
Réflexions (French

The characteristic of extraordinary merit in a
man can be seen where those who envy him the
most are nevertheless obliged to praise him.

Le monde récompense plus souvent les apparences du mérite que le mérite même.
FRANÇOISE, DUC DE LA ROCHEFOUCAULD
Réflexions (French,

The world more often pays tribute to the
appearance of merit than to merit itself.

MIGHT
see also Force, Nationhood, Power.

As-sarīr kan ḍāq yaga' al-ḥajarāni
ARAB PROVERB

The weakest goes to the wall (*lit.* when the bed's
too narrow, it's the outside one who falls off).

La justice sans la force est impuissante; la force sans la justice est tyrannique.

BLAISE PASCAL:
Pensées (French)

Justice without force is impotent; force without justice is tyranny.

Le pouvoir est ma croix.

VICTOR HUGO:
Cromwell (French)

The cross I bear is power.

Es ehret der Knecht nur den Gewaltsamen.

FRIEDRICH HÖLDERLIN:
Menschenbeifall (German)

Slaves only admire the powerful.

Es gibt nur ein Recht in der Welt, und dieses Recht liegt in der eigenen Stärke.

ADOLF HITLER:
Munich, 22 September 1928 *(German)*

There is only one kind of right in this world, and right lies vested in one's own strength.

Kraft ist oberstes Gesetz.

ADOLF HITLER:
Mein Kampf (German)

Power is the supreme law.

Wer nicht die Kraft hat, dem nutzt das 'Recht an sich' gar nichts.

ADOLF HITLER
(German)

If you have no power, then having right on your side is useless.

Was Hände bauten, können Hände stürzen.

J. C. F. VON SCHILLER:
Wilhelm Tell (German)

What hands have built hands can destroy.

Zur Macht gelangt nur, wer die Macht begehrt.

ERICH KÄSTNER:
Das Ohnmächtige Zwiegespräch (German)

The only people who attain power are those who crave for it.

Aphrōn d', hos k' ethelēi pros kreissonas antipherizein.
Nikēs te steretai pros t' aiskhesin algea paskhei

HESIOD:
Works and Days (Greek)

He who strives with the stronger is a fool, for he loses the contest and reaps both shame and hurt.

Chi è cagione che uno diventi potente, ruina.

NICCOLÒ MACHIAVELLI:
The Prince (Italian)

He who causes another to become powerful is ruined himself.

Conscia succumbent audito verbere terga.

CLAUDIAN:
In Eutropium (Latin)

At the crack of the whip, the back that has felt its blows will yield.

Plus potest qui plus valet.

LATIN PROVERB
(quoted in Plautus; *Truculentus) (Latin)*

The stronger will triumph.

MIND
see also Freedom, Intellect, Marriage, Old age, Slaves.

Deux choses instruisent l'homme de toute sa nature: l'instinct et l'expérience.

BLAISE PASCAL:
Pensées (French)

The whole of man's nature is learnt from two things: instinct and experience.

Corpora obnoxia sunt et adscripta dominis, mens quidem est sui iuris.

ST. THOMAS AQUINAS:
Summa Theologica (quoting Seneca: *De Beneficiis*)
(Latin)

The body is a slave and subject to a master; but the mind is free.

MISFORTUNE
see also Adversity, Disaster, Fate, Fortune, Freedom, Greatness, History, Hope, Leadership, Life, Moderation, Self-knowledge.

Al-jōza 'l-naḳḍāna, al-bulād al-ji'āna, ad-dābbe 'l-'atlāna, al-kiswe 'l-gamyāna, ad-dulma 's-sūdāna

ARAB PROVERB

A shrew of a wife, a starving town, sick cattle, old clothes, and darkness on your way.

Nous avons tous assez de force pour supporter les maux d'autrui.
FRANÇOIS, DUC DE LA ROCHEFOUCAULD:
Réflexions (French)

We always have enough strength to endure other people's misfortunes.

Les flûtes sauvages du malheur.
ST.-JOHN PERSE:
Vents (French)

The wild flutes of misfortune.

Un malheureux cherche l'autre.
FRENCH PROVERB

Unhappy people seek out each other.

L'expérience apprend à l'homme que le malheur toujours le guette
RAYMOND QUENEAU:
Une Histoire Modèle (French)

Man knows from experience that misfortune is never far away.

J'ai vu sous le soleil tomber bien d'autres choses
Que les feuilles des bois et l'écume des eaux,
Bien d'autres s'en aller que le parfum des roses
Et le chant des oiseaux.
ALFRED DE MUSSET:
Souvenir (French)

In the light of day I have seen fall many things other than the leaves of the trees and the foam of the water – many other things have disappeared beside the scent of the roses and the song of the birds.

Was muss geschehn, mag's gleich geschehn!
GERMAN PROVERB

Whatever must come, let it come quickly!

Aiol' anthrōpōn kaka
AESCHYLUS:
The Suppliant Maidens (Greek)

Many are the troubles of mankind.

Philoi, kakōn men hostis empeiros kurei,
Epistatai brotoisin hōs hotan kludōn
Kakōn epelthēi panta deimainein philei
AESCHYLUS:
The Persians (Greek)

Friends, anyone who has suffered knows that when we are overwhelmed with trouble, we fear everything.

Euphēmon ēmar ou prepei kakangelōi
Glōssēi miainein
AESCHYLUS:
Agamemnon (Greek)

A happy day should not be spoilt by news of ill-fortune.

Miseria una uni quidem hominist adfatim.
PLAUTUS:
Trinummus (Latin)

One misfortune is sufficient for any man.

MOCKERY
see also Ridicule.

Ou gar gelasthai tlētōn ex ekhthrōn philai
EURIPIDES:
Medea (Greek)

I will not tolerate the taunts of my foes.

Oukoun gelōs hēdistos eis ekhthrous gelan?
SOPHOCLES:
Ajax (Greek)

Is not mocking one's enemy the most delightful pursuit?

o hay nada en el mundo que moleste más a un
ombre que el que no se le tome en serio.

> PALACIO VALDÉS:
> *La Hija de Natalia (Spanish)*

othing in the world annoys a man more than
ot being taken seriously.

MODERATION
see also Greed, Responsibilities,
Self-control, Wealth.

hayr al-umūr al-wasat

> ARAB PROVERB

middle course is always best.

'Rien de trop' est un point
ont on parle sans cesse, et qu'on n'observe
oint.

> JEAN DE LA FONTAINE:
> *Rien de Trop (French)*

veryone talks ceaselessly about not overdoing
ings, and no-one does anything about it.

a modération des personnes heureuses vient
u calme que la bonne fortune donne à leur
umeur.

> FRANÇOIS, DUC DE LA ROCHEFOUCAULD:
> *Réflexions (French)*

oderation in people who are contented comes
om that calm that good fortune lends to their
pirit.

a modération est comme la sobriété: on vou-
rait bien manger davantage, mais on craint de
e faire mal.

> FRANÇOIS, DUC DE LA ROCHEFOUCAULD:
> *Réflexions (French)*

oderation is like sobriety: we should like to eat
ore, but we fear to make ourselves ill.

ui borne ses désirs est toujours assez riche.

> FRENCH PROVERB

e who curbs his desires will always be rich
nough.

uand le malheur ne serait bon
u'à mettre un sot à la raison,

Toujours serait-ce à juste cause
Qu'on le dit bon à quelque chose.

> JEAN DE LA FONTAINE:
> *Le Mulet se Vantant de sa Généalogie (French)*

Even if misfortune is only good for bringing a
fool to his senses, it would still be just to deem it
good for something.

Petit pluie abat grand vent.

> FRENCH PROVERB

A little rain allays great dust.

Früh ins Bett und früh heraus,
Frommt dem Leib, dem Geist, dem Haus.

> GERMAN PROVERB

Early to bed, early to rise, makes a man healthy,
wealthy and wise (*lit.* early to bed, early to rise,
benefits the belly, the mind, and the home).

Wo Mässigung ein Fehler ist, da ist Gleichgül-
tigkeit ein Verbrechen.

> GEORG CHRISTOPH LICHTENBERG:
> *Aphorismen (German)*

If moderation is a fault, then indifference is a
crime.

Tōn gar metriōn prōta men eipein
Tounoma nikai, khrēsthai te makrōi
Lōista brotoisin

> EURIPIDES:
> *Medea (Greek)*

Moderation, instead of excess, is the most
acceptable to mortals.

Houtō to lian hēsson epainō
Tou mēden agan

> EURIPIDES:
> *Hippolytus (Greek)*

I believe moderation to be preferable to
extremes in all things.

Mēdan agan

> DELPHIC MAXIM
> (Greek)

No excess!

Mēden huper to metron

> GREEK PROVERB

Nothing beyond due measure.

Metron d'epi pasin ariston

PYTHAGORAS:
Golden Verses (Greek)

Moderation in all things is excellent.

Chi va piano va sano e va lontano.

ITALIAN PROVERB

He who goes gently, goes safely and will go far.

Est modus in rebus.

HORACE:
Satires (Latin)

There is measure in all things.

Uti, no abuti.

LATIN PROVERB

Use – don't abuse!

Ne quid nimis.

LATIN PROVERB

Not too much of anything.

Postremo modus muliebris nullust.

PLAUTUS:
Poenulus (Latin)

Moderation does not appeal to women.

Miratur, quibus ille disciplinis
Tantam sit sapientiam assecutus,
Quem tres cauliculi, selibra farris,
Racemi duo tegula sub una
Ad summam prope nutriant senectam

SUETONIUS:
De Grammaticis (Latin)

We can but wonder by what training he has attained such a degree of wisdom that three small cabbages, half-a-pound of meal and two clusters of grapes beneath one roof suffice for him when he is well-nigh at life's end!

¡Qué muda la virtud por el prudente!
¡Qué redundante y llena de ruido
Por el vano, ambicioso y aparente!

Attrib. ANDRÉS FERNÁNDEZ DE ANDRADA:
Epístola Moral (Spanish)

How silent is virtue in those who are circumspect! How superfluous and full of noise it shows in those who are vain, ambitious and affected!

MODESTY
see also Women.

La fausse modestie est le plus décent de tous les mensonges.

S. R. N. CHAMFORT:
Maximes et Pensées (French)

False modesty is the seemliest of all lies.

La modestie est la vertu des tièdes.

JEAN-PAUL SARTRE:
Le Diable et le Bon Dieu (French)

Modesty is characteristic of lukewarm friends.

Amolior et amoveo nomen meum.

LIVY:
History (Latin)

I pass over and lay no stress on my name.

Sram chestnyĭ litse devȳ velmi ukrashaet,
egda ta nichesozhe ne lepo derzaet.

SIMEON POLOTSKY:
Deva (Russian)

Chaste modesty greatly adorns a maiden's face when she refrains from whatever is unbecoming.

MONARCHY
see also Kings, Leadership, Statesmen.

La monarchie est le meilleur ou le pire des gouvernements.

VOLTAIRE:
Brutus (French)

Monarchy is the best or the worst of governments.

MONEY
see also Advice, Avarice, Borrowing, Bribery, Corruption, Friendship, Honesty, Illness, Law, Lending, Poverty, Reputation, Success, Time.

Al-filūs fī-hā 'afrīt

ARAB PROVERB

Money disappears like magic.

Ar-rājil illī mā luh-sh fulūs mā luh-sh aṣḥāb

ARAB PROVERB

He that has no money has no friends.

Al māl ishtaghala lō kana dirhuma
ARAB PROVERB

Money is a worry, even only a farthing.

L'or est comme l'esprit de la société.
PAUL VALÉRY:
La Soirée avec Monsieur Teste (French)

Gold is the spirit of society.

L'argent qu'on possède est l'instrument de la liberté; celui qu'on pourchasse est celui de la servitude.
J. J. ROUSSEAU:
Les Confessions (French)

Our own money is the tool of liberty; the money we pursue is the tool of bondage.

L'argent des sots est le patrimoine des gens d'esprit.
FRENCH PROVERB

The money of fools is the heritage of great minds.

A quoi lui servait son argent puisqu'elle se privait de tout?
MME LA COMTESSE DE SÉGUR:
Un Bon Petit Diable (French)

What good was her money since she deprived herself of everything?

Touchez pas au grisbi!
FRENCH SLANG EXPRESSION

Don't lay a finger on the money!

Sein Geld hebt er in seinem Herzen auf, die Schläge zählen es.
ELIAS CANETTI:
Aufzeichnungen, 1942 (German)

He heaps up his money in his heart where the heart-beats can count it.

Khrusos de kreissōn muriōn logōn brotois
EURIPIDES:
Medea (Greek)

Among mankind money is far more persuasive than logical argument.

All' ouk esti ge khrēmatōn ōnion alupia megalophrosunē eustatheia tharraleotēs autarkeia
PLUTARCH:
Moralia (Greek)

Money cannot buy peace of mind, greatness of spirit, serenity, confidence, or self-sufficiency.

Multos   iam   lucrum   lutulentos homines reddidit;
Est etiam ubi profecto damnum praestet facere quam lucrum.
PLAUTUS:
Captivi (Latin)

Love of gain has contaminated many people. There are even occasions when it is better to lose than to gain.

Imperat aut servit collecta pecunia cuique.
HORACE:
Epistles (Latin)

Money hoarded is for each a master or a servant.

Clausum possidet arca Iovem.
PETRONIUS:
Satyricon (Latin)

Money can achieve anything (*lit.* a strongbox holds Jupiter confined).

Necesse est facere sumptum qui quaerit lucrum.
PLAUTUS:
Asinaria (Latin)

To get money you must spend it.

Semper tu ad me cum argentata accedito querimonia.
PLAUTUS:
Pseudolus (Latin)

Always bring money along with your complaints.

Aurum per medios ire satellites
Et perrumpere amat saxa, potentius
Ictu fulmineo.
HORACE:
Odes (Latin)

Gold loves to make its way through the midst of sentinels and to break through rocks, for it is mightier than the thunderbolt.

Quid enim differt, bara-
throne
Dones quidquid habes an numquam utare
paratis?

HORACE:
Satires (Latin)

What is the difference whether you squander all
you have, or never use your savings?

Vincant divitiae.
JUVENAL:
Satires (Latin)

Let money (i.e. bribery or corruption) carry the
day.

Ergo sollicitae tu causa, Pecunia, vitae,
Per te immaturum mortis adimus iter,
Tu vitiis hominum crudelia pabula praebes,
Semina curarum de capite orta tuo.

PROPERTIUS:
Elegies (Latin)

So, Money, it is you who are responsible for life's
anxieties; you who force us to take the road to
early death; you who foster and encourage
man's vices; the seeds of ambition spring from
your stock.

Pecunia una regimen est rerum omnium.
LATIN PROVERB

Money alone is the ruling principle of the world.

Være sig selv paa Grundlag af Guld,
Det er som at bygge sit Hus paa Sandet.
HENRIK IBSEN:
Peer Gynt (Norwegian)

Building one's life on a foundation of gold is just
like building a house on foundations of sand.

Oro es lo que oro vale.
SPANISH PROVERB

Money is what it will buy.

Dios es omnipotente, y el dinero es su teniente.
SPANISH PROVERB

God is all-powerful, and money is his lieutenant.

Por dinero baila el perro.
SPANISH PROVERB

The dog will dance for money.

Que las mujeres discretas
No habemos de pretender
Sino dinero, que amores
No valen nada sin él.

TIRSO DE MOLINA
Marta la Piadosa (Spanish)

Without money we do not have to pretend with
prudent women, for affairs are worthless without it.

MOON
see also Home, Midnight, Night, Sky, Sleep Solitude.

A měsíc v řece kdy se houpá,
Ten noční chodec napilý
Modravou parou, z vod jež stoupá.

ANTONIN SOVA
U řek (Czech)

On the river the moon is reeling, that rover of the
night-time, drunk with the bluish haze which
rises from the water.

De groote maan
Kogelend voortgaat langs den stroeven dag
Der nacht.

HERMAN GORTER:
De School der Poëzie (Dutch)

The great full moon goes rolling onward
through the sterner glow of the night.

La lune peignait ses cheveux avec un démêloir
d'ébène qui argentait d'une pluie de vers
luisants les collines, les prés el les bois.

ALOYSIUS BERTRAND:
Gaspard de la Nuit: Le Fou (French)

The moon combed its tresses with a broad-
toothed comb of ebony, releasing a silver shower
of glow-worms on the hills, the meadows and the
woods.

Oh! qu'il est doux, quand l'heure tremble au
clocher, la nuit, de regarder la lune qui a le nez
fait comme un carolus d'or!

ALOYSIUS BERTRAND:
Gaspard de la Nuit: Le Clair de Lune (French)

How marvellous it is at night, when time
trembles in the belfry, to look at the moon
which has the face of a gold sovereign.

orsqu'à minuit la lune brille dans le ciel
omme un écu d'argent sur une bannière d'azur
emée d'abeilles d'or!

ALOYSIUS BERTRAND:
Scarbo (French)

At midnight the moon shines in the sky like a
ilver coin on an azure banner spangled with
golden bees!

Et puis, comme une lampe aux rayons blancs et
doux,
La lune, d'un feu pur inondant sa carrière,
Semble ouvrir sur le monde une immense
paupière,
Pour chercher son Dieu jeune, égaré parmi
nous.

MARCELINE DESBORDES-VALMORE:
Révélation (French)

And then, like a lamp with clear white rays, the
moon, with a pure fire flooding its course, seems
to open a vast eyelid on the world, seeking its
young God lost among us.

C'était, dans la nuit brune,
Sur le clocher jauni,
La lune,
Comme un point sur un i.

ALFRED DE MUSSET:
Ballade à la Lune (French)

At dusk, over the yellowing bell-tower, it was the
moon, like the dot on an 'i'.

Ah! la belle pleine Lune,
Grosse comme une fortune!

JULES LAFORGUE:
Complainte de la Lune en Province (French)

Ah! the beautiful full moon, fat as a fortune!

Voyez! la lune monte à travers ces ombrages.
Ton regard tremble encor, belle reine des nuits;
Mais du sombre horizon déjà tu te dégages
Et tu t'épanouis.

ALFRED DE MUSSET:
Souvenir (French)

Look! the moon is climbing through these
shadows. Beautiful queen of the night, your gaze
still trembles. But you are already disengaging
yourself from the dim horizon and showing
yourself clearly.

Der Mond ist wie ein schlafendes Kind, die
goldnen Locken sind ihm im Schlaf über das
liebe Gesicht heruntergefallen.

GEORG BÜCHNER:
Leonce und Lena (German)

The moon is like a sleeping child whose golden
locks have fallen over his beloved face.

Der Mond von einem Wolkenhügel
Sah kläglich aus dem Duft hervor.

J. W. VON GOETHE:
Willkommen und Abschied (German)

From a bank of clouds the moon shone dismally
through the vapour.

Der Mond schöpft alle Schwere
Aus See und Berg und Baum.
In einer grossen Leere
Schweben Zeit und Raum.

HANNS JOHST:
Die Gute Nacht (German)

The moon smoothes all severities out of sea
and mountain and tree. Time and space are
suspended in a great vacuum.

Füllest wieder Busch und Tal
Still mit Nebelglanz,
Lösest endlich auch einmal
Meine Seele ganz.

J. W. VON GOETHE:
An den Mond (German)

You fill again the silent copse and dale with
misty gleam, freeing at last my entire soul.

Ma tu, luna, abbellir godi co 'l raggio
Le ruine ed i lutti.

GIOSUÈ CARDUCCI:
Classicismo e Romanticismo (Italian)

You delight, O Moon! to clothe in silver the old
ruins and the scenes of ancient battle.

E queta sovra i tetti e in mezzo agli orti
Posa la luna, e di lontan rivela
Serena ogni montagna.

GIACOMO LEOPARDI:
La Sera del Di' di Festa (Italian)

Peacefully the moon pauses over the rooftops,
and hovers by the orchards, lighting each
distant mountain in a picture of calm.

Ts'ki mireba chiji ni mono koso kanashkere,
wagami h'tots no aki ni wa aranedo
OHOYE NO CHISATO:
Waga (Japanese)

What countless times I have looked at the moon.
She has made me calm, but she has also
saddened me once autumn has come.

Aki-kaze ni tanabiku kumo no tahe-ma yori
more idsuru ts'ki no kage no sayakesa
SAKYO NO TAIU AKISUKE:
Waga (Japanese)

Through the opening rifts in the clouds, which
the winds of autumn have spread thinly over the
sky, the beauty of the moonlight and its shadows
glint out.

Aki no umi ni
Utsureru tsuki wo
Tachi-kayeri
Nami wa arayedo,
Iro mo kawarazu
KIYOWARA FUKAYABU:
Waga (Japanese)

As the waves tumble over each other, they wash
the moon as it is reflected in the autumn sea, but
its beauty remains unchanged.

Ista luce feminea collustrans cuncta moenia et
udis ignibus nutriens laeta semina.
APULEIUS:
Metamorphoses (Latin)

[The moon's] feminine light sharply bringing
out the city walls, and with her damp fires
nourishing the happy seed.

Nareszcie księżyc srebrną pochodnię zaniecił,
Wyszedł z boru i niebo i ziemię oświecił.
ADAM MICKIEWICZ:
Pan Tadeusz (Polish)

At last the moon lit its silver torch, emerged
from the forest, and illumined the heavens and
the earth.

Belÿĭ prizrak lunÿ
Smotrit v dushu moyu i bÿluyu pechal'
Naryazhaet v zabÿtÿe snÿ
YAKOV POLONSKY:
Kolokol'chik (Russian)

The moon's white spectre looks into my soul,

and clothes my past sadness in forgotten
dreams.

Con una sonrisa
Firme, contemplando a muchos
Frente a frente, presidiendo
Redondeas tu nocturno
Señorío.
JORGE GUILLÉN
Esta Luna (Spanish)

Firmly smiling and looking mankind straight
in the eyes, you preside over and round your
nightly domain.

Luna que reluces,
Blanca y plateada,
Toda la noche alumbres.
Luna que Reluces (Spanish)

Shining moon, white and silvery, you illuminate
all the night.

Nadie come naranjas
Bajo la luna llena.
Es preciso comer
Fruta verde y helada.

FEDERICO GARCÍA LORCA:
La Luna Asoma (Spanish)

No-one eats oranges below a full moon. It is
necessary to eat green and icy fruit.

MORALS AND MORALITY
see also Purpose, War, Wrong.

Quand la législation s'affaiblit, les moeurs
dégénèrent.
J. J. ROUSSEAU:
Du Contrat Social (French)

When legislation grows weak, morality degener-
ates.

La vraie morale se moque de la morale.
BLAISE PASCAL:
Pensées (French)

True morality mocks at morals.

La moralité n'est autre chose que l'unité de
l'être.
MARIE JEAN GUYAU:
*Esquisse d'une Morale sans Obligation ni Sanction
(French)*

Morality is but the unity of the human being.

Il n'y a point de principe de morale qui n'ait son inconvénient.

DENIS DIDEROT:
Le Neveu de Rameau (French)

There is no moral precept that does not have something inconvenient about it.

Nous avons tous trop souffert, anges et hommes,
De ce conflit entre le Pire et le Mieux.

ARTHUR RIMBAUD:
Crimen Amoris (French)

Both angels and men have suffered too much from this struggle between the worst and the best.

Jeder Mensch hat auch seine moralische 'Backside', die er nicht ohne Not zeigt, und die er solange als möglich mit der Hosen des guten Anstandes zudeckt.

GEORG CHRISTOPH LICHTENBERG:
Aphorismen (German)

Every man has his moral backside as well, which he does not expose unnecessarily, but keeps covered as long as possible with the trousers of decorum.

Alle Moralität des Menschen hat ihren Grund in der Aufmerksamkeit, d.h. im tätigen Einfluss der Seele auf die materiellen Ideen im Denkorgan.

J. C. F. VON SCHILLER:
Werke (German)

All man's morality springs from his attention, *i.e.* the active influence of the soul on the material ideas in his organ of thought.

Reue und Verzweiflung über ein begangenes Verbrechen zeigen uns die Macht des Sittengesetzes nur später, nicht schwächer.

J. C. F. VON SCHILLER:
Werke (German)

Contrition and despair over having committed a crime only later, but no less forcibly, reveal the power of the moral law.

Persona privata non potest inducere efficaciter ad virtutem.

ST. THOMAS AQUINAS:
Summa Theologica (Latin)

A private person is not able to compel right living.

Quod non vetat lex, hoc vetat fieri pudor.

SENECA:
Troades (Latin)

What the law does not forbid, shame forbids to be done.

Vivere si recte nescis, decede peritis.

HORACE:
Epistles (Latin)

If you don't know how to live aright, make way for those who do.

MORTALITY
see also Death, Mankind.

Nicht ist es gut
Seellos von sterblichen
Gedanken zu seyn.

FRIEDRICH HÖLDERLIN:
Andenken (German)

It is not good to be unmoved by mortal thoughts.

Horō gar hēmas ouden ontas allo plēn
Eidōl' hosoiper zōmen ē kouphēn skian

SOPHOCLES:
Ajax (Greek)

We live, but we remain phantoms, nought but shadows.

Hōs hēmera klinei te kanagei palin
Hapanta tanthrōpeia

SOPHOCLES:
Ajax (Greek)

Everything mortal can be raised up or laid low in a single day.

Homines autem cum sint mortales in perpetuum durare non possunt.

ST. THOMAS AQUINAS:
On Princely Government (Latin)

Men, being mortal, cannot live for ever.

Vive memor, quam sis aevi brevis.

HORACE:
Satires (Latin)

Live mindful of how brief your life is.

Vitae summa brevis spem nos vetat incohare
longam.

HORACE:
Odes (Latin)

The span of our short life forbids us to embark
on lasting hopes.

Et querimur, cito si nostrae data tempora vitae
Diffugiunt?

JACOPO SANNAZARO:
Poems (Latin)

Do we complain if our life's allotted span quickly
passes?

Damnati ac morituri in terrae claudimur omnes
Carcere.

ST. THOMAS MORE:
On the Vanity of this Life (Latin)

Condemned and doomed to die, we are all shut
up in the prison of this world.

Recidunt omnia in terras et oriuntur e terris.

CICERO:
De Natura Deorum (Latin)

All things fall back into the earth and also arise
from the earth.

Aciram vat' ayam kāyo paṭhavim adhisessati
Chuddho apetaviññāṇo nirattham va kaliṅg-
aram

Dhammapada: Cittavaggo (Pali)

Alas, before long this body will lie on the earth,
despised, bereft of consciousness, as useless as a
burnt faggot.

MOTHERS
see also Children, Husbands,
Nostalgia, Parents.

Tebki lēk akhtak kāba tafūt,
Tebki lēk martak daḵshi 'd-dabūt,
Tebki lēk ummak yōmit tamūt

ARAB PROVERB

When you are dead your sister's tears will dry as
time goes on, your widow's tears will cease in
another's arms, but your mother will mourn you
till the day she dies.

Galb al-wālide 'ale 'l maulūd, galb al-maulūd
'ale 'l wālide

ARAB PROVERB

The mother once protected her son; now she is
protected by him (*lit.* the parent's heart to the
child, and the child's to the parent).

Man wisse wohl, wie es öppe gehe, wenn zwei an
einer Feuerplatte zusammenkämen.

JEREMIAS GOTTHELF:
Anne Bäbi Jowäger (German)

Everyone knows how it goes when two stand at
the same hearth (Jowäger is explaining why he
did not marry until after the death of his
mother).

Niech przyjaciele moi w nocy się zgromadzą
I biedne serce moje spalą w aloesie,
I tej, która mi dała to serce, oddadzą:
Tak się matkom odpłaca świat – gdy proch
odniesie.

JULIUSZ SLOWACKI:
Testament Mój (Polish)

Let my friends gather by night and burn my
poor heart on a pyre of aloes, rendering it back to
her who gave it, for dust is the coin with which
the world repays our mothers.

Do ciebie, Matko moja, twarz obrócę,
Do ciebie znowu tak jak anioł biały,
Z obłędnych krajów – położyć się wrócę,
U twoich biednych stóp – bez szczęścia –
chwały,
Lecz bez łzy próżnej

JULIUSZ SLOWACKI:
Beniowski (Polish)

I shall turn my face to you, Mother. To you
again, like a white angel, from the lands of my
insanity, I shall return to lay myself at your poor
feet, without happiness or fame, nor yet with
empty tears.

MOTIVES
see also Emotion, Feelings, Passion,
Right and wrong.

Tout nostre raisonnement se reduit à céder au
sentiment.

BLAISE PASCAL:
Pensées (French)

All our reasoning ends in surrender to feeling.

la concupiscence et la force sont les sources de
toutes nos actions: la concupiscence fait les vol-
ontaires, la force, les involontaires.

BLAISE PASCAL:
Pensées, Adversaria (French)

All our actions spring from concupiscence or
force: concupiscence begets the voluntary, force
begets the involuntary actions.

J'appelais l'homme: l'animal capable d'une action gratuite. Et puis après j'ai pensé de con-
raire: que c'était le seul être incapable d'agir
gratuitement.

ANDRÉ GIDE:
Le Promethée Mal Enchainé (French)

I defined man as an animal capable of selfless
deeds. Later I changed my mind, feeling that he
was the only being incapable of acting without
motive.

MOURNING
see also Death, Widows and widowers.

Heu pietas! heu prisca fides invactaque bello
Dextera.

VIRGIL:
Aeneid (Latin)

Mirrour of ancient faith in early youth!
Undaunted worth; Inviolable truth!

(*tr.* Dryden)

Quo sequar? aut quae nunc artus avulsaque
membra
Et funus lacerum tellus habet?

VIRGIL:
Aeneid (Latin)

Where shall I follow you? Your corpse defiled,
your mangled limbs – where are they?

MURDER

C'est la fatalité qui a pris la forme de mes mains.
JEAN GENET:
Haute Surveillance (French)

It is fate that took the form of my hands ('Yeux-
Verts' speaking of his feelings while strangling a
girl).

Mit gewaltsamer Hand
Löset der Mord auch das heiligste Band.

J. C. F. VON SCHILLER:
Braut von Messina (German)

With violent hand, murder loosens the holiest
bond.

Ecclesia abhorret a sanguine.

LATIN PROVERB

The Church abhores bloodshed.

MUSIC
see also Colour, Liberal arts, Poetry.

Uuen soiton suoriak-i,
Uuen kuun kulettajaksi,
Uuen päivän päästäjäksi

The Kalevala (Finnish)

Once more play the entrancing harp, lighting
anew the shining moonbeams, and reviving the
radiant sunshine (referring to the wonderful
playing of Väinämöinen, the inventer of the first
harp).

Soitto on suruista tehty,
Murehista muovaeltu

The Kalevala (Finnish)

Every chord vibrating with grief, and every note
attuned to sadness (referring to the origin of the
harp).

Je croyais entendre
Une vague harmonie enchanter mon sommeil
Et près de moi s'épandre un murmure pareil
Aux chants entrecoupés d'une voix triste et
tendre.

CHARLES BRUGNOT:
Les Deux Genii (French)

I thought I heard a faint harmony bewitching
my sleep, and nearby grew a similar theme, with
a sad and tender voice intersecting the melodies.

On a toujours estimé la Musique des anciens
estre la plus divine, d'autant qu'elle a esté
composée en un siecle plus heureux, et moins

entaché des vices qui regnent en ce dernier age de fer.

PIERRE DE RONSARD:
Livre de Meslanges (preface) *(French)*

We have always thought classical music the most divine, inasmuch as it was composed in happier times, and is less besmirched with the vices that reign in this age of strife.

La Musique à sa date, est venue balayer cela.

STÉPHANE MALLARMÉ:
Le Mystère dans les Lettres (French)

Music has come at the appointed time to sweep away all that.

La récompense la plus agréable qu'on puisse recevoir des choses que l'on fait, c'est de les connues, de les voir caressées d'un applaudissement qui vous honore.

MOLIÈRE:
Le Bourgeois Gentilhomme (French)

The most pleasing reward we can receive for our creations is to have their worth recognised and to have the honour of seeing them distinguished by applause (a dancing master, discussing their compositions with a music master).

Die Tonkunst begrub hier einen reichen Besitz, Aber noch viel schönere Hoffnungen.

FRANZ GRILLPARZER:
inscription on Schubert's memorial stone
(German)

Music has buried great riches here, but even finer hopes.

Musik, das Hohlmass des Menschen.

ELIAS CANETTI:
Aufzeichnungen, 1956 *(German)*

Music, the measure of mankind.

Kaitoi tade men kerdos akeisthai
Molpaisi brotous

EURIPIDES:
Medea (Greek)

How valuable music could be if it could cure the sorrows of mankind!

To tekhnion hēmas diatrephei

SUETONIUS
Nero (Greek

A humble art (*i.e.* music) gains us our dail bread (favourite saying of Nero's).

Cit binni lib i cech mí
cuislennaig no chornairi,
isí mo chobais in-díu
ro-cúala céol bad binniu.

IRISH SONG *(Gaelic*

Though you at all times take pleasure in th playing of pipes or hornblowers, I declare today that I have heard music that could give me mor pleasure.

Musices seminarium accentus.

LATIN PROVER

Accent is the seed-bed of melody.

¡Oh música del hombre y más que el hombre,
Último desenlace
De la audaz esperanza!

JORGE GUILLEN
El Concierto (Spanish

Music! man's music, and yet so much more thar man! The last unfolding of breathless hope!

Aquí la alma navega
Por un mar de dulzura, y finalmente
En él así se anega,
Que ningún accidente
Extraño o peregrino oye o siente.

FRAY LUIS DE LEÓN
Oda a Francisco Salinas (Spanish

Here the soul sails through a sea of sweetness in which it is finally submerged, so that it neither hears nor feels any strange or foreign sensation.

MUTABILITY
see also Change.

Dis es ton auton potamon ouk an embaiēs

GREEK PROVERF

The same situation never recurs (*lit.* one cannot set foot in the same river twice).

N

NAMES

Les choses les plus simples et les plus impor-
tantes n'ont pas toutes un nom.

PAUL VALÉRY:
Mauvaises Pensées (French)

Not all the most simple and important of things
have a name.

Eikos de malista hēmas heurein ta orthōs
keimena peri ta aei onta kai pephukota.
Espoudasthai gar entautha malista prepei tēn
thesin tōn onomatōn. Isōs d' enia autōn kai
hupo theioteras dunameōs ē tēs tōn anthrōpon
etethē

PLATO:
Cratylus (Greek)

We are most likely to find the correct names in
the nature of the eternal and absolute; for there
the names ought to have been given with the
greatest care, and perhaps some of them were
given by a power more divine than is that of
men.

NATIONHOOD
see also Fatherland, Law, Liberty, Misery, Patriotism, People, the State.

Die Nation, die die meiste Spannkraft hatte, war
auch allezeit die freiste und glücklichste.

GEORG CHRISTOPH LICHTENBERG:
Aphorismen (German)

The nation with the most vigour has always
been the freest and the luckiest.

Die Kraft eines Volkes nicht in erster Linie in
seinen Waffen liegt, sondern in seinem Willen.

ADOLF HITLER:
Mein Kampf (German)

In the first instance the strength of a nation lies
not in its weapons, but in its will.

Alle Macht kommt vom Volke.

GERMAN PROVERB

All might comes from the people.

A niechaj narodowie wżdy postronni znają,
Iż Polacy nie gęsi, iż swój język mają.

MIKOŁAJ REJ *(Polish)*

Let neighbouring countries forever know that
Poles are not geese but have their own language.

NATURE
see also Art, Boredom, Civilisation, Equality, Fortune, Freedom, Golden age, Government, Imitation, Joy, Necessity, Society, the Soul, Spring, the Universe.

Aux faux soupçons la nature est sujette,
Et c'est souvent à mal que le bien s'interprète.

MOLIÈRE:
Le Tartuffe (French)

Human nature is subject to false suspicions, and
good is often misinterpreted as evil.

Il y a deux procureurs généraux, l'un à votre
porte, qui châtie les délits contre la société; la
nature est l'autre. Celle-ci connaît de tous les
vices qui échappent aux lois.

DENIS DIDEROT:
Le Neveu de Rameau (French)

There are two Attorneys General: one is on your
threshold ready to chastise offences against
society. Nature is the other – she sees all the
vices that escape the law.

Que peu de temps suffit pour changer toutes
choses!
Nature au front serein, comme vous oubliez!
Et comme vous brisez dans vos métamorphoses
Les fils mystérieux où nos coeurs sont liés!

VICTOR HUGO:
Tristesse d'Olympia (French)

How little time it takes to change everything!
Nature, with your serene brow, how you forget!
and how you, in your metamorphoses, break the
threads by which our hearts are linked!

La Nature est un temple où de vivants piliers
Laissent parfois sortir de confuses paroles.

CHARLES BAUDELAIRE:
Correspondances (French)

Nature is a temple whose living pillars sometimes give forth a babel of words.

L'insensibilité de l'azur et des pierres.

STÉPHANE MALLARMÉ:
Tristesse d'Été (French)

The indifference of the rocks and the azure sky.

Mais l'homme fait la guerre aux forêts
pacifiques;
L'ombrage sur les monts recule chaque jour;
Rien ne nous restera des asiles mystiques
Où l'âme va cueillir la pensée et l'amour.

VICTOR DE LA PRADE:
La Mort d'un Chêne (French)

Man makes war on the peaceful forests, and
each day the shadows on the mountains retreat.
Nothing will remain for us of the mystic refuges
where we could garner thought and love.

Tout ce monde visible n'est qu'un trait imperceptible dans l'ample sein de la nature.

BLAISE PASCAL:
Pensées (French)

The whole visible world is but an imperceptible
speck in the ample bosom of nature.

[La Nature]: c'est une sphère infinie, dont le
centre est partout, la circonférence nulle part.

BLAISE PASCAL:
Pensées (French)

Nature is an infinite sphere of which the centre is
everywhere, and the circumference nowhere.

La Nature paraît se servir des hommes pour ses
desseins, sans se soucier des instruments qu'elle
emploie, à peu près comme les tyrans qui se
défont de ceux dont ils se sont servis.

S. R. N. CHAMFORT:
Maximes et Pensées (French)

Nature appears to make use of mankind for her
projects without caring for the instruments she
uses, somewhat like tyrants who destroy those
who have been of service to them.

Comment ai-je pu exister si longtemps hors de
nature et sans m'identifier à elle?

GÉRARD DE NERVAL
Aurélia (French)

How is it that I have been able to exist for so long
apart from nature, and without identifying myself with her?

Pour les progres à réaliser, il n'y a que la nature

PAUL CÉZANNE
Lettres (French)

To make progress in understanding there is only
nature.

O leite meinen Gang
Natur!

J. W. VON GOETHE
Der Wandrer (German)

O Nature, guide my steps!

In der Natur ist alles einzeln.

GERMAN PROVERB

Everything in nature is separate.

Die ganze Natur ist ein gewaltiges Ringen zwischen Kraft und Schwäche.

ADOLF HITLER
to Heinrich Brüning *(German)*

The whole of nature is a mighty struggle between strength and weakness.

Wo fass ich dich, unendliche Natur?

J. W. VON GOETHE
Faust (German)

Boundless Nature, where shall I grasp thee?

Wir sehen in der Natur nicht Wörter, sondern
immer nur Anfangsbuchstaben von Wörtern
und wenn wir alsdann lesen wollen, so finden
wir, dass die neuen sogenannten Wörte
wiederum bloss Anfangsbuchstaben von andern
sind.

GEORG CHRISTOPH LICHTENBERG
Aphorismen (German)

In nature we see not words but always just the
initial letters of words, and if we then try to read
them, we discover that the new so-called words
are again only the initials of others.

Der ganzen modernen Weltanschauung liegt die
Täuschung zugrunde, dass die sogennanten
Naturgesetze die Erklärungen der Natur-
erscheinungen seien.

LUDWIG WITTGENSTEIN:
Tractatus Logico-philosophicus (German)

The whole modern concept of the world is
founded upon the illusion that the so-called laws
of nature are the explanations of natural
phenomena.

Wo ist er nun, der grosse Traum der Erde,
Der Traum von Vogelflug und Pflanzensein –
Die Dinge blieben doch, ihr altes Werde,
Ihr alter Tod und ach, ihr altes Nein.

GÜNTER EICH:
March Day (German)

Where is it now, that great dream of the earth,
the dream of birdflight and fruitful herb – in all
things there remain the ancient growth, the
ancient death and, alas, the ancient *No*.

Panta phusis dunatai

GREEK PROVERB

Nature can achieve everything.

Homologoumenōs tēi phusei zēn

STOIC MAXIM
(Greek)

Live in accordance with nature.

Chi vuol veder quantunque po natura
E 'l ciel tra noi, venga a mirar costei.

FRANCESCO PETRARCÁ;
Sonnets (Italian)

He who wishes to see how much nature and the
heavens can achieve among us should come to
gaze upon her.

Ma da natura
Altro negli atti suoi
Che nostro male o nostro ben si cura.

GIACOMO LEOPARDI:
Sopra un Basso Relievo Antico Sepolcrale (Italian)

Nature, in her actions, has in mind some other
aim than our harm or benefit.

Non ha natura al seme
Dell 'uom più stima o cura
Che alla formica.

GIACOMO LEOPARDI:
La Ginestra (Italian)

Nature has no more care or praise for human
souls than for the ants.

O natura, o natura,
Perché non rendi poi
Quel che prometti allor? perché di tanto
Inganni i figli tuoi?

GIACOMO LEOPARDI:
A Sylvia (Italian)

Ah Nature! why do you not fulfill your early
promises? Why do you deceive your sons so
bitterly?

Natura beatis omnibus esse dedit, si quis
cognoverit uti.

CLAUDIAN:
In Rufinum (Latin)

Nature has given the chance of happiness to all,
if only they knew how to use it!

Natura est motus principium per se non per
accidens.

BOETHIUS:
Contra Eutychen (Latin)

Nature is the principle of movement of its own
accord and not accidentally.

Sumus sapientes, quod naturam optimam
ducem tamquam deum sequimur eique
paremus.

CICERO:
De Senectute (Latin)

We are wise because we follow nature as the best
of guides, and obey her as a goddess.

Dociles natura nos edidit.

SENECA:
Epistles (Latin)

At our birth nature made us teachable.

Natura abhorret vacuum.

LATIN PROVERB

Nature abhores a vacuum.

Natura non facit saltus.

LATIN PROVERB

Nature does not play leapfrog.

Omnium quidem rerum natura, quantum in nutrimentum sui satis sit, apprehendit.

SENECA:
Natural Questions (Latin)

Nature takes from the earth as much as is sufficient for its nourishment.

Quid enim aliud est natura quam deus?

SENECA:
De Beneficiis (Latin)

What else is nature but God?

Natura genetrix.

LATIN PROVERB

Nature is our mother.

Locuples ac divina natura, quo maiorem sui pareret admirationem ponderatioraque sua essent beneficia, neque uni omnia dare nec rursus cuiquam omnia voluit negare.

CORNELIUS NEPOS:
Fragments (Latin)

Opulent and divine nature, in order to win greater admiration and make a better distribution of her gifts, has chosen neither to give everything to one man, nor, on the contrary, to refuse everything to anyone.

Ne to, chto mnite vȳ, priroda:
Ne slepok, ne bezdushnȳĭ lik –
V neĭ est' dusha, v neĭ est' svoboda,
V neĭ est' lyubov', v neĭ est' yazȳk.

FËDOR TYUTCHEV:
Nature Is Not What You Think (Russian)

Nature is not what you think! She is not a mould, or an image without a soul. She has a soul, she has freedom, she has love, and she can speak.

NECESSITY
see also Possessions, Ways and means.

Al-a'ma gāḍī, al-maghaṣūb rāḍī

ARAB PROVERB

Needs must when the devil drives (*lit.* the blind man goes straight forward, a man under compulsion agrees to anything).

Nécessité est mère de l'industrie.

FRENCH PROVERB

Necessity is the mother of ingenuity.

La neciessità è maestra e tutrice della natura.

LEONARDO DA VINCI
Literary Works (Italian)

Necessity is the mistress and tutor of nature.

Necessitas ante rationem est.

CURTIUS RUFUS
Opera (Latin)

Necessity knows no law.

Necessitas plus posse quam pietas solet.

SENECA
Troades (Latin)

Necessity is often a greater force than love.

Necessitas dat legem, non ipsa accipit.

LATIN PROVERB

Necessity prescribes the law; she does not observe it herself.

Necessitati quodlibet telum utile est.

LATIN PROVERB

Necessity finds any weapon serviceable.

Feriis caret necessitas.

PALLADIUS RUTILIUS TAURUS
(Latin)

Necessity knows no law (*lit.* necessity has no need of rest).

Il-bżonn iġagħlek tagħmel kollox.

MALTESE PROVERB

Necessity makes you do everything.

Quien no llora, no mama.

SPANISH PROVERB

The child that does not cry is not suckled.

A falta de pan, buenas son tortas.

SPANISH PROVERB

If there's no bread, cakes are very good.

NEIGHBOURS
see also Public opinion, Temptation.

ăr-ak al-qarīb wa-lā a<u>kh</u>ū-k al-ba'īd

ARAB PROVERB

▲ near neighbour [may be of more service] than distant brother.

▶ēma kakos geitōn, hosson t' agathos meg' ▶neiar

HESIOD:
Works and Days (Greek)

▶ad neighbours are a burden, but good ones are ▲ blessing.

Vicinis bonus esto.

MARCUS CATO:
De Agricultura (Latin)

▶e a good neighbour.

Nam tua res agitur, paries cum proximus ardet.

HORACE:
Epistles (Latin)

Lt *is* your concern if your neighbour's house is on ▲re.

Al hijo de tu vecino limpiale las narices y mételo ▶n tu casa.

SPANISH PROVERB

Treat your neighbours' children as your own ▲ *lit.* if your neighbour's son comes, wipe his nose ▲nd receive him into your home).

Quien ha buen vecino, ha buen amigo.

SPANISH PROVERB

A good neighbour is a good friend.

NIGHT
see also Dawn, Evening, Horror,
Moon, Wind, Worry.

Stil, achter dooven spiegelbrand
Vangt ijmker nacht den dagverloren zwerm
De sterrebijen aan den hemelberm
In de gekorfde schaduw van zijn hand.

PETER CORNELIS BOUTENS:
Perelaar (Dutch)

Still, screened by the mirror-fire's last glimmer,
▶beekeeper night gathers in the daylost swarm of
star-bees straying on heaven's rim, within the hive-like shadows of his hand.

La nuit mélancolique achevait de descendre
Et semblait sur le parc avec lenteur tomber,
Comme d'un fin tamis une légère cendre,
En noyant les contours qu'elle allait dérober.

SULLY-PRUDHOMME:
Le Bonheur (French)

Sad night completed its descent and seemed to fall slowly on the park, like a gentle layer of ashes sifting through a fine screen, drowning the contours it was about to conceal.

Le crépuscule ami s'endort dans la vallée
Sur l'herbe d'émeraude et sur l'or du gazon.

ALFRED DE VIGNY:
La Maison du Berger (French)

The friendly dusk settles down to sleep in the valley, covering the emerald grass and the golden turf.

Oh! la terre, murmurai-je à la nuit, est un calice embaumé, dont le pistil et les étamines sont la lune et les étoiles!

ALOYSIUS BERTRAND:
Gaspard de la Nuit: La Chambre Gothique (French)

The earth, I murmured to the night, is like a preserved calyx, of which the pistil and the stamens are the moon and the stars.

Reveillez-vous, gens qui dormez,
Et priez pour les trépassés!

FRENCH NIGHTWATCHMAN'S CALL

Sleepers, awake! and pray for the dead.

Gelassen stieg die Nacht ans Land,
Lehnt träumend an der Berge Wand;
Ihr Auge sieht die goldne Waage nun
Der Zeit in gleichen Schalen stille ruhn.

EDUARD MÖRIKE:
Um Mitternacht (German)

Calmly night spreads across the land, leaning dreamily against the mountain wall. Now her eyes see the golden Libra, time balancing evenly in the silent scales.

Nachtgrau, das um mich schweigt
Voll inneren Dämmerlichtes wie ein Traum.

Ein stiller See, der in dem ruhigen Raum
Hoch über mir bis an die Decke steigt.
> WILHELM VON SCHOLZ:
> *Die Nacht (German)*

The grey night that keeps silence around me is
full of twilight shafts as in a dream; a calm sea
that in the peaceful room reaches high above me
to the ceiling.

Tiefe Nacht ist drauss und drinnen,
Tiefe Nacht in euren Sinnen,
Tiefe Nacht allumgetan.
> ALBRECHT SCHAEFFER:
> *Die Lange Nacht (German)*

Dark night is in and outdoors, dark night is in
our senses, dark night is complete.

Der Wald aber rühret die Wipfel
Im Traum von der Felsenwand.
Denn der Herr geht über die Gipfel
Und segnet das stille Land.
> JOSEPH VON EICHENDORFF:
> *Nachts (German)*

In the forest the treetops stir in their dream of
walls of rock. Then the Lord comes over the
mountain peaks, and blesses the silent land.

Zur Nachtzeit wachsen den Gassen,
Den Winkeln heimliche Ohren.
Das Dunkel steht gelassen
Und horchend unter Toren.
> MAX DAUTHENDEY:
> *Das Dunkel (German)*

At night-time the alleys are thronged, and the
corners have secret ears. The dark stands
patiently, listening at doors.

Wenn des Mondes still lindernde Tränen
Lösen der Nächte verborgenes Weh,
Dann wehet Friede. In goldenen Kähnen
Schiffen die Geister im himmlischen See.
> CLEMENS BRENTANO:
> *Sprich aus der Ferne (German)*

When the quiet soothing tears of the moon loose
the night's secret sorrow, then peace prevails,
and the spirits set forth in golden skiffs on a
heavenly sea.

Die Luft ging durch die Felder,
Die Ähren wogten sacht,
Es rauschten leis die Wälder,
So sternklar war die Nacht.
> JOSEPH VON EICHENDORFF
> *Mondnacht (German*

The breeze drifted through the fields, the tips of
the corn waved gently, the woods rustled peace
fully, so starry bright was the night.

Nox et solitudo plenae sunt diabolo.
> LATIN PROVER

Night and solitude are full of devils.

Těngah malam sudah těrlampau,
Dinihari bělum lagi tampak,
Budak-budak dua kali jaga;
Orang muda pulang běrtandang;
Orang tua běrkaleh tidor;
Ěmbun jantan rintek-rintek
> *Hikayat Maalim Dewa (Malay*

The midnight hour was long past, but daylight
was not yet visible. Twice had waking children
risen and sunk again in sleep. Truant youth
were homeward bound; their elders all wrapped
in sleep.

Kogda dlya smertnogo umolknet shumnȳi den'
I na nemȳe stognȳ grada
Poluprozrachnaya nalyazhet noch' ten'
I son, dnevnȳkh trudov nagrada.
> ALEKSANDR SERGEEVICH PUSHKIN
> *Vospominanie (Russian*

When noisy day is stilled for mortal man, and
over the wide and silent city streets spread
night's translucent shadow, and sleep, reward
for the day's toil.

Svyataya noch' na nebosklon vzoshla,
I den' otradnȳi, den' lyubeznȳi
Kak zolotoï pokrov ona svila,
Pokrov, nakinutȳi nad bezdnoï.
> FĒDOR TYUTCHEV
> *Holy Night (Russian*

Holy night has risen in the heavens, rolling up
the kind, comforting day like a golden cloth – a
cloth thrown over the abyss.

La noche sosegada
En par de los levantes de la aurora,
La música callada,
La soledad sonora.

ST. JOHN OF THE CROSS:
Canciones entre el Alma y el Esposo (Spanish)

The peaceful night accompanying the dawn's
stirring, the barely perceptible music, and the
pleasing solitude.

Noche que en tu amoroso y dulce olvido
Escondes y entretienes los cuidados
Del enemigo día y los pasados
Trabajos recompensas al sentido.

FRANCISCO DE LA TORRE:
Noche (Spanish)

Night that, in your kind and sweet neglect, allay
and conceal our daily burdens, and reward our
senses for their past efforts.

Todo esto viene en medio del silencio profundo
En que la noche envuelve la terrena ilusión.

RUBÉN DARÍO:
Nocturno (Spanish)

All this comes in the midst of the profound
silence in which night enwraps the earthly
illusion.

NIGHTINGALE
see also Birds.

Le chant du rossignol est, dans la nuit sereine,
Comme un appel aux dieux de l'Ombre souter-
raine,
Mais non, hélas! aux roses dont le parfum
s'accroît
De ne pouvoir mourir, d'un souffle, à cette voix!

PAUL FORT:
Philomèle (French)

In the serenity of the night the song of the
nightingale is like a call to the gods of the
subterranean world, but not, alas! — to the roses
whose scent grows from not being able to die at
the first breath of that voice!

NOSTALGIA
see also Memories.

Mais où sont les neiges d'antan?

FRANCOIS VILLON:
Ballade des Dames du Temps Jadis (French)

Where are the snows of yesteryear?

Oui, je me souviens du passé,
Du berceau vide où j'ais laissé
Mon rêve à peine commencé,
Et de ma mère.

CASIMIR DELAVIGNE:
Sonnet (French)

Yes, I remember the past, the empty cradle
where I left a dream I had hardly begun – and
my mother.

O mihi praeteritos referat si Iuppiter annos!

LATIN EXPRESSION

Would that Jupiter would give me back the
years already gone!

NOVELTY

Rien n'est nouveau sous le soleil.

FRENCH PROVERB

There is nothing new under the sun.

Nous voulons, tant ce feu nous brûle le cerveau,
Plonger au fond du gouffre, Enfer ou Ciel,
qu'importe?
Au fond de l'Inconnu pour trouver du *nouveau!*

CHARLES BAUDELAIRE:
Le Voyage (French)

This fire so scorches our brain, that we want to
plunge deep into the gulf, whether heaven or
hell, who cares? To find something *new* in the
depths of the unknown!

L'esprit de nouveauté est capable d'abattre les
édifices les plus solides.

MICHEL SERVIN:
Les Réguliers (French)

The spirit of innovation is capable of demolish-
ing even the most solid of walls.

Pereant qui nostra ante nos dixerunt.

AELIUS DONATUS:
(commenting on Terence's 'Nullum est iam
dictum, quod non dictum sit prius' – Nothing
can be said nowadays which has not already
been said – *Eunuchus*, as recorded by
St. Jerome in his commentary on the Book of
Ecclesiastes). *(Latin)*

May they perish who have said these things
before we could!

O

OBEDIENCE
see also America, Duty, Kings.

Obéissez aux puissances. Si cela veut dire: Cédez à la force, le précepte est bon, mais superflu.

J. J. ROUSSEAU:
Du Contrat Social (French)

Obey authority! If that means yield to force, the precept is good but superfluous.

L'obéissance est un métier bien rude.

PIERRE CORNEILLE:
Nicomède (French)

Obedience is a hard profession.

Gehorsam ist des Christen Schmuck.

J. C. F. VON SCHILLER:
Der Kampf mit dem Drachen (German)

Obedience is the adornment of Christ.

Peitharkhia gar esti tēs eupraxias
Mētēr, gunē sōtēros

AESCHYLUS:
The Seven against Thebes (Greek)

Obedience is the mother of success, and the wife of security.

Anceps quaestio et in utramque partem a prudentibus viris arbitrata est.

AULUS GELLIUS:
Attic Nights (Latin)

It is a difficult question that has been answered both ways by wise men (discussing whether, on being exactly instructed to do something, one has the right to alter the instructions to improve the success and advantages of the project on behalf of the man who gave the original instruction).

OBLIVION
see also History, Memory, Sleep, Time.

Ve zlatém víně ztopíme
tyranský rozmar paměti.

KAREL TOMAN:
'Sentimentální Pijáci' in Torso Života (Czech)

We shall drown the tyrant whim of memory in golden wine.

Le monde ordinaire a la pouvoir de ne pas songer à ce qu'il ne veut pas songer.

BLAISE PASCAL:
Pensées (French)

Ordinary people are able to expunge from their minds those things they do not want to think about.

Ces arbres et ces prairies enseignent à haute voix la plus belle de toutes, l'oubli de ce qu'on sait.

ALFRED DE MUSSET:
On ne Badine pas avec l'Amour (French)

These trees and meadows teach us clearly the best of all things – to forget what we know.

Aisoi, apustoi

GREEK PROVERB

Out of sight, out of mind.

Io voglio io voglio adagiami
In un tedio che duri infinito.

GIOSUE CARDUCCI
All Stazione (Italian)

I long unconsciously to sink lost in languid eternal slumber.

Procul a Jove, procul a fulmine.

LATIN PROVERB

Out of sight, out of mind (*lit.* far from Jupiter, far from the thunderbolt).

Vixere fortes ante Agamemnon
Multi; sed omnes illacrimabiles

rgentur ignotique longa
octa, carent quia vate sacro.

> HORACE:
> *Odes (Latin)*

here have been many brave men before
gamemnon; but they have all vanished in the
ong night, unknown and unwept, because they
cked a sacred bard.

Lethaei ad fluminis undam
ecuros latices et longa oblivia potant.

> VIRGIL:
> Aeneid *(Latin)*

1 Lethe's lake they long oblivion taste
f future life secure, forgetful of the past
> (*tr.* Dryden).

1as se o sereno ceo me concedera
Qualquer quieto, humilde e doce estado,
Onde com minhas Musas só vivera.
em ver-me em terra alheia degredado.

> LUIS DE CAMÕES:
> *Mas se O Sereno (Portuguese)*

f only the peaceful heavens would grant me
ome quiet, humble and pleasant place in life
/here, no more in exile, I could live with my
1use.

Dichoso aquel que apartado de los negocios y
bre de todo cuidado cultiva los campos de sus
adres!

> ARMANDO PALACIO VALDÉS:
> *La Novela de un Novelista (Spanish)*

Iappy is he who, far from business and free
om all care, cultivates the lands of his
refathers!

OFFENCE

lus l'offenseur est cher, et plus grande est
offense.

> PIERRE CORNEILLE:
> *Le Cid (French)*

`he dearer the offender is to us, the greater his
ffence.

Demus itaque operam, abstineamus offensis.

> SENECA:
> *Epistles (Latin)*

et us be careful not to give offence.

Calces deteris!

> PLAUTUS:
> *Mercator (Latin)*

You are treading on my heels!

Non quicquid nos offendit, et laedit.

> SENECA:
> *Epistles (Latin)*

What annoys us does not necessarily harm us.

OFFICE
see also Greatness, Leadership.

Il n'est pas toujours bon d'avoir un haut emploi.

> JEAN DE LA FONTAINE:
> *Les Deux Mulets (French)*

It is not always good to hold high office.

Chacun à son metier doit toujours s'attacher.

> JEAN DE LA FONTAINE:
> *Le Cheval et le Loup (French)*

Everyone should stick to his trade.

D'un magistrat ignorant
C'est la robe qu'on salue.

> JEAN DE LA FONTAINE:
> *L'Âne Portant des Reliques (French)*

We salute the uniform, not the man.

Couvertes de l'honnêteté publique.

> J. J. ROUSSEAU:
> *Lettre à d'Alembert (French)*

Covered in public honesty.

Petere honorem pro flagitio more fit.

> PLAUTUS:
> *Trinummus (Latin)*

Nowadays a disgraceful background is no
hindrance to seeking office.

Tribunus ambustus.

> CICERO:
> *Oratio pro Milone (Latin)*

The singed tribune of the people (Cicero, jest-
ingly referring to the tribune of the people,
Munacius Plancus, at whose suggestion the
enraged populace set fire to the Senate-house).

Magistratus facit hominem.

LATIN PROVERB

The office makes the man.

Vivat et urbanis albus in officiis.

MARTIAL:
Epigrams (Latin)

Let him live pale from the cares of public office.

Neque enim sexum in imperiis discernunt.

TACITUS:
Agricola (Latin)

For in appointing their leaders [the Britons] do not discriminate by sex.

OLD AGE
see also Advice, Contentment, Judgment, Marriage, Time, Wisdom, Youth.

J'obeis à la loy que la Nature a faite.

PIERRE DE RONSARD:
Sonnets (French)

I obey the law laid down by Nature (referring to his old age).

La jeunesse se flatte, et croit tout obtenir;
La vieillesse est impitoyable.

JEAN DE LA FONTAINE:
Le Vieux Chat et la Jeune Souris (French)

Youth flatters itself, believing it can get everything it wants; old age is merciless.

En vieillissant on devient plus fou et plus sage.

FRANÇOIS, DUC DE LA ROCHEFOUCAULD:
Réflexions (French)

As we get old we become at the same time more foolish and wiser.

Peu de gens savent être vieux.

FRANÇOIS, DUC DE LA ROCHEFOUCAULD:
Réflexions (French)

Few people know how to be old.

Les femmes regardaient Booz plus qu'un jeune homme,

Car le jeune homme est beau, mais le vieillard est grand.

VICTOR HUGO
Booz Endormi (French)

The women looked at Booz more than at young man, for a young man is handsome, but the old are magnificent.

Il fera comme fait un cassé mortepaye,
Qui confinant ses jours dans quelque vieux chasteau
Après avoir pendu ses armes au rateau,
Inutile à soymesme enrouille de paresse
Avecques son harnois les ans de sa vieillesse.

PIERRE DE RONSARD
Discours au Roy (closing lines) *(French)*

He will be like a retired soldier who, living out his remaining years in some old castle, hangs up his arms and, feeling useless, lets the years of his old age, together with his harness, rust up with idleness.

La course de nos jours est plus qu'à demi faite;
L'âge insensiblement nous conduit à la mort.

MARQUIS DE RACAN
Stances sur la Retraite (French)

Our life's span is more than half completed, and old age imperceptibly leads us to our death.

En prenant des anneés on devient plat ou fou, et j'ai une peur atroce de mourir comme un sage.

ALFRED DE MUSSET
Il faut qu'une Porte soit Ouverte ou Fermée (French)

As the years go on one becomes either dull or mad, and I have a terrible fear of dying like a sage!

Ouwê war sint verswunden alliu mîniu jâr?

WALTHER VON DER VOGELWEIDE
Elegy (or *Palinode*) *(German)*

Alas, where have they vanished, all the years I knew?

Smikra palaia sōmat' euazei rhopē

SOPHOCLES
Oedipus Tyrannus (Greek)

One touch will despatch an old man.

Kai su gerōn ei kai mōros

SUETONIUS:
Divus Claudius (Greek)

You are both an old man and a fool!

Aithbe damcen bés mora;
sentu fom-dera croan;
toirsi oca cía do-gnéo,
sona do-tét a loan.

ANONYMOUS NINTH-CENTURY IRISH POET

Ebbtide has come to me as to the sea; old age
makes me bleed; though I may sorrow over this,
its tide returns happily.

La vecchiezza, ove fosse
Incolume il desio, la speme estinta,
Secche le fonti, del piacer, le pene
Maggiori sempre, e non più dato il bene.

GIACOMO LEOPARDI:
Il Tramonto della Luna (Italian)

Old age, where desire remains intact but hope
extinct, where the fountains of pleasure run dry,
and pain grows always greater, and good is no
longer granted.

Hana no ira wa
Utsurinikeri na
Itazura ni
Waga mi yo ni furu
Nagame seshi ma ni

ONO NO KOMACHI:
Waga (Japanese)

Alas! the flowers have lost their colours, while I
uselessly spend my aging days in these pitiful
rains.

Oi-raku no
Komu to shiri-seba
Kado sashite
Nashi to kotayete
Awazara-mashi wo

Kokin Shū (Japanese)

When old age approaches, how wonderful it
would be to lock the door and refuse to admit
him!

Nagaraheba mata konogoro ya shinobaren ushi
to mishi you zo ima wa koishki

FUJIWARA NO KYOSKE-ASON:
Waga (Japanese)

Suffering grows with my years, and my misery
increases the more.

Quid est autem turpius quam senex vivere inci-
piens?

SENECA:
Epistles (Latin)

Is there anything worse than beginning to live
when you are old?

Potest frugalitas producere senectutem.

SENECA:
Epistles (Latin)

Old age can be brought on by frugality.

Nihil habeo quod accusem senectutem.

CICERO:
De Senectute (Latin)

I have no reason to reproach old age (quoting
Georgias of Leontini replying to someone who
asked him why he chose to remain alive for so
long – he lived on until he was 107).

Rugaque in antiqua fronte senilis erit.

OVID:
Tristia (Latin)

The wrinkles of old age will come in time upon
thy brow.

Eheu fugaces, Postume, Postume
Labuntur anni.

HORACE:
Odes (Latin)

Alas, O Postumus, the years glide swiftly by!

Iam venient rugae, quae tibi corpus arent.

OVID:
Ars Amatoria (Latin)

Now come the wrinkles that plough furrows over
your body.

Atque equidem memini – fama est obscurior annis.

VIRGIL:
Aeneid (Latin)

I call to mind (but time the tale has worn).

(*tr.* Dryden)

Nos ignoremus quid sit matura senectus,
Scire aevi meritum, non numerare decet.

AUSONIUS:
Poems (Latin)

Let us not know what ripe old age will bring but only accept its rewards.

Resistendum senectuti est.

CICERO:
De Senectute (Latin)

Old age must be resisted (by watching over one's health, taking moderate exercise, eating moderately etc.).

Nihil est otiosa senectute iucundius.

CICERO:
De Senectute (Latin)

Nothing is more enjoyable than a leisured old age (that is, if one has reserves of study and learning).

Ut diu vivitur, bene vivitur.

LATIN PROVERB,
quoted in Plautus: *Trinummus*

By living long we learn to live.

Senectus ipsast morbu'.

TERENCE:
Phormio (Latin)

Age is itself a malady.

Obrepit non intellecta senectus.

JUVENAL:
Satires (Latin)

Old age creeps on us unperceived.

Mihi solitudo et recessus provincia est.

CICERO:
Ad Atticum (Latin)

My province is solitude and retirement.

Frigidus obsistit circum praecordia sanguis.

VIRGIL:
Georgics (Latin)

The cold blood (*i.e.* old age) round my heart now hinders me.

Omnia fert aetas, animum quoque.

VIRGIL:
Bucolics (Latin)

Age carries all things, even the mind, away.

Solve senescentem mature sanus equum, ne
Peccet ad extremum ridendus et ilia ducat.

HORACE:
Epistles (Latin)

Be wise in time and turn loose the ageing horse, lest at last he stumble amid jeers and burst his wind.

Complectamur illam [senectutem] et amemus;
plena est voluptatis, si illa scias uti.

SENECA:
Epistles (Latin)

Let us cherish and love old age, for it is full of pleasure if we know how to use it.

[Dixi] miseram esse senectutem quae se oratione defenderet.

CICERO:
De Senectute (Latin)

I have said that old age can be wretched if it needs to defend itself with words (that is, since it cannot draw on the comfort of past achievements).

Satukan hangat dan dingin,
Tinggalkan loba dan ingin,
Hanchor děndak sapěrti lilin,
Mangka-nya dapat kěrja-mu lichin.

HAMZAH OF BARUS:
Sha'ir Dagang (Malay)

When heat and cold have become the same, and greed and desire but useless terms, and you yourself are like wax resolved in the flame, then smooth enough you will find the rest of your life.

En elli gefr honum engi friŏ,
þótt honum geirar gefi

OLD NORSE PROVERB

Old age gives no quarter, even if spears do.

ammel Ørn sin Fjærham fælder,
ammel Støder gaar og hælder,
ammel Kjærring mister Tænder,
ammel Knark faar visne Hænder, –
Iver og en faar vissen Sjæl.

HENRIK IBSEN:
Peer Gynt (Norwegian)

ge makes eagles lose their feathers, makes old
geys' footsteps fail, sets an old crone's teeth
ecaying, gives an old man withered hands –
nd they all get withered souls.

athā daṇḍena gopālo gāvo pāceti gocaram
vaṁ jarā ca maccū ca āyuṁ pācenti pāṇinam
Dhammapada: Daṇḍavaggo (Pali)

ust as a cowherd drives, with his staff, the cows
to the pasture, so old age and death drive us
to a new existence.

hizn' nasha v starosti – iznoshennӱi khalat:
sovestno nosit' ego, i zhal' ostavit'.

PËTR VYAZEMSKY:
Zhizn' (Russian)

Our old age is like a worn-out dressing-gown; it
hames us to wear it, yet we cannot bring our-
elves to throw it away.

Ne rasti trave
Posle oseni;
Ne tsvesti tsvetam
Zimoï po snegu!

ALEKSEI KOL'TSOV:
Esnya (Russian)

Grass does not grow once autumn is past;
lowers do not bloom in the snowy winter!

La gallina vieja hace buena sopa.
SPANISH PROVERB

The old hen makes good soup.

No le quiere mal quien le hurta al viejo lo que ha
de cenar.
SPANISH PROVERB

No ill-will is shown to the old man if his supper is
stolen from him.

OMENS
see also Dreams, Oracles, Warnings.

Nec pro ostento ducendum, si pecudi cor
defuisset.

SUETONIUS:
Divus Iulius (Latin)

It should not be regarded as a portent, if a beast
has no heart (Caesar, rejecting the implications
of unfavourable omens).

Bono animo estote! nobis adluxit.

SUETONIUS:
Vitellius (Latin)

Be of good cheer! To us light is given! (Vitellius,
commenting on the meaning of his dining-
room's catching fire the night he was first hailed
as Emperor).

OPINION
see also Advice, Force, Knowledge,
Public opinion, Reputation.

L'opinion est la reine du monde.
BLAISE PASCAL:
Pensées (French)

Opinion is queen of the world.

Prouver que j'ai raison serait accorder que je
puis avoir tort.

P. A. C. DE BEAUMARCHAIS:
Le Mariage de Figaro (French)

To prove I am right would be to admit that I
could be wrong (Figaro's fiancée's reason for not
explaining why she dislikes something).

Allos allo legei
GREEK PROVERB

Some say one thing, others another.

To gar orthousthai gnōman odunai
EURIPIDES:
Hippolytus (Greek)

How unpleasant it is to have one's opinions
corrected!

To men gar talēthes doxazein kalon, to de pseudesthai aiskhron

PLATO:
Theaetetus (Greek)

It is good to hold a true opinion, but disgraceful to be deceived.

Numquam enim in praestantibus in republica gubernanda viris laudata est in una sententia perpetua permansio.

CICERO:
Letter to Lentulus (Latin)

Never has an undeviating persistence in one opinion been reckoned as a merit in those distinguished men who have steered the ship of state.

La opinión popular le importa muy poco a los gobiernos.

JACINTO BENAVENTE:
La Escuela de las Princesas (Spanish)

Public opinion matters very little to governments.

OPPORTUNITY
see also Temptations, Thieves and theft, Time.

Wa-qaddaysh tibqā furaṣ 'and al-wāḥid wa-lā yitfikkirsh

ARAB PROVERB

How many opportunities present themselves to a man without his noticing them?

Sikitnā luh dakhal bi-ḥumāruh

ARAB PROVERB

Give a man an inch, and he will take a mile (*lit.* we said nothing to him and he came in with his donkey).

Al-gharqān yimsik fī qashāya

ARAB PROVERB

A drowning man will clutch at a straw.

Une jument qui veut courir trouve toujours un cavalier.

JACQUES AUDIBERTI:
La Poupée (French)

A filly who wants to run will always find a rider.

Cueillez dès aujourd'hui les roses de la vie.

PIERRE DE RONSARD
Sonnet pour Hélène (French

Gather ye rosebuds while ye may (*lit.* gathe today the roses of life).

Les moments sont très chers pour les perdre ex paroles.

JEAN RACINE
Bajazet (French

These moments are too precious to lose them i talk.

Il faut qu'une porte soit ouverte ou fermée.

ALFRED DE MUSSET
title of one of his one-act plays *(French*

Either a door is open or it's closed.

Kai tōnde kairon hostis ōkistos labe

AESCHYLUS
The Seven against Thebes (Greek

Delay not to seize the hour!

Kairos gar, hosper andrasin
Megistos ergou pantos est' epistatēs

SOPHOCLES
Electra (Greek

Seize the hour, for opportunity is our best leader in all ventures.

Hēdu gar ti ktēma tēs nikēs labein

SOPHOCLES:
Philoctetes (Greek

It is delightful to have victory within one's grasp.

Fronte capillata, post est Occasio calva.

LATIN PROVERB

Seize time by the forelock! (*lit.* the head of opportunity has locks in front, but is bald at the back).

Carpe diem, quam minimum credula postero.

HORACE:
Odes (Latin

Seize the day; trust the morrow as little as possible.

n liquida nat tibi linter aqua.
LATIN PROVERB

'ou have a favourable opportunity (*lit.* your
▸oat floats in liquid waters).

Nunc ipsa vocat res.
Iac iter est.
VIRGIL:
Aeneid (Latin)

The hour is ripe, and yonder lies the way.

▸tat sua cuique dies.
VIRGIL:
Aeneid (Latin)

:ach man has his day.

)ccasio facit furem.
LATIN PROVERB

)pportunity makes the thief.

Jno saltu duos apros capere.
PLAUTUS:
Casina (Latin)

To kill two birds with one stone (*lit.* to capture
wo boars with one leap).

In ipso articulo.
TERENCE:
Adelphoe (Latin)

In the nick of time.

Lupo agnum eripere.
LATIN PROVERB

To snatch meat from a dog's mouth (*lit.* to
snatch the lamb from the wolf).

Lupus observavit, dum dormitaret canes.
PLAUTUS:
Trinummus (Latin)

The wolf watched for his opportunity while the
dog slept.

Quae cuique est fortuna hodie, quam quisque
secat spem.
VIRGIL:
Aeneid (Latin)

Whatever the fortune of each today, whatever
the hope each pursues.

Adveniet justum pugnae, ne arcessite, tempus.
VIRGIL:
Aeneid (Latin)

There shall come a lawful time for battle – do
not anticipate it.

Occasio aegre offertur, facile amittitur.
LATIN PROVERB

Opportunity is slow to offer, easy to miss.

Cada broma quiere su tiempo y lugar.
SPANISH PROVERB

Everything has a time and a place.

ORACLES
see also Omens, Warnings.

Un oracle jamais ne se laisse comprendre.
PIERRE CORNEILLE:
Horace (French)

An oracle takes care never to be understood.

ORATORY
see also Eloquence, Speech, Words.

Er sagt was das Herz seiner Zuhörer zu hören
wünscht.
Otto Strasser, 1930 (speaking of Hitler)
(German)

He says what his hearers in their hearts want to
hear.

Cavendum est, ne arcessitum dictum putetur.
CICERO:
De Oratore (Latin)

One should take care lest an expression be
considered far-fetched.

Loqui e lintre.
LATIN PROVERB

To speak from a boat (said of one who sways his
body to and fro when speaking).

Ponendus est ille ambitus, non abiciendus.
CICERO:
De Oratore (Latin)

The period must be brought gradually to a
close, not broken off suddenly.

ORDER
see also Providence, Society.

Ordnung führt zu allen Tugenden! Aber was
führt zur Ordnung?

> GEORG CHRISTOPH LICHTENBERG:
> *Aphorismen (German)*

Order leads to all virtues. But what leads to
order?

Sinn ist Ordnung, und Ordnung ist doch am
Ende Übereinstimmung mit unserer Natur.

> GEORG CHRISTOPH LICHTENBERG:
> *Aphorismen (German)*

Sense is order, and order – in the end – is i
harmony with our nature.

OXFORD

Nur eine Luststadt!

> Professor Willemovitz-Moellendor
> (viewing Oxford from the top c
> Magdalen Tower) *(German*

Only a fun city!

P

PAIN
see also Death, Despair, Language, Life, Old age, Pleasure, Self-indulgence, Sorrow.

Misstrauen gegen den Schmerz: es ist immer ein eigener Schmerz.

ELIAS CANETTI:
Aufzeichnungen, 1944 *(German)*

Distrust of pain is always a pain of its own.

Das leiseste Zucken des Schmerzes, und rege es sich nur in einem Atom, macht einen Riss in der Schöpfung von oben bis unten.

GEORG BÜCHNER:
Dantons Tod (German)

The slightest twinge of pain, be it perceptible only in an atom, makes a crack in creation from top to bottom.

Wir haben der Schmerzen nicht zu viel, wir haben ihrer zu wenig, denn durch den Schmerz gehen wir zu Gott ein!

GEORG BÜCHNER, on his death bed
(German)

We haven't too much pain, we have too little, for through pain we enter into God.

Uscir di pena
È diletto fra noi.

GIACOMO LEOPARDI:
La Quiete dopo la Tempesta (Italian)

The end of pain we take as happiness.

Avara pena, tarda il tuo dono
In questa mia ora
Di sospirati abbandoni.

SALVATORE QUASIMODO:
Oboe Sommerso (Italian)

Miser pain, delay your gift in this hour of abandon I have so long desired!

Assai felice
Se respirar ti lice
D'alcun dolor: beata
Se te d'ogni dolor morte risana.

GIACOMO LEOPARDI:
La Quiete dopo la Tempesta (Italian)

You can be happy indeed if you have breathing-space from pain; and you can be blessed all the more if death should heal you of the pain you fear!

Pro medicina est dolor dolorem qui necat.

LATIN PROVERB

The pain that kills pain acts as medicine.

Cuivis dolori remedium est patientia.

LATIN PROVERB

Endurance is the cure for any pain.

Bene perdis gaudium ubi dolor pariter perit.

LATIN PROVERB

We are content to forgo joy when pain is also lost.

Der staar skrevet: det er ikke grejdt at forstaa,
Hvor Skoen trykker, naar en ikke har den paa.

HENRIK IBSEN:
Peer Gynt (Norwegian)

You can't tell where the shoe is pinching unless you've got it on.

PAINTERS AND PAINTING
see also Art and artists.

Le Peintre donne une âme à une figure, et le Poète prête une figure à un sentiment et à une idée.

S. R. N. CHAMFORT:
Maximes et Pensées (French)

The painter gives a soul to a figure, and the poet lends a figure to a feeling and to an idea.

La peinture est sans doute l'art dans lequel la sensation de l'impuissance nous est le plus facilement donnée par l'artiste.

PAUL VALÉRY:
Choses Tues (French)

Painting is undoubtedly the art in which the feeling of impotence is most easily conveyed to us by the artist.

Male gut und schnell!

Advice given to Walter Sickert by his father
(German)

Paint well and quickly!

Das Bild ist ein Modell der Wirklichkeit.

LUDWIG WITTGENSTEIN:
Tractatus Logico-philosophicus (German)

A picture is a model of reality.

Che finge figura,
Se non può essar lei, non la può porre.
DANTE:
Convivio (last treatise) *(Italian)*

Whoever paints a figure, unless he can *be* it, cannot set it down.

Pictoribus atque poetis
Quidlibet audendi semper fuit aequa potestas.
HORACE:
Ars Poetica (Latin)

Painters and poets have always had the equal right to dare all.

PALINDROMES

Esope reste ici et se repose

(French)

Aesop stops here for a rest

L'âme des uns jamais n'use de mal

(French)

People's souls never make use of evil

Signa te, signa, temere me tangis et angis!

(Latin)

Cross thyself, cross thyself, thou plaguest and vexeth me without need!

Roma tibi subito motibus ibit amor!

(Latin)

Rome, so dear to thee, will soon by my efforts be in sight!

(The two palindromes above were said in exasperation by the Devil who, in the form of a mule, was being ridden by a bishop on his way to Rome).

Subi dura a rudibus

(Latin)

To undergo harshness by rods

Sator Arepo tenet opera rotas

(Latin)

The sower Arepo carries out his work with the aid of wheels

This is also a word square:

```
SATOR
AREPO
TENET
OPERA
ROTAS
```

Odo tenet mulum

(Latin)

Odo holds the mule

Madidam mappam tenet Anna

(Latin)

Anna holds the soaked towel

Llad dad dall

(Welsh)

Holy blind father

Lladd dafad ddall

(Welsh)

Kill a blind sheep

PARADISE

J'ai cru à des paradis et je ne les ai jamais vus de ma vie.

ALBERT CAMUS
Carnets (French)

I have always believed in the existence of paradises, but I have never seen any of them during my lifetime

Le paradis perdu n'est pas celui qu'on pense.
> PAUL GILSON:
> *La Romance des Capitales (French)*

The paradise that is lost is not what one thinks it
is.

Srotha téithmilsi tar tír,
rogu de mid ocus fín.
doíni delghaidi cen on,
combart cen peccad, cen chol.
> ANONYMOUS NINTH-CENTURY IRISH POET *(Gaelic)*

Gentle sweet streams water the earth; the best of
mead and wine is drunk; the inhabitants are fine
and peerless; conception there is without sin or
guilt.

Jeg stængte for mit Paradis
Og tog dets Nøgle med.
> HENRIK IBSEN:
> *Peer Gynt (Norwegian)*

I locked my gate to Paradise and took away the
key.

PARDON

Nous nous pardonnons tout, et rien aux autres
hommes.
> JEAN DE LA FONTAINE:
> *La Besace (French)*

We pardon everything in ourselves, but nothing
in other people.

Les fréquentes grâces annoncent que, bientôt,
les forfaits n'en auront plus besoin.
> J. J. ROUSSEAU:
> *Du Contrat Social (French)*

Frequent pardons mean that crime will soon
need them no longer.

PARENTS
see also Children, Families, Mothers.

Beitet unz iuwer jugent zergê:
Swaz ir in tuot, daz rechent iuwer jungen.
> WALTHER VON DER VOGELWEIDE:
> *Die Veter habent ir Kint erzogen (German)*

Just wait till your youth is gone! What you did to
them, your children will do to you!

Eutukhōs men, all' homōs
Ta tōn tekontōn ommath' hēdiston blepein
> SOPHOCLES:
> *Oedipus Tyrannus (Greek)*

I flourished away from home, but missed that
best of all things – the sight of my parents.

Tois tekousi gar
Oud' ei ponei tis, dei ponou mnēmēn ekhein
> SOPHOCLES:
> *Oedipus Coloneus (Greek)*

Work, if work it be, is nothing if it is done for our
parents' sake.

Alla mēn kai makheitai ge pan zōon diapheron-
tōs parontōn hōn an tekēi
> PLATO:
> *The Republic (Greek)*

Any creature fights better if its young are
present.

Qui nihil aliud nisi quod sibi soli placet
Consulit advorsum filium, nugas agit:
Miser ex animo fit, factius nihilo facit.
> PLAUTUS:
> *Trinummus (Latin)*

The father who subordinates his son's interests
to his own convenience is a fool: he himself loses,
and the situation remains unimproved.

PARIS

On ne guérit pas de Paris.
> FRENCH PROVERB

We never get tired of Paris.

Paris vaut bien une messe.
> Henri IV, at the time of his final
> conversion to Catholicism *(French)*

Paris is well worth a mass.

Tout Paris les condamne, et tout Paris les court.
> VOLTAIRE:
> *Lettres Philosophiques (French)*

The whole of Paris condemns them, and the
whole of Paris runs after them (speaking of the
current Paris stage).

PARTING
see also Applause, Farewell, Love.

Vaert wel mijn lief, mijn leven:
Hoe kranck is, laes! 't vermoghen by de
Menschen;
In Godt bestaet het geven

Van 't luck, en heyl, dat wy den and 'ren
wenschen.
> GERBRAND ADRIAENSZOON BREDERO:
> *Adieu-Liedt (Dutch)*

Farewell my love, my life! How weak, alas, is the
power of man. God alone can grant the fortune
and good luck we wish each other.

Laat alles zijn
Voorbij, gedaan, verleden,
Dat afschied tusschen ons
En diepe kloven spant.
> GUIDO GEZELLE:
> *Ego Flos (Dutch)*

Let all things that still divide us now, like
chasms standing between us, be over past and
gone, departed.

Keine Ferne macht dich schwierig,
Kommst geflogen und gebannt.
> J. W. VON GOETHE:
> *Selige Sehnsucht (German)*

No distance is an obstacle to you; you come
flying and enchanted.

Hono-bono to
Akashi no ura no
Asa-giri ni
Shima kakure-yuku
Fune wo shi zo omou
> *Kokin Shū (Japanese)*

The night has hardly drifted away from Akashi
Bay, and already in the morning haze the boat
that carries my longings disappears behind that
island.

Ai-mite no nochi no kokoro kurabureba, mukshi
wa mo no wo omowazari keru
> CHIU-NAGON ATSUTADA:
> *Waga (Japanese)*

After we had parted I searched my heart, finding I was overwhelmed with sadness.

Tak inogda razluki chas
Zhivee sladkogo svidan'ya.
> ALEKSANDR SERGEEVICH PUSHKIN;
> *The Last Flowers (Russian)*

The hour of parting can sometimes be more
vivid than a sweet tryst.

PASSION
see also Absence, Emotions, Feelings, Jealousy, Love, Poets and poetry, Wisdom.

La durée de nos passions ne dépend pas plus de
nous que la durée de notre vie.
> FRANÇOIS, DUC DE LA ROCHEFOUCAULD:
> *Réflexions (French)*

The duration of our passions does not depend on
us any more than the length of our lives.

Men skal De ăndigt dø, da lev forinden!
Vær min i Herrens vårlige Natur.
> HENRIK IBSEN:
> *Love's Comedy (Norwegian)*

If die you must, then live beforehand, be mine in
the springtime of God's earth.

Yathā agāraṁ ducchannaṁ vuṭṭhi
samativijjhati
Evam abhāvitaṁ cittaṁ rāge samativijjhati
> DHAMMAPADA: *Yamakavaggo (Pali)*

Passion makes its way into an untrained mind
just as rain will break through a poorly-thatched
house.

Na kahāpaṇavassena titti kāmesu vijjati
Appassādā dukhā kāmā iti viññāya paṇḍito
> DHAMMAPADA: *Buddhavaggo (Pali)*

Even a shower of gold cannot secure satisfaction
of our passions. He who realises that passions
give brief enjoyment and can produce much
distress, is wise.

El hombre es fuego, la mujer, estopa; llega el
diable y sopla!
> SPANISH PROVERB

Man is fire, woman tow; along comes the Devil
and blows!

PATIENCE
see also Prudence.

La patience est l'art d'espérer.
> LUC DE CLAPIERS, MARQUIS DE VAUVENARGUES:
> *Réflexions et Maximes (French)*

Patience is the art of hoping.

Facilis mea
'arumper aure verba patienti excipe.

SENECA:
Hercules Furens (Latin)

.isten patiently to me for a little while.

'aciencia y barajar!

SPANISH PROVERB

'atience! and shuffle the cards!

;iertas cosas acabarían con la paciencia del
anto Job que resucitase.

PARDO BAZÁN;
Los Pazos de Ulloa (Spanish)

;ertain things would put an end even to the
aintly Job's patience, if he were alive.

'ara el que viene del cielo es la paciencia; para el
ue del suelo, la prudencia.

BALTASAR GRACIÁN:
Oráculo Manual y Arte de Prudencia (Spanish)

'atience is the virtue of the angels; for us, here
n earth, prudence will do.

PATRIOTISM
see also Duty, Fatherland, Nationhood,
the People.

\lbe vous a nommé, je ne vous connais plus.

PIERRE CORNEILLE:
Horace (French)

Jow that Alba has selected you, I no longer
.now you (Horace's famous words spoken to his
riend Curiace when he discovers that the war
etween Alba and Rome is to be settled by
•ersonal combat between Horace and his
)rothers and Curiace and his brothers).

\vant que d'être à vous, je suis à mon pays.

PIERRE CORNEILLE:
Horace (French)

√ly duty to my country exceeds my duty to you
Horace's words to his wife Camille just before
ie leaves for battle).

Mourir pour le pays n'est pas un triste sort:
C'est s'immortaliser par une belle mort.

PIERRE CORNEILLE:
Le Cid (French)

Dying for one's country is not a bad fate – you
become immortal through a fine death.

Je sers mon empereur, et je sais mon devoir.

PIERRE CORNEILLE:
Héraclius (French)

I serve my Emperor, and I know my duty.

Je suis une brave poule de guerre –
Je mange peu et produis beaucoup.

Legend beneath a French poster
of World War I showing a chicken
on an inordinate number of eggs.

I am a fine wartime chicken – I eat little and
produce much!

Es gibt einen Weg zur Freiheit. Seine Meilens-
teine heissen: Gehorsam, Fleiss, Ehrlichkeit,
Ordnung, Sauberkeit, Nüchternheit, Wahrhaf-
tigkeit, Opfersinn und Liebe zum Vaterlande!

Notice in Sachsenhausen concentration
camp in World War II *(German)*

There is one way to freedom: its milestones are
obedience, diligence, uprightness, order, clean-
liness, temperance, truthfulness, self-sacrifice,
and love of the Fatherland.

La migliore fortezza che sia è non essere odiato
dal populo.

NICCOLÒ MACHIAVELLI:
The Prince (Italian)

The best fortress is to be found in the love of the
people.

L'armi, qua l'armi: io solo
Combatterò, procomberò sol io.

GIACOMO LEOPARDI:
All'Italia (Italian)

Weapons, give me weapons, and I alone will
fight, and fall alone!

Eran trecento: eran giovani e forti
E sono morti.

MERCANTINI:
La Spigolatrice di Sapri (Italian)

They were three hundred; they were young and
strong; and now they are dead (referring to the
Sicilian patriot Pisacane and his band).

Prima divelte, in mar precipitando,
Spente nell'imo strideran le stelle,
Che la memoria e il vostro
Amor trascorra o scemi.

GIACOMO LEOPARDI:
All'Italia (Italian)

Stars will fall screaming into the deep sea before
the memory of your devotion is lost.

Qui per virtutem, periit, at non interit.

PLAUTUS:
Captivi (Latin)

He who dies in a worthy cause does not perish
completely.

Dulce et decorum est pro patria mori.

HORACE:
(Odes) (Latin)

It is sweet and glorious to die for one's country.

Urbi pater est, urbique maritus.

LUCAN:
Pharsalia (Latin)

Not only is he the father of the city – he is its
husband.

Si patriae volumus, si nobis vivere cari.

HORACE:
Epistles (Latin)

If we would live dear to our country, and dear to
ourselves!

Urbis terrarum divitias accipere nolo pro
patriae caritate.

CORNELIUS NEPOS:
Epaminondas (Latin)

I would not take all the riches of the world in
exchange for my love of my country.

Sztandar jest ważny. Nie dłoń
Co drzewce trzyma.

MARJAM HEMAR
Inwokacja (Polish)

What matters is the banner, not the hand that
holds the shaft!

Poetom mozhesh' tỹ ne bỹt',
No grazhdaninom bỹt' obyazan.

NIKOLAI ALEKSEEVICH NEKRASOV
Patriotism (Russian)

It is possible not to be a poet, but it is essential to
be a citizen.

Oho, fatše lena,
La bo-ntat'a rona,
Le be le khotso.

LESOTHO NATIONAL ANTHEM (Sotho

Oh, beloved country! dear to all our fathers
Peace shall dwell in thee!

PATRONAGE
see also Loyalty.

Elle est notre guide fidèle,
Notre félicité vient d'elle.

JEAN RACINE
motto for the Maison Royale de
St. Louis à St. Cyr (probably referring to
Madame de Maintenon) *(French*

She is our faithful guide; we owe our happiness
to her.

PEACE
see also Commonweal, Government,
Liberty, Night, Patriotism, Printing, War.

Caarle cuuluisin cuningas,
Tule cullainen cotihin,
Tuoppas raha tullessansi!

BARTHOLDUS VHAEL
Valitusruno (Finnish)

Charles! most famed among the monarchs of the
world, come back to your old beloved land, and
restore peace by your beloved presence!

La paix est fort bonne de soi,
J'en conviens; mais de quoi sert-elle
Avec des ennemis sans foi?

JEAN DE LA FONTAINE
Les Loups et les Brebis (French)

Peace, I agree, is alright in itself; but what use is
it with enemies who are faithless?

'as soll all der Schmerz und Lust?
isser Friede,
omm, ach komm in meine Brust!

J. W. VON GOETHE:
Wanderers Nachtlied (German)

'hat matters all the joy and pain? Sweet peace,
me into my breast!

erpe khairōn

GREEK EXPRESSION

o in peace!

' populi amavano la quiete, e per questo
navono e' principi modesti.

NICCOLÒ MACHIAVELLI:
The Prince (Italian)

eople like tranquillity, and therefore they like
eaceful princes.

bi solitudinem faciunt, pacem appellant.

TACITUS:
Agricola (quoted in J. J. Rousseau:
Du Contrat Social) *(Latin)*

Vhen men create a desert they call it peace.

unc patimur longae pacis mala.

JUVENAL:
Satires (Latin)

Ve are now suffering the evils of a prolonged
eace.

ilitis in galea nidum fecere columbae.

PETRONIUS:
Poems (Latin)

oves have nested in the soldier's helmet.

eati pacifici.

Motto of James I of England *(Latin)*

lessed are the peacemakers.

aritur pax bello.

LATIN PROVERB

eace is won by war.

At nobis, pax alma, veni spicamque teneto
Profluat et pomis candidus ante sinus.

TIBULLUS:
Elegies (Latin)

Come to us, kindly peace! bring ears of grain,
and let apples pour forth from your bright
bosom!

Pacis Amor deus est; pacem veneramur
amantes.

PROPERTIUS:
Elegies (Latin)

Peace has love as its god; peace is what we lovers
worship.

Sarcula nunc durusque bidens et vomer
aduncus,
Ruris opes, niteant, inquinet arma situs,
Conatusque aliquis vagina ducere ferrum
Adstrictum longa sentiat esse mora.

OVID:
Fasti (Latin)

Now the hoes, the hard mattocks and beaked
plough shares the wealth of the countryside! Let
them shine, while weapons grow dirty with
mould! Let anyone who tries to draw his blade
from its sheath find it held hard by long idleness!

THE PEOPLE
see also Crowds, Leadership, Nationhood, Patriotism, Public opinion, Silence, Society.

Ich bin zu dem Leuten freundlich. Ich setze
Einen steifen Hut auf nach ihrem Brauch.
Ich sage: es sind ganz besonders riechende Tiere
Und ich sage: es macht nichts, ich bin es auch.

BERTOLT BRECHT:
Vom Armen B.B. (German)

I am friendly to people. I put on a top hat as is
their custom. I say: there are some very strange-
smelling animals round here. And then I say: it
doesn't matter – I'm one of them.

Chi fonda in sul populo fonda in sul fango.

ITALIAN PROVERB
(quoted in Niccolò Machiavelli: *The Prince*)

He who builds on the people, builds on mud.

Nel mondo non è se non vulgo.

NICCOLÒ MACHIAVELLI:
The Prince (Italian)

The world consists only of the vulgar.

Tene magis salvum populus velit an populum
tu,
Servet in ambiguo qui consulit et tibi et urbi
Iuppiter.

HORACE:
Epistles (Latin)

May Jupiter, who takes thought for you and for
Rome, keep it a secret whether the people are
more concerned for your welfare, or you for the
people's!

Ad populi salutem.

LATIN EXPRESSION

For the people's benefit.

Pro bono publico.

LATIN EXPRESSION

For the good of the people.

Vox populi, vox Dei.

LATIN PROVERB

The voice of the people is the voice of God.

PERFECTION
see also Faults, Happiness, Truth.

Vollkommenheit des Menschen liegt in der
Übung seiner Kräfte durch Betrachtung des
Weltplans.

J. C. F. VON SCHILLER:
Works (German)

Man's perfection consists in his exercising his
powers by contemplating the plan of the
universe.

Quod in omni mundo optimum sit, id in perfecto
aliquo atque absoluto esse debere.

CICERO:
De Natura Deorum (Latin)

A perfect and complete being is bound to possess
that which is best in all the world.

!Oh perfeccion: dependo
Del total más allá,
Dependo de la cosas!

JORGE GUILLÉN:
Más Allá (Spanish)

Oh, Perfection! All that surpasses me, lying
beyond me, sustains me! I depend on the things
of this world!

PERFUME
see also Sensation.

Si vous adoptez cette fragrance, vos problèmes
d'amour n'existent pas!

JEAN HONORÉ FRAGONARD,
to a nobleman who was having difficulties
with his mistress *(French)*

If you use this perfume your love problems will
vanish!

Les parfums sont les plus grands traîtres du
monde. Ils annoncent, ébauchent et dénoncent
les desseins les plus délicieux.

PAUL VALÉRY:
Lust (French)

Perfumes are the greatest traitors in the world.
They herald, they outline, and they declare the
most delicious of intentions.

PERMISSIVENESS
see also Honesty.

Fay ce que vouldras.

FRENCH PROVERB

Do what you like.

Proclivior usus in peiora datur
Suadetque licentia luxum
Inlecebrisque effrena favet.

CLAUDIAN:
*Panegyricus de Quarto Consulatu
Honorii Augusti (Latin)*

The easiest way often leads to worse; liberty
begets licence, and, when uncontrolled, fosters
vice.

PERSONALITY
see also Individualism, Temperament.

C'est quand on prend les hommes au sérieux
que les bêtises commencent.
> JEAN GIONO:
> *Arcadie . . . Arcadie . . . (French)*

The stupidities begin when one takes men
seriously.

Je vous dis que chacun, vis-à-vis de soi, se réduit
à peu près à ce qu'il se dit, et ce qu'il se dit à ce
qu'il sait se dire.
> PAUL VALÉRY:
> *Discours à Saint-Denis* (variété IV) *(French)*

I tell you that each of us, privately, is pretty well
limited to what he says to himself, and what he
says to himself is limited to what he is capable of
saying.

Nous vivons contrefaits, plutôt que de ne pas
ressembler au portrait que nous avons tracé de
nous d'abord.
> ANDRÉ GIDE:
> *Les Caves du Vatican (French)*

We live counterfeit lives in order to resemble the
idea we first had of ourselves.

Mache mich bitter.
Zähle mich zu den Mandeln.
> PAUL CELAN:
> *Zähle die Mandeln (German)*

Make me bitter. Count me among the almonds.

Höchstes Glück der Erdenkinder
Sei nur die Persönlichkeit.
> J. W. VON GOETHE:
> *Der West-östliche Divan (German)*

The highest happiness of earth's children is
nothing but personality.

Hätte Gott mich anders gewollt, so hätt' er mich
anders gemacht.
> J. W. VON GOETHE, in his old age
> *(German)*

If God had wanted me otherwise, he would have
created me otherwise.

Gott schafft die Tiere, der Mensch schafft sich
selber.
> GEORG CHRISTOPH LICHTENBERG:
> *Aphorismen (German)*

God creates the animals, man creates himself.

Und wenn wir dachten, wir hätten's gefunden
Und, was er sei, nun ganz empfunden,
Wie wurd' er so schnell uns wieder neu!
> C. M. WIELAND:
> *An Psyche (German)*

When we believed we had captured him and
really found out what he was, how swiftly he
changed into something new! (referring to
Goethe's chameleon-like nature).

Avrei voluto sentirmi scabro ed essenziale
Siccome i ciottoli che tu volvi,
Mangiati dalla saledine.
> EUGENIO MONTALE:
> *Mediterraneo (Italian)*

I should like to have felt myself rough and
fundamental, like the pebbles you are turning
over, eaten by the salt tides.

Magis quis veneris quam quo interest.
> SENECA:
> *Epistles (Latin)*

Personality is more important than surround-
ings.

Nihil enim silens, ac si cuperet, faciebat.
> MARTIANUS CAPELLA:
> *Liber de Nuptiis Mercurii et Philologiae (Latin)*

She did nothing silently, unless it suited her
(referring to Rhetoric's giving Philologia a noisy
kiss).

PERSUASION

Epei tous kharientas esti kai parēgorēsai
> PLUTARCH:
> *Moralia (Greek)*

Reasonable men are open to persuasion.

PHILOLOGY
see also Language, Philosophy.

Utinam essem bonus grammaticus. No aliunde
discordiae in religione pendent quam ab
ignoratione grammaticae.

JOSEPH JUSTUS SCALIGER:
Scaligerana (Latin)

I wish I were a good philologist. All controver-
sies in religion arise from ignorance of the
critical approach of philology.

Quae philosophia fuit, facta philologia est.

SENECA:
Epistles (Latin)

What was philosophy has been made into
philology.

PHILOSOPHERS
see also Philosophy, Revolution, Wisdom.

Les philosophies valent ce que valent les
philosophes. Plus l'homme est grand, plus la
philosophie est vrai.

ALBERT CAMUS:
Carnets, 1935–1937 (French)

Philosophies are worth just as much as their
creators. The greater the philosopher, the more
true his philosophy.

C'est le philosophe qui n'a rien et qui ne
demande rien.

DENIS DIDEROT:
Le Neveu de Rameau (French)

It's the philosopher who has nothing and asks
for nothing.

C'est un philosophe dans son espèce. Il ne pense
qu'à lui; le reste de l'univers lui est comme d'un
clou à soufflet.

DENIS DIDEROT:
Le Neveu de Rameau (French)

He's a philosopher in his way: he thinks only of
himself, the rest of the universe counting for
nothing with him.

Qu'est ce qu'un Philosophe? C'est un homme
qui oppose la Nature à la Loi, la raison à l'usage,
sa conscience à l'opinion, et son jugement à
l'erreur.

S. R. N. CHAMFORT
Maximes et Pensées (French

What is a philosopher? He is a man who
contrasts nature with law, reason with usage
his conscience with public opinion, and his
judgment with error.

Le premier pas dans la carrière philosophique
est de se cuirasser contre le ridicule.

ERNEST RENAN
Avenir de la Science (French

The first step in one's career as a philosopher is
to arm oneself against ridicule.

Tout porte à croire qu'il existe un certain point
de l'esprit d'où la vie et la mort, le réel et
l'imaginaire, le passé et le futur, le communicable et l'incommunicable, le haut et le bas
cessent d'être perçus contradictoirement. Or,
c'est en vain qu'on chercherait à l'activité sur-
réaliste un autre mobile que l'espoir de détermi-
nation de ce point.

ANDRÉ BRETON:
Second Manifeste du Surréalisme (French)

Everything leads us to believe that there is a
certain point in the intellect where life and
death, the real and the imaginary, the past and
the future, the communicable and the incommunicable, the high and the low, cease to be
deemed contradictory. Hence it would be useless to search for another motive for surrealism
than the hope of determining what this point
may be.

Die meisten Philosophen haben eine zu geringe
Vorstellung von der Variabilität menschlicher
Sitten und Möglichkeiten.

ELIAS CANETTI:
Aufzeichnungen, 1943 (German)

Most philosophers have too narrow a concept of
the variety of man's habits and possibilities.

Ton de dē eukherōs ethelonta pantos
mathēmatos geuesthai kai asmenōs epi to man-

thanein ionta kai aplēstōs ekhonta, touton d' en dikēi phēsomen philosophon

PLATO:
The Republic (Greek)

He who enjoys every kind of learning and eagerly studies and hungers for still more knowledge can justly be termed a true philosopher.

Ean mē, ēn d' egō, ē hoi philosophoi basileusōsin en tais polesin ē hoi basileis te nun legomenoi kai dunastai philosophēsōsi gnēsiōs te kai hikanōs kai touto eis tauton xumpesēi, dunamis te politikē kai philosophia, tōn de nun poreuomenōn khōris eph' hekateron hai pollai phuseis ex an ankēs apokleisthōsin, ouk esti kakōn paula, ō phile Glaukōn, tais polesi, dokō d' oude tōi anthrōpinōi genei

PLATO:
The Republic (Greek)

There is no end to trouble for the state or for mankind until the philosophers rule, or until kings and rulers take up the study of philosophy properly and seriously, and until politics and philosophy work together and those who follow only the one or the other are excluded from government.

Neque enim continuo verae sapientiae sunt amatores quicumque appellantur philosophi.

ST. AUGUSTINE:
De Civitate Dei (Latin)

Those who are called philosophers are not necessarily lovers of true wisdom.

Primum vivere, deinde philosophari.

LATIN PROVERB

First to learn how to live, and then to philosophise.

Sunt ex terra homines, non ut habitatores sed spectatores rerum superarum et caelestium.

CICERO:
De Natura Deorum (Latin)

There are men of the earth who live, not as dwellers thereon, but as observers of things divine and heavenly.

Abnormis sapiens.

HORACE:
Satires (Latin)

The independent philosopher.

De filosofía habla, en queriendo, y no habla mal, toda persona de imaginación y viveza.

DON JUAN VALERA:
El Comendador Mendoza (Spanish)

Any keen and imaginative person can talk, if he wishes, about philosophy, and he will not talk badly.

PHILOSOPHY
see also Philology, Philosophers, Politics, Thought and thinking, Truth.

La seule philosophie est peut-être après tout de tenir bon longtemps.

STÉPHANE MALLARMÉ:
letter to John H. Ingram, 8 November 1885
(French)

The only philosophy after all is perhaps to keep well for as long as possible.

La Philosophie, ainsi que la Médecine, a beaucoup de drogues, très peu de bons remèdes, et presque point de spécifiques.

S. R. N. CHAMFORT:
Maximes et Pensées (French)

Like medicine, philosophy has many drugs, very few good remedies, and practically no specifics.

Philosopher, c'est douter.

MONTAIGNE:
Essays (French)

To philosophise is to doubt.

La philosophie sera toujours le fait d'une imperceptible minorité.

ERNEST RENAN:
Etudes d'Histoire Religieuse (French)

Philosophy will always be the activity of a tiny minority of people.

Les âmes boiteuses, les bastardes et vulgaires, sont indignes de la philosophie.

MONTAIGNE:
Essays (French)

Twisted souls, bastards and common people are unworthy of philosophy.

Se moquer de la philosophie, c'est vrayement philosopher.

BLAISE PASCAL:
Pensées, Adversaria (French)

True philosophy scoffs at philosophy.

La philosophie triomphe aisément des maux passés et des maux à venir, mais les maux présents triomphent d'elle.

FRANÇOIS, DUC DE LA ROCHEFOUCAULD:
Réflexions (French)

Philosophy triumphs easily over past and future evils, but is herself defeated by the evils of today.

Die Philosophie ist keine Lehre, sondern eine Tätigkeit.

LUDWIG WITTGENSTEIN:
Tractatus Logico-philosophicus (German)

Philosophy is not a body of doctrine but an activity.

Die Philosophie hat ihrem Zeitalter der Universalität, dem Zeitalter der grossen Kompendien selbst ein Ende gesetzt, sie musste ihre brennendsten Fragen aus ihrem logischen Raum entfernen oder, wie Wittgenstein sagt, ins Mystische verweisen.

HERMANN BROCH:
James Joyce und die Gegenwart (German)

Philosophy has itself set an end to the age of universality and to the age of great compendia. It must remove its most burning questions from their logical context or, as Wittgenstein says, banish them into mysticism.

Ou gar allē arkhē philosophias ē hautē

PLATO:
Theaetetus (Greek)

There is no other start to philosophy but wonder.

Doloris medicinam a philosophia peto.

CICERO:
Academica (Latin)

I seek a cure for my grief from philosophy.

Numquam igitur laudari satis digne philosophia poterit, cui qui pareat omne tempus aetatis sine molestia possit degere.

CICERO:
De Senectute (Latin)

Philosophy can never be praised as much as it deserves, since it enables the man who obeys its precepts to pass every season of life free from worry.

Sed a philosophia cum mater avertit monens imperaturo contrariam esse.

SUETONIUS:
Nero (Latin)

Nero's mother turned him from the study of philosophy, warning him that it was a drawback to one who was destined to rule.

PHOTOGRAPHY
see also Painters and painting.

Sin-sya zitsu-va butsu-zo-sya-no gwa-ni site, kwo-ki-va sono fude nari

MATSUKI KO-AN: *Waga (Japanese)*

Photography is the Creator's painting – his paintbrush is the light.

PIETY

Tres bien l'empleie, pas nel pert.

LE MYSTERE D'ADAM *(French)*

He who serves God cannot lose by his service.

En cette foi je veux vivre et mourir.

FRANÇOIS VILLON:
Ballade (French)

In this faith may I live and die.

Ou gar eusebeia sunthnēiskei brotois

SOPHOCLES:
Philoctetes (Greek)

Though men die, piety lives on.

In specie autem fictae simulationis . . . pietas inesse non protest.

CICERO:
De Natura Deorum (Latin)

Piety cannot exist in mere outward show and pretence.

PLANNING
see also Action.

Die schönsten Plän sind schon zuschanden
geworden durch die Kleinlichkeit von denen, wo
sie ausführen sollten, denn die Kaiser selber
können ja nix machen, sie sind angewiesen auf
die Unterstützung von ihre Soldaten und dem
Volk, wo sie grad sind.

BERTOLT BRECHT:
Mutter Courage und ihre Kinder (German)

The finest plans are often spoilt through the
pettiness of those who are supposed to carry
them out, since even emperors can do nothing
without the support of their soldiers and
hangers-on.

Malum est consilium quod mutari non potest.
LATIN PROVERB

It's an ill plan that cannot be changed.

PLAY

Der Mensch spielt nur, wo er in voller Be-
deutung des Worts Mensch ist, und er ist nur da
ganz Mensch, wo er spielt.

J. C. F. VON SCHILLER:
*Über die Ästhetische Erziehung des Menschen
(German)*

Man plays only where he is, in the full sense of
the word, a man, and he is a whole man only
where he plays.

PLAYWRITING

Vous n'avez rien fait, si vous n'y faites reconnaître les gens de vôtre siècle.

MOLIÈRE:
La Critique de l'Ecole des Femmes (French)

In comedy you achieve nothing if you do not
provide recognisable portraits of the people of
your time.

Etudiez la cour et connoissez la ville.

NICOLAS BOILEAU:
Art Poétique (French)

Study the court and know the town (Boileau's
advice to a dramatist).

Castigat ridendo mores.
Inscription on a bust of Molière at the house
(rue de la Tonnelerie, Paris) where he lived.
(Latin)

In comedy he castigated the customs of his day.

Quando he de escrivir una comedia,
Encierro los preceptos con seis llaves.

LOPE DE VEGA:
*Arte Nuevo de Hazer Comedias en este Tiempo
(Spanish)*

When I have to write a comedy, I lock up all the
rules with six keys.

PLEASURE
see also Cost, Enjoyment, Excess,
Grief, Hunters and hunting, Life, Love,
Old age, Patience, Self-indulgence.

jak vesele dovedem žít a pít,
tak vesele na poli padnem.

PETR BEZRUČ:
'Kyjov' in *Slezské Písně (Czech)*

Happy as we live and drink our fill, so happily
we shall go to meet our end.

Le sentiment de la fausseté des plaisirs présents,
et l'ignorance de la vanité des plaisirs absents
causent l'inconstance.

BLAISE PASCAL:
Pensées (French)

Awareness of the unreality of present pleasures,
and ignorance of the vanity of absent pleasures,
unsettle us.

Fi de plaisir
Que la crainte peut corrompre!

JEAN DE LA FONTAINE:
Le Rat de Ville, et le Rat des Champs (French)

To hell with pleasure that's haunted by fear!

En général l'enfant comme l'homme, et
l'homme comme l'enfant, aime mieux s'amuser
que s'instruire.

DENIS DIDEROT:
Le Neveu de Rameau (French)

In general, children, like men, and men, like
children, prefer entertainment to education.

Le vin et la paresse
Se partagent mon coeur.
> P. A. C. DE BEAUMARCHAIS:
> *Le Barbier de Séville (French)*

My heart is divided between drinking and idleness.

Il n'est pas honteux à l'homme de succumber sous la douleur, et il luy est honteux de succumber sous le plaisir.
> BLAISE PASCAL:
> *Pensées (French)*

There is no disgrace in yielding to pain, but it is shameful to yield to pleasure.

L'homme, sans plaisir,
Vivrait comme un sot,
Et mourrait bientôt.
> P. A. C. DE BEAUMARCHAIS:
> *Le Barbier de Séville (French)*

Without pleasure man would live like a fool and soon die.

Les plus doux plaisirs doivent avoir leur fin.
> LABICHE & MARC-MICHEL:
> *Un Chapeau de Paille d'Italie (French)*

There must be an end even to the sweetest pleasures.

Les hommes peuvent avoir plusieurs sortes de plaisirs. Le véritable est celui pour lequel ils quittent l'autre.
> MARCEL PROUST:
> *Sodome et Gomorrhe (French)*

People can have many different kinds of pleasure. The real one is that for which they will forsake the others.

Le Dieu du Monde,
C'est le Plaisir.
> GÉRARD DE NERVAL:
> *Chanson Gothique (French)*

It is pleasure that is the god of this world.

Plaisir vaporeux fuira vers l'horizon
Ainsi qu'une sylphide au fond de la coulisse.
> CHARLES BAUDELAIRE:
> *L'Horloge (French)*

Misty pleasure will flee toward the horizon, just like a sylph gliding off-stage.

Es läuft auf eins hinaus, an was man seine Freude hat, an Leibern, Christusbildern, Blumen oder Kinderspielsachen.
> GEORG BÜCHNER:
> *Dantons Tod (German)*

It's all one, whether we find our pleasure in our bodies, or in crucifixes, in flowers or children's toys.

Jenes süsse Gedränge der leichtesten irdischen Tage.
> J. W. VON GOETHE:
> *Euphrosyne (German)*

Those sweet crowded hours of lightfooted earthly days.

Horos tou megethous tōn hēdonōn hē pantos tou algountos hupexairesis
> EPICURUS:
> *Sententiae (Greek)*

The summit of pleasure is the elimination of all that gives pain.

Nam nunc mores nihil faciunt quod licet, nisi quod lubet.
> PLAUTUS:
> *Trinummus (Latin)*

It's usual nowadays to ignore what should be done in favour of what pleases us.

Tardum est differre quod placet.
> PETRONIUS:
> *Satyricon (Latin)*

Waiting for one's pleasures is weary work.

Nocet empta dolore voluptas.
> HORACE:
> *Epistles (Latin)*

Pleasure bought with pain is harmful.

Voluptas commendat rarior usus.
> JUVENAL:
> *Satires (Latin)*

Rarity gives zest to pleasure.

Nec lusisse pudet, sed non incidere ludum.
HORACE:
Epistles (Latin)

The shame lies not in having a fling, but in not cutting it short.

Brevis hic est fructus homullis;
Iam fuerit neque post umquam revocare licebit.
LUCRETIUS:
De Rerum Natura (Latin)

Short is poor man's pleasure here; soon it's gone, with no possibility of recall.

Que da mão a boca
O sabor se troca;
Trocam-se as vontades.
FRANCISCO DE SÁ DE MIRANDA:
Dialogo de Duas Moças (Portuguese)

Pleasures can swiftly lose their artifice, and change from joy to pain.

No todo el monte es orégano.
SPANISH PROVERB

The mountain side is not all marjoram.

Grand plazer e chico duelo es de todo ome querido.
SPANISH PROVERB

Much pleasure and little grief is every man's desire.

PLOTS
see also Traps.

La ruse la mieux ourdie
Peut nuire à son inventeur,
Et souvent la perfidie
Retourne sur son auteur.
JEAN DE LA FONTAINE:
La Grenouille et le Rat (French)

The best-laid plot can injure its maker, and often a man's perfidy will rebound on himself.

Hotan takhus tis houpibouleuōn lathrai
Khorēi, takhun dei kame bouleuein palin
SOPHOCLES:
Oedipus Tyrannus (Greek)

If the plotter lurks with swift intent, let the counterplot be ready just as speedily.

POETS AND POETRY
see also Elocution, Eloquence, Painters and painting, Patriotism, Women.

Un million ne vaut certainement pas un beau poème.
STÉPHANE MALLARMÉ:
letter to Leo d'Orfer, 30 June 1888 (French)

A fine poem is certainly worth more than a million francs.

Le mensonge et les vers de tout temps sont amis.
JEAN DE LA FONTAINE:
Contre Ceux qui ont le Goût Difficile (French)

Lies and poetry have always been friends.

Les dieux eux-mêmes meurent,
Mais les vers souverains
Demeurent
Plus forts que les airains.
THÉOPHILE GAUTIER:
L'Art (French)

The gods themselves die, but the finest poems survive, stronger than bronze.

Le poète se fait voyant par un long, immense et raisonné dérèglement de tous les sens.
ARTHUR RIMBAUD:
letter to Georges Izambard (French)

The poet makes himself perceptive by a long, vast and carefully thought out derangement of all the senses.

La poésie est semblable à l'amandier: ses fleurs sont parfumées et ses fruits sont amers.
ALOYSIUS BERTRAND:
Gaspard de la Nuit: Foreword (French)

Poetry is like an almond-tree: its blossom is perfumed but its fruit is bitter.

Telle, aimable en son air, mais humble dans son style,
Doit éclater sans pompe, une élégante idylle.
NICOLAS BOILEAU:
L'Art Poétique (French)

Thus, lovely in its appearance but humble in its style, should an elegant idyll shine without pomp.

Le poète est le personnage le plus vulnérable de la création. En effet, il marche sur les mains.
PAUL VALÉRY:
Mauvaises Pensées (French)

Poets are the most vulnerable of people in creation. In fact, they walk on their hands.

Dans sa création, le poète tressaille.
VICTOR HUGO:
Les Contemplations (French)

The poet trembles as he composes.

Les philosophes savent que les poètes ne pensent pas.
ANATOLE FRANCE:
Les Torts de l'Histoire (French)

Philosophers know that poets don't think.

Les plus désespérés sont les chants les plus beaux,
Et j'en sais d'immortels qui sont de purs sanglots.
ALFRED DE MUSSET:
La Nuit de Mai (French)

The most beautiful poems are those filled with despair, and I know of immortal lines that are nothing but sobs.

Poésie, heure des grands, route d'exil et d'alliance, levain des peuples forts et lever d'astres chez les humbles.
SAINT-JOHN PERSE:
Pour Dante (French)

Poetry, hour of the great, way of exile and union, leaven of strong people and creator of stars among the humble!

Le poète est semblable au Prince des Nuées
Qui hante le ciel et se rit de l'archer;
Exilé sur le sol au milieu des huées,
Ses ailes de géant l'empêchent de marcher.
CHARLES BAUDELAIRE:
L'Albatros (French)

The poet resembles the Prince of the Clouds who haunts the skies and mocks the bowman; exiled on earth, beset by booing, his giant wings prevent his walking.

Seulement, sachons n'existerait pas le vers: lui, philosophiquement remunère le défaut des langues, complètement supérieur.
STÉPHANE MALLARMÉ:
Crise des Vers: Variations sur un Sujet (French)

We know that the poem does not exist that philosophically makes good the defects of languages and is completely superior to them.

Rime, qui donnes leurs sons
Aux chansons,
Rime, l'unique harmonie
Du vers, qui, sans tes accents
Frémissants,
Serait muet au génie.
CHARLES-AUGUSTIN SAINTE-BEUVE:
A la Rime (French)

Rhyme, giving sounds to songs!
Rhyme, the unique harmony of verse which, without your quivering accents, would render genius mute.

La poésie seule peut récupérer l'homme.
GIUSEPPE UNGARETTI
(French)

Poetry alone can restore a man.

Il n'y a point de bel air dont on ne puisse faire un beau récitatif, et point de beau récitatif dont un habile homme ne puisse faire un bel air.
DENIS DIDEROT:
Le Neveu de Rameau (French)

There is no melody for which one cannot write a good recitative; and no recitative for which a skilful man cannot compose a melody.

La première étude de l'homme qui veut être poète est sa propre connaissance entière.
ARTHUR RIMBAUD:
Lettre du Voyant (French)

The first study of aspiring poets should be the whole of their own knowledge.

Oh! la nuance seule fiance
Le rêve au rêve et la flûte au cor!
PAUL VERLAINE:
Art Poétique (French)

O, only a touch blends the dream to the dream, and the flute to the horn.

n cest sonet coind' e leri
auc motz e capuig e doli,
ue serant verai e cert
an n'aurai passat la lima.

ARNAUT DANIEL:
Sonnets (French)

n this gracious, sweet little melody, I fashion
ords, carpenter and plane them, so that they
ill be true and certain when I have passed the
le over them.

oesie und Wissenschaft erschienen als die
rössten Widersacher.

J. W. VON GOETHE:
Zur Morphologie (German)

oetry and science appear as sworn enemies.

Venn ich nicht sinnen oder dichten soll,
o ist das Leben mir keinen Leben mehr.

J. W. VON GOETHE:
Tasso (German)

Not to meditate or to be a poet would mean not
o live at all.

ine notwendige Operation des Dichters ist
dealisierung seines Gegenstandes, ohne welche
r aufhört seinen Namen zu verdienen.

J. C. F. VON SCHILLER
in a review of G. A. Bürger: *Gedichte) (German)*

The idealisation of his subject is a necessary
actic for the poet; without this he can scarcely
laim to be a poet.

leilige Gefässe sind die Dichter.

FRIEDRICH HÖLDERLIN:
Buonaparte (first line) (German)

oets are sacred vessels.

edes vollkommene Gedicht ist Ahnung und
Gegenwart, Sehnsucht und Erfüllung zugleich.

HUGO VON HOFMANNSTHAL:
Gespräch über Gedichte (German)

very complete poem is, at the same time, pre-
nonition and presence, longing and fulfilment.

Mit Gott und Weltall spiel ich kühne Spiele!
Der Dichter wird Jongleur – er wirft im Nu
Der allerzartesten Gegenstände viele

Hoch durch die Luft – es glückt ihm Coup auf
Coup,
Denn alle kehrn zurück zu ihm, dem Ziele . . .
Gott ist die Welt – und Gott und ich sind Du!

OTTO ERICH HARTLEBEN:
Der Dichter (German)

I am playing a daring game with God and the
universe! The poet becomes a juggler, throwing
many very delicate objects rapidly high in the
air. He is delighted when one by one they all
come back to him, to their goal. God is the
world, and God and I are you!

Es liegen in den verschiedenen poetischen
Formen geheimnisvolle grosse Wirkungen.

J. W. VON GOETHE:
Conversations with Eckermann (German)

Within the different poetic forms there lie
hidden great forces.

In Erstaunen setzen, ist das nicht die Natur des
Poeten?

ERNST PENZOLDT:
Der Delphin (German)

Is it not the very nature of poets to astound?

Schlechten gestümperten Versen genügt ein
geringer Gehalt schon, während die edlere Form
tiefe Gedanken bedarf.

AUGUST, GRAF VON PLATEN
(German)

Certainly, poor bungled verse will make do with
trivial contents while the nobler forms need
deeper ideas.

Tois men gar paidarioisin
Esti didaskalos hostis phrazei, toisin d' hēbōsi
poiētai
Panu dē dei khrēsta legein hēmas

ARISTOPHANES:
The Frogs (Greek)

What the schoolmaster is to his pupils, the poets
are to youth. Thus poets must be strictly moral
in their teaching.

A makar, hostis eēn keinon khronon idris aoidēs.
Mousaōn therapōn, hot' akēratos ēn eti leimōn.
Nun d' hote panta dedastai, ekhousi de peirata
tekhnai,

Huatatoi hōste dromou kataleipometh', oude
pēi esti
Pantē paptainonta neozuges harma pelassai
CHOERILUS OF SAMOS:
from a lost epic on the Persian wars *(Greek)*

Oh! the bards of olden ages, blessed bards in
song-craft skilled,
Happy henchmen of the Muses, when the field
was yet untill'd.
All the land is now apportion'd, bounds to all
the Arts belong;
Left the last of all the poets, looking keenly,
looking long,
I can find no bright new chariot for the
race-course of my song.
(tr. Sir John Sandys)

Poiētēs ou proteron hoios t' esti poiein prin an
entheos genētai
GREEK PROVERB

A poet cannot write poems until he is inspired.

Ou gar aoidas
Amblunein aiōn, k'ēn ethelēi, dunatai
GREEK PROVERB

Even if he wished to do so, Time could not fade
the impact of poetry.

Phusis, thelēsis, epimelei', eutaxia,
Sophous tithēsi k'agathous. Etōn de toi
Arithmos ouden allo plēn gēras poiei
attrib. SIMYLUS *(Greek)*

Nature, goodwill, effort and grace make men
[poets] wise and good. Length of years will make
them older men, but nothing more.

Ekhthairō to poiēma to kuklikon
CALLIMACHUS:
Epigrams (Greek)

I hate all epics!

Hē men gar poiēsis mallon ta katholou,
Hē d' historia ta kath' hekaston legei
ARISTOTLE:
Poetics (Greek)

Poetry tends to express the universal, and
history the particular.

Non domandarci la formula che mondo poss
aprirti,
Sì qualche sorta sillaba e secca come un ramo.
EUGENIO MONTALE
Ossi di Seppia (Italian

Don't ask for a formula that will open up th
world to you − ask only for some crooke
syllable, dry like a withered branch!

Invenias etiam disiecti membra poetae.
HORACE
Satires (Latin

May you find the limbs of a dismembered poet!

Castum esse decet poetam
Ipsum, versiculos nihil necesset.
CATULLUS
Poems (Latin

The true poet should be chaste himself; hi
verses need not be.

Non scribit, cuius carmina nemo legit.
MARTIAL
Epigrams (Latin

A man whose poems no-one reads cannot b
called a poet.

Nihil cum fidibus graculo.
LATIN PROVER

Ignorant people have nothing to do with poetr
(*lit.* a jackdaw has nothing to do with a lyre).

Carmina proveniunt animo deducta sereno.
OVID
Tristia (Latin

Like a fine thread, poetry flows from a mind a
peace.

Sit ius liceatque perire poetis.
HORACE
Ars Poetica (Latin

Let poets have the right and power to destroy
themselves.

Me pedibus delectat claudere verba.
HORACE
Satires (Latin

My own delight is to write verse (*lit.* to shut up
words in feet).

Quodsi me lyricis vatibus inseres
Sublimi feriam sidera vertice.

HORACE:
Odes (Latin)

If you will put me among the lyric bards, I shall strike the stars with my head.

Ridentur mala qui componunt carmina; verum
Gaudent scribentes et se venerantur et ultro,
Si taceas, laudant quidquid scripsere beati.

HORACE:
Odes (Latin)

Bad poets are laughed at; but then they love their own writings and admire themselves. If you are silent, they are not backward in praising whatever they have written, for they are happy in their own conceit.

Divina opici rodebant carmina mures.

JUVENAL:
Satires (Latin)

Barbarian mice were gnawing at divine poems.

Scribendi recte sapere est et principium et fons.

HORACE:
Ars Poetica (Latin)

The source and fount of good writing is wisdom.

Papirets Digtning hører Pulten til,
Og kun den levende er Livets eje

HENRIK IBSEN:
Et Vers (Norwegian)

Paper poems can stay in the desk – to live, your poetry must be lived through.

At digte – det er at holde
Dommedag over sig selv.

HENRIK IBSEN:
Et Vers (Norwegian)

Writing poetry is to hold judgment on your soul!

I że poezja jest to nerwów drżenie
W takt namiętnościom

CYPRIAN KAMIL NORWID:
Sława (Polish)

Poetry is the quivering of nerves in time with the passions.

Ot veka iz terniĭ
Poeta zavetnȳĭ venok

VALERY BRYUSOV:
Poetu (Russian)

From time immemorial, the poet's treasured crown has been one of thorns.

Poet
    vsegda
        dolzhnik vselennoĭ,
Platyashchiĭ
    ha gore
        protsenty
            i peni

VLADIMIR MAYAKOVSKY:
Razgovor s Fininspektorom o Poezii (Russian)

Poets are always in debt to the universe, paying interest and fines on sorrow.

No lish' bozhestvennȳĭ glagol
Do slukha chutkogo kosnĕtsya,
Dusha poeta vstrepenĕtsya,
Kak probudivshiĭsya orĕl

ALEKSANDR SERGEEVICH PUSHKIN:
The Poet (Russian)

Once the poet's acute ear hears the divine word, his soul responds like an eagle aroused.

Bolyashchiĭ dukh vrachuet pesnopen'e.
Garmonii tainstvennaya vlast'
Tyazhĕloe iskupit zabluzhden'e
I ukrotit buntuyushchuyu strast'

EVGENY BARATYNSKY:
Muza (Russian)

Poetry is the cure for unhappy souls. Harmony's mysterious power redeems grievous faults and curbs rebellious passion.

Aquel que illumina las palabras opacas
Por el occulto fuego originario.

LUIS CERNUDA:
A un Poeta Muerto (F.G.L.) (Spanish)

He who illuminates opaque words with their original hidden fire.

Un famoso poeta es menos inventor que descubridor.

JORGE LUIS BORGES *(Spanish)*

A famous poet is a discoverer, rather than an inventor.

POLITICS
see also Leadership, Mankind, Philosophers.

La politique et le sort des hommes sont formés par des hommes sans idéal et sans grandeur. Ceux qui ont une grandeur en eux ne font pas de politique.

ALBERT CAMUS:
Carnets, 1937–1939 (French)

Politics and the fate of mankind are fashioned by men who lack ideals and greatness. Those who have greatness in them do not take part in politics.

Was den politischen Enthusiasten bewegt, ist nicht was er siehet, sondern was er denkt.

J. C. F. VON SCHILLER:
Werke (German)

The political idealist is moved not by what he sees but by what he thinks.

Si igitur principalior scientia est quae est de nobiliori et perfectiori, necesse est politicam inter omnes scientias practicas est principaliorem et architectonicam omnium aliarum, utpote considerans ultimum et perfectum bonum in rebus humanis.

ST. THOMAS AQUINAS:
Commentary on the Politics of Aristotle (Latin)

If then, the most important science is that which treats of the noblest and most perfect things, it must follow that politics is the most important of all practical sciences, and the keystone of them all; for it treats of the highest and perfect good in human affairs.

POSSESSIONS
see also Blessings, Danger, Gains, Law, Poverty, Time, Wealth.

Le droit de premier occupant, si faible dans l'état de nature, est respectable à tout homme civil.

J. J. ROUSSEAU:
Du Contrat Social (French)

The right of the first occupant, so little respected in nature's realm, is accepted by every civilised man.

Ce qui est bon à prendre, est bon à garder.

FRENCH PROVER

What is good to take, is good to keep.

L'usage seulement fait la possession.

JEAN DE LA FONTAIN
L'Avare qui a Perdu son Trésor (French

True possession lies in use.

Il vaut mieux pour moi, n'avoir que peu
Mais l'avoir seul.

ANDRÉ GID
Le Roi Candaule (Frencl

I prefer to have few possessions but to be the sole possessor.

Tout homme a naturellement droit à tout ce qu lui est nécessaire; mais l'acte positif qui le ren propriétaire de quelque bien l'exclut de tout l reste.

J. J. ROUSSEAU
Du Contrat Social (French

Naturally everyone has a right to what he needs but the very act that makes him its owne renders it inaccessible to everyone else.

Bien mal acquis ne profite jamais.

FRENCH PROVER

Ill-gotten gains never prosper.

Mos alos es
En tal deves
Res mas ieu non s'en pot jauzir;
Aissi l'ai claus
De pens venaus
Que nuills no lo.m pot envazir.

MARCABRU
D'Aisso lau Dieu (French

My private property is in such a prohibite enclosure that no-one but I can take pleasure i it: I have so closed it round with deceivin thought, that no-one can invade it.

Mais am un ort
Serrat e fort
Qu'hom ren no m'en puesca emblar
Que cent parras

us en puegz plas
u'autre las tenh' ez ieu las guar.
> PEIRE D'ALVERNHE:
> *Be m'es plazen (French)*

prefer a locked strong garden, where nothing
n be stolen from me, to a hundred parcels of
nd high up on the open plain, where another
ight own them and I only be permitted to look
them.

uod tuomst meumst, omne meumst autem
om.
> PLAUTUS:
> *Trinummus (Latin)*

hat's yours is mine, and of course all mine is
urs.

ix ea nostra voco.
> Motto of the Earls of Warwick

scarcely call these things our own.

bi quisque habeant quod suomst.
> PLAUTUS:
> *Curculio (Latin)*

et each man keep what is his own.

ihil amplius nostrum est; quod nostrum di-
mus, artis est.
> CICERO:
> *De Finibus (Latin)*

othing more is our own; what we call our own
convention.

l que tiene mujer hermosa ó castillo en frontera
viña en carretera, nunca le falta guerra.
> SPANISH PROVERB

e who has a handsome wife, a castle on the
ontier, or a vineyard on the highway, will
ever lack for quarrels.

POVERTY
see also Aspiration, Charity, Freedom, Hunger, Law, Possessions, Wealth.

est dur d'être gueux, tandis qu'il y a tant de
ts opulents aux dépens desquels on peut vivre.
> DENIS DIDEROT:
> *Le Neveu de Rameau (French)*

t is hard to be poor when there are so many rich
ols at whose expense one could live.

Frappant chez les pauvres – Dieu a mis la
complaisance à côté du désespoir comme le
remède à côté du mal.
> ALBERT CAMUS:
> *Carnets, 1935–1937 (French)*

Knocking at the door of the poor, God has put
kindliness at the side of despair, like putting the
remedy close to the sickness.

La pauvreté met le crime au rabais.
> S. R. N. CHAMFORT:
> *Maximes et Pensées (French)*

Poverty brings down the price of crime.

Tous les gueux se réconcilient à la gamelle.
> DENIS DIDEROT:
> *Le Neveu de Rameau (French)*

Every beggar reconciles himself to a tin cup.

Sans argent l'honneur n'est qu'une maladie.
> JEAN RACINE:
> *Les Plaideurs (French)*

Honour, without money, is nought but a
sickness.

Povrete est agreable a Dieu, car povrete est vraie
souffisance sanz desirier autre chose.
> JACQUES LE GRAND:
> dedication to the Duc de Berry of his *Livre des Bonnes Moeurs (French)*

Poverty is acceptable to God, for poverty is true
sufficiency without desiring any other thing.

Il n'est pas du bon ordre de n'avoir pas toujours
de quoi manger.
> DENIS DIDEROT:
> *Le Neveu de Rameau (French)*

It is most unsatisfactory not always to have
something to eat.

On doit toujours avoir l'air utile quand on n'est
pas riche.
> LOUIS-FERDINAND CÉLINE:
> *Voyage au Bout de la Nuit (French)*

If you aren't rich, you should always look useful.

Was Grosshaus sündigt, muss Kleinhaus
bussen.
GERMAN PROVERB

The poor man must suffer for the rich man's
transgressions.

Ich bin ze lange arm gewesen âne mînen danc.
WALTHER VON DER VOGELWEIDE:
Ich hân mîn Lêhen (German)

I have been poor too long against my will.

Penian gar oukh homologein aiskhron, all' ergōi
mē diapheugein aiskhrion
THUCYDIDES:
History (Greek)

Not to admit poverty is a disgrace – but not to
get away from it by work is a greater disgrace.

Penēs legōn talēthes ou pisteuetai
GREEK PROVERB:

When a poor man speaks the truth he is not
believed.

Garibi hathao!
Mrs. Gandhi's electioneering slogan
(Hindi)

Get rid of poverty!

Il pastor romano non vuole pecora senze lana.
ITALIAN PROVERB

The Roman shepherd does not want sheep without wool.

Mastru Giuanne est bennidu
A Bonorva a caddu e a sedda.
Gesus, ite nue niedda
Hat battidu pro nos dare!
SARDINIAN FOLK SONG *(Italian)*

Master John (*i.e.* poverty) has come to Bonorva
with horse and saddle. Jesus! what a black cloud
he has brought to give us!

Honesta res est laeta paupertas.
SENECA:
Epistles (quoting Epicurus, fragment) *(Latin)*

Contented poverty is an honourable state.

Aliquid cotidie adversus paupertatem, aliqui
adversus mortem auxilii compara.
SENEC
Epistles (Lati

Add each day something to fortify you again
poverty and death.

Inops audacia tuta est.
PETRONIU
Satyricon (Latin

A beggar can risk everything safely.

Infantem nudum cum te natura creavit,
Paupertatis onus patienter ferre memento.
Catonis Disticha (Lati

Since nature created you a naked infant, r
member to bear patiently the burden of poverty

Pauperis est numerare pecus.
OVI
Metamorphoses (Lati

Only the poor man counts his flock.

Ploratur lacrimis amissa pecunia veris.
JUVENA
Satires (Lati

Tears that lament lost wealth are unfeigned.

Is est immunis, cui nihil est qui munus fungatu
suom.
PLAUTU
Trinummus (Lati

The real 'part-with-nothing' is the man that ha
nothing with which to do his part.

Cantabit vacuus coram latrone viator.
JUVENA
Satires (Lati

A wayfarer with empty pockets will sing in th
face of a robber.

Paupertas non est vitium.
LATIN PROVER

Poverty is not a crime.

aupertatis pudor et fuga.

HORACE:
Epistles (Latin)

he avoidance and dread of poverty.

obreza no es vileza, mas es ramo de picardía.

SPANISH PROVERB

overty's no sin – but it's a branch of knavery.

ltirez y pereza, llaves de pobreza.

SPANISH PROVERB

ride and laziness are the keys of poverty.

POWER
ee also **Ambition, Existence, Forgiveness, Government, Ill-gotten gains, Innocence, Kings, Might, Money, Pride, Tyranny, Unity, Violence.**

a puissance qui vient de l'amour des peuples st sans doute la plus grande.

J. J. ROUSSEAU:
Du Contrat Social (French)

ower that derives from a nation's love is, no oubt, the greatest.

rincipatus virum ostendit.

BIAS OF PRIENE:
Apothegms (quoted in St. Thomas Aquinas:
Princely Government) *(Latin)*

ower proves a man.

iolente nemo imperia continuit diu, moderata urant.

SENECA:
Troades (Latin)

o-one can maintain ungoverned power for ng, but if it is controlled it will last.

octes atque dies niti praestante labore,
d summas emergere opes rerumque potiri.

LUCRETIUS:
De Rerum Natura (Latin)

ee night and day men strain with wondrous toil
rise to utmost power and grasp the world.

Si quantum cuperem possem quoque.

HORACE:
Epistles (Latin)

If I only had power equal to my longing.

PRAISE
see also Candour, Merit, Vanity.

On ne donne les louanges que pour en profiter.

FRANÇOIS, DUC DE LA ROCHEFOUCAULD:
Réflexions (French)

We only praise where we can derive some advantage by it.

Il y a des reproches qui louent et des louanges qui médisent.

FRANÇOIS, DUC DE LA ROCHEFOUCAULD:
Réflexions (French)

Some reproaches praise, just as some praise vilifies.

C'est un grand signe de médiocrité de louer toujours modérément.

LUC DE CLAPIERS, MARQUIS DE VAUVENARGUES:
Réflexions et Maximes (French)

It's a sure sign of mediocrity always to praise moderately.

Tois idiois epainois allotrios epetai psogos aei kai gignetai telos adoxia tēs kenodoxias tautēs

PLUTARCH:
Moralia (Greek)

Self-praise always involves criticism from others – thus vainglory has an inglorious end!

Kai mēn epainon ge ton para tōn dusōpountōn kibdēlon onta

PLUTARCH:
Moralia (Greek)

The praise that comes from suitors is false coin.

In tenui labor, at non
Tenuis gloria.

VIRGIL:
Georgics (quoted in Ausonius) *(Latin)*

Though slight the task, not slight the praise.

Ut laus est cerae, mollis cedensque sequatur.
PLINY:
Epistles (Latin)

Praise is like wax; it becomes soft and melts away.

PRAYER
see also Despair, Devotion, Enjoyment, Humility, Mankind.

Par des voeux importuns nous fatiguons les dieux.
JEAN DE LA FONTAINE:
L'Homme et la Puce (French)

We wear out the gods with importunate pleas.

Bete, Herr,
Bete, zu uns,
Wir sind nah.
PAUL CELAN:
Tenebrae (German)

Pray, Lord, pray to us – we are here.

Beruf ist mirs, zu rühmen Höhers.
FRIEDRICH HÖLDERLIN:
Die Prinzessin Auguste von Homburg (German)

My profession is to glorify the highest.

Domine dirige nos.
Motto of the Corporation of the
City of London *(Latin)*

O Lord, guide us!

Di meliora duint!
LATIN EXPRESSION

The Gods forbid! (*lit.* may the Gods grant better things!)

PRIDE
see also Government, Ingratitude, Jealousy, Moderation, Poverty.

Kibr al-insān yiqtil-uh
ARAB PROVERB

Pride will have a fall (*lit.* a man's arrogance will slay him).

Ar-rūḥ al-kabīre, gayyalat fī beit al-haddād
ragadat fī beit al-ma'tūq
ARAB PROVER

Pride is not a characteristic of a true aristocra
(*lit.* pride takes the siesta with the blacksmith
and sleeps the night with the freed slave).

Al hidim awwelah zo'om 'agābah khijle
ARAB PROVER

Pride comes before a fall (*lit.* clothes when ne
make you swagger, when old make yo
ashamed).

Lad lysets knive skrabe bort
Mit inderste sure hovmod.
BENNY ANDERSEN
Morgenbøn (Danish

Let knives of light scrape away my core of sou
pride!

La tulipe est parmi les fleurs ce que le paon es
parmi les oiseaux. L'une est sans parfum, l'autr
est sans voix: l'une s'enorgueillit de sa robe
l'autre de sa queue.
Le Jardin des Fleurs Rares et Curieuses (French

The tulip is, among flowers, what the peacock i
among birds. A tulip lacks scent, a peacock ha
an unpleasant voice. The one takes pride in it
garb, the other in its tail.

L'orgueil se dédommage toujours, et ne per
rien lors même qu'il renonce à la vanité.
FRANÇOIS, DUC DE LA ROCHEFOUCAULD
Réflexions (French

Pride always makes up for things, even when i
renounces vanity.

L'orgueil ne veut pas devoir, et l'amour-propr
ne veut pas payer.
FRANÇOIS, DUC DE LA ROCHEFOUCAULD
Réflexions (French

Pride never wants to owe, and self-respect neve
wants to pay.

J'aime, je l'avoûrai, cet orgueil généreux
Qui jamais n'a fléchi sous le joug amoureux.
JEAN RACINE
Phédre (French

I admit I love this generous pride that has neve
given way under the yoke of love.

L'orgueil chez les puissants et chez les misérables.

VICTOR HUGO:
Une Terre au Flanc Maigre (French)

Pride exists both among the powerful and among the weak.

L'eau et le temps sont les deux plus puissant dissolvants que je connaisse: l'un fend la pierre, l'autre l'amour-propre.

ALEXANDRE DUMAS:
Les Quarante-Cinq (French)

Time and water are the two most powerful solvents I know: one breaks up pride, the other stones.

Roi ne puis, prince ne daigne, Rohan je suis.

Motto of the Rohan family *(French)*

King I cannot be; prince I do not deign to be; I am a Rohan.

Tis d' ou semnos akhtheinos brotōn;

EURIPIDES:
Hippolytus (Greek)

Who does not detest a haughty man?

Secundas fortunas decent superbiae.

PLAUTUS:
Stichus (Latin)

Pride sits well on those whom fortune favours.

In solitudine cito subrepit superbia.

ST. JEROME:
letter to Rusticus *(Latin)*

In solitude pride quickly creeps in.

PRIESTS
see also Revolution.

Los curas son la gente que se toma más trabajo en el mundo para no trabajar.

RAMÓN J. SENDER:
Requiem por un Campesino Español (Spanish)

Priests are people who create much work by not working.

Los curas son las únicas personas a quienes todo el mundo llama padre, menos sus hijos, que los llaman tíos.

SPANISH PROVERB

Priests are the only people whom everyone calls father, except their sons who call them uncle.

PRINCIPLES

Sacrifier sa vie est peu de chose, dit Iégor. Accepter de rester vivant et sacrifier sa pensée, là commence le dévouement.

CHARLES PLISNIER:
Faux Passeports: 'Iégor' (French)

There's nothing in sacrificing one's life, said Iégor. But to consent to stay alive and sacrifice one's beliefs . . . that's where self-sacrifice begins! (in discussing communism).

Nihil equidem ut retionem vitae beatae veritatemque deseram.

CICERO:
De Natura Deorum (Latin)

For no consideration would I forsake the principles of happiness and truth.

Contra principium negantem non est disputandum.

MEDIEVAL TAG *(Latin)*

First principles cannot be questioned.

Si quid novisti, rectius istis,
Candidus imperti; si nil, his utere mecum.

HORACE:
Epistles (Latin)

If you can better these principles, tell me; if not, join me in following them.

PRINTING

Die Druckkunst ist eine internationale Kunst, sie gehört allen Völkern und ist ein wirksames Instrument für den Weltfrieden. Wenn aber der Friede wirklich ein Produkt gegenseitigen Verstehens ist, dann gibt es kein Werk eines

Menschen, das sich besser dazu eignen würde um dieses Verständnis zu fördern, als die Druckerpresse.

RAYMOND BLATTENBERGER:
Manuale Typographicum (German)

Printing is an international art — it belongs to the people of all nations and is an effective instrument for world peace. For, if peace really is the product of mutual understanding, then there is no work of man that is better designed to promote that understanding than the printing press.

Miraris Lector, Magnus cum dormit Homerus,
Connivere aliquo tempore Chalcographos?
Qui sunt maiores naevi, mea penna notavit,
Ipse tua lima corrige, quaeso, leves.

LAURENCE HUMPHREY:
Iesuitismi Pars Prima (preface) *(Latin)*

If Homer occasionally nods, can you wonder, dear reader, that printers too should sometimes drowse? I myself have corrected the more important errors; please do the same with the more trivial ones.

Rogo, ut artificem, quem elegeris, ne in melius quidem sinas aberrare.

PLINY:
Epistles (Latin)

I ask that the copier you choose should not depart from the original, even to improve it!

PRIORITIES
see also Second-best.

Voor je met de inslag iets kan doen, moet je eerst de schering hebben.

DUTCH PROVERB

Before you can do anything with the woof, you must first have the warp.

Nemo cum sarcinis enatat.

SENECA:
Epistles (Latin)

No man can swim ashore and take his baggage with him.

¿Que aprovecha el candil sin mecha?

SPANISH PROVERB

What use is a candle without a match?

PROBLEMS

Magna ista, quia parvi sumus, credimus.

SENECA:
Natural Questions (Latin)

We believe that these problems of ours are great because we ourselves are small.

Saepe ego audivi eum primum esse virum qui ipse consulat quid in rem sit, secundum eum qui bene monenti oboediat.

LIVY:
History (Latin)

I have often heard that the outstanding man is he who thinks deeply about a problem, and the next is he who listens carefully to advice.

PROCRASTINATION
see also Action, Hesitation, Truth.

Mēd' anaballesthai es t' aurion es te enēphin

HESIOD:
Works and Days (Greek)

Don't put things off till tomorrow or the day after!

In crastinum differo res severas.

CORNELIUS NEPOS:
Pelopidas (Latin)

Serious matters can wait until tomorrow.

Obró mucho el que nada dejó para mañana.

BALTASAR GRACIÁN:
Oráculo Manual y Arte de Prudencia (Spanish)

He who puts off nothing till tomorrow has done a great deal.

PROGRESS
see also Effort.

Toujours la nuit! jamais l'azur! jamais l'aurore!
Nous marchons. Nous n'avons point fait un pas encore!
Nous rêvons ce qu'Adam rêva.

VICTOR HUGO
Horror (French)

Always night! never blue skies! never dawn! We march — but so far we have not progressed an inch! We still dream what Adam dreamt!

PROMISES
see also Disillusion, Gratitude, Lies, Temptation, Untrustworthiness.

Wa'd bilā waf'ā adāwa bilā sabab
ARAB PROVERB

Promising and not fulfilling causes needless enmity.

PROSPERITY
see also Adversity, Envy, Liberty.

Bona quae veniunt nisi sustineantur opprimunt.
LATIN PROVERB

Prosperity must be sensibly restrained or it crushes you.

Desinat elatis quisquam confidere rebus.
CLAUDIAN:
In Rufinum (Latin)

Put not your trust in prosperity.

PROTEST

Pros ta kentra mē laktizetō
GREEK EXPRESSION

To kick against the pricks.

Advorsum stimulum calces iactare.
or
Calcitrare contra stimulum.
LATIN PROVERBS

To kick against the pricks.

Tacitus apud me gemebam.
THOMAS JAMES,
Bodley's first librarian (Latin)

I groaned silently to myself (speaking of the need for a union-catalogue of the Oxford libraries, which he himself eventually provided in his *Ecloga Oxonio Cantabrigiensis*)

La peor rueda del carro es la que más rechina.
SPANISH PROVERB

It's the worst wheel of the wagon that screeches the loudest.

PROVIDENCE
see also Chance, Destiny, Wisdom.

la Providence
Sait ce qu'il nous faut mieux que nous.
JEAN DE LA FONTAINE:
Jupiter et le Métayer (French)

Providence knows what is good for us better than we do.

Divina providentia omnibus rebus ordinem imponit.
ST. THOMAS AQUINAS:
Summa contra Gentiles (Latin)

Divine providence imposes an order on all things.

PRUDENCE
see also Caution, Patience, Resourcefulness, Virtue.

Nous en avions assez, prudence, de tes maximes à bout de fil à plomb, de ton épargne à bout d'usure et de reprise.
ST.-JOHN PERSE:
Vents (French)

We have had enough, Prudence, of your maxims weighted to a plumb-line, of your thrift threadbare beyond mending!

La prudence n'est pas dans les jeunes gens.
MOLIÈRE:
Don Juan (French)

Young people know nothing of prudence.

Ex praeterito praesens prudenter agit ni futura actione deturpet.
Inscription on Titian's *Allegory of Prudence*
(Latin)

From the example of the past, mankind today acts prudently to avoid imperilling the future.

PUBLIC OPINION
see also Opinion, Reputation, Silence, Wisdom.

Il y a des siècles où l'opinion publique est la plus mauvaise des opinions.
S. R. N. CHAMFORT:
Maximes et Pensées (French)

There are times when public opinion is the worst of all opinions.

Houtō tous pelas mallon aidoumetha, ti pote
peri hēmōn phronēsousin, ē heautous

MARCUS AURELIUS:
Meditations (Greek)

We take more notice of our neighbours' opinions
of us than of our own.

Vilia miretur vulgus.

OVID:
Amores (Latin)

Let base-conceited wits admire vile things! (*tr.*
Christopher Marlowe).

PUNISHMENT
see also Evil, Hell.

La fréquence des supplices est toujours un signe
de faiblesse ou de paresse dans le gouvernement.

J. J. ROUSSEAU:
Du Contrat Social (French)

Frequent punishments are always a sign of
weakness or laziness on the part of the government.

Qui aime bien châtie bien.

FRENCH PROVERB

He who truly loves will chastise well.

Le fléau qui bat le grain se bat lui-même.

FRENCH PROVERB

The flail that beats the grain beats itself.

Hoti d' ouk estin aiskhiōn oude lupousa pou
mallon hetera kolasis ē tous ex heautōn kaka
paskhontas di hautous horan

PLUTARCH:
Moralia (Greek)

No punishment is more galling or shameful than
to see one's own children suffer on one's
account.

Si stimulos pugnis caedis, manibus plus dolet.

PLAUTUS:
Truculentus (Latin)

If you beat a stick with your fists, it is your hands
that will suffer.

PURITY
see also Chastity, Innocence, Moderation.

Ganz unbefleckt geniesst sich nur das Herz.

J. W. VON GOETHE:
Iphigenie auf Tauris (German)

Only if it is quite immaculate can the heart enjoy
itself.

Otium naufragium castitatis.

LATIN PROVERB

Idleness is the ruin of chastity.

Sincerum est nisi vas, quodcumque infundis
acescit.

HORACE:
Epistles (Latin)

If the vessel is unclean, whatever you pour in
turns sour.

Res est arduissima vincere naturam . . . mentem
esse puram.

THE ARCHPOET (so-called):
Fragment *(Latin)*

It is a most arduous task to overcome nature and
to be pure in mind.

PURPOSE
see also Ambition, Determination, Right
and Wrong, Ways and means.

La fin justifie les moyens.

FRENCH PROVERB

The end justifies the means.

Pierre qui roule n'amasse pas mousse.

FRENCH PROVERB

A rolling stone gathers no moss.

Qui veut la fin veut les moyens.

FRENCH PROVERB

Where there is a will there is a way (*lit.* he who
desires the end desires the means).

Aber der Mensch hat noch ein Bedürfnis mehr, als zu leben und sich wohl sein zu lassen.

J. C. F. VON SCHILLER:
Werke (German)

There is more to life than just existing and having a pleasant time.

Infatuatum sal ad nihilum est utile.

ST. JEROME:
Letter to Heliodorus (Latin)

Salt that has lost its flavour is useless.

Galgo que muchas liebres levanta ninguna mata.

SPANISH PROVERB

The greyhound that starts many hares kills none.

No se puede repicar y andar en la procesión.

SPANISH PROVERB

You can't ring the bells and, at the same time, walk in the procession.

Q

QUARRELS
see also Kings, Love, Possessions, Women.

Qui entre nus comencera bargaigne,
Tres bien l'achat, ke dreiz est qu'il s'en pleigne.
Le Mystère d'Adam (French)

He who begins a quarrel, let him pay dearly for
it, for it is right that he should have to lament.

N'allons donc point chercher à faire une
querelle,
Pour un affront qui n'est que pure begatelle.
MOLIÈRE:
Sganarelle (French)

Don't let's try to quarrel over an offence which is
but a trifle (Sganarelle, trying to persuade himself that being cuckolded does not warrant a
duel).

R

RACE

L'homme occidental sait maintenant qu'il n'est
plus le seul représentant de l'espèce humaine
digne de considération.
RAYMOND QUENEAU:
Présentation de l'Encyclopédie (French)

Western man now knows that he is no longer the
sole representative of the human race worthy of
esteem.

RAIN
see also Autumn.

Dharatī jaisa gagana kē nēhā;
Palaṭi bharai barakhā ritu mēhā
MALIK MUHAMMAD JĀYASĪ:
Padumāvatī (Avadhi)

The earth is in love with the heavens, and in the
rainy season the clouds return and fill it with
water.

Pauvre oiseau que le ciel bénit!
Il écoute le vent bruire,
Chante, et voit des gouttes d'eau luire
Comme des perles dans son nid!
VICTOR HUGO:
Contemplations (French)

Poor bird, blessed of heaven! you hear the wind,
and as you sing you see the drops of water
gleaming like pearls in your nest!

Des arcs-en-ciel tendus comme des brides
Sous l'horizon des mers, à des glauques
troupeaux!
ARTHUR RIMBAUD:
Le Bateau Ivre (French)

Rainbows stretching like bridles under the
ocean horizons, on those sea-green flocks.

Ao-yagi no
Yeda ni kakareru
Haru-same wa,
Ito mote-nukeru
Tama ka to zo miru
THE LADY ISE:
Waga (Japanese)

The spring rain hanging on the branches of the
willows looks like pearls threaded on gossamer.

E ua e te ua
Takamingomingo noa
Ki Papa-tu-a-nuku
Nga tohu o te po
NGA-PUHI:
He Walata-putorino (Maori)

Rain on, rain on, now here, now there, over the
broad earth – the signs of final darkness.

RAPACITY

... Tantum ... curamus frigora, quantum ...
numerum [ovium] lupus.

VIRGIL:
Eclogues (Latin)

We care as much about the kid as the wolf does
about the number of sheep.

Quiconque est loup agisse en loup.

JEAN DE LA FONTAINE:
Le Loup devenu Berger (French)

A wolf cannot conceal that he is a wolf.

REACTIONS

Je me presse de rire de tout, de peur d'être obligé
d'en pleurer.

P. A. C. DE BEAUMARCHAIS:
Le Barbier de Séville (French)

I hasten to laugh at everything, for fear of being
obliged to weep.

Ut ridentibus arrident, ita flentibus adsunt
Humani voltus.

HORACE:
Ars Poetica (Latin)

As men's faces smile on those who smile, so they
respond to those who weep.

Haec, si displicui, fuerint solatia nobis;
Haec fuerint nobis praemia, si placui.

MARTIAL:
Epigrams (Latin)

If I have caused displeasure, these things could
be my consolation; if I have caused pleasure,
they could be my reward.

Es más difícil estar a la altura de la circunstan-
cias que au-dessus de la mêlée.

ANTONIO MACHADO:
Works (Spanish)

It is more difficult to rise to the occasion than to
stand above the conflict.

REALITY
see also Art and artists, Painters and painting, Sophistry, Sorrow, World.

To men pantelōs on pantelōs gnōston, mē on de
mēdamēi pantēi agnōston

PLATO:
The Republic (Greek)

What is entirely real is perfectly knowable, but
what is completely unreal is wholly unknow-
able.

REASON
see also Adoration, Emotion, Love, Mediocrity, Memory, Motives, Persuasion, Vanity, Wisdom, Youth.

C'est la raison et non les sens qu'il faut con-
sulter.

NICOLAS MALEBRANCHE:
Entretiens sur la Métaphysique (French)

We must always consult reason and not our
senses.

La raison nous commande bien plus impérieuse-
ment qu'un maistre.

BLAISE PASCAL:
Pensées (French)

Reason commands us far more imperiously than
any master.

La raison du plus fort est toujours la meilleure.

JEAN DE LA FONTAINE:
Le Loup et l'Agneau (French)

The reason of the strongest is always the best.

Nous n'avons pas assez de force pour suivre
toute notre raison.

FRANÇOIS, DUC DE LA ROCHEFOUCAULD:
Maximes (French)

We haven't enough strength to observe completely the dictates of our reason.

On ne souhaite jamais ardemment ce qu'on ne
souhaite que par raison.

FRANÇOIS, DUC DE LA ROCHEFOUCAULD:
Maximes (French)

Reason alone is insufficient to make us en-
thusiastic in any matter.

Er nennt's Vernunft und braucht's allein,
Nur tierischer als jedes Tier zu sein.

J. W. VON GOETHE:
Faust (Prologue to Heaven) *(German)*

He calls it reason but only uses it to be more beastly than any animal.

Die Vernunft sieht jetzt über das Reich der dunklen, aber warmen Gefühle so hervor wie die Alpenspitzen über die Wolken. Sie sehen die Sonne reiner und deutlicher, aber sie sind kalt und unfruchtbar.

GEORG CHRISTOPH LICHTENBERG:
Aphorismen (German)

Reason stands out above the realm of the obscure but warm emotions, like the Alpine peaks above the clouds. They see the sun more clearly and distinctly, but they are cold and sterile.

Hē deinon hōi dokēi ge kai pseudē dokein

SOPHOCLES:
Antigone (Greek)

How dangerous can false reasoning prove!

Theoi phuousin anthrōpois phrenas,
Pantōn hos' esti ktēmatōn hupertaton

SOPHOCLES:
Antigone (Greek)

Reason, heaven's greatest gift, is given to mankind by the gods.

Mēden thaumazein

GREEK MAXIM

Marvel at nothing!

O forza vindice
De la ragione!

GIOSUE CARDUCCI:
A Satana (Italian)

Oh, the vindictive force of reason!

Quid enim ratione timemus aut cupimus?

JUVENAL:
Satires (Latin)

When did reason ever direct our desires or our fears?

An melior ullus auctor est quam ratio?

LAURENTIUS VALLA
Confutatio Prior in Benedictum Morandum Bononiensem (Latin

What better authority can there be than reason?

Fuera de los límites de la racionalidad está lo irracional

MIGUEL DE UNAMUNO
(Spanish

Outside the limits of reason lies the irrational.

REASSURANCE

Estai panta kalōs

SUETONIUS:
Domitianus (Greek)

All will be well (the words of a raven, perched on the Capitol, interpreted as presaging Domitian's approaching death).

REBUKE

Crudelis est in re adversa obiurgatio.

LATIN PROVERB

Rebuke is cruel in adversity.

RECONCILIATION

Im Lieben und in Hassen
Wie einig waren wir!
Wenn alle dich verlassen,
Kehrst du zurück zu mir!

MAX HERRMANN-NEISSE:
Verlassen (German)

How united we were in both in love and in hate! When everyone deserted you, you turned back to me!

Ne, pueri, ne tanta animis assuescite bella,
Neu patriae validas in viscera vertite vires.

VIRGIL:
Aeneid (Latin)

Embrace again, my sons, be foes no more;
Nor stain your country with her children's gore

(*tr.* Dryden)

REDEMPTION
see also Aspiration, Atonement, Effort, Repentance.

Il n'y a point de méchant qu'on ne pût rendre bon à quelque chose.
> J. J. ROUSSEAU:
> *Du Contrat Social (French)*

There is not a single ill-doer who could not be turned to some good.

Substantia animae hominis vel homo cum eo per quod substanciatur, fit propinquius ad intelligenciam agentem et hic est finis ultimus et vita alia.
> AL-FARABI:
> *De Intellectu et Intellecto* (12th century translation) *(Latin)*

Man, with that essence of mind through which he is fulfilled, is drawn nearer to the active intellect, and this is his ultimate end – a new life.

Hartóse el gato de carne, y luego se hizo fraile.
> SPANISH PROVERB

The cat had its fill of meat and then turned friar.

No hay mal que por bien no venga.
> SPANISH PROVERB

There is nothing so bad that good may not come of it.

REINCARNATION

On ne saurait nier que de toutes les hypothèses religieuses, la réincarnation est la plus plausible, et celle qui choque le moins nôtre raison.
> MAURICE MAETERLINCK:
> *La Mort (French)*

We cannot deny that, of all religious hypotheses, reincarnation is the most acceptable and the least offensive to our reason.

RELATIONS
see also Children, Families, Neighbours, Parents.

C'est sans les oublier qu'on quitte ses parents;
L'hymen n'efface point ces profonds caractères.
> PIERRE CORNEILLE:
> *Horace (French)*

When we leave our relations we don't forget them – marriage cannot efface such deep ties.

Mâc hilfet wol, friunt verre baz.
> WALTHER VON DER VOGELWEIDE:
> *Man Hôchgemâc (German)*

Kinsmen may help, but friends do so much better.

Heus proxumus sum egomet mihi.
> TERENCE:
> *Andria (Latin)*

My closest relation is myself.

Værst er ens egne Frænder.
> NORWEGIAN PROVERB

One's own relations are always the worst.

RELIGION
see also Atheism, Modesty, Philology, Truth.

Par tout pays, la Religion dominante, quand elle ne persécute point, engloutit à la longue toutes les autres.
> VOLTAIRE:
> *Lettres Philosophiques (French)*

In every country the dominant religion, when it does not persecute other religions, in the long run engulfs them all.

Mettre [la Religion] dans l'esprit et dans le coeur par la force et par les menaces, ce n'est pas y mettre la Religion mais la terreur.
> BLAISE PASCAL:
> *Pensées (French)*

Putting religion into people's hearts and souls by force or menaces does not induce religion but terror.

Un Anglais, comme homme libre, va au Ciel par le chemin qui lui plaît.
> VOLTAIRE:
> *Lettres Philosophiques (French)*

The English, being a free people, go to Heaven by whatever road it pleases them to use!

Nostre religion est si divine qu'une autre religion divine n'en a que le fondement.
> BLAISE PASCAL:
> *Pensées (French)*

Our religion is so sacred that it is the basis of all others.

Les religions disparaîtraient avec le bonheur des hommes.

> RAYMOND QUENEAU:
> *Une Histoire Modèle (French)*

Religions tend to disappear with man's good fortune.

La Théologie se retrouve un peu partout.

> PAUL VALÉRY:
> *Monsieur Teste* (preface) *(French)*

Theology has a tendency to turn up occasionally everywhere.

Der Glaube an einen Gott ist Instinkt, er ist dem Menschen natürlich, so wie das Gehen auf zwei Beinen.

> GEORG CHRISTOPH LICHTENBERG:
> *Aphorismen (German)*

Belief in a god is instinctive; to mankind it is as natural as walking on two legs.

Die meisten Religionen machen die Menschen nicht besser, aber vorsichtiger.

> ELIAS CANETTI:
> *Aufzeichnungen*, 1952 *(German)*

Most religions do not make men better, only warier.

REMEDIES

Ho trōsas iasetai

> GREEK PROVERB
> (quoted in Suetonius' *Divus Claudius*) *(Greek)*

He who dealt the wound will heal it.

Ubi turpis est medicina, sanari piget.

> SENECA:
> *Oedipus (Latin)*

When the medicine is foul-tasting, it is loathsome to be cured.

Al catarro, con el jarro.

> SPANISH PROVERB

A cold is best cured with a decanter.

REMEMBRANCE
see also Memories.

Un souvenir heureux est peut-être sur terre
Plus vrai que le bonheur.

> ALFRED DE MUSSET
> *Souvenir (French*

A happy memory is perhaps more truthful than good fortune on this earth.

Souvente me souvene.

> Motto of Henry Stafford
> duke of Buckingham, 1483 *(French*

Remember me often.

THE RENAISSANCE

La renaissance, loin d'être, comme on l'a dit, un égarement de l'esprit moderne, fourvoyé après un idéal étranger, n'est que le retour à la vraie tradition de l'humanité civilisée.

> ERNEST RENAN
> *Averroès (French*

The Renaissance, far from being, as has been said, an aberration of the modern spirit led astray after a foreign ideal, is only the return of civilised humanity to the true tradition.

Dall' Italia soltanto il classicismo poteva sperare il suo rinascimento, dall' unica terra dove il vecchio mondo classico in rovine, superava in grandezza e maestà il giovane medio evo.

> HORTIS:
> *Studi sulle Opere Latine del Boccaccio (Italian*

Only in Italy could classicism hope to achieve its renaissance, in the one country where the old classical world lay in ruins, but towered over the young Middle Ages in grandeur and majesty.

REPENTANCE
see also Evil, Redemption.

Le tard repentir ne guarist le dommage.

> PIERRE DE RONSARD:
> *Sonnets (French*

Late repentance does not cure the harm.

idelissimus est ad honesta ex paenitentia
ansitus.

SENECA:
Natural Questions (Latin)

he most dependable change towards integrity
omes from repentance.

REPROACH

ous l'avez voulu, vous l'avez voulu, George
andin!

MOLIÈRE:
George Dandin (French)

ou asked for it, George Dandin! (Dandin
eproaches himself for allowing himself to be
utwitted by his in-laws).

REPROOF

alei kai mē thingane

GREEK PROVERB

cold me, but hands off!

egre reprehendas quod sinas consuescere.

ST. JEROME:
Epistles (Greek)

ou censure this with difficulty because you
ave allowed it to become customary.

REPUTATION
see also Ancestors, Appearance,
Fame, Generosity, Genius, Glory,
Materialism, Patriotism, Respect, Wealth.

l-jawāb yit'irif min 'inwān-uh

ARAB PROVERB

he letter is known from its address.

Jul n'est prophète en son pays.

Aucun n'est prophète chez soi.

FRENCH PROVERB

No-one is a prophet in his own country.

Qui a bon renom de se lever le matin peut
ormir jusqu'à midi.

ALPHONSE DAUDET:
Tartarin sur les Alpes (French)

Ie who has a reputation for early rising can
leep till noon.

Bonne renommée valait mieux que ceinture
dorée.

FRENCH PROVERB

A good reputation is better than wealth.

Je ne considère les gens après leur mort que par
leurs ouvrages.

VOLTAIRE:
Letters Philosophiques (French)

After their death I only weigh up people by their
works.

Ce que nous nous rapellons de notre conduite
reste ignoré de notre plus proche voisin; ce que
nous avons oublié avoir dit, ou même ce que
nous n'avons jamais dit, va provoquer l'hilarité
jusque dans une autre planète.

MARCEL PROUST:
Le Côté de Guermantes (French)

What we remember of our conduct remains
ignored by our closest neighbour; but what we
have forgotten we have said, or even what we
have never said, will provide cause for laughter
even into the next world.

Outoi biou moi tou makraiōnos pothos,
Pheronti tēnde baxin

SOPHOCLES:
Oedipus Tyrannus (Greek)

If my reputation is injured, I no longer wish to
go on living.

Ti dēta doxēs ē ti klēdonos kalēs
Matēn rheousēs ōphelēma gignetai

SOPHOCLES:
Oedipus Coloneus (Greek)

What is the use of fame or good reputation? How
empty they are!

Bona fama in tenebris proprium splendorem
tenet.

LATIN PROVERB

A good name keeps its brightness even in dark
days.

Bona opinio hominum tutior pecunia est.

LATIN PROVERB

There is more safety in men's good opinion than
in money.

Exegi monumentum aere perennius
Regalique situ pyramidum altius.

HORACE:
Odes (Latin)

I have built a monument more lasting than
bronze, and loftier than the regal grace of the
pyramids.

Omnia post obitum fingit maiora vetustas;
Maius ab exsequiis nomen in ora venit.

PROPERTIUS:
Elegies (Latin)

Antiquity makes everything more impressive
after death. One's name comes grandly into
men's mouths once the funeral is over.

Tu recte vivis, si curas esse quod audis.

HORACE:
Epistles (Latin)

You live right, if you are careful to be what
people call you.

Omnis bonos bonasque adcurare addecet,
Suspicionem et culpam ut ab se segregent.

PLAUTUS:
Trinummus (Latin)

All decent men and women should take care to
stay completely free from suspicion and guilt.

Tertium seculum non videt eum hominem
quem vidit primum.

MARCUS TERENTIUS VARRO:
De Lingua Latina (Latin)

The third generation cannot look on a man in
the same way that the first generation saw him.

Non enim hominum interitu sententiae quoque
occidunt.

CICERO:
De Natura Deorum (Latin)

When men die their doctrines do not perish with
them.

Na cāhu, na ca bhavissati, na c'etarahi vijjati
Ekantaṁ nindito poso ekantaṁ vā pasaṁsito
Dhammapada: Khodhavaggo (Pali)

No-one receives or ever will receive unqualified
blame or praise.

De dinero y calidad, la mitad de la mitad.

SPANISH PROVER[B]

Reports of wealth or worth are best halved – an[d]
then halved again.

RESENTMENT

Voilà un joli commencement du règne!

Tsar Nicolas, commenting bitterly on th[e]
Decembrist rising of 1825 at St. Petersbur[g]
(French[)]

Here's a fine beginning to our reign!

Chi crede che ne' personaggi grandi e' benefiz[i]
nuovi faccino dimenticare le iniurie vecchi[e]
s'inganna.

NICCOLÒ MACHIAVELL[I]
The Prince (Italian[)]

He who thinks that among great men ne[w]
benefits cause old resentments to be forgotte[n]
makes a great mistake.

Utinam p[opulus] R[omanus] unam cervicen[e]
haberet!

SUETONIUS[:]
Gaius Caligula (Latin[)]

I wish the Roman people had but a single neck[.]

RESIGNATION
see also Self-knowledge, Sorrow.

A son pas de lieuse de gerbes s'en va la vie san[s]
haine ni rançon.

ST.-JOHN PERSE[:]
Nocturne (French[)]

As the binder of corn sheaves steps forth, her lif[e]
runs on without hate or ransom.

Melius quidquid erit pati.

HORACE[:]
Odes (Latin[)]

Better to accept whatever happens.

Durum: sed levius fit patentia
Quidquid corrigere est nefas.

HORACE[:]
Odes (Latin[)]

Hard; but what it is forbidden to put righ[t]
becomes lighter by acceptance.

Feriat iam, quem volet.

SUETONIUS:
Domitianus (Latin)

Well, let fate now strike whom it will!

RESOLUTION
see also Courage.

Hier baet geen deizen neen, wy zyn te hoogh geklommen.

JOOST VAN DER VONDEL:
Lucifer (Dutch)

Recoil were vain here; no! we've climbed too great a height.

Andiam pur noi audacemente a questa
Impresa, e non manchiam noi a noi stessi.
La Fortuna, in cui man son l'human'opre,
Gli animosi, i gagliardi aita sempre,
Et a chi teme, vien del tutto meno.

GIAMBATTISTA CINTHIO GIRALDI:
Selene (Italian)

Let us therefore approach this enterprise with resolution and see that we do ourselves justice. Fortune, in whom rest the affairs of men, always helps the spirited and the courageous, but completely fails the faint-hearted.

Tutissimum est inferre, cum timeas, gradum.

SENECA:
Hippolytus (Latin)

When in fear, it is safest to force the attack.

Nu er jeg stålsat: jeg følger der bud
Der byder i højden at vandre!

HENRIK IBSEN:
On the Vidde (Norwegian)

Now I am steel-set: I follow the call to the clear radiance and glow of the heights.

Jeg går til Frihed gennem Døgnets Ørk,
For mig er Fremkomst selv i Havets Fjære.

HENRIK IBSEN:
Love's Comedy (Norwegian)

I go to freedom through disdain's parched sand. There will be a path for me over the waves.

Intet – eller Alt!

NORWEGIAN PROVERB

All or nothing!

RESOURCEFULNESS
see also Caution, Prudence.

Epi duoiē ankurain hormein

GREEK EXPRESSION

To have two strings to one's bow (*lit.* to be moored with two anchors).

Cogitato, mus pusillus quam sit sapiens bestia,
Aetatem qui non cubili uni umquam committit suam,
Quin, si unum obsideatur, aliud iam perfugium elegerit.

PLAUTUS:
Truculentus (Latin)

Consider what a canny beast the timid mouse is. He does not put his trust in just one hole, but has already made another for use if the first one is blocked.

RESPECT
see also Caution, Prudence.

Was ist der Mensch ohne Verehrung, und was hat die Verehrung aus dem Menschen gemacht!

ELIAS CANETTI:
Aufzeichnungen, 1943 (German)

What is man without respect? but what has respect made of man!

Askeitai dē to aei timōmenon, ameleitai de to atimazomenon

PLATO:
The Republic (Greek)

What we respect we always do, but what we do not respect we ignore.

Numquam erit alienis gravis qui suis se cocinnat levem.

PLAUTUS:
Trinummus (Latin)

He who carries no weight in his own home will never be respected abroad.

Diligimus pariter pariterque timemus.

CLAUDIAN:
Epithalamium (Latin)

We love thee, yet we fear thee.

Qui colitur, et amatur.

SENECA:
Epistles (Latin)

Respect means love.

Estímese si quisiere que le estimen.

SPANISH PROVERB

If you want to be respected, you must respect yourself.

Nunca bien venerará la estatua en el ara el que la conoció tronco en el huerto.

BALTASAR GRACIÀN:
Oráculo Manual y Arte de Prudencia (Spanish)

The image on the altar will never be properly revered by the man who knew it when it was but a tree trunk in the garden.

RESPONSIBILITIES

On n'est point forcé de charger un homme d'un plus grand fardeau qu'un homme ne peut porter.

J. J. ROUSSEAU:
Du Contrat Social (French)

There is no need to lay on any man burdens too great for him to bear.

Être directeur, c'est être dirigé.

RAYMOND QUENEAU:
Présentation de l'Encyclopédie (French)

Being a director means you must submit to direction.

Sumite materiam vestris, qui scribitis, aequam
Viribus et versate diu, quid ferre recusent,
Quid valeant umeri.

HORACE:
Ars Poetica (Latin)

Writers! choose a subject equal to your abilities; think carefully what your shoulders may refuse and what they are capable of bearing.

Boni pastoris est tondere pecus, non deglubere.

LATIN PROVERB

It is the part of a good shepherd to shear his flock, not to skin it!

REST

Meriggiare pallido e assorto
Presso un rovente muro d'orto.

EUGENIO MONTALE
Meriggiare Pallido e Assorto (Italian

To rest at noon, pallid and absorbed, next to scorching garden wall.

RESTLESSNESS
see also Aspiration, Bustle, Uncertainty.

Tout le malheur des hommes vient d'une seul chose, qui est de ne savoir pas demeurer e repos, dans une chambre.

BLAISE PASCAL
Pensées (French

All mankind's unhappiness derives from on thing: his inability to know how to remain i repose in one room.

Wo wird einst des Wandermüden
Letzte Ruhestätte sein?

HEINRICH HEINE
Wo? (German

Where will the travel-weary find his last restin place?

Bleiben ist nirgends.

RAINER MARIA RILKE
Duineser Elegien (German

Abiding is nowhere.

Romae rus optas; absentem rusticus urbem
Tollis ad astra levis.

HORACE
Satires (Latin

In Rome you long for the country. In the country you praise to the skies the distant town

RETICENCE

Le silence des grands est la leçon des petits!

LABICHE AND MARTIN
La Poudre aux Yeux (French

The reticence of the great provides an example for the lowly!

REVELATION

Hélas! l'Evangile a passé! l'Evangile! l'Evangile!
J'attends Dieu avec gourmandise.
ARTHUR RIMBAUD:
Une Saison en Enfer (French)

Alas! the Gospel has faded! I await God with greed.

Tendono alla chiarità le cose oscure.
EUGENIO MONTALE:
Poesia (Italian)

Dark things reach out toward brightness.

Pande oculos, pande stellatae frontis honorem.
MARC-ANTOINE MURET:
Juvenilia (Latin)

Open your eyes, reveal the splendour of your glorious face!

REVENGE
see also Anger, Hesitation, Vengeance.

Quitte à quitte.
FRENCH EXPRESSION

Tit for tat.

Schwarze Milch der Frühe wir trinken sie abends.
PAUL CELAN:
Todesfuge (German)

We drink the black milk of morning at evetide.

Mein Handwerk ist Wiedervergeltung – Rache ist mein Gewerbe.
J. C. F. VON SCHILLER:
Die Räuber (German)

My occupation is retaliation; revenge is my trade.

O über mich Narren, der ich wähnete, die Welt durch Greuel zu verschönen und die Gesetze durch Gesetzlosigkeit aufrecht zu halten. Ich nannte es Rache und Recht.
J. C. F. VON SCHILLER:
Die Räuber (German)

How stupid to think I could improve the world by atrocity, and uphold the law by lawlessness. I called it revenge and right.

Intus habes, quem poscis!
OVID:
Metamorphoses (Latin)

He whom you want you have within you (Procne's terrible answer to Tereus, when he asks for his son Itys – Procne has slain Itys, and Tereus has unwittingly eaten his flesh).

La sangre es más dulce que la miel.
SPANISH PROVERB

Blood is sweeter than honey.

Todo se paga.
MEXICAN PROVERB

Everything is paid.

REVOLUTION
see also War.

Toutes les révolutions civiles et politiques ont eu une patrie et s'y sont renfermées.
ALEXIS DE TOCQUEVILLE:
L'Ancien Régime et la Révolution (French)

Every civil or political revolution has had a fatherland to which it has confined itself.

Ce n'est pas toujours en allant de mal en pis que l'on tombe en révolution.
ALEXIS DE TOCQUEVILLE:
L'Ancien Régime et la Révolution (French)

It does not always happen that, in going from bad to worse, a revolution occurs.

La Révolution. Je suis un homme d'affaires. La Révolution est une affaire comme les autres.
JACQUES AUDIBERTI:
La Poupée (prologue) (French)

Revolution? I'm a business man. Revolution is business like anything else! (The plutocrat Moren is emphasising his contempt for the revolutionaries).

Il y a eu, dans la révolution française, deux mouvements en sens contraire qu'il ne faut pas confondre: l'un favorable à la liberté, l'autre favorable au despotisme.
ALEXIS DE TOCQUEVILLE:
De la Démocratie en Amérique (French)

In the French Revolution there were two conflicting movements that should not be confused: one favourable to liberty, the other to despotism.

Je voudrais voir le dernier des Rois étranglé avec le boyau du dernier des Prêtres!
Anonymous (quoted in S. R. N. Chamfort:
Caractères) *(French)*

I should like to see the last of the kings strangled with the guts of the last of the priests!

Ils avaient peur de faire peur.
Léo Blum, speaking in the Sorbonne, in 1948, about the revolutionaries of 1848 *(French)*

They were afraid of frightening people.

Die Philosophen haben die Welt nur verschieden interpretiert; es kommt aber darauf an, sie zu verändern.
KARL MARX:
Thesen über Feuerbach (German)

All that philosophers have done is interpret the world in different ways. It is our job to change it!

Proletarier aller Länder, vereinigt euch!
KARL MARX:
Communist Manifesto (German)

Citizens of the world, unite!

Die Revolution ist wie Saturn, sie frisst ihre eignen Kinder.
GEORG BÜCHNER:
Dantons Tod (German)

Revolution is like Saturn – it eats its own children.

Friede den Hütten! Krieg den Pallästen!
GEORG BÜCHNER:
Der Hessische Landbote (opening words) *(German)*

Peace to the cottages! War on the palaces!

Ich studierte die Geschichte der Revolution. Ich fühlte mich wie zernichtet unter dem grässlichen Fatalismus der Geschichte.
GEORG BÜCHNER:
letter to Minna Jaegle, 10 March 1834 *(German)*

I studied the history of the [French] revolution – I felt as if I were crushed by the terrible fatalism of history.

Marci Catonis est: unum ex omnibus Caesarem ad evertendam rem publicam sobrium accessisse.
SUETONIUS:
Divus Iulius (Latin)

Marcus Cato used to say that Julius Caesar was the only man who undertook to overthrow the state when sober.

Venid a ver la sangre por las calles!
PABLO NERUDA:
Coro (Spanish)

Come and see the blood in the streets!

La revolución renance siempre, como un fénix Llameante en el pecho de los desdichados.
LUIS CERNUDA:
La Visita de Dios (Spanish)

Revolution, like a phoenix, is always reborn, rising like a flame from the bodies of the wretched.

RIDICULE
see also Mockery, Philosophers.

Le ridicule déshonore plus que le déshonneur.
FRANÇOIS, DUC DE LA ROCHEFOUCAULD:
Réflexions (French)

Ridicule dishonours more than dishonour itself.

Satius est rideri quam derideri.
PETRONIUS:
Satyricon (Latin)

It is better to give rise to laughter than to ridicule.

RIGHT AND WRONG
see also Justice, Might, Purpose, Wrong.

Le besoin d'avoir raison, marque d'esprit vulgaire.
ALBERT CAMUS:
Carnets, 1935–1937 *(French)*

The need to be right is the mark of a vulgar spirit.

Das Recht wohnet beim Überwältiger, und die Schranken unserer Kraft sind unsere Gesetze.
J. C. F. VON SCHILLER:
Die Räuber (German)

Right is in the hands of the conqueror, and the limits of our strength are our laws.

Als man hörte vom Rechte der Menschen, das
allen gemein sei,
Von der begeisternden Freiheit und von der
löblichen Gleichheit!

> J. W. VON GOETHE:
> *Hermann und Dorothea (German)*

We heard of the rights of man that should be
common to all; the freedom that inspires; and
equality worthy of praise!

Honesta turpitudo est pro causa bona.

> LATIN PROVERB

The end justifies the means (*lit.* foul is fair when
the cause is good).

Sua sponte recte facere quam alieno metu.

> TERENCE:
> *Adelphoe (Latin)*

To do right of one's own will, rather than
through fear of others.

Quamvis non rectum quod iuvat rectum putes.

> LATIN PROVERB

It may not be right but, if it pleases, think it so.

Nam si violandum est ius, regnandi gratia violandum est; aliis rebus pietatem colas.

> CICERO:
> *De Officiis (Latin)*

If wrong is ever done, it should be for the sake of
ruling; in all else you should foster a sense of
duty.

RISK
see also Soldiers.

Tout homme a droit de risquer sa propre vie
pour la conserver.

> J. J. ROUSSEAU:
> *Du Contrat Social (French)*

Every man has the right to risk his own life in
order to save it.

Nam mimima commoda non minimo sectantis
discrimine similes aiebat esse aureo hamo pis-
cantibus, cuius abrupti damnum nulla captura
pensari posset.

> SUETONIUS:
> *Divus Augustus (Latin)*

[Augustus] likened such as grasped at slight
gains with no slight risk, to those who fished
with a golden hook, the loss of which, if it were
carried off, could not be made good by any
catch.

RIVERS
see also Spring, Streams, Summer.

Les rivières sont des chemins qui marchent.

> BLAISE PASCAL:
> *Pensées, Adversaria (French)*

Rivers are moving roads.

Quis color ille vadis, seras cum propulit umbras
Hesperus, et viridi perfundit monte Mosellam!
Tota natant crispis iuga motibus et tremit
absens
Pampinus, et vitreis vindemia turget in undis.

> AUSONIUS:
> *Mosella (Latin)*

What a glow was on the shallows, when the
shades of evening fell,
And the verdure of the mountain bathed the
breast of fair Moselle!
In the glassy stream reflected, float the hills in
wavy line,
Swells the vintage, sways the trembling tendril
of the absent vine.

> (*tr.* Sir John Sandys)

Despues de años mil vuelve el rio a su cubil.

> SPANISH PROVERB

After a thousand years the river returns to its
original bed.

ROME
see also Antiquity.

Rome est une ville où il y a plus de sbires que de
citadins, plus de moines que de sbires.

> FRENCH POPULAR SAYING

Rome is a city where there are more cops than
citizens, and more priests than cops.

Je trouve Rome plus vaillante avant qu'elle feuste sçavante.

> MONTAIGNE:
> *Essays (French)*

I think Rome was more spirited before it became so learned.

Rome n'est plus dans Rome, elle est toute où je suis.

> PIERRE CORNEILLE:
> *Sertorius (French)*

Rome is no longer just in Rome; it is there wherever I am!

Salve, dea Roma! Chi diconósceti
Cerchiato ha il senno di fredda tenebra,
E a lui nel reo cuore germoglia,
Torpida la selva di barbarie.

> GIOSUE CARDUCCI:
> *Nell' Annuale della Fondazione di Roma (Italian)*

Hail, Rome divine! Let the cold mists of night enclose the man who knows thee not! Let a crop of barbarous weeds spring up in his base heart!

Optima nutricum nostris lupa Martia rebus
Qualia creverunt moenia lacte tuo!

> PROPERTIUS:
> *Elegies (Latin)*

O, she-wolf of Mars, best of nurses for us, what a city grew from your milk!

Quamdiu stabit Coliseus, stabit et Roma; quando cadet Coliseus, cadet et Roma; quando cadet Roma, cadet et mundus.

> Roman prophecy recorded by
> the Venerable Bede *(Latin)*

While the Coliseum stands, Rome shall stand; when it falls, Rome shall fall and, with it, the whole world.
(While stands the Coliseum, Rome shall stand;
When falls the Coliseum, Rome shall fall;
And when Rome falls – the world.

> Byron: *Childe Harold's Pilgrimage*)

Roma vorax hominum, domat ardua colla virorum,

Roma ferax febrium, necis est uberrima frugum,
Romanae febres stabili sunt jure fideles.

> ST. PETER DAMIANI:
> *Fragment (Latin)*

Rome devours men; she tames the stiff necks of men; she abounds in torments. Rome is most fruitful of the excellence of men now dead. Roman strife is founded on stable law.

Ut iure sit gloriatus marmoream se relinquere, quam latericiam accepisset.

> SUETONIUS:
> *Divus Augustus (Latin)*

[Augustus] could justly boast he had found [Rome] built of brick, and he had left it in marble.

Par tibi, Roma, nihil, cum sis prope tota ruina;
Quam magni fueras integra, fracta doces.

> RADULFUS TORTARIUS:
> *Ruinae Romae* (opening lines) *(Latin)*

Nothing is equal, Rome, to you, even when you are nearly all ruins. It is they who show how great you were when you were whole.

Buscas en Roma a Roma ¡oh peregrino!
Y en Roma misma a Roma no la hallas:
Cadáver son las que ostentó murallas,
Y, tumba de sí propio, el Aventino.

> FRANCISCO DE QUEVEDO Y VILLEGAS:
> *A Roma Sepultada en sus Ruinas (Spanish)*

Pilgrim! you seek Rome in Rome, but you cannot find her: the famous walls are a corpse, and the Aventine is its own tomb.

ROSES
see also Misfortune, Spring.

Mignonne, allons voir si la rose,
Qui ce matin avait déclose
Sa robe de pourpre au soleil,
A point perdu cette vesprée
Les plis de sa robe pourprée,
Et son teint au vôtre pareil

> PIERRE DE RONSARD:
> *A Cassandre (French)*

Dearest, let us go to see if the rose which this morning unfolded its crimson robe to the sun has already this evening lost the folds of its robe, and its blush so like your own.

ROYAL PREROGATIVE
see also Kings.

De par le roi, défense à Dieu
De plus fréquenter en ce lieu.

> Eighteenth-century notice at St. Médard
> Cemetery (quoted in Voltaire:
> *Philosophical Dictionary: Convulsions*) *(French)*

By order of the King, God is forbidden to
frequent this place.

Toute justice émane du Roy.
Si veut le Roy, veut la loi.
Une foi, une loi, un Roy.

> LUDWIG II OF BAVARIA:
> *Diary*, 1869 *(French)*

All justice derives from the King. If it is the wish
of the King, that is the law. One faith, one law,
one King!

RUMOUR
see also Calumny, Reputation.

Il y a un démon qui met des ailes a certaines
nouvelles et qui les lâche comme des aigles dans
l'espace.

> ALEXANDRE DUMAS:
> *La Dame de Monsoreau (French)*

There is a demon who puts wings on certain
tales and launches them like eagles out into
space.

Alla takhumoron
Gunaikogēruton ollutai kleos

> AESCHYLUS:
> *Agamemnon (Greek)*

Rumours spread by women have short lives.

Nullam ego rem citiorem apud homines esse
quam famam reor.

> PLAUTUS:
> *Fragment (Latin)*

I know nothing swifter in life than the voice of
rumour.

S

SACRIFICE
see also Soldiers.

Jō jehi lāgi sahai tapa jōgū;
Sō tehi kē saṁga mānai bhōgū

MALIK MUHAMMAD JĀYASĪ:
Padumāvatī (Avadhi)

He who endures penance and hardships for
another delights in that person's company.

Mex aim o il estre mendis
Et vivre d'erbes et de glan,
Qu'avoir le reigne au roi Otran.

BÉROUL:
Le Roman de Tristan (French)

Rather would I be a beggar and live on herbs
and acorns [with Iseut] than have Otran's
kingdom.

SADNESS
see also Grief, Love, Sorrow.

La tristesse est un état de péché.

ANDRÉ GIDE:
La Porte Étroite (French)

Sadness is a state of sin.

Sur les ailes du Temps la tristesse s'envole.

JEAN DE LA FONTAINE:
La Jeune Veuve (French)

Sadness flies away on the wings of time.

Ainsi, parfois, quand l'âme est triste, nos
pensées
S'envolent un moment sur leurs ailes blessées,
Puis retombent soudain.

VICTOR HUGO:
Tristesse d'Olympio (French)

Thus sometimes, when we are sad, our thoughts
fly away for a moment on their damaged wings,
and as suddenly return.

Ah! sous une feinte allégresse
Ne nous cache pas ta douleur!
Tu plais autant par ta tristesse
Que par ton sourire enchanteur

GÉRARD DE NERVAL:
Romance (French)

Do not conceal your sadness from us under a
pretended gaiety! You please as much by your
sorrow as by your enchanting smile.

Tristitia est hominis a majore ad minorem perfectionem.

SPINOZA:
Ethics (Latin)

In mankind sadness ranges from great to minor
perfection.

Dolendi voluptas.

LATIN PHRASE

The luxury of grief.

SAILORS
see also Fishermen, Sea.

Eh bien, tous ces marins – matelots, capitaines,
Dans leur grand Océan à jamais engloutis,
Partis insoucieux pour leurs courses lointaines,
Sont morts absolument comme ils étaient
partis –
Allons! c'est leur métier, ils sont morts dans
leurs bottes!

TRISTAN CORBIÈRE:
La Fin (French)

Ah well, all these sailors – seamen, captains,
engulfed for ever in their Ocean – embarked
carefree for their distant voyages, but were completely dead from the movement they set out –
Come! it's their trade! They died with their
boots on!

SAMPLING
see also Judgment.

Arkei d' ha mellēsis

GREEK PROVERB

A taste is enough (*i.e.* one can draw one's own
conclusions concerning the whole).

SANCTUARY

Tes yeux cherchent en vain, tu ne peux
échapper,
Et Dieu de toutes parts a su t'envelopper.
JEAN RACINE:
Athalie (French)

Your gaze searches in vain! you cannot escape,
and God encircles you on every side (when
Athalie has at last reached the sanctuary of the
Temple).

Ou toi mēpote s' ek tōnd' hedranōn, ō geron,
akonta tis axei
SOPHOCLES:
Oedipus Coloneus (Greek)

Never shall anyone drive you from this resting-
place against your will.

Kreisson de purgou bōmos, arrekton sakos
AESCHYLUS:
The Suppliant Maidens (Greek)

An altar is a sure shield, stronger than a fortress.

SCIENCE
see also Language, Poets and poetry.

Répertoire de la nature et du ciel.
STÉPHANE MALLARMÉ:
Le Mystère dans les Lettres (French)

A repertory of nature and the heavens.

Mon cher enfant, j'ai tant aimé les sciences dans
ma vie que cela me fait battre le coeur.
JEAN-BAPTISTE BIOT:
(to the young Pasteur when he showed
him his first great discovery). *(French)*

My dear chap, I have loved science so much
during my life that this makes my heart pound.

SEA
see also Fishermen, Sailors, Waves.

Et la mer s'apaisait comme une urne écumante
Qui s'abaisse au moment où le foyer pâlit,
Et, retirant du bord sa vague encore fumante,
Comme pour s'endormir, rentrait dans son
grand lit.
ALPHONSE DE LAMARTINE:
L'Occident (French)

And the sea calmed down, just as a foaming urn
subsides when the hearth cools, and withdrew
its waves still smoking from the shore, as if to
drop off to sleep, taking once again to its great
bed.

Oh! combien de marins, combien de capitaines
Qui sont partis joyeux pour des courses
lointaines,
Dans ce morne horizon se sont évanouis!
VICTOR HUGO:
Océano Nox (French)

How many sailors, how many captains have
happily set sail on distant voyages, and have
perished beyond that gloomy horizon!

La mer n'est pas comme une chose, ni comme
une montagne. C'est une personne vivante, que
j'aime, qui me parle et à qui je parle. Elle a des
sentiments, des passions, elle sait rire et se
mettre en colère. Quelquefois elle ne m'aime
pas. Elle n'aime personne.
J. M. G. LE CLÉZIO:
L'Inconnu sur la Terre (French)

The sea is not like a thing or a mountain. It is a
living person whom I love; who speaks to me
and to whom I speak. It has feelings, passions,
and knows how to laugh and to get angry.
Sometimes it does not love me; it does not love
anyone.

Thalassa kluzei panta tanthrōpōn kaka
EURIPIDES:
Iphigeneia in Tauris (Greek)

The sea washes away all mortal evils.

Pasa thalassa thalassa
ANTIPATER OF THESSALONICA:
Epigrams (Greek)

Every part of the sea is dangerous.

Navigare necesse est,
Vivere non est necesse.
HANSEATIC PROVERB *(Latin)*

Navigation is essential; life is not.

Avidum mare est exitio nautis.
LATIN PROVERB

The greedy sea means death to sailors.

O litus vita mihi dulcius, O mare! felix
Cui licet ad terras ire subinde meas!

PETRONIUS:
Satyricon (Latin)

O sea shore sweeter to me than life! O sea, happy
am I who may come at last to go to my own
lands!

Faħħar il-baħar u ibqa' fuq l-art!

MALTESE PROVERB

Praise the sea and remain on dry land!

Mar pavoroso, mar tenebroso,
Profundo mar!
Furias eternas, furias eternas,
Nas ondas negras ha cavernas
Com monstros verdes a ulular.

ABILIO GUERRA JUNQUEIRO:
Fallam Casebres de Pescadores (Portuguese)

O sea of dread, darkened by gloom, fathomless
sea! Rave on endlessly! In the caves of your
black waters green monsters howl eternally!

Quem as haverá de passar
Senão quem a vontade pôs
Onde a não póde tirar?

BERNARDIM RIBEIRO:
Romance (Portuguese)

Who shall cross the sea but he whose heart is set
on a course from which he cannot escape?

Pevuchest' est' v morskikh volnakh,
Garmoniya v stikhiïnÿkh sporakh

FËDOR TYUTCHEV:
There is a Melody (Russian)

There is a melody in the waves of the sea, and
harmony in the strife of the elements.

Kak khorosho tÿ, o more nochnoe, –
Zdes' luchezarno, tam sizo-temno . . .
V lunnom siyanii, slovno zhivoe,
Khodit, i dÿshit, i bleshchet ono

FËDOR TYUTCHEV:
Kak Khorosho Tÿ (Russian)

How beautiful you are, O night sea – radiant
here, darkly blue-grey there, moving and
breathing and glittering in the moonlight, just
like a living creature.

Iz tuchi s tucheï v bezumnom spore
Roditsya shkval, –
Pod nim zÿbuchiï v pustÿnnom more
Vskipaet val

INNOKENTY ANNENSKY:
Decrescendo (Russian)

A squall blows up from the mad struggle
between the clouds and, below on the open
sea, great billows develop.

Olas gigantes que os rompéis bramando
En las playas desiertas y remotas,
Envuelto entre las sábanas de espuma,
¡Llevadme con vosotros!

GUSTAVO ADOLFO BÉCQUER:
Rimas (Spanish)

Giant waves, breaking noisily on far-off desert
shores, wrapped in sheets of foam, take me with
you!

¡Qué semejante
El viaje del mar al de la muerte,
Al de la eterna vida!

JUAN RAMÓN JIMÉNEZ:
Nocturno Soñado (Spanish)

How similar is an ocean voyage to the voyage of
death, the voyage of eternal life!

SECOND-BEST
see also Compromise, Priorities.

La poule ne doit point chanter devant le coq.

FRENCH PROVERB

The hen should not crow when the cock is there.

Tel brille au second rang qui s'éclipse au
premier.

VOLTAIRE:
La Henriade (French)

He who effaces himself in the first rank, may well
shine in the second.

Ich aber soll zum Meissel mich erniedern,
Wo ich der Künstler könnte sein?

J. C. F. VON SCHILLER:
Werke (German)

Why should I demean myself to be a chisel,
when I could be the artist?

Vertentem sese frustra sectabere canthum,
Cum rota posterior curras et in axe secundo.

PERSIUS:
Satires (Latin)

Thou, like the hindmost chariot-wheels, art
curst
Still to be near, but ne'er to be the first.

(*tr.* Dryden)

SECRETS

Les véritables secrets d'un être lui sont plus
secrets qu'ils ne le sont à autrui.

PAUL VALÉRY:
Choses Tues (French)

A man's genuine secrets are more secret to him
than to anyone else.

Rien ne pèse tant qu'un secret.

JEAN DE LA FONTAINE:
Les Femmes et le Secret (French)

Nothing is harder to keep than a secret (*lit.*
nothing weighs more than a secret).

L'oiseau cache son nid, nous cachons nos
amours.

VICTOR HUGO:
Les Contemplations: L'Hirondelle

The bird hides its nest, we hide our loves.

Secreta tegatur.

AUSONIUS:
Opuscala (Latin)

Let secret things remain hidden.

Los secretos ni oirlos ni decirlos.

SPANISH PROVERB

Don't listen to secrets – and don't tell them!

SELF-CONTROL

Ce serait avoir gagné beaucoup dans la vie que
de savoir rester toujours parfaitement naturel et
sincère avec soi-même, de ne croire aimer que ce
qu'on aime véritablement, et de ne pas pro-
longer par amour-propre et par émulation vaine
des passions déjà expirées.

CHARLES AUGUSTIN SAINTE-BEUVE:
Causeries du Lundi (French)

We gain a great deal in life if we learn how to
remain perfectly natural and sincere towards
ourselves, and only to love what we truly love,
and not – out of pride and false emulation – to
prolong passions already dead.

De triste coeur chanter joyeusement.

CHRISTINE DE PISAN:
Fragment (French)

Though sad at heart, to sing joyfully.

Je suis maître de moi comme de l'univers.

PIERRE CORNEILLE:
Cinna (French)

I am master of myself as well as of the universe!

Von der Gewalt, die alle Wesen bindet
Befreit der Mensch sich, der sich überwindet.

J. W. VON GOETHE:
Die Geheimnisse (German)

The man who masters himself is delivered from
the force that binds all creatures.

Zuweilen muss Man auch einem Blick in sich
selbst thun.

ADALBERT STIFTER:
Der Nachsommer (German)

From time to time we must look inside ourselves.

Si ipse animum pepulit, dum vivat victor
victorum cluet.

PLAUTUS:
Trinummus (Latin)

The man who masters his own soul will for ever
be called conqueror of conquerors.

Qui animum vincunt, quam quos animus,
semper probiores cluent.

PLAUTUS:
Trinummus (Latin)

He who conquers his feelings, rather than let
himself be conquered by them, will always be
known as a man of probity.

Spernere mundum, spernere neminem,
Spernere se ipsum, spernere se sperni.

ST. BERNARD:
(adopted as a motto by St. Philip Neri) *(Latin)*

Despise the world, despise nobody, despise
yourself, despise being despised!

SELF-DECEPTION
see also Deceit, Praise, Right and wrong.

Chacun se trompe ici-bas.
On voit courir après l'ombre
Tant de fous.
> JEAN DE LA FONTAINE:
> *Le Chien qui Lâche sa Proie pour l'Ombre (French)*

In this world, everyone deceives himself – we see so many fools chasing after shadows.

Ich weiss nicht, was in mir das andere belügt.
> GEORG BÜCHNER:
> *Dantons Tod (German)*

I cannot tell what part of me deceives the other.

To gar exapatasthai auton huph' autou pantōn khalepōtaton
> PLATO:
> *Cratylus (Greek)*

The worst of all deceptions is self-deception.

Ipsi sibi somnia fingunt.
> VIRGIL:
> *Eclogues (Latin)*

They invent their own dreams.

SELF-HELP
see also Self-knowledge.

Aide-toi, le Ciel t'aidera.
> JEAN DE LA FONTAINE:
> *Le Chartier Embourbé (French)*

Heaven helps those who help themselves.

Hilf dir selbst, so hilft dir Gott.
> GERMAN PROVERB

God helps those who help themselves.

Ein rechter Schütze hilft sich selbst.
> J. C. F. VON SCHILLER:
> *Wilhelm Tell (German)*

An accurate marksman helps himself.

Die Axt im Haus erspart den Zimmermann.
> J. C. F. VON SCHILLER:
> *Wilhelm Tell (German)*

An axe at home saves hiring a carpenter.

Dei facientes adiuvant.
> MARCUS TERENTIUS VARRO:
> *De Re Rustica (Latin)*

The gods help those who help themselves.

Ne quid expectes amicos, quod tute agere possies.
> QUINTUS ENNIUS:
> *Saturae* quoted in
> Aulus Gellius: *Attic Nights) (Latin)*

Don't ask of your friends what you yourself can do.

Al que madruga, Dios le ayuda.
> SPANISH PROVERB

God helps those who help themselves (*lit.* God helps those who rise betimes).

SELF-INDULGENCE

Proxumum quod sit bono quodque a malo longissume,
Id volo.
> PLAUTUS:
> *Captivi (Latin)*

I seek the utmost pleasure and the least pain.

SELF-INTEREST
see also Gratitude, Relations.

Nostre propre interest est encore un merveilleux instrument pour nous crever les yeux agréablement.
> BLAISE PASCAL:
> *Pensées (French)*

Our own interests are still a wonderful instrument for dazzling our eyes in a most pleasant manner.

On veut toujours son bien, mais on ne le voit pas toujours.
> J. J. ROUSSEAU:
> *Du Contrat Social (French)*

We always want our own well-being, but we do not always see what that is.

Jeder glaubt,
Es sei auch schicklich, was ihm nützlich ist.
J. W. VON GOETHE:
Tasso (German)

Everyone believes that what suits him is the
right thing to do.

Zweckmässigkeit gewährt uns unter allen Ums-
tänden Vergnügen, sie beziehe sich entweder
gar nicht auf das Sittliche, öder sie widerstreite
demselben. Wir geniessen dieses Vergnügen
rein, so lange wir uns keines sittlichen Zwecks
errinern, dem dadurch widersprochen wird.
J. C. F. VON SCHILLER:
Werke (German)

Expediency always pleases us, whether it bears
no relationship to morality or is in direct conflict
with it. We can unreservedly enjoy this satisfaction as long as we are not reminded of any moral
purpose which might be at variance with it.

Hercle, mihi tecum cavendum est!
PLAUTUS:
Mostellaria (Latin)

Heavens, with you I must look after myself!

Canis caninam non est.
LATIN PROVERB

Dog won't eat dog.

Nam fere maxima pars morem hunc homines
habent: quod sibi volunt,
Dum id impetrant, boni sunt;
Sed id ubi iam penes sese habent,
Ex bonis pessimi ed fraudulentissimi
Fiunt.
PLAUTUS:
Captivi (Latin)

Usually most people are very good as long as
they need something from you. Once they have
it, however, they turn into frauds and wretches
of the worst kind.

Tunica propior palliost.
LATIN PROVERB
(quoted in Plautus: *Trinummus*) *(Latin)*

Your shirt is closer than your coat.

Gana tiene de coles quien besa al hortelano.
SPANISH PROVERB

She who kisses the market-gardener has a liking
for cabbages.

SELF-KNOWLEDGE
see also Personality, Self-control, Wisdom.

Il faut entrer en soi-même armé jusqu'aux
dents.
PAUL VALÉRY:
Quelques Pensées de Monsieur Teste (French)

To penetrate one's own being, one must go
armed to the teeth.

Se connaître n'est pas s'amender.
PAUL VALÉRY:
Choses Tues (French)

Knowing oneself does not necessarily imply
improving oneself.

Que l'homme maintenant s'estime son prix.
BLAISE PASCAL:
Pensées (French)

Let each man now establish his own worth.

Ne t'attends qu'à toi seul!
JEAN DE LA FONTAINE:
*L'Alouette et ses Petits, avec le Maître d'un Champ
(French)*

Never depend on anyone except yourself!

Où est le temps, miroir, où je pouvais me regarder des heures en bâillant? Où sont les hommes
qui me regardaient me regarder sans même oser
respirer? Maintenant on est au boulot.
JEAN GENET:
Les Paravents (French)

Mirror! what has happened to the time when I
could look at myself for hours? Where are the
men who watched me looking at myself, without
daring to breathe? Now that's all over!

Il s'en faut bien que nous ne connaissions toutes
nos volontés.
FRANÇOIS, DUC DE LA ROCHEFOUCAULD:
Maximes (French)

Its just as well that we do not know all our
whims and fancies.

Wohin wir nur sehen, so sehen wir bloss uns.
GEORG CHRISTOPH LICHTENBERG:
Aphorismen (German)

Wherever we look, we can see ourselves all too clearly.

Erkenne dich selbst!
RICHARD WAGNER
(title of one of his essays) *(German)*

Know thyself!

Was einem angehört, wird man nicht los, und wenn man es wegwürfe.
J. W. VON GOETHE:
Maximen und Reflexionen (German)

If something really belongs to you, you cannot lose it even if you throw it away.

Gnōthi seauton
GREEK PROVERB
(attributed to Chilon)

Know yourself!

To gar esleussein oikeia pathē,
Mēdenos allou parapraxantos,
Megalas odunas hupoteinei
SOPHOCLES:
Ajax (Greek)

What fate can be worse than to know we have no-one but ourselves to blame for our misfortunes!

E quelle difese solamente sono buone, sono certe, sono durabili, che dependono da te proprio e dalla virtú tua.
NICCOLÒ MACHIAVELLI:
The Prince (Italian)

The only defences that are good, certain, and lasting, are those that depend on yourself alone and on your own ability.

Noscenda est mensura sui.
JUVENAL:
Satires (Latin)

A man must know his own limitations.

Primum argumentum compositae menti existimo posse consistere et secum morari.
SENECA
Epistles (Latin)

I believe that the prime indication of a well-ordered mind is a man's ability to remain in one place and to linger in his own company.

Ipse mihi theatrum.
LATIN EXPRESSION

Myself my own entertainment.

Rarum est enim ut satis se quisque vereatur.
QUINTILIAN:
Institutiones Oratoriae (Latin)

We seldom respect ourselves enough.

Magister mihi exercitor animus nunc est.
PLAUTUS:
Trinummus (Latin)

This mind of mine is a trainer that certainly works me hard.

Nej, i dybet maa jeg ned;
Der er fred fra evighed.
HENRIK IBSEN:
The Miner (Norwegian)

No! in the depths, down I must bore. There is peace for eternity.

Principio es de corregirse el conocerse.
SPANISH PROVERB

Self-knowledge is the beginning of self-improvement.

Más sabe el necio en su casa, que el sabio en la ajena.
SPANISH PROVERB

The ignorant man in his own house knows more than the educated man in someone else's house.

SELFLESSNESS

Ātmany asati cātmīyaṁ kuta eva bhaviṣyati
Nirmamo nirahaṅkāraḥ sámād manīnayoh
Mādhyamika-kārikā (Pali)

When the idea of 'self' disappears, the notion of

mine' also vanishes, and we free ourselves from
the idea of 'I' and 'mine'.

SELF-SACRIFICE

Qui veut conserver sa vie aux dépens des autres
doit la donner aussi pour eux quand il faut.

J. J. ROUSSEAU:
Du Contrat Social (French)

He who wishes to preserve his life at another's
expense, should also, when necessary, be prepared to give up his own life for another's sake.

Was man aufgibt, hat man nie verloren.

GERMAN PROVERB

That which a man sacrifices is never lost.

Per te gittammo l'anima
Ridenti al fato nero

GIOSUE CARDUCCI:
*Per il Quinto Anniversario della Battaglia di Mentana
(Italian)*

Fearlessly we cast down our lives for thee and
smile at black fate.

Quanto quisque sibi plura negaverit,
Ab dis plura feret.

HORACE:
Odes (Latin)

The more a man denies himself, the more will he
receive from the gods.

SENSATIONS
see also Life, Reason.

Nayana bayana nāsika au sravanā,
Cārihum samga jiu hai avanā.
Jēmvana dēkhā nayana sirānē;
Jībha savāda bughuti rasa mānē.
Nāsika sabai bāsanā pāī;
Sravanahi kā sēvata pahunāī.
Ehi kaham hōi nāda tēm pōkhū,
Taba cārihum kara hōi samtōkhū.

MALIK MUHAMMAD JĀYASĪ:
Padumāvatī (Avadhi)

Man is born with eyes, tongue, nose and ears.
The eyes are pleased at the sight of a feast; the
tongue enjoys so many delightful delicacies.
Fragrance pleases the nose. What is the delight
of the ears? – they are nourished by sound. So,
all four gain satisfaction.

Les quatre expressions de la matière par rapport
à l'homme, le son, la couleur, le parfum, la
forme, ont une même origine.

HONORÉ DE BALZAC:
Louis Lambert (French)

The four manifestations of matter in relation to
mankind – sound, colour, scent, and form – have
a common origin.

Comme de longs échos qui de loin se confondent
Dans une ténébreuse et profonde unité,
Vastes comme la nuit et comme la clarté,
Les parfums, les couleurs et les sons se
répondent.

CHARLES BAUDELAIRE:
Les Fleurs du Mal (French)

Like the long-drawn-out echoes that merge in
the distance in a sombre and profound unity,
vast as the night and the light, perfumes, colours
and sounds answer each others' calls.

Nihil est in intellectu quod non prius in sensu.

LATIN PROVERB

Nothing reaches the intellect before making its
appearance in the senses.

SERVICE
see also Duty, Fortune.

Hippos me pherei, basileus me trephei

GREEK PROVERB

I am carried by a horse, I am fed by a king.

Makar, hostis eudaimōn
Teletas theōn eidōs
Biotan hagisteuai kai
Thiaseuetai psukhan

EURIPIDES:
The Bacchae (Greek)

Blessed he who fortunately knows the ways of
the gods, serves them faithfully, and is one of
their mystic communion.

Ta men metria kai preponta dei prothumōs
hupourgein tois axiousi mē dusōpoumenous all'
hekontas

PLUTARCH:
Moralia (Greek)

To those who ask for them we must render
reasonable and proper services – not at their
insistence, but because we choose to do so.

Hena hekaston en deoi epitēdeuein tōn peri tēn polin, eis ho autou hē phusis epitēdeiotatē pephukuia eiē

> PLATO:
> *The Republic (Greek)*

Each citizen should play his part in the community according to his individual gifts.

Humanum curare genus quis terminus umquam praescripsit?

> CLAUDIAN:
> *Panegyricus dictus Manlio Theodoro Consuli (Latin)*

What boundary ever set limits to the service of mankind?

SHARING

Koinos Hermēs
or
Hermēs koinos

> GREEK PROVERB

Share and share alike.

SILENCE
see also Language, Night, Personality, the Unmentionable, Women.

Du silence universel on doit présumer le consentement du peuple.

> J. J. ROUSSEAU:
> *Du Contrat Social (French)*

Universal silence must be taken to imply the consent of the people.

Le bel teisir est curteisie.

> FRENCH PROVERB

Fine silence is courteous.

Voulez-vous qu'on croye du bien de vous? N'en dites pas.

> BLAISE PASCAL:
> *Pensées (French)*

If you want others to have a good opinion of you, say nothing.

La bouche garde le silence
Pour écouter parler le coeur.

> ALFRED DE MUSSET:
> *La Nuit de Mai (French)*

The mouth keeps silent to hear the heart speak.

Boshaft wie goldene Rede beginnt diese Nacht
Wir essen die Äpfel der Stummen.

> PAUL CELAN
> *Spät und Tief (German*

Mischievously as golden conversation begin this night. We are eating the apples of silence.

Mē toi khlidēi dokeite mēd' authadiai
Sigan me. Sunnoiai de daptomai kear,
Horōn emauton hōde prouseloumenon

> AESCHYLUS
> *Prometheus Bound (Greek*

If I am silent, do not think me proud o stubborn. My heart is torn at my treatment here

All' aiskhron eipein kai siōpēsai baru

> ARISTOPHANES
> *Lysistrata (Greek*

It is difficult to remain silent, but worse to speak

Dum tacet haec loquitur.

> LATIN PROVER

His very silence speaks volumes.

Est et fideli tuta silentio merces.

> HORACE
> *Odes (Latin*

This is a sure reward for trusty silence.

Ubi non licet tacere, quid cuiquam licet?

> SENECA
> *Oedipus (Latin*

Where silence is not allowed, what then i permissible?

El silencio es salud.

> Motto on the Obelisk in the
> Avenida 9 de Julio, Buenos Aires *(Spanish*

Silence is health.

SIMPLICITY

Tout ce qui est vrai n'est pas naïf, mais tout ce qui est naïf est vrai, mais d'une vérité piquante et rare.

> DENIS DIDEROT
> *Pensées Detachées sur la Peinture (French*

Not everything that is true is simple, but every-

:hing simple is true, but of an unusual and rare
.ruth.

Simplifier, c'est exagérer ce qui reste.

ANDRÉ GIDE:
Journal, 1889–1939 *(French)*

If you simplify one item, you exaggerate the rest.

Ach, dass die Einfalt, dass Unschuld nie
Sich selbst und ihren heil'gen Wert erkennt!

J. W. VON GOETHE:
Faust (German)

Ah, that simplicity and innocence never recognise themselves and their sacred worth!

Naiv muss jedes wahre Genie sein.

J. C. F. VON SCHILLER:
Über Naive und Sentimentalische Dichtung (German)

Every true genius is bound to be naïve.

Gott hat den Menschen einfach gemacht, aber
wie er gewickelt und sich verwickelt ist schwer
zu sagen.

J. W. VON GOETHE:
letter to Charlotte von Stein, 11 December 1778
(German)

God made man simple, but how he changed and
got complicated is hard to say.

Wohl dem! Selig muss ich ihn preisen,
Der in der Stille der ländlichen Flur,
Fern von des Lebens verworrenen Kreisen,
Kindlich liegt an der Brust der Natur.

J. C. F. VON SCHILLER:
Werke (German)

Happy is he, and I call him blessed, who leans
like a child in pastoral fields on nature's breast,
far from the madding crowd.

Aevo rarissima nostro
Simplicitas.

OVID:
Ars Amatoria (Latin)

Simplicity, most rare in our age.

Naturalia non sunt turpia.

LATIN PROVERB

What is natural is not shameful.

Nihil facilius.

LATIN EXPRESSION

Nothing easier.

SIN
see also Death, Evil, Existence, Fallibility, Law, Redemption.

Il n'y a de péché que s'il y a connaissance.

MICHEL SERVIN:
Les Réguliers (French)

Sin only exists where it is recognised.

Le salaire du péché est dans le péché même.

MICHEL SERVIN:
Les Réguliers (French)

The wages of sin are in the sin itself.

Quelle âme est sans défaute!

ARTHUR RIMBAUD:
Faim (French)

What soul is without sin!

J'ai mal lorsque je pense que je suis là devant
Dieu, les mains vides; c'est le péché qui s'est
détourné de moi, pas moi du péché.

LIANE DE POUGY:
Mes Cahiers Bleus (French)

I feel devastated when I think of going before
God with empty hands. It is sin that has turned
away from me, not I from sin.

Die Sünde ist im Gedanken. Ob der Gedanke
That wird, ob ihn der Körper nachspielt, das is
Zufall.

GEORG BÜCHNER:
Dantons Tod (German)

Our transgression is in our thoughts. It is pure
chance if these thoughts become deeds, if they
materialise.

Ut queant laxis   Resonare fibris
Mira gestorum   Famuli tuorum
Solve polluti   Labii reatum
Sancte Johannes
Paul, deacon of the church at Aquilea (c770):
Hymn to John the Baptist (Latin)

Oh holy John, pardon the sins of an unclean lip,
that your servants may pour forth the wonders
of thy works to loosened strings.

Initium est salutis notitia peccati.

> SENECA:
> *Epistles* (citing Epicurus: *Fragment*) *(Latin)*

Knowledge of sin is the beginning of salvation.

Peccantem damnare cave: nam labimur omnes:
Aut sumus, aut fuimus, vel possumus esse quod
hic est.

> An old abbot to his monks
> (quoted in Hearne's *Collections* *(Latin)*

Don't condemn the sinner! We are, or we were,
or we could be as this man is.

Tengo sed de pecados.

> ANTONIO MIRA DE AMESCUA:
> *El Esclavo del Demonio (Spanish)*

I am thirsty for sin.

SINCERITY

La sincérité est une ouverture de coeur.

> FRANÇOIS, DUC DE LA ROCHEFOUCAULD:
> *Réflexions (French)*

Sincerity is an opening of the heart.

Respue quod non es.

> PERSIUS:
> *Satires (Latin)*

Cast off everything that is not yourself.

Multoque melius est e duobus inperfectis rus-
ticitatem sanctam habere quam eloquentiam
peccatricem.

> ST. JEROME:
> *Letter to Nepotian (Latin)*

Of the two imperfections, a holy clumsiness is
much better than a sinful eloquence.

Los sinceros son amados, pero engañados.

> SPANISH PROVERB

Sincere people are loved – but deceived.

SINGING

Qui chante son mal enchante.

> FRENCH PROVERB

Who sings of his woes, enchants.

Qe sembl' oire sec al soleill
Ab son chantar magre dolen,
Q'es chans de vieilla porta-seill.

> GIRAUT DE BORNELH
> *Chansons (French*

He looks like a sun-dried wine-skin, with his thi
doleful singing, a song of an old hag carrying
pail.

Omnibus hoc vitium est cantoribus, inter
amicos
Ut numquam inducant animum cantare rogat
Iniussi numquam desistant.

> HORACE
> *Satires (Latin*

All singers have the same fault – if their friend
want them to sing, they don't want to; but whe
unasked, they never stop!

Skabt for Sang er Nattan sval;
Sangen er vor fælles Sfære.

> HENRIK IBSEN
> *Peer Gynt (Norwegian*

Night's cool hours are meant for nothing; sing
ing is our common sphere.

La peregrina voz y el claro acento
Por la dulce garganta despedido,
Con el suave efecto del oído
Bien pueden suspender cualquier tormento.

> JUAN DE TASIS
> *A una Señora que Cantaba (Spanish*

The wonderful voice and clear modulation com
ing from so sweet a throat, with its sweet effec
on our hearing, could well soothe any anguish.

SINGLE-MINDEDNESS
see also Achievement.

Heis hekastos hen men an epitēdeuma kalō
epitēdeuoi, polla d' ou, all' ei touto epikheiroi
pollōn ephaptomenos pantōn apotunkhanoi an
hōst' einai tou ellogimos

> PLATO
> *The Republic (Greek)*

Each man is capable of doing one thing well. I
he attempts several, he will fail to achieve
distinction in any.

equaquam satis in re una consumere curam.

> HORACE:
> *Satires (Latin)*

is by no means enough to spend all one's care
a a single point.

SKILL

l-ghazzāla tighzil bi-rijl ḥumāra

> ARAB PROVERB

good spinner can spin with a donkey's leg.

SKY

ee also **Autumn, Clouds, Dawn, Evening,
Spring.**

s nuages couraient sur la lune enflammée
mme sur l'incendie on voit fuir la fumée
les bois étaient noirs jusques à l'horizon.

> ALFRED DE VIGNY:
> *La Mort du Loup (French)*

he clouds scudded across the flaming moon,
st as one sees the smoke stream forth in a
nflagration, and the woods were black as far
one could see to the horizon.

ellis fulgentibus apta caeli domus.

> LUCRETIUS:
> *De Rerum Natura (Latin)*

he abode of heaven studded with glittering
ars.

uid potest esse tam apertum, tamque pers-
cuum, cum caelum suspeximus caelestiaque
ntemplati sumus, quam aliquod esse numen
aestantissimae mentis quo haec regantur?

> CICERO:
> *De Natura Deorum (Latin)*

ooking up at the heavens and contemplating
e stars, what could be more obvious or clear
an that some power of superior intelligence
ists that controls all these things?

ec frustra signorum obitus speculamur et
tus,
emporibusque parem diversis quattuor
num.

> VIRGIL:
> *Georgics (Latin)*

is not aimless to watch the rising and setting of
the stars, and the year divided into its four equal
seasons.

SLAVES
see also **Freedom, Honour, Hope,
Human nature, Liberty, Might, Mind,
Patriotism.**

En Grèce, il y avait des hommes libres parce
qu'il y avait des esclaves.

> ALBERT CAMUS:
> *Carnets, 1939–42 (French)*

There were free men in Greece because there
were slaves there.

Ei sōma doulon, all' ho nous eleutheros

> GREEK PROVERB

If the body is enslaved, at least the mind is free.

No pierde la esclavitud de su vileza, aunque se
desmienta con la nobleza del sujeto.

> BALTASAR GRACIÁN:
> *Oráculo Manual y Arte de Prudencia (Spanish)*

The nobility of a slave does not wipe out the
disgrace of slavery.

SLEEP
see also **Conscience, Contentment, Idleness,
Lullabies, Night, Oblivion.**

Zuweilen liebt auch klares Auge den Schatten
Und versuchet zu Lust, eh' es die Noth ist, den
Schlaf.

> FRIEDRICH HÖLDERLIN:
> *Brod und Wein (German)*

At times even wide-awake eyes, before need be,
seek the shadows and the pleasure of sleep.

Schlafe, schlafe – überm Weiher
Zieht der Mond die blasse Bahn.
In dein Schloss aus Traum und Wahn
Trittst du nun zu trunkner Feier.

> WILLI FEHSE:
> *Schlaflied (German)*

Sleep! sleep! the moon draws its pale track
across the pond. In the castle of your dreams
and fancies, you are now tripping to the drunken
festival.

Hupnon te lēthēn tōn kath' hēmeran
Kakōn dedōsin

EURIPIDES:
The Bacchae (Greek)

Through sleep, he (*i.e.* Bacchus) grants us oblivion from our daily worries.

En d' ho pankratēs hupnos
Luei pedēsas, oud' aei labōn ekhei

SOPHOCLES:
Ajax (Greek)

Even irresistible sleep cannot hold the sleeper for ever – it must eventually relinquish him.

Perfugium videtur omnium laborum et sollicitudinum esse somnus.

CICERO:
De Divinatione (Latin)

Sleep is regarded as a refuge from every toil and care.

Es la almohada sibila muda, y el dormir sobre los puntos vale más que el desvelarse debajo de ellos.

BALTASAR GRACIÁN:
Oráculo Manual y Arte de Prudencia (Spanish)

The pillow is a silent Sybil, and it is better to sleep on things than to lie awake under their load.

Suäve Sueño, tu, qu'en tardo buelo
Las alas perezosas blandamente
Bates, d'adormideras coronado
Por el puro, adormido i vago cielo,
Ven al 'ultima parte d'Ocidente.

FERNANDO DE HERRERA:
Canción (Spanish)

Sweet sleep! crowned with poppies, beating softly your idle wings in tardy flight through the wide clear sky, to the furthest point of the West.

'Tiemblo ante al sueño lúgubre
Que nunca acaba . . .'
Duerme y no te acongojes
Que hay un mañana;
¡Duerme!

MIGUEL DE UNAMUNO:
Duerme, Alma Mía (Spanish)

'I tremble before the sad sleep that never ends . . .' Go to sleep and do not torture yourself. Morning is certain. Sleep!

SMOKE

Lignus melaina, aiolē puros kasis

AESCHYLU
The Seven against Thebes (Gree

Black smoke, the flickering sister of fire.

SMOKING

Il n'est rien d'égal au tabac; c'est la passion d honnêtes gens, et qui vit sans tabac, n'est pa digne de vivre.

MOLIÈR
Don Juan (Frenc

There's nothing quite like tobacco; it's th favourite of decent fellows, and he who liv without tobacco is not worthy of going on living

Le tabac inspire des sentiments d'honneur et vertu à tous ceux qui en prennent.

MOLIÈR
Don Juan (Frenc

Tobacco inspires sentiments of honour an virtue among all those who take it.

O gioia la nube leggera!

ERMANNO WOLF-FERRAR
Il Segreto di Suzanna (Italia

Oh, what joy that light cloud inspire (Suzanna's expression of delight at the joys smoking).

SNOW
see also Nostalgia, Storms, Summer, Winter.

La grande roseraie blanche de toutes neiges à l ronde.

ST.-JOHN PERSI
Neiges (Frenc

The great white rose-garden of all the surround ing snows.

Der Schnee nicht mehr die Wege verlässt,
Der Winter hängt weiss an den Dornen fest.

anch Ast unter der Last zerbricht,
nd die Berge liegen im Licht.
> MAX DAUTHENDEY:
> *Der Schnee (German)*

he roads are no longer free of snow; winter
angs white on the thorns; many a bough breaks
nder its icy burden, and the mountains glitter
the sunlight.

o blanco está sobre lo verde,
 canta.
ieve que es fina quiere
er alta.
> JORGE GUILLÉN:
> *La Nieve (Spanish)*

he green is carpeted with white, and the snow
ngs. Snow that is fine loves to be deep.

SOCIETY
see also Character, Citizenship, Law, Mankind, Money, the State, Virtue.

a société serait une chose charmante, si on
intéressait les uns aux autres.
> S. R. N. CHAMFORT:
> *Caractères et Anecdotes* (Appendix I) *(French)*

ociety would be a delightful thing if only people
ere interested in each other.

,'ordre social est un droit sacré qui sert de base
tous les autres.
> J. J. ROUSSEAU:
> *Du Contrat Social (French)*

ocial order is a sacred right on which all others
re based.

es grands vendent toujours leur société à la
anité des petits.
> S. R. N. CHAMFORT:
> *Caractères et Anecdotes* (Appendix I) *(French)*

he great always sell their society for the sake of
he vanity of the lower classes.

)ans la nature, toutes les espèces se dévorent;
outes les conditions se dévorent dans la société.
> DENIS DIDEROT:
> *Le Neveu de Rameau (French)*

n nature all species devour each other; all
lasses devour each other in society.

Tout a son vrai loger dans ce monde.
> DENIS DIDEROT:
> *Le Neveu de Rameau (French)*

Everyone has his own true perch in this world.

Il faut recommencer la société humaine.
> S. R. N. CHAMFORT:
> *Caractères et Anecdotes (French)*

We shall have to start human society all over
again.

Man ist nicht bloss ein einzelner Mensch, man
gehört einem Ganzen an, und auf das Ganze
haben wir beständig Rücksicht zu nehmen, wir
sind durchaus abhängig von ihm.
> THEODORE FONTANE:
> *Effi Briest (German)*

Man is not just an individual, he belongs to the
whole; we must always take heed of the whole,
for we are completely dependent on it.

In foro infimo boni homines atque dites
ambulant.
> PLAUTUS:
> *Curculio (Latin)*

The better classes of society and the wealthy
come and go in the lowest part of the market-
place.

No vivimos en época estable. Los fenómenos
sociales, a cual más inesperado y sorprendente,
se suceden sin tregua.
> BENITO PÉREZ GALDÓS:
> *El Amigo Manso (Spanish)*

We no longer live in a stable society. Social
phenomena, each more unexpected and surprising, ceaselessly succeed each other.

SOLDIERS
see also Battles, War.

Soldaten sehn sich alle gleich
Lebendig und als Leich.
> WOLF BIERMANN:
> *Soldat, Soldat (German)*

Dead or alive, soldiers are all alike.

Der Soldat allein ist der freie Mann.
> J. C. F. VON SCHILLER:
> *Wallensteins Lager (German)*

The only free man is a soldier.

Non enim possunt militares pueri dauco exducier.
> PLAUTUS:
> *Truculentus (Latin)*

You can't rear soldiers' sons on carrots.

Hvo intet ejer, lettvindt vover.
Naar man af Verden raader knappt
Den Stribe Muld man skygger over,
Man till Kanonmad er som skabt.
> HENRIK IBSEN:
> *Peer Gynt (Norwegian)*

The man who possesses nothing can light-heartedly take chances. Those whose all is no more than the scrap of earth they stand on, are the fittest by far for sacrifice and cannon-fodder.

SOLITUDE
see also Contentment, Grief, Marriage, Night, Old age, Pride.

Jeg er egentlig bedst
Når jeg er helt alene.
> BENNY ANDERSEN:
> *Godhed (Danish)*

I am actually at my best when I'm all alone.

La solitude est un produit qu'on fait partout.
> PAUL VALÉRY:
> *Lust (French)*

Solitude is a product that is made everywhere.

La gloire ne sait point ma demeure ignorée,
Et je chante tout seul ma chanson éplorée,
Qui n'a charmes que pour moi.
> CHARLES BRUGNOT:
> *Ode (French)*

Glory remains unaware of my neglected dwelling where alone I sing my tearful song which has charms only for me.

Wie gern er in einer Welt wäre, in der er nicht existiert.
> ELIAS CANETTI
> *Aufzeichnungen*, 1951 *(German*

How happy one would be in a world in which one did not exist!

Ich schaue auf und schau hinein
Ins stille Mondesangesicht
Und senk das Haupt und bin allein
Wozu denn Nacht und Sang?
> RUDOLF H. BINDING
> *Allein (German*

I look up and I look into the peaceful face of the moon; and sink my head and am alone. What price then night and song!

Deduke men a selanna
Kai Plēiades, mesai de
Nuktes para d' erkhet' ōra,
Egō de mona kateudō
> SAPPHO
> *Poems (Greek*

The moon and the Pleiades have set. It is midnight, time passes, and I lie alone.

Wabinureba
Mi wo uki-gusa no
Ne wo taete
Sasu mizu araba
Inan to zo omou
> ONO NO KOMACHI
> *Waga (Japanese*

How sad it is to be rootless, floating on the water to whose first flurry I may well yield.

Negeki tsutsu litori nuru yo-no akuru ma-va,
Ika-ni lisasiki mono-to ka-va siru
> SHŪ-I-SHŪ
> *(Japanese*

Do you know how long it is from nightfall till dawn when sighs prevent your sleep as you lie alone?

Só vae e sem companhia,
Que os seus fôra elle deixar;

Que quem não leva descanso
Descansa em só caminhar.

BERNARDIM RIBEIRO:
Romance (Portuguese)

Alone, far from his friends, he goes without company; for he who finds no solace, takes comfort in walking alone.

SOPHISTRY

Poteron ēdē touto saphes, hoti tōn goētōn esti tis, mimētēs ōn tōn ontōn

PLATO:
The Sophist (Greek)

[The sophist] is a kind of juggler, an imitator of reality.

SORROW
see also Adversity, Consolation, Disillusion, Grief, Joy, Life, Love, Misfortune, Music, Poets and poetry, Sadness, Suffering, Tears, Time, Wine, Worry.

Bolest, jako velký pták,
na mém srdci těžce sedí.
Nehýbe se.

OTAKAR THEER:
Všemu na Vzdory (Czech)

Sorrow, like a mighty bird, weighs upon my heart and moves not.

La douleur qui se tait n'en est que plus funeste.

RACINE:
Andromaque (French)

Silent sorrow is only the more profound.

Considerez qu'on doute, mon Dieu, quand on souffre,
Que l'oeil qui pleure trop finit par s'aveugler,
Qu'un être que son deuil plonge au plus noir du gouffre.
Quand il ne vous voît plus, ne peut vous contempler.

VICTOR HUGO:
A Villequier (French)

Just think, God, that some people do not realise, in their sorrow that eyes which weep too much become blind, that the mourner, plunged into the black depths of grief, loses sight of you and can no longer contemplate you.

Je t'adore à l'égal de la voûte nocturne,
O vase de tristesse, ô grande taciturne.

CHARLES BAUDELAIRE:
Spleen et Idéal (French)

I adore you, vessel of sorrow, no less than night's vault, O deeply silent one!

La seule chose qui nous console de nos misères est le divertissement, et cependant c'est la plus grande de nos misères, car c'est cela qui nous empêche principalement de songer à nous, et qui nous fait perdre insensiblement.

BLAISE PASCAL:
Pensées (French)

The only thing that consoles us in our misery is distraction; but that is the greatest of our miseries for it prevents us from thinking out our affairs and, imperceptibly, makes us losers.

Deinon men to palai keimenon ēdē kakon epegeirein

SOPHOCLES:
Oedipus Coloneus (Greek)

To revive a forgotten sorrow is cruel.

Khronos malaxei, nun d' eth' hēbai soi kakon

EURIPIDES:
Alcestis (Greek)

Time will cure you, but now is your grief still young.

Pas d' odunēros bios anthrōpōn,
Kouk' esti ponōn anapausis

EURIPIDES:
Hippolytus (Greek)

The life of mankind is full of woe, with never a moment's grace.

Ti dēt' an algoiēs ep' exeirgasmenois?

SOPHOCLES:
Ajax (Greek)

There is no sense in crying over spilt milk (*lit.* why bewail what is done and cannot be recalled?)

All' ou to poiein, ō beltiste, klaiein kai dakruein,
to de pauein lupoumenous kai klaiontas semnon
estin

PLUTARCH:
Moralia (Greek)

What is admirable is not making men sorrow
and weep, but putting an end to their troubles.

Sotto

Ogni clima, ogni ciel, si chiamo indarno
Felicità, vive tristezza e regna.

GIACOMO LEOPARDI:
Al Conte Carlo Pepoli (Italian)

Under all skies, all weathers, man's happiness
lies always elsewhere; sorrow lives and reigns.

Che sicura non è la sventura,
Ma sicuro pur troppo e il dolor.

PIETRO METASTASIO:
Il Trionfo di Clelia (Italian)

No matter how certain and sure the adventure,
even more sure and certain will be the sorrow.

Infandum, regina, jubes renovare dolorem.

VIRGIL:
Aeneid (Latin)

Too cruel, lady, is the pain you bid me thus
revive again.

Flebunt amici et bene noti mortem meam,
Nam populus in me vivo lacrimavit satis.

Epitaph for the tragedian Pupius
(Latin)

My friends and important men will weep for my
death; for my audiences have shed enough tears
in my lifetime.

Sabba dukkha, sabba anatta, sabba anikka.

BUDDHA:
(Pali)

Sorrow is everywhere; in man there is no abiding
entity, in things no abiding reality.

THE SOUL

**see also Beauty, Conscience, Honour,
Humility, Liberty, Life, Love, Mankind,
Morals and morality, Music, Nature,
Old age, Self-control, Sympathy,
Thought and thinking, Truth,
Understanding, Worry.**

Ziel van mijn ziel! Leven, dat in mij woont,
Veelnamige Mysterie, die ik noem
Mijn Ik, mijn Zelf, mijn Wezen.

ALBERT VERWEY
Cor Cordium (Dutch)

Soul of my soul! Life that dwells within me
Many-named mystery that I name my ego, my
self, my being!

L'âme doit se raidir plus elle est menacée,
Et contre la fortune aller tête baissée,
La choquer hardiment, et, sans craindre la
mort,
Se presenter de front à son plus rude effort.

PIERRE CORNEILLE
Médée (French)

The more it is threatened, the soul must brace
itself and breast the storm with head down
battling with it and, without fear of death, face
boldly its worst efforts.

Mon âme, haquenée boiteuse des fatigues du
jour, repose maintenant sur la litière dorée des
songes.

ALOYSIUS BERTRAND:
Gaspard de la Nuit: Le Nain (French)

My soul, a nag lamed by the weariness of life,
rests now on the gilded litter of dreams.

Toute âme est une mélodie, qu'il s'agit de
renouer.

STÉPHANE MALLARMÉ:
Crise de Vers (French)

Every soul is a melody which needs renewing.

L'esprit est toujours la dupe du coeur.

FRANÇOIS, DUC DE LA ROUCHEFOUCAULD:
Maximes (French)

The soul is always the dupe of the heart.

l importe à toute la vie de sçavoir si l'âme est
mortelle ou immortelle.

BLAISE PASCAL:
Pensées (French)

Our very life depends on our knowing whether
he soul is mortal or immortal.

Les revendications de l'âme sur la chair sont
extrêmes. Qu'elles nous tiennent en haleine! Et
qu'un mouvement très fort nous porte à nos
limites, et au-delà de nos limites!

ST.-JOHN PERSE:
Vents (French)

The demands of the soul on the flesh are
extreme. They leave us breathless. So strong an
impulse may fully extend us, and even push us
beyond our limits!

Mon âme est tellement ouverte à toutes sortes
d'idées, de goûts et de sentiments; elle reçoit si
avidement tout ce qui se présente!

XAVIER DE MAISTRE:
Voyage autour de ma Chambre (French)

How open my soul is to all sorts of ideas, tastes
and sentiments; it receives so avidly everything
that is brought to its notice!

Die schöne Seele hat kein anderes Verdienst, als
dass sie ist.

J. F. C. VON SCHILLER:
Über Anmut und Würde (German)

A beautiful soul has no other merit than its
existence.

Es ist, dünkt mich, eine sehr unphilosophische
Idee, unsere Seele bloss als ein leidendes Ding
anzusehen; nein, sie leihet auch den Gegens-
tänden.

GEORG CHRISTOPH LICHTENBERG:
Aphorismen (German)

To my way of thinking, it's a very unphilosophi-
cal idea to think of the soul as just suffering – no!
it borrows all the circumstances as well!

Ich bin mein Himmel und meine Hölle.

J. F. C. VON SCHILLER:
Die Räuber (German)

I am my own heaven and hell!

Die Natur gab die Schönheit des Baues, die
Seele gibt die *Schönheit* des Spiels.

J. F. C. VON SCHILLER:
Über Anmut und Würde (German)

We derive beauty of structure from nature, and
beauty of motion from the soul.

Des Menschen Seele
Gleicht dem Wasser:
Vom Himmel kommt es,
Zum Himmel steigt es,
Und wieder nieder
Zur Erde muss es,
Ewig wechselnd.

J. W. VON GOETHE:
Gesang der Geister über den Wassern (German)

The soul of man is like water: it comes from
heaven, and climbs to heaven again. And then
down to earth it must go, eternally changing.

Zwei Seelen wohnen, ach! in meiner Brust!

J. W. VON GOETHE:
Faust (German)

Two souls dwell, alas! within my breast!

Ploutos ho **tēs** psukhēs ploutos monos estin
alēthēs

LUCIAN:
Dialogues (Greek)

The wealth of the soul is the only true wealth.

Kai tēn opsin hautos houtos anēr anapsai phēsin
tēn phusin en hēmin hopōs hupo theas tōn en
ouranōi pheromenōn kai thaumatos aspazesthai
kai agapan ethizomenē to euskhēmon hē psukhē
kai tetagmenon apekhthantai tois anarmostois
kai planētois pathesi kai pheugēi to eikēi kai hōs
etukhen hōs kakias kai plēmmeleias hapasēs
genesin

PLUTARCH:
Moralia (Geeek)

Nature kindled vision in us so that the soul,
beholding the heavenly motions and wondering
at the sight, should grow to accept and cherish
all that moves in stateliness and order, and thus
come to hate discordant or errant passions, and
to shun the aimless and haphazard as sources of
all vice and jarring error.

All' an emoi peithōmetha, nomizontes athana-
ton psukhēn kai dunatēn panta men kaka
anekhesthai, panta de agatha

> PLATO:
> *The Republic (Greek)*

If you will accept my leadership, we shall believe
in the soul's immortality, and that it can withstand the extremes of both good and evil.

Tautēi oun tithemai kai egō pant' andra, hos an
agathos ēi, daimonion einai kai zōnta kai tele-
utēsanta, kai orthōs daimona kaleisthai

> PLATO:
> *Cratylus (Greek)*

Thus I assert that every good man, living or
dead, is of spiritual nature, and is rightly called a
spirit.

Emoi men gar ou phainetai, ho an khrēston ēi
sōma, touto tēi hautou aretēi psukhēn agathēn
poiein, alla tounantion psukhē agathē tēi hautēs
aretēi sōma parekhein hōs hoion te beltiston

> PLATO:
> *The Republic (Greek)*

To my mind, a sound and healthy body does not
necessarily imply a good soul, but a good soul by
its very nature will produce the finest of bodies.

l'animo che vince ogni battaglia,
Se col suo grave corpo non s'accascia.

> DANTE:
> *Inferno (Italian)*

The soul, that conquers in every battle if it is not
weighed down by its heavy body.

Animus facit nobilem.

> SENECA:
> *Epistles (Latin)*

The soul alone raises us to nobility.

Modus quo corporibus adhaerent spiritus com-
prehendi ab hominibus non potest, et hoc tamen
homo est.

> ST. AUGUSTINE:
> *De Civitate Dei (Latin)*

How the spirit is attached to the body is incom-
prehensible to man, and yet this is what man is.

Dicuntur ... tenebrescere animam sapientia
luce privatam.

> ST. AUGUSTINE
> *De Civitate Dei (Latin)*

The soul becomes dark when deprived of th
light of wisdom.

Aliquem habeat animus quem vereatur.

> SENECA
> *Epistles (Latin)*

Let the soul have someone it can reverence.

Es el alma quien padece y no el cuerpo.

> PALACIO VALDÉS
> *Marta y María (Spanish)*

It is the soul, not the body, that suffers.

SPEECH
see also Animals, Oratory, Thought and thinking, Understanding, Words.

To de g' ap' ekeinēs rheuma dia tou stomato
ion meta phthongou keklētai logos?

> PLATO
> *The Sophist (Greek)*

Is not speech the stream flowing from the soul
which the mouth makes audible?

Logos dunastēs megas

> GORGIAS OF LEONTINI
> *Helena (Greek)*

Speech is a mighty ruler.

SPRING
see also Autumn, Birds, Enjoyment.

Le Printemps adorable a perdu son odeur!

> CHARLES BAUDELAIRE
> *Le Goût du Néant (French)*

My beloved spring has lost her scent!

Rivière, fontaine et ruisseau
Portent en livrée jolie
Gouttes d'argent d'orfévrerie;
Chacun s'habille de nouveau.
Le temps a laissé son manteau.

> CHARLES D'ORLÉANS
> *Rondel (French)*

Rivers, fountains and streams have all put on a
sweet livery of jewelled silver drops; each dresses

in new clothes, and the weather has laid aside its winter coat.

Comme on voit sur la branche au mois de mai la rose
En sa belle jeunesse, en sa première fleur,
Rendre le ciel jaloux de sa vive couleur,
Quand l'aube de ses pleurs au point du jour l'arrose.

PIERRE DE RONSARD:
Sonnet pour Marie (French)

Just as one sees in May the rose in all the beauty of its first youth, its first bloom rendering the heavens jealous of its piercing colour, while the dawn of its tears sprinkles its petals at the beginning of the day.

O printemps! petit oiseau de passage, nôtre hôte d'une saison qui chante mélancoliquement dans le coeur du poète et dans la ramée du chêne!

ALOYSIUS BERTRAND:
Gaspard de la Nuit: Encore un Printemps (French)

Spring! little bird of passage, our guest for a season that sings sadly in the poet's heart and in the green oak boughs.

Déjà les beaux jours, la poussière,
Un ciel d'azur et de lumière,
Les murs enflammés, les longs soirs.

GÉRARD DE NERVAL:
Avril (French)

Already we have fine days, dust, blue skies, sunlight, heat-drenched walls, and long evenings.

Autet e bas entre.ls prims fuoills
Son nou de flors e rams li renc,
E no.i ten mut bec ni gola
Nuills auzels, anz brai' e chanta
Cadahus
En son us.

ARNAUT DANIEL:
Canzoni (French)

High and low among the first leaves, the country is new again with flowers and foliage; no bird is silent, but calls and sings, each in his own way.

Botono.ill vim
E l'aussor cim
Son de color

De mainta flor
E verdeia la fuoilla,
E.il chan e.il braill
Son a l'ombraill
Dels auzels per la bruoilla.

ARNAUT DANIEL:
Canzoni (French)

The osiers are in bud; the tops of the trees are tipped with bloom, the leaves are green; and from the depths of the green come bird voice and song.

Can l'erba fresch' e'lh folha par
E la flors boton' el verjan,
E.l rossinhols autet e clar
Leva sa votz e mou so chan,
Joi ai de lui, e joi ai de la flor,
E joi de me e de midons major.

BERNARD DE VENTADOUR:
Canso (French)

When the fresh grass and foliage appear, and bloom covers the branches, and the nightingale lifts up his voice so high and clear and begins his song, I have joy for him, for the flowers, for myself, and best of all, for my lady.

L'airs clars e.l chans dels auzelhs
La flors fresc' e.l fuelha
Que s'espan per los brondelhs.

PEIRE D'ALVERNHE:
L'Airs Clars (French)

Clean air; bird song; fresh flowers; and the leaves unfurling on the twigs.

Lancan folhon bosc e jarric,
E.lh flors pareis e.lh verdura
Pels vergers e pels pratz,
E.lh auzel, c'an estat enic,
Son gai desotz los folhatz,
Autresi.m chant e m'esbaudei
E reflorisc e reverdei
I folh segon ma natura.

BERNARD DE VENTADOUR:
Canso (French)

When the woods and groves are covered with green, and grass and flowers appear in the orchards and meadows, and the birds who were sad are now gay among the foliage, then I also sing and exult, I bloom again and flourish, as is my wont.

Le soleil revient d'exil;
Tous les nids sont en querelle.
L'air est pur, le ciel léger,
Et partout on voit neiger
Des plumes de tourterelle.

FRANÇOIS COPPÉE:
Sérénade du 'Passant' (French)

The sun returns from its exile; all the birds are at
odds with each other. The air is pure, the
heavens clear, and everywhere the turtledoves
shed their snowy plumage.

Nun blühn die Bäume seidenfein
Und Liebe duftet von den Zweigen.
Du musst mir Mutter und Vater sein
Und Frühlingsspiel und Schätzelein
Und ganz mein eigen.

ELSE LASKER-SCHÜLER:
Frühling (German)

Now the silken blossoms on the branches exhale
their fragrance. You must be mother and father
to me, and my love and games of spring, and all
my own.

Zart birgt den Bach entlang der Bast
Die jungen Schellen blau und braun,
Und ein Magd zwickt Ast um Ast
Vom Baum und steckt den Bohnenzaun.

THEODOR KRAMER:
März (German)

Along the stream the bark tenderly conceals the
young blue and brown buds; a young girl twists
off branch after branch and makes them into a
beanframe.

So die bluomen ûz dem grase dringent,
Same si lachen gegen der spilnden sunnen,
In einem meien an dem morgen fruo,
Und diu kleinen vogellin wol singent
Ín ir besten wîse die si kunnen
Waz wünne mac sich dâ gelîchen zuo?

WALTHER VON DER VOGELWEIDE:
Das Bessere Spiel (German)

When the flowers grow through the grass, as if
laughing at the playful sunshine early on a May
morning; and the little birds are singing as
beautifully as they can; with what rapture then
can we compare all this?

Uns will schiere wol gelingen,
Wir suln sîn gemeit,

Tanzen lachen unde singen,
Âne dörperheit.
We wer waere unfrô?
Sît die vogele alsô schône
Singent in ir besten dône,
Tuon wir ouch alsô!

WALTHER VON DER VOGELWEIDE
Maiwunder (German

What we venture in Maytime surely must suc
ceed. Let us dance, laugh and jump then in a
orderly manner. If we were not joyful, hov
would the birds rehearse their best efforts? An
so we should do too!

Gaia de kuaneē khloerēn estepsato poiēn,
Kai phuta thēlēsanta neois ekomēse petēlois

MELEAGER
Garland (Greek

The dark earth garlands herself in green her
bage, and the plants, bursting into leaf, wav
their newborn tresses.

Seinnid crot caille ceól;
con-greinn seól síd slán;
síatair denn do cech dinn,
dé do loch linn lán.

Anonymous tenth-century Irish poet *(Gaelic*

Woodland music plays; the sail swells – perfec
peace; colour blows from every peak, and there
is a drift of haze from the lake.

Marzo è un bambino in fasce che già ride.

ROCCO SCOTELLARO:
Le Viole Sono dei Fanciulli Scalzi (Italian

March is a child in swaddling clothes whc
already laughs.

Hisakata no
Hikari nodokeki
Haru no hi ni
Shizu-gokoro naku
Hana no chiruran

KI NO TOMONORI:
Waga (Japanese

Why does the blossom go on falling without
cease on such a beautiful sun-drenched spring
day?

Ame sosogu
Hanatachibana ni

aze sugite
amahototogisu
umo ni naku nari

FUJIWARA SHUNZEI:
Waga (Japanese)

he fragrant orange blossoms, shimmering in
e rain, are stirred by the breeze, and the first
ngs of the wood-thrush float in clouds among
e hills.

am nec prata rigent nec fluvii strepunt
iberna nive turgidi.

HORACE:
Odes (Latin)

ook! no more are the meadows stiff; no torrents
ome swollen with winter snow.

olvitur acris hiems grata vice veris et Favoni.
HORACE:
Odes (Latin)

Vinter's grip has relaxed, and spring's quicken-
ng winds are welcome back.

ipi-wharau-roa!
awekawea!
e tangi iho nei
arere o Mahuru;
Vhiti mai! whiti mai!

NGA-PUHI:
He Walata-putorino (Maori)

hining cuckoo! Long-tailed cuckoo! Messen-
ers of spring singing down to me! Come here
nd be welcome!

) prado as flores brancas e vermelhas
stá suavemente presentando.

LUIS DE CAMÕES:
Canta Agora, Pastor (Portuguese)

he meadow shows its red and white flowers,
oftly fair.

ara que são, Maio,
antas alegrias,
ois teus longos dias
assam como raio?

FRANCISCO DE SÁ DE MENESES:
O Rio Leça (Portuguese)

) May! What are all your joys for, when your
ng days go by as quick as lightning?

Ulŷbkoĭ yasnoyu priroda
Skvoz' son vstrechaet utro goda:
Sineya bleshchut nebesa.
Eshchë prozrachnÿe, lesa
Kak budto pukhom zeleneyut.

ALEKSANDR SERGEEVICH PUSHKIN:
Eugen Onegin (Russian)

Nature, smiling happily, sleepily greets the
morning of the year. The sky, now blue, glistens,
and the bare woods are covering themselves
with a soft green veil.

Que por mayo era, por mayo,
Cuando hace la calor,
Cuando los trigos encañan
Y están los campos en flor,
Cuando canta la calandria
Y responde el ruiseñor,
Cuando los enamorados
Van a servir al amor.

Romance del Prisionero (Spanish)

It was in the month of May when it gets hot, and
the fields are in flower and the wheat is beginning to ripen, when the lark sings and the nightingale replies, when lovers join in love's service.

Este mesmo órrido suelo
Reverdece, i pomposo su riqueza
Muestra, i del blanco marmol la dureza
Desata de Favonio el tibio buelo.

FERNANDO DE HERRERA:
Soneto (Spanish)

This same vast earth is green again, and proudly
shows its wealth, and the warm westerly winds
come to change the white marble surface of the
earth.

Abril venía, lleno
Todo de flores amarillas:
Amarilla el arroyo,
Amarillo el vallado, la colina,

JUAN RAMÓN JIMÉNEZ:
Primavera Amarilla (Spanish)

April came, full of golden flowers. The streams
were golden, and so were the hills and meadows.

STARS
see also Dawn, Evening, Liberal arts, Love, Night, Sky, Sun.

L'étoile au coeur de feu qui tressaille et palpite
Paraissait écouter avec étonnement

La lyre si puissante et pourtant si petite
Qui vibrait au gosier de son terrestre amant.
SULLY-PRUDHOMME:
Le Bonheur (French)

The star at the heart of the fire which quivered
and throbbed appeared to listen with astonish-
ment to so powerful and yet so small a lyre which
vibrated in the throat of its earthly lover.

Die Sternbilder waren als Ratschläge gedacht,
doch niemand hat sie verstanden.
ELIAS CANETTI:
Aufzeichnungen, 1955 (German)

The constellations were consulted for advice,
but no one understood them.

Wie schimmernde Thränen sind die Sterne
durch die Nacht gesprengt.
GEORG BÜCHNER:
Dantons Tod (German)

How like the stars are to shimmering teardrops
sprinkled through the night.

Hespere, panta pherōn hosa phainolis eskedas'
auōs,
Phereis ouin, phereis aiga,
Phereis apu materi paida
SAPPHO:
Poems (Greek)

O Evening-star, that brings home all things
which had been driven apart by dawn, you bring
the sheep, you bring the goat, you bring the
child back to its mother ('Hespere, panta phereis' became a proverb).

Aiola nux
GREEK EXPRESSION

Star-spangled night.

Suadentque cadentia sidera somnos.
VIRGIL:
Aeneid (Latin)

The setting stars invite repose.

Astra regunt mundum, sed regit astra deus.
LATIN PROVERB

The stars rule the world, but god controls the
stars.

Na stoge sena noch'yu yuzhnoï
Litsom ko tverdi ya lezhal,
I khor svetil, zhivoï i druzhnÿi,
Krugom raskinuvshis', drozhal.
AFANASY FE᷈
Na Stoge Sena (Russian

On a southern night I lay on a hayrick searchin᷈
the heavens, and the choir of stars was sprea᷈
out in a circle, live and trembling in harmony.

Ves el lucero de la tarde
Latiendo en fulgor solitario.
LUIS CERNUDA᷈
Tiempo de Vivir, Tiempo de Dormir (Spanish

Look at that evening star, beginning to throb i᷈
splendid isolation!

Quien mira el gran concierto
De aquestos resplandores eternales,
Su movimiento cierto,
Sus pasos desiguales,
Y en proporción concorde tan iguales.
FRAY LUIS DE LEON᷈
Noche Serena (Spanish

Who looks at the splendour of this great concer᷈
of eternal stars, with their planned movement᷈
their uneven step, but with one great ordere᷈
scheme to follow.

THE STATE
see also Commonweal, Government, Injustice, Justice, Kings, Law, Monarchy, Opinion.

Chaque génération tente de formuler sa propre
conception de l'Etat et de la Société.
J. P. MAYER (in his introduction to his edition
of A. de Tocqueville's *De la Démocratie
en Amérique) (French)*

Each generation tries to formulate its own con-
cepts of the state and of society.

L'état social est ordinairement le produit d'un᷈
fait, quelquefois des lois, le plus souvent de ces
deux causes réunies; mais une fois qu'il existe,
on peut le considérer lui-même comme la cause
première de la plupart des lois, des coutumes et

des idées qui règlent la conduite des nations; ce qu'il ne produit pas, il le modifie.

ALEXIS DE TOCQUEVILLE:
De la Démocratie en Amerique (French)

The state is usually the product of a deed, sometimes of laws, but more often of both these causes together. Once the state exists, we can consider it to be the first cause of the majority of laws, of customs, and of the ideas which control the conduct of nations. What it does not itself produce, it modifies.

Es ist der Gang Gottes in der Welt, dass der Staat ist: sein Grund ist die Gewalt der sich als Wille verwirklichenden Vernunft.

G. W. F. HEGEL:
Grundlinien der Philosophie des Rechts (German)

The state is the progress of God in the world: its foundation is the power deriving from the intention to realise commonsense.

Hē polis hapantōn tōn politōn koinē estin
GREEK PROVERB

The state is the common property of all citizens.

Tis gar toiaut' an ouk an orgizoit' epē
Kluōn, ha nun su tēnd' atimazeis polin?

SOPHOCLES:
Oedipus Tyrannus (Greek)

Who can control his wrath when he hears your insolent scorn of the state?

Ekhomen oun ti meizon kakon polei ē ekeino, ho an autēn diaspai kai poiēi pollas anti mias? ē meizon agathon tou ho an xundēi te kai poiēi mian?

PLATO:
The Republic (Greek)

What worse can befall a state than to be rent apart and have its unity destroyed? What greater fortune can it have than its secure unity?

Ita mihi salvam ac sospitem rem p[ublicam] sistere in sua sede liceat atque eius rei fructum percipere, quem peto.

SUETONIUS:
Divus Augustus (Latin)

May it be my privilege to establish the state in a firm and secure position, and to reap from that the fruit I desire (from an edict of Augustus).

STATESMEN
see also Kings, Leadership, Monarchy.

Khrē legein ta kairia
Hostis phulassei pragos en prumnēi poleōs
Oiaka nōmōn, blephara mē koimōn hupnōi

AESCHYLUS:
The Seven against Thebes (Greek)

The ever-watchful man at the helm of state, and guiding its fortune, must declare what is to be done.

STATISTICS

Man hat behauptet, die Welt werde durch Zahlen regiert: das aber weiss ich, dass die Zahlen uns belehren, ob sie gut oder schlecht regiert werde.

J. W. VON GOETHE:
in conversation with Eckerman, 31st January 1830 (the motto of *The Statesman's Year-Book*, since its inception in 1864) *(German)*

It has been said that figures rule the world; maybe. I am quite sure that it is figures which show us whether it is being ruled well or badly (*tr.* S. H. Steinberg).

STEADFASTNESS

Fortitudo et fidelitas.
Motto of the royal burgh of Dumbarton
(Latin)

Fortitude and faith.

Per fas et nefas.
LATIN EXPRESSION

Through right and wrong.

STORMS
see also Clouds, Sea.

Burya mgloyu nebo kroet,
Vikhri snezhnÿe krutya;
To, kak zver', ona zavoet,
To zaplachet, kak ditya

ALEKSANDR SERGEEVICH PUSHKIN:
Zimniĭ Vecher (Russian)

Darkness envelops the storm-ridden sky; the snow descends in a whirlwind; at one moment the storm howls like a wild beast; at the next it screams like a child.

Lyublyu grozu v nachale maya,
Kogda vesenniĭ, pervyĭ grom,
Kak bў rezvyasya i igraya,
Grokhochet v nebe golubom

FЁDOR TYUTCHEV:
Vesennyaya Groza (Russian)

I love the thunderstorms of May's beginning –
spring's first playful thunders rumble frolicking
in the blue of the heavens.

STRATEGY
see also Cunning, War.

Ath-tha'lab yistikhabbạ wa-ba'dayn yirja'
thānī wa-yighishsh illī yijrī warāh

ARAB PROVERB

The fox runs then turns back, and so baffles his
pursuers.

STREAMS
see also Rivers, Spring.

Ce ruisseau, dont l'onde tremblante
Réfléchit la clarté des cieux,
Paraît dans sa course brillante
Etinceler de mille feux.

GÉRARD DE NERVAL:
Stances Élégiaques (French)

This stream, whose trembling ripple reflects the
clear blue of the skies, appears in its sparkling
course to glitter with a thousand fires.

La Voulzie, est-ce un fleuve aux grandes îles?
Non;
Mais, avec un murmure aussi doux que son
nom,
Un tout petit ruisseau coulant visible à peine;
Un géant altéré le boirait d'une haleine.

HÉGÉSIPPE MOREAU:
La Voulzie (French)

Is the Voulzie a river with large islands? No! it is
quite a small stream whose current is hardly
visible, and whose song is as sweet as its name. A
thirsty giant could drink it up in a single
swallow.

SUCCESS
see also Achievement, Failure, Faults, Obedience, Victory.

Les succès produirent les succès, comme
l'argent produit l'argent.

S. R. N. CHAMFORT:
Maximes et Pensees (French)

Success breeds success, just as money breeds
money.

Der Erfolgreiche hört nur noch Händek-
latschen. Sonst ist er taub.

ELIAS CANETTI:
Aufzeichnungen, 1942 *(German)*

Success listens only to applause – to all else it is
deaf.

Er ging auf wie ein Meteor und schwindet wie
eine sinkende Sonne.

J. C. F. VON SCHILLER,
in his own review of the production of *Die Räuber*
(German)

He rose like a meteor, and departs like a setting
sun.

Ein Diadem erkämpfen ist gross. Es wegwerfen
ist göttlich.

J. C. F. VON SCHILLER:
Fiesco (German)

To fight for and gain a crown is greatness. To
reject it is godlike.

Hora, ponou toi khōris ouden eutukhei

SOPHOCLES:
Electra (Greek)

Success is dependent on effort.

Kai enthade kai en tēi khilietei poreiai, hēn
dielēluthamen, eu prattōmen

PLATO:
The Republic (closing words) *(Greek)*

So both here and in our thousand-year journey
we shall succeed.

Me non profiteor, secutum esse prae me fero.

CICERO:
De Natura Deorum (Latin)

I do not profess to have attained success, though
I do claim to have attempted it.

Si dives, qui sapiens est,
Ct sutor bonus et solus formosus et est rex,
Cur optas quod habes?

HORACE:
Satires (Latin)

If the wise man is rich, and a good cobbler, and
outstandingly handsome, and a king, why crave
what you have already?

SUCCOUR
see also Neighbours.

Adelphos andri pareiē

GREEK PROVERB
(quoted in Plato's *Republic*)

Let a brother help a man.

SUFFERING
see also Adversity, Language, Mankind,
Misfortune, Sorrow, War, Women.

Het leed der menschheid laat mij vaak niet
slapen.

HENRIETTE ROLAND HOLST:
Tusschen Tijd en Eeuwigheid (Dutch)

Man's sorrow often will not let me sleep.

Souffrir, c'est donner à quelque chose une attention suprême.

PAUL VALÉRY:
La Soirée avec Monsieur Teste (French)

Suffering means giving your complete attention
to one thing.

Quand on souffre, on fait souffrir les autres.

DENIS DIDEROT:
Le Neveu de Rameau (French)

When we suffer, we make others suffer.

La souffrance ne donne pas de droits.

ALBERT CAMUS:
Carnets, 1935–1937 (French)

Suffering gives us no special rights.

Plutôt souffrir que mourir.

JEAN DE LA FONTAINE:
La Mort et le Bucheron (French)

Better suffer than die.

Il faut apprendre de la vie à souffrir la vie.

FRENCH PROVERB

We must learn from life how to suffer it.

Nos pleurs et notre sang sont l'huile de la lampe
Que Dieu nous fait porter devant le genre
humain!

ALPHONSE DE LAMARTINE:
Ferrare (French)

Our blood and tears are the oil of the lamp that
the Lord makes us carry before the human race!

J'aime la majesté des souffrances humaines;
Vous ne recevrez pas un cri d'amour de moi.

ALFRED DE VIGNY:
La Maison du Berger (French)

I love the majesty of human suffering; you will
not get a cry of love from me!

Der Menschheit ganzer Jammer fasst mich an.

J. W. VON GOETHE:
Faust (German)

The whole suffering of mankind seizes me.

Die unbegrenzte Welt, voll Leiden überall, in
unendlicher Vergangenheit, in unendlicher
Zukunft.

ARTHUR SCHOPENHAUER:
Die Welt als Wille und Vorstellung (German)

The limitless universe, full of suffering everywhere, in the infinite past, in the infinite future.

Wirkliches Leiden, aber gestattet kein äs-
thetisches Urteil, weil es die Freiheit des Geistes
aufhebt.

J. C. F. VON SCHILLER:
Werke (German)

Real suffering hinders aesthetic judgment, for it
inhibits the mind's freedom.

Aber ich, wär ich allmächtig, sehen Sie, ich
könnte das Leiden nicht ertragen – ich würde
retten, retten!

GEORG BÜCHNER:
Woyzeck (German)

But I, if I were all-powerful, you see, I shouldn't
be able to bear the suffering – I should save,
save!

Mokhthein de brotoisin anankē

EURIPIDES:
Hippolytus (Greek)

Suffering is the lot of all mankind.

Felix qui patitur quae numerare potest.

OVID:
Tristia (Latin)

Happy the man who can count his sufferings.

SUMMER
see also Evening, Rest, Sun.

Ten blijdsten tide vanden jare,
Dat alle voghele singhen clare,
Ende die nachtegale openbare
Ons maket hare bliscap cont.

HADEWIJCH:
Die Veertiende Sanc (Dutch)

In the blithest season of the year, when all the
birds are singing clear, and the nightingale, for
all to hear, proclaims her joy to us.

Midi, roi des étés, épandu sur la plaine,
Tombe en nappes d'argent des hauteurs du ciel
bleu.
Tout se tait. L'air flamboie et brûle sans haleine;
La terre est assoupie en sa robe de feu.

LECONTE DE LISLE:
Midi (French)

Noon, that summer king, spread over the plain,
falls in silver sheets from the heights of the blue
sky. Everything is quiet. The air blazes and
burns breathlessly. The earth drowses in its
fiery robe.

Voici que vient l'été, la saison violente!

GUILLAUME APOLLINAIRE:
Zone (French)

Here comes the summer! the violent season!

Quand revient l'été superbe,
Je m'en vais au bois tout seule,
Je m'etends dans la grande herbe,
Perdu dans ce vert linceul.

GÉRARD DE NERVAL:
Les Papillons (French)

When magnificent summer comes round again,
I go off all alone to the woods, lie down on the
rich grass, and am lost in its green shroud.

Es ist ein eigenes, erquickendes Labsal, die rein
Luft des heiteren Sommers zu athmen.

ADALBERT STIFTER
Der Nachsommer (German

It is a unique, refreshing restorative, to breath
the pure air of bright summer.

Die grossen Tage stehn, bedeckt vom Staube,
Verweilend, breit und still im ebnen Land.
In ihren heissen Händen reift die Traube,
Vergilbt das Feld, verbrennt das Gartenland.

FRITZ DIETTRICH
Heisser Sommer (German

The great days remain, covered in dust, linger
ing broad and peaceful over the level land. I
their hot hands the clusters of grapes ripen, th
fields turn yellow, and the gardens are scorched.

Ich hoer aber die vogel singen,
In dem walde suoze erklingen,
Dringen/ siht man bluomen durch daz gras.
Was/ diu sumerwunne in leide
Nú hât aber diu liebe heide
Beide/ bluomen unde rôsen rôt.

GOTFRIT VON NIFEN
Bitte um Trost (German)

I hear the birds singing sweetly through the
woods. You can see flowers blooming through
the grass. A hint of early summer, with heather
now in flower and roses red.

Touto men niphostibeis
Kheimōnes ekkhōrousin eukarpōi therei

SOPHOCLES:
Ajax (Greek)

Snow-covered winter yields to summer in all its
wealth.

Nunc frondent silvae, nunc formosissimus
annus.

VIRGIL:
Eclogues (Latin)

Now the forest is clothed with verdure, now the
year is at its most beautiful.

Okh, leto krasnoe! Lyubil bӯ ya tebya,
Kogda b ne znoĭ, da pӯl', da komarӯ, da mukhi.

ALEKSANDR SERGEEVICH PUSHKIN:
Osen (Russian)

Beautiful summer! How fond of you I could be,

were it not for the heat, the dust, the mosquitoes, and the flies!

Lenivo dȳshit polden' mglistȳĭ;
Lenivo katitsya reka;
I v tverdi plamennoĭ i chistoĭ
Lenivo tayut oblaka.

FĒDOR TYUTCHEV:
Noon (Russian)

Lazily breathes the misty noon; lazily flows the river; lazily melt away the clouds in the pure and fiery heavens.

La verdura del prado, la olor de las flores,
Las sombras de los árbores de temprados sabores
Refrescáronme todo, e perdí los sudores.

GONZALO DE BERCEO:
Milagros de Nuestro Señora (Spanish)

The green of the meadows, the scent of the flowers, the shade of the trees and the fragrant showers, refresh me and everything in its labours.

SUN
see also Dawn, Evening, Insignificance, Spring, Summer, Trees.

Na rahai chapā sūruja paragāsū;
Dēkhi kaṁvala mana bhaeu bigāsū

MALIK MUHAMMAD JĀYASĪ:
Padumāvatī (Avadhi)

The brilliance of the sun does not remain hidden; at its sight the heart of the lotus has bloomed.

V zářných slunných dnech
ožije oblouk hodin v průčelí,
a po něm rozmarný a veselý
stín času tančí
a recituje vážně nebesům:
sine sole nihil sum

KAREL TOMAN:
Sluneční Hodiny (Czech)

On glowing sunlit days the sundial's arc that fronts the place returns to life. Freakishly and gaily time's shadow dances, and solemnly recites to the sky: Without the sun I am nothing!

Ce soir un soleil fichu gît au haut du coteau
Gît sur le flanc, dans les genêts, sur son manteau.
Un soleil blanc comme un crachat d'estaminet
Sur une litière de jaunes genêts,
De jaunes genêts d'automne.

JULES LAFORGUE:
L'Hiver qui Vient (French)

This evening a beastly sun lies high above the hill, lies in its cloak on the slopes among the broom. A white sun, like the spittle on a barroom floor, over a litter of young broom, the yellow broom of autumn.

Quand, ainsi qu'un poète, il descend dans les villes,
Il ennoblit le sort des choses les plus viles,
Et s'introduit en roi, sans bruit et sans valets,
Dans tous les hôpitaux et dans tous les palais.

CHARLES BAUDELAIRE:
Le Soleil (French)

When like a poet, he visits the towns, he ennobles the fate of even the most vile of things, and introduces himself royally – but without fanfares or flunkeys – into all the hospitals as well as all the palaces.

Le temps a laissé son manteau
De vent, de froidure et de pluie,
Et s'est vêtu du broderie
De soleil luisant, clair et beau.

CHARLES D'ORLÉANS:
Rondel (French)

Time has left off its coat of wind, cold and rain; and is decked out in embroidery of gleaming sun, clear and beautiful.

Halie kai phaos hameras

EURIPIDES:
Alcestis (Greek)

O sun! that lights up the sky.

Harmata men tade lampra tethrippōn
Hēlios ēdē lampei kata gēn,
Astra de pheugei pur tod' ap' aitheros
Eis nukhth' hieran

EURIPIDES:
Ion (Greek)

The blazing chariot of the sun chases the stars as they flee into the sacred night, and brings light once again to the earth.

Ou gar an pōpote eiden ophthalmos hēlion
hēlioeidēs mē gegenēmenos

PLOTINUS:
Enneads (Greek)

The eye would never have beheld the sun had it
not been sunlike.

Benigno è il sol; de gli uomini al lavoro
Soccorre e alegro l'ama;
Per lui curva la vasta mèsse d'oro
Freme e la falce chiama.

GIOSUE CARDUCCI:
Classicismo e Romanticismo (Italian)

The sun is kind: he scorns no man's work. His
beams are warm and hale. Through him the
rustling acres of golden corn can bow to the
reaper's scythe.

Sol, quasi flagitator, astat usque ad ostium.

PLAUTUS:
Mostellaria (Latin)

The sun, like a creditor, stands eternally at the
door.

¡Oh sol con madejas de oro
Que de la noche el silencio
Rompes y enjudas mi lloro,
Desde aquí te reverencio
Y como el indio te adoro!

TIRSO DE MOLINA:
Marta la Piadosa (Spanish)

Oh Sun! with your golden tresses – you break
night's silence and dry my tears, since when I
adore and reverence you, as do the Indians.

De los dorados límites de Oriente
Que ciñe el rico en perlas Oceano,
Al término sombroso de Occidente,
Las orlas de tu ardiente vestidura
Tiendes en pompa, augusto soberano,
Y el mundo bañas en tu lumbre pura.

JOSÉ DE ESPRONCEDA:
El Sol (Spanish)

From the golden limits of the east, by the ocean
richly girdled with pearls, to the darkened edges
of the west, the fringes of your gleaming gar-
ments shine in splendour, august and majestic,
and you bathe all the world in your pure fires.

El sol tiende los rayos de su lumbre
Por montes y por valles, despertando
Las aves y animales y la gente:
Cuál por el aire claro va volando,
Cuál por el verde valle o alta cumbre
Paciendo va segura y libremente,
Cuál con el sol presente
Va de nuevo al oficio,
Y al usado ejercicio
Do su natura o menester le inclina.

GARCILASO DE LA VEGA:
Eclogues (Spanish)

The sun extends its splendour over mountains
and valleys, waking birds and animals and
people. Some fly through the clear air, others
through the green valleys or over the high sum-
mits, safely and peacefully grazing; some, now
that the sun is up, go to their usual work to
which nature or necessity has accustomed them.

SURVIVAL
see also Endurance.

C'est folie
De compter sur dix ans de vie.

JEAN DE LA FONTAINE:
Le Charlatan (French)

It's madness to count on ten more years of life!

S'il vit, il aura de l'eage.

RABELAIS:
Gargantua (French)

If he lives he will have years.

Pour gagner du bien, le savoir-faire vaut mieux
que le savoir.

P. A. C. DE BEAUMARCHAIS:
Le Mariage de Figaro (French)

To gain one's living, craftiness is better than
pure knowledge.

Qui vivra verra.

FRENCH PROVERB

He who survives will see the outcome.

Die grossen Worte aus den Zeiten, da Geschehen noch sichtbar war, sind nicht für uns.
Wer spricht von Siegen? Überstehn ist alles.

RAINER MARIA RILKE:
Requiem für Wolf, Graf von Kalckreuth (German)

Those great words from the time when events

were still visible are not for us. Who speaks of victory? Survival is everything.

Ind ráith d'éis cech ríg ar úair,
Ocus int ślúaig foait i n-úir.
IRISH PROVERB *(Gaelic)*

The fort survives after each king in turn, and the hosts sleep in the ground.

Morieris, orieris, eris, is (*or* es).
Schoolboy tag *(Latin)*

Thou shalt die; thou shalt rise again; thou shalt exist; thou art on thy way (*or* thou existest now).

Immortalia ne speres, monet annus et almum
Quae rapit hora diem.
HORACE:
Odes (Latin)

The year and the hour which snatch the kindly day from us, warn you not to hope for immortality.

SUSPICION
see also Belief, Jealousy, Reputation.

La méfiance
Est mère de la sûreté.
JEAN DE LA FONTAINE:
Le Chat et un Vieux Rat (French)

Suspicion is the mother of safety.

Gnōmēi d' adēlōi mē me khoris aitiō
SOPHOCLES:
Oedipus Tyrannus (Greek)

Do not condemn me on suspicion alone, without giving me a chance to refute it!

Quia me vestigia terrent,
Omnia te adversum spectantia, nulla retrorsum.
Belua multorum es capitum.
HORACE:
Epistles (Latin)

How your footprints scare me. They all lead into your den; but none leads back! You are a monster of many heads (referring to the Roman crowds).

Suspicio est in pectore alieno sita.
PLAUTUS:
Trinummus (Latin)

Suspicion is stored in the thoughts of others.

SYMPATHY
see also Common interests, Compassion, Hardships, Reactions.

Hypocrite lecteur, – mon semblable, – mon frère!
CHARLES BAUDELAIRE:
Les Fleurs du Mal (last line of preface) *(French)*

Hypocritical reader! my double! my brother!

Donner et reçevoir, c'est faire vivre l'âme.
VICTOR HUGO:
Les Contemplations: La Vie aux Champs (French)

Giving and receiving makes the soul come alive.

Managem ist unmaere
Swaz einem andern werre:
Der sî ouch bî den liuten swaere.
WALTHER VON DER VOGELWEIDE:
Zwô Fuoge Hân Ich Doch (German)

Some people are indifferent to what troubles others; so let them be obnoxious to other people.

Konnt' ich dies Herz verhärten,
Das der Himmel fühlend schuf!
J. C. F. VON SCHILLER:
Die Jungfrau von Orleans (German)

Can I harden this heart which heaven has made so susceptible!

Lacrimis adamanta movebis.
OVID:
Ars Amatoria (Latin)

You can move a heart of stone with tears.

T

TALENTS

So ist jede schöne Gabe
Flüchtig wie des Blitzes Schein,
Schnell in ihrem düstern Grabe
Schliesst die Nacht sie wieder ein.

J. C. F. VON SCHILLER:
Die Gunst des Augenblicks (German)

Thus every fine talent is as fleeting as a flash of
lightning, soon to be buried by night in a gloomy
grave.

Es bildet ein Talent sich in der Stille,
Sich ein Charakter in dem Strom der Welt.

J. W. VON GOETHE:
Tasso (German)

A talent forms itself in isolation, a character in
the stream of the world.

Sutor ne supra crepidam [indiceret].

LATIN PROVERB

Let the cobbler stick to his last.

Omnis sibi malle melius esse quam alteri.

LATIN PROVERB

Every man prefers greater advantage for himself
than for others.

TASTE

Le goût est fait de mille dégoûts.

PAUL VALÉRY:
Choses Tues (French)

Taste is formed from a thousand dislikes.

El libro de los gustos está escrito en blanco.

SPANISH PROVERB

The book of good taste is written in white.

TAXES

Die, für die die Gabe bestimmt ist,
Verlangen Opfermut.

BERTOLT BRECHT:
Die das Fleisch Wegnehmen vom Tisch (German)

Those for whom gifts are destined demand
sacrifices.

Ein jeder wird besteuert nach Vermögen.

J. C. F. VON SCHILLER:
Wilhelm Tell (German)

Everyone will be taxed according to his means.

Casi casi es preciso poner al contribuyente
delante de una horca para que pague.

BENITO PÉREZ GALDÓS:
Miau (Spanish)

To make a taxpayer pay up, it's practically
essential to put him before a gallows.

TEACHING
see also Learning, Logic.

Obest plerumque iis qui discere volunt auc-
toritas eorum qui se docere profitentur.

CICERO:
De Natura Deorum (Latin)

The authority of those who profess to teach is
often a positive hindrance to those who desire to
learn.

Gaudeo discere, ut doceam.

SENECA:
Epistles (Latin)

I delight in learning so that I can teach.

TEARS
see also Grief, Laughter, Life, Poverty, Sorrow, Suffering, Sympathy.

Ah! laissez-les couler, elles me sont bien chères,
Ces larmes que soulève un coeur encor blessé!

Ne les essuyez pas, laissez sur mes paupières
Ce voile du passé!

> ALFRED DE MUSSET:
> *Souvenir (French)*

Let them flow, they are very dear to me, these
tears rising from a heart still wounded! Don't
dry them; leave this veil of the past on my
eyelids.

Molli verriano a questi pianti i sassi,
E benigne le Tigri a questi preghi.

> GIAMBATTISTA CINTHIO GIRALDI:
> *Didone (Italian)*

These tears could soften stones; these entreaties
could tame tigers.

Lacrimas non sponte cadentes
Effudit, gemitusque expressit pectore laeto.

> LUCAN:
> *Pharsalia (Latin)*

Despite his will, hot tears fell from his eyes, and
groans came from his joyful breast.

Mollissima corda
Humano generi dare se natura fatetur,
Quae lacrimas dedit; haec nostri pars optima
sensus.

> JUVENAL:
> *Satires (Latin)*

When Nature gave tears to man she proclaimed
that he was tender-hearted; and tenderness is
the best quality in man.

Y en lluvias tan extrañas
Sartas de perlas hizo les pestañas.

> LUIS VÉLEZ DE GUEVARA:
> *Reinar Después de Morir (Spanish)*

With such rare showers of tears, she made her
eyelashes strings of pearls.

Salid fuera sin duelo,
Salid sin duelo, lágrimas, corriendo.

> GARCILASO DE LA VEGA:
> *Eclogues (Spanish)*

Pour forth and flow abundantly, tears!

TEMPERAMENT
see also Character, Personality.

Ich binn wie immer bald leidlich bald unleid-
lich.

> J. W. VON GOETHE:
> letter to Johanna Fahlmer, 31 October 1773
> *(German)*

As always, I am bearable at one moment,
unbearable the next.

Ich gleiche ziemlich einem Chamaeleon.

> J. W. VON GOETHE,
> in an application – at the age of 14 – to join a
> boys' club. *(German)*

I am something of a chameleon.

TEMPERANCE
see also Moderation.

A Potsdam, les totaux absteneurs,
Comme tant d'autres titotalleurs,
Sont gloutons, monivores,
Nasirubicolores,
Grands manchons et terribles duffeurs.

> *Punch*, 1877 *(French)*

In Potsdam the total abstainers, like so many
other teetotallers, are gluttonous, greedy, red-
nosed, fat-necked, and terrible duffers.

Pheu tines hudōr
Pinousin, maniēn sōphrona mainomenoi

> ANTIGONUS OF CARYSTUS:
> *Fragment (Greek)*

Alas for those who drink water – they are mad,
but with a temperate madness.

TEMPTATION
see also Devils.

In paradyzen nestlen slangen:
De slangen hangen boven 't hooft,
Daer goude en blozende appels hangen:
Dies wacht uw vingers, wacht uw hant,
Noch vat de doot niet met uw tant.

> JOOST VAN DEN VONDEL:
> *Joseph in Egypten (Dutch)*

There are snakes in paradise; they hang waiting
overhead among the golden apples. So guard
your fingers, watch your hand – don't seize on
death with greedy tooth!

Hominem etiam frugi flectit saepe occasio.

LATIN PROVERB

Opportunity can often sway even an honest man.

Montes auri pollicens.

TERENCE:
Phormio (Latin)

Promising mountains of gold.

Ut canis a corio numquam absterrebitur uncto.

HORACE:
Satires (Latin)

Like a dog that can never be frightened away from the greasy hide (*i.e.* to which pieces of fat still adhere).

Entre santa y santo, pared de cal y canto.

SPANISH PROVERB

Between a holy woman and a holy man, erect a stone wall.

Cierra tu puerta y harás a tu vecina buena.

SPANISH PROVERB

Lock your door and preserve your neighbour's honour.

TERROR
see also Fear.

Qui terret, plus ipse timet.

CLAUDIAN:
Panegyricus de Quarto Consulatu Honorii Augusti (Latin)

He who terrorises is himself the more terrified.

THEORY
see also Action.

Grau, teurer Freund, ist alle Theorie,
Und grün des Lebens goldner Baum.

J. W. VON GOETHE:
Faust (German)

My dear friend, grey is the colour of theory, but green the golden tree of life!

THIEVES AND THEFT
see also Crime, Moderation, Opportunity, Poverty, Trust.

Al-māl as-sāyib yi'allim as-sirqa

ARAB PROVERB

Opportunity makes the thief (*lit.* neglected property teaches theft).

À vilain vilain et demi.

FRENCH PROVERB

Set a thief to catch a thief.

Mal prend aux volereaux de faire les voleurs.

JEAN DE LA FONTAINE:
Le Corbeau voulant Imiter l'Aigle (French)

The petty thief who would emulate thieves comes to a sorry end.

Si un voleur vole l'autre, le diable s'en rit.

FRENCH PROVERB

The devil laughs if a thief steals from another thief.

Die Hölle des Diebs ist die Angst vor Dieben.

ELIAS CANETTI:
Aufzeichnungen, 1951 (German)

Hell for thieves is the fear of being robbed.

Pack schlägt sich, Pack verträgt sich.

GERMAN PROVERB

Thieves may squabble, but they stick together.

Ein Fuchs riecht den andern.

GERMAN PROVERB

Set a thief to catch a thief (*lit.* one fox smells out another).

Dōs agathē, harpax de kakē, thanatoio doteira

HESIOD:
Works and Days (Greek)

Giving is good; but theft evil, bringing death in its train.

Perdat hic aeternum qui vult hinc tollere regnum.

LATIN PROVERB

Let him who tries to take it away be banned from the kingdom of heaven for ever.

Occasio facit furem.
LATIN PROVERB

Opportunity makes the thief.

Min Fader var Tyv;
Hans Søn maa stjæle.
HENRIK IBSEN:
Peer Gynt (Norwegian)

My father stole – his son must steal.

Qué buena cara tiene mi padre el día que no
hurta.
SPANISH PROVERB

What a happy face my father has on the days he
doesn't have to go out stealing!

El hurtar es cosa linda si colgasen por la pretina.
SPANISH PROVERB

Stealing would be a pleasant occupation if they
only hanged you round your waist.

Al entendido, un buen entendedor.
SPANISH PROVERB

Set a thief to catch a thief (*lit.* to the understanding person, a person of good understanding).

Los ladrones, por lo regular, es gente bien
informada.
JACINTO BENAVENTE Y MARTÍNEZ:
La Honradez de la Cerradura (Spanish)

Thieves are generally very well informed.

THOUGHT AND THINKING
see also Action, Greatness, Language, Laughter, Laziness, Logic, Materialism, Morals and morality, Mortality, Philosophy, Sadness, Sin, Words.

Toute la dignité de l'homme est en la pensée.
BLAISE PASCAL:
Pensées (French)

The whole dignity of man lies in the power of
thought.

L'objet propre, unique et perpétual de la pensée
est: *ce qui n'existe pas.*
PAUL VALÉRY:
Mauvaises Pensées (French)

The particular, unique and perpetual pursuit of
thought is the non-existent!

La pensée est toujours en avant. Elle voit trop
loin, plus loin que le corps qui est dans le
présent.
ALBERT CAMUS:
Carnets, 1937–39 *(French)*

Thought is always in advance; it can see too far
ahead, outstripping our bodies which are in the
present.

La pensée console de tout.
S. R. N. CHAMFORT:
Maximes et Pensées (French)

There is consolation for everything in thought.

Der Gedanke ist der sinnvolle Satz.
LUDWIG WITTGENSTEIN:
Tractatus Logico-philosophicus (German)

A thought is a meaningful proposition.

Alles, was überhaupt gedacht werden kann,
kann klar gedacht werden.
LUDWIG WITTGENSTEIN:
Tractatus Logico-philosophicus (German)

Everything that can be thought at all can be
thought clearly.

Denken ist danken.
GERMAN PROVERB

To think is to thank.

Der Beweis ist das Erb-Unglück des Denkens.
ELIAS CANETTI:
Aufzeichnungen, 1942 *(German)*

Argument is the hereditary misfortune of
thought.

Es genügt nicht zu denken, man muss auch
atmen. Gefährlich die Denker, die nicht genug
geatmet haben.

ELIAS CANETTI:
Aufzeichnungen, 1960 *(German)*

Thought is not enough; man must also breathe.
Dangerous the thinker who has not breathed
enough!

Die Gesamtheit der wahren Gedanken sind ein
Bild der Welt.

LUDWIG WITTGENSTEIN:
Tractatus Logico-philosophicus (German)

The totality of true thought is a picture of the
world.

Mein Kind, ich hab' es klug gemacht:
Ich habe nie über des Denken gedacht.

J. W. VON GOETHE:
Zahme Xenien (German)

My child, I have been very wise – I have never
thought about thinking.

Oukoun dianoia men kai logos tauton. Plēn ho
men entos tēs psukhēs pros hautēn dialogos
aneu phonēs gignomenos tout' auto hēmin
epōnomasthē, dianoia;

PLATO:
The Sophist (Greek)

Is it not true that thought and speech are the
same, thought being thus named because it is
the silent inner conversation of the soul with
itself?

Optimae conceptiones non possunt esse, nisi ubi
scientia et ingenium est.

DANTE:
De Vulgari Eloquio (Latin)

The best thoughts can only exist where knowledge and genius are to be found.

Hablar sin pensar es tirar sin encarar.

SPANISH PROVERB

To speak without thinking is to shoot without
first taking aim.

El sentir es libre; no se puede ni debe violentar.

BALTASAR GRACIÁN:
Oráculo Manual y Arte de Prudencia (Spanish)

Thought is free; it cannot and should not be
coerced.

THREATS

Te ad terram, scelus, adfligam!

PLAUTUS:
Persa (Latin)

Scoundrel, I shall dash you to the earth!

THRIFT

Ei thesaurōi tis entukhoi, plousiōteros an eiē,
oikonomikoteros d' ou

GREEK PROVERB

If a man should discover a treasure, he would be
the richer, but not necessarily more thrifty.

TIME
See also Grief, Hesitation, Impermanence,
Life, Love, Moon, Night, Poets and poetry,
Pride, Sadness, Sorrow, Sun.

Een grijsaert sijt ghij Tijt, en proefden noyt
twegelt
Van t geene datse Liefd' en soete weerlieft
hieten.

PIETER CORNELISZ HOOFT:
Sonnet (Dutch)

Time, you are a greybeard and have never
known the glow of what we call love and love's
shared tenderness.

O temps, suspends ton vol! et vous, heures
propices,
Suspendez votre cours!
Laissez-nous savourer les rapides délices
Des plus beaux de nos jours!

ALPHONSE DE LAMARTINE:
Le Lac (French)

Time! suspend your flight! Propitious hours,
suspend your course! Let us savour the swift
delights of the most beautiful of our days!

Oh! oui! le Temps a reparu; le Temps règne en
souverain maintenant, et avec le hideux vieillard est revenu tout son démoniaque cortège de

Souvenirs, de Regrets, de Spasmes, de Peurs, d'Angoisses, de Cauchemars, de Colères et de Névroses.

CHARLES BAUDELAIRE:
La Chambre Double (French)

Ah, yes, Time has reappeared and now reigns supreme; and with the hideous old man has returned all his devilish retinue of Memories, Regrets, Spasms, Fears, Anguishes, Nightmares, Wraths and Neuroses.

Le temps aux plus belles choses
Se plait à faire un affront,
Et saura faner vos roses
Comme il a ridé mon front.

PIERRE CORNEILLE:
Stances à la Marquise (French)

Time has a way of insulting the most beautiful things, and will fade your rosy cheeks just as he has wrinkled my brow.

Le Temps m'engloutit minute par minute,
Comme la neige immense un corps pris de roideur.

CHARLES BAUDELAIRE:
Le Goût du Néant (French)

Minute after minute time engulfs me, just as a vast snowfall will cover a frozen body.

Souviens-toi que le Temps est un joueur avide
Qui gagne sans tricher, à tout coup! c'est la loi!

CHARLES BAUDELAIRE:
L'Horloge (French)

Remember that time is an avid gambler who has no need to cheat to win every time – that's the law!

Le temps est un grand maître, il règle bien des choses.

PIERRE CORNEILLE:
Sertorius (French)

Time is a great master who regulates things well.

Tout passe, tout lasse.

FRENCH PROVERB

Everything passes; everything gets tired.

Tout est affaire de chronologie.

MARCEL PROUST:
Le Temps Retrouvé (French)

Everything is a matter of chronology.

Die Zeit wird Herr.

J. W. VON GOETHE:
Faust (German)

Time is lord.

Immer zierlicher die Uhren, immer gefährlicher die Zeit.

ELIAS CANETTI:
Aufzeichnungen, 1960 (German)

Ever more graceful the clocks, ever more dangerous time!

An den langen Tischen der Zeit
Zechen die Krüge Gottes.

PAUL CELAN:
Die Krüge (German)

The pitchers of God tipple at Time's long table.

Es bringt die Zeit ein anderes Gesetz.

GERMAN PROVERB

Time brings a different law.

Zeit ist teuer.

GERMAN PROVERB

Time is money (*lit.* costly).

Die Zeit ist blind und blickt uns an.

ERICH KÄSTNER:
Das Riesenspielzug (German)

Blind time is staring at us.

Aiōn panta pherei

GREEK PROVERB

Time brings everything.

Ho te khronos legetai trimerēs einai

SEXTUS EMPIRICUS:
Outlines of Pyrrhonism (Greek)

They say that time can be divided into three parts (*i.e.* past, present and future).

Omnia aliena sunt, tempus tantum nostrum est.
SENECA:
Epistles (Latin)

Nothing is ours except time.

Omnia tempus edax depascitur, omnia carpit.
LATIN PROVERB

Voracious time devours all, destroys all.

Damna fleo rerum, sed plus fleo damna dierum:
quisque potest rebus succurrere, nemo diebus.
LATIN PROVERB

Possessions dwindle: I mourn their loss. But I
mourn the loss of time much more; for anyone
can save his purse, but none can win back lost
time.

Est quoque cunctarum novitas carissima rerum.
OVID:
Ex Ponto (Latin)

The opportune time is the most valuable.

[Tempus] etiam saevas paulatim mitigat iras
Hoc minuit luctus maestaque corda levat.
OVID:
Tristia (Latin)

Time gradually softens even fierce anger; it
lessens grief and relieves the sorrowing heart.

Nihil non aut lenit aut domat diuturnitas.
LATIN PROVERB

There's nothing that time does not either soothe
or quell.

Quicquid aetatis retro est, mors tenet
SENECA:
Epistles (Latin)

We cannot repair the wasted time of the past.

Perfecto temporis orbe.
VIRGIL:
Aeneid (Latin)

When the circle of time was finished.

Quicquid transit temporis, perit.
SENECA:
Epistles (Latin)

All past time is lost time.

Fugit irreparabile tempus.
VIRGIL:
Georgics (Latin)

Time passes irrevocably.

Iż-żmien jagħti parir.
MALTESE PROVERB

Time gives good advice.

Tiden tærer og Elven skjær.
HENRIK IBSEN:
Peer Gynt (Norwegian)

Time destroys and the stream cuts through.

Reka vremën v svoëm stremlen'i
Unosit vse dela lyudeï
I topit v propasti zabven'ya
Narodÿ, tsarstva i tsareï
GAVRIL ROMANOVICH DERZHAVIN:
Na Tlennost' (Russian)

The river of the ages carries away all the works
of men in its course, and drowns peoples, king-
doms and kings in the abyss of oblivion.

U menya ostaëtsya odna zabota na svete:
Zolotaya zabota, kak vremeni bremya izbÿt'
OSIP MANDEL'SHTAM:
Sëstrÿ (Russian)

The one golden aim I wish to achieve in this
world is to free myself from time's burden.

Peor es que todo ande.
FEDERICO GARCÍA LORCA:
Quimera (Spanish)

The worst thing is that everything goes on and
on!

Intacto aun, enorme,
Rodeo el tiempo.
JORGE GUILLÉN:
Más Allá (Spanish)

Still whole and tremendous, time sweeps on.

Con qué ligeros pasos vas corriendo!
Oh cómo te me ausentas, tiempo vano!
LUIS DE CARRILLO Y SOTOMAYOR:
A la Ligereza y Pérdida del Tiempo (Spanish)

With what light steps you flow past me! How can you leave me behind, arrogant time!

TIMIDITY
see also Ignorance

Nemo timendo ad summum pervenit locum.
LATIN PROVERB

Faint heart never won fair lady (*lit.* fear never brought one to the top).

TOLERANCE

Khalli 'n-nās yākulū 'aysh
ARAB PROVERB

Live and let live (*lit.* let people eat bread).

TOMORROW
see also Anticipation, Events, Future, Procrastination.

Discipulus est prioris posterior dies.
LATIN PROVERB

Tomorrow is today's pupil.

TRADITION

Le blason des deuils épars sur de vains murs.
STÉPHANE MALLARMÉ:
Toast Funèbre (French)

The blazon of sparse mourning on the empty walls.

Plus l'institution des choses est ancienne, plus il y a d'idiotismes; plus les temps sont malheureux, plus les idiotismes se multiplient.
DENIS DIDEROT:
Le Neveu de Rameau (French)

The greater the age of the customs, the more idiocy; the more wretched the times, the more the idiocies multiply.

Le déracinement est de loin la plus dangereuse maladie des sociétés humaines, car il se multiplie lui-même.
SIMONE WEIL:
L'Enracinement (French)

Uprooting is by far the most dangerous of the ills of human society, for it perpetuates itself.

Patrious paradokhas, has th' homēlikas khronōi
Kektēmeth', oudeis auta katabalei logos,
Oud' ei di' akrōn to sophon hēurētai phrenōn
EURIPIDES:
The Bacchae (Greek)

Our ancestral traditions, traditions as old as time itself, cannot be overturned by argument, however subtle the approach.

To auto aideis aisma
GREEK EXPRESSION

Ever the old tune.

Adiuvare nos possunt non tantum qui sunt, sed qui fuerunt.
SENECA:
Epistles (Latin)

We can get help from the dead as well as from the living.

Aut famam sequere aut sibi convenientia finge.
HORACE:
Ars Poetica (Latin)

Either follow tradition or invent what is self-consistent.

Auspicium melioris aevi.
Motto of the Order of St. Michael
and St. George *(Latin)*

Token of a better age.

De entre tus piedras seculares, tumba
De remembranzas del ayer glorioso,
De entre tus piedras recogió mi espíritu
Fe, paz y fuerza.
MIGUEL DE UNAMUNO:
Salamanca (Spanish)

My spirit draws faith, peace and strength from your age-old stones, the monument to memory of the glorious past.

TRANSLATION

Un traducteur ne doit pas répondre des sentiments de son auteur; tout ce qu'il peut faire,
c'est de prier Dieu pour sa conversion.

VOLTAIRE:
Lettres Philosophiques (French)

A translator is not responsible for the opinions of
his author; all he can do is to pray God for his
conversion.

Oude gar pantōs tēn autēn diasōzei dianoian
methermēneuomena ta onomata all' esti tina,
kai kath' hekaston ethnos idiōmata, adunata eis
allo ethnos dia phōnēs sēmainesthai

IAMBLICHUS:
De Mysteriis (Greek)

It is by no means always the case that translated
terms preserve the original concept; indeed,
every nation has some idiomatic expressions
that are impossible to render perfectly in the
language of another.

Si non circa vilem patulumque moraberis
orbem.

HORACE:
Ars Poetica (Latin)

If you do not dally down the open easy paths
(referring to pedestrian word-for-word trans-
lating).

Le quitó mucho de su natural valor, y lo mismo
haran todos aquellos que los libros de verso
quisieran volver en otra lengua.

MIGUEL DE CERVANTES:
Don Quixote (Spanish)

It lost much of its true worth; and the same
happens when people try to translate books of
verse into another language.

TRAPS
see also Plots.

Wer andern eine Grube gräbt, fällt selbst hinein.
GERMAN PROVERB

He who digs a pit for another will fall in it
himself.

TRAVEL
see also Restlessness.

Kull ad-durūb tiwaddī ilạ aṭ-ṭahūn
ARAB PROVERB

All roads lead to Rome (*lit.* all roads lead to the
mill).

Heureux qui, comme Ulysse, a fait un beau
voyage;
Ou comme celui-là qui conquit la toison,
Et puis est retourneé, plein d'usage et raison,
Vivre entre ses parents le reste de son âge!

JOACHIM DU BELLAY:
Sonnet des 'Regrets' (French)

Happy the man who, like Ulysses, has made a
fine voyage, or has won the Golden Fleece, and
then returns, experienced and knowledgeable,
to spend the rest of his life among his family!

Il n'y a que les Européens au monde qui
voyagent par curiosité.

JEAN CHARDIN:
Voyages en Perse (French)

It is only Europeans who travel out of sheer
curiosity.

Pour moi,
L'Europe est comme une seule grande ville
Pleine de provisions et de tous les plaisirs
urbains,
Et le reste du monde
M'est la campagne ouverte où, sans chapeau,
Je cours contre le vent en poussant des cris
sauvages!

VALÉRY LARBAUD:
Poésies d'A. O. Barnabooth (French)

As I see it, Europe is like a single great city full of
provisions and the pleasures of the town; whereas the rest of the world is like the open country,
where hatless I can run against the wind with
savage cries!

Il faut avoir le pied marin
Pour utiliser le métropolitain.

RAYMOND QUENEAU:
Adaptation (French)

To use the underground effectively, you must
have a nautical instinct.

Nocte die tutum carpe, viator, iter.
        Virgil (in a schoolboy couplet) *(Latin)*

Wayfarer, now follow your course night and day without fear.

Caelum, non animum, mutant, qui trans mare currunt.
                                    HORACE:
                            Epistles (Latin)

Those who go overseas find a change of climate, not a change of soul.

En largo camino paja pesa.
                            SPANISH PROVERB

On a long journey even a straw weighs heavy.

TREACHERY
see also Deceit, Peace, Plots.

Vuoi tu, che il finger ti succieda? Fingi
Fede et amor, et sotte habbi il coltello
A dar l'ultimo colpo a chi ti crede,
Sí tosto, che l'occasion ti s'offra.
                GIAMBATTISTA CINTHIO GIRALDI:
                            Altile (Italian)

If you want your deceit to succeed, pretend love and loyalty; keep a dagger under your cloak, ready to administer the coup de grâce, at the first opportunity, to the man who trusts you!

TREES
see also Forests, Love, Maturity, Night, Spring, Summer, Woodlands.

O chêne, je comprends ta puissante agonie!
Dans sa paix, dans sa force, il est dur de mourir;
A voir crouler ta tête, au printemps rajeunie,
Je devine, ô géant! ce que tu dois souffrir.
                        VICTOR DE LAPRADE:
                    La Mort d'un Chêne (French)

Alas, oak, I understand your mighty agony; in your strength and peace it is hard to die. Seeing your head roll, rejuvenated, on the springtime earth, I know, o giant, what you must be suffering.

Ce vieux chêne a des marques saintes;
Sans doute qui le couperait

Le sang chaud en découlerait,
Et l'arbre pousserait des plaintes.
                        TRISTAN L'HERMITE:
                Le Promenoir des Deux Amants (French)

This old oak has holy marks; no doubt if it were cut down warm blood would trickle out, and the tree would groan in pain.

Ecoute, bûcheron, arreste un peu le bras:
Ce ne sont pas des bois que tu jettes à bas;
Ne vois-tu pas le sang, lequel dégoutte à force,
Des nymphes, qui vivaient dessous la dure
écorce?
La matière demeure et la forme se perd!
                        PIERRE DE RONSARD:
                        Forêt Coupée (French)

Woodman! stay your hand for a moment! Listen! That is not just wood that you fling down there. Can't you see the blood being squeezed out of the nymphs who live under the hard bark? The matter remains, but the form has gone!

Wer möchte ohne den Trost der Bäume leben?
                                GÜNTER EICH:
                    Ende eines Sommers (German)

Who wants to live without the comfort of trees?

            Lo más alto
De un árbol – hoja a hoja
Soleándose, dándose,
Todo actual – me enamora.
                            JORGE GUILLEN:
                        Más Allá (Spanish)

The topmost point of a tree – leaf after leaf aloft in the sunlight, yielding to the sun, everything real, delights me.

TRIVIALITIES

Parvum parva decent.
                                HORACE:
                            Epistles (Latin)

Little things please little minds (*lit.* suit a little person).

TRUST
see also Friendship, Greatness, Kings, Prosperity.

Difficil'è via piú ch'altri non stima,
Il trovar vera fede in core humano.

GIAMBATTISTA CINTHIO GIRALDI:
Altile (Italian)

It is much more difficult than you can imagine to find a heart that is truly to be trusted.

Etiam in peccato recte praestatur fides.

LATIN PROVERB

There is trust even among thieves.

Male creditis hosti.

OVID:
Fasti (Latin)

You do ill to trust the foe.

TRUTH
see also Action, Art, Belief, Corruption, Flattery, Frankness, Honesty, Ignorance, Imagination, Opinion, Poverty, Principles, Simplicity, Wine.

Honte à toi qui la première
M'as appris la trahison,
Et d'horreur et de colère
M'as fait perdre la raison!

ALFRED DE MUSSET:
La Nuit d'Octobre (French)

Shame on you that you should be the first to tell me of this treason and, through horror and anger, have made me lose my reason!

La vérité est le fondement et la raison de la perfection et de la beauté.

FRANÇOIS, DUC DE LA ROCHEFOUCAULD:
Réflexions (French)

Truth is the foundation and justification for perfection and beauty.

Rien n'est beau que le vrai.

FRENCH PROVERB

Only truth is beautiful.

La certitude est le propre de la vérité qui se prouve par l'opinion ferme et unique.

FRENCH PROVERB

Certainty is the characteristic of truth, which proves itself by resolute personal opinion.

Craindre la vérité comme le feu, dont elle a les propriétés. Rien n'y résiste.

PAUL VALÉRY:
Mauvaises Pensées (French)

Beware of truth as you would fire – they both have the same properties. Nothing can resist them.

La vérité est devant nous, et nous ne comprenons plus rien.

PAUL VALÉRY:
Eupalinos (French)

Truth confronts us, and we can no more understand anything.

Mon âme en toute occasion
Développe le vrai caché sous l'apparence.

JEAN DE LA FONTAINE:
Un Animal dans la Lune (French)

My soul will always discover the truth concealed below the surface.

Le plus bas nous paraît le plus vrai.

DENIS DE ROUGEMONT:
L'Amour et l'Orient (French)

The lowest appears to us the truest.

Toute vérité n'est pas bonne à dire.

P. A. C. DE BEAUMARCHAIS:
Le Mariage de Figaro (French)

Not every truth is fit to be told.

Toute vérité n'est pas bonne à croire.

P. A. C. DE BEAUMARCHAIS:
Le Mariage de Figaro (French)

Not every truth is palatable.

On avale à pleine gorgée le mensonge qui nous flatte, et l'on boit goutte à goutte une vérité qui nous est amère.

DENIS DIDEROT:
Le Neveu de Rameau (French)

We swallow whole-heartedly any lie that flatters us, but we sip reluctantly at any truth we find harsh.

Rien n'est beau que le vrai, le vrai seul est aimable.

NICOLAS BOILEAU DESPRÉAUX:
Epitres (French)

Truth alone is beautiful and lovable.

Die Treue, sie ist doch kein leere Wahn.

J. C. F. VON SCHILLER:
Die Bürgschaft (German)

Truth is no empty illusion.

Die Wahrheit is das Ganze.

G. W. F. HEGEL
(German)

Truth is the whole.

Glaube keinem, der immer die Wahrheit spricht.

ELIAS CANETTI:
Aufzeichnungen, 1942 (German)

Do not believe those who always speak the truth.

Was wir als Schönheit hier empfunden
Wird einst als Wahrheit uns entgegen gehn.

J. C. F. VON SCHILLER:
Werke (German)

The beauty we found in this world we shall encounter as truth in the next.

Die Wahrheit finden wollen ist Verdienst, wenn man auch auf dem Wege irrt.

GEORG CHRISTOPH LICHTENBERG:
Aphorismen (German)

There is merit in seeking the truth, even if one strays on the way.

Mit der Wahrheit ist das wie mit einer stadtbekannten Hure. Jeder kennt sie, aber es ist peinlich, wenn man ihr auf der Strasse begegnet.

WOLFGANG BORCHERT:
Draussen vor der Tür (German)

Truth is like a well-known whore. Everyone knows her, but it is embarrassing to encounter her on the street.

Durch zweier Zeugen Mund wird alle Wahrheit kund.

GERMAN LEGAL RULE

Agreement between the statements of two independent witnesses is taken to be sufficient proof of truth.

Einmal werd ich die Wahrheit sagen – das meint man, aber die Lüge ist ein Egel, sie hat die Wahrheit ausgesaugt.

MAX FRISCH:
Andorra (German)

Once I used to tell the truth – I meant to, but lying is a leech that has sucked truth dry.

Ta toi kal' en polloisi kallion legein

EURIPIDES:
Hippolytus (Greek)

Truth grows in grace the wider it is voiced.

Ouk estin oute zōgraphos, out' andriantopoios hostis toiouton an kallos plaseien hoion hē alētheia ekhei

GREEK PROVERB

No painter or sculptor could mould or depict a beauty such as truth is mistress of.

Pan soi phrasō t'alēthes oude krupsomai

SOPHOCLES:
Trachiniae (Greek)

I shall tell you everything and withhold nothing.

Tōi gar alēthei khalepainein ou themis

PLATO:
The Republic (Greek)

It is not seemly to resent the truth.

Quae veritati operam dat oratio incomposita esse debet et simplex.

SENECA:
Epistles (Latin)

Speech which devotes its attention to truth should be plain and without adornment.

Felices animae, quibus haec cognoscere primum
Inque domos superas scandere cura fuit!

OVID:
Fasti (Latin)

Happy the souls who first took pains to know
these mysteries, and to scale the heavenly home!
(*i.e.* the sacredness of the search for truth).

Veritas odit moras.

SENECA:
Oedipus (Latin)

Truth hates delays.

Veritas odium parit.

LATIN PROVERB

Truth brings forth hatred.

Quod verum est, meum est.

SENECA:
Epistles (Latin)

Whatever truth there is, is mine.

Patet omnibus veritas.

SENECA:
Epistles (Latin)

Truth lies open to us all.

Homini praeposuit veritatem.

ST. AUGUSTINE:
De Civitate Dei (Latin)

He has laid truth before men.

Nec modus est ullus investigandi veri nisi
inveneris.

CICERO:
De Finibus (Latin)

There is no limit to investigating the truth, until
you discover it.

Sed ut hoc pulcherrimum esse iudico, vera videre, sic pro veris probare falsa turpissimum est.

CICERO:
Academica (Latin)

But just as I deem it supremely honorable to
hold true views, so it is supremely disgraceful to
approve falsehoods as true.

Philosophia veritatem quaerit, theologia in
venit, religio possidet.

GIOVANNI PICO DELLA MIRANDOLA
letter to Aldus Manutius, 1490 (*Opera*) (*Latin*

Truth is sought by philosophy, found b
theology, and possessed by religion.

Sandhed i sin Overdrift
Er en bagvendt Visdomsskrift.

HENRIK IBSEN
Peer Gynt (Norwegian)

Truth, if it's exaggerated, is no more than wis
dom turned upside down.

Sige sin Kjærlighedslykke Godnatt –
Alt for at finde det sandes Mysterium, –
Det er den ægte Forskers Kriterium!

HENRIK IBSEN:
Peer Gynt (Norwegian)

Bidding adieu to love's soft promptings, to solve
the mystery of truth! That is the test of a real
enquirer!

Tāpāc chedāc ca nikaṣāt suvarṇam iva
paṇḍitaiḥ
Parīkṣya bhikṣavo grāhyaṁ madvaco na tu
gauravāt

Jñānasāra-samuccaya (Pali)

Just as the wise test gold by burning, cutting and
rubbing it with a touchstone, so you must only
believe what I say after examining my words,
and not merely accept them out of regard for me.

Paramārtho hi āryāṇāṁ tūṣṇīmbhāvaḥ

Mādhyamika Vṛtti (Pali)

For the noble, the highest truth is silence.

Anakṣarasya dharmasya śrutiḥ kā deśanā ca kā
Śrūyate deśyate cāpi samāropād anakṣaraḥ

Mādhyamika Vṛtti (Pali)

How can the truth, which is inexpressible, be
taught and heard? Yet it is through attribution
that it is taught and heard.

Asāre sāramatino sāre cāsāradassino
Te sāraṁ nādhigacchanti
micchāsaṁkappagocarā

Dhammapada: Yamakavaggo (Pali)

Those who imagine truth in untruth, and see

untruth in truth, never arrive at truth, but follow
only their own desires.

⋯stina v vine

Truth lies in wine.

No todas las verdades se pueden decir: unas
porque me importan a mí, otras porque al otro.
BALTASAR GRACIÁN:
Oráculo Manual y Arte de Prudencia (Spanish)

Not all truths can be told; some must be concealed in my own interest, others in that of my
fellows.

La mentira es siempre la primera en todo;
arrastra necios por vulgaridad continuada. La
verdad siempre llega la última y tarde, cojeando
con el tiempo.
BALTASAR GRACIÁN:
Oráculo Manual y Arte de Prudencia (Spanish)

Falsehood is always first in the field in everything. It drags fools along with the strength of
their own obstinate vulgarity. Truth is always
the last to arrive, limping along on time's arm.

Son la verdad y Dios, Dios verdadero.
Ni eternidad divina los separa,
Ni de los dos alguna fué primero.
FRANCISCO DE QUEVEDO:
Epístola Satírica y Censoria (Spanish)

Truth and God are God in truth; they are not
divided by divine eternity; and neither of them
takes precedence.

TWILIGHT
see also Evening, Night.

Bénis plutôt ce Dieu qui place un crépuscle
Entre les bruits du soir et la paix de la nuit!
ALPHONSE DE LAMARTINE:
La Vigne et la Maison (French)

Blessed be God who has inserted the twilight
between the noises of the evening and the peace
of the night!

A l'heure où le soleil se couche, où l'herbe est
plaine
Des grands fantomes noirs des arbes de la plaine
Jusqu'aux lointains coteaux rampant et
grandissant,
Quand le brun laboureur des collines descend
Et retourne à son toit.
VICTOR HUGO:
Mugitusque Boum (French)

At the time of the setting sun; when the grass is
full of the great black shadows of the trees of the
plain which creeps and stretches as far as the
distant hills, when the suntanned labourer
comes down from the slopes and returns to his
home.

C'est le moment crépusculaire.
J'admire, assis sous un portail,
Ce reste de jour dont s'éclaire
La dernière heure du travail.
VICTOR HUGO:
Saison des Semailles – Le Soir (French)

It is the twilight hour when, seated in the porch,
I can admire the remains of the day which lights
the last hour of toil.

Le plus beau de ce jour chante avant de mourir.
PAUL VALÉRY:
Lust (French)

The most beautiful part of this day is singing
before her death.

TYRANNY
see also Freedom, Government, Justice,
Might, Nature, Power, Revolution.

La tyrannie consiste au désir de domination,
universel et hors de son ordre.
BLAISE PASCAL:
Pensées (French)

Tyranny is a universal and extravagant desire
for domination.

Quand on tue un tyran, lui fait-on voir le fer?
VICTOR HUGO:
Cromwell (French)

When we kill a tyrant, must we make him see the
sword?

Ce qui me répugne le plus en Amérique, ce n'est pas l'extrême liberté qui y règne, c'est le peu de garantie qu'on y trouve contre la tyrannie.
ALEXIS DE TOCQUEVILLE:
De la Démocratie en Amérique (French)

What I find most repugnant about America is not the extreme liberty that prevails there, but the lack of guarantee to be found against tyranny.

La tyrannie se sert ordinairement de l'arbitraire, mais au besoin elle sait s'en passer.
ALEXIS DE TOCQUEVILLE:
De la Démocratie en Amérique (French)

Tyranny usually makes use of the arbitrary; but if need be, it can make do without it.

Es ehret der Knecht nur den Gewaltsamen.
FRIEDRICH HÖLDERLIN:
Menschenbeifall (German)

Servile spirits admire only the masterful.

Hubris phuteuei turannon
SOPHOCLES:
Oedippus Tyrannus (Greek)

The tyrant is born of insolence.

Alla katthanein kratei.
Pepaitera gar moira tēs turannidos
AESCHYLUS
Agamemnon (Greek

Death is preferable – it is a milder fate than tyranny.

Necesse est quod tyrannis sit pessimum.
ST. THOMAS AQUINAS
On Princely Government (Latin

It follows that tyranny is the worst form of government.

Omnes enim et habentur et dicuntur tyranni qui potestate utuntur perpetua in ea civitate quae libertate usa est.
CORNELIUS NEPOS
Contra Miltiade (Latin

All those who enjoy perpetual power in a state that has experienced liberty are regarded as and called tyrants.

U

UBIQUITY

Alibi atque alibi.
LATIN COLLOQUIAL EXPRESSION

At one time here, at another time there.

Ubique.
Motto of the Royal Artillery *(Latin)*

Everywhere.

Hic et ubique.
SHAKESPEARE:
Hamlet (Latin)

Here and everywhere.

UNCERTAINTY

Die Unruhe und Ungewissheit sind unser Theil.
J. W. VON GOETHE:
letter to Sophie von La Roche, 1774 *(German)*

Unrest and uncertainty are our lot.

UNDERSTANDING
see also Knowledge, the Soul, Wisdom.

Je tiens impossible de connoistre les parties sans connoistre le tout.
BLAISE PASCAL:
Pensées (French)

I maintain that it is impossible to understand the parts without understanding the whole.

Einen Menschen recht zu verstehen, müsste man zuweilen der nämliche Mensch sein, den man verstehen will.
GEORG CHRISTOPH LICHTENBERG:
Aphorismen (German)

To understand a man completely, you would sometimes have to be that person.

Epistēmēs gar oute nomos oute taxis oudemia kreittōn
PLATO:
Laws (Greek)

No law or ordinance is mightier than understanding.

Uma niwa notte miyo, hito niwa sotte miyo.
JAPANESE PROVERB

Know a horse by riding him; a person, by associating with him.

Defendimus etiam insipientem multa comprendere.
CICERO:
Academica (Latin)

We maintain that even the unwise man can understand many things.

Dictum sapienti sat est.
LATIN PROVERB

A word to the wise is sufficient.

Quae natura negabat
Visibus humanis, oculis ea pectoris hausit.
OVID:
Metamorphoses (Latin)

Those things that nature denied to human sight, she revealed to the eyes of the soul.

Ex vultibus tamen hominum mores colligo, et cum spatientum vidi, quid cogitet scio.
PETRONIUS:
Satyricon (Latin)

From a man's face I can read his character; if I see him walk, I know his thoughts.

THE UNEXPECTED

Nur das Unerwartete macht glücklich, aber es muss auf viel Erwartetes stossen, das es zerstreut.

ELIAS CANETTI:
Aufzeichnungen, 1951 *(German)*

Only the unexpected can bring good fortune, but it must come up against much of the expected and disperse it.

Polla metaxu pelei kulikos, kai kheileos akrou
GREEK PROVERB

There's many a slip 'twixt cup and lip.

Para doxan polla pollois dē egeneto
PLATO:
The Republic (Greek)

The unexpected often happens.

UNIQUENESS

Si je ne vaux pas mieux, au moins je suis autre.
J. J. ROUSSEAU:
Les Confessions (French)

I may not amount to much, but at least I am unique.

UNITY
see also Anger, Co-operation, Victory.

Toute puissance est faible à moins que d'être unie.

JEAN DE LA FONTAINE:
Le Vieillard et ses Enfants (French)

All power is feeble unless it is united.

Tous pour un, un pour tous!
ALEXANDRE DUMAS:
Les Trois Mousquetaires (French)

All for one, one for all!

L'Union fait la Force.
The Belgian national motto
(French)

Unity creates strength.

Unitate fortior.
Motto of the North Yorkshire
County Council *(Latin)*

Stronger in unity.

Virtus unita magis est efficax ad effectum inducendum, quam dispersa vel divisa.

ST. THOMAS AQUINAS:
On Princely Government (Latin)

A power united is more efficient than one dispersed or divided.

Manifestum est, quod plures multitudinem nullo modo conservant, si omnino dissentirent.

ST. THOMAS AQUINAS:
On Princely Government (Latin)

It is clear that many persons will never succeed in achieving unity in the community if they differ among themselves.

Tria juncta in uno.
Motto of the Guards Club
(Latin)

Three united as one.

THE UNIVERSE
see also Eternity, Mankind, Perfection, World.

Je sais que le fruit tombe au vent qui le secoue,
Que l'oiseau perd sa plume et la fleur son parfum;
Que la création est une grande roue
Qui ne peut se mouvoir sans ecraser quelqu'un;
Les mois, les jours, les flots des mers, les yeux qui pleurent,
Passent sous le ciel bleu:
Il faut que l'herbe pousse et que les enfants meurent,
Je le sais, ô mon Dieu!

VICTOR HUGO:
A Villequier (French)

I know that the fruit falls from the branch as the wind shakes it, that birds lose their feathers and flowers their perfume; that creation itself is a great wheel that cannot move without crushing someone. The months, the days, the waves, and the eyes that weep, pass under the blue heavens. That grass must grow, and children die, I understand, O Lord!

Tu gardes les coeurs de connaître
Que l'univers n'est qu'un défaut
Dans la pureté du Non-Etre!
PAUL VALÉRY:
Ebauche d'un Serpent (French)

You keep our hearts from knowing that the universe is only a defect in the purity of non-being! (the serpent is addressing the sun).

Das allgemeine Verhältniss erkennet nur Gott.
GERMAN PROVERB

Only God understands the universe.

Das Universum ist kein reiner Abdruck eines Ideals, wie das vollendete Werk eines menschlichen Künstlers.
J. C. F. VON SCHILLER:
Werke (German)

The universe is no clear impression of an ideal, like the complete work of some human artist.

M'illumino
D'immenso.
GIUSEPPE UNGARETTI:
Mattina (Italian)

I illuminate myself with immensity.

Così, tra questa
Immensità s'annega il pensier mio:
E il naufragar m'è dolce in questo mare.
GIACOMO LEOPARDI:
L'Infinito (Italian)

So, among this immensity my thought is drowned; and sweet it is to me to be a shipwreck in this sea.

Naturam primum studeat cognoscere rerum.
LUCRETIUS:
De Rerum Natura (Latin)

Let man's first study be the knowledge of the nature of the universe.

THE UNMENTIONABLE

Wovon man nicht sprechen kann, darüber muss man schweigen.
LUDWIG WITTGENSTEIN:
Tractatus Logico-philosophicus (German)

What we cannot speak about we must consign to silence.

UNTRUSTWORTHINESS
see also Lies, Peace, Women.

Hē glôss' homōmokh', hē de phrēn anōmotos
EURIPIDES:
Hippolytus (Greek)

It was my tongue that swore; my heart is unsworn.

UNWORTHINESS

Sella Chunradi habet Ascensoria Caroli.
MEDIAEVAL LATIN PROVERB

The throne of Conrad II (*c.* 990–1039, Holy Roman Emperor) is reached by the stairway of Charlemagne (meaning that no-one was worthy to succeed Charlemagne).

UPRIGHTNESS

Ipse decor, recte facti si praemia desint non movet et gratis paenitet esse probum.
OVID:
Ex Ponto (Latin)

Even the glory of a good deed, if it lacks reward, leaves men unmoved. Unrewarded uprightness brings them regret.

Is probus est quem paenitet quam probus sit et frugi bonae.
PLAUTUS:
Trinummus (Latin)

The only upright man is he who knows his shortcomings.

V

VALUE
see also Judgment.

Les choses ne valent que ce qu'on les fait valoir.
> MOLIÈRE:
> *Les Précieuses Ridicules (French)*

Things are only worth what you make them worth.

Proba mers facile emptorem reperit, tam etsi in abstruso sitast.
> PLAUTUS:
> *Poenulus (Latin)*

Good merchandise, even when hidden, soon finds buyers.

VANITY
see also Flattery, Fools, Loquacity, Moderation, Praise, Pride.

L'amour-propre est le plus grand de tous les flatteurs.
> FRANÇOIS, DUC DE LA ROCHEFOUCAULD:
> *Réflexions (French)*

Vanity is the greatest of all flatterers.

La vanité nous fait faire plus de choses contre notre goût que la raison.
> FRANÇOIS, DUC DE LA ROCHEFOUCAULD:
> *Réflexions (French)*

Vanity can make us do more things against our better judgment than reason can.

La vanité n'est que d'être sensibles a l'opinion probable des autres sur nous.
> PAUL VALÉRY:
> *Mauvaises Pensées (French)*

Vanity is only being sensitive to what other people probably think of us.

Les grandes et les petits ont mesmes accidans.
> BLAISE PASCAL:
> *Pensées (French)*

Great and small suffer the same mishaps.

Vain veut dire vide.
> FRENCH PROVERB

Vain means empty.

Quand on renonce à la vanité, il n'en faut pas faire à deux fois.
> P. C. DE C. DE MARIVAUX:
> *La Fausse Suivante (French)*

If you renounce vanity, you don't have to do it twice.

La sotte vanité jointe avecque l'envie,
Deux pivots sur qui roule aujourd'hui notre vie.
> JEAN DE LA FONTAINE:
> *Le Bûcheron et Mercure (French)*

Stupid vanity in league with envy – the two pivots on which our life revolves.

Sic leve, sic parvum est, animum quod laudis avarum
Subruit aut reficit.
> HORACE:
> *Epistles (Latin)*

So light, so small a circumstance can depress or raise up the spirit that longs for praise.

Vellem tam formosus esse, quam Maecius sibi videtur.
> SUETONIUS:
> *Domitianus (Latin)*

How I wish I were as fine looking as Maecius thinks he is (Domitian commenting on vanity).

Vsya zhizn' est' tsarstvo suetẏ,
I, dunoven'e smerti chuya,
Mẏ uvyadaem, kak tsvetẏ
> ALEKSEI TOLSTOY:
> *Ioann Damaskin (Russian)*

The whole of life is a country of vanity, and when we sense the breath of death, we wither away like flowers.

El león daria la mitad de su vida por un peine.
RAMÓN GÓMEZ DE LA SERNA:
Greguerías (Spanish)

The lion would give half his life for a comb.

VARIETY
see also Diversity.

Vivificat vitam varietas.
LATIN PROVERB

Variety is the spice of life.

VEGETARIANISM

Eines kann ich den Fleischessen prophezeien:
Die Gesellschaft der Zukunft wird vegetarisch
leben.
ADOLF HITLER
(German)

One thing I can prophecy to the flesh-eaters
of today: the society of the future will be
vegetarian.

VENGEANCE
see also Clemency, Revenge.

Tombe sur moi le ciel, pourvu que je me venge!
PIERRE CORNEILLE:
Rodogune (French)

Let me have vengeance, even if the heavens fall
on me!

Qui vindicet, ibit!
CLAUDIAN:
*Panegyricus de Quarto Consulatu Honorii Augusti
(Latin)*

The avenger will come!

Vindex sequetur!
SENECA:
Medea (Latin)

The avenger will pursue!

Qui asinum non potest, stratum caedit.
PETRONIUS:
Satyricon (Latin)

He who cannot reach the perpetrator avenges
himself on the innocent (*lit.* he who cannot beat
his donkey, beats the saddle).

Ja go zemszczę lepiej od ognia i wojny,
Lepiej niź sto tysięcy wroga,
Lepiej od Boga.
JULIUSZ SŁOWACKI:
Lilla Weneda (prologue) *(Polish)*

I shall avenge him better than fire and war,
better than a hundred thousand of the enemy,
better than God.

Ojo por ojo y diente por diente.
SPANISH PROVERB

An eye for an eye, and a tooth for a tooth.

Venganza, sólo sois vos
Ley del mundo sin prudencia.
TIRSO DE MOLINA:
Escarmientos para el Cuerdo (Spanish)

Vengeance, you are but the law of an imprudent
world!

VENICE

Venetia, Venetia, chi non te vede non te pregia,
Ma che t'ha troppo velato te dispregia.
ITALIAN PROVERB

Venice! he who never saw you cannot prize you;
he who has seen too much of you must despise
you!

VICE
see also Hypocrisy, Illness, Inadequacy, Kings, Money, Nature, Permissiveness, the Soul, Wisdom.

Le vice ne blesse les hommes que par intervalle;
les caractères apparents du vice les blessent du
matin au soir.
DENIS DIDEROT:
Le Neveu de Rameau (French)

Vice only wounds people from time to time;
but its visible characteristics affect them from
morning to night.

Le vice a été pour moi un vêtement, maintenant
il est collé à ma peau.
ALFRED DE MUSSET:
Lorenzaccio (French)

I wore vice like a garment; now it is stuck to my
skin.

Quand les vices nous quittent, nous nous flat-
tons de la créance que c'est nous qui les quittons.
FRANÇOIS, DUC DE LA ROCHEFOUCAULD:
Réflexions (French)

When our vices abandon us we flatter ourselves
with the belief that we abandoned them.

Nos vertus ne sont le plus souvent que des vices
déguisés.
FRANÇOIS, DUC DE LA ROCHEFOUCAULD:
Réflexions (French)

Very often our virtues are only vices in disguise.

Tous les vices à la mode passent pour vertus.
MOLIÈRE:
Don Juan (French)

All fashionable vices pass for virtues.

Le vice est de n'en pas sortir, non pas d'y entrer.
ARISTIPPUS
(as recounted by Montaigne in his *Essays*)
(French)

The vice lies not in entering, but in not coming
out (Aristippus, to his pupils, who blushed on
seeing him go into the house of a prostitute).

S'als malvatz no fos tan grans guaucx,
Avoleza ia no fora.
PEIRE D'ALVERNHE:
Belh m'es qu'ieu fass' huey Mays un Vers (French)

If vice were not such a great delight to the
wicked, it would never exist!

Utcunque defecere mores,
Dedecorant bene nata culpae.
HORACE:
Odes (Latin)

Vice will stain the noblest race and the paternal
stamp efface (*tr.* Conington) (*lit.* wherever laws
of conduct fail, vice mars the well-born).

Etiam sine magistro vitia discuntur.
SENECA:
Natural Questions (Latin)

Vices can be learnt, even without a teacher.

Nos multa alligant, multa debilitant.
SENECA:
Epistles (Latin)

We are fettered and weakened by many vices.

Area scelerum.
CICERO:
Epistles (Latin)

Where vices have full scope.

VICTORY
see also Achievement, Effort, Opportunity, Steadfastness, War.

Une victoire racontée en détail, on ne sait plus ce
qui la distingue d'une défaite.
JEAN-PAUL SARTRE:
Le Diable et le Bon Dieu (French)

Once you hear the details of a victory, it is hard
to distinguish it from a defeat.

Nos exaequat victoria caelo.
LUCRETIUS:
De Rerum Natura (Latin)

Victory puts us on a level with heaven.

Veni, vidi, vici.
JULIUS CAESAR:
Bellum Civile (Latin)

I came, I saw, I conquered.

Ibi semper est victoria ubi concordia est.
LATIN PROVERB

Where there is unity, there lies victory.

VIGOUR

Eti moi menos empedon estin
HOMER:
Iliad; Odyssey (Greek)

As yet my strength is unimpaired.

VILLAINS
see also Crime, Thieves and theft.

Emoi gar hostis adikos ōn sophos legein
Pephuke, pleistēn zēmian ophliskanei
EURIPIDES:
Medea (Greek)

To me a wicked man who is also eloquent seems
the most guilty of them all (*tr.* Vellacott).

Kakou gar andros dōr' onēsin ouk ekhei
EURIPIDES:
Medea (Greek)

No fortune springs from the gifts of a villain.

VIOLENCE
see also Force, Wealth.

La violence, c'est bon pour ceux qui n'ont rien à perdre.
JEAN-PAUL SARTRE:
Le Diable et le Bon Dieu (French)

Violence suits those who have nothing to lose.

Qui enim per violentiam dominium surripit non efficitur vere praelatus vel dominus.
ST. THOMAS AQUINAS:
Commentary on the Sentences of Peter Lombard (Latin)

He who achieves power by violence does not truly become lord or master.

Iuvenile vitium est regere non posse impetum.
SENECA:
Troades (Latin)

Ungoverned violence is a fault of youth.

VIRGIL

Questi son gli occhi della nostra lingua.
FRANCESCO PETRARCA:
Trionfo della Fama (Italian)

These are the eyes of our language (referring to Virgil and Cicero).

Virgilium vatem melius sua carmina laudent.
Inscription in a library *(Latin)*

Virgil is lauded best in Virgil's lays.

VIRGINS
see also Chastity, Purity.

La verginella è simile alla rosa
Ch'in bel giardin su la nativa spina
Mentre sola e sicura si riposa,
Né gregge né pastor se le avicina.
LUDOVICO ARIOSTO:
Orlando Furioso (Italian)

A virgin is like a rose growing in a garden, defended by its thorns, and safe from the shepherd and his flock.

VIRTUE
see also Crime, Duty, Envy, Greatness, Hypocrisy, Idleness, Illness, Inadequacy, Leadership, Moderation, Order, Patriotism, Smoking, Vice, Wisdom, Work.

La naissance n'est rien où la vertu n'est pas.
MOLIÈRE:
Don Juan (French)

Birth counts for nothing if virtue is not there.

La vertu se fait respecter, et le respect est incommode; la vertu se fait admirer, et l'admiration n'est pas amusante.
DENIS DIDEROT:
Le Neveu de Rameau (French)

Virtue commands respect, and respect is uncomfortable; virtue demands admiration, and admiration is boring.

On loue la vertu, mais on la hait, mais on la fuit, mais elle gèle de froid, et dans ce monde il faut avoir les pieds chauds.
DENIS DIDEROT:
Le Neveu de Rameau (French)

We praise virtue, but we hate it and flee from it; virtue is freezing cold, and in this world we have to keep our feet warm.

Les belles actions cachées sont les plus estimables.
BLAISE PASCAL:
Pensées (French)

Good deeds, when concealed, are the most admirable.

Gens liberes, bien nez, bien instruictz, conversans en compaignies honnestes, ont par nature un instinct et aguillon, qui tousjours les poulse à faictz vertueux et retire de vice, lequel ilz nommoient honneur.
RABELAIS:
Gargantua (French)

Men that are free, well-born, well-bred, and conversant with honest company, have naturally an instinct and a spur which prompts them to virtuous actions and withdraws them from vice, and which is called honour.

La vertu est le premier titre de noblesse.
MOLIÈRE:
Don Juan (French)

Virtue is nobility's highest title.

Tēs d' aretēs hidrōta theoi proparoithen
ethēkan
Athanatoi
HESIOD:
Works and Days (Greek)

The immortal gods have decreed that virtue cannot be attained without sweat.

Aretēn hēn te labein khalepon
THEOGNIS:
Fragment (Greek)

Virtue is not easily achieved.

Dizesthai biotēn, aretēn d' hotan, ēi bios ēdē
PHOCYLIDES:
Fragment (Greek)

Look first for a living, and then for virtue when you are well established.

To sōphron hōs hapantakhou kalon,
Kai dexan esthlēn en brotois karpizetai
EURIPIDES:
Hippolytus (Greek)

How beautiful is virtue wherever one finds it, and the good reputation it earns for itself.

Ou didakton estin hē aretē
GREEK PROVERB

Virtue is not a thing that can be taught.

To kalon kai to aiskhron
GREEK EXPRESSION

Virtue and vice.

Ou gar estin ho ti meizon anthrōpos apolauein theou pephuken ē to mimēsei kai diōxei tōn en ekeinōi kalōn kai agathōn eis aretēn kathistasthai
PLUTARCH:
Moralia (Greek)

Man is fitted to derive from God no greater blessing than to become settled in virtue

through copying and aspiring to the beauty and the goodness that are his.

O tlēmon aretē, logos ar' ēsth' egō de se hōs ergon ēskoun
Brutus' dying words
(quoted from a Greek tragedy) (Greek)

Woeful virtue, you are after all nothing but a word – yet I was practising you as a reality!

Rectique cultus pectora roborant.
HORACE:
Odes (Latin)

Virtue arms the robust mind.

Virtuosa igitur vita est congregationis humanae finis.
ST. THOMAS AQUINAS:
On Princely Government (Latin)

The object of human society is a virtuous life.

Vile latens virtus.
CLAUDIAN:
Panegyricus de Quarto Consulatu Honorii Augusti (Latin)

Hidden virtue has no value.

Virtutes discere vitia dediscere est.
SENECA:
Epistles (Latin)

Learning virtue means unlearning vice.

Honestum et turpe.
LATIN EXPRESSION

Virtue and vice.

Virtus, repulsae nescia sordidae,
Intaminatis fulget honoribus.
HORACE:
Odes (Latin)

True worth, that never knows ignoble defeat, shines with undimmed glory.

Probitas laudatur et alget.
JUVENAL: Satires (Latin)

Virtue is praised, and yet freezes (i.e. is neglected).

Cassis tutissima virtus.

> Motto of the original sixteenth-century ship,
> *The Golden Hind,* and that of Sir Christopher
> Hatton, the major shareholder in Francis
> Drake's venture to circumnavigate
> the world *(Latin)*

Virtue is the safest helmet.

Nihil est enim virtute amabilius.

> CICERO:
> *De Natura Deorum (Latin)*

Nothing is more worthy of love than virtue.

Gratior et pulchro veniens in corpore virtus.

> VIRGIL:
> *Aeneid (Latin)*

Virtue is the more welcome when it comes in an acceptable guise.

Nec vero hominis natura perfecta est, et efficitur tamen in homine virtus.

> CICERO:
> *De Natura Deorum (Latin)*

Man's nature is not perfect, yet virtue may be realised in man.

Ipsa quidem Virtus pretium sibi.

> CLAUDIAN:
> *Panegyricus Dictus Manlio Theodoro Consuli (Latin)*

Virtue is its own reward.

Cum virtute congruere semper.

> CICERO:
> *De Officiis (Latin)*

Always keep in line with virtue.

Cum bonis ambula.

> LATIN PROVERB

Walk in the ways of good.

Domat omnia virtus.

> LATIN PROVERB

Virtue conquers everything.

Vilius argentum est auro, virtutibus aurum.

> HORACE:
> *Epistles (Latin)*

Silver is worth less than gold, gold less than virtue.

Virtus difficilis inventu est, rectorem ducemque desiderat.

> SENECA:
> *Natural Questions (Latin)*

Virtue is difficult to find – it needs a director and a guide.

Dum modo morata recte veniat, dotata est satis.

> PLAUTUS:
> *Aulularia (Latin)*

As long as she is wise and good, a girl has sufficient dowry.

¡Qué muda la virtud por el prudente!
¡Qué redundante y llena de ruido
Por el vano, ambicioso y aparente!

> Attrib. Andrés Fernández de Andrada:
> *Epístola Moral (Spanish)*

How silent is virtue in the prudent! How redundant, and full of noise it is in the ambitious, flashy and frivolous!

VULNERABILITY

Mish kull marra tislam al-jarra

> ARAB PROVERB

The pitcher eventually gets broken.

Tant va la cruche à l'eau qu'enfin elle se brise.

> FRENCH PROVERB
> (quoted in Molière: *Don Juan*) *(French)*

The jug goes so often to the well that eventually it will break.

Pulmo hominis facile deficit.

> CLAUDE GALIEN:
> *De Facultatibus (Latin)*

A man's lungs easily fail him.

Si el cántaro da en la piedra, o la piedra en el cántaro, mal para el cántaro.

> SPANISH PROVERB

No matter whether the pitcher hits the stone, or the stone the pitcher, it is the pitcher that will suffer.

WAR

see also Arms, Battles, Belligerence, Civil War, Discord, Laments, Law, Peace, Soldiers.

Quand les riches se font la guerre, ce sont les pauvres qui meurent.

> JEAN-PAUL SARTRE:
> *Le Diable et le Bon Dieu (French)*

When the rich make war, it's the poor who die.

Jeder Krieg enthält alle früheren.

> ELIAS CANETTI:
> *Aufzeichnungen, 1951 (German)*

Every war includes all earlier wars.

Wir führen einen Kampf auf Leben und Tod und können zur Zeit keine Geschenke machen.

> ADOLF HITLER:
> letter to Franco, 1940 *(German)*

We are conducting a life and death struggle and can make no concessions to time.

Von allen Religionen des Menschen ist der Krieg die zäheste; aber auch sie lässt sich auflösen.

> ELIAS CANETTI:
> *Aufzeichnungen, 1942 (German)*

War is man's toughest religion; but even war loosens its grip.

Will vom Krieg leben
Wird ihm wohl müssen auch etwas geben.

> BERTOLT BRECHT:
> *Mutter Courage und ihre Kinder (German)*

He who would live off war must eventually yield something in return.

Der Krieg wird seinen Mann ernähren.

> BERTOLT BRECHT:
> *Mutter Courage und ihre Kinder (German)*

War provides a livelihood for her husband.

Die Sieg und Niederlagen der Grosskopfigen oben und der von unten fallen nämlich nicht immer zusammen, durchaus nicht. Es gibt sogar Fälle wo die Niederlag für die Untern eigentlich ein Gewinn ist für sie. Die Ehr ist verloren, aber nix sonst.

> BERTOLD BRECHT:
> *Mutter Courage und ihre Kinder (German)*

Leaders' victories and defeats are not always victories and defeats for their followers. Definitely not. There have even been cases where a defeat proved a victory for the underlings. They only lost their honour – nothing else at all!

So wie die Welt nicht von Kriegen lebt, so leben die Völker nicht von Revolutionen.

> ADOLF HITLER:
> *Mein Kampf (German)*

Just as the world does not live by war, so can people live without revolutions.

Lokhou d' exebain' Arēs

> EURIPIDES:
> *Troades (Greek)*

War stalked forth from its hiding-place.

Iustum enim est bellum quibus necessarium, et pia arma ubi nulla nisi in armis spes est.

> NICCOLÒ MACHIAVELLI:
> *The Prince (Latin)*

War is just when it is necessary; arms are permissible when there is no hope except in arms.

Quaeritur belli exitus,
Non causa.

> SENECA:
> *Hercules Furens (Latin)*

We are investigating the outcome, not the cause, of a war.

Quis furor est atram bellis accersere Mortem.

> TIBULLUS:
> *Elegies (Latin)*

How mad it is to summon grim death by means of war!

Numina nulla premunt: mortali urgemur ab hoste
Mortales.

VIRGIL:
Aeneid (Latin)

No gods assail us; we are mortals fighting with mortals.

Diu apparandum est bellum ut vincas celerius.

LATIN PROVERB

To win a war quickly takes long preparation.

Proelium quidem aut bellum suscipiendum omnino negabat, nisi cum maior emolumenti spes quam damni metus ostenderetur.

SUETONIUS:
Divus Augustus (Latin)

[Augustus] used to say that a war or a battle should not be begun under any circumstances unless the hope of gain was clearly greater than the fear of loss.

Ducis in consilio posita est virtus militum.

LATIN PROVERB

A soldier's valour hangs upon his general's strategy.

Ad arma!

LATIN EXPRESSION

To arms!

Bella viri pacemque gerant quis bella gerenda.

VIRGIL:
Aeneid (Latin)

Leave peace and war to men whose business it is to fight.

Nobis ad belli auxilium pro nomine tanto
Exiguae vires.

VIRGIL:
Aeneid (Latin)

Though great our name, small is our strength for war.

Heu, quibus ille
Iactatus fatis! quae bella exhausta canebat!

VIRGIL:
Aeneid (Latin)

Alas! how harried by fate he has been! What wars he told of, endured to the end!

Militare non est delictum, sed propter praedam militare peccatum est.

ST. MAXIMUS, BISHOP OF TURIN:
Works (Latin)

It is not wrong to perform military service; but to serve for booty is sinful.

Ferox gens, nullam esse vitam sino armis rati.

LIVY:
History (Latin)

A savage tribe, believing life worthless without war.

Tidak-kah děngar bunyi
Gěnděrang pěrang di-Tukasan
Palu taboh-tabohan?
Hari dinihari, bulan pun terang

*Hikayat raja-raja pasai
(Malay)*

Do you not hear the thudding of the war-drums at Tukasan, beaten thud on thud at the dawn of day in the light of the moon?

De spøker i nye menn.

NORDAHL GRIEG:
De Beste (Norwegian)

Ghosts looming through the minds of new men (referring to the war dead).

Ante el sufrimiento, la sangre y la muerte del hombre, los preceptos morales se desvanecen en nada.

RAFAEL MARTÍNEZ NADAL:
El Publico (Spanish)

In the face of suffering, blood and death, moral principles fade away into nothing.

WARNINGS
see also Dreams, Omens, Oracles.

Quamvis acerbus qui monet nulli nocet.

LATIN PROVERB

The warning voice, however sharp, harms none.

Quodsi quis monitis tardas adverterit auris,
Heu referet quanto verba dolore meo!

PROPERTIUS:
Elegies (Latin)

Anyone slow to heed my warnings will repeat
my words, alas, with what deep pain!

WASTE

Caligare in sole.

LATIN PROVERB
(quoted in Quintilian: *Institutiones Oratoriae*)

To grope in broad daylight.

Perdendi finem nemo nisi egestas facit.

LATIN PROVERB

Only want sets a limit to waste.

Addere calcaria sponte currenti.

LATIN PROVERB
(quoted in Pliny's *Epistles*)

To spur a willing horse.

WATER
see also Pride, Wine.

Ariston hudōr

PINDAR:
Olympian Odes (Greek)

Water is best.

WAVES
see also Sea.

Chaque flot est un ondin qui nage dans le
courant.

ALOYSIUS BERTRAND:
Gaspard de la Nuit: Ondine (French)

Each wave is a water-sprite swimming in the
current.

Les marées reviennent chaque jour avec les
gazettes.

RAYMOND QUENEAU:
Les Marées (French)

The tides turn up each day like the newspapers.

WAYS AND MEANS
see also Achievement, Skill, Necessity, Purpose.

Il faut casser des oeufs pour faire une omelette.

FRENCH PROVERB

To make an omelette we have to break eggs.

Allōi hēlōi ekkrouein ton hēlon

LUCIAN:
Dialogues (Greek)

To drive out one nail by another.

Dokō men, ouden rhēma sun kerdei kakon

SOPHOCLES:
Electra (Greek)

The end justifies the means.

WEALTH
see also Avarice, Contentment, Friendship, Greatness, Honesty, Knowledge, Marriage, Materialism, Money, Possessions, Poverty, Prosperity, Reputation, Society, the Soul, Thrift, Wisdom.

At-taḥānī mā yighannī fagri

ARAB PROVERB

Wishing does not make a poor man rich.

Toutes les occupations des hommes sont à avoir
du bien.

BLAISE PASCAL:
Pensées (French)

Mankind's one objective is to amass wealth.

Les richesses font les riches.

FRENCH PROVERB

Money begets money (*lit.* riches make riches).

L'or est tout, et le reste, sans or, n'est rien.

DENIS DIDEROT:
Le Neveu de Rameau (French)

Gold is everything; without gold there's
nothing!

Le plus riche des hommes, c'est l'econome. Le plus pauvre, c'est l'avare.

S. R. N. CHAMFORT:
Maximes et Pensées (French)

The richest man is the most economical. The poorest man is the miser.

Quoi qu'on fasse, on ne peut se déshonorer quand on est riche.

DENIS DIDEROT:
Le Neveu de Rameau (French)

No matter what you do, you can't dishonour yourself when you are rich.

L'or, même à la laideur, donne un teint de beauté.

NICOLAS BOILEAU:
Satires (French)

Gold lends a touch of beauty even to the ugly.

Das Leben der Reichen ist ein langer Sonntag.

GEORG BÜCHNER:
Der Hessische Landbote (German)

The life of the rich is one long Sunday.

Tois gar plousiois polla paramuthia phasin einai

GREEK PROVERB
(quoted in Plato's *Republic*)

The rich have many consolations.

Makarios hostis ousian kai noun ekhei

GREEK PROVERB

Happy is he who has both wealth and common-sense.

Ploutōi d' aretē kai kudos opēdei

HESIOD:
Works and Days (Greek)

Wealth brings virtue and fame.

Khrēmata d' oukh harpakta, theosdota pollon ameinō

HESIOD:
Works and Days (Greek)

God-given wealth is far better than wealth obtained by violence.

Oiomai se kai dia touto hēdion ploutein hoti peinēsas khrēmatōn peploutēkas

XENOPHON:
Cyropaedia (Greek)

I believe you enjoy your wealth so much more since it was only after you longed for riches that you became wealthy.

Ison toi ploutousin hotōi polus arguros esti kai khrusos . . . kai hōi mona tauta paresti, gastri te kai pleurēis kai posin habra pathein

SOLON:
Fragment (Greek)

Equal surely is the wealth of him who has much gold and silver . . . to that of him who has only this – comfort in stomach, and sides, and feet.

Ta khrēmata kai ktōmenous euphrainei tous anthrōpous kai kektēmenous hēdion poiei zēn

GREEK PROVERB

Riches both make men happy while they are acquiring them, and give them a more pleasant life when they have acquired them.

Tauta moi diplē merimna phrastos estin en phresin,
Mēte khrēmatōn anandrōn plēthos en timēi sebein
Mēt' akhrēmatoisi lampein phōs hoson sthenos para

AESCHYLUS:
The Persians (Greek)

Two thoughts have been much on my mind: we should not respect riches without men; and men without riches remain in obscurity.

Come ricco tu sei, tu sei pregiato.

GIAMBATTISTA CINTHIO GIRALDI:
Euphimia (Italian)

Once you are rich you will find yourself very highly esteemed.

Infirmi animi est pati non posse divitias.

SENECA:
Epistles (Latin)

To be unable to bear riches shows an unbalanced mind.

Nemo nascitur dives.

SENECA:
Epistles (Latin)

No-one is born rich.

Multis parasse divitias non finis miseriarum fuit
sed mutatio.

SENECA:
Epistles (quoting Epicurus: *Fragment*) *(Latin)*

For many men, the acquisition of wealth does
not end their troubles, it only changes them.

Quod habes ne habeas et illuc quod non habes
habeas, malum,
Quandoquidem nec tibi bene esse pote pati
neque alteri.

LATIN SONG
(quoted in Plautus: *Trinummus*)

May you lose what you've got and get what you
lack; it does no good to either of us.

Non dominantur opes.

CLAUDIAN:
*Panegyricus de Tertio Consulatu Honorii
Augusti (Latin)*

Wealth holds no sway.

Assem habeas, assem valeas.

PETRONIUS:
Satyricon (Latin)

Your wealth is estimated by your possessions.

Quis sit divitiarum modus, quaeris? Primus
habere quod necesse est, proximus quod sat est.

SENECA:
Epistles (Latin)

You ask what is the proper limit for wealth? It is,
first, to have what is necessary; and, second, to
have what is enough.

Ser rico es la mayor calamidad que puede pesar
sobre un hombre.

SPANISH PROVERB

To be rich is the greatest disaster that can afflict
a man.

Madre, yo al oro me humillo;
El es mi amante y mi amado,

Pues de puro enamorado,
De contino anda amarillo.

FRANCISCO DE QUEVEDO:
Letrilla Lĩrica (Spanish)

Mother, I have given in to wealth: he is my lover,
and I his. Thus from pure affection comes a
golden stream!

WIDOWS AND WIDOWERS
see also Families, Grief, Mourning.

N'oppose plus ton deuil au bonheur où j'aspire,
Ton visage est-il fait pour demeurer voilé?
Sors de ta nuit funèbre, et permets que j'admire
Les divines clartés des yeux qui m'ont brûlé . . .

FRANÇOIS MAYNARD:
La Belle Vieille (French)

Don't parry my aspiration with your mourning!
Must your features remain veiled? Come forth
from the night of the dead and let me admire
those splendid eyes whose glance has already
singed me.

Ti gar pleon aneri kēdeus mounōi huper gaiēs,
oikhomenēs alokhou?

GREEK PROVERB

Once his wife is dead, what but grief is left for a
husband?

Viuda lozana, ó casada ó sepultada ó
emparedada.

SPANISH PROVERB

A buxom widow should get herself married, or
buried, or shut away in a convent.

Cuando el que buen siglo aya seía en este portal,
Daba sombra a la casas e reluzié la cal';
Mas do non mora ome, la casa poca val.

JUAN RUIZ:
Libro de Buen Amor (Spanish)

When your late husband used to sit in this
doorway, he lent dignity and radiance to the
whole street. But a house without a husband is
worth little.

WIND
see also Autumn.

Tout sur terre appartient aux princes, hors le
vent

VICTOR HUGO:
La Rose de l'Infante (French)

Everything in the world belongs to the princes,
except the wind!

Der Wind, das einzige Freie in der Zivilisation.
ELIAS CANETTI:
Aufzeichnungen, 1943 (German)

The wind is the only thing in civilisation to enjoy
freedom.

Wenn es in den alten Apfelbäumen rauscht, ist
es anders.
Und wenn es in Tannenwipfeln rauscht, ist es
anders.
Wenn es über Felder braust, ist es anders.
Wenn es im Weidenbusche rauscht, ist es
anders.

PETER ALTENBERG:
Geräusche (German)

It's different when it rushes through the old
apple-trees; and it's different again when it rus-
tles across the tops of the pine trees. It's different
when it storms across the fields; and it's different
when it rushes through the hedges.

Jakieś dzikie pradzieje śpiewa, śpiewa, zamiera,
U szyb wisi, całuje, do pokoju się wdziera.
Potem płacząc opada, zrozpaczony, zmęczony,
Zawierusza się w nocy, bijąc korne pokłony.

JULJAN TUWIM:
Wiatr ją Prosi (Polish)

It sings of the savage events of time immemorial;
sings, dies away, hangs at the window, kisses,
and tries to break into the room. Then, weeping,
it falls, plunged into despair, worn out, and
strays into the night, bent in humble bowing.

Pĕrtama angin si-charek kafan,
Kĕdua angin tajam tĕmilang,
Ketiga angin puting bĕliong,
Kĕĕmpat bĕdil bĕrjanggut,
Kĕlima payong 'Ali,

Kĕĕnam si-lautan tulang
Kĕtujoh si-hampar rĕbah

Hikayat Maalim Dewa (Malay)

Wind that could tear a dead man's shroud, wind
as sharp as a spade's edge, wind as keen as the
tip of an axe, wind that swoops like bearded
shot, wind umbrella-like in form, wind that fills
the sea with bones, wind that levels all before it.

Con tal vehemencia el viento
Viene del mar, que sus sones
Elementales contagian
El silencio de la noche.

LUIS CERNUDA:
El Viento y el Alma (Spanish)

So strongly comes the wind from the sea, that its
elemental sounds infect night's silence.

WINE
see also Contentment, Drinking,
Enjoyment, Oblivion, Truth.

Le vin coule en la bouche,
Le vin ce sent, se touche
Et se boit; je l'aime mieux
Que musique, fleurs et cieux.

FRENCH FOLK SONG

Wine pours into our mouths; you can smell it,
feel it and drink it. I prefer it to music, flowers or
the heavens.

Un bon bouveur doit au premier coup reconnaître le cru, au second la qualité, au troisième
l'année.

ALEXANDRE DUMAS:
La Dame de Monsoreau (French)

At the first sip a good drinker will recognise the
vineyard, at the second the quality, and at the
third the year.

Ah! bouteille, ma mie,
Pourquoi vous videz-vous?

MOLIÈRE:
Le Médecin Malgré Lui (French)

Ah, bottle, my friend! – why have you emptied
yourself?

Vom donnernden Gott kommet die Freude des Weins.

> FRIEDRICH HÖLDERLIN:
> *Brod und Wein (German)*

The enjoyment of wine comes from the thunderous god.

Isan d' es te ton olbion
Ton te kheirona dōk' ekhein
Oinou terpsin alupon

> EURIPIDES:
> *The Bacchae (Greek)*

Both to the rich and the poor he gave wine, the happy antidote for sorrow.

Pinōmen. Koinos pasi limēn Aidēs

> LEONIDAS OF TARENTUM:
> *Epigrams (Greek)*

Let us all drink, and reach the harbour of Hell!

Oinos elenkhei
Ton tropon

> CALLIAS OF ARGOS:
> Fragment *(Greek)*

Wine is the test of character.

Quid non ebrietas dissignant?

> HORACE:
> *Epistles (Latin)*

What miracles can a wine-cup not work!

Bonum vinum laetificat cor humanis.

> LATIN PROVERB

The human heart rejoices in good wine.

Vitigeni latices in aquai fontibus audent
Misceri.

> LUCRETIUS:
> *De Rerum Natura (Latin)*

The vine's juices venture boldly to intermingle with the water.

Non vinum viris moderari, sed viri vino solent.

> PLAUTUS:
> *Truculentus (Latin)*

Men should control the effects of wine, not wine men.

Dissipat Euhius
Curas edaces.

> HORACE:
> *Odes (Latin)*

Bacchus dispels growing cares.

In vino veritas.

> LATIN PROVERB

Truth emerges when you're drunk (*lit.* in wine, truth).

Merum sobrio male olet.

> LATIN PROVERB

Fragrant wine smells bad to the sober man.

El vino bueno es caro y el malo hace daño.

> SPANISH PROVERB

Good wine is dear; bad wine will do you no good.

El amigo y el vino, antiguo.

> SPANISH PROVERB

Friends and wine should be old.

El agua, para los bueyes: el vino, para los reyes.

> SPANISH PROVERB

Water for oxen, wine for kings.

WINE
see also Autumn, Home, Snow, Spring.

Ouvre plus grande la fenêtre;
L'air est si calme, pur et frais,
Que les ormeaux et que les hêtres
Sont tous vêtus et tout drapés,
De branche en branche, de neige blanche.

> FRANCIS VIELÉ-GRIFFIN:
> *Matinée d'Hiver (French)*

Open the window wider; the air is so fresh and pure and calm, that the elms and the beech trees are all decked and draped, branch by branch, with white snow.

L'oiseau s'en va, la feuille tombe,
L'amour s'éteint, car c'est l'hiver.

> THÉOPHILE GAUTIER:
> *La Dernière Feuille (French)*

The birds abandon us, the leaves fall, and love is quenched, for it is winter.

L'hiver est une maladie.
ALFRED DE MUSSET:
Il faut qu'une Porte soit Ouverte ou Fermée (French)

Winter is a disease.

Er quant s'embla.l foill del fraisse
E.l ram s'entressecon pel som
(Que per la rusca no.i poja
La dolz' umors de la saba)
E.ill aucel son de cisclar mut
Pel freit que par que.ls destrenga.
RAIMBAUT D'AURENGA:
Cars Douz (French)

When the leaf is stolen from the ash, and on the crests of the tree-tops the boughs are withering, and the cold has brought the birds' song to an end.

Ar vei bru, escur, trebol cel
Don per l'air vent' e giscl' e plou,
E chai neus e gels e gibres,
E.l sol qu'era cautz, ferms e durs
Es sa calors teun' e flaca,
E fuelh e flors chai jos dels rams
Si que en plais ni en blaca
Non aug chans, ni critz mas dins murs.
RAIMBAUT D'AURENGA:
Ar Vei Bru (French)

Now I can see sombre, dark and stormy skies, bringing gale and rain and howling gusts throughout the land. Snow, ice and frost beset us. The sun, once hot and strong, yields little heat; the boughs are denuded of blossom and leaf, and no birdsong comes from the hedges and woodlands.

Möhte ich verslâfen des winters zît!
WALTHER VON DER VOGELWEIDE:
Uns hât der Winter Geschât über al (German)

If only I could sleep away the winter time!

Weh mir, wo nehm ich, wenn
Es Winter ist, die Blumen und wo
Den Sonnenschein
Und Schatten der Erde?
Die Mauer stehn
Sprachlos und kalt, im Winde
Klirren die Fahnen.
FRIEDRICH HÖLDERLIN:
Hälfte des Lebens (German)

Woe is me! when winter comes, where shall I find the flowers, the sunshine, and the shady places? The walls stand speechless and cold. The weathercock jangles in the wind.

Die gleiche weisse Decke aller Strassen,
Hüllt und bedeckt die Mühsal auf der Erde.
Es stirbt ein Jahr, lautlos, entsühnt, gelassen,
Gibt dem Geschicke heim, was dauern werde.
ERWIN G. KOLBENHEYER:
Wintersonnenwende (German)

The same white blanket covers all the streets and adorns the hardship of the world. The old year dies without a sound, absolved and tired, handing back to fate something to regret.

Gáeth ard úar;
ísel grían;
gair a rith;
ruirthech rían.
Anonymous ninth or tenth century
Irish poet *(Gaelic)*

The wind is high and cold; the sun low; its course is short; the sea runs strongly.

Poutru pobelevshiĭ dvor,
Kurtinȳ, krovli i zabor,
Na stëklakh legkie uzorȳ,
Derev'ya v zimnem serebre,
Sorok vesëlȳkh na dvore
I myagko ustlannȳe gorȳ
Zimȳ blistatel'nȳm kovrom.
Vsë yarko, vsë belo krugom
ALEKSANDR SERGEEVICH PUSHKIN:
Eugen Onegin (Russian)

In the morning the whitened yard, flower beds, roofs and fence; delicate patterns on the window panes; the trees in winter silver, gay magpies outside, and the hills softly overspread with winter's brilliant carpeting. All is bright, all is white around.

Ya el rigor importuno i grave ielo
Desnuda los esmaltes i belleza
De la pintada tierra, i con tristeza
S'ofende en niebla oscura el claro cielo.
FERNANDO DE HERRERA:
Soneto (Spanish)

The unseasonable cold and the heavy frost strip the enamel and the beauty of the earth's painted landscape, and the clear skies are besmirched by dark clouds.

WISDOM

see also Advice, Beauty, Common sense, Compromise, Distrust, Enjoyment, Folly, Future, Greatness, Idealism, Ignorance, Judgment, Language, Leadership, Love, Mankind, Mediocrity, Moderation, Old age, Philosophers, Poets and poetry, the Soul, Truth, Understanding.

Le monde est plein de gens qui ne sont pas plus sages.

JEAN DE LA FONTAINE:
La Grenouille qui se veut faire aussi Grosse que le Boeuf (French)

The world is full of people who are not wise enough.

La Sagesse nous envoye à l'enfance.

BLAISE PASCAL:
Pensées (French)

Wisdom sends us back to our childhood.

La sagesse:
C'est un trésor qui n'embarrasse point.

JEAN DE LA FONTAINE:
Les Souhaits (French)

Wisdom is a treasure whose possession never embarrasses us.

C'est une grande folie de vouloir être sage tout seul.

FRANÇOIS, DUC DE LA ROCHEFOUCAULD:
Réflexions (French)

It's foolish to want to be the only wise one.

Nous ne vivons que deux moments:
Qu'il en soit un pour la sagesse.

VOLTAIRE:
A Madame du Châtelet (French)

In our lives we only live two moments – let one be for wisdom.

Apprenez à connaître, enfants qu'attend l'effort,
Les inégalités des âmes et du sort.

VICTOR HUGO:
Les Contemplations: le Maître d'Études (French)

Learn to recognise, children on the brink of discovery, the injustices of minds and of chance.

La sagesse est la connaissance en tant qu'elle modère toutes choses, et particulièrement elle-même.

PAUL VALÉRY:
Mauvaises Pensées (French)

Wisdom is understanding in that it moderates everything, particularly itself.

Il y a plus de fous que de sages, et dans le sage même, il y a plus de folie que de sagesse.

S. R. N. CHAMFORT:
Maximes et Pensées (French)

There are more fools than wise men, and even among the wise there is more stupidity than wisdom.

De vains prestiges forment un lieu passager; il n'y a que la sagesse qui le rende durable.

J. J. ROUSSEAU:
Du Contrat Social (French)

Empty reputations find only a temporary resting place; only wisdom can make it lasting.

Les passions font *vivre* l'homme; la sagesse le fait seulement *durer*.

S. R. N. CHAMFORT:
Maximes et Pensées (French)

Passion makes a man live; wisdom only makes him last!

Scharfsinn ist ein Vergrösserungsglas, Witz ein Verkleinerungsglas.

GEORG CHRISTOPH LICHTENBERG:
Aphorismen (German)

Wisdom is a magnifying glass, wit a reducing glass.

Der wîse minnet niht sô sêre,
Alsam die gotes hulde und êre.

WALTHER VON DER VOGELWEIDE:
Swer Houbetsünde und Schande Tuot (German)

A wise man loves nothing so much as God's grace and honour.

Der Weise vergisst seinen Kopf.

ELIAS CANETTI:
Aufzeichnungen, 1951 (German)

The wise man would forget his own head.

Bestünde nur die Weisheit mit der Jugend
Und Republiken ohne Tugend,
So wär die Welt dem höchsten Ziele nah.

J. W. VON GOETHE:
Faust (subsequently omitted) *(German)*

If only youth had wisdom, if only there were
republics without virtue, the world would be
closer to its highest goal!

Thaumazo kai autos palai tēn emautou sophian
kai apistō

PLATO:
Cratylus (Greek)

I have been admiring my own wisdom all day; I
just cannot believe it! (said by Socrates).

Sophias phthonēsai mallon ē ploutou kalon
GREEK PROVERB

It is better to envy wisdom than riches.

Nomōn ekhesthai panta dei ton sōphrona
GREEK PROVERB

A wise man should observe the law in all things.

To sophon d' ou sophia

EURIPIDES:
The Bacchae (Greek)

Cleverness is not wisdom.

To thaumazein arkhē esti tēs sophias
GREEK PROVERB

Wonder is the beginning of wisdom.

Ē ouk haper epistēmones, tauta kai sophoi?
PLATO:
Theaetetus (Greek)

Is not wisdom based on being well-informed?

Pros tas tukhas gar tas phrenas kektēmetha
EURIPIDES:
Hippolytus (Greek)

A reputation for wisdom depends very much on
luck.

Pollōi to phronein eudaimonias
Prōton huparkhei

SOPHOCLES:
Antigone (Greek)

Wisdom is the most important part of happiness.

Phamen oudena hontina ou ta men hauton
hēgeisthai tōn allōn sophōteron, ta de allous
heautou

PLATO:
Theaetetus (Greek)

Everyone believes himself wiser than others in
some things, but admits that others are wiser
than he in other things.

Qui ipse sibi sapiens prodesse nequit nequid-
quam sapit.

ENNIUS:
Medea (Latin)

He whose wisdom cannot help him gets no good
from being wise.

Corporis exigui vires contempnere noli:
Consilio pollet cui vim natura negavit.
Catonis Disticha (Latin)

Don't despise the strength of a weak body –
wisdom flourishes in him to whom nature has
denied strength.

Sapiens quidem pol ipsus fingit fortunam sibi:
Eo non multa quae nevolt eveniunt, nisi fictor
malust.

PLAUTUS:
Trinummus (Latin)

A wise man builds his own destiny – so not much
happens to him that he does not want, unless he
be a poor builder.

Virtus est vitium fugere et sapientia prima stul-
titia caruisse.

HORACE:
Epistles (Latin)

To flee vice is the beginning of virtue; to rid
oneself of folly is the beginning of wisdom.

Sapere aude!

HORACE:
Epistles (Latin)

Dare to be wise!

Non aetate, verum ingenio apiscitur sapientia;
Sapienti aetas condimentum, sapiens aetati
cibust.

PLAUTUS:
Trinummus (Latin)

Wisdom is got by character, not by age – age
merely spices wisdom; wisdom is the very
substance of age.

Tota philosophorum vita commentatio mortis
est.

CICERO:
Tusculan Disputations (Latin)

A wise man's life is all one preparation for death.

Mihi satis apparet propter se ipsam appetenda
sapientia.

SERVATUS LUPUS:
Epistles (Latin)

It is quite clear to me that wisdom must be
sought for its own sake.

Sapientis est ordinare.

ST. THOMAS AQUINAS:
Commentary on the Nichomachean Ethics (Latin)

The proper task of the wise is to bring order into
everyday affairs.

Vultu an natura sapiens sis, multum interest.

PUBLILIUS SYRUS:
Sententiae (Latin)

To appear wise is not the same as being born
wise.

Sapientia est potissima perfectio rationis.

ST. THOMAS AQUINAS:
Commentary on the Nichomachean Ethics (Latin)

Wisdom is the highest perfection of reason.

Nullas recipit prudentia metas.

CLAUDIAN:
Panegyricus dictus Manlio Theodoro Consuli (Latin)

Wisdom is boundless.

Ubi ego multum mirari soleo, cum pulchros
dicant non esse nisi sapientes, quibus sensibus
corporis istam pulchritudinem viderint, qual-
ibus oculis carnis formam sapientiae decusque
conspexerint.

ST. AUGUSTINE:
De Civitate Dei (Latin)

I never cease to wonder when men say that only
the wise are beautiful, with what physical senses
they have seen that particular beauty, and with
what eyes they have beheld the form of the flesh
and the loveliness of wisdom.

Itaque sapiens numquam potentium iras
provocabit.

SENECA:
Epistles (Latin)

A wise man will never provoke the anger of those
in power.

Nihil invitus facit sapiens.

SENECA:
Epistles (Latin)

Wise men do nothing against their will.

Is cadit ante senem qui sapit ante diem.

LATIN PROVERB

He dies young who is wise before his time.

Loquaris ut plures, sapias ut pauci.

LATIN PROVERB

Speak as the many, think as the few.

Selo yathā ekaghano vātena na samīrati,
Evam dhammāni sutvānā vippasīdanti paṇḍitā
Dhammapada: Paṇḍitavaggo (Pali)

Just as solid rocks are not shaken by the wind, so
wise men are not moved by either blame or
praise.

Śakunānām ivākāśe matsyānām iva codake
Yathā padam na dṛśyeta tathā jñānavidam
gatiḥ
Dhammapada: Arahantavaggo (Pali)

Just as the paths of the birds or the fish are
invisible, so is the path of the possessors of
wisdom.

Dalo dve doli providenie
Na vȳbor mudrosti lyudskoĭ;
Ili nadezhdu i volnenie,
Il' beznadezhnost' i pokoĭ

EVGENY BARATYNSKY:
Dve Doli (Russian)

Providence offers human wisdom the choice of
two fates – hope and agitation, or calm and
despair.

Aquel es sabio que los sabios aman.

LOPE DE VEGA:
Égloga a Claudio (Spanish)

Only he is wise whom wise men love.

Nadie es sabio por lo que supo su padre.

SPANISH PROVERB

No man gains wisdom through his father's experience.

WITCHCRAFT
see also Magic.

Haeresis est maxima opera maleficarum non
credere.

Written on the title-page of the *Malleus
Maleficarum: the Hammer of Witches (Latin)*

To disbelieve in witchcraft is the greatest of
heresies.

WIVES
see also Husbands, Marriage, Widows and widowers.

Domōn agalma

GREEK EXPRESSION

Jewel of my home.

Vitium uxoris aut tollendum aut ferendum est.

VARRO:
Menippean Satires (Latin)

A wife's faults must either be put down or put up
with.

Teper' mȳ mozhem spravedlivo
Skazat', chto v nashi vremena
Suprugu vernaya zhena,
Druz'ya moi, sovsem ne divo

ALEKSANDR SERGEEVICH PUSHKIN:
Count Nulin (Russian)

It can justly be said that, in these times, it is not
unusual for a wife to be faithful to her husband.

El consejo de la mujer es poco, y el que no lo
toma es loco.

SPANISH PROVERB

A wife's advice is of little value, but he who does
not take it is a fool.

Mi mujer tiene un geniecito que ya ya.

RAMÓS CARRIÓN:
La Careta Verde (Spanish)

My wife has a temper that words cannot express.

Triste está la casa donde la gallina canta y el
gallo calla.

SPANISH PROVERB

Sad is the home where the hen crows and the
cock is silent.

Quien más no puede, con su mujer se acuesta.

SPANISH PROVERB

He who can't do any better goes to bed with his
own wife.

¡Si tu mujer quiere que te tires de un balcón,
pide a Dios que sea bajo!

SPANISH PROVERB

If your wife tells you to throw yourself over a
balcony, pray God it be a low one!

WOMEN
see also Adultery, Appearance, Beauty, Betrayal, Constancy, Contentment, Crime, Cunning, Devotion, Disillusion, Emotion, Fickleness, Marriage, Moderation, Modesty, Rumour.

Al-bitt al-fatā awwel-hā garad ākhir-hā 'asal

ARAB PROVERB

A young girl is at first [bitter as] acacia fruit, but
in the end she is as sweet as honey.

An-nisē hamman wa-ghamman

ARAB PROVERB

Women are a trouble and a worry.

Quelle injustice aux dieux d'abandonner aux femmes
Un empire si grand sur les plus belles âmes.
Et de se plaire à voir de si faibles vainqueurs
Régner si puissamment sur les plus nobles coeurs!

PIERRE CORNEILLE:
Horace (French)

How unfair of the gods to abandon so great an empire over the finest spirits to such frail conquerors, and to take pleasure in watching them rule so powerfully over the noblest hearts (Horace commenting on his wife Sabine's eloquence as she pleads with him to put her to death).

La femme est toujours femme, et jamais ne sera que femme, tant qu'entier le monde durera.

MOLIÈRE:
Le Dépit Amoureux (French)

Women will always be women, and never anything but women, as long as this world holds together.

Toutes les femmes sont des garces.

FRENCH PROVERB

All women are trollops.

Le travers des femmes est de ne jamais penser à l'avenir.

DENIS DIDEROT:
Ceci n'est pas un Conte

The fault of women is that they never think of the future.

O Femme! femme! femme! créature faible et décevante.

P. A. C. DE BEAUMARCHAIS:
Le Mariage de Figaro (French)

O woman! feeble and deceiving creature!

Si Dieu n'avait fait la femme
Il n'aurait pas fait la fleur.

VICTOR HUGO:
Les Contemplations: Les Femmes sont sur la Terre
(French)

If God had not created woman, he would not have created flowers.

C'est un sexe engendré pour damner tout le monde.

MOLIÈRE:
L'Ecole des Maris (French)

Women were born to bring the whole world to perdition.

Les femmes aiment beaucoup qu'on les appelle cruelles.

P. A. C. DE BEAUMARCHAIS:
Le Barbier de Séville (French)

Women are very pleased when you accuse them of being cruel.

Il y a des hommes, il y a une femme.

EDMOND DE GONCOURT
(French)

There are many different types of men, there is only one woman.

Rien ne coûte si cher que les femmes qui ne coûtent rien.

ALFRED DE MUSSET:
Bettine (French)

The costliest women are the ones who cost nothing.

Il faut choisir d'aimer les femmes ou de les connaître: il n'y a pas de milieu.

FRENCH PROVERB

You can either love women or know them; there's no middle way.

Les femmes enfin ne valent pas le diable.

MOLIÈRE:
Le Dépit Amoureux (French)

Women just aren't worth it!

Elle éblouit comme l'Aurore
Et console comme la Nuit.

CHARLES BAUDELAIRE:
Tout Entière (French)

She dazzles like the dawn, and comforts like the night.

La tête d'une femme est comme la girouette
Au haut d'une maison, qui tourne au premier
vent.

MOLIÈRE:
Le Dépit Amoureux (French)

A woman's head is like the weathercock on the
top of a house, which turns at the first breeze.

Maint poète a souvent poursuivi dans diverses
liaisons l'image d'une femme unique.

CHARLES BAUDELAIRE:
note in his translation of Edgar
Alan Poe's *Eleanora (French)*

Many a poet has often, in various affairs,
pursued the image of a unique woman.

Une femme d'esprit est un diable en intrigue.

MOLIÈRE:
L'Ecole des Femmes (French)

A witty woman is a devil in intrigue!

Une femme est l'amour, la gloire et l'espérance;
Aux enfants qu'elle guide, à l'homme consolé,
Elle élève le coeur et calme la souffrance,
Comme un esprit des cieux sur la terre exilé.

GÉRARD DE NERVAL:
Une Femme est l'Amour (French)

Woman is love, glory and hope. To the children
whom she guides, to the man she has consoled,
she lifts up their hearts and calms their suffering,
like a heavenly body that has been exiled on
earth.

Règle générale, dès que les jeunes filles se
marient, elles négligent les beaux-arts.

LABICHE AND MARTIN:
La Poudre aux Yeux (French)

As a general rule young women give up art as
soon as they are married.

Das Ewig-Weibliche
Zieht uns hinan.

J. W. VON GOETHE:
Faust (German)

The Eternal-Feminine draws us onward.

Waz hât diu werlt ze gebenne
Liebers dan ein wîp,

Daz ein sende herze baz gefreuwen müge?

WALTHER VON DER VOGELWEIDE:
Waz hât diu Werlt? (German)

What dearer thing can the world contribute
than a woman who can gladden a longing heart?

Hütet Euch vor Weibertücken!

Libretto of *The Magic Flute*, opera by
W. A. Mozart *(German)*

Watch out for women's tricks!

Hora ge men dē k'an gunaixin hōs Arēs
Enestin. Eu d' exoistha peiratheisa pou

SOPHOCLES:
Electra (Greek)

By now you will have discovered that women too
can be militant.

Ei ara tais gunaixin epi tauta khrēsometha kai
tois andrasi, tauta kai didakteon autas

PLATO:
The Republic (Greek)

If women are expected to do the same work as
men, we must teach them the same things.

Khrēn ar' allothen pothen brotous
Paidas teknousthai, thēlu d' ouk einai genos.
Khoutōs an ouk ēn ouden anthrōpois kakon

EURIPIDES:
Medea (Greek)

If women did not exist, and children could be
produced without them, mankind would be rid
of its troubles.

Hos de gunaiki pepoithe, pepoith' d' ge
phēlētēisin

HESIOD:
Works and Days (Greek)

He who trusts a woman trusts a deceiver.

Ouden gunaikos kheiron, oude tēs kalēs

MENANDER:
Fragment (Greek)

There is nothing worse than a woman – even a
good woman!

Gunē de thēlu kapi dakruois ephu
> EURIPIDES:
> *Medea (Greek)*

Women are but women – tears are their portion.

Gunai, gunaixi kosmon hē sigē pherei
> SOPHOCLES:
> *Ajax (Greek)*

Women! your sex's finest adornment is silence.

Peithon gunaixi, kaiper ou stergōn, homōs
> GREEK PROVERB

Though you love them not, give way to women!

Pasa gunē kholos estin
> PALLADAS OF ALEXANDRIA:
> *Epigrams (Greek)*

Every woman is a source of annoyance.

Orgē tou Dios esti gunē
> GREEK PROVERB

Woman is the wrath of Zeus.

Hē de gunē pur
Asbeston, phlogeron, pantot' anaptomenon
> PALLADAS OF ALEXANDRIA:
> *Epigrams (Greek)*

Women are fire, unquenchable, flaming, ever alight.

Melei gar andri, mē gunē bouleuetō,
T'axōthen
> AESCHYLUS:
> *The Seven against Thebes (Greek)*

Affairs outside the home are the province of men – it is not for women to advise on them.

Gunaikes esmen, philophron allēlais genos,
Sōizein te koina pragmat' asphalestatai
> EURIPIDES:
> *Iphigeneia in Tauris (Greek)*

We are women, each others' friends, loyal keepers of each others' secrets.

Ou gar all' anēr mēn ek domōn
Thanon potheinos, ta de gunaikos asthenē
> EURIPIDES:
> *Iphigeneia in Tauris (Greek)*

Families can ill spare a man (by death); women are not such a loss.

In céin marat-sam re lá
De ní scarat mná re baís
> Anonymous eleventh-century Irish poet
> *(Gaelic)*

Women will not cease from folly as long as they live in the light of day.

Ogni donna mi fa palpitar.
> Libretto of *The Marriage of Figaro,* opera
> by W. A. Mozart (spoken by Cherubino)
> *(Italian)*

Every woman makes my heart beat faster!

Donne ch'avete intelletto d'Amore.
> DANTE:
> *Vita Nuova (Italian)*

Ladies who understand love.

Mulier saevissima tunc est, cum stimulos odio pudor admovet.
> JUVENAL:
> *Satires (Latin)*

Never is a woman so savage as when her hatred is goaded by shame.

Ecastor mulier recte olet, ubi nihil olet.
> PLAUTUS:
> *Mostellaria (Latin)*

The woman who has the best perfume is she who has none.

Namque est feminea tutor unda fide.
> PENTADIUS:
> *Epigrams (Latin)*

A sea-wave is more trustworthy than a woman's word.

Varium et mutabile semper femina.
> VIRGIL:
> *Aeneid (Latin)*

Woman is always a variable and changeable thing.

Mulieri nimio male facere levius onus est quam bene.
PLAUTUS:
Truculentus (Latin)

For a woman, doing wrong is much less burdensome than doing right.

Neque mulier, amissa pudicitia, alia abnuerit.
TACITUS:
Annals (Latin)

A woman who has sacrificed her modesty can refuse nothing.

Nascitur ad fructum mulier prolemque futuram.
CLAUDIAN:
In Eutropium (Latin)

Woman is born that she may have children and perpetuate the human race.

Femina consilio prudens, pia, prole beata,
Auxit amicitiis, auxit honore virum.
Inscription on Queen Eleanor's tomb in Westminster Abbey *(Latin)*

She was a devout woman, a wise adviser, blessed in her children; she was rich in friends, and highly esteemed by mankind.

Nil melius muliere bona, nil quam mala peius,
Omnibus ista bonis praestat et illa malis.
ABELARD:
Monita ad Astrolabium (Latin)

Nothing is better than a good woman; nothing is worse than a bad one. The former outstanding in all virtues, the latter in all vices.

La mujer y el melón, bien maduritos.
SPANISH PROVERB

Both women and melons are best when fairly ripe.

Sólo es dichoso en mujeres aquel de quien caso no hacen.
SPANISH PROVERB

He who is ignored by women is most fortunate.

Compuesta no hay mujer fea.
SPANISH PROVERB

A well-turned-out woman is never ugly.

La muger por ser chica, por eso non es pior;
Con doñeo es más dulçe que açúcar nin flor.
JUAN RUIZ:
De las Propiedades que las Dueñas Chicas han (Spanish)

A little woman is none the worse for being little; to converse with her is sweeter far than sugar or flowers.

Do son todas mugeres nunca mengua renzilla.
SPANISH PROVERB

Where they are all women there is never any lack of quarrelling.

WORDS
see also Action, Advice, Authorship, Dictionaries, Education, Elocution, Frankness, Grammar, Kings, Knowledge, Language, Loquacity, Love, Mathematics, Philology, Speech, War.

'Cherchez les effets et les causes,'
Nous disent les rêveurs moroses.
Des mots! des mots! cueillons les roses.
THÉODORE DE BANVILLE:
A Adolphe Gaïffe (French)

'Look for causes and effects', urge our morose dreamers. Words! words! let's gather in our roses!

Regarde ce chaos depuis que les mots ont quitté les choses!
Y. BERGER:
Le Sud (French)

Look at the chaos now that words no longer represent the things they name.

Les mots ont fini de jouer,
Les mots font l'amour.
ANDRÉ BRETON:
Les Pas Perdus (French)

Words have finished flirting; now they are making love.

La brèche ouverte au coeur de l'armée de nos ennemis les mots.
TRISTAN TZARA:
L'Homme Approximatif (French)

The open breach in the heart of the army of our enemies; words!

Die Doggen der Wortnacht.

PAUL CELAN:
Abend der Worte (German)

The hounds that bay at the blackness of speech.

Nahme Schall und Rauch,
Umnebelnd Himmels Glut.

J. W. VON GOETHE:
Faust (German)

Words are mere sound and smoke, dimming the heavenly light.

Menschen durch Worte am Leben erhalten, – ist das nicht beinahe schon so, wie sie durch Worte erschaffen?

ELIAS CANETTI:
Aufzeichnungen, 1945 (German)

Keeping people alive by means of words – is this not almost the same as creating through words?

Lasst uns niederfahren
In der Sprache der Engel
Zu den zerbrochenen Ziegeln Babels.

PETER HUCHEL:
Lasst uns Niederfahren (German)

Let us go down, in the language of the angels, to the broken bricks of Babel.

Polla toi smikroi logoi
Esphēlan ēdē kai katōrthōsan brotous

SOPHOCLES:
Electra (Greek)

Fortune has often depended on a word or so.

Arkhē paideuseōs hē tōn onomatōn episkepsis

ANTISTHENES:
Fragment (Greek)

The beginning of education lies in the exploration of the meaning of words.

Phusei tōn onomatōn ouden estin

ARISTOTLE:
De Interpretatione (Greek)

No word is by nature.

Ogni uome sa che la parola è mezzo di rappresentare il pensiere; ma pochi si accorgono che la progressione, l'abbondanza e l'economia del pensiero son effetti della parola.

UGO FOSCOLO:
Essays (Italian)

Everyone knows that words are the means of representing thought; but few are aware that the progress, abundance and economy of thought are the effects of words.

Tu, enim, Caesar, civitatem dare potes hominibus, verbo non potes!

SUETONIUS:
De Grammaticis (Latin)

You, Caesar, can confer citizenship upon a man, but not upon a word! (Marcus Pomponius Marcellus, criticising the use of a word in one of Tiberius's speeches.)

Non verba me adnumerare lectori putavi oportere, sed tamquam appendere.

CICERO:
De Optimo Genere Oratorum (Latin)

The reader should have regard not to the number of my words, but to their weight or force.

Sahassam api ce vācā anatthapadasaṁhitā
Ekam atthapadaṁ seyyo yaṁ sutvā
upasammati

Dhammapada: Sahassavaggo (Pali)

One sensible word, on hearing which we become peaceful, is better than a thousand utterances of meaningless words.

Una palabra nueva, terminada en ismo, que no la conociera nadie, era para él un regalo de los dioses.

PIO BAROJA:
La Dama Errante (Spanish)

A new word ending in 'ism', that no-one else knew, was to him a heaven-sent gift.

WORK
see also Cost, Idleness, Laziness, Life, Parents, Priests, Women.

Fi 'l-ḥaraka baraka

ARAB PROVERB

Work is good (*lit.* in activity there is good fortune).

Ālāt al-ghinā ba'ad ash shibe'
ARAB PROVERB*

Work before play (*lit.* musical instruments after satisfying one's hunger).

Travaillez, prenez de la peine.
C'est le fonds qui manque le moins.
JEAN DE LA FONTAINE:
Le Laboureur et ses Enfants (French)

Work hard! it's the surest source of gain.

L'homme est né pour le travail.
FRENCH PROVERB

Man was born for work.

On ne peut travailler pour autrui sans travailler aussi pour soi.
J. J. ROUSSEAU:
Du Contrat Social (French)

We cannot work for others without working for ourselves.

Das Werk, glaubt mir, das mit Gebet beginnt,
Das wird mit Heil und Ruhm und Sieg sich krönen!
HEINRICH VON KLEIST:
Prinz Friedrich von Homburg (German)

Believe me, the enterprise that begins with a prayer will end with prosperity, fame and triumph.

Arbeit ist das halbe Leben,
Und die andre Hälfte auch.
ERICH KÄSTNER:
Bürger, Schont eure Anlagen (German)

Work is half one's life – and the other half, as well!

Es leben die Sterblichen
Von Lohn und Arbeit.
FRIEDRICH HÖLDERLIN:
Abendphantasie (German)

Mortals live by work and wages.

Tōn ponōn pōlousin hēmin panta, tagath' hoi theoi
GREEK PROVERB

The gods sell us all things at the price of labour.

Erdoi tēn emathen tis
GREEK PROVERB

Let every man ply his own trade.

Tēs Aretēs hidrōta theoi proparoithen ethēkan
HESIOD:
Works and Days (Greek)

The gods rank work above virtue.

Ergon d' ouden oneidos, aergiē de t' oneidos
HESIOD:
Works and Days (Greek)

Work is no reproach; the reproach is idleness.

Sic fiet, ut minus ex crastino pendeas, si hodierno manum inieceris.
SENECA:
Epistles (Latin)

You will not be so dependent on tomorrow if you make an effort today.

Labor ipse voluptas.
LATIN PROVERB

Work is joy itself.

Labor omnia vincit improbus.
VIRGIL:
Georgics (Latin)

Unremitting toil overcomes every difficulty.

Generosos animos labor nutrit.
SENECA:
Epistles (Latin)

Work is food for noble minds.

WORLD
see also Civilisation, Eternity, Happiness, History, Nature, the Universe, Wisdom.

Il n'y a que l'inutilité du premier déluge qui empêche Dieu d'en envoyer un second.
S. R. N. CHAMFORT:
Caractères et Anecdotes (French)

It's only the futility of the first deluge that prevents God's sending a second.

Le monde va finir. La seule raison pour laquelle
il pouvait durer, c'est qu'elle existe.

> CHARLES BAUDELAIRE:
> *Journaux Intimes (French)*

The end of the world is coming. The only reason
for its continuing is that it already exists.

Le monde est sombre, ô Dieu! l'immuable
harmonie
Se compose des pleurs aussi bien que des chants;
L'homme n'est qu'un atome en cette ombre
infinie,
Nuit où montent les bons, où tombent les
méchants.

> VICTOR HUGO:
> *A Villequier (French)*

Oh God, the world is sombre. The immutable
harmony of the world is made of tears as well as
song. Man is but an atom in this infinite darkness, a night where the good ascend, and the
wicked fall.

Die Welt und das Leben sind Eins.

> LUDWIG WITTGENSTEIN:
> *Tractatus Logico-philosophicus (German)*

The world and life are one.

Die Welt ist die Gesamtheit der Tatsachen,
nicht der Dinge.

> LUDWIG WITTGENSTEIN:
> *Tractatus Logico-philosophicus (German)*

The world is the totality of facts, not of things.

Die Welt ist unabhängig von meinem Willen.

> LUDWIG WITTGENSTEIN:
> *Tractatus Logico-philosophicus (German)*

The world is independent of my will.

Die gesamte Wirklichkeit ist die Welt.

> LUDWIG WITTGENSTEIN:
> *Tractatus Logico-philosophicus (German)*

The sum total of reality is the world.

Diu werlt ist ûzen schoene, wîz grüene unde rôt,
Und innân swarzer varwe, vinster sam der tôt.

> WALTHER VON DER VOGELWEIDE:
> *Elegy (or Palinode) (German)*

The world is beautiful outside: white, green, and
red; but inside it is black and dark as death.

Die Welt ist rund. Denn dazu ist sie da.
Ein Vorn und Hinten gibt es nicht.
Und wer die Welt von hinten sah,
Der sah ihr ins Gesicht!

> ERICH KÄSTNER:
> *Die Welt ist Rund (German)*

The world is round – that's why it's there! It has
no front, and no back. He who saw it from
behind was really looking at its face!

Allah braucht nicht mehr zu schaffen,
Wir erschaffen seine Welt.

> J. W. VON GOETHE:
> *Wiederfinden (German)*

Allah need do no more: *we* are creating his
world!

Die Erde, diese allgemeine Wiege, hatte nun
ein gutes halbes Hundertmillionen Kinder von
allerlei Stand eingewiegt.

> GEORG CHRISTOPH LICHTENBERG:
> *Aphorismen (German)*

Earth, that universal cradle, has already rocked
well over fifty million children of all kinds in its
arms.

Noch ein Endlichstes zu wissen!
Welt ist Traum und Traum wird Welt.

> GEORG BERNECK:
> *Letzte Sehnsucht (German)*

Still something ultimate to learn! the world is a
dream, and dreams become the world.

Il dolce mondo.

> Phrase often used by Dante
> *(Italian)*

The sweet world.

La vita che sembrava
Vasta è più breve del tuo fazzoletto.

> EUGENIO MONTALE:
> *Le Occasioni (Italian)*

Life that seemed so vast is a tinier thing than
your handkerchief.

Deoque tribuenda, id est mundo.

> CICERO:
> *De Natura Deorum (Latin)*

This must be attributed to God; that belongs to
the world.

Cuanto más achiquemos nuestro mundo, más dueños seremos de él.

JACINTO BENAVENTE:
Titania (Spanish)

The more we reduce the size of our world, the more we shall be its master.

El mundo ha sido siempre de una suerte;
Ni mejora de seso ni de estado.

LOPE DE VEGA:
Égloga a Claudio (Spanish)

The world has always been the same; it gets neither better nor worse.

El mundo es un valle de lágrimas y mientras más pronto salís de él.

BENITO PÉREZ GALDÓS:
Miau (Spanish)

The world is a vale of tears; the sooner you leave it, the better!

Si Dios no hubiera descansado el domingo habría tenido tiempo de terminar el mundo.

GABRIEL GARCÍA MÁRQUEZ:
La Viuda de Montiel (Spanish)

If God had not rested on Sunday, he could have completed the world.

El mundo está mal hecho.

GABRIEL GARCÍA MÁRQUEZ:
La Viuda de Montiel (Spanish)

The world is a botched job (*lit.* the world is badly made).

WORRY
see also Adversity, Care, Philosophy, Sleep, Sorrow.

Das Sorgenschränkchen, das Allerheiligste der innersten Seelenökonomie, das nur des Nachts geöffnet wird.

GEORG CHRISTOPH LICHTENBERG:
Aphorismen (German)

The little worry locker, the holy of holies of the innermost workings of the soul, which is opened only during the night.

Ahi, ahi, s'asside
Su l'alte prue la negra cura, e sotto

Ogni clima, ogni ciel, si chiama indarno
Felicità, vive tristezza e regna.

GIACOMO LEOPARDI:
Al Conte Carlo Pepoli (Italian)

Alas, alas, black care sits forever high upon the prow. In all climates, under all skies, man's happiness is always somewhere else. Sorrow lives and reigns.

WORTHLESSNESS

Un grand vaurien est un grand vaurien, mais n'est point une espèce.

DENIS DIDEROT:
Le Neveu de Rameau (French)

A great big good-for-nothing is a great big good-for-nothing – but he does not constitute a species.

Les gens qui ne veulent rien faire de rien, n'avancent rien, et ne sont bons à rien.

P. A. C. DE BEAUMARCHAIS:
Le Mariage de Figaro (French)

People who don't want to do anything at all, gain nothing and are good for nothing.

Harena sine calce.

LATIN EXPRESSION

Salt that has lost its savour (*lit.* sand without lime).

WRONG
see also Evil, Indignation, Kings, Right and wrong, Women.

Kalon men ton adikeonta kōluein. Ei de mē, mē xunadikein

DEMOCRATES:
Fragment (Greek)

You should either stop other people doing wrong, or avoid taking part in wrongdoing.

En sophoisi gar
Tad' esti thnētōn, lanthanein ta mē kala

EURIPIDES:
Hippolytus (Greek)

The advice of wise men is to sweep moral lapses under the carpet.

Y

YOUTH

see also Beauty, Behaviour, Idealism, Joy,
Judgment, Life, Old age, Parents, Poets and
poetry, Prudence, Silence, Violence,
Wisdom.

Qui me rendra ces jours où la vie a des ailes
Et vole, vole ainsi que l'alouette aux cieux.
MARCELINE DESBORDES-VALMORE:
L'Impossible (French)

Who will give me back those days when life had
wings and flew just like a skylark in the sky?

La jeunesse est un temps pendant lequel les
conventions sont, et doivent être, mal comprises: ou aveuglement combattues, ou aveuglement obéies.
PAUL VALÉRY:
Monsieur Teste (preface) *(French)*

Youth is a time when the conventions are rightly
misunderstood; they are either blindly obeyed,
or blindly challenged.

La jeunesse est une ivresse continuelle: c'est la
fièvre de la raison.
FRANÇOIS, DUC DE LA ROCHEFOUCAULD:
Réflexions (French)

Youth is a time of unending ecstasy; it is reason
in a fever.

Ma jeunesse ne fut qu'un ténébreux orage,
Traversé çà et là par de brillants soleils.
CHARLES BAUDELAIRE:
Les Fleurs du Mal (French)

My youth was nought but a shadowy storm, shot
here and there by brilliant flashes of sunshine.

Poète, prends ton luth; le vin de la jeunesse
Fermente cette nuit dans les veines de Dieu.
ALFRED DE MUSSET:
La Nuit de Mai (French)

Poet, take up your lute; this night the wine of
youth ferments in God's veins.

Adorable et terrible, éblouissante et douce,
Tu m'apparus, Jeunesse, une rose à la main!
GABRIEL VICAIRE:
Jeunesse (French)

Adorable and terrifying, sweet but dazzling, you
appeared before me, youth, with a rose in your
hand!

Je n'ai vu luire encor que les feux du matin.
ANDRÉ CHÉNIER:
La Jeune Captive (French)

So far I have seen only the flames of morning.

On peut toujours être heureux
Quand l'avenir a les yeuz bleus.
PAUL GILSON:
Absent Minded (French)

We can always be happy when the future has
blue eyes.

J'ai vu le temps où ma jeunesse
Sur mes lèvres était sans cesse
Prête à chanter comme un oiseau.
ALFRED DE MUSSET:
Le Poète (French)

I have seen times when my youth was ever on
my lips, ready to sing like a bird.

Gib meine Jugend mir zurück!
J. W. VON GOETHE:
Faust (preface) *(German)*

Give me back my youth!

Erloschen sind die heitern Sonnen,
Die meiner Jugend Pfad erhellt.
J. C. F. VON SCHILLER:
Die Ideale (German)

Gone is the brilliant sunshine that illuminated
the paths of my youth.

.n Deinem Alter, mein liebes Kind, hat noch fast
edes Jahr sein eigenes Gesicht: denn die Jugend
ässt sich nicht ärmer machen.

THEODOR STORM:
Immensee: ein Brief (German)

At your time of life, dear boy, nearly every year
till brings its own particular experience – for
youth is apt to turn everything to the best
account.

Getauft geimpft gefirmt geschult.
Gespielt hab ich mit Bombensplittern
Und aufgewachsen bin ich zwischen
Dem Heiligen Geist und Hitlers Bild.

GÜNTER GRASS:
Kleckerburg (German)

Baptised, vaccinated, educated, confirmed, I
played with bomb splinters and grew up
between the Holy Ghost and Hitler's portrait.

Mokhthos gar oudeis tois neois skēpsin pherei

EURIPIDES:
Iphigeneia in Tauris (Greek)

Youth knows no bounds to adventure.

Nea gar phrontis ouk algein philei

EURIPIDES:
Medea (Greek)

Youth and grief are ill-assorted.

Hai neotētes
Aphrones, hai poliai d' empalin andranees

GREEK PROVERB

Youth is foolish, old age feeble.

Saita sakura ni
Naze koma tsunagu
Koma ga isameba
Hana ga chiru.

JAPANESE FOLKSONG

Why tether your young horse to a tree in
blossom? As he prances the flowers will fall!

Bushi no ko wa kutsuwa no oto no me o samasu.

JAPANESE PROVERB

The child of a warrior awakes at the sound of a
bride.

Parcendum est teneris.

JUVENAL:
Satires (Latin)

Be gentle with the young.

Ratione non vi vincenda adulescentia est.

LATIN PROVERB

Youth must be mastered not by force but by
reason.

Dum vernat sanguis, dum rugis integer annus.

PROPERTIUS:
Elegies (Latin)

While the blood yet courses through your
veins, and your years are free from wrinkles.

Spas og Spilopper er Ungdoms Kriterium!

HENRIK IBSEN:
Peer Gynt (Norwegian)

Jokes and fun are what youth is known by!

Vi er Børn af Våren
Bag den skal ikke komme nogen Høst.

HENRIK IBSEN:
Love's Comedy (Norwegian)

We are born of spring, and never shall autumn
come to us.

Solov'ëm zalëtnym
Yunost' proletela,
Volnoï v nepogodu
Radost' proshumela

ALEKSEI KOL'TSOV:
Gor'kaya Dolya (Russian)

My youth has swept by like a passing nightingale; happiness has echoed past like a wave in
bad weather.

Z

ZEAL

Sedulitas autem stulte quem diligit urget.
HORACE:
Epistles (Latin)

Zeal is foolish to worry those it loves.

THE ZODIAC
see also Astronomy, Stars.

Accipe divisas hominis per sidera partes sing-
ulaque in propriis parentia membra figuris, in
quis praecipuas tote de corpore vires exercent.
MANILIUS:
Astronomica (Latin)

Learn now how the parts of the human body are
distributed among the signs, and behold each
member plainly allocated to its own constella-
tion. In the parts of the body so distributed, the
signs exercise the powers that concern that part,
out of the whole body, that belongs to them.

LIST OF HEADWORDS

INDEX OF AUTHORS AND THEIR WORKS